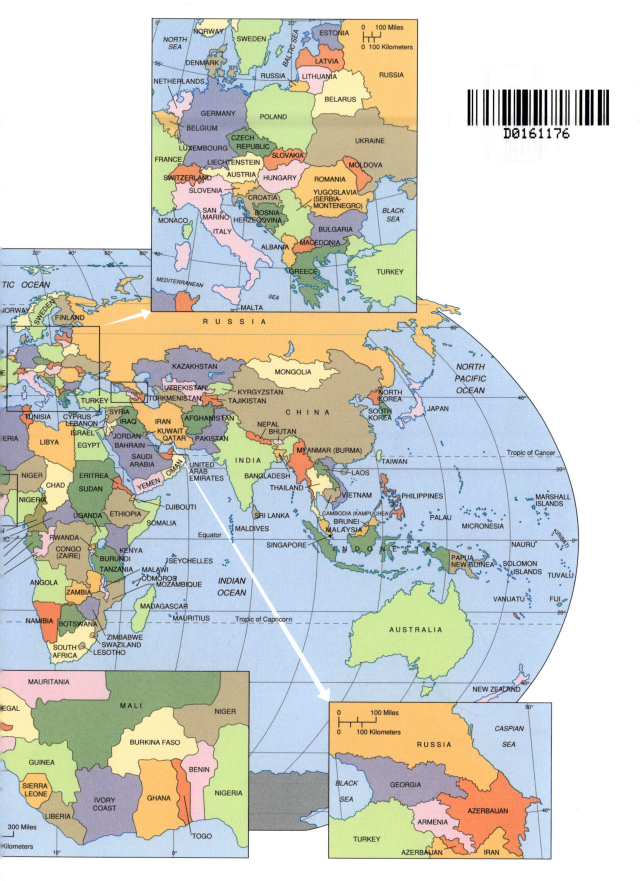

INTERNATIONAL MANAGEMENT

Text and Cases

McGRAW-HILL ADVANCED TOPICS IN GLOBAL MANAGEMENT

F O U R T H   E D I T I O N

INTERNATIONAL MANAGEMENT

Text and Cases

Paul W. Beamish
Ivey Business School
The University of Western Ontario

Allen J. Morrison
Ivey Business School
The University of Western Ontario

Philip M. Rosenzweig
IMD

Andrew C. Inkpen
Thunderbird, The American Graduate School of International Management

Irwin
McGraw-Hill

Boston   Burr Ridge, IL   Dubuque, IA   Madison, WI   New York   San Francisco   St. Louis
Bangkok   Bogotá   Caracas   Lisbon   London   Madrid
Mexico City   Milan   New Delhi   Seoul   Singapore   Sydney   Taipei   Toronto

McGraw-Hill Higher Education

*A Division of The **McGraw-Hill** Companies*

INTERNATIONAL MANAGEMENT

This book is printed on acid-free paper.

domestic   1 2 3 4 5 6 7 8 9 0 FGR/FGR 9 0 9 8 7 6 5 4 3 2 1 0 9
international 1 2 3 4 5 6 7 8 9 0 FGR/FGR 9 0 9 8 7 6 5 4 3 2 1 0 9

ISBN   0-07-229072-2

Vice president/Editor-in-chief: *Michael W. Junior*
Publisher: *Craig S. Beytien*
Senior sponsoring editor: *Jennifer Roche*
Marketing manager: *Kenyetta Giles Haynes*
Project manager: *Christine Parker*
Production supervisor: *Michael R. McCormick*
Freelance design coordinator: *Mary Christianson*
Photo research coordinator: *Sharon Miller*
Supplement coordinator: *Rose M. Range*
Freelance cover designer: *the Visual*
Compositor: *Electronic Publishing Services, Inc., TN*
Typeface: *10/12 Times Roman*
Printer: *Quebecor Printing Book Group/Fairfield*

Library of Congress Cataloging-in-Publication Data

International management : text and cases / Paul Beamish . . . [et al.].
  — 4th ed.
     p.   cm. — (McGraw-Hill advanced topics in global management)
   Rev. ed. of: International management / Paul W. Beamish. 3rd ed.
1997.
   Includes index.
   ISBN 0-07-229072-2
   1. International business enterprises—Management.
  2. International business enterprises—Management Case studies.
  I. Beamish, Paul W., 1953–   . II. Series.
  HD62.4.B4   2000
  658'.049—dc21   99-31818

INTERNATIONAL EDITION   ISBN 0-07-116934-2
Copyright © 2000. Exclusive rights by The McGraw-Hill Companies, Inc. for manufacture and export.
This book cannot be re-exported from the country to which it is consigned by McGraw-Hill.
The International Edition is not available in North America.

http://www.mhhe.com

to our children
Katie, Christine, Alexander & Daniel Beamish
Robert, Andrew, Rachel & William Morrison
Thomas & Caroline Rosenzweig
Anne & Carly Inkpen

International Management is intended as an *international,* international-management book. The first three editions were used in over 200 universities and colleges in over 20 countries. The fourth edition, we hope, will have even wider usage. Why our optimism with this edition? In brief, it is because the book focuses on issues of international management common and important to businesspeople everywhere.

International Management is about how firms become and remain international in scope. It is about the experiences of firms of all sizes, from many countries, as they come to grips with an increasingly competitive global environment. It is about the practice of management when a home-market perspective is no longer enough to achieve and sustain success. Through carefully selected comprehensive case studies and integrated text material, this book bridges both the internationalization process and multinational management.

Many texts focus on ongoing management issues in the world's larger MNEs—the lower-right-hand cell in the following matrix. This is an important area, but one that presupposes a body of knowledge that most students do not possess. Our text takes a broader view, examining small and medium-sized firms as well as large MNEs, and the process of internationalization as well as the challenges of ongoing management in multinationals.

	Internationalization	Ongoing Multinational Management
Small/Medium-Sized Firms	Smaller domestic firms moving abroad	Global niche competitors
Larger MNEs	Larger firms moving into more markets	Large, full-scale global competitors

The first half of *International Management* helps to demystify international business so a meaningful study of multinational management can occur. We focus on *internationalization*—developing an awareness of the impact of international forces on the firm's future and establishing and conducting transactions with firms internationally. We provide an understanding about the basic modes of involvement and deciding when each is most appropriate. For each mode, both inward- and outward-looking perspectives can be considered: licensing (as licensor and licensee), trade (exporting and importing), joint ventures (with foreign companies abroad and at home), and subsidiaries (establishing foreign affiliates and as part of a foreign-controlled affiliate). As the left-hand cells in the matrix suggest, these issues are relevant for firms of all sizes.

In the second half of the book, focus is on how to establish a balance between the sometimes conflicting demands of the multinational headquarters, the multinational subsidiary, and the governments of all the countries in which the MNE operates. The cases are not limited to the experiences of the world's largest MNEs—they are also about smaller companies that must be global to survive and about the management of small subsidiaries. Nor are the cases solely focussed on the experience of MNEs from one country. In 1970, two-thirds of the world's largest companies were from the U.S.A. Now only about one-quarter are U.S.-headquartered.

International Management is intended for use in international business and international management courses at the undergraduate, graduate, and executive levels. It can serve as the basis for an overarching course that deals with internationalization and multinational management, or for courses in each. The chapters of text material can (and should) be supplemented with readings of the instructor's choice. Many of the suggested supplementary readings are from *Journal of International Business Studies,* which provides blanket permission to photocopy articles for classroom use at no charge.

In response to suggestions from the users and reviewers of the third edition, this edition contains more cases (31 versus 28) and more chapters of text (13 versus 12). Of the 31 cases, 18 are new to the fourth edition while others have been significantly revised and updated. The new cases were selected on the basis of managerial relevance, overall fit with suggested themes, availability, and the evaluations we received from a survey of the faculty users of the third edition. In regard to text material, there is an entirely new chapter on Global Leadership, while all other chapters have been revised and updated. All but one of the chapters were (co)authored by us or one of our current or past colleagues. This has allowed us the opportunity to shape the body of text material into an integrated whole.

The cases in *International Management* have been extensively classroom-tested by us and colleagues around the world in executive, MBA, and undergraduate programs. One measure of their quality is that a number of them have been translated—into Japanese, French, Chinese, Spanish, Russian, and Indonesian. As well, several have won awards. For example, the Russki Adventures and Brent Spar cases received EFMD Case Competition Awards.

A videotape containing material relevant to a number of the cases is available from McGraw Hill. Use of the video is preferable but not essential.

Acknowledgments

The individual we most wish to acknowledge is Harold Crookell, a coauthor on the first edition. He passed away suddenly in 1991 and is sorely missed by all who knew him. His spirit of intellectual curiosity and dedication to the improvement of international management permeate this volume.

The authors are deeply indebted to a number of colleagues and institutions for the intellectual and financial support we have received:

Faculty Contributors of Cases/Chapters

Stewart Black, Center for Global Assignments and University of Michigan
James Bowey, Bishop's University
Andrew Delios, Hong Kong University of Science and Technology
Charles Dhanaraj, Indiana University
Joseph DiStefano, Ivey Business School
Bud Johnston, Ivey Business School
Peter Killing, IMD
Masaaki (Mike) Kotabe, Temple University
Henry W. Lane, Ivey Business School
Donald Lecraw, Ivey Business School
Isiaih Litvak, York University
Shigefumi Makino, Chinese University of Hong Kong
Arvind Phatak, Temple University
Thomas A. Poynter, Principal, The Transitions Group, Inc.
David Sharp, Ivey Business School
Ulrich Steger, IMD

Research Associates or Assistants

Azimah Ainuddin, Harry Cheung, Chang Choi, Gayle Duncan, Anthony Goerzen, Katherine Johnston, Lambros Karavis, Joyce Miller, Mary Schweinsberg, Tanya Spyridakis, S.M. Steele, Ian Sullivan, Matthias Winter, Shari Ann Wortel.

Institutional Contributors

Richard Ivey School of Business, The University of Western Ontario, London, Canada
IMD—International Institute for Management Development, Lausanne, Switzerland
Thunderbird, The American Graduate School of International Management, Arizona, U.S.A.
The World Bank, Washington, D.C.

The following persons provided detailed reviews on this or an earlier edition:

Lance Brouthers, University of Texas—San Antonio
Ellen Cook, University of San Diego
F. Derakhshan, CSUSB
George Gore, University of Cincinnati

David Hopkins, University of Denver
Carol Howard, University of Hawaii at Manoa
Stephen Jenner, San Diego State University
Robert Moran, American Graduate School of International Management
Cynthia Pavett, University of San Diego
John Stanbury, University of Indiana—Kokomo
Kenneth R. Tillery, Middle Tennessee State University
Robert Vidal, University of Cincinnati
Leland Wooton, Southern Methodist University

Input on the cases contained in the various editions has been received from:

Rafiq Ahmen, A. Ali, Joe Anderson, William J. Arthur, John Banks, Edgar Barrett, Brad Brown, Marie Burkhead, Jafor Chowdhury, Susan Crockett, Chris Demchak, John Dutton, L.R. Edleson, Nick Fry, Sanjay Goel, Robert Grosse, Ruth Gunn, S.D. Guzell, Steven H. Hanks, Louis Hébert, Mary Howes, S. Kumar Jain, Dale Kling, R. Kustin, Neng Liang, Clair McRostie, Alan Murray, Behnam Nakhai, Kent Neupert, R.F. O'Neil, Y.S. Paik, Less Palich, S. Porth, Rich Pouder, Mohammad Pourheydarian, Krishnan Ramaya, Kathy Rehbein, Lawrence Rhyne, Kendall Roth, Carol Sanchez, Bill Scheela, Jason Schweizer, Hendrick Seturie, Trudy Somers, William C. Sproull, John Stanbury, Phil Van Auken, Tom Voight, William A. Ward, Marion White, Georgie Willcox, Patrick Woodcock, and George Yates.

We are grateful to all of these individuals and have tried to be as responsive as possible to their suggestions.

Finally, we wish to express our appreciation to our colleagues at Ivey. Richard Ivey School of Business is the second-largest producer of management case studies in the world. Seventeen of the 31 cases in this edition originated at Ivey. Any ongoing undertaking of this magnitude requires a great deal of financial and intellectual support. We receive this at Ivey.

Paul W. Beamish
Allen J. Morrison
Philip M. Rosenzweig
Andrew C. Inkpen

C O N T E N T S

PART III

MULTINATIONAL MANAGEMENT

PAUL W. BEAMISH is Associate Dean–Reasearch and the Royal Bank Professor in International Business at the Richard Ivey School of Business, The University of Western Ontario, London, Canada. From 1993 to 1997 he served as editor-in-chief of the *Journal of International Business Studies* (JIBS). He is the author or coauthor of over 100 publications in the international strategy area and series editor of 32 volumes of cases for China. He has consulted and managed training activities in the public and private sectors, and he regularly acts as a joint venture facilitator for firms contemplating an alliance. His work has received awards from the Academy of Management, Academy of International Business, European Foundation for Management Development, and the Administrative Sciences Association of Canada. Before joining Ivey's faculty in 1987, he worked for Procter & Gamble Company of Canada and Wilfrid Laurier University.

ALLEN J. MORRISON is Associate Dean–Executive Development and an Associate Professor of International Management at the Richard Ivey School of Business, The University of Western Ontario. Dr. Morrison has also been a Visiting Professor at the Anderson School at UCLA, and Professor of International Mangement at Thunderbird, The American Graduate School of International Management. Dr. Morrison's research and teaching interests center on multinational strategy and global leadership. He has authored or coauthored numerous articles and case studies, and seven books including *Global Explorers: The Next Generation of Leaders* (Routledge, 1999). His views have been cited in such publications as *USA Today, Newsweek, Fortune,* and *Wall Street Journal.* Dr. Morrison holds an M.B.A. degree from Ivey and a Ph.D. from the University of South Carolina.

PHILIP M. ROSENZWEIG is a professor at IMD in Lausanne, Switzerland. Before that, he was on the faculty of the Harvard Business School (1990 to 1996). His research has explored a number of aspects of international management, including organization design, human resource management, cross-cultural management, and ethical issues in foreign investment. He has published many case studies and articles that have appeared in *Academy of Management Review, Management Science, Journal of International Business Studies, California Management Review,* and *European Management Journal.* He is also active in international executive education, recently teaching in Japan, France, the Netherlands, Hungary, Peru, and the United Arab Emirates. He completed his Ph.D. at the Wharton School of the University of Pennsylvania, and has an M.B.A. from UCLA. He was employed by Hewlett-Packard Co. from 1980 to 1986.

ANDREW C. INKPEN is an Associate Professor of Management at Thunderbird, The American Graduate School of International Management in Glendale, Arizona. He holds a Ph.D. in Business from Ivey. He has also been on the faculties of Temple University and the National University of Singapore. His research and teaching deal with the management of multinational firms, with a particular focus on strategic alliances, knowledge management, and organizational learning. He is the author or coauthor of more than 30 articles in journals such as *Academy of Management Review, Academy of Management Executive, California Management Review, Strategic Management Journal,* and *Journal of International Business Studies.* He is actively involved in international executive education and consulting. Before entering academe, he worked in public accounting and qualified as a Chartered Accountant in Canada.

I TEXT

1 THE INTERNATIONALIZATION PROCESS

Firms become international in scope for a variety of reasons—some proactive and some reactive. Collectively these include a desire for continued growth, an unsolicited foreign order, domestic market saturation, the potential to exploit a new technological advantage, and so forth. The dominant reason, however, relates to performance. There is clear evidence that among the largest multinational enterprises (MNEs), a strong correlation exists between improved performance and degree of internationalization (see Exhibit 1–1). Geographic scope is positively associated with firm profitability, even when controlling for the competing effect of the possession of proprietary assets. There is intrinsic value in internationalization itself.

Internationalization is the process by which firms increase their awareness of the influence of international activities on their future, and establish and conduct transactions with firms from other countries. International transactions can influence a firm's future in both direct and indirect ways. Business decisions made in one country, regarding such things as foreign investments and partnership arrangements, can have significant impact on a firm in a different country—and vice versa. The impact of such decisions may not be immediately and directly evident. The development of an awareness and appreciation for the role of foreign competition becomes an integral—and sometimes overlooked—part of the internationalization process. Internationalization has both *inward-looking* and *outward-looking* dimensions. The outward-looking perspective incorporates an awareness of the nature of competition in foreign markets, and includes the following modes of activities:

a. Exporting.

b. Acting as licensor to a foreign company.

c. Establishing joint ventures outside the home country with foreign companies.

d. Establishing or acquiring wholly owned businesses outside the home country.

This chapter was prepared by Paul W. Beamish.

EXHIBIT 1–1   MNE Performance and Degree of Internationalization*

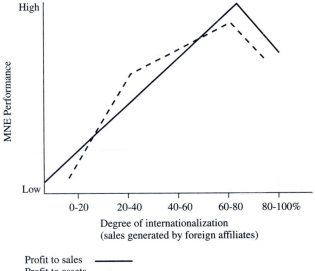

Degree of internationalization
(sales generated by foreign affiliates)

Profit to sales ————
Profit to assets – – – –

* Data are based on the 100 largest U.S. MNEs and the 100 largest European MNEs.

Source: J. M. Geringer, Paul W. Beamish, and R. daCosta, "Diversification Strategy and Internationalization: Implications for MNE Performance," *Strategic Management Journal,* Vol. 10, 1989, pp. 109–19.

These outward-oriented elements are similar to those in the stages model of international expansion. The stages model is an outward-looking perspective developed to reflect the commonly observed pattern of increased commitment to international business. In the stages model,[1] a firm might progress from (*a*) indirect/ad hoc exporting—perhaps from unsolicited export orders—to (*b*) active exporting and/or licensing to (*c*) active exporting, licensing, and joint equity investment in foreign manufacture to (*d*) full-scale multinational marketing and production.

These are, of course, broad-based stages. In practice, there are many more subcategories. Within exporting, for example, firms may start with order-filling only. Soon after, however, they may be confronted with questions of whether to use exporting middlemen who take ownership (distributors) or those who are commissioned agents; and whether to export directly (either through the firm's own sales force, an export department, or a foreign sales company) or indirectly (through brokers or export agents). From a service sector perspective, comparable issues exist, such as whether to use management contracts or to develop in-house capability.

---

[1]See Franklin R. Root, *Entry Strategies for International Markets* (Lexington, Mass: Lexington Books, 1987), p. 19.

EXHIBIT 1–2   The Foreign Direct Investment of MNEs

Choosing the Scale of Investment, Type of Partner, and Ownership Arrangement

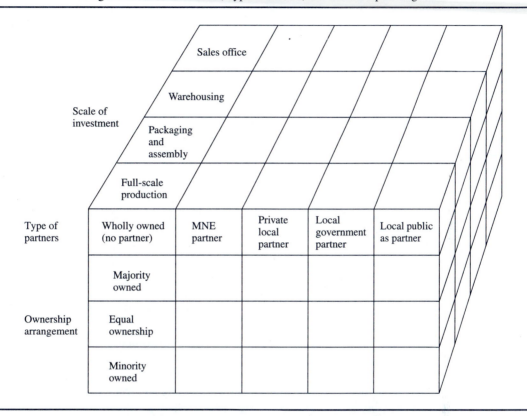

Note: While full-scale production via a wholly owned subsidiary is the most commonly studied form of MNE foreign direct investment (FDI), it is only one of at least 80 (5 × 4 × 4) regularly used forms of FDI.

Similarly, if an investment is to be made, there are questions regarding scale of investment (sales office, warehouse, packaging and assembly, or full-scale production), level of ownership (wholly, majority equity, equal, minority equity), and type of partner. As Exhibit 1–2 illustrates, there are numerous variations on the types of foreign direct investment possible.

Another way of considering the various forms of foreign investment (and there are over 300,000 subsidiaries around the world) is illustrated in Exhibit 1–3. Each of these four forms has merit, although generally greenfield and joint venture tend to be superior performers versus acquisitions (because here there is a tendency to pay too much and/or to have integration problems.)

The sequential approach in the stages model is intuitively appealing in that it suggests that as firms develop experience and confidence with international business, they will be willing to increase the scale of their investment and commitment in some sort of predictable

---

EXHIBIT 1–3   **Forms of Foreign Investment**

	Partially Owned	Wholly Owned
Existing Business	Capital Participation	Acquisition
New Business	Joint Venture	Greenfield

---

fashion. The stages model also implies that over time, the firm's international operations will evolve toward modes such as wholly owned subsidiaries that promise greater risk (due to the required scale of investment) with the offsetting ability to exert greater control.

Not all firms follow such a path. Some start and stay with a particular mode or some skip stages, while others even change modes to a direction opposite to that suggested by the stages model. So while the stages model provides a useful way to organize our discussion, it is by no means reflective of, or appropriate for, all firms' approaches to international business. It is a descriptive model. It reflects what firms often do, not what they must or ought to do.

We also observe the formation of firms that, by necessity or design, are international from inception. These so-called born globals can take many forms, depending on the number of countries involved and the number of value chain activities that must be coordinated. Firms that are international from inception are often led by entrepreneurs who are able to overcome not just the liabilities of newness and size, but the liability of being foreign. Many firms do not originate with both international business competency and confidence. (See Exhibit 1–4).

Internationalization affects firms in equally important ways from an inward perspective, which incorporates an awareness of the impact of global competitors on the ability of domestically oriented firms to compete. The related modes of activity include:

a. Importing/sourcing.
b. Acting as licensee from a foreign company.
c. Establishing joint ventures (JVs) inside the home country with foreign companies.
d. Managing as the wholly owned subsidiary of a foreign firm.

All of these modes and influences are relevant to the internationalization process and all are often overlooked. There are numerous reasons for considering importing rather than purchasing domestically, for considering foreign licensors or joint venture partners rather than strictly local ones, or if selling an entire business, considering foreign purchasers as an alternative to becoming the subsidiary of a domestic firm. Drawing upon resources and alternatives that are present elsewhere can help the firm see new opportunities, improve its bargaining power with local firms, make more informed decisions, and compete better at home.

EXHIBIT 1–4   Types of International New Ventures

Few Activities Coordinated across Countries (Primarily Logistics)	New International Market Makers	
	Export/Import Start-up	Multinational Trader
Coordination of Value Chain Activites	i	ii
	iii	iv
Many Activities Coordinated across Countries	Geographically Focused Start-up	Global Start-up

Few	Many

Number of Countries Involved

Source: B. M. Oviatt and P. McDougall, "Toward a Theory of International New Ventures," *Journal of International Business Studies,* Vol. 25, No. 1, 1994, p. 59.

Many firms have an appreciation for the nature and degree of competition in one or more foreign markets. Yet often they will not aggressively seek out markets that differ in language, geographic proximity, cultural similarity, and so forth. Some have suggested that for certain products, the world is a single market. The so-called Triad market (Japan, North America, and western Europe) is made up of over 630 million buyers with similar tastes.[2] This view raises a number of issues to be explored in later chapters. Which products/services would fall into this category? How would a firm know that it may have a *globally* competitive product/service? If it did, how could it take the product/service effectively to numerous distant markets? To complicate this even further, we must consider how the answers to these and other questions change over time. For example, many of the reasons for making a foreign investment in the 1970s are different today (see Exhibit 1–5). The nonstatic nature of the environment is simultaneously one of the greatest attractions and frustrations for the international manager.

In terms of the new entrant to international business, how do managers make the decision to get involved internationally using *any mode*? Individual managers and groups of managers often possess distinct attitudes toward international business. These can range from being home-country oriented (ethnocentric),[3] to host-country oriented (polycentric), to world oriented (geocentric). There are two major risks associated with an ethnocentric,

---

[2]See Kenichi Ohmae, *Beyond National Borders* (Homewood, Ill.: Dow Jones-Irwin, 1987).

[3]See H. V. Perlmutter, "The Tortuous Evolution of the Multinational Corporation," *Columbia Journal of World Business,* January/February 1969, pp. 9–18; H. V. Perlmutter & D. A. Heenan, "How Multinational Should Your Top Managers Be?" *Harvard Business Review,* Vol. 6, 1974, pp. 121–32; S. J. Kobrin, "Is There a Relationship between a Geocentric Mind-Set and Multinational Strategy?" *Journal of International Business Studies,* Vol. 3, 1994, pp. 493-511; and J. Calof and P. Beamish, "The Right Attitude for International Success," *Business Quarterly,* Vol. 59, No. 1, 1994, pp.105–10.

EXHIBIT 1–5   Some Variables Influencing the Location of Value Added Activities by MNEs in the 1970s and 1990s

Type of FDI	In the 1970s	In the 1990s
A. Resource Seeking	1. Availability, price, and quality of natural resources. 2. Infrastructure to enable resources to be exploited, and products arising from them to be exported. 3. Government restrictions on FDI and/or on capital and dividend remissions. 4. Investment incentives, e.g., tax holidays.	1. As in the 1970s, but local opportunities for upgrading quality of resources and the processing and transportation of their output are a more important locational incentive. 2. Availability of local partners to jointly promote knowledge and/or capital-intensive resource exploitation.
B. Market Seeking	1. Mainly domestic, and occasionally (e.g., in Europe) adjacent regional markets. 2. Real wage costs; material costs. 3. Transport costs; tariff and nontariff trade barriers. 4. As A.3 above, but also (where relevant) privileged access to import licenses.	1. Mostly large and growing domestic markets, and adjacent regional markets (e.g., NAFTA, EU, etc.). 2. Availability and price of skilled and professional labor. 3. Presence and competitiveness of related firms, e.g., leading industrial suppliers. 4. Quality of national and local infrastructure, and institutional competence. 5. Less spatially related market distortions, but increased role of agglomerative spatial economies and local service support facilities. 6. Macroeconomic and macro-organizational policies as pursued by host governments. 7. Increased need for presence close to users in knowledge-intensive sectors. 8. Growing importance of promotional activities by regional or local development agencies.
C. Efficiency Seeking	1. Mainly production cost related (e.g., labor, materials, machinery, etc.). 2. Freedom to engage in trade in intermediate and final products. 3. Presence of agglomerative economies, e.g., export processing zones. 4. Investment incentives, e.g., tax breaks, accelerated depreciation, grants, subsidized land.	1. As in the 1970s, but more emphasis placed on B2, 3, 4, 5 and 7 above, especially for knowledge-intensive and integrated MNE activities, e.g., R&D and some office functions. 2. Increased role of governments in removing obstacles to restructuring economic activity, and facilitating the upgrading of human resources by appropriate educational and training programs. 3. Availability of specialized spatial clusters, e.g., science and industrial parks, service support systems etc.; and of specialized factor inputs. Opportunities for new initiatives by investing firms; an entrepreneurial environment, and one which encourages competitiveness enhancing cooperation within and between firms.

(continued)

EXHIBIT 1–5   *(concluded)*

Type of FDI	In the 1970s	In the 1990s
D. Strategic Asset Seeking	1. Availability of knowledge-related assets and markets necessary to protect or enhance ownership-specific advantages of investing firms—and at the right price. 2. Institutional and other variables influencing ease or difficulty at which such assets can be acquired by foreign firms.	1. As in the 1970s, but growing geographical dispersion of knowledge-based assets, and need of firms to harness such assets from foreign locations, makes this a more important motive for FDI. 2. The price and availability of "synergistic" assets to foreign investors. 3. Opportunities offered (often by particular subnational spatial units) for exchange of localized tacit knowledge, ideas and interactive learning. 4. Access to different cultures, institutions and systems; and different consumer demands and preferences.

Source: John H. Dunning. "Location and the Multinational Enterprise: A Neglected Factor?" *Journal of International Business Studies,* Vol. 29, No. 1, p. 53, 1998.

or home-country, focus. The first of these is a lack of awareness and appreciation for opportunities that exist external to the domestic market. The counterpoint to these potential opportunities is the potential threat of foreign competition in the home market. Numerous businesses have been hurt as a result of the naive view that if a product or service is NIH (not-invented-here), it won't be effective.

Relevant to all of the various perspectives and modes of involvement is the firm's need for methods of coming to grips with various international cultures. Firms do not typically have the resources available to develop a detailed understanding of numerous cultures. Yet to compete internationally, some degree of understanding is required. But how much? And which cultures does it make more sense to try to learn about?

There are still business people who persist in believing that international competition cannot affect them because they are too small, or because they are solely focused on the local market. Foreign competition affects every sector of every economy. Education is an important consideration at each stage of the internationalization process.

In the balance of this chapter, some of the issues we will deal with in the subsequent chapters and cases will be briefly considered.

The Global Business Environment

A key element of the internationalization process concerns *where* an organization chooses to do business outside its country. Many firms conduct an incomplete analysis of potential markets. This is due, in part, to a lack of awareness regarding global demographics.

Many criteria are available for assessing market compatibility. Chapter 2 provides some introductory material on population, gross national product, country growth rates, and so forth. Basic statistics on countries are included. This material is particularly useful when the firm is looking at opportunities on a worldwide (see Cameron case), regional (see Palliser case), or national (see Technophar in Vietnam case) basis.

The World of International Trade

Chapter 3 presents an overview of the international trade environment, with particular emphasis on the need to appreciate the role of foreign competition in both the home market and foreign markets. A great deal of emphasis is placed on demystifying the nature of international business, in part through an overview of the trade framework.

The trade framework considers social, technological, economic, and political (STEP) environments, which make any country more or less attractive for international investment and trade. As part of this analysis, the distinctions between comparative and competitive advantage, theories of international trade, and the nature of exchange rates are reviewed.

Managing Export Operations

Exporting can often be the basis for all or part of an entire course on international marketing. This is because, as both the Neilson in Mexico case and the Selkirk case demonstrate, the export decision process is complex, requiring resolution of a number of fundamental questions. Firms of any size are faced with the same questions of where to expand (at home or abroad); if exporting, to which markets; the best way to enter these markets (i.e., what distribution arrangement, method of pricing, level of promotion, whether to adapt the product, and so forth); and the ongoing management of their foreign export operations. These questions are considered in detail in Chapter 4.

Global Sourcing Strategy

The decision to import a good or service must be made in the context of whether it would be better to purchase locally or to produce the product oneself. A firm with a home-country orientation may not even consider the possibility of importing. Not surprising, larger firms tend to have an advantage over smaller ones because they possess more resources with which to assess the importing alternative.

An excellent set of production and sourcing decisions that firms confront would include:[4]

1. From where should the firm supply the target market?
2. To what extent should the firm *itself* undertake production (degree of integration)?
3. To the extent that it does not, what and where should it buy from others?
4. To the extent that a firm opts to do at least some manufacturing, how should it acquire facilities?
5. Should the firm produce in one plant or many, related or autonomous?

---

[4]See R. D. Robinson, *Internationalization of Business* (Chicago: The Dryden Press, 1984).

6. What sort of production equipment (technology) should it use?
7. What site is best?
8. Where should research and development be located?

Importing should be a significant area of investigation, yet even purchasing texts frequently devote only limited space to international considerations. Of all the parts in the internationalization process, either from an outward or inward perspective, importing may well be the most underresearched. Although there has been recent progress[5] much work remains. Chapter 5 deals with global sourcing strategy. It emphasizes logistical management of the interface of R&D, manufacturing, and marketing activities on a global basis.

Licensing

Our knowledge of international licensing is incomplete but growing. There are unresolved issues regarding the types of firms that license-out; the predominant industries that are involved; the revenues generated; the extent to which they consider alternatative modes; the countries they license to; whether they tend to consider it a stage in an internationalization process (or an end in itself); the costs of negotiating, administering, and policing license agreements; the frequency with which they lose proprietary advantages after licensing out; the most common terms in their license agreements; the areas in which there is the most disagreement; and so forth. Despite these limitations, we do know that firms license out their technology, trademarks, or other proprietary advantages in order to generate additional profits. Further, we know that licensing involves billions of dollars annually.

For the licensor, licensing is a chance to exploit its technology in markets that are too small to justify larger investments or in markets that restrict imports or FDI, or as a means of testing and developing a market. Firms are far more willing to license their peripheral technologies than their core technologies: no one wants to create a future competitor.

For the licensee, there are two principal advantages of licensing. The first is that it permits the acquisition of technology more cheaply than by internal development. Second, it allows the firm to acquire a technology that, when combined with other skills already present, permits it to diversify. It is important for technology buyers to (a) develop a minimum level of technical competence, (b) know their needs, and (c) consider alternative modes such as JVs.[6] This latter point is particularly relevant in the Cameron case.

While there are typically lower levels of commitment associated with a licensing strategy, there are nonetheless risks for both parties. For the licensor there are the risks of losing a technological advantage, reputation, and potential profits. For the licensee, there are the risks that the technology will not work as expected or will cost more to implement than anticipated. Chapter 6 provides an introduction to the whole area of licensing.

[5]See M. Leenders and D. Blenkhorn, *Reverse Marketing* (New York: The Free Press, 1988).

[6]See J. Peter Killing, "Technology Acquisition: License Agreement or Joint Venture?" *Columbia Journal of World Business,* Autumn 1980, pp. 38–46.

The Design and Management of International Joint Ventures

International joint ventures are alliances formed by organizations from two or more countries. They are formed for a variety of reasons: to mesh complementary skills from different organizations, to assure or speed market access, to leapfrog a technological gap, to strategically respond to more intense competition, and so forth.

Joint ventures do not have to be physically located outside your home country to be "international." For an American, for example, an auto plant in the United States co-owned by American and Japanese partners is an "international" joint venture. In fact, given differences in language, culture, and management practices, such a joint venture would have greater international complexity than, for example, an American-Canadian joint venture physically located in Canada.

Joint ventures are one of many forms of cooperation, each of which has unique characteristics in terms of (a) whether it is equity-based, (b) the length of the agreement, (c) whether a whole range of resources and rights is transferred, (d) the method of resource transfer, and (e) the typical compensation method (see Exhibit 1–6). As the cases note, many firms often overlook the potential use of alternative cooperative approaches.

Chapter 7 considers why companies create joint ventures as well as providing some guidelines for their successful design and management. This serves as a useful basis for the internationalization case study Nora-Sakari, which looks at a proposed alliance. While this and other cases deal with proposals, they differ significantly in terms of country, scale, alliance type, motives for formation, and partner choice.

Before any investment occurs—joint venture or otherwise—there is of course a need to be clear why the investment is occurring, why the particular market is being chosen, and whether now is the appropriate time (Exhibit 1–7). With these and the mode question resolved, we can consider the issues which more typically characterize the management of multinational enterprises.

International Strategy Formulation

Chapter 8 looks at how international firms formulate product-market strategy to maximize the international competitiveness of the firm. The chapter and cases examine the pressures that exist for the multinational firm both to achieve global efficiencies and to be locally responsive. These pressures are easy to understand but difficult to deal with simultaneously.

At the same time as managers identify the incentives to become more international, they begin to run up against the sovereign interests of the various countries they may wish to do business in. The local governments will often use regulations to further their own interests in such things as employment, where production occurs, development of local businesses, foreign exchange controls, and so forth. This orientation must be balanced against the multinational's interest in operating efficiently and coordinating its global activities.

If this were not enough, there are also pressures to adapt products to local conditions, perhaps organize to reflect a unique environment, and be generally responsive to the variety of differences that can exist between regions, countries, and cultures. Not surprisingly, subsidiary managers will often have very different ideas about how a subsidiary can best

EXHIBIT 1–6   A Typology of International Industrial Cooperation Modes*

Form of Cooperation	Equity or Nonequity	Length of Agreement	Transfer of Resources and Rights	Method of Transfer	Typical Compensation Method†
1. Wholly owned foreign subsidiaries	Equity	Unlimited	Whole range?	Internal to firm	Profits
2. Joint ventures	Equity	Unlimited	Whole range?	Internal to firm	Fraction of shares/dividends
3. Foreign minority holdings	Equity	Unlimited	Whole range?	Internal to firm	Fraction of shares/dividends
4. "Fade-out" agreements	Equity	Limited	Whole range? (for limited period)	Internal to firm changing to market	Fraction of shares/dividends
5. Licensing	Nonequity	Limited by contract	Limited range	Mixed**	Royalty as percent of sales
6. Franchising	Nonequity	Limited by contract	Limited + support	Market	Royalty as percent of sales and markups on components
7. Management contracts	Nonequity	Limited by contract	Limited	Market	Lump sum. Royalty.
8. Technical training	Nonequity	Limited	Small	Market	Lump sum
9. Turnkey ventures	Nonequity	Limited	Limited in time	Market	Lump sum
10. Contractual joint ventures	Nonequity	Limited	Specified by contract	Mixed	Function of the change in the costs and revenues of the venture, firm, or dominant partner
11. International subcontracting**	Nonequity	Limited	Small	Market	Markups
12. Strategic buyer-supplier coalitions**	Nonequity	Limited by contract but long-term	Limited + support	Mixed	Markups. Respective decreased costs/ increased revenues.

*Adapted from Peter J. Buckley and Mark Casson, *The Economic Theory of the Multinational Enterprise* (New York: St. Martin's Press, 1985), except where noted with double asterisk (**).

†Derived primarily from F. Contractor and P. Lorange, *Cooperative Strategies in International Business* (Lexington, MA: D. C. Heath, 1988).

be managed. These in turn must be reconciled with the headquarters perspective and sovereignty concerns. All of the cases dealing with multinational management can be reviewed from these three perspectives. As you would expect, substantial overlap often exists.

The Impact of Globalization on the Organization of Activities

A major reason for the rise of multinational enterprises is their demonstrated ability to organize business activities on a multicountry basis. Organization involves both geographic configuration and international coordination and integration.

EXHIBIT 1–7   But Before the Alliance...

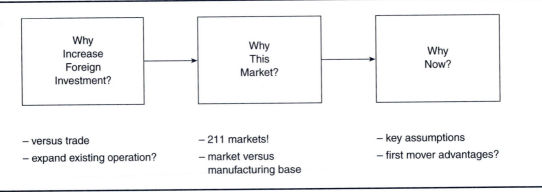

Chapter 9 introduces the organization structures through which international companies carry out their activities. The structures considered include the international division, area division, global product division, and the transnational option. Each structure represents a compromise—an attempt to balance the inherent strengths and weaknesses of the form chosen. Each structure must reconcile ease of administration with customer responsiveness, and parent company versus subsidiary perspectives. All of this must be done in the context of the sovereign concerns of different national governments, and sometimes widely different cultures.

The Evolving Multinational

Most multinationals undertake a series of foreign market entries over the course of years. Not surprisingly, they evolve in very different ways in order to reflect market complexity and the need to differentiate various subsidiaries.

The focus of Chapter 10 is on the evolving multinational enterprise. This evolving nature is considered along three dimensions: geographic, a line of business, and function. Insights are offered regarding factors that facilitate or impede evolution.

Emphasis then shifts to the ways in which evolution along these dimensions can be integrated. Of particular emphasis here is the way in which knowledge can be leveraged.

The Global Manager

Chapter 11 identifies and describes the skill set of the global manager. Effective global executives require the ability to develop and use global strategic skills, manage change and transition, manage cultural diversity, design and function in flexible organization structures, work with others and in teams, communicate, and learn and transfer knowledge in an organization. This list can be viewed as a daunting challenge—or a lifelong opportunity.

The process of developing managers with these abilities involves human resource management policies and the managing of international assignments. This in turn is linked to selection, training, and repatriation.

Managing Government Intervention

Chapter 12 looks at how to manage under conditions of both government regulation and government intervention, and at political risk. The first section reviews some of the major sources of trade regulation which affect both the exporter and the foreign investor. As such this chapter may be equally relevant at the time entry strategies are being considered.

The relationship between a nation's sovereignty (and what it deems as its "rightful interventions") and multinational enterprises continues to be an important one for international managers. The Enron Development Corporation case, for example, focuses on the implications of the cancellation of a multibillion-dollar power plant project in India.

The Global Leader

Finding people to lead (versus administer) the operations of multinational enterprises is the key challenge for international success. Most senior executives in the larger MNEs feel that there are both insufficient numbers of global leaders and too many leaders who do not possess the needed capabilities! This concluding chapter explores some of the strategies that can be used to develop global leaders, including the importance of travel, teams, training, and transfers.

Conclusion

The chapters and cases that follow deal with issues of both internationalization and ongoing multinational management. They are intended to help build an understanding of the impact of global competition; an appreciation for the various modes of involvement; and a sensitivity to, and experience with, international management.

Supplementary Reading

Anderson, O. "On the Internationalization Process of Firms: A Critical Analysis." *Journal of International Business Studies,* Vol. 24, No. 2, 1993.

Beamish, Paul W. "The Role of Alliances in International Entrepreneurship" in R. Wright (ed) *Research in Global Strategic Management,* Greenwich CT. JAI Press, (in press).

Calof, Jonathan, and Paul W. Beamish. "Adapting to Foreign Markets: Explaining Internationalization." *International Business Review,* Vol. 4, No. 2, 1995, pp.115–31.

Delios, Andrew, and Paul W. Beamish. "Geographic Scope, Product Diversification and the Corporate Performance of Japanese Firms." *Strategic Management Journal* (in press) 1999.

Eriksson, Kent, Jan Johanson, Anders Majkgård, and D. Deo Sharma. "Experiential Knowledge and Cost in the Internationalization Process." *Journal of International Business Studies,* Vol. 28, No. 2, 1997.

Forsgren, M. *Managing the Internationalization Process.* London: Routledge, 1989.

Johanson, Jan, and Jan-Erik Vahlne. "The Internationalization Process of the Firm—A Model of Knowledge Development and Increasing Foreign Market Commitments." *Journal of International Business Studies,* Spring-Summer 1977.

———. "The Mechanism of Internationalization." *International Marketing Review,* Vol. 7, No. 4, 1990, pp. 11–24.

Kogut, B., and H. Singh. "The Effect of National Culture on the Choice of Entry Mode." *Journal of International Business Studies,* Fall 1988.

Leenders, M., and D. Blenkhorn. *Reverse Marketing.* New York: The Free Press, 1988.

Ohmae, Kenichi. *Beyond National Borders.* Homewood, Ill.: Dow Jones-Irwin, 1987.

Reuber, A. R., and E. Fischer. "The Influence of the Management Team's International Experience on the Internationalisation Behavior of SMEs. " *Journal of International Business Studies,* Vol. 28, No. 4, 1997, pp. 807–25.

Robinson, Richard D. *Internationalization of Business.* Chicago: The Dryden Press, 1984.

Root, Franklin R. *Entry Strategies for International Markets.* Lexington, Mass.: Lexington Books, 1987.

Sullivan, Daniel. "Measuring the Degree of Internationalization of a Firm," *Journal of International Business Studies,* Vol. 25, No. 2, 1994, pp. 325–42

Welch, L. S., and R. Luostarinen. "Internationalization: Evolution of a Concept." *Journal of General Management,* Winter 1988.

2 THE GLOBAL BUSINESS ENVIRONMENT

Effective international management starts with a knowledge of key variables in the global economic environment. In any industry in any country, managers must have an overall knowledge of the wheres, whats, whys, and hows of the countries and regions of the world. This knowledge starts with the size and growth rates of country markets; their populations; their trade volumes, compositions, and growth rates; their natural resource bases and labor costs; and their financial positions. This knowledge can be used as an initial way to identify the threats and opportunities that might arise in their international operations. It can assist them to identify countries and regions to which they might export, from which they might import, and in which they might invest in production operations.

Although we live in the "information age," often we are ignorant of these basic facts: Which countries have the highest income (gross national product) per person in the world? Which are the 10 most populous countries in the world? Which countries with populations over five million grew the fastest over the past 10 years? Which countries have the largest markets? Which countries have the largest volumes of international trade? Which countries have had the highest growth rates in their trade volumes over the past decade? Which countries are among the top 10 as sources for foreign direct investment? As host countries?

The purpose of this chapter is to present data—population, GNP, purchasing power parity, and international trade statistics—to respond to some of these questions. It also highlights the problems and limitations of the data and shows how the data can be used by international managers to begin to address some of the basic decisions of international management. In subsequent chapters additional data on trade and foreign investment will be presented. It should be emphasized, however, that these publicly available data are only a start. Once the relevant publicly available data have been gathered, additional data often must be gathered, sometimes by first-hand research; all the data must be interpreted, and decisions reached using these data as inputs. There is the story of a salesperson who went to one country to

---

This chapter was prepared by Paul W. Beamish.

investigate the market for shoes. The summary of the trip report was: "No market here; no one wears shoes." Several years later another salesperson went to the same country. The summary of this trip was: "Huge market here; no one wears shoes."

Population

From a year 2000 base of six billion people, earth's population is expected to grow to 8.5 billion by the year 2025. These people are unevenly distributed, with over half the world's population in Asia Pacific countries and only 5 percent in North America. About one in six people are currently located in the 53 high-income countries where per capita GNP is $9,636 or more (Exhibit 2–1). This portion will drop to one in eight in the decades ahead. These population trends have enormous implications for global employment. For example, the current movement of high-volume, semiskilled manufacturing jobs from high-income to low-income countries can only increase. Real wages in low-income countries with large and/or fast-growing populations, such as India, the Philippines, Indonesia, Bangladesh, Kenya, Syria, and Nicaragua, will likely not rise dramatically. They will be low-wage countries into the foreseeable future. Exports of low-cost, labor-intensive products from these countries will continue to exert pressure on producers of competing products in high-income countries.

High population growth rates also have implications for the types of products that are and will be in demand. In 48 countries, 45 percent of the population is under the age of 15; in 62 countries, 3 percent or less of the population is over 65 years old. Conversely, in 24 countries, less than 25 percent of the population is less than 15 years old; and for 32 countries, at least 10 percent of the population is at least 65 years old.

Substantial variability exists among countries with respect to the concentration of the population within the country. In many African countries, over 90 percent of the population is in rural areas. In other countries—such as Singapore, England, Australia, the Netherlands, Venezuela, Uruguay, and Germany—over 85 percent of the population lives in urban areas. Urban concentrations provide an opportunity for international managers to focus their efforts on geographically concentrated consumers and access the country's labor force. Nowhere is this truer than in the metropolitan areas where the population exceeds 10 million: Mexico City, Tokyo-Yokohama, São Paulo, New York, Calcutta, Shanghai, Bombay, Jakarta, Manila, Buenos Aires, Seoul, Rio de Janeiro, Los Angeles, and London. Beyond the concentration of the population in urban centers are the growth rates of these centers. In 15 countries, the urban population is growing faster than 6 percent per year. These high growth rates have implications for growth in demand for products and services to support the infrastructure, such as equipment and services to provide electricity, housing, roads, transportation, telecommunications, and all types of environmental cleanup. On the other hand, they have implications for the availability of urban labor.

One of the trends of the last decades is the increasing number of people who go abroad to find jobs and to increase incomes. Over 80 million people work outside their home country. International migration of this magnitude has a major impact on overall trade and balance of payments when the funds that workers remit to their home countries are considered. For example, the World Bank has estimated that Filipino workers abroad remit $8 billion per year, compared to exports of about $13.5 billion.

EXHIBIT 2–1   Statistics on 211 Countries

Economy	Population Thousands 1997	GNP $ Millions 1997[a]	GNP per Capita $ 1997[a]	GNP per Capita PPP[b] International $ 1997	GNP per Capita Average Annual Real Growth % 1990–97
Afghanistan	24,965	..	..[c]	..	..
Albania	3,324	2,540	760	2,170[d]	2.2
Algeria	29,318	43,927	1,500	4,250[d]	−1.6
American Samoa	62	..	..[e]	..	..
Andorra	64	..	..[f]	..	..
Angola	11,659	3,012	260	820[d]	−10.0
Antigua and Barbuda	66	489	7,380	8,650	1.8
Argentina	35,677	319,293	8,950	10,100	4.2
Armenia	3,787	2,112	560	2,540	−10.7
Aruba	89	..	..[f]	..	−0.6
Australia	18,532	382,705	20,650	19,510	2.4
Austria	8,072	225,373	27,920	22,010	1.1
Azerbaijan	7,600	3,886	510	1,520	−16.0
Bahamas, The	289	..	..[f]	..	−2.0
Bahrain	620	..	..[e]	..	2.6
Bangladesh	123,633	44,090	360	1,090	3.3
Barbados	265	..	..[e]	..	−0.9
Belarus	10,267	22,082	2,150	4,820	−5.6
Belgium	10,190	272,382	26,730	23,090	1.3
Belize	230	614	2,670	4,080	0.3
Benin	5,796	2,227	380	1,260	1.7
Bermuda	63	..	..[f]	..	..
Bhutan	737	315	430	..	2.0
Bolivia	7,767	7,564	970	2,810	2.0
Bosnia and Herzegovina	2,346	..	..[c]	..	..
Botswana	1,533	5,070	3,310	7,430	1.3
Brazil	163,689	784,044	4,790	6,350	1.9
Brunei	308	..	..[f]	..	−2.1
Bulgaria	8,312	9,750	1,170	3,870	−2.0
Burkina Faso	10,474	2,579	250	1,000[d]	0.8
Burundi	6,435	924	140	620[d]	−5.9
Cambodia	10,480	3,162	300	1,290[d]	2.7
Cameroon	13,936	8,610	620	1,770	−3.3
Canada	30,287	594,976	19,640	21,750	0.8
Cape Verde	401	436	1,090	2,950[d]	1.0
Cayman Islands	36	..	..[f]	..	..
Central African Republic	3,418	1,104	320	1,310[d]	−1.0
Chad	7,153	1,629	230	950[d]	1.0
Channel Islands	148	..	..[f]	..	..
Chile	14,622	70,510	4,820	12,240	6.4
China	1,227,177	1,055,372	860	3,070	10.0
Hong Kong, China	6,502	163,834	25,200	24,350	3.3
Colombia	40,042	87,125	2,180	6,570	2.6
Comoros	518	209	400	1,530[d]	−3.1
Congo, Dem. Rep.	46,709	5,201	110	760[d]	−9.6

EXHIBIT 2–1   *(continued)*

Economy	Population *Thousands* *1997*	GNP *$ Millions* *1997ᵃ*	GNP per Capita		
			$ *1997ᵃ*	*PPPᵇ* *International* *$ 1997*	*Average* *Annual Real* *Growth* *% 1990–97*
Congo, Rep.	2,708	1,827	670	1,290	−2.9
Costa Rica	3,464	9,275	2,680	6,510	2.3
Côte d'Ivoire	14,211	10,152	710	1,690	0.9
Croatia	4,768	19,343	4,060	4,930	2.7
Cuba	11,059	..	..ʰ	..	..
Cyprus	747	..	..ᶠ	..	2.6
Czech Republic	10,304	53,952	5,240	10,380	−0.3
Denmark	5,284	184,347	34,890	23,450	2.5
Djibouti	636	..	..ʰ	..	..
Dominica	74	225	3,040	4,020	0.7
Dominican Republic	8,107	14,148	1,750	4,690	3.5
Ecuador	11,937	18,785	1,570	4,700	0.9
Egypt, Arab. Rep.	60,348	72,164	1,200	3,080	2.8
El Salvador	5,928	10,704	1,810	2,860	3.5
Equatorial Guinea	420	444	1,060	..	12.1
Eritrea	3,773	852	230	1,040ᵈ	2.9
Estonia	1,458	4,899	3,360	5,090	−2.8
Ethiopia	59,750	6,507	110	500	2.2
Faeroe Islands	44	..	..ᶠ	..	..
Fiji	815	2,007	2,460	3,860	0.4
Finland	5,140	127,398	24,790	19,660	0.9
France	58,607	1,541,630	26,300	22,210	1.0
French Guiana	157	..	..ᶠ	..	..
French Polynesia	224	..	..ᶠ	..	..
Gabon	1,153	4,752	4,120	6,560	−0.1
Gambia, The	1,181	407	340	1,440ᵈ	−0.6
Georgia	5,427	4,656	860	1,980	−14.9
Germany	82,071	2,320,985	28,280	21,170	0.7
Ghana	17,985	6,982	390	1,610ᵈ	1.4
Greece	10,522	122,430	11,640	12,540	1.0
Greenland	56	..	..ᶠ	..	..
Grenada	96	300	3,140	4,760	1.3
Guadeloupe	427	..	..ᵉ	..	..
Guam	146	..	..ᶠ	..	..
Guatemala	10,519	16,582	1,580	4,060	1.5
Guinea	6,920	3,830	550	1,790	2.7
Guinea-Bissau	1,137	264	230	..	1.0
Guyana	848	677	800	2,800ᵈ	12.9
Haiti	7,492	2,864	380	1,260ᵈ	−4.4
Honduras	5,986	4,426	740	2,260	1.0
Hungary	10,155	45,760	4,510	6,970	0.2
Iceland	271	..	..ᶠ	..	0.4
India	962,378	357,391	370	1,660	4.3
Indonesia	200,390	221,533	1,110	3,390	5.9

EXHIBIT 2–1 *(continued)*

Economy	Population Thousands 1997	GNP $ Millions 1997[a]	GNP per Capita		
			$ 1997[a]	PPP[b] International $ 1997	Average Annual Real Growth % 1990–97
Iran, Islamic Rep.	60,929	108,614	1,780	5,690	1.9
Iraq	21,847	..	..[h]	..	..
Ireland	3,661	65,137	17,790	17,420	5.6
Isle of Man	76	..	..[e]	..	..
Israel	5,836	94,402	16,180	17,680	2.6
Italy	57,523	1,160,444	20,170	20,100	1.0
Jamaica	2,554	3,956	1,550	3,330	0.8
Japan	126,091	4,812,103	38,160	24,400	1.4
Jordan	4,437	6,755	1,520	3,350	2.8
Kazakhstan	15,801	21,317	1,350	3,530	−7.4
Kenya	28,612	9,654	340	1,160	−0.3
Kiribati	83	76	910	..	−0.6
Korea, Dem. Rep.	22,893	..	..[h]	..	..
Korea, Rep.	45,991	485,209	10,550	13,430	6.0
Kuwait	1,809	..	..[f]	..	17.5
Kyrgyz Republic	4,635	2,211	480	2,180	−9.7
Lao PDR	4,849	1,924	400	1,300	3.9
Latvia	2,465	5,995	2,430	3,970	−7.3
Lebanon	4,146	13,900	3,350	6,090	4.9
Lesotho	2,014	1,368	680	2,490[d]	2.5
Liberia	2,886	..	..[c]	..	..
Libya	5,201	..	..[e]	..	..
Liechtenstein	31	..	..[f]	..	..
Lithuania	3,706	8,360	2,260	4,140	−7.1
Luxembourg	422	..	..[f]	..	0.2
Macao	448	..	..[f]	..	..
Macedonia, FYR	1,997	2,187	1,100	3,180[d]	−2.1
Madagascar	14,148	3,575	250	900	−1.6
Malawi	10,276	2,129	210	700	0.8
Malaysia	21,667	98,195	4,530	7,730	5.8
Maldives	256	301	1,180	3,340[d]	4.3
Mali	10,290	2,656	260	720	0.3
Malta	375	3,498	9,330	13,380[d]	3.0
Marshall Islands	60	97	1,610	..	..
Martinique	393	..	..[f]	..	..
Mauritania	2,461	1,093	440	1,650[d]	1.5
Mauritius	1,148	4,444	3,870	9,230	3.7
Mayotte	108	..	..[e]	..	..
Mexico	94,349	348,627	3,700	8,110[d]	0.2
Micronesia, Fed. Sts.	111	213	1,920	..	−1.8
Moldova	4,312	1,974	460	1,450	−10.8
Monaco	32	..	..[f]	..	..
Mongolia	2,542	998	390	1,490[d]	−1.4
Morocco	27,310	34,380	1,260	3,210	0.2

EXHIBIT 2–1   *(continued)*

Economy	Population Thousands 1997	GNP $ Millions 1997[a]	GNP per Capita $ 1997[a]	GNP per Capita PPP[b] International $ 1997	GNP per Capita Average Annual Real Growth % 1990–97
Mozambique	16,630	2,405	140	690[d]	2.6
Myanmar	43,893	..	..[c]	..	..
Namibia	1,623	3,428	2,110	5,100[d]	1.1
Nepal	22,321	4,863	220	1,090	2.2
Netherlands	15,607	403,057	25,830	21,300	1.9
Netherlands Antilles	210	..	..[f]	..	..
New Caledonia	202	..	..[f]	..	..
New Zealand	3,761	59,539	15,830	15,780	1.2
Nicaragua	4,677	1,907	410	1,820[d]	1.6
Niger	9,799	1,962	200	830[d]	−1.9
Nigeria	117,897	33,393	280	860	0.7
Northern Mariana Islands	54	..	..[f]	..	..
Norway	4,404	158,973	36,100	24,260	3.8
Oman	2,256	..	..[e]	..	−0.4
Pakistan	128,457	64,638	500	1,580	2.0
Palau	17	..	..[e]	..	..
Panama	2,719	8,373	3,080	6,890	3.0
Papua New Guinea	4,501	4,185	930	..	2.5
Paraguay	5,085	10,183	2,000	3,860	0.0
Peru	24,371	63,672	2,610	4,580	4.6
Philippines	73,527	88,372	1,200	3,670	1.6
Poland	38,650	138,909	3,590	6,510	4.2
Portugal	9,945	109,472	11,010	14,180	2.0
Puerto Rico	3,827	..	..[e]	..	..
Qatar	721	..	..[f]	..	−5.3
Reunion	678	..	..[f]	..	..
Romania	22,554	31,787	1,410	4,270	−0.1
Russian Federation	147,307	394,861	2,680	4,280	−7.9
Rwanda	7,895	1,680	210	650	−5.7
Samoa	174	199	1,140	3,570[d]	0.7
São TomJ and Principe	138	40	290	..	−1.7
Saudi Arabia	20,066	143,430	7,150	10,540[d]	−2.5
Senegal	8,790	4,777	540	1,690	0.0
Seychelles	78	537	6,910	..	1.7
Sierra Leone	4,748	762	160	410	−5.7
Singapore	3,104	101,834	32,810	29,230	6.7
Slovak Republic	5,383	19,801	3,680	7,860	0.3
Slovenia	1,986	19,550	9,840	11,880	4.2
Solomon Islands	403	350	870	2,270[d]	1.0
Somalia	8,775	..	..[c]	..	..
South Africa	40,604	130,151	3,210	7,190[d]	−0.2
Spain	39,323	569,637	14,490	15,690	1.3
Sri Lanka	18,552	14,781	800	2,460	4.0
St. Kitts and Nevis	41	256	6,260	7,770	4.0
St. Lucia	159	558	3,510	5,030	2.8

EXHIBIT 2–1   *(concluded)*

Economy	Population Thousands 1997	GNP $ Millions 1997[a]	GNP per Capita $ 1997[a]	GNP per Capita PPP[b] International $ 1997	Average Annual Real Growth % 1990–97
St. Vincent & the Grenadines	112	272	2,420	4,060	1.8
Sudan	27,737	7,917	290	1,370[d]	3.7
Suriname	412	544	1,320	..	−0.5
Swaziland	958	1,458	1,520	3,690	−0.6
Sweden	8,849	231,905	26,210	19,010	0.2
Switzerland	7,088	305,238	43,060	26,580	−0.5
Syrian Arab Republic	14,895	16,643	1,120	3,000	3.3
Taiwan	21,800	285,259[i]	13,233	..	5.7
Tajikistan	6,017	2,010	330	1,100	−16.1
Tanzania	31,316	6,632	210	620	0.9
Thailand	60,602	165,759	2,740	6,490	5.9
Togo	4,345	1,485	340	1,460[d]	−1.2
Tonga	98	177	1,810	..	1.4
Trinidad and Tobago	1,307	5,553	4,250	6,460	0.5
Tunisia	9,215	19,433	2,110	5,050	2.0
Turkey	63,745	199,307	3,130	6,470	2.3
Turkmenistan	4,658	2,987	640	1,410	−14.6
Uganda	20,317	6,608	330	1,160[d]	4.4
Ukraine	50,698	52,625	1,040	2,170	−12.6
United Arab Emirates	2,580	..	..[f]	..	−3.8
United Kingdom	59,009	1,231,269	20,870	20,710	1.9
United States	267,636	7,783,092	29,080	29,080	1.7
Uruguay	3,266	20,035	6,130	9,110	3.5
Uzbekistan	23,667	24,236	1,020	..	−5.6
Vanuatu	177	238	1,340	3,230 d	−3.5
Venezuela	22,777	79,317	3,480	8,660	−0.2
Vietnam	76,711	24,008	310	1,590	6.1
Virgin Islands (U.S.)	117	..	..[f]	..	..
West Bank and Gaza	2,570	..	..[h]	..	..
Yemen, Rep.	16,072	4,405	270	720	−1.5
Yugoslavia, FR (Serb./Mont.)	10,614	..	..[h]	..	..
Zambia	9,443	3,536	370	910	−0.9
Zimbabwe	11,468	8,208	720	2,240	−0.7

.. Not available

Note: Figures in italics are for years other than those specified; 0 or 0.0 means zero or less than half the unit shown and not known more precisely.

[a]Calculated using the World Bank Atlas method.

[b]Purchasing power parity.

[c]Estimated to be low income ($785 or less).

[d]Estimate is based on regression; others are extrapolated from the latest International Comparison Programme survey.

[e]Estimated to be upper middle income ($3,126 to $9,655).

[f]Estimated to be high income ($9,656 or more).

[g]Data for GNP are GDP.

[h]Estimated to be lower middle income ($786 to $3,125).

[i]1997 figures. Source: Taipei Economic and Cultural Office.

Countries

The 1991 *World Bank Atlas* provided statistics on 185 countries and territories. The 1999 *World Bank Atlas* provided statistics on 210 countries and territories. Country proliferation is relevant not just to mapmakers and statisticians. It has obvious and immediate implications for multinational enterprises and international traders and their need to coordinate with national governments, to define territorial scope of operations, to analyze foreign exchange rates, and so forth.

Country proliferation seems likely to continue. In 1993, the Czechoslovakian federation was split into the Czech Republic and Slovakia. Yugoslavia now comprises a variety of countries. Separatist elements exist in many of the countries of Africa and Asia, such as Indonesia, the Philippines, and India. Whether due to differences in culture, ethnic origin, language, or religion, this trend complicates the life of the international manager.

Beyond the proliferation in the number of countries, many countries are also highly diverse in terms of religion, ethnic groups, language, and income level. This diversity has implications for effective management practices in all the functional areas as well as general management in many countries. The department of geodesy and cartography of the state geological committee of the Russian Academy of Sciences has devised an "Ethnic and Linguistic Homogeneity Index" of most of the countries of the world. The index ranges from 100 for North and South Korea to 7 for Tanzania. This index gives some idea of the diversity facing international managers within each country.[1]

Economic Development

Global economic activity continues to be dominated by a small number of countries. Yet the ranks of the traditional G7 nations (the United States, Japan, Germany, France, Italy, United Kingdom, Canada), the countries with the largest economies as measured by GNP, are under challenge. As of 1997, when measured using purchasing power parity, China, Indonesia, India, Mexico, and Brazil have economies that are larger than that of Canada and some of the other G7 countries.

The economic figures for many countries can serve as a useful approximation of reality, while for others they are notoriously inaccurate. Some countries intentionally understate their GNP to attract development aid. Others simply have poor tracking mechanisms. As well, wars and insurrections can dramatically reduce—or increase—economic activity.

The data on GNP are designed to capture the volume of goods and services produced and consumed in a country. Hence, GNP is a first rough measure of market size. In 1997, the GNP of countries ranged from $7.8 trillion for the United States to $4.8 trillion for Japan, $2.3 trillion for Germany, down to $40 million for São Tomé and Principe.

Beyond the *size* of an economy, its growth rate is also important, since it signals the speed at which markets are growing. Many of the fastest-growing economies continue to be concentrated on the Asia-Pacific Rim. The "Asian flu" of the late 1990s did not uniformly

---

[1]See *The New Book of World Rankings* and *The CIA World Factbook* (referenced at the end of this chapter) for these and other interesting statistics.

affect every country in the region. And many of the slowest-growing economies continue to be concentrated on the African continent. Many of the economies that have experienced negative growth have been concentrated in central and eastern Europe. Within the geographical regions, however, growth is far from uniform.

GDP (or GNP) per capita figures can give an indication of the income levels of countries. Income levels in turn can indicate the types of products that may be in demand and wage levels. These figures must be interpreted with care, however. They have three major faults. GNP is a measure of the goods and services that are produced by the economy and sold via the market *as recorded by the government.* For developing countries, many goods and services are produced for self-consumption or bartered. Government reporting systems often do not record these transactions or the transactions of small producers. The so-called subculture economies (SCEs) often include indigenous peoples, people who do not participate in the official economy, people who produce mostly for themselves and their families, and those working under ill-structured manufacturing environments (for example, producers of handicrafts, cultural products, handmade clothing, and so on). In some countries, 20 to 30 percent of the population works in the SCE. A similar problem exists to a lesser extent in many high-income countries.

In addition to the SCE, the production and consumption of illegal goods and services are not reported to the government, and, hence, do not appear in GNP statistics. Neither does production and consumption of goods and services that are not reported to the government in order to avoid sales and income taxes. Studies of several countries estimate that this "underground economy" may equal as much as 20 to 30 percent of reported GNP.

A second problem arises when GNP is compared among countries. The GNP of the United States is expressed in dollars, that of Japan in yen, Germany in deutsche marks, and so on. Comparisons need to be made using a common measure. Most often a country's GNP in domestic currency is converted into U.S. dollars *at the prevailing exchange rate* (or using an average of the past several years). But unless the exchange rate is maintained at its long-run equilibrium value, this conversion can give misleading results. For example, from 1990 to 1994 the Philippine peso rose from 28 per dollar to 24.5 per dollar and the Philippine GNP in pesos rose from 1,077 billion to 1,694 billion. These numbers led to a rise in GNP (expressed in dollars) from $38 billion to $66.4 billion, a 75 percent increase in GNP and a 60 percent increase in GNP per capita in just four years. If U.S. inflation over this period of a total of about 15 percent is subtracted to give real growth expressed in dollars, these numbers are reduced to 60 percent and 45 percent. Yet real growth in the Philippine GNP and GNP per capita *totalled* 10.4 percent and 1.4 percent, respectively, over this period. The problem here and in other intercountry comparisons is that the real exchange rate of the Philippines appreciated by about 50 percent over the period.[2]

The final problem is that prices for the same product may not be the same among countries when expressed in a common currency. If a cup of coffee costs 5 cents in India and 5 dollars in Japan, one cup of coffee produced in India would add 5 cents to GNP, but the same cup of coffee produced in Japan would add 5 dollars to Japan's GNP. This effect lowers the GNP (and, hence, the GNP per capita) figures for countries with low prices relative to ones

---

[2]See Chapter 3 for a description of the real exchange rate. This has particularly important implications in periods of rapid fluctuations. For example, in early 1999 the Philippine peso had declined to 38 per dollar.

with high prices. This problem can be addressed by restating GNP figures of each country with the same prices for all goods and services. This method is called the purchasing power parity (PPP). If PPP is applied to relatively expensive high-income countries, it usually leads to a fall in reported GNP per capita. Using 1997 data, the GNP per capita of Switzerland on a PPP basis was $26,580 compared to $43,060 using the standard method. This implies that goods and services in Switzerland were on average 48 percent more expensive than in the United States.[3] When the price differences are removed, Switzerland's GNP falls by 62 percent. Using the PPP, in 1997, U.S. GNP per capita of $29,080 was the second highest in the world (after Singapore) among countries with populations over one million, followed by Switzerland, Japan, and Hong Kong. Conversely, the GNP per capita levels of low-income countries are raised under the PPP method, in some cases by as much as much as a factor of six.

The PPP method also addresses the problem of changing exchange rates, since it uses common prices in all countries. GNP measured at PPP gives a more realistic measure of the size of a country's markets and its income levels. Notice that it leads to a compression of the range of GNP per capita figures, i.e., the income gap between the richest and the poorest countries is reduced, as is the gap between the incomes of high income countries.

A word of caution is necessary here. The PPP method uses cost comparisons for *average* consumers. It is not an appropriate measure to use when considering overseas operations or the living expenses of expatriate managers. For example, China's GNP per capita in 1997 as reported by the World Bank was $860 and its PPP GNP per capita was $3,070. This implies a price differential of nearly four times. Yet, for an expatriate manager living in Beijing compared with costs in Des Moines, Iowa, housing, car, food, and education expenses are all substantially higher, with only a few items being markedly less expensive.

Beyond the average level of income, the distribution of income around this level also has important implications for international management. China's reported GNP per capita was $860 in 1997. Even adjusting for purchasing power parity to $3,070, China still appears to have a low level of income and, hence, little demand for luxury products. Yet Shanghai traffic is chronically jammed, and in the jam are a high proportion of luxury automobiles.

Growth in GNP and GNP per capita reflects rising demand and rising income levels and, hence, market opportunities. These growth figures are usually more accurate than the data on the levels themselves. Increasing demand not only makes a country more attractive as a trade destination or investment site, it may also facilitate entry. Existing suppliers may face capacity constraints. Sales by a new competitor, although reducing the market shares of existing firms, may not reduce their absolute sales volumes. Hence, competitive reaction may be muted.

Some firms have been more astute than others at responding to the changing income levels in certain countries. Phillips has the major share of the electric lamps sold in Indonesia. As electricity is extended into the countryside, it has introduced 15-watt bulbs priced at less than half the price of its 100-watt bulbs (even though the delivered cost is almost

---

[3]The news magazine *The Economist* regularly publishes its "Big Mac Index," which compares prices of a Big Mac among a number of countries as a measure of relative prices. Switzerland regularly has the highest-priced Big Macs, when converted to dollars, suggesting it is the most overvalued currency.

the same) to fit the income levels, demand characteristics, and voltage levels in these areas. Over time, it introduces higher-priced, higher wattage bulbs as income levels rise and as the people become accustomed to using (Phillips) electric lighting.

To this point, the analysis has been based on the *past* performance of the economy. This analysis is useful for many purposes, such as market size, income distribution, and wage rates. But as with many areas of business management and strategy, some indications of future performance are also useful. Forecasting growth has proven to be difficult at best for economists. Two organizations, the World Economic Forum and the Institute for Management Development, each construct a "World Competitiveness Report," which rank countries based on hundreds of factors that are thought to contribute to future growth. The overall rankings for each are in Exhibit 2–2. There are some significant differences between the two sets

EXHIBIT 2–2   World Competitiveness Rankings

Economy	World Economic Forum Ranking	IMD Ranking	Economy	World Economic Forum Ranking	IMD Ranking
Singapore	1	2	China	28	24
Hong Kong SAR	2	3	Israel	29	25
United States	3	1	Iceland	30	19
United Kingdom	4	12	Indonesia	31	40
Canada	5	10	Mexico	32	34
Taiwan	6	16	Philippines	33	32
Netherlands	7	4	Jordan	34	—
Switzerland	8	7	Czech Republic	35	38
Norway	9	6	Argentina	36	31
Luxembourg	10	9	Peru	37	—
Ireland	11	11	Egypt	38	—
Japan	12	18	Vietnam	39	—
New Zealand	13	13	Turkey	40	33
Australia	14	15	Italy	41	30
Finland	15	5	South Africa	42	42
Denmark	16	8	Hungary	43	28
Malaysia	17	20	Greece	44	36
Chile	18	26	Venezuela	45	43
Korea	19	35	Brazil	46	37
Austria	20	22	Colombia	47	44
Thailand	21	39	Slovakia	48	—
France	22	21	Poland	49	45
Sweden	23	17	India	50	41
Germany	24	14	Zimbabwe	51	—
Spain	25	27	Russia	52	46
Portugal	26	29	Ukraine	53	—
Belgium	27	23			

Note: The World Economic Forum ranked 53 countries; IMD ranked 46 countries.

Sources: World Economic Forum, *The Global Competitiveness Report 1998.* IMD, *The World Competitiveness Yearbook 1998.*

of rankings: the UK is ranked fourth by one method, twelfth in the other; Canada is fifth in one ranking, tenth in another; Japan is twelfth in one ranking, eighteenth in the other. But there is a rough correspondence between the two rankings. Beyond these overall rankings, the two reports also rank countries based on natural resource availability, labor costs and quality, political stability, tax rates, and so on. These reports can provide a wealth of data on current and future economic conditions in many countries in the world.

Overall economic development has improved dramatically in the past 25 years—including the standard of living in the developing countries. Per capita incomes have grown nearly one and a half percent per year for the five billion people in the developing countries. This has brought real progress in the quality of life: infant mortality has dropped, life expectancy has risen, primary school enrollments and adult literacy have improved, food production growth has exceeded population growth, and so forth.

None of this is to suggest that there is not still substantial need for further economic development. Arguably the world's greatest scandal is that over a billion people in the developing world live in extreme poverty—subsisting on less than $1.00 a day. Since "a rising tide *does* float all boats," the effective international manager can have a positive impact on this situation.

Trade, Natural Resources, and Foreign Investment

An analysis of the trade volumes, growth rates, composition, and destinations and sources can provide useful insights into emerging sources of supply, shifting comparative and competitive advantage, and new markets. Trade as a percentage of GNP is very important to some countries, such as Hong Kong, Ireland, the Netherlands, and Taiwan.[4] For other countries—particularly those with large domestic markets such as the United States, Japan, and Brazil—trade as a percentage of GNP is much lower. Over the past decade, growth in trade has been highest in many of the countries of the Asia-Pacific Rim and has stagnated in many of the countries of Africa (see Exhibit 2–3).

By the mid-1990s, the United States still accounted for the largest share of world merchandise trade, with approximately 12.6 percent of world exports and 16.2 percent of world imports, followed by Germany and Japan (Exhibit 2–3). The United States also had by far the largest share of world trade in commercial services (Exhibit 2–4). Over the past two decades, the trade exposure of the United States, defined as exports plus imports as a percentage of GDP, has increased. But by the mid-1990s, the trade exposure of the United States was still below that of most major countries.

Over the past decades, there have been three trends in the trade of manufactured products. The volume of trade in manufactured products has risen dramatically. The number of source countries has risen as well. And the composition of the trade of many countries has

---

[4]Again there is a problem with these figures. International trade takes place in international currencies. Hence there is *not* a problem with understating it or overstating it based on differing prices, the PPP problem described above. GDP and GNP figures, however, are over- and understated because of differing prices. This tends to overstate the trade exposure of low-cost, usually developing, countries and understate the trade exposure of high-cost countries such as Switzerland and Japan.

EXHIBIT 2–3   Leading Exporters and Importers in World Merchandise Trade, 1997
($ billions and percentage)

Rank				1997		Rank				1997	
1990	*1993*	*1997*	*Exporters*	*Value*	*Share*	*1990*	*1993*	*1997*	*Importers*	*Value*	*Share*
2	1	1	United States	$688.7	12.6%	1	1	1	United States	899.0	16.2%
1	2	2	Germany	511.7	9.4	2	2	2	Germany	441.4	7.8
3	3	3	Japan	421.0	7.7	3	3	3	Japan	338.7	6.0
4	4	4	France	289.5	5.3	5	4	4	United Kingdom	308.2	5.5
5	5	5	United Kingdom	281.6	5.2	4	5	5	France	268.4	4.8
6	6	6	Italy	238.2	4.4	12	9	6	Hong Kong	213.3	3.8
8	7	7	Canada	214.4	3.9	6	7	7	Italy	208.1	3.7
7	8	8	Netherlands	193.8	3.5	8	6	8	Canada	200.9	3.6
11	10	9	Hong Kong	188.2	3.4	7	8	9	Netherlands	177.2	3.4
15	12	10	China	182.7	3.3	10	10	10	Belgium-Luxembourg	155.8	2.8
9	9	11	Belgium-Luxembourg	168.2	3.1	14	13	11	Korea	144.6	2.6
13	11	12	Korea	136.2	2.5	18	11	12	China	142.4	2.5
18	14	13	Singapore	125.0	2.3	15	12	13	Singapore	132.4	2.4
12	15	14	Taiwan	121.9	2.2	11	14	14	Spain	122.7	2.1
21	17	15	Mexico	110.4	2.0	21	16	15	Mexico	113.2	2.0
17	16	16	Spain	104.3	1.9	16	17	16	Taiwan	113.2	2.0
16	18	17	Sweden	82.7	1.5	24	40	17	Malaysia	79.0	1.4
26	19	18	Malaysia	78.4	1.4	13	15	18	Switzerland	76.0	1.3
14	13	19	Switzerland	76.2	1.4	20	19	19	Australia	65.9	1.2
20	21	20	Russia	66.3	1.2	17	20	20	Sweden	65.4	1.2
22	22	21	Australia	62.9	1.2	30	27	21	Brazil	65.0	1.2
20	23	22	Austria	58.6	1.1	19	18	22	Austria	64.8	1.2
31	27	23	Thailand	57.4	1.1	22	21	23	Thailand	63.6	1.1
28	26	24	Indonesia	53.5	1.0	9	22	24	Russia	48.8	.9
29	29	25	Ireland	53.1	1.0	31	23	25	Turkey	48.6	.9
25	24	26	Brazil	53.0	1.0	23	24	26	Denmark	44.6	.8
19	20	27	Saudi Arabia	52.8	1.0	—	36	27	Poland	42.3	.8
25	25	28	Denmark	48.9	.9	32	25	28	Indonesia	42.0	.7
24	28	29	Norway	47.7	.9	29	28	29	India	40.4	.7
27	31	30	Finland	40.8	.7	33	31	30	Ireland	39.2	.7
35	32	31	India	33.9	.6	—	35	31	Philippines	38.0	.7
30	30	32	South Africa	30.3	.6	26	29	32	Norway	35.5	.6
—	34	33	Turkey	26.2	.5	27	30	33	Portugal	33.5	.6
38	38	34	Poland	25.8	.5	37	34	34	South Africa	32.9	.6
—	39	35	Argentina	25.5	.5	38	32	35	Israel	30.8	.5
—	—	36	Philippines	25.3	.5	25	37	36	Finland	30.7	.5
—	—	37	United Arab Emirates	25.0	.5	—	39	37	Argentina	30.3	.5
38	35	38	Portugal	23.2	.4	—	—	38	United Arab Emirates	27.8	.5
36	37	39	Venezuela	23.1	.4	28	26	39	Saudi Arabia	27.3	.5
—	—	40	Czech. Rep.	22.8	.4	—	—	40	Czech. Rep.	27.2	.5
			Total	$5,069.2	92.8%				Total	$5,079.1	90.2%
			World	$5,464.0	100.0%				World	$5,630.0	100.0%

Sources: WTO, *Annual Report 1998.* World Bank, *World Tables,* 1995.

EXHIBIT 2–4   **Leading Exporters and Importers in World Trade in Commercial Services, 1997 ($ billions and percentage)**

Rank (1990)	Rank (1993)	Rank (1997)	Exporters	1997 Value	1997 Share	Rank (1990)	Rank (1993)	Rank (1997)	Importers	1997 Value	1997 Share
1	1	1	United States	$229.9	17.5%	2	1	1	United States	$150.1	11.6
3	4	2	United Kingdom	85.5	6.5	1	2	1	Japan	122.1	9.4
2	3	3	France	80.3	6.1	3	5	3	Germany	120.1	9.3
4	5	4	Germany	75.4	5.7	6	7	4	Italy	70.1	5.4
6	7	5	Italy	71.7	5.5	5	4	5	United Kingdom	68.6	5.3
5	2	6	Japan	68.1	5.2	4	3	6	France	62.1	4.8
7	8	7	Netherlands	48.5	3.7	7	10	7	Netherlands	43.9	3.4
8	10	8	Spain	43.6	3.3	9	13	8	Canada	35.9	2.8
14	18	9	Hong Kong	37.3	2.8	8	6	9	Belgium-Luxembourg	32.1	2.5
9	6	10	Belgium-Luxembourg	34.0	2.6	33	23	10	China	30.0	2.3
13	13	11	Singapore	30.4	2.3	19	21	11	Korea	29.0	2.2
12	14	12	Canada	29.3	2.2	18	14	12	Austria	27.4	2.1
10	11	13	Austria	28.5	2.2	11	12	13	Spain	24.3	1.9
11	9	14	Switzerland	25.6	2.0	13	9	14	Taiwan	24.1	1.9
19	17	15	Korea	25.4	1.9	22	30	15	Hong Kong	22.7	1.8
27	20	16	China	24.5	1.9	10	15	16	Sweden	19.5	1.5
23	24	17	Turkey	19.2	1.5	23	8	17	Singapore	19.4	1.5
20	19	18	Australia	18.2	1.4	30	20	18	Brazil	19.0	1.5
15	15	19	Sweden	17.6	1.3	—	26	19	Russia	18.7	1.4
22	16	20	Taiwan	17.0	1.3	15	17	20	Australia	18.2	1.4
21	22	21	Thailand	15.9	1.2	25	25	21	Thailand	17.2	1.3
32	29	22	Philippines	15.1	1.2	26	28	22	Malaysia	16.8	1.3
31	30	23	Malaysia	14.5	1.1	—	24	23	Indonesia	16.1	1.2
17	21	24	Norway	14.2	1.1	37	27	24	Ireland	15.0	1.2
—	34	25	Russia	13.5	1.0	17	22	25	Norway	14.5	1.1
18	23	26	Mexico	11.2	0.9	12	16	26	Switzerland	14.1	1.1
25	28	27	Egypt	9.6	0.7	—	—	27	Philippines	14.1	1.1
30	31	28	Israel	8.3	0.6	16	18	28	Saudi Arabia	13.9	1.1
36	37	29	Brazil	7.9	0.6	21	19	29	Mexico	11.5	0.9
28	27	30	Portugal	7.5	0.6	28	32	30	Israel	10.9	0.8
—	—	31	Czech. Rep.	7.0	0.5	—	37	31	Turkey	8.1	0.6
29	35	32	Finland	6.8	0.5	24	29	32	Finland	8.1	0.6
36	37	33	Indonesia	6.8	0.5	—	—	33	Egypt	7.2	0.6
37	36	34	Ireland	6.0	0.5	34	36	34	Portugal	6.1	0.5
—	—	35	Ukraine	4.9	0.4	31	34	35	South Africa	6.0	0.5
34	40	36	South Africa	4.9	0.4	38	33	36	Argentina	6.0	0.5
—	—	37	Hungary	4.8	0.4	—	—	37	Czech. Rep.	5.3	0.4
38	25	38	Saudi Arabia	4.5	0.3	—	35	38	Venezuela	5.1	0.4
—	—	39	New Zealand	4.3	0.3	36	39	39	New Zealand	4.9	0.4
—	—	40	Colombia	4.0	0.3	—	—	40	Kuwait	4.3	0.3
			Total	$1,181.7	90.1%				Total	$1,162.5	89.7%
			World	$1,311.5	100.0%				World	$1,295.9	100.0%

Sources: WTO, *Annual Report 1998.* World Bank, *World Tables,* 1995.

changed. These trends have been driven by the spread of product and process technology, the fall of transportation costs relative to production costs, and the reduction of tariff and nontariff barriers to trade (until the past five years). Rising real wages in some high-income countries and in the NICs (newly industrializing countries) have led to labor-intensive products being produced in lower-income countries. Nontariff barriers to trade, such as quotas, have also provided incentives for firms to move production to countries that have not had quotas imposed on them. For example, one U.S. importer of jeans compared a list of all the countries on which the United States imposed quotas on jeans and a list of all low-wage countries. He then went to several countries in southern Africa (which did not face quotas) to find firms with supply capabilities. He now imports jeans from Botswana.

Another influence on the volume, patterns, and composition of trade has been the change in the trade strategies of many developing countries—most notably China, Brazil, and Mexico, and more recently India and Indonesia—toward export promotion. The large populations of these countries and the rapid growth of their labor forces imply that real wages will continue to be low for many years into the future. Hence, unlike the NICs, they should remain low-cost producers of labor-intensive products for many years to come.

Trade in services has increased as a percentage of international trade and there is every likelihood that this trend will continue in the future. The United States leads the world in exports of services: financial services, visual and audio media, shipping, insurance, advertising, and so on. In the coming decades, tourism is likely to be the highest growth sector in trade. Already trade in tourism is the major export of many countries (Exhibit 2–4).

Over the past decades, the relative value of unprocessed natural resources in international trade has declined. But, over the past decade, a combination of technology transfer and relatively low labor and, in some instances, land costs has led to a rapid increase in the number of countries that have begun to export fresh and processed agricultural and fishery products. These products have often been sold as "off brands" or "house brands" to price-sensitive consumers in high-income countries. Examples are: canned sardines, tuna fish, and pineapple (Thailand and Indonesia), orange juice (Brazil), apple juice (many countries), and fresh flowers (several countries in South America, and Africa). In the years to come, it is likely that this trend will continue and that greater volumes of an increased variety of agricultural products will be exported from a wider number of countries. The other factor in trade in agricultural products over the past 15 years has been the transformation of the EU (European Union) as a whole from the largest importer to the largest exporter of agricultural products. (This development was the root cause of one of the major points of friction in the Uruguay round of the GATT negotiations. See Chapter 4.)

Foreign direct investment has become one of the major means by which companies operate internationally and by which countries are linked. Foreign direct investment (FDI) influences not only the flow of capital but also the flows of product and process technology and trade patterns and volumes. Foreign investment often flows in response to market opportunities, factor costs (such as wages), natural resource availability and cost, the political and economic stability of countries, and the international debt position of the host country. Inflows of FDI not only affect the flows of imports into a country but often, at a later time, affect its exports. Hence, monitoring the volumes and industry composition of FDI is often an early warning signal concerning future exports.

Several other features of FDI flows are of note. They are highly concentrated among a relatively few countries. About three-fourths of the flows of FDI are among the high-income countries, especially within the Triad of Europe, Japan, and North America. Of the FDI that flows to lower-income countries, about two-thirds is concentrated among 10 countries. FDI flows tend to be more volatile over time, both in aggregate and at the country level, than are GDP, domestic investment, and trade. FDI flows declined from 1979 to 1982 as world economic growth stagnated. Starting in 1986, however, FDI boomed, growing at 28.3 percent annually through 1990, compared with growth rates of 13 percent for merchandise exports and 12 percent for nominal GDP. This increase was largely fueled by substantial increases in outward investment from Japan. In the early 1990s, FDI outflows declined, but they have recovered over the 1993 to 1995 period. By 1995 estimated global sales generated by foreign subsidiaries of multinational enterprises (MNEs) totaled $7 trillion, compared with world exports of goods and services (excluding factor payments) of $5.8 trillion. About a third of international trade is estimated to be intrafirm, i.e., between subsidiaries of MNEs in different countries.

Another feature of FDI is that the number of firms that have become multinational enterprises (MNEs) has increased steadily over the decades, and the number of home countries in which MNEs are based has increased as well. These trends have increased the complexity of the world competitive environment. In the second half of the 1980s, Japan became the largest source country for FDI, overtaking the United States and Britain. In the mid-1990s, the United States regained first place among outward investing countries. The United States also became the largest host country for inward FDI (Exhibit 2–5).

The Environment

The days of uncontrolled international economic growth with little consideration for the environment are over. For example, in 1993, progress on signing a North American Free Trade Agreement was in jeopardy due to U.S. concerns over whether Mexico would legislate (and enforce) environmental protection.

For the multinational enterprise and its managers, the task of doing business internationally has become more complicated as everyone becomes aware of the impact of economic development on the environment. Waste creation (and disposal), water supply and use, air quality, overfishing and overlogging, acid rain, and so forth variously affect businesses no matter where they are located. As an example, in the Philippines some Japanese companies have complained that new environmental standards for new investments are more stringent than they are in Japan—and that even if they were willing to bear the costs of meeting them, the government does not have the equipment to test for compliance to these standards. In addition, the number of constituencies that multinational firms are potentially answerable to has increased dramatically with the heightened awareness of our interconnectedness. This has raised both ethical and legal problems for MNEs. As but one of many examples, some countries have relatively loose standards for water discharge from rayon plants to encourage investment, employment, and output in this industry and allow supplying its downstream textile industry at low cost. What are the legal and ethical responsibilities

---

EXHIBIT 2–5   FDI Statistics

	France	*Germany*	*Japan*	*United Kingdom*	*United States*	*Developing Economies*
Outflows of FDI (1991-1996, $ billions)	143	139	126	185	376	203
Share of FDI outlflows (1985-1990, percent)	9	8	18	16	14	7
Share of FDI outflows (1991-1996, percent)	9	9	8	12	24	13
Inward stock of FDI (1996, $ billions)	168	171	18	345	645	918
Percentage of world total, inward FDI stock (1996)	5	5	1	11	20	28
Outward stock of FDI (1996, $ billions)	206	288	330	356	794	282
Percentage of world total outward FDI stock (1996)	6	9	10	11	25	9

Source: United Nations, *World Investment Report,* 1997.

of MNEs when choosing their technology in undertaking such an investment? Both MNEs and national governments are increasingly trying to balance economic growth and environmental management.

Summary

These are only a few of the facts that are useful and relevant for international managers. They can provide but a start for an understanding of the international environment in which international managers must operate. Beyond these basics, an international manager needs more product-specific information. For example, if the manager works for a garment producer, information on the top exporters and importers and the growth rates of these imports and exports of textiles and garments is needed. Which country had the largest increase in garment exports over the past 10 years? Which country's exports are most highly concentrated in garments? Which countries are gaining comparative advantage in textiles and garments and which ones are losing it? How are markets and production of textiles segmented worldwide? And so on.

Also, as described in more detail in the next chapters, increasing international trade and investment are no longer undertaken on a country-by-country basis, but rather are undertaken on a regional, even global basis. This complicates the analysis manyfold.

An incredible amount and variety of data are available to managers. Knowledge of appropriate international data and the skills to interpret these data are an important start in reaching effective international management decisions.

Supplementary Reading

CIA. *The CIA World Factbook* (Washington, D.C.: CIA, annual editions; also available on CD-ROM and at http://www.odci.gov/cia).

Dreifus, Shirley B., and Michael Moynihan. *The World Market Atlas.* New York: Business International Corporation, annual editions.

IMD. *The World Competitiveness Yearbook 1998.* Lausanne: IMD, 1998; a summary is also available at http://www.imd.ch/wcy.html.

Kidron, Michael, and Ronald Segal. *The State of the World Atlas.* 5th ed. New York: Penguin Books, 1995.

Kurian, George. *The New Book of World Rankings.* 3rd ed. New York: Facts on File, 1991.

Tsai, Terence. *The Fight to Be Green: The Struggle for Corporate Environmentalism in China and Taiwan.* London: Macmillan Press, 1999 forthcoming.

The World Bank. *The World Bank Atlas.* Washington, D.C.: The World Bank, annual editions.

World Economic Forum. *Global Competitiveness Report 1998.* Geneva: World Economic Forum, 1998.

3 THE WORLD OF INTERNATIONAL TRADE

International trade has been carried on between countries and geographical regions for thousands of years. Over the centuries, international trade, although periodically interrupted by wars and natural disasters, has gradually expanded, usually at a faster pace than the expansion of world output. The impetus for the existence and expansion of international trade is the same as that for any commercial transaction: value creation. International trade creates value for both producers and consumers. International trade increases demand for exportable products, thereby raising prices and volumes. It increases the supply of importable products, thereby reducing prices and increasing product availability and variety for consumers. International trade increases the efficiency of resource allocation worldwide, reduces production costs through economies of scale, and lowers input costs.

International trade can also lead to increased exposure for both firms and countries to the forces in the international economy: changes in prices and demand in export markets, changes in prices and supply of imported products, and changes in exchange rates. The increased openness to the international economic environment can increase the variability of a firm's profits and of a nation's GNP growth rate and hence increase the risks of a firm's operations and reduce the stability of a country's economy. International trade can also lead to disruption and restructuring as domestic firms are forced to compete with less expensive or higher-quality imported products. On the other hand, international trade can allow firms to diversify away from dependence on demand in one country and can allow a country to diversify its economy through exports.

Every major firm is affected by international trade in one way or another: as an exporter; as an importer; as a competitor with imports; or as a financial institution involved in trade finance, foreign exchange markets, and international debt management. Similarly, the economies and firms in every country are impacted by international trade flows—and there is every likelihood that these effects will increase into the foreseeable future.

This chapter was prepared by Andrew C. Inkpen.

A knowledge of international trade—the forces behind it and the means by which it is carried out—is essential to all business managers, not just to those directly engaged in international business operations. International trade, exporting and importing, is often the first form of international operations for firms in the manufacturing, natural resource, energy, and agricultural sectors. In 1997, world merchandise trade exceeded $5.3 trillion, up from less than $5 trillion in 1995. The dollar value of world commercial services exports was $1.3 trillion in 1997.

International trade is inextricably linked with foreign direct investment, international technology transfer, and international finance: international trade often leads to foreign direct investment, which in turn often changes trade flows and patterns. Trade also leads to international financial flows, and in turn trade is affected by foreign exchange availability and exchange rate movements. Technology transfer is often accomplished through international trade in capital goods, and, in turn, technology transfer leads to trade in raw materials and semifinished and final products.

The International Trade Environment in the Late 1990s

In the 1970s, international trade was one of the major driving forces behind world economic expansion. The real value (the volume) of world exports expanded nearly threefold (10.2 percent per year on average) between 1970 and 1980 (from $700 billion to $2 trillion in constant 1980 dollars). This expansion was fostered by falling tariff and nontariff barriers to trade in most countries, decreased transportation and communication costs, and by the export-oriented growth strategies of many countries during this period. During the global recession in the early 1980s, world trade declined in real terms by a greater amount than did world GDP. The decline in world trade worsened the recession in many countries. From 1985 to 1995, however, the average annual increase in world merchandise export *volume* was 6 percent. The *volume* of world merchandise exports grew by 9.5 percent in 1997, the second-highest rate recorded in more than two decades. The dollar value of world merchandise exports rose 3 per cent in 1997, which was somewhat less than the 4 percent rate recorded in 1996. (See Exhibit 3–1 for the growth rates in international trade and world GDP.)

Measured in terms of combined merchandise imports and exports, the United States is the largest trading nation in the world, with 12.6 percent of world exports and 16.1 percent of world imports in 1997. The relative trading power of the United States, which had fallen over the past several decades, improved in the 1990s. The positions of Italy, Canada, the Netherlands, and Belgium also have improved, while those of Russia, Saudi Arabia, and Sweden have fallen. Until the Asian financial crisis, the most dramatic changes have come from export-oriented newly industrializing countries (NICs), and in particular, Asian countries such as South Korea, Malaysia, Singapore, Taiwan, and Thailand. In 1997, imports of Indonesia, South Korea, and Thailand declined and Malaysia showed no change. On a combined basis, in 1997 Indonesia, Malaysia, the Philippines, South Korea, and Thailand experienced a 3 percent decline in imports after a 30 percent increase in 1995 and an 8 percent increase in 1996. The future evolution of the economies of these countries most affected by the crisis is still uncertain. Strong currency depreciations may contribute to rapid export growth.

EXHIBIT 3–1   Growth in the Volume of World Merchandise Exports and GDP, 1987–97

Annual Percentage Change

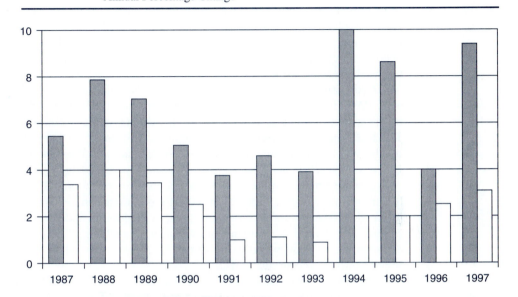

Source: World Trade Organization.

The rise in the real value of the U.S. dollar from 1978 through early 1985 had a severe negative impact on U.S. exporters and import-competing industries.[1] The fall of the U.S. dollar from 1985 to 1988 led to a strong recovery of U.S. exports and a reduction in the growth rate of imports. Export volume increased by 68 percent from 1985 to 1991, while import volume increased by 20 percent. This situation led to increased trade deficits as import growth exceeded export growth. The rise in the value of the dollar in the mid-1990s contributed to further trade deficits. By 1998, the merchandise trade deficit of the U.S. had increased to $211 billion. In 1998, the U.S. economy was expanding while the economies of its major trading partners such as Germany, France, and Japan continued with slow or negative growth.

Until the early 1980s, the U.S. current account was roughly in balance. Since 1982, however, its trade deficits have led to substantial current account deficits totaling $1,260 billion over the 1982 to 1995 period. In 1999 alone, the U.S. current account deficit was in the range of $200 billion. Current account deficits translate roughly into surpluses on the capital account. Hence, the United States went from being a net creditor with the rest

---

[1]The concept of the "real value" of a currency is treated further on in this chapter. In short, the real value of a country's currency (its real exchange rate) increases (decreases) if changes in its nominal exchange rate are greater (less) than the differential inflation rates between it and its trading partners (when exchange rates are expressed in terms of the amount of foreign currency that can be purchased with one unit of domestic currency).

of the world of about $400 billion to a net debtor of about $900 billion in 1994. If the United States is to stop going further and further into debt with the rest of the world, its trade balance (about $250 billion in 1999 alone) will have to improve in the next decade following its deterioration in the 1990s. The trade deficit will have to become a trade surplus to compensate for the interest and dividends on its accumulated international debt and net inward foreign direct investment. The longer this reversal from a trade deficit to a trade surplus is delayed, the greater the eventual surplus will have to be—otherwise U.S. international indebtedness will continue to rise.

As the trade deficit in the United States declined starting in the late 1980s through the early 1990s, its trading partners had to absorb about a $90 billion annual turnaround on their trade accounts through increased import growth rates and decreased export growth rates. This had a depressing effect on their economies, while at the same time it spurred U.S. economic growth. The deterioration of the U.S. trade account throughout the 1990s reduced U.S. economic growth and increased growth for its trading partners. If the U.S. trade deficit is to become a trade surplus, the trade accounts of its partners will have to accommodate this through substantial increases in import growth rates and a slowing of export growth rates. Most developing countries are not in a position to increase imports or decrease exports; they have debt problems of their own. If anything, their goals are to accelerate export growth. The oil exporters will not absorb it; oil prices will be stable at best, and U.S. imports of oil will continue to rise.

That leaves Japan, some European countries, Canada, and the NICs of Asia such as Taiwan, South Korea, Singapore, and Hong Kong to make the adjustment. However, with slowing growth in Japan and other Asian countries hit by financial crisis, a reduction of Asian exports is unlikely. And no country wants to reduce export or increase import growth rates for fear of reducing its own economic growth rate. One reaction to the U.S. trade and international debt problems has been a rise in protectionism, as each country has tried to shift the adjustment costs onto someone else. From 1980 to 1988, the percentage of U.S. imports under some form of nontariff restraint rose from 8 to 24 percent. These trade restraints cost U.S. consumers tens (some say hundreds) of billions of dollars per year. The United States has also enacted trade legislation that requires the government each year to assemble a "hit list" of countries that are not dealing fairly with American exports, investments, or intellectual property (patents and trademarks). This list is then used as a basis of negotiations with these countries, and in the event the outcomes of these negotiations are not satisfactory, to impose trade sanctions. The rancor of the trade disputes between the U.S. and Japan, China, and even Canada was in part due to the United States' mounting trade deficits.

Major political leaders may also have significant implications for the world trade environment. The Uruguay round of GATT negotiations resulted in the establishment of the World Trade Organization (WTO) and produced some of the most basic changes to the GATT since it was implemented in 1947. In North and South America, the Free Trade Area of the Americas (FTAA) is under negotiation among 34 nations in the American hemisphere for completion in 2005. Yet in the political campaign of 1996, NAFTA itself came under attack by some U.S. politicians as being detrimental to U.S. interests.

The gains from the negotiation and implementation of trading agreements such as GATT, NAFTA, and FTAA can be great. Most of the reductions in protection were in the manufacturing sector. Services received almost no liberalization, while agriculture received some limited reduction in protection.

Liberalization in the agriculture sector would affect the European Union to a large degree. Prior to the conclusion of the Uruguay round, trade-distorting policies in the European Union under the Common Agricultural Policy (CAP) turned the EU from the largest net importer of food products to the largest net food exporter in less than two decades. The CAP cost the EU between $40 billion and $50 billion per year in direct subsidies. The CAP cost consumers in the EU countries roughly an equal amount in higher prices and added 4 percent to the unemployment rate in Europe. In the late 1980s, it precipitated the largest trade war in 40 years, as the United States and Canada responded to agricultural subsidies in Europe with massive increases in the subsidies to their own farmers.[2]

The Uruguay round of the GATT resulted in some reductions in agriculture protection. Nontariff barriers to trade in agriculture were converted to tariff equivalents, which were scheduled for reduction in the future. The extension of GATT over trade in agricultural products was important in placing agricultural trade under firmer international regulations, and for setting the stage for future gains over time and in later negotiations. The establishment of the WTO also helps to alleviate fears of the development of a "fortress Europe" for exporters from Japan and North America.

Prior to the Uruguay round, North America's other large trading partner, Japan, had reduced its explicit tariff and nontariff barriers to trade on most products to levels below those in most other countries and had ceased its policy of undervaluing its exchange rate (to increase exports and reduce imports). In the first half of the 1990s, the yen continued its appreciation against major currencies in the world, and especially against the U.S. dollar. Japan's real exchange rate appreciated by over 60 percent from 1985 to 1994. By the end of 1995, 100 yen could purchase $1 U.S., a marked change from the 240 yen required for $1 U.S. in 1985. Over the next few years the yen declined in value against the U.S. dollar, dropping as low as 147 yen to the dollar in 1998. Over this period, Japan continued to run ever-increasing merchandise trade surpluses.

Although the value of Japanese exports increased only 2 percent in 1997, Japanese imports declined 6 percent, leading to a merchandise trade surplus of $83 billion. These mounting trade surpluses have often brought Japan's trading policies under the scrutiny of its major trading partners.

Japan's domestic market structure and its international trade are dominated by large trading houses and industrial groups. Its distribution channels for manufactured products have proven difficult at best for Western exporters to penetrate. The Japanese government has also continued to follow a mercantilist trade strategy toward high-technology trade products in emerging industries, such as telecommunications and computers, through a combination of direct subsidies, market protection, and government purchasing regulations. Under duress, Japan has agreed to replace quantitative restrictions on rice imports with tariffs, but the replacement process has been slow and the initial tariffs were on the order of 700 percent.

One view of Japan's future trade and economic strategies has been graphically expressed by Mr. Morita (chairman of the board of Sony) and Mr. Ishihara (an elected official) in *The*

---

[2]Prior to reform in 1992, direct agricultural subsidies took up to two-thirds of the European Union budget. Direct agricultural subsidies *per farmer* in 1989 were about $10,000 in the EU, $16,000 in Canada and Japan, $21,000 in the United States, and $30,000 in Sweden. (As quoted in Clayton Yeuter, "Back 40 Blues," *The World in 1990* (London, Economist Publications, 1990). Even after EU reform, half the EU budget in 1998 went to subsidizing farming, an industry employing only about 5 percent of the EU's working population.

Japan That Can Say "No." They foresee a Japan that is largely independent of U.S. economic and political pressures and has reoriented itself toward leading a trading bloc of the countries of the Asia-Pacific Rim, including China. Although there have been proposals for the formation of a formal East Asian trading bloc with Japan as a major player, as yet these have not come to fruition. The Asian financial crisis has resulted in many new questions about Asian integration and trade. However, Japan's foreign direct investment and trade activities in Southeast and East Asia are contributing to the economic integration of the national economies of this region.

Among developing countries, there are also major pressures on the trade system. In general throughout the 1980s and the 1990s, the governments of most developing countries moved toward a more liberal position in international trade, both to expand exports and to open their economies to imports. Developing countries have often faced export markets made difficult to penetrate by tight regulations, and this difficulty has contributed to pressure and discontent with the international trade system on the part of developing countries, particularly as it applies to trade in labor-intensive products such as textiles, clothing, and footwear.

The conditions of trade established during the Uruguay round help to alleviate some of the pressure and discontent with international trade. Developing countries such as Indonesia, Malaysia, the Republic of Korea, and Thailand stand to benefit most from the new trading agreements. These countries, which are highly competitive exporters of textiles and clothing, have been committed to the liberalization of trade in agriculture and manufacturing. The elimination of the Multifibre Arrangement (a voluntary export restraint agreement), for example, enables these countries to expand their production of low-cost, labor-intensive products. Countries in South Asia (India, Nepal, Pakistan, and Bangladesh) are similarly expected to benefit from the Uruguay round; however, China, Taiwan, and Russia are not expected to gain as much because they are not WTO members.

There are other areas of uncertainty—both opportunity and risk—for firms engaged in international trade: the drive for modernization and deregulation in the economies of the People's Republic of China and in India; continued economic and political reforms in the eastern European countries; the reversion of Hong Kong to Chinese political control; and the emergence of Japan as a leading country for technology generation, trade, international capital, and foreign direct investment. Yet, it is within this environment that firms must compete in world trade markets if they are to survive, much less prosper.

In short, the pressures on the international trading system are enormous. This is the world of international trade.

A Framework for International Trade

The international trading environment is complex and ever changing. To manage international trade operations within this environment, a framework of analysis is useful. A framework can be used to disentangle the many factors that drive international flows of goods and services. This section presents one possible framework for analyzing a firm's international trade environment.

To simplify the exposition of this framework, the initial viewpoint will be of a firm with production operations in a single country as it analyzes trade operations with another country. Although this viewpoint is obviously unrealistic in a world of global competition with complex trading arrangements and in which some 33 percent of international trade is carried out by multinational enterprises (MNEs) at the intrafirm level, it can serve as a reasonable starting point for our analysis. Further on, this simple framework is expanded to include multicountry and multifirm trade. Subsequent chapters will describe global sourcing and the complex trade and investment relationships that exist within and between multinational enterprises.

An Overview of the Trade Framework

A Framework for Trade Analysis

1. The Social, Technological, Economic, and Political (STEP) system and how this system affects the firm's comparative and competitive advantage.
2. Countries abroad as markets for exports and sources of imports.
3. Tariff and nontariff barriers to trade and government incentives to promote trade.
4. Linking producers and buyers through trade intermediaries.

The Step System and Comparative and Competitive Advantage

Each firm operates within the social, technological, economic, and political (STEP) environment of the country in which it produces. The STEP environment has a strong influence on the firm: the cost, quality, and range of products it produces, domestic demand for its products, the product and process technology it uses, its efficiency and scale of operations, the cost and availability of natural resources and factor inputs, such as capital and labor, the range of support industries, and how and where it markets its products. The firm's STEP environment influences the *comparative* advantage of the products it produces relative to products produced by other firms abroad. The firm's STEP environment may also influence its *competitive* advantage in the national market and abroad. Trends in this STEP environment relative to the trends in the STEP environment of other countries have a strong influence on a firm's ability to enter or to continue international trading operations.[3]

For example, Singapore's rapid economic development over the past 20 years has led to a substantial rise in real wages relative to those in most other countries. In response to this change in Singapore's comparative advantage in labor-intensive products, firms in the export-oriented, labor-intensive garment industry became less and less competitive on world markets, that is, they lost their comparative advantage arising from Singapore's past relatively low labor costs and high worker efficiency. In response to this change, some firms have changed their *comparative* advantage in the production of low-cost, low-quality, standardized garments to a *comparative* advantage in high-quality designer garments (based on Singapore's relatively low-wage skilled workers). Alternatively, other firms have invested abroad. To do this, they have utilized their competitive advantage in managing a low-wage labor force and in their channels of distribution from Singapore to other

---

[3]See Paul Beamish, "European Foreign Investment: Why Go to Canada," *European Management Journal,* Vol. 14, No. 1, 1996, for an application of the STEP analysis.

lower-wage countries onto export markets. Firms that could not respond to these changes in Singapore's comparative advantage with changes in their competitive advantage have gone out of business. Changes in all the elements of the STEP system in which the firm operates can have similar effects on its ability to export or to compete with imports. In other countries, social pressures have led to implementation of strict environmental protection measures. These measures have changed the comparative advantage of heavy, pollution-intensive industries in these countries, such as steel, chemicals, and pulp and paper. Government policies and economic forces can influence the location of technology generation and its diffusion within the country and worldwide by subsidizing these industries in a number of ways. These policies have changed the comparative advantage of some countries in technology-intensive industries.

The STEP system in which a firm operates—and how it responds to and influences comparative and competitive advantage—forms the first block in the analytical framework. This emphasis on the effects of a firm's external environment on its ability to trade is not meant to be deterministic, however. A firm can develop a competitive advantage that enables it to export even though the STEP system in its home country places it at a comparative disadvantage. Kaufman Shoes in Canada exports work boots and after-ski boots worldwide. Kaufman has developed a competitive advantage based on quality, style, and design that has allowed it to compete internationally even though the shoe industry as a whole in Canada is at a comparative disadvantage in international trade. Similarly, in the mid-1980s, Proton component televisions were developed in Taiwan by contracting for state of the art, U.S. design technology. By this means it developed a competitive advantage at the very top end of the line in televisions, despite Taiwan's comparative disadvantage in state-of-the-art technology generation (as opposed to technology transfer and adaptation). For both these firms, however, the STEP systems in which they operate do not foster their competitive advantage, rather they detract from it. Kaufman must constantly strive to maintain its competitive advantage in quality, design, and style over firms in lower-wage countries whose skills on these dimensions are increasing year by year. Similarly, when Proton failed to continue to upgrade its technology by further purchases from abroad, firms in Japan, the United States, and Europe with in-house technology generation capabilities (which Proton lacked) matched its quality at a lower price.

A competitive advantage based on government subsidies (when the country does not have and cannot develop a comparative advantage in the firm's products) is always at risk if funding for these programs is reduced or they are terminated. The budget constraints under which many countries are operating in the 1990s have placed, and will continue to place, pressure on subsidies that come out of the government budgets. As an extreme example, Indonesia has fostered the development of a mainframe aircraft producer, IPTN, through heavy direct government subsidies and a monopoly on the captive market in Indonesia. When these subsidies were terminated and the domestic market dried up, IPTN faced extreme difficulties. A similar conclusion would hold for agribusiness firms in Europe and Japan, for example, which rely on heavy government protection and subsidies.

Conversely, a country may have a comparative advantage in a product, but producers in the country may not be able to turn it into a competitive advantage either in export markets or in their domestic market. This situation often results when the governments in other countries are heavily subsidizing or protecting their own producers. Exports of palm-oil-based products in Southeast Asia are impeded by subsidies and barriers to trade in the United States and Europe designed to protect domestic producers of vegetable oils; sugar producers in the Philippines have often faced world prices below their production costs, even though the Philippines has a comparative advantage in sugar; U.S. exports of computers, telecommunications equipment, and aircraft are impeded by national programs in Europe, Brazil, Japan, and elsewhere.

Market Identification

For a firm with both a comparative and a competitive advantage that gives it the potential to undertake ongoing exports, the next step in the analysis is to identify markets abroad to which it can export its product. This step entails analysis of trends in demand arising from changes in population, income levels, and consumer preferences in potential export markets. If there is a demand for the firm's products in a market, the supply capabilities of domestic firms and other exporters worldwide to meet this demand at lower prices or higher quality must be assessed. For example, paper consumption in Japan has risen rapidly with the rise in Japan's GNP and consumer incomes. Concerns with environmental pollution have placed restrictions on the ability of its pulp manufacturers to increase output to meet this demand. This trend toward an imbalance between demand and supply has created the potential for increased exports to Japan for both pulp and paper products. Japanese pulp and paper firms have also responded to this trend by locating production facilities abroad to produce pulp for their downstream paper production facilities. For a pulp and paper producer in North America, the analysis would then revolve around the issue of whether these developments present an opportunity to increase exports to Japan. The analysis of export markets forms the second block in the framework.

Impediments to Trade

The third block of analysis concerns the impediments to trade flows, both natural ones, such as transportation costs, and measures governments have taken to impede or to facilitate the linking of producers and buyers through international trade. Government policies to restrict and to promote trade can have a decisive influence on (1) trade flows, (2) the competitive position of firms in export markets, (3) the availability and price of imports, and (4) the ability of firms to compete with imports. Hence, an analysis of the level and trends in tariff and nontariff barriers to trade is an essential component of the international trade framework. Governments can also facilitate exports directly by such measures as concessional export financing, export subsidies, differential taxation of export earnings, and financing for export market development.

Trade Intermediaries

If the firm has a competitive advantage *and* if there is demand for its product in an export market *and* if government intervention in the international trade system (or through movements in real exchange rates) does not prevent the producer from accessing buyers in the export market, the final area of analysis concerns the linkages of producers in one country to buyers in the export market. A competitive product and a receptive market are not enough; the product must somehow be transported from the factory to the point of shipment (port or airport) to export market, be received in the export market, clear customs, move through distribution channels to the point of sale, be sold to the customer, and be serviced after sale. International channels of distribution are often long, multilayered, complex, difficult to analyze and understand, and expensive to access or to develop. Channel costs may represent three times the production cost of a product.

Marketing in a country with which a producer is not familiar can present substantial problems as well. The success or failure of a firm's export initiative may stand or fall on the pricing, promotion, advertising, and distribution policies it follows in export markets. These subjects are examined in more detail in the next chapter.

The framework presented above may seem quite complicated at first, but it represents the bare bones of the international trading system in which exporters and importers must manage their trade operations. Each block in this analytical framework is examined in more detail in the next sections of this chapter and in the following chapter.

Comparative and Competitive Advantage

It is important for managers of firms engaged in international trade to understand the driving forces behind the international flow of goods and services. As with any form of voluntary exchange between independent, value-maximizing agents, international trade takes place when value is created for the participants in the transaction above the value they can receive through alternative uses of their resources. Put more bluntly, trade must be profitable for both the seller and the buyer or it will not continue—at least over the long run.

For the exporter, the value of international trade comes from some combination of higher prices, increased volume, decreased costs (through economies of scale and learning by doing), and the effects of international trade on product quality and design. For the importer, value may be created through lower prices, greater variety, increased quality, and diversification of sources of supply. International trade operations may also affect the risks faced by importers and exporters alike: risks may be decreased by diversifying sales among several markets and sources among several producers; risks may be increased through greater exposure to the effects of trade restrictions, exchange rate movements, and demand, supply, and price fluctuations in foreign markets. Managers of international trade operations must balance the effects of international trade on both profits and risks in order to maximize the value of the firm through its international trade operations.

Managers must bear in mind that the goal of international trade operations is to increase the value of the firm; exports for exports' sake (except in the short run to gain market share) are not the goal. Similarly, for countries, the goal of international trade is not to increase exports (and to decrease imports), but rather to increase national income through international trade. Exports in general and of a specific product are *not* "good" in and of themselves, and imports in general or of specific products are *not* "bad." Yet this view often seems to be the presumption behind the policies of governments around the world as they try to promote exports and to impede imports in general and of specific products.

In fact, exports might be considered "bad." A nation's resources—labor, capital, technology, natural resources—are used to produce exports, but consumers abroad receive the benefits of consuming them and they reduce the supply of goods available for domestic consumption. Imports could be considered "good." They are produced using the resources of other countries, but are consumed domestically and they increase the goods and services available for domestic use. Exports are only "good" to the extent that the receipts from export sales allow a country to finance imports or to service its accumulated international debt. Similarly, accumulating foreign exchange reserves is beneficial only to the extent that these reserves may allow a country to smooth out the effects of short-term fluctuations in export receipts and import payments and to import products in the future. These facts are difficult for individuals and governments to accept.

This view of value creation as the driving force behind international trade raises the question of what factors lead a firm (or a country) to produce a product for export or to import a product from abroad. How and why is value created when some products are exported and others imported? To understand the answer to this most fundamental question of international trade requires a (short) digression into the theory of international trade. Understanding this theory is important to managers. International trade theory can be thought of as the fundamental tides beneath the turbulent waves of day-to-day international trade activity. Understanding both the tides and the waves of international trade is important for managers engaged in international trade operations.

Absolute and Comparative Advantage

Consider the two countries, A and B, which produce two products, X and Y, with labor as the only input to the production process. Before trade, country A produces and consumes 16 units of product X, using 8 hours of labor and produces and consumes 4 units of product Y using 4 hours of labor. Country B produces and consumes 4 units of X using 4 hours of labor and produces and consumes 4 units of Y using 2 hours of labor (Exhibit 3–2). In country A, the price of Y relative to X would be 2 (since it takes twice as long to produce a unit of Y as it does to produce a unit of X); in country B the price ratio is 1/2 (since it takes half as long to produce a unit of Y as it does to produce a unit of X). Country A has an *absolute* advantage in product X; country B has an absolute advantage in product Y. If the two countries are opened to trade, country A will tend to specialize in product X and country B will tend to specialize in product Y. If there is total specialization, country A could produce 24 units of X (12 hours times 2 units per hour) and country B could produce 12 units of Y (6 hours times 2 units per hour), compared to total production of 20 units of X and 8 units of Y with no trade. With international trade, both more X and more Y are produced and consumed and both countries are better off. Under trade, the price of Y relative to X will fall somewhere between 2 and 1/2.

The gains from trade may not be shared equally, however. For country A, producers and workers in the Y industry and heavy consumers of product X have lost; the Y producers have gone out of business, the Y workers have had to shift to the production of X and X consumers are facing higher prices for X. Producers and workers in the X industry and heavy consumers of Y have won. The same applies to country B; producers and workers in the X industry and heavy consumers of X have won. Overall, however, both countries

EXHIBIT 3–2   Absolute Advantage

	Output		Output/Hour		
	X	Y	X	Y	*Labor Hours*
Country A	16	4	2	1	12
Country B	4	4	1	2	6
Total output (no trade)	20	8			
Total output (trade)	24	12			

have gained, since there is more output to be consumed in both countries. The distribution of the gains among the two countries is also uncertain. In general, the smaller the country and the greater its absolute advantage in one product relative to the absolute advantage of the other country, the greater its share of the gains. A small, natural-resource-intensive country like New Zealand has more to gain from trade than a large country with a more balanced economy such as the United States.

Now consider two other countries, *C* and *D,* producing *X* and *Y* (Exhibit 3–3). Country *C* produces 12 units of *X* in 3 hours and 4 units of *Y* in 2 hours; country *D* produces 7 units of *X* in 7 hours and 7 units of *Y* in 7 hours. Notice that country *D* is less efficient in producing *both* products. But trade is still possible and yields gains. With trade, country *C* will specialize in *X,* while country D will specialize in *Y,* since the ratio of *C*'s efficiency in *X* relative to *Y* is higher than that in *D.* If there is total specialization, then country *C* could produce 20 units of *X* and country *D* could produce 14 units of *Y.* Before trade, total production was just 19 units of *X* and 11 units of *Y.* The important point here is: even if one country is more efficient in *both* products, there are still gains for each country through trade. In this example, since country *D* is less efficient than country *C* in both products, with trade, although both countries have gained, incomes will still be higher in *D* than in *C.* To be more concrete, even if both steel producers and garment producers in the United States were more productive than steel and garment producers in India, there would still be gains for both countries if the United States produced steel and India produced garments. This is the theory of *comparative* advantage.

For managers, there are two lessons to be learned from this analysis. It is important to understand what factors contribute to the comparative advantage of both country *C* in product *X* and country *D* in product *Y.* The reason is *not* that producers in country *C* are more or less efficient than those in country *D.* The important factor is the *ratio* of the efficiency in the two industries in country *C compared* to their *ratio* in country *D.* If, through technology generation or transfer, education programs, and so on, producers of product *X* in country *D* improve their efficiency to above 2 units per hour (and assuming that all other producers do not increase their efficiencies), then country *D* would become a net exporter of *X, even though* there had been no changes in the relative efficiency of producers in country *C and* even through producers of *X* in country *C* were still more efficient than those in country *D.* Such a situation has occurred in such products as orange and apple juices, canned pineapples, tomatoes, and cut flowers. Producers in developing countries have

EXHIBIT 3–3   **Comparative Advantage**

	Output		Output/Hour			
	X	Y	X	Y	*Labor Hours*	*Py/Px*
Country C	12	4	4	2	5	2
Country D	7	7	1	1	14	1
Total output (no trade)	19	11				
Total output (trade)	20	14				

increased their efficiencies through transfer of agricultural technology and reduced transportation costs over the past decade to the point where they have a comparative advantage in these products. In analyzing the effects of trade on an industry, the important factor is the comparison of these two ratios among trading partners and how they change over time.

Pineapple producers and canners in Hawaii are the most efficient in the world. Yet over time, the efficiency of producers in other countries has increased rapidly, and first Taiwan, then Thailand, and more recently Indonesia have displaced Hawaiian producers from the market and forced them to close. A similar situation has occurred for garment producers in North America. They are highly efficient and their efficiency has increased over time relative to many other manufacturing industries. Yet the efficiency of garment manufacturers in low-wage countries has increased even more rapidly compared to the efficiency of other producers in these countries. The result has been the gradual decline of garment manufacturers in North America and the rise of exports from first Japan, then from Korea, Taiwan, and Hong Kong, and more recently from Thailand, India, China, Turkey, and Indonesia.

Although the theories of absolute and comparative advantage as presented above involve only two countries producing two products and using one factor of production with a constant return-to-scale production function, they can be generalized to many countries, many products, many factors' inputs, and diminishing returns to scale. The conclusions of this more complicated analysis generally are the same as those for the simple analysis presented above: trade enhances the welfare of both countries, but the distribution of these gains among participants within each country and among the countries is not uniform. The more complicated theories also show that:

1. Trade improves the relative welfare of the factors of production that are used intensively in the exported product. For example, if a country exports steel (a capital-intensive product), the welfare of those who have capital will be improved relative to those who supply labor.

2. If labor and capital are immobile among sectors, then the returns to the factors of production (labor and capital) in the exporting industry will improve relative to those in the importing sector.

3. The welfare of consumers of the export products will decline relative to consumers of imported products (since prices of the exported product will rise relative to the imported product). For example, if a country exports food and

imports consumer durables, the welfare of the poor, whose budgets contain a relatively high proportion for food, will decline relative to the rich, who can afford consumer durables.

4. Countries will tend to export products that use their relatively inexpensive and abundant factors of production intensively. For example, a country in which labor is relatively inexpensive compared to capital will export labor-intensive products and import capital-intensive ones.

5. Trade brings about an equalization of the returns to factors of production; that is, trade tends to equalize capital costs and wage rates among countries over time.

The overriding conclusion of this analysis is that a country will *always* have a comparative advantage in some product groups. The product groups may change over time, however. A situation will never arise in which a country will lose comparative advantage in almost all product groups and not gain it in others. High wages do not make a country noncompetitive on export markets. They make it uncompetitive in labor-intensive products. A deteriorating trade deficit is *not* a sign of a loss of comparative advantage. As discussed below, it is a sign that the country's real exchange rate has risen to an inappropriate level. The U.S. trade deficit in the 1980s was *not* due to the loss of its comparative advantage. The United States still had a comparative advantage in some products (although the products in which it had a comparative advantage might have changed). The U.S. trade problems came largely from an appreciation of its real exchange rate over the 1977–85 period. Over this period the real exchange rate of the U.S. dollar rose by almost 50 percent against the currencies of its trading partners. The exchange-rate appreciation had the effect of pricing products in which the United States had a comparative advantage out of world markets.

New Theories of International Trade

The theories of absolute and comparative advantage are most easily used to explain *inter*industry trade, that is, trade in which one country exports a product of industry X and imports a product of industry Y. But much of international trade is composed of *intra*industry trade, that is, trade among countries in products in the same industry. France both exports and imports garments; the United States both exports and imports steel; England both exports and imports consumer electronics, and so on. In fact, a majority of the trade in manufactured products among high-income countries is composed of intraindustry trade.[4]

There are basically two explanations for intraindustry trade. The first is well within the framework of comparative advantage as presented above. France exports high-quality, high-fashion garments and imports low-quality, standard ones; the United States imports standard steels and exports specialized steels; England imports mass-market consumer electronics and exports state-of-the-art ones, and so on. Each country, then, is exporting the

---

[4]The percentage of intraindustry trade in international trade depends on the definition used for "industry": the broader the definition, the greater the percentage. For example, the percentage of intraindustry trade in "textiles and garments" is higher than it would be for "men's T-shirts."

products that make intensive use of its relatively abundant factors of production (fashion designers, steel technologists, and sound engineers).

This is only part of the explanation, however. In industries in which there are economies of scale in production, R&D, distribution, advertising, and sales operations, a firm may be able to establish a *competitive* advantage in the domestic and international market. Duralex glasses, Bally shoes, YKK zippers, and Heineken beer are examples of products that have successfully established a sustainable competitive advantage based on cost or product differentiation.

Once a firm has achieved a competitive advantage based on cost or product differentiation (through branding, R&D, design, or service), it may be able to use its current competitive position to erect barriers to entry for other, later entrants. One way to do this is to signal implicit or explicit threats to potential competitors that the firm will lower prices or increase volumes if entry does occur. If incumbent firms were to follow through with these threats of retaliation, new entrants might find themselves in an untenable position. To gain market share they would have to price below established producers (due to brand loyalty), yet, initially, their costs would be high due to their initial small market share (and hence production volumes) and their limited experience. Barriers to entry are especially high in industries in which there are large economies of scale (implying high up-front capital investments), large initial R&D expenditures, and high cost to establishing a brand name. In such industries, if incumbent firms are far down on the learning curve, operating at efficient scale, or have a considerable degree of brand loyalty, these threats may be sufficiently "credible" to dissuade potential entrants from starting production.

Clusters of Interconnected Companies

There is another set of conditions that some groups of firms and whole industries in some countries have been able to develop which has allowed them to achieve and sustain a competitive advantage in world trade. Rarely is a firm a free-standing entity that can produce all the necessary inputs for production, perform all the design and R&D for product development, and provide all the marketing and after-sales services by itself. Firms most often rely on a wide variety of suppliers for inputs, outside design and R&D firms for design and product development, and a wide range of sales and after-sales support firms. In some regions and some countries, industry clusters have developed over time. Ideas are exchanged among personnel of these firms. A trade infrastructure is built up to support them, with elements internal to the firms, in separate support firms, and in transportation and communications systems. The demand by this cluster of firms for specific job skills is met in part by in-house training and in part by government programs that set up an education system to provide workers with those skills. This view of how international competitive advantage can be created and sustained has been most forcefully presented by Michael Porter in *The Competitive Advantage of Nations*. In the first chapter of this book a list of 100 industry clusters is presented for 10 countries. To pick a few examples: food additives and furniture in Denmark; cutlery and printing presses in Germany; ceramic tiles, footwear, and wool fabrics in Italy; air-conditioning machinery, musical instruments, and forklift trucks in Japan; pianos, travel goods, and wigs in Korea; ship repair in Singapore; mining equipment, environment control equipment, and refrigerated shipping in Sweden;

dyestuffs, heating controls, and survey equipment in Switzerland; confectionery, auction-eering, and electrical generation equipment in the United Kingdom; and detergents, agri-cultural chemicals, and motion pictures in the United States. In Canada (not covered in Porter's book), a similar situation exists for packaging equipment. Often these industries are clustered geographically as well as nationally.

Porter concludes that among the firms and supporting infrastructure in these clusters there are substantial economies of scale, positive spillover effects (externalities), and inter-linkages that promote both competition and cooperation. Rivals compete intensely to win and retain customers. Without vigorous competition, a cluster will fail. Porter argues that clusters affect competition in three broad ways: first, by increasing the productivity of com-panies in the area; second, by driving the direction and pace of innovation, which drives future productivity growth; and three, by stimulating the formation of new businesses, which expands and strengthens the cluster itself.

Porter argues in his later work that in the new economics of competition, what mat-ters most in all industries is not inputs and scale but productivity. Based on this argument, there is no such thing as a low-tech industry. There are only low-tech companies that fail to use world-class technology to enhance productivity and innovation. An important impli-cation for global competition is that locational factors such as low wages and taxes lose their importance in the absence of efficient infrastructure, sophisticated suppliers, and other cluster benefits that can offset savings from low input costs. As global competition changes the nature of traditional comparative advantages, a growing number of multina-tionals are moving their headquarters to more vibrant clusters. For example, when the two pharmaceutical firms, Pharmacia of Sweden and Upjohn of the United States, merged in 1995, a decision was made to locate the head office in London. A few years later the firm relocated to New Jersey, the most competitive location for the pharmaceutical industry.

The unique competitive conditions created by clusters cannot be replicated in another country or region unless a similar cluster is developed. Such development can be extremely difficult, since the whole of the cluster is greater than the sum of its parts. Hence, substantial parts of the cluster must exist before the individual firms can compete internationally. Porter also concludes that it is possible for countries to foster the upgrading of clusters through government action to influence demand patterns, education and training programs, indus-try protection, and trade promotion. For example, at one time the United States, the United Kingdom, and Sweden had clusters in shipbuilding. But first Japan and more recently Korea have been able to develop clusters in these industries and outcompete them internation-ally. Similar shifts in the location of clusters have occurred in cars, semiconductors, apparel, and footwear.

Porter cautions that governments should not be involved in choosing among clusters and instead should focus on strengthening productivity in existing clusters. There are var-ious examples of concerted attempts to develop clusters that have not been successful. For example, in the late 1970s and early 1980s as wages rose in Japan, the apparel industry there tried to develop a sustainable competitive advantage in high-fashion clothing. The design schools of Europe were flooded with students from Japan and Japanese high-fashion houses were developed. Despite the success of some firms, such as Hanae Mori and Isye Myake, the clothing industry in Japan has continued to decline. Porter also acknowledges that the concentration of Japanese industry in the Tokyo and Osaka region, and the consequent inef-ficiencies due to congestion, is the result of a powerful and intrusive central government.

"First-mover advantages" and the presence of industry clusters can be overcome by new entrants with sufficient resources to bear the initial losses entry entails.[5] Such strategic moves by individual firms can be assisted by government policy, which can give a firm a "deep pocket" to finance its initial losses on entry or that can give it a protected domestic market for initial sales. This situation may have occurred for firms in Japan and some of the newly industrializing countries. This view of the driving force behind international trade in these types of products gives credence, at least in theory, to government intervention in international trade both to protect existing national firms in such industries from attack by new entrants and to assist new national firms as they break into the market.

Two trends have reinforced the ability of firms and industrial clusters to establish a sustainable competitive advantage based on economies of scale and product differentiation, and two trends have lessened their ability. National incomes per capita, wages, and capital costs among countries in the upper third of the world income distribution have tended to become more homogeneous over time and the importance of endowments of many natural resources has declined. Among these countries, competitive advantage has become based less on relative factor endowments and costs and more on firm-specific ownership advantages—such as economies of scale, management, technology, brand names—as well as on highly developed support industries, education, worker skills, and trade infrastructure. As incomes have risen, buyers have become more discriminating in their purchases as to style, quality, fashion, design, and performance. Consumers have also come to value a wider range of products with a wider range of product attributes. These trends have increased the ability of producers to differentiate their products entering international trade. In the United States, shoes made by Bally (produced in Italy and Switzerland) compete with shoes from Gucci (Italy), Church (England), and Alden (United States) at the top end of the market in the $200 plus range. But shoes from Indonesia and China are demanded in the $10 to $20 price range.

The increasingly rapid pace of technology transfer and diffusion has led to a growing number of firms (in a growing number of countries) possessing or having access to more or less the same product and process technology. In industries in which technological ability (including design and quality control) has become more widely diffused, competition may once again become based on relative factor costs. Falling transportation costs and trade barriers have also accentuated the force behind comparative advantage. Many firms have become multinational enterprises. These firms, to the extent that relative factor costs are still important, can rationalize production and sales on a global basis. Increasingly, however, knowledge-intensive products, in which manufacturing labor and materials account for a limited amount of product cost, are becoming more important. As a result, in industries such as software and entertainment and even automobiles, the idea of moving production to a low-cost location makes little sense.

---

[5]This may have been the case of Great Giant Pineapple (GGP), a subsidiary of Genung Sewu, a large conglomerate in Indonesia. Initially GGP priced 15 percent below the producer in Thailand with the worst reputation for quality *and* graded all its pineapple rings as "Grade C" to ensure that in delivering at least the quality described in the contract (and usually higher quality), it could keep its name among buyers as living up to its contract. By 1989, with its reputation established and with 8 percent of the world market, GGP was pricing above the Thai producer with the best reputation *and* was selling grades A and B slices. By 1996, GGP had 15 percent of the world market for canned pineapple.

The Benefits of Trade

The overwhelming conclusion of all the theories of international trade is that trade creates value for *all* the participants. The more open a country is to trade, the better off it will be in the long run. In the short run, there may be adjustment problems for some sectors and some firms within these sectors, but, overall, all countries win. In Chapter 2, "world competitiveness rankings" were given for a number of countries. This should *not* be interpreted to mean that, as in a sports contest, some countries will win and others lose in international competition through trade and foreign investment. Individual companies may win or lose, but at the national level, countries all win by opening up to trade (and foreign investment). A more apt comparison is with dancing, rather than a sports contest. The closer we dance together, the greater the benefits will be for both partners (although there may be some stumbling and hurt toes as we learn to dance together).

These newer theories of the driving forces behind international trade have several implications for managers. It is necessary to analyze which of the forces will predominate in the industry in which the firm operates, that is, can the firm establish a sustainable competitive advantage based on some proprietary ownership advantage that will allow it to operate internationally, or will the forces of comparative advantage predominate? Governments may intervene in the market to assist firms in some industries to "create" their own comparative and competitive advantage. In theory, governments can increase national welfare by protecting firms in this type of industry from trade competition while they are still struggling to gain scale efficiency, undertake R&D, differentiate their products, and promote exports. Many governments around the world have "targeted" manufacturers of products such as computers, biotechnology, aircraft, telecommunications, robotics, ceramics, and fiber optics for protection and incentives during their developmental stages. For firms in these industries, government policies at home and in competing countries may be the key to competitive success in export as well as in domestic markets.

A word of warning is needed, however. Often, management and governments have focused their attention on the "hot" industries on the cutting edge of technology when they have tried to identify the "winners of tomorrow" in export markets. For many, even most, of the industries in which firms have achieved a sustainable competitive advantage, technology of the bubbling test tube and whizzing computer variety is *not* the norm. German firms export knives and garden equipment; English firms export razors, combs, cookies, and candy; Swiss firms export shoes, textiles, and cereals; American firms export textiles and clothing and processed food products; Canadian firms export packaging machinery, feed mixers, dental drills, and garbage cans; Japanese firms export zippers, disposable lighters, and books; and Swedish firms export saws and scissors. These firms have all achieved a sustainable competitive advantage in export markets, based not on "high" technology but on design, quality, and marketing expertise.[6]

---

[6]See Porter, *The Competitive Advantage of Nations,* Chapter 1, Table 1.2, pp. 27–28, for a complete list of the 100 industries that he and his coauthors studied. In particular note that many of the firms and the industries that have been able to establish a competitive advantage are not particularly high-tech. Rather, their competitive advantage is based on quality, design, innovation, and so on.

Firms that enter the hot industries based on government incentives may find themselves caught in a worldwide subsidy war in which competitive advantage is based more on which governments are willing to subsidize the most and which governments ultimately flinch from the mounting costs of these subsidies. If several governments continue to subsidize their "national champions," worldwide overcapacity may exist in the long run, prices will remain below costs, and the ultimate winners will be consumers in importing countries.

Real Exchange Rates

Beyond comparative and competitive advantage, there are two important factors that influence trade flows: the real exchange rate and demand conditions over the business cycle. The concept of the "real exchange rate" is a difficult one to master and to use. But the influence of real exchange rates on trade flows is so great that it should be mastered. Everyone is familiar with exchange rates in general. If we travel abroad we change our domestic currencies into the currencies of the countries that we visit at the prevailing exchange rate. For example, in early 1999, one U.S. dollar could be changed into 120 yen or into 1.52 Canadian dollars. This is the *nominal* exchange rate. The nominal exchange rate is important for international business. A Canadian importer receives a shipment from the United States with payment in dollars. Canadian dollars must then be converted into U.S. dollars at the prevailing exchange rate and sent to the United States. In early 1999, the Canadian importer would have to pay $1.52 to buy one U.S. dollar. This is a straightforward transaction and easy to understand. If the nominal exchange rate between the U.S. dollar and the Canadian dollar falls to $1.60, the importer will have to pay $1.60 Canadian to buy one U.S. dollar. Such a fall of the Canadian dollar can have important implications for the prices the importer must charge when the product is sold or on its profit margins if prices cannot be changed.

The "real" exchange rate is more difficult to understand, but it is of even greater importance in many instances. The concept of the real exchange rate can be illustrated with a stylized example. In year one, assume that U.S. and Japanese producers of machine tools are making normal economic profits; the landed, duty-paid price of a U.S. machine tool in Japan is $100,000; the nominal exchange rate is 100 yen = $1; and the price of comparable machine tools *in yen* is 10,000,000. The U.S.-produced machine tool is then competitive in Japan (since $100,000 = 10,000,000 yen and exports take place). Over the next year, inflation in the United States is 10 percent and in Japan it is only 3 percent, *and* the *nominal* exchange rate remains at 100 yen = $1. What has happened to the ability of the U.S. producer to export to Japan? If the total costs of the U.S. producer (including a normal profit) have risen by the average rate of U.S. inflation, its costs would be $100,000 × 1.10 = $110,000 = 11,000,000 yen. The price of Japanese competitors *in yen* has risen by the Japanese rate of inflation to 10,000,000 × 1.03 = 10,300,000. Hence, the U.S. producer must either cut prices in dollars to $103,000 and severely reduce its profit margins or the Japanese importer will not be able to sell the product in competition with Japanese-made products.

In this example, although the *nominal* exchange rate has remained constant, the ability of the U.S. producer to export to Japan has declined due to differing inflation rates between Japan and the United States. The real exchange rate is a measure of this loss of competitive ability due to differing inflation rates (and hence changing relative costs). In this example, the *real* exchange rate has *risen* by about 7 percent. The real exchange rate can be thought of as an index number. In the example, if it were 100 in year one, it would have risen to 106.8 (1.10/1.03 × 100) in year two. (For small percentage inflation rates, the calculation can be simplified to: the real exchange rate in year two = 100 + U.S. inflation − Japanese inflation rate = 100 + 10 − 3 = 107.) In order for the U.S. producer to remain competitive, the *nominal* exchange rate in this example would have had to fall by 6.36 percent to 93.6 (1.03/1.10 − 1 = 0.0636), more or less the inflation rate differential. If this had occurred, then the *real* exchange rate would have remained constant.

Just as a rise in the real exchange rate reduces the competitive ability in export markets of national producers, it also increases the competitive ability of producers abroad to export to the domestic market. Hence, all else equal, a rise in the real exchange rate leads to reduced export growth rates and increased import growth rates. Conversely, a fall in the real exchange rate leads to increased export growth rates and reduced import growth rates. Notice that this effect is *independent* of either comparative or competitive advantage of the nation or of its firms.

For managers engaged in international trade operations, an analysis of movements of the real exchange rates is crucial for determining success in export markets and success in competing with imports. In the mid-1980s, the United States had a comparative advantage in sophisticated machine tools, but its currency was overvalued by almost 50 percent (i.e., its real exchange rate has moved from 108 in to 154). U.S. producers found themselves priced out of export markets on the one hand and under threat of import competition on the other.

Estimates of the real exchange rate of major trading countries are available on a monthly basis from many sources, most notably the *International Financial Statistics Yearbook* (published by the International Monetary Fund).[7] For example, over the 1978 to 1996 period (with 1990 indexed as 100), the real exchange rate of the U.S. dollar rose from 108.8 in 1978 to as high as 156.5, fell to 91.9 in 1995, and rose to 96.9 in 1996. The effects of these movements in the U.S. real exchange rate on U.S. exporters and firms that compete with imports were dramatic—and completely swamped out any effects of relative competitive ability due to "Japanese management," technological superiority, product quality differentials, or national trade strategies, factors which have figured prominently in the press as causes of the U.S. trade deficit.

Exhibit 3–4 displays the real exchange rate of the U.S. dollar from 1975 to 1996 and the U.S. trade balance *lagged by two years* (i.e., from 1977 to 1998). The lag was included since imports and exports respond to changes in the real exchange rate with a lag. Firms take time to switch among sources of supply on the international market and to fill export and import orders. With the fall of the dollar in 1985, U.S. exports began to expand rapidly and import growth was reduced. From 1985 to 1991, U.S. export volume increased by 68 percent and import volume increased by 26 percent. Over the same period, export and import volumes in Japan increased 65 and 17 percent, respectively; for Germany the figures were

---

[7]See the technical notes in the IMF publication for a description of how the various measures of real exchange rates have been calculated.

EXHIBIT 3–4   U.S. Real Exchange Rates, 1975–96, and Balance of Trade, 1977–98

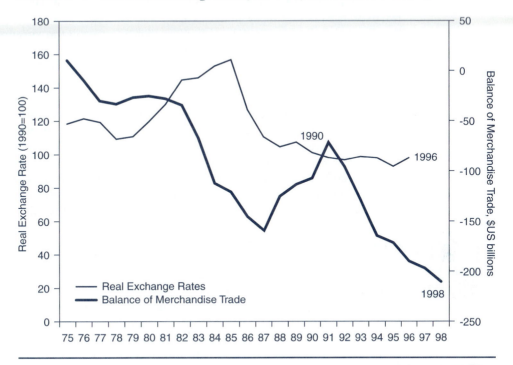

Note: The trade balance in billions of dollars (right-hand scale) is lagged behind the real exchange rate (left-hand scale, with 1990=100).

Source: IMF, *International Financial Statistics Yearbook,* 1998.

24 and 61 percent.[8] This dramatic reversal of the fortunes of U.S., Japanese, and German exporters was largely the result of the changes in the real exchange rates of these countries.[9]

In Japan, the situation was roughly the reverse of that in the United States. From an index of 82.8 in 1985, its real exchange rate rose to 116.6 in 1988, declined to 100 in 1990, rose continuously to a high of 166.7 in mid-1995, and then fell dramatically to 124 in mid-1996. These real exchange rate movements have had a significant effect on Japanese firms and the economy as a whole. Major Japanese firms have had to downsize and lay off workers, relocate production abroad, and increase productivity substantially. This restructuring and redeployment of resources was one of the major factors that contributed to the slow growth of the Japanese economy in the mid-1990s.

[8]These figures are for the overall exchange rates, not the bilateral ones between the United States and Japan or Germany. The fluctuations of these rates were higher still. Similarly, the trade statistics are for total, not bilateral, trade. If the bilateral trade figures had been given, both the change in real exchange rates and the change in export growth rates would have been substantially greater.

[9]Demand conditions also influence international trade and are an important factor in explaining post-1991 changes in the U.S. balance of trade. This point is discussed at the end of this chapter.

As part of this block of the analysis, the key role of the level and potential movements of the real exchange rate between the two countries must be assessed. The IMF publishes real exchange rates for many countries in the *International Financial Statistics Yearbook.* For those countries for which data are not available, a rough approximation of the movement of the real exchange rate can easily be made. Essentially, if the inflation rate in one country exceeds that of another, in order for its real exchange rate to remain constant, its nominal exchange rate must devalue by the inflation rate differential. In the example above, the U.S. inflation rate was 7 percent higher than that in Japan. So, for the real exchange rate to remain constant, the yen would have to appreciate against the dollar by about 7 percent. If it did not, but rather appreciated by only 2 percent, then the real value of the dollar would have risen by about 5 percent.

An increase in a country's real exchange rate has many of the same effects as a reduction in its tariff rate: it makes market access easier as the prices of imports relative to domestic production fall. A fall in the real exchange rate has the opposite effect. It is difficult to overemphasize the importance of movements of the real exchange rate of the home country and potential destination countries for international trade flows and for the success of import and export operations.

The importance of the real exchange rate holds for large and small countries and for high-income and developing countries alike.[10] In the early 1990s, foreign investors perceived that the Philippines had a relatively stable government. Foreign direct and portfolio investment began to pour into the Philippines. At the same time, transfers from abroad (largely by Filipino overseas workers) accelerated. The consequent 25 percent rise in the real exchange rate of the Philippines from 1991 to 1995 led to a reduction in export growth, an increase in import growth, and a reduction in manufacturing employment of 16 percent, despite a surge of foreign investment.

Real exchange rates may change for several reasons. If there is a gap between investment demand and domestic savings, real interest rates will rise and capital will flow in from abroad, thereby driving up the real exchange rate. The inevitable imbalances that this appreciation of the real exchange rate will cause will lead to mounting external debt and eventually to an unwillingness of investors abroad to hold more debt. Capital inflows will decline and the real exchange rate will fall. For the United States, high investment demand (due to an expanding economy) and a low savings rate (due to low personal savings and large government deficits) led to high real interest rates, capital inflows, a rise in the real exchange rate, and a deterioration of U.S. trade accounts from 1977 to 1985. Over the 1985 to 1988 period, private investors outside the United States became increasingly reluctant to hold more U.S. dollar denominated debt, capital inflows from these sources declined, and the real exchange rate declined.

Similarly, short-term government macroeconomic policy (to reduce inflation, for example) may lead to relatively high interest rates and an appreciation of the real exchange rate. Over the 1986 to 1991 period, Canada's real exchange rate rose by 27 percent in response to a government policy of halting inflation by setting high interest rates. The

---

[10]The exception to this generalization is when a country counteracts movements in its real exchange rate by additional offsetting export promotional measures and import impeding measures. Korea is one example of a country which through 1985 was able to follow such a policy.

policies worked, but at the expense of the trade sector. Once inflation was reduced and the government relaxed its monetary policies in 1991, the real exchange rate fell significantly, dropping from 100 in 1990 to 83 in 1996.

Real exchange rates may also increase (decrease) if a country's terms of trade (the ratio of unit export prices to unit import prices) move in its favor (against it). If this change is permanent, then the real exchange rate will remain at this higher level. For example, if the decline in oil prices over the 1981–88 period were permanent, the real exchange rates of oil-exporting countries would have to fall permanently in order for them to maintain their trade accounts at a sustainable level. In fact, the real exchange rates of oil exporters, such as Saudi Arabia and Bahrain, did fall from 40 to 50 percent with the decline in oil prices in the mid-1980s through the early 1990s.

A country's real exchange rate can also appreciate if some valuable natural resource is discovered within the country. For example, when natural gas was discovered in Holland's offshore waters, its real exchange rate rose as this gas was exported. The rise in Holland's real exchange rate caused manufacturers in Holland to be priced out of export markets for manufacturing products and led to a decline in its manufacturing sector, the so-called Dutch disease. If a country's productivity increases relative to that of its trading partners, its real exchange rate will rise, unless the government acts to hold it down by accumulating foreign exchange reserves and investing abroad. In this case, the country will generate ever-increasing trade surpluses until the time when it lets its exchange rate rise to an appropriate level. This phenomenon occurred in such countries as Japan, South Korea, and Taiwan over the 1985 to 1988 period. Singapore is an interesting example of a country that has resisted this pressure to revalue its currency. From 1985 to 1996, it maintained the real exchange rate of the Singapore dollar while at the same time accumulating $71 billion in foreign exchange reserves by 1997 ($23,000 per capita, by far the largest per capita foreign exchange reserves in the world outside the oil-exporting countries). In the future, despite the unwillingness of the Singapore government to revalue its currency, its real value will have to rise.

The examples given above should not lead to a conclusion that real exchange rates are highly volatile. The real exchange rates of Switzerland and Austria have not changed by more than 15 percent over the past decade. Real exchange rates move dramatically only in response to strong economic forces, such as the financial crisis in Asia in the late-1990s. It is, however, important to identify those times when real exchange rates move away from their long-run equilibrium position and to make appropriate decisions regarding trade and investment.

The theory and evidence from international finance show that over the short run the foreign exchange market is "perfect," i.e., that investors on average cannot make economic profits in speculating in foreign exchange. Over the longer term, however, it is possible to forecast movements in the real exchange rate (and hence the nominal exchange rate) when the real exchange rate is significantly above or below its long-run equilibrium value. The long run is the appropriate time frame for those engaged in international trade (a long-term investment in export markets) and foreign direct investment. Although it is impossible to "beat" the foreign exchange market consistently over the short term, from time to time it is both possible and necessary to predict the direction of real and nominal exchange rate movements accurately over the longer term. This task is part of an international manager's job.

For managers, there are several implications of this analysis of the effects of movements in real exchange rates on the competitive advantage of their firms. First, they must try to determine if changes in real exchange rates are short- or long-term. The effects of short-term movements in real exchange rates on their competitive ability should be taken into account when making such decisions as whether to change the volume and prices of their exports in response to exchange-rate movements or to absorb the impact of these changes on the profitability of export operations.

In the early 1980s, with the rise of the real value of the U.S. dollar, Japanese car producers increased their market penetration by pricing aggressively in dollars (while still maintaining their profit levels in yen). When the combination of increased imports and the recession led to layoffs and losses in the U.S. car industry, the U.S. government was induced to negotiate restraint agreements on cars from Japan. Japanese car manufacturers responded to volume restrictions by raising prices on existing models and by introducing new models at even higher prices (to clear the market) and made enormous profits in the U.S. market. With the fall of the dollar in 1985, the Japanese were faced with a dilemma: either raise U.S. prices dramatically and lose market share or have profit levels decline. A similar dilemma was faced by Japanese consumer electronics firms. Both groups of firms did raise prices, but not to the extent of the decline of the dollar against the yen. The result was that by the early 1990s most Japanese car and consumer electronics firms were running operating losses (partially offset by nonoperating profits on their portfolio investments of their previous profits). Over the longer term, when the Japanese saw that the real value of the yen would remain high, they upgraded product quality, increased efficiency, laid off workers, and invested heavily abroad.

The second implication for managers is that identification of times when their home country's real exchange rate is above its long-run equilibrium level and when a destination country's real exchange rate is below this level can assist in identifying export market opportunities, since, unless the change is permanent, ultimately overvalued and undervalued exchange rates will move back to their equilibrium levels. Third, identification of short- and long-run movements of real exchange rates in the future can assist in identification of threats and opportunities arising from international markets.

Another implication of real exchange-rate movements goes beyond international trade into both portfolio and direct investment management. As mentioned above, the rise of the U.S. dollar through 1985 was largely fueled by huge inflows of investment in U.S. financial instruments: short- and long-term bonds and stock purchases. These investors used their relatively cheap foreign currencies to buy relatively expensive dollars to make these investments. When the dollar fell, the value of these investments in terms of foreign currencies fell as well. For these investors, the good news was that they earned relatively high returns (interest and stock appreciation and dividends) in dollars; the bad news was that they lost substantial capital when they converted their depreciated U.S. dollars into their national currencies. Japanese financial institutions were reported to have lost upward of $40 billion (in terms of yen).

For direct investors in plant and equipment, the situation was somewhat different. They too converted relatively cheap foreign currencies to buy relatively expensive dollars. And they were hurt when the dollar declined. On the other hand, as the dollar fell, the cost competitiveness of their investments increased (just as it did for U.S. manufacturers), and hence profits rose above projections. However, these profits were in dollars.

For all these reasons, a close watch should be kept on movements of real exchange rates. Further, forecasts of real exchange-rate movements should be made. Although this forecasting exercise is difficult, it can be extremely useful. And not to forecast is to miss opportunities and to court trouble. All else equal, for real exchange rates, what goes up must come down, and vice versa.

One of the problems in this analysis, however, is to decide whether a rise in the real exchange rate is a movement back toward equilibrium or away from equilibrium. A good starting point can be found by determining a time period when the country's trade is roughly balanced, then counting back two years (to account for lag effects) and defining this level as 100. Movements away from 100 in the real exchange rate will tend to be movements away from equilibrium, which eventually will be reversed. Other indications of an *overvalued* real exchange rate are persistent and worsening trade deficits, high real interest rates, unusual capital inflows, and chronic international debt problems. For countries with a high concentration of exports in a particular natural resource product, such as oil or natural gas, a long-term shift (up or down) will put pressure on the real exchange rate (up or down). Conversely, for countries with persistent trade surpluses, mounting foreign exchange reserves, and burgeoning international investments, there will be pressures for the real exchange rate to rise.

Demand

The final factors influencing international trade (both imports and exports) are demand conditions over the business cycles in the domestic market and in export markets, and source countries for imports. If the domestic economy is expanding relative to the economies of other countries, exporters will tend to divert production to the domestic market, where demand and prices are rising. Producers abroad, faced with slack demand at home, will tend to try to push excess production onto export markets. For example, the large Japanese trade surplus in 1998 was in part due to the *fall* of the yen over the past few years. But it was also influenced by the deceleration of the growth rate of the Japanese economy and import demand there and the increase in import demand in the United States as the U.S. economy expanded.

Summary

The first step in a firm's analysis of its international trade position is to analyze the forces in the national economy that give rise to some form of comparative advantage or disadvantage. The exporter must also analyze what competitive advantage the firm has or can develop, based either on the country's comparative advantage or on "ownership advantages"—such as economies of scale, marketing, management, and R&D—which cannot easily be duplicated by other competitors worldwide. In general, the more closely a firm's competitive advantage is aligned with the country's comparative advantage, the more easily it can develop, maintain, and increase its competitive advantage. In Thailand there is a saying, "It's easier to help an elephant get up when it's getting up than it is to hold it up when it wants to lie down." Our youth culture phrases this as "Go with the flow." These sayings apply to international trade.

Supplementary Reading

Cline, William R. *American Trade Adjustment: The Global Impact.* Policy Analysis in International Economics Series No. 26. Washington, D.C.: Institute for International Economics, 1989.

Jackson, John. *The World Trading System.* Cambridge, MA: MIT Press, 1992.

Kreinen, Mordechai E. *International Economics: A Policy Approach.* Fort Worth, TX: Dryden Press, 1998.

Krugman, Paul R., and Maurice Obstfeld. *International Economics: Theory and Practice.* 4th ed. Reading, MA: Addison-Wesley, 1997.

Porter, Michael E. "Clusters and the New Economics of Competition." *Harvard Business Review,* November-December 1998, pp. 77–90.

———. *The Competitive Advantage of Nations.* New York: Free Press, 1990.

Scherer, F. M., and Richard S. Belous *Unfinished Tasks: The New International Trade Theory.* New York, Ottawa, and London: The British-North American Committee, 1995.

Thurow, Lester. *Head to Head: The Coming Economic Battle Among Japan, Europe, and America.* New York: William Morrow and Company, 1992.

Vernon, Raymond, and Debora Spar. *Beyond Globalism: Remaking American Foreign Economic Policy.* New York: Macmillan, Free Press, 1989.

The World Competitiveness Yearbook 1999. Lausanne, Switzerland: IMD, 1999.

World Trade Organization, *www.wto.org.* Geneva, Switzerland: 1999.

4   MANAGING EXPORT OPERATIONS

In Chapter 3, the STEP framework was introduced. This framework can be used by managers to analyze a firm's comparative and competitive advantage in export markets. A firm's competitive advantage can be moderated by movements in the real exchange rate and in demand conditions abroad. The second block of analysis centers on the analysis of export markets to assess their potential demand for the firm's products. The firm may have a product with a competitive advantage, but it also needs to identify a market in which users value its product above the products that are currently available in the market from domestic producers and exporters from other countries. One procedure for accomplishing this analysis involves three steps. Initially, the analysis will focus on single-country markets, but later on in the chapter regional and global markets will be brought into the analysis.

Step 1: Segment World Markets

Market segmentation lies at the heart of marketing for many products, especially the differentiated products that have become increasingly important in international trade. This chapter, however, is not the place for an elaborate description of market segmentation techniques; this can be found in introductory marketing textbooks.

In segmenting markets in countries abroad, several fundamental questions must be addressed: Is there a market segment in the potential export market that will value the product characteristics of the exporter's product? Is this segment large enough to justify the costs of exporting? Is this segment adequately served by existing domestic producers or other exporters? Can it be accessed by the exporter?

Markets can be segmented in a number of ways. The two most important are product quality and product features. Both of these two segmentation techniques have implications for product price. Typically, the higher the quality and the greater the number of distinctive product features, the higher the costs of production and marketing and the higher the

---

This chapter was prepared by Paul W. Beamish.

price. One of the characteristics of international markets is the wide range of quality and product characteristics that are in demand by some groups of potential buyers. As examples, sweaters sell for $8 at a discount store, while across town at a fashionable store sweaters are sold for over $1,000; name-brand ballpoint pens, such as Cross or Mount Blanc, sell for $70 to $200, while Bic pens are sold for 50 cents—sometimes in the same store.

Initially, in the 1960s, Japanese automobile firms entered the U.S. market by following a niche strategy aimed at the low end of the market. They targeted buyers with low incomes, buyers who wanted a second car, and buyers who were more interested in basic transportation than in quality or features. Over time, these Japanese producers have upgraded their products to compete in ever higher priced segments of the market. On the other hand, in the 1980s, when Honda entered the U.S. market for products using small, gas-powered engines—such as lawn mowers, outboard motors, and generators—it chose the very high end of the market to cater to high-income consumers who wanted dependability, quality, unique design, and high performance and had the money to pay for these features. When Samsung entered China with color televisions, a key issue was which segment to target.

Market segments often differ between countries in the number, size, and characteristics by which they are segmented. In the United States, markets may be segmented regionally, whereas in Japan there may be few regional differences. Markets in a populous country, such as the United States, may have more segments (with enough demand in each segment to make the segmentation effort pay off) than in less populous countries. The proportion of the market in each segment often differs among countries. For consumer products, differences in the age distribution of the population, income level and growth, and the distribution of income may affect segment size and relative importance.

If, for example, the exporter's product is of high quality or has unique design features, one starting point would be to segment countries by GNP per capita (as a proxy for personal disposable income) and then to focus on countries with high GNP per capita. This crude segmentation could be refined, however, by examining the income distributions of both the initial target group and lower-income countries (that had been left out of the group) to identify countries with a disproportionately high percentage of high-income or high-wealth residents, such as many of the countries in South America and some of the countries in the Asia-Pacific region. If the exporter's product were most appropriate for one age group, trends in these countries in the age distribution of the population could then be examined. For products appropriate for older people, Japan and some European countries would stand out; for the youth market, certain South American countries; for infants, certain African countries, Canada, and the United States.

Consumer tastes also influence segment size. Consumers in Japan, for example, place considerable value on product quality and design features and often prefer to buy a limited number of high-quality, high-priced products, rather than a large number of low-quality, low-priced products. Countries could also be grouped by weather conditions—average temperature and range, and amount of rainfall—for products whose performance and appropriateness are dependent on these conditions. For tropical countries, both packaging and product may have to be changed to be more resistant to humidity and high temperatures. As an example, Tetra packs for juices and milk are more prevalent in tropical countries, particularly lower-income ones where refrigeration is not widespread.

For industrial machinery and inputs, the level and dispersion of wages and technical skills and the composition of industrial output affect the size and importance of market segments. Very high technology, highly automated, but flexible machinery might be targeted at northern Europe, Japan, and Canada; somewhat more standardized, mass-production machinery might be directed at the newly industrializing countries; and older, standardized machinery targeted at the developing countries. For example, Husky Injection Moulding has been able to extend the life of its product line by selling its highest-priced, most-advanced, high-speed equipment to the United States, Europe, and Japan, while at the same time selling its older, much cheaper, slower equipment to countries in which demand is lower. Similarly, countries could be segmented according to their natural resource and agricultural bases by exporters of production equipment for mining and agriculture or for processing of these products.

Fast growth often leads to strains on infrastructure. In some emerging markets, for example, the demand for electricity has grown 8–10 percent a year for the last decade, leading to a huge demand for electrical generating equipment and services. Similar demand growth can be found in fast-growing countries for construction and earth-moving equipment, water distribution and treatment facilities, telecommunications equipment, sewage treatment equipment, pollution control equipment, and garbage handling and processing equipment. In many developing countries privatization of many basic infrastructure operations has led to a burgeoning demand for investment in these services.

Once the potential export destinations have been placed in groups with higher and lower priority, the market potential in each country needs to be examined in more detail. Part of this analysis has already been accomplished in the analysis of the previous block, when the firm's sustainable competitive advantage was identified. The consumers and industrial buyers that value the firm's product in the home country and give it a competitive advantage there are often similar to the ones that will value it in export markets. The consumer segment that values a firm's high-quality pots and pans in the home market may be the same as the consumer segment in export markets. As well, in many cases firms with export potential will have received (and sometimes filled) unsolicited orders from customers or importers abroad. The problem, then, is to discover if there is sufficient demand in these export markets to justify a more concerted export marketing effort. After payment of transportation costs, agents' fees, and tariffs, the price the firm must charge to be profitable in an export market may have risen several-fold above the price that its normal target segment is willing to pay. Then the problem is to determine if there are sufficient potential purchasers in the segment who can and are willing to buy in this price range and if the firm's product will have a competitive advantage in this segment. For example, a pots and pans manufacturer in the United States may have a competitive advantage in the large middle segment of the U.S. market, but in Japan it will have to aim at the top end of the market, a smaller segment. Yogurt sells for 50 cents a container in Australia, but yogurt exported from Australia to Indonesia sells there for $2 a container while Häagen-Dazs ice cream sells for $10 a pint.

Three conditions may be particularly important in this type of analysis: (1) emerging demand met by innovations in product technology in one country that are mirrored in other countries, (2) the deregulation and restructuring of markets, and (3) government policies and programs. As examples, changing energy prices have led to emerging demand for vehicles powered by natural gas in many countries. Compressed natural gas units to power vehicles developed in response to demand conditions in one country may face the same demand conditions in other countries. The restructuring of markets in Japan in response to rising incomes and efforts by the Japanese government to open up the country to international trade has presented opportunities for many exporters to penetrate channels of distribution (such as door-to-door sales, large discount stores, and catalog sales), and to increase sales of heavily branded luxury products.

Identification of emerging product and segment demand is a prime tool of export marketing. It is often easier to penetrate a rapidly growing market or segment of the market than to penetrate markets and segments in which demand is stagnant. In these more dynamic markets and segments, existing suppliers may be experiencing problems with expanding capacity, or they may have grown complacent as their sales have boomed. At least part of the success of the Airbus during the 1980s stemmed from the capacity problems experienced by Boeing in the face of escalating demand for civilian aircraft. In buoyant markets and segments, existing suppliers may be less prone to retaliate against a new exporter. Although existing suppliers may lose market share to the newcomer, their sales levels will continue to increase. In emerging markets and segments, the distribution system may also be in a state of flux, and traditional buyer-seller relationships may be weaker than in slower-growing markets and segments.

Step 2: Select an Entry Strategy to Promote Sustainable Competitive Advantage

Once a viable segment of the market has been selected, the next step is to determine the best strategy by which to penetrate this segment. Strategy formulation does not end with matching product characteristics to market segments. It should include channels of distribution, sales and advertising techniques, service before and after sales, and so on. Some producers give substantial support to wholesalers and retailers. They provide fast delivery, inventory support, and technical assistance and training before the sale and repair and maintenance support after the sale. On the other hand, some firms have been successful in export markets by providing a lower level of these services to their distribution networks and to consumers and, instead, competing more on the basis of price.

Having a different strategy than the major competitors in the market also has advantages. Large entrenched producers with strong brand images may find it difficult to respond to exporters following a strategy that differs from their own. A similar situation exists in many markets for entrants at the bottom end of the market. The branded major producers may not be able to respond without damaging their brand images.

The final, and arguably the most important, decision in a firm's export strategy is whether to sell a standardized product worldwide or whether to tailor products and the entire marketing mix to meet individual country requirements. There is no one right or wrong answer to this problem. The correct answer depends on a host of considerations, such as the ability and capacity of the firm to modify products, the R&D and design costs of modifications, and the effects on production, inventory, and distribution costs of producing and marketing a more diverse set of products.

In the past, exporters in different countries tended to follow one of three different strategies. In general, firms in Japan tended to export one standardized product to all markets;

firms in the United States tended to follow a product life-cycle strategy by first introducing a new product in the U.S. market and later exporting it as demand by other countries became more similar to U.S. demand; and firms in Europe tended to be more responsive to local market conditions and to view each market as a separate entity. These generic strategies tended to converge and overlap during the 1980s, as firms tried to incorporate all the strengths of flexibility to respond to individual market needs, global marketing to gain economies of scale, and international learning to access and supply worldwide product and process innovations. As examples, Toyota, after initially selling the same car in Canada as it did worldwide, now tailors its cars sold in Canada to better withstand diverse weather conditions: extremes of heat and cold and prolonged exposure to salt. Kodak introduced a new line of film first in Japan, then in Europe, and only a year later in the United States.

Export strategies can be changed over time in response to changing exchange rates and consumer preferences. Initially, Japanese car firms exported inexpensive standard cars that competed on price, not quality, design, or features. Over time, they broadened their product line to access consumers with different preferences to increase market share.

In general, most exporters would prefer to follow a standard product and marketing-mix strategy worldwide. Such a strategy reduces production, logistics, and inventory costs, complexity, market and product research and development, and managerial time. Such a strategy is obviously more appropriate for some products than for others. If demand characteristics are similar in many potential export markets, then a standardized product approach is often most appropriate, and vice versa. The same Pringles potato chips are exported all over the world. On the other hand, U.S. cookie, ketchup, and cereal manufacturers have had to modify the sugar content of their product for export to Europe. The key question to be addressed is the extent to which demand will be increased through product and marketing-mix changes (at constant prices) and to what extent differentiation will lead to higher costs, higher prices, and decreased demand. Usually, tailoring a product for individual markets through product modification will increase market share. Unless the full costs of this tailoring can be recouped in higher prices or increased demand, however, following this strategy will not be successful, where success is defined in terms of profits on export markets.[1] Even for the same product, different companies can successfully follow different strategies. In personal health care products, for example, Ponds sells the same face cream worldwide, while other producers tailor their products to individual markets, based on such characteristics as skin color, texture, and weather conditions. P&G sells Tide laundry detergent in bars in many developing countries, where most washing is done by hand. But it also sells its standard powdered detergent. Philips sells the same lighting products worldwide. But firms from Taiwan sell lower-quality lighting products at lower prices to developing countries.[2]

---

[1]See Adrian Ryans, "Strategic Market Entry Factors and Market Share Achievement in Japan," *Journal of International Business Studies,* Fall 1988.

[2]Ironically, Philips' expensive, but long-life, energy-efficient "new lighting" fluorescent lamps (which it developed for high-income markets) face severe problems in some developing countries. The problem is not competition with lower-price products; the problem is that to achieve energy efficiency and long life, the voltage tolerances on these products make them inappropriate for countries with problems in voltage swings and low voltage.

A company may follow a combination of both strategies for one product. It can sell a standard product in markets of one group of countries and tailor its product for another group of countries. Similarly, a company may follow a standard product strategy for one product and a tailored product strategy for another. Coca-Cola, for example, follows a standard product strategy for Coke, but a tailored product strategy for Fanta by which it sells a wide range of flavors in some countries.

Step 3: Take a Long-Run Perspective

Export markets are not built overnight. Building and maintaining a sustainable competitive advantage in any one export market, let alone worldwide, is an investment (although for accounting purposes it must unfortunately be treated as a current cost). The initial R&D, channel development, and advertising (all necessary to launch a product) are best viewed as investments, not current costs. So, too, should the costs of entering export markets be viewed as investments. They are investments whose payoffs come only over time. A firm must invest the time and the money in export markets. It must gain expertise in export operations and in identifying export markets; identify, select, and manage channels of distribution into those markets; gain the technical expertise to modify products for export markets; and develop on-the-ground experience in an export market. As well, often initial losses are incurred to penetrate markets through low prices. All these costs are *investments* in export markets, not expenses.

This characterization of the initial stages of export marketing as an investment strengthens the value of the systematic approach to export operations outlined in this framework. The costs of undertaking the research involved in using this framework to analyze export opportunities are low, compared with the costs of investment in product and process R&D, channels of distribution, and market development that often follow a decision to enter an export market.

Factors That Impede and Facilitate Trade

If a firm's product has a competitive advantage in export markets and if there is a country market or a segment within that market that values the product sufficiently above the products of competing suppliers to offset the costs of exporting, attention can be turned to the factors that may impede or facilitate access to this demand. These factors can be divided into natural and government-imposed ones. The latter are discussed in Chapter 12 in greater detail. Natural factors include transportation costs and the cost of doing business in a different country. Government-imposed factors include impediments such as tariff and nontariff barriers to trade and undervalued exchange rates. On the other hand, governments of the exporting country can also facilitate trade through export incentives, concessional financing for exports, information services, sponsored trade fairs, and export missions.

Over the decades, transportation, communications, and travel costs have fallen, thereby reducing some of the natural impediments to trade and world competition. National differences have also decreased due to the convergence of income levels in many countries, mass media, and travel (and arguably the spread of English as the language of international business). National differences in language, culture, social values, and political systems, however, can still represent major barriers to trade, especially for a new exporter. Many Canadian firms have experienced difficulty in operating in the United States even though the two countries seem to be quite similar. The Japanese language is a major barrier to exporting to and operating in Japan. People differ among countries in how they relate to each other and in how they do business. These differences act as impediments to trade. Lack of knowledge and expertise in doing business abroad in general and in specific export markets is a key barrier to trade. It is a key impediment for firms in their efforts to realize the potential competitive advantage of their products. Conversely, having this knowledge and expertise is a key competitive strength, but one that can be developed only at considerable cost. The manager of a large Japanese trading company in Singapore has stated that the company is not much interested in its operations in Singapore. The Singapore economy and government regulations are too open, transparent, and straightforward. This company largely left Singapore to new, smaller firms who competed fiercely with each other and made small profits. The manager preferred operations in Indonesia, where markets and government regulation were complex and filled with "anomalies," which, once understood, led to substantial profits.

Channels of Distribution and Export Marketing

The last block of analysis involves identifying the means by which the product can be moved from the producer to the ultimate buyer.

Four characteristics of the channels of distribution that link producers in one country with buyers in another are especially important:

1. International channels of distribution are usually more complex and have more layers than do channels in the national market. A typical channel for the domestic market would be: producer–wholesaler–retailer. For export it might be: producer–export agent–import agent–major wholesaler–small wholesaler–retailer.

2. The costs of international channels are usually higher than those of domestic channels, so a higher percentage of the final price to the buyer comes from the costs of building, accessing, and operating through international channels of distribution.

3. An exporter may have to operate through different types of channels of distribution on export markets than it uses in its domestic market. For example, in the domestic market, its scale of operations or the value of close customer contact may argue for an in-house distribution and sales system all the way to the ultimate purchaser. To set up such a system in an export market might be prohibitively expensive, given planned export volumes. Conditions in export markets might be such that expertise in local marketing techniques (which the firm does not possess) may be more important than product knowledge. Regulations in the export market may hinder or even prohibit a firm from entering into distribution and sales operations. Conversely, in a firm's domestic market, there may be a well-developed system of independent distributors for the firm's

product, whereas in the export market such a distribution system may not exist or company personnel may not have the skills required to distribute and sell the firm's product effectively.

4. International channels of distribution are often also the source of information to the firm about conditions in its export markets, and how and why its product is succeeding or failing in these markets. In such a situation, a firm must either integrate forward into distribution and sales, place some of its personnel in the export market, or develop close ties and good information flows between itself and its distributors abroad.

For these four reasons, a firm's strategy toward, and management of, its international channels of distribution are usually relatively more important, more costly, and more difficult for export marketing than are its channels for marketing in the domestic market. A firm can have a competitive product, but if it chooses the wrong channel of distribution or mismanages its relationships with the channel, its export performance will be reduced below potential. As well, exporters, particularly new exporters, have less expertise with international channels of distribution than they have with the channels in their national markets.

Firms entering export operations are often caught in a bind when they select their channels of distribution. The more closely the channel matches the one they use in their domestic market, the greater their expertise at managing the channel, and the higher the probability of success. On the other hand, the more appropriate the channel is for the export market, the higher the probability of export success. The implications of these two generalizations on the factors influencing export success for channel selection may differ, however. A firm may use an in-house wholesale and retail system in the domestic economy, but access to a similar system in an export market may not be available, purchasing one may be too expensive, or the firm may not want to risk investing so much capital outside its home country. In this situation, it must turn to independent agents or distributors to gain access to the export market. Similarly, a firm may use direct selling in the domestic market, but such an approach may be inappropriate in the export market.

There is a wide variety of possible channels of distribution from which an exporter may choose: brokers, factors, manufacturer's representatives, export agents, wholesalers, retailers, import jobbers, trading houses, and so on. These trade intermediaries can be characterized in two dimensions. The first dimension is ownership of the goods: agents who act on the firm's behalf for a fee versus distributors who pay for, take title to, and sell the goods on their own behalf. The second dimension is channel control: a direct approach (in which the firm owns and operates the channels) versus an indirect approach (in which the channels are independent of the firm).

Selection among these four basic alternative combinations (and the many different types of organizations within each type) is a difficult but important task. The decision will rest on such criteria as the size, capabilities, and resources of the exporter; its strategy in the export market; the degree of risk it is willing to undertake; the extent of its current and future export sales; the importance of coverage, penetration, control, and information feedback; and the differences between the export market and the domestic market.

Conflicts can easily arise between exporters and independent (indirect) channels over many issues. Often importers desire sole import rights for the product in the country.

Exporters want sole product rights—that is, for the importer to carry no competing products. There can be conflicts over pricing, cost sharing for advertising and service, margins, new product introduction, and so on. The benefits of using indirect channels are that typically resource costs are lower and the independent channels may have superior firsthand knowledge of, and access to, customers in the export market. The major costs are in loss of control, less ability to push goods through the channels by discounts, promotions, and direct selling or to pull goods through the channels through control of advertising. Use of indirect channels usually reduces information flows and reduces knowledge acquisition of market information when compared with direct channels. The costs and benefits of using direct (company-owned) channels tend to be the reverse of the costs and benefits of indirect channels: initially less firsthand knowledge of, and expertise in, the market; less access to customers, greater up-front costs on the one hand, but fewer conflicts, increased control, and greater information flows on the other.

Often an exporter's success with using indirect (independent) channels of distribution rests on whether its bargaining power is greater or less than that of its independent agent/distributor. Superior bargaining power can rest with either side and largely depends on which side provides the most value, which side faces the greatest range of alternatives, and which side needs the other the most. The importance of channels of distribution and the difficulty in accessing them in Japan often tip the balance of bargaining power in favor of independent agents and distributors in Japan. Yet American firms have been able to access these channels or to develop their own through direct selling and in-house distribution and sales networks. Whatever channels are chosen and whatever the relative bargaining power, the complexity and the length of international channels of distribution add to their cost.

Pricing in Export Markets

Product pricing is an important and difficult decision in any market. Four pricing strategies can be identified that are unique to export markets: (1) requiring prices in export markets that yield higher returns than are available in domestic markets; (2) pricing to yield similar returns in domestic and export markets; (3) pricing to yield lower returns, or even losses, in export markets—at least in the short run; (4) and pricing to sell production in excess of the needs of the domestic market so long as these sales make a contribution to fixed overhead and profit.

The first pricing strategy is often based on the belief that export operations are more risky relative to domestic sales, and they often entail hidden costs that are not picked up by standard accounting systems. Under this viewpoint, the prices and profits recorded on export sales must be higher than those for domestic markets if exports are to be undertaken.

The second strategy is based on the viewpoint that export markets do not differ from domestic markets. This strategy is often taken by experienced exporters, for whom there is little differentiation between export and domestic sales. It is also taken by new and inexperienced exporters, who take an "if they order it, we'll ship it" attitude toward export markets.

The third strategy reflects an approach that views export markets as the potential growth markets of the future. These are the markets in which the firm must operate if it is to survive in the long run. These aggressive exporters are willing to take short-term losses to buy market share, to develop products that are appropriate for export markets, and to achieve economies of scale. They believe that in the long run, once their position in export markets has been established, their costs will be lowered and they will be able to earn satisfactory returns. This strategy, however, may make the firm vulnerable to antidumping action by domestic competitors in the export market and subject to antidumping duties.

The final strategy reflects a view of export markets as a dumping ground for production in times of excess capacity. Although this type of export does make a contribution to profits, firms that view export markets in this way cannot be regarded as true export marketers.

Whatever pricing strategy is chosen, the relatively high fixed costs per unit that are typical of international distribution channels have a significant effect on the ability of the firm to use price as a competitive weapon. To take an extreme case, often the costs of international distribution are a fixed amount *per unit* (due to transportation costs based on weight or volume, tariffs levied on a per unit basis, and channel costs/fees on a per unit basis). They do not vary with cost or price. Then a change of 10 percent at the producer price level may only change the price faced by the buyer by 2 percent. Yet a 10 percent reduction in price may reduce the producer's margins over direct costs by 50 percent. Buyer response to such a price cut would have to be enormous for this price cut to be worthwhile.

At least some of the costs of distribution are indeed set with respect to the producer's selling price, such as inventory costs, some agents' fees, and some components of tariff charges. Sales taxes are usually based on the landed, duty-paid price of the product. They vary with price. But there is also a fixed component due to the fixed transportation costs per unit. Most of the fees charged by independent agents are usually based on producer prices, as are the markups taken through the channels of distribution. Despite these portions of the price paid by purchasers that varies with the producer prices, in export marketing there is usually a higher component in final prices that varies with the number of units sold than for domestic marketing. This characteristic of export marketing must be taken into consideration by firms in their export marketing pricing strategies.

Stages of Export Market Involvement

For firms operating solely in the domestic market, starting a new business or introducing a new product are major strategic moves and are undertaken only after careful research, analysis, and consideration. The decision to enter export operations at all or in a particular export market is more often quite haphazard and made by chance, or the decision itself may go unnoticed. Most frequently, a firm will enter export operations based on an unsolicited order from abroad, or an offer from an agent or importer abroad to represent the firm or sell its products. Other unplanned entries into export marketing may come from internal factors, such as overproduction, declining domestic sales, and excess capacity. Such external events as competitive pressures, "follow the leader" behavior, government-sponsored trade fairs, and funded export missions may also lead to unplanned entry into export markets.

Most firms initially develop, produce, and market products for their domestic markets without regard for export markets. They may even turn down orders from abroad. If a firm continues to receive unsolicited orders, it may move toward filling orders as they are received, despite the problems of documentation and payment that may arise. Gradually, the firm may develop management expertise in the basic mechanics of exporting, and these orders begin to become a significant part of sales. In this situation, a firm may begin to explore why these orders have been received. It may try to determine if there is a potential to increase sales to the firms that have already placed orders and to other firms in the same export market.

In the next stage of export involvement, the firm begins to evaluate the impact of export sales on its performance in a more systematic way. If it finds this impact to be positive, it may begin to change its export operations to increase their effectiveness. It is at this stage when a systematic analysis of exporting, as described in these chapters, can be of value. In the final stage, exports become a major, even the deciding, factor in the firm's strategy and operations. For firms at this stage, products are often developed and introduced in relationship to export markets as well as the domestic market.

This process of internationalization may be short-circuited at any stage if the results of export operations are not seen as favorable. Such a decision may be incorrect if the firm has not really given export operations the same attention that it has given domestic markets. Conversely, a firm may have no choice but to start at some more advanced stage. The domestic market may be too small to support any operations at all, much less a scale-efficient one. Increasingly, however, the evolution of the international trading environment has forced more and more firms at a faster and faster pace through these stages of internationalization to become full-fledged export marketers. Table 4–1 summarizes many of the key conceptual issues for each of the major export stages according to various features.

Trade Intermediaries

Import Traders

The topic of importing has received relatively little attention in books on international marketing or international business. Yet for every export, there is an import. And arm's-length importing still represents the majority of imports. This section focuses on "pure" importers, i.e., importers who purchase products abroad for resale. The important topic of sourcing imports for use as inputs in the production process is the subject of the next chapter.

This section is quite brief, since much of the basic framework of analysis has already been presented. However from the perspective of the importer, the export framework presented earlier cannot simply be turned inside out. As Table 4–2 points out, the assumed importer behaviors associated with the relevant export decisions are not identical with actual importer behavior. An importer assesses the comparative and competitive advantages of producers outside the home market; assesses the evolving demand and supply characteristics of the home market to look for gaps in markets or segments of markets that these producers' products could fill; assesses the impediments to connecting producers abroad with buyers in the home market and the factors that might facilitate this linkage; and assesses the channels of distribution that might be used to link producers abroad with buyers in the home market. An importer could either have the objective to resell the imported products (an import marketer) to other buyers or to use these products as raw or semifinished materials, or as components in its own final products (an import purchasing manager).

TABLE 4–1   Conceptual Issues Emerging from Export Development Models

	Export Stages		
Model Features	*Pre-Engagement*	*Initial*	*Advanced*
(i) Facilitators and Inhibitors:			
Managerial characteristics	A number of objective and subjective managerial parameters might act as inhibitors in the firm's export engagement.	Certain managerial characteristics, such as cosmopolitan, multilingual and educated management, might facilitate the involvement of firms in export activities.	Management quality and dynamism is an important facilitator in advanced export operations.
Management style	The firm's management style applies only to the domestic business situation and it is rather institutionalized and structured.	The decisionmaker approaches export marketing in a rather informal, disjointed, and unplanned manner.	With the establishment of appropriate systems and processes relating to foreign business, decision-making styles tend to become more formalized, continuous, and structured.
Organizational determinants	Certain organizational determinants might prevent the engagement of the firm in foreign operations.	Some organizational factors, particularly those relating to the firm's competitive advantages, might facilitate the engagement of the firm in international operations.	The firm capitalizes on differential advantages, such as possession of unique products, competitive prices, and technological intensiveness, to gain a foothold in foreign markets.
Organizational resources	There is typically a limited number of corporate resources that are used exclusively for domestic operations.	The firm gradually commits small amounts of financial, human, and allied resources to international operations, due to the high uncertainty prevailing in foreign markets.	An increasing amount of organizational resources is released to export operations, but their allocation is based upon real market conditions and strategic preferences.
(ii) Information needs and acquisition:			
Information requirements	There is limited or no knowledge about export operations: firms actively seeking to export want information about foreign market possibilities.	The firm has limited experience and knowledge about exporting and, therefore, seeks information of a more experiential and general nature.	As the firm gains more experience and exposure to export activities, it searches for more objective and specific information.
Information acquisition	Lack of information about exporting results in high levels of uncertainty in international markets compared to the domestic market.	The availability of information about export business and foreign marketing practices is still limited, thus creating considerable uncertainty.	The firm gradually obtains more export-related information, particularly of an experiential nature, leading to reduced levels of uncertainty regarding overseas markets.
(iii) Stimuli and barriers:			
Stimulating forces	The nonexporting firm is not responsive to various export stimuli to which it is exposed due to managerial, organizational, or environmental constraints.	The firm is more likely to be motivated in international business by reactive and external factors, exemplifying passive and tactical thinking toward exporting.	The export stimulation of the firm is more likely to occur due to proactive and internal factors, indicating an aggressive and strategic approach to international business.

(continued)

TABLE 4–1 *(concluded)*

Model Features	Export Stages		
	Pre-Engagement	Initial	Advanced
Barrier factors	The would-be exporter is exposed to a number of export barriers, the most important being its inability to locate/analyze foreign markets.	The firm experiences obstacles that are related mainly to difficulties in understanding the mechanics and day-to-day activities of exporting.	Export obstacles are associated mainly with strategic marketing issues and external constraints in foreign markets.
(iv) Market selection, entry/expansion:			
Market selection	The firm deals exclusively with the domestic market from where it might choose to serve specific segments.	The firm selects few countries that are more psychologically close to its home business and, therefore, easier and less costly to penetrate.	The firm gradually expands its foreign operations to a greater number of host countries that are psychologically more distant.
Entry mode	The firm uses only domestic distribution methods since its goods are sold exclusively in the home market.	The firm enters foreign markets via indirect export methods, such as export merchants, trading companies, resident buyers, and export agents.	The firm distributes its products to overseas markets using direct export methods, such as agents, distributors, and sales branches.
Market expansion	The firm is likely to undergo an extraregional expansion, that is, expansion within regions of its own country base.	Limited corporate resources, fear of the unknown, and other barriers are responsible for the firm adopting a concentrated foreign market focus.	As the firm acquires more resources, seeks to exploit more foreign opportunities, and gains expertise in handling export problems, it spreads to a large number of markets.
(v) Marketing strategy:			
Marketing control	The firm maintains full or partial control over the elements of the marketing mix, because it deals exclusively with the domestic market.	The firm is highly dependent on overseas buyers' guidelines and actions with regard to product, pricing, distribution, and promotional requirements in foreign markets.	The firm gradually internalizes and ultimately gains full control of the elements of the export marketing mix strategy.
Marketing adaptations	The firm's marketing strategy is relatively standardized as it deals exclusively with local customers.	The firm is more likely to adopt more standardized export marketing strategies.	Considerable adaptations in the elements of the marketing mix are likely to take place, particularly as regards products and promotion.

Source: L. C. Leonidou and C. S. Katsikeas, "The Export Development Process: An Integrative Review of Empirical Models," *Journal of International Business Studies,* Vol. 27, No. 3, 1996, pp. 532–33.

Pure importers usually have an "ownership advantage" related to the domestic market in which they operate, such as knowledge of the domestic market, ownership of or access to the channels of distribution, or expertise in evaluating government regulation of imports, or business practices in the domestic market. Importers typically possess one of two other ownership advantages: knowledge and expertise in operations in one or more foreign countries or knowledge and expertise in the production capabilities of some product or range of

TABLE 4–2   Understanding Importer Behavior

Relevant Export Decisions	Assumed Importer Behavior	Actual Importer Behavior
Export initiation	• Exporters export to importers. • Importers lured into importing when exporters offer better deals.	• "Global" importers recruit, select, train exporters. • Buyers forced into importing when existing vendors failed to meet task-requirement and nontask expectations.
Export targeting	• Importers search the world for best exporters. • Best vendors included in choice set via screening analysis. • Best importers always available, "out there"; no deadline in targeting.	• Importers search heuristically to minimize cognitive effort and risk. • Choice set limited by accessibility in bilateral search and discovery. • Search terminated when "good enough" vendor found.
Export entry	• Vendor evaluation is transaction-based, process objective, and analytical. • Vendor evaluation compensatory, all relevant factors considered. • Best vendor chosen on the merits of export proposal (bid). • Export strategy based on 4Ps.	• Vendor evaluation is relationship-based, previous association important. • Vendor evaluation judgmental based on available info. and cognitive heuristics. • Qualified vendor chosen for non-task-related benefits. • More than 4Ps at work.
Export management	• Exporters are the prime movers of international trade. • Importers implement export strategy formulated/supported by exporters. • Export marketing decision controlled by exporters.	• World markets are increasingly "buyer's markets"; much international exchange is buyer-coordinated importing rather than producer-initiated exporting. • Importers have strategies of their own. • Importers may take control of export marketing decisions in importer-led international exchange.

Source: N. Liang and A. Parkhe, "Importer Behavior: The Neglected Counterpart of International Exchange," *Journal of International Business Studies,* Vol. 28, No. 3, 1997, p. 523.

products worldwide. The knowledge of domestic conditions allows importers to create value for producers abroad relative to the value they could access by exporting directly to buyers in the domestic economy. Knowledge of production capabilities worldwide allows them to create value for domestic producers (for imported inputs) and domestic retailers relative to the value they would receive if they tried to search out these products for themselves.

Pure importers are market connectors; they create value through linking producers abroad to buyers in the domestic market. If they do not continue to create value after the initial link has been made, producers abroad may begin to sell directly to the buyers in the domestic market. Similarly, purchasers in their domestic market will make direct connections with producers abroad.

Export Traders

In the section on export operations, the viewpoint of an export producer, rather than a pure export trader, was taken. This was done since in most respects the analysis of the international trade environment is the same from both perspectives. The major difference between the producer-exporter and the export trader is that the latter has the opportunity to buy products from (or act as an agent for) different producers in the same or different industries. In this respect, an export trader shares many of the same characteristics as an import trader. The "ownership advantages" of export traders typically lie in knowledge of markets in particular countries or in knowledge of worldwide markets for particular products. They are also market connectors and face the same problems as pure importers once they have linked domestic producers with buyers in export markets.

Trading Houses

In some cases, pure import operations and pure export operations may be joined together within the same firm: the trading house. Typically, however, a trading house will specialize in either exports or imports. The exception to this generalization is found in the large trading houses in Japan, Hong Kong, and Korea and to some extent in Europe and in firms that specialize in trading such commodities as energy products, minerals, and agricultural products.

Import and export operations also exist together in some export producers. These firms may need to source inputs for their production operations and to fill out their product lines from abroad and to export their output as well. As discussed below, some export sales are contingent on reciprocal imports under various forms of countertrade. These operations can be handled by this type of department as well.

In summary, managers of export operations or those about to engage in export operations need to address five questions:

1. Does our product and firm have a sustainable competitive advantage in export markets and, if so, why?
2. What are the export markets and the segments of those markets that will value our product sufficiently (relative to other competing products) to offset our costs of production and distribution?
3. Should the firm export a standard product with a standard marketing mix worldwide or should it tailor its products and marketing mix to individual export markets?
4. What natural and government-imposed trade barriers impede linking production in one country to purchase in another, and what factors might facilitate this linkage?
5. What are the most appropriate channels of distribution for our product to achieve our goals in export markets?

Global Trade and Investment

So far, the viewpoint of exporting has been one of a producer-exporter or importer or a trade intermediary exporting products to one country market. This viewpoint, although useful to present the basics of international trade, is highly simplistic and may give a false impression of international trade. This basic model can be extended to encompass a more realistic view of world trade. The model of international trade presented so far can be extended to make it more realistic in three ways.

First, as tariff and nontariff barriers to trade have fallen globally and as free trade areas have developed, firms often now analyze trade opportunities on a regional, even global, basis: exports to Belgium may not be of interest, but exports to Belgium as a gateway to Europe as a whole make a much more interesting proposition.

Second, exports are often not sent directly from one home production site to an export market abroad. Rather, inputs are sourced in a number of countries and assembled in other countries, and the final product is sold in yet other countries. Japanese car producers manufacture parts in Japan and ship them for assembly in Europe, in North America, and in developing countries. In turn they source some parts in these countries for use in Japan and in their assembly operations abroad.

Third, trade has become intricately linked with foreign investment, joint ventures, licensing, franchising, contract production, and component sourcing. These topics are described in later chapters. In particular there is a strong link between trade and foreign investment. A large component of international trade is carried out by multinational enterprises (MNEs). About a third of all world trade in manufactured products is through MNEs. Most U.S. merchandise exports were undertaken by U.S. MNEs or affiliates of foreign-owned MNEs operating in the United States. A similar situation prevailed in the United Kingdom. Japanese MNEs accounted for over 40 percent of exports from and 60 percent of imports to Japan. A considerable proportion of the trade conducted by MNEs is within the firm (i.e., between units of the MNE located in different countries).

Is the analytical framework developed so far useful for analyzing trade by MNEs? What then are the differences between trade via or within MNEs and arm's-length trade? The answer to the first question is yes, but with some modifications. By definition, an MNE has investments and (usually) production operations in more than one country. At the headquarters level of the MNE, basic decisions are made about where different activities along the value-added chain are located geographically. For example, one U.S. manufacturer of scientific instruments performs R&D and product design in the United States and produces the key high-quality, low-tolerance components there. It exports raw materials to its subsidiary in Puerto Rico for production of lower-tolerance, labor-intensive standard components. Components from its U.S. and Puerto Rican facilities are exported to Malaysia for assembly. The finished instruments are then exported to Singapore for inspection and then to Ireland for final testing. The final products are then re-exported all over the world at the direction of the head office. Managers in the head office then balance production costs and capabilities with transportation costs in an effort to minimize the costs of production, transportation, and inventories. They also search out markets for the firm's products worldwide. At the conceptual level, their analysis and activities are similar to the ones described in the framework for export operations, but on a larger and more complex scale. For managers at the subsidiary level, however, trade is performed at the direction of the head office staff. At the subsidiary level, although managers are engaged in export and import operations, the volume, type, and destination of the subsidiary's exports are controlled from the head office.

As international business has evolved over the decades, the forms of international involvements have increased in number and complexity. Besides exports, a firm utilizes its core skills to service markets abroad via investment in production facilities in another country, by licensing its product or process technology, or by contract production. In the early 1990s, IKEA, the Swedish household products company, decided to move some of its product sourcing to Southeast Asia. To accomplish this move, it tried to avoid equity participation in production facilities. Rather, it formed long-term relationships with producers who it determined had the basic production and management capabilities to produce to its design and quality specifications. It now distributes and sells these products worldwide. IKEA, however, engages in extensive training with its suppliers. It also will supply equipment and train producers in its use. In exchange, it receives price concessions on its future purchases. IKEA supplies these producers with the designs and needed imported inputs. Although IKEA's contract suppliers both import inputs and export their output, for all intents and purposes they are not engaged in international trade.

Countertrade

A special form of exporting is countertrade, the linked exchange of goods for goods in international trade. From the mid-1970s to the mid-1980s, countertrade expanded rapidly. In the 1990s, however, the growth of countertrade slowed with the changes in the former "second world." Nonetheless, countertrade still remains an important feature of international trade, particularly in certain industries and countries. Further, it is a way of dealing with currency volatility.

The term *countertrade* covers eight types of trade operation:

1. Barter: The simultaneous exchange of goods without money.
2. Counterpurchase: The assumption by the exporter, through a separate but linked contract, of an obligation to import some percentage of the price of the goods exported in the form of goods purchased in the importing country.
3. Compensation or buyback: The agreement by an exporter of plant and equipment to buy back some portion of output of the goods produced by the equipment it exports from the importing firms.
4. Production sharing: Similar to buyback, but used in mining and energy projects, where the developer is paid out of a share of the production of the mine or well.
5. Industrial offsets: An obligation undertaken by the exporter to produce or assemble part of the product and source parts in the importing country. Exporting from the importing country may also be undertaken as part of an industrial offset arrangement.
6. Switches: An undertaking by the exporter to import goods from a third country with which the importing country has developed a trade surplus in its "clearing account" under a bilateral trade agreement.
7. Unblocking funds: The use of suppliers' credits that cannot be repatriated due to foreign exchange controls (blocked funds) in the importing country to purchase goods there for export.

8. Debt for equity swaps: The conversion of international debts owed by the importing country to equity in some operation there.

Countertrade contracts can be very complicated and costly to negotiate and to execute. They are filled with pitfalls for the unwary exporter. Only 1 in 10 countertrade arrangements is ever finalized. For an inexperienced exporter or an exporter who is not familiar with countertrade, the best course of action is to seek the advice and support of an experienced countertrader. Many exporters have been caught unaware when countertrade demands are introduced in the negotiation process of a trade arrangement.

Countertrade contracts have nine important characteristics:

1. The timing of the flow of goods (will the export precede, be simultaneous with, or follow the countertraded import?).
2. The duration of the contracts (within what time period must the matching import be made?).
3. The countertrade percent (what percent of the export price must be taken back in countertraded products?).
4. Voluntary or mandatory countertrade.
5. The penalties for noncompliance with the countertrade contract.
6. The product requirements for the linked imports (is the exporter free to choose any goods to fulfill the countertrade obligation or must the exporter source from an approved list?).
7. Whether the countertraded goods must be incremental to the exporter's previous purchases in the importing country.
8. Country destination of the linked imports (can they be sold to any country or must their final destination be the exporter's home country?).
9. Whether the exporting firm itself must fulfill the countertrade obligation or whether it can transfer it to another party.

Each of these provisions is subject to negotiations between the exporter and the importer or the importing country's government. As can be appreciated from the preceding description of countertrade operations, they require exporters to develop a new set of skills—often at great cost in terms of management time, risks, and failed and unprofitable countertrade arrangements. Essentially, countertrade requires a "double coincidence of needs": the importer needs the exporter's product, and the exporter either needs products from the importer or the importing country or can identify buyers who do. In general, countertrade is an inefficient form of trade. It creates costs and risks for both importers and exporters and reduces the value created by international trade. In general, using money to facilitate trade is much more efficient than countertrade.

Major Project Development

The importance of major project development in international trade and investment increased during the 1990s, and there is every prospect that it will continue to increase into the future. These projects are often for infrastructure development such as electricity generation, telecommunications, water and sewage treatment facilities, and even roads and ports. These major projects are of three types: turnkey projects; build, operate, and transfer projects; and build, operate, and own projects.

In a turnkey project, the project manager undertakes to construct a major project, such as a smelter or electrical generating plant, and then turn it over to its owners when it is in full operation. Turnkey projects offer exporters a means of increasing their exports dramatically by one sale. Turnkey projects differ on two dimensions: self-engineered versus construction to specification; fixed price versus cost plus. In the self-engineered project, the exporter undertakes to meet certain performance requirements set by the importer, but the actual equipment and plant design is left up to the exporter. For example, the exporter might undertake to construct a pipeline with the capacity to pump a specified quantity of natural gas per day from one location to another. The size and thickness of the pipe and the power and number of the pumping stations are left to the discretion of the exporter; the exporter bears the risk of not meeting the performance requirements. In construction to specification, the exporter undertakes to construct the project to the importer's specifications. As long as these are met, the risk of performance failure rests with the importer.

Both self-engineered and construction to specification contracts can be undertaken on a fixed-price or a cost-plus basis. On a cost-plus contract, the risk of cost overruns lies with the purchaser. With a fixed-price contract, the risk lies with the exporter. Usually the purchaser specifies in the bid documents the types of contract to be undertaken. An inexperienced, risk-averse purchaser may choose a fixed-price, self-engineered contract to shift the risk to the exporter. This type of contract usually leads to a higher bid price, since the exporter must be compensated for the increased risk it undertakes.

For turnkey projects, bids are usually submitted by a small number of exporters or groups of exporters. The importer typically screens the bidders prior to the actual bid to eliminate bidders who lack the required technical skills to undertake the contract. In this situation, with only a few bidders, the higher an exporter bids, the greater the expected profits, but the lower the probability of winning the bid. Assessing the trade-off between higher profits and decreased probability of winning the bid is one of the key factors in turnkey operations. Often, after the bids have been opened, the importer will go back to the exporters and try to negotiate with those with the lowest bids to get them to reduce their bids by playing one against the other.

Build, operate, and transfer (BOT) and build, operate, and own (BOO) projects have many of the same features as turnkey projects. Firms bid for the right to construct the project. BOT and BOO projects of course differ from turnkey projects in that the winning firm also operates the facility after it is completed, hence there is an element of foreign direct investment in these types of projects. For BOT projects, ownership is limited to a certain time period, at which time the project is to be transferred to another organization, usually the host country government. For both BOT and BOO projects, output prices and volume over time are often specified.

Exports, Imports, and International Finance

Three important aspects of international finance need to be understood by every exporter and importer: the effect of the real exchange rate on competitive advantage, the effect of variations in the nominal exchange rate on export and import profitability, and the effect of trade on financing needs and sources.

Movements in the nominal exchange rate can have a dramatic impact on the profitability of international trading operations. Take the case of an importer in Canada sourcing from the United States. The importer buys a machine worth $100,000 for sale to a Canadian company with a 10 percent markup over landed cost with delivery six months later. If, over this six-month period, the U.S. dollar appreciates against the Canadian dollar by 2 percent, the importer's gross profit margin is reduced by 20 percent.

An importer has several options through which to handle this risk. It can insist that the U.S. exporter price the machine in Canadian dollars and set its markup based on this price. This alternative simply shifts the exchange rate risk back onto the U.S. exporter and may result in a higher purchase price. The importer may decide to bear the risk and hope that the Canadian dollar does not fall, or even that it may rise. In this case, the importer may try to shift the cost of this risk onto the ultimate customer by increasing its selling price. This action, however, may result in the loss of the sale.

Alternatively, the importer may use some type of currency hedge to eliminate the exchange-rate risk. At the time of the sale, the importer can exchange the Canadian dollar equivalent of $100,000 U.S. (minus the six-month interest rate) into U.S. dollars and place them in a six-month financial asset. When the machine is shipped, the importer can then cash in the U.S. dollar-denominated financial asset and pay for the purchase. Alternatively, the importer could also enter the foreign exchange market and buy $100,000 U.S. six months forward at the six-month forward rate prevailing at the time. When the machine is shipped in six months, it can exercise its forward contract for U.S. dollars at the exchange rate that was set six months before. The forward market for currencies (in this example, U.S. and Canadian dollars) is exactly the same as the spot market for foreign exchange. The rate is set by the supply and demand for U.S. and Canadian dollars six months forward. Buying dollars forward obligates the purchaser to exercise the contract in six months at the rate set at the time of the purchase in the forward market for foreign exchange.

By either of these two methods, the importer can be certain of the Canadian dollar cost of the U.S. import. The importer can then price to the ultimate purchaser in terms of this Canadian dollar price. A Canadian producer that sources inputs in the United States could follow the same procedure before making a purchase in order to be able to compare the Canadian dollar price of the import with the prices of other inputs in the Canadian market.

There is another aspect of international trade that has important implications for corporate finance: the effect of international trade on working capital requirements. For international trade, in most cases there is a longer time period between when a product is produced and the time the ultimate purchaser receives it. Someone must finance the capital requirements and pay the capital costs of these larger inventories of final products: the producer, the exporter, the importer, or some financial intermediary. Who finances these inventory costs depends on the financial strength of the importer and the exporter. For example, the exporter can demand payment when the goods are shipped through an irrevocable letter of credit that is discharged when the goods are loaded on the international carrier. In this case, the importer must arrange the financing for the period from the time the goods are exported until they are sold and the importer receives payment. Similarly, the importer could demand that payment be made only when the goods arrive in the destination country. Whichever party finally agrees to finance this inventory, arranging the finance often proves to be difficult and costly.

The problem lies with the valuation and security of the goods from the viewpoint of whoever is going to finance them. If, for example, the importer rejects the goods when they arrive as being not to specification or damaged, what is their value and how can it be recovered? As an extreme example, an American producer of customized vehicles received an order from Libya for ambulances that were to be specially modified for desert conditions. The size of the order was several times the net worth of the company. Who would finance such a specialized product by such a country? The sale fell through for lack of financing.

An alternative approach is to require that the importer open an irrevocable letter of credit for the amount of the purchase. The exporter is then paid via this letter when the goods are shipped. This shifts the financing costs onto the importer. It also shifts other problems onto the importer, since the importer has already paid for the products. The products may be of unacceptable quality, or not to specification, or the order may not be complete, or the product may be damaged during shipping. These problems can be addressed through the use of inspection and certification firms that act on behalf of the importer and through buying insurance.

The importance of export financing as an export tool has grown over the years as more and more importers and importing countries have experienced problems in accessing foreign exchange to pay for imports. The debt situation in many countries has further increased the importance of export financing in export marketing. A firm may have a competitive product, there may be demand for the product in an export market, but trade may be blocked unless some means is found to finance the sale.

The governments of most European countries and the United States, Japan, and Canada have set up government-owned and funded institutions to provide export financing. The interest rates and the terms and conditions on the loans provided by these institutions are designed to promote exports from their countries. When firms from different countries bid on an export contract, there is a tendency for these government-backed banks to make the terms of the loans more and more favorable in order to win the contract for the exporter they are supporting. Interest rate wars can easily break out. To prevent this situation from occurring, an informal agreement has been reached among them that they will not provide funds at rates below their own cost of capital. This agreement has proven impossible to enforce, however. The cost of capital of these banks is difficult to calculate and varies over time and among countries. Exporters often exert pressure through the government for these banks to make their terms more favorable so that they can win the export contract. Governments themselves often have an interest in promoting exports of certain products or exports to certain countries.

Summary

In the previous chapter, a framework was developed to analyze international trade operations. In that chapter, the factors that influence comparative and competitive advantage and the effect of real exchange rates on export performance were described. This chapter started off where the previous chapter ended. It described how to analyze export markets and various strategies for entering those markets. As the final block in the analysis, it described how the producer itself might enter export markets and use various pricing strategies in export markets. Beyond direct exports by the firm, there are also several types of trade intermediaries through which a firm can export, such as importers and exporters and trading houses. The basic model was then extended to the more complex forms of trade that are currently prevalent: the linkages between trade, joint ventures, foreign direct investment, licensing, and contract production. The model was also extended to regional trade and trade, investment, production, and sales in several countries along the value-added chain.

The last section of the chapter dealt with several special topics, such as countertrade, turnkey, BOT, and BOO projects, and trade finance. These two chapters cover the basics of international trade operations.

In the future, there is every prospect that a higher and higher percentage of world output will be traded internationally. For firms in many industries, the question is not, "Should we trade internationally?" They have no choice if they are to maintain and enhance their competitive position. Rather, the question is, "How can we trade more effectively?" Expertise in international trade will become an increasingly important skill for managers to acquire.

Supplementary Reading

Czinkota, Michael R., and Ilkka A. Ronkainen. *International Marketing.* 5th ed. Fort Worth, TX.: Dryden Press, 1998.

Harper, Timothy. *Cracking the New European Markets.* New York: John Wiley & Sons, 1990.

JETRO. *Selling in Japan. The World's Second Largest Market.* Tokyo: JETRO, 1985.

Peng, Mike W., and Anne Ilinitch. "Export Intermediary Firms: A Note on Export Development Research." *Journal of International Business Studies,* Vol. 29, No. 3, 1998 pp. 609–20.

Preeg, Ernest. *Traders in a Brave New World: The Uruguay Round and the Future of the International Trading System.* Chicago: University of Chicago Press, 1995.

Quelch, John A., and Christopher A. Bartlett. *Global Marketing Management.* 4th ed. Reading, MA: Addison-Wesley Publishing Company, Inc., 1999.

Renner, Sandra L., and W. Gary Winget. *Fast-Track Exporting.* New York: AMACOM, 1991.

Ricks, David. *Blunders in International Business.* Cambridge, MA: Basil Blackwell, 1993.

Schaffer, Matt. *Winning the Countertrade War: New Export Strategies for America.* New York: John Wiley & Sons, 1989.

Thorelli, Hans B., and S. Tamer Cavusgil, eds. *International Marketing Strategy.* 3rd ed. Elmsford, NY: Pergamon Press, 1995.

Triller, Lawrence W. *Going Global: New Opportunities for Growing Companies to Compete in World Markets.* Homewood. IL: Business One Irwin, 1991.

Weiss, Kenneth D. *Building an Export/Import Business.* New York: John Wiley & Sons, 1991.

5 GLOBAL SOURCING STRATEGY

R&D, MANUFACTURING, AND MARKETING INTERFACES

During the last decade or so, international business has experienced a major metamorphosis of an irreversible kind. The pendulum of international trade has already shifted from cross-Atlantic to cross-Pacific. Such a shift has a lot to do with U.S. and Japanese multinational companies engaged in global sourcing strategy across the Pacific. Gone are the days when international business meant the one-way expansion of U.S. companies to the rest of the world. Also gone are the days when European and Japanese companies simply exported to, or manufactured in, the United States. Today, executives of the same companies have come to accept a new reality of global competition and global competitors. An increasing number of companies from around the world, particularly from the United States, western Europe, and Japan, are competing head-on for a global dominance. Global competition suggests a drastically shortened life cycle for most products, and no longer permits companies a polycentric, country-by-country approach to international business. If companies that have developed a new product do follow a country-by-country approach to foreign market entry over time, a globally oriented competitor will likely overcome their initial competitive advantages by blanketing the world markets with similar products in a shorter period of time.

A frequently used framework to describe cross-national business practices is the international product cycle theory. The theory has provided a compelling description of dynamic patterns of international trade of manufactured products and direct investment as a product advances through its life cycle. According to the theory, changes in inputs and product characteristics toward standardization over *time* determine an optimal production location at any particular phase of the product's life cycle.

However, three major limitations of the international product cycle theory have to be borne in mind:

This chapter was prepared by Masaaki Kotabe of Temple University.

1. **Increased pace of new product introduction and reduction in innovational lead time,** which deprive companies of the age-old polycentric approach to global markets,

2. **Predictable sourcing development during the product cycle,** which permits a shrewd company to outmaneuver competition, and

3. **More active management of locational and corporate resources on a global basis,** which gives a company a preemptive first-mover advantage over competition.

One successful example of such globally oriented strategy is Sony. Sony developed transistorized solid-state color TVs in Japan in the 1960s and marketed them initially in the United States before they were introduced in the rest of the world including the Japanese market. Mass marketing initially in the United States and then throughout the world in a short period time had given this Japanese company a first-mover advantage as well as economies of scale advantages. In contrast, EMI provides a historic case example of the failure to take advantage of global opportunities that existed. This British company developed and began marketing CAT (computerized axial tomography) scanners in 1972, for which its inventors won a Nobel Prize. Despite an enormous demand for CAT scanners in the United States, the largest market for state-of-the-art medical equipment, EMI failed to export them to the United States immediately and in sufficient numbers. Instead, the British company slowly, and probably belatedly, began exporting them to the United States in the mid-1970s, as if to follow the evolutionary pattern suggested by the international product cycle model. Some years later, the British company established a production facility in the United States, only to be slowed down by technical problems. By then, EMI was already facing stiff competition from global electronics giants including Philips, Siemens, General Electric, and Toshiba. Indeed, it was General Electric that in a short period of time blanketed the U.S. market and subsequently the rest of the world with its own version of CAT scanners that were technologically inferior to the British model.

In both cases, technology diffused quickly. Today, quick technological diffusion has virtually become a matter of fact. Without established sourcing plans, distribution, and service networks, it is extremely difficult to exploit both emerging technology and potential markets around the world simultaneously. General Electric's swift global reach could not have been possible without its ability to procure crucial components internally and on a global basis. As a result, the increased pace of new product introduction and reduction in innovational lead time calls for more proactive management of locational and corporate resources on a global basis. In this chapter, we emphasize logistical management of the **interfaces** of R&D, manufacturing, and marketing activities on a global basis—which we call **global sourcing strategy**—and also the importance of the ability to procure major components of the product in-house such that companies can proactively standardize either components or products. Global sourcing strategy requires a close coordination among R&D, manufacturing, and marketing activities across national boundaries.[1]

There always exist conflicts in the tug-of-war of differing objectives among R&D, manufacturing, and marketing. Excessive product modification and proliferation for the sake of satisfying the ever-changing customer needs will forsake manufacturing efficiency

---

[1]Masaaki Kotabe, *R&D, Manufacturing, and Marketing Interfaces* (New York: Quorum Books, 1992).

and have negative cost consequences, barring a perfectly flexible computer-aided design (CAD) and computer-aided manufacturing (CAM) facility. CAD/CAM technology has improved tremendously in recent years, but the full benefit of flexible manufacturing is still many years away.[2] Contrarily, excessive product standardization for the sake of lowering manufacturing costs will also be likely to result in unsatisfied or undersatisfied customers. Similarly, innovative product designs and features as desired by customers may indeed be a technological feat but might not be conducive to manufacturing. Therefore, topics such as product design for manufacturability and components/product standardization have become increasingly important strategic issues today. It has become imperative for many companies to develop a sound sourcing strategy in order to exploit most efficiently R&D, manufacturing, and marketing on a global basis.

Extent and Complexity of Global Sourcing Strategy

In this chapter, we introduce subject matters not ordinarily covered in an international management textbook. It is our strong belief that managers should understand and appreciate the important roles that product designers, engineers, and production managers, and purchasing managers, among others, play in corporate strategy development. Strategy decisions cannot be made in the absence of these people. The overriding theme throughout the chapter is that successful management of the interfaces of R&D, manufacturing, and marketing activities determines a company's competitive strengths and, consequently, its market performance. Now we will look at logistical implications of this interface management.

Toyota's global operations illustrate one such world-class case. The Japanese carmaker is equipping its operations in the United States, Europe, and Southeast Asia with integrated capabilities for creating and marketing automobiles. The company gives the managers at those operations ample authority to accommodate local circumstances and values without diluting the benefit of integrated global operations. Thus, in the United States, Calty Design Research, a Toyota subsidiary in California, designs the bodies and interiors of new Toyota models, including Lexus and Solara, a sporty new coupe. Toyota has technical centers in the United States and in Brussels to adapt engine and vehicle specifications to local needs. Toyota operations in Southeast Asia supply each other with key components to foster increased economies of scale and standardization in those components—gasoline engines in Indonesia, steering components in Malaysia, transmissions in the Philippines, and diesel engines in Thailand.

Undoubtedly, those multinational companies, including Toyota, not only facilitate the flow of capital among various countries through direct investment abroad but also significantly contribute to the world trade flow of goods and services as well. Multinational companies combine this production and distribution to supply those local markets hosting their foreign subsidiaries, and then export what remains to other foreign markets or back to their parent's home market.

Let us revisit the significance of multinational companies' foreign production relative to their exports from their home base. U.S. multinational companies are the most experienced

---

[2]*The Economist,* "A Survey of Manufacturing Technology," March 5, 1994, pp. 3–18.

in the industrialized world and sell over three times as much overseas through their subsidiaries as they export to the world. For U.S. multinationals, the 3:1 ratio of foreign sales to exports has remained largely unchanged since the mid-1960s. This ratio for European multinationals had grown from 3:1 in the 1970s to 5:1 by 1990. Similarly, the ratio for Japanese multinationals had increased from 1:1 in mid-1970s to 2.5:1 by 1990. Also, both American and Japanese subsidiaries sell over 20 percent of their foreign sales in third-country markets (including their home markets), while European subsidiaries in the United States and Japan sell approximately 10 percent in third-country markets.[3]

As a result, the total volume of international trade among the Triad regions (i.e., North America, Europe, and Japan) alone increased more than 10-fold in 20 years to well over $500 billion in 1995 from $44.4 billion in 1970, or approximately by four times in real terms. This phenomenal increase in international trade is attributed largely to foreign production and trade *managed* by multinational companies.

Two notable changes have occurred in international trade. First, the last 25 years have observed a decline in the proportion of trade between Europe and the United States in the Triad regions, and conversely an increase in trade between the United States and Japan, and in particular, between Europe and Japan. It strongly indicates that European countries and Japan have found each other increasingly important markets above and beyond their traditional markets of the United States. Second, newly industrialized countries (NICs) in Asia, including South Korea, Taiwan, Hong Kong, and Singapore, have dramatically increased their trading position vis-à-vis the rest of the world. Not only have these NICs become prosperous marketplaces, but more significantly they have become important manufacturing and sourcing locations for many multinational companies.

From the sourcing perspective, U.S. companies were procuring a less expensive supply of components and finished products in NICs for sale in the United States. As a result, U.S. bilateral trade with NICs has increased 60-fold to $130 billion in 1995 from $1.8 billion in 1970, of which the United States accounts for more than 90 percent. Trade statistics, however, do not reveal anything other than the amount of bilateral trade flows between countries. It is false to assume that trade is always a business transaction between independent buyers and sellers across national boundaries. It is equally false to assume that a country's trade deficit in a certain *industry* equates with the decline in the competitiveness of *companies* in that industry. As evidenced above, an increasing segment of international trade of components and finished products is strongly influenced by multinational companies' foreign direct investment activities.

Trends in Global Sourcing Strategy

Over the last 20 years or so, gradual yet significant changes have taken place in global sourcing strategy. The cost-saving justification for international procurement in the 1970s and 1980s was gradually supplanted by quality and reliability concerns in the 1990s. However, most of the changes have been in the way business executives think of the scope of global

---

[3]Dennis J. Encarnation, "Transforming Trade and Investment, American, European, and Japanese Multinationals across the Triad" (paper presented at the Academy of International Business Annual Meetings, November 22, 1992).

sourcing for their companies and exploit various opportunities available from it as a source of competitive advantage. Peter Drucker, a famed management guru and business historian, once said that sourcing and logistics would remain the darkest continent of business—the least exploited area of business for competitive advantage. Naturally, many companies, regardless of their nationality, that have a limited scope of global sourcing are at a disadvantage over those that exploit it to the fullest extent in a globally competitive marketplace.

Trend 1: The Decline of the Exchange Rate Determinism of Sourcing

Since the mid-1970s, exchange rates have fluctuated rather erratically over time. If the dollar appreciates, U.S. companies would find it easy to procure components and products from abroad. Such was the case in the mid-1980s when the dollar appreciated precipitously. The appreciation of the dollar was reflected in the surge of U.S. imports. Contrarily, if the dollar depreciates, U.S. companies would find it increasingly difficult to depend on foreign supplies as they have to pay higher dollar prices for every item sourced from abroad. In these scenarios, companies consider the exchange rate determining the extent to which they can engage in foreign sourcing.

However, this exchange rate determinism of sourcing is strictly based on price factor alone. Indeed, a recent study shows that exchange rate fluctuations have little impact on the nature of sourcing strategy for crucial components.[4] Foreign sourcing also occurs for noncost reasons such as quality, technology, and so on. First of all, since it takes time to develop overseas suppliers for noncost purposes, purchasing managers cannot easily drop a foreign supplier even when exchange rate changes have an adverse effect on the cost of imported components and products. Second, domestic suppliers are known to increase prices to match rising import prices following exchange rate changes. As a result, switching to a domestic supplier may not ensure cost advantages. Third, many companies are developing long-term relationships with international suppliers—whether those suppliers are their subsidiaries or independent contractors. In a long-term supply relationship, exchange rate fluctuations may be viewed as a temporary problem by the parties involved. Finally, some companies with global operations are able to shift supply locations from one country to another to overcome the adverse effects of exchange rate fluctuations. Obviously, these factors other than cost have kept many U.S. companies from reducing their dependence on foreign supplies of components and finished products.[5]

Trend 2: New Competitive Environment Caused by Excess Worldwide Capacity

The worldwide growth in the number of manufacturers has added excess production capacity in most industries. The proliferation of manufacturers around the world in less sophisticated, less capital-intensive manufactured products is much greater than in more complex, knowledge-intensive products such as computers. Thus, there has been a tremendous downward pressure on prices of many components and products around the world. Although the

---

[4]Janet Y. Murray, "A Currency Exchange Rate-Driven vs. Strategy-Driven Analysis of Global Sourcing," *Multinational Business Review,* Vol. 4, No. 1, Spring 1996, pp. 40–51.

[5]*Business Week,* "Guess Who Isn't Buying American: For Many U.S. Companies, Imported Goods Are Cheaper and Better-Made," November 2, 1992, pp. 26–27.

ability to deliver a high volume of products of satisfactory quality at a reasonable price was once the hallmark of many successful companies, an increasing number of global suppliers have eventually rendered the delivery of volume in an acceptable time no longer a competitive weapon. There has since occurred a strategic shift from *price* and *quantity* to *quality* and *reliability* of products as a determinant of competitive strength.[6] According to a recent survey (See Exhibit 5–1), better product and component quality, lower price, unavailability of item domestically, and more advanced technology abroad are among the most important reasons for increased sourcing from abroad.[7]

Trend 3: Innovations in and Restructuring of International Trade Infrastructure

Advances in structural elements of international trade have made it easier for companies to employ sourcing for strategic purposes. The innovations and structural changes that have important influences on sourcing strategy are (1) the increased number of purchasing managers experienced in sourcing, (2) improvements made in transportation and communication (e.g., fax), (3) new financing options, including countertrade (see Chapter 4), offering new incentives and opportunities for exports from countries without hard currency, (4) manufacturing facilities diffused throughout the world by globally minded companies, and (5) neighboring country sourcing opportunities. For example, maquiladora plants on the Mexican side of the U.S. border provide a unique form of sourcing option to manufacturers operating in the United States. Similarly Hong Kong–based companies may source out of nearby Shenzhen.

Trend 4: Enhanced Role of Purchasing Managers

During the last 10 to 15 years, manufacturers were under pressure to compete on the basis of improved cost and quality as just-in-time (JIT) production was adopted by a growing number of companies. JIT production requires close working relationships with component suppliers and places an enormous amount of responsibility on purchasing managers. Furthermore, sourcing directly from foreign suppliers requires greater purchasing know-how and is riskier than other alternatives that use locally based wholesalers and representatives. Locally based representatives are subject to local laws and assume some of the currency risk associated with importing. However, now that purchasing managers are increasingly making long-term commitments to foreign suppliers, direct dealings with suppliers is justified. According to one major survey, the dominant form of purchasing from abroad was to buy directly from foreign sources.[8] The finding suggests that purchasing managers are confident about their international know-how and that they may be seeking long-term sourcing arrangements.

---

[6]Martin K. Starr and John E. Ullman, "The Myth of Industrial Supremacy," in Martin K. Starr, ed., *Global Competitiveness* (New York: W. W. Norton and Co., 1988).

[7]Hokey Min and William P. Galle, "International Purchasing Strategies of Multinational U.S. Firms," *International Journal of Purchasing and Materials Management,* Summer 1991, pp. 9–18.

[8]Somerby Dowst, "International Buying: The Facts and Foolishness," *Purchasing,* June 25, 1987.

EXHIBIT 5–1	Key Factors for Sourcing from Abroad

Factor
Very Important
1. Better quality
2. Lower price
3. Unavailability of items in the U.S.
Important
4. More advanced technology abroad
5. Willingness to solve problems
6. More on-time delivery
7. Negotiability
8. Association with foreign subsidiary
Neutral
9. Geographical location
10. Countertrade requirements
11. Government assistance

Source: Adapted from Hokey Min and William P. Galle, "International Purchasing Strategies of Multinational U.S. Firms," *International Journal of Purchasing and Materials Management,* Summer 1991, p. 14.

Trend 5: Trend toward Global Manufacturing

During the 1980s, while U.S. companies continued to locate their operations in various parts of the world, companies from other countries such as Japan, Germany, and Britain expanded the magnitude of their foreign manufacturing operations at a much faster pace. Foreign share of manufacturing in the United States increased from 5.2 percent in 1977 to some 15 percent recently. As a global company adds another international plant to its network of existing plants, it creates the need for sourcing of components and other semi-processed goods to and from the new plant to existing plants. Global manufacturing adds enormously to global sourcing activities either within the same company across national boundaries or between independent suppliers and new plants.

In the late 1980s, U.S. companies increased sourcing from abroad, which represents a strategic expansion and rationalization over time. In response to slow productivity growth in the United States relative to other major trading nations in the 1980s, U.S. parent companies' technology has been increasingly transferred directly to their foreign affiliates for production instead of in the form of equipment and components for local modification in the foreign markets. Mature companies are increasingly assigning independent design and other R&D responsibilities to satellite foreign units so as to design a regional or world product. As a result, foreign affiliates have also developed more independent R&D activities to manufacture products for the U.S. markets in addition to expanding local sales.[9]

---

[9]Masaaki Kotabe and K. Scott Swan, "Offshore Sourcing: Reaction, Maturation, and Consolidation of U.S. Multinationals," *Journal of International Business Studies,* Vol. 25, First Quarter, 1994, pp. 115–40.

Potential Pitfalls in Global Sourcing

Global sourcing strategy requires close coordination of R&D, manufacturing, and marketing activities, among others, on a global basis. However, while national boundaries have begun losing their significance both as a psychological and as a physical barrier to international business, the diversity of local environments still plays an important role not as a facilitator, but rather as an inhibitor, of optimal global strategy development. Now the question is to what extent successful multinational companies can circumvent the impact of local environmental diversity.

Indeed, we still debate the very issue raised more than 20 years ago: counteracting forces of "unification versus fragmentation" in developing operational strategies. As early as 1969, Fayerweather[10] wrote emphatically:

> What fundamental effects does (the existence of many national borders) have on the strategy of the multinational firm? Although many effects can be itemized, one central theme recurs, that is, their tendency to push the firm toward adaptation to the diversity of local environments which leads toward fragmentation of operations. But there is a natural tendency in a single firm toward integration and uniformity which is basically at odds with fragmentation. Thus the central issue...is the conflict between unification and fragmentation—a close-knit operational strategy with similar foreign units versus a loosely related, highly variegated family of activities.

The same counteracting forces have since been revisited in such terms as "standardization versus adaptation" (1960s), "globalization versus localization" (1970s), "global integration versus local responsiveness" (1980s), and, most recently, "scale versus sensitivity" (1990s). Terms have changed, but the quintessence of the strategic dilemma that multinational companies face today has not changed and will probably remain unchanged for many years to come.

One thing that has changed, however, is the *ability* and *willingness* of these companies to integrate various activities on a global basis in an attempt either to circumvent or to nullify the impact of differences in local markets to the extent possible. It may be more correct to say that these companies have been increasingly compelled to take a global view of their businesses, due primarily to increased competition, particularly among the Triad regions of the world: namely, North America, western Europe, and Japan. Remember "If you don't do it, somebody else will at your expense." This contemporary view of competitive urgency is shared by an increasing number of executives of multinational companies, irrespective of nationality.

The lack of competitive urgency can indeed be a problem. In his *Business Not As Usual,* for instance, Mitroff[11] was very critical of the lack of this competitive urgency in the U.S. automobile industry in the 1970s and 1980s. He argued that the automobile industry minimized the need for constant innovation and its adoption into the working design

---

[10]John Fayerweather, *International Business Management: Conceptual Framework* (New York: McGraw-Hill, 1969), pp. 133–4.

[11]Ian I. Mitroff, *Business Not As Usual: Rethinking Our Individual, Corporate, and Industrial Strategies for Global Competition* (San Francisco, CA: Jossey-Bass, Inc, 1987).

of cars until it was forced on it by foreign competition. Not surprisingly, the result was an extreme isolation from the rest of the world—"a tunnel vision of the worst kind" (p. 84). This is not an isolated incident, however. Mitroff's indictment arguably applies to other industries, such as machine tool and electronics, in the United States.

In contrast, the last 25 years have seen a tremendous growth and expansion of European and Japanese multinational companies encroaching on the competitive strengths of U.S. multinational companies in almost all the markets around the world. While U.S. multinational companies have subsidiaries all over the world, they have been somewhat reluctant to develop an integrated and well-coordinated global strategy that successful European and Japanese multinational companies have managed to establish. At the core of an integrated global strategy lies the companies' ability to coordinate manufacturing activities with R&D, engineering, and marketing on a global basis. Indeed, European and Japanese multinational companies have heavily invested in, and improved upon, their strengths in manufacturing that many U.S. multinational companies have ignored. As a result, U.S. companies tend to have ill-coordinated manufacturing strategy that results in a poor match between their manufacturing system capability and markets.

This functional mismatch has been traced to U.S. management's strategic emphasis having drifted away from manufacturing to marketing and to finance over the years. U.S. management's attention was focused on marketing in the 1960s, followed by a preoccupation with finance in the 1970s, culminating in the merger and acquisition craze of the 1980s—aptly called, "paper entrepreneurship."[12]

As a result, manufacturing management gradually lost its influence in the business organization. Production managers' decision-making authority was reduced such that R&D personnel prepared specifications with which production complied and marketing imposed its own delivery, inventory, and quality conditions, but not productivity considerations. In a sense, production managers gradually took on the role of outside suppliers within their own companies. Production managers' reduced influence in the organization led to a belief that manufacturing functions could be transferred easily to independent operators and subcontractors, depending upon the cost differential between in-house and contracted-out production. Thus, in order to lower production costs under competitive pressure, U.S. multinational companies turned increasingly to *outsourcing* of components and finished products from newly industrializing countries such as South Korea, Taiwan, Singapore, Hong Kong, Brazil, and Mexico, among others. Akio Morita, a co-founder of Sony, a highly innovative Japanese electronics company, chided such U.S. multinational companies as "hollow corporations" which simply put their well-known brand names on foreign-made products and sell them as if the products were their own.[13]

However, we should not rush to a hasty conclusion that outsourcing certain components and/or finished products from foreign countries will diminish a company's competitiveness. Many multinational companies with plants in various parts of the world are exploiting not only their own competitive advantages (e.g., R&D, manufacturing, and marketing skills) but also the locational advantages (e.g., inexpensive labor cost, certain skills,

---

[12]Robert Reich, *The Next American Frontier* (New York: Times Books, 1983).

[13]*Business Week,* "Special Report: The Hollow Corporation," March 3, 1986, pp. 56–59.

mineral resources, government subsidy, and tax advantages) of various countries. Thus, it is also plausible to argue that these multinational companies are in a more advantageous competitive position than are domestic-bound companies.

Then, isn't the "hollowing-out" phenomenon indicative of a superior management of both corporate and locational resources on a global basis? What is wrong, if anything, with Caterpillar Tractor Company procuring more than 15 percent of components for its tractors from foreign suppliers? How about Honeywell marketing in the United States the products manufactured in its European plants? Answers to these questions hinge on a company's ability and willingness to integrate and coordinate various activities.

Value Chain and Functional Interfaces

The design of global sourcing strategy is based on the interplay between a company's competitive advantages and the comparative advantages of various countries. Competitive advantage influences the decision on what activities and technologies a company should concentrate its investment and managerial resources in, relative to its competitors in the industry. Comparative advantage affects the company's decision on where to source and market, based on the lower cost of labor and other resources in one country relative to another. As shown in Exhibit 5–2, the value chain concept offers a general framework for understanding what it takes to manage the interrelated value-adding activities of a company on a global basis.[14] A company is essentially made up of a collection of activities that are performed to design, manufacture, market, deliver, and support its product. This set of interrelated corporate activities is called the value chain. Therefore, to gain competitive advantage over its rivals in the marketplace, a company must perform these activities either at a lower cost or in such a way as to offer differentiated products and services, or accomplish both.

The value chain can be divided into two major activities performed by a company: (1) *primary activities* consisting of inbound logistics (procurement of raw materials and components), manufacturing operations, outbound logistics (distribution), sales, and after-sale service, and (2) *support activities* consisting of human resource management, technology development, and other activities that help promote primary activities. Competing companies constantly strive to create value across various activities in the value chain. Of course, the value that a company creates is measured ultimately by the price buyers are willing to pay for its products. Therefore, the value chain is a useful concept that provides an assessment of the activities that a company performs to design, manufacture, market, deliver, and support its products in the marketplace.

Five continuous and interactive steps are involved in developing such a global sourcing strategy along the value chain.[15]

---

[14]Michael E. Porter, ed., *Competition in Global Industries* (Cambridge, MA: Harvard Business School Press, 1986).

[15]Richard D. Robinson, ed., *Direct Foreign Investment: Costs and Benefits* (New York: Praeger Publishers, 1987).

1. Identify the separable links (R&D, manufacturing, and marketing) in the company's value chain,
2. In the context of those links, determine the location of the company's competitive advantages, considering both economies of scale and scope,
3. Ascertain the level of transaction costs (e.g., cost of negotiation, cost of monitoring activities, and uncertainty resulting from contracts) between links in the value chain, both internal and external, and selecting the lowest cost mode,
4. Determine the comparative advantages of countries (including the company's home country) relative to each link in the value chain and to the relevant transaction costs, and
5. Develop adequate flexibility in corporate decision making and organizational design so as to permit the company to respond to changes in both its competitive advantages and the comparative advantages of countries.

In this chapter, we focus on the three most important interrelated activities in the value chain: namely, R&D (i.e., technology development, product design, and engineering), manufacturing, and marketing activities. Management of the interfaces, or linkages, among these value-adding activities is a crucial determinant of a company's competitive advantage. A basic framework of management of R&D, manufacturing, and marketing interfaces is outlined in Exhibit 5–2. Undoubtedly, these value-adding activities should be examined as holistically as possible, by linking the boundaries of these primary activities. Thus, global sourcing strategy encompasses management of (1) the interfaces among R&D, manufacturing, and marketing on a global basis and (2) logistics identifying which production units will serve which particular markets and how components will be supplied for production.

R&D/Manufacturing Interface

Technology is broadly defined as know-how composed of product technology (the set of ideas embodied in the product) and process technology (the set of ideas involved in the manufacture of the product or the steps necessary to combine new materials to produce a finished product). However, executives tend to focus solely on product-related technology as the driving force of the company's competitiveness. Product technology alone may not provide the company a long-term competitive edge over competition unless it is matched with sufficient manufacturing capabilities.[16]

An earlier example of EMI's CAT (computerized axial tomography) scan technology represents a classic case of such a product technology orientation. EMI developed and slowly began marketing CAT scanners in Britain in 1972. This British company's CAT scanner represented the state-of-the-art technology that was inherently difficult to manufacture. As a result, the company was not able to manufacture fast enough to meet an increased demand for CAT scanners in the United States, the largest market for this device. It was then General Electric, Toshiba, Philips, and Siemens that took advantage of the void

---

[16]Bruce R. Guile and Harvey Brooks, *Technology and Global Industry: Companies and Nations in the World Economy* (Washington, DC: National Academy Press, 1987).

EXHIBIT 5–2   R&D, Manufacturing, and Market Interfaces

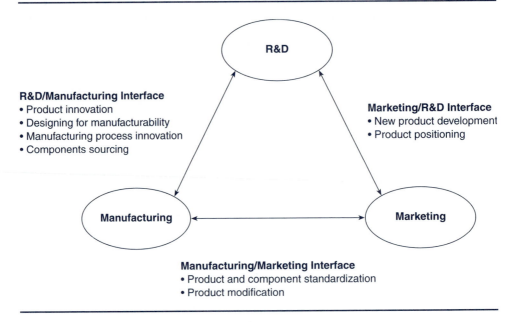

R&D/Manufacturing Interface
- Product innovation
- Designing for manufacturability
- Manufacturing process innovation
- Components sourcing

Marketing/R&D Interface
- New product development
- Product positioning

Manufacturing/Marketing Interface
- Product and component standardization
- Product modification

---

in competition and swiftly captured the market with their own CAT scanners, which were technologically inferior to, but more easily manufacturable than, the original British model.

Similar cases exist throughout history. The British discovered and developed penicillin, but it was a small U.S. company, Pfizer, which improved on the fermentation (i.e., manufacturing) process and, as a result, became the world's foremost manufacturer of penicillin. The first jet engine was developed in Britain and Germany, but it was again U.S. companies, Boeing and Douglas, that improved on the technology and eventually dominated the jet plane market.

Ignoring manufacturing as a strategic weapon, many companies have historically placed emphasis on product innovations (i.e., product proliferation and modifications). However, as technological leads over foreign competition have evaporated, there will be fewer products that companies can export simply because no one else has the technology to manufacture the products. Stressing the historical linkage of imitation and product innovations, it is contended that imitation (manufacturing process learning), followed by more innovative adaptation, leading to pioneering product design and innovation, forms the natural sequence of industrial development. In other words, product innovation and manufacturing activities are intertwined so that continual improvement in manufacturing processes can enable the company not only to maintain product innovation-based competitiveness but also to improve its product innovative abilities in the future.

These examples amply suggest that manufacturing processes should also be innovative. To facilitate the transferability of new product innovations to manufacturing, a team of product designers and engineers should strive to design components so that they are conducive to manufacturing without undue retooling required and that components may be used interchangeably for different models of the product. Low levels of retooling requirements and interchangeability of components are necessary conditions for efficient sourcing strategy on a global scale. If different equipment and components are used in various manufacturing plants, it is extremely difficult to establish a highly coordinated sourcing plan on a global basis.

Manufacturing/Marketing Interface

There exists a continual conflict between manufacturing and marketing divisions. It is to the manufacturing division's advantage if all the products and components are standardized to facilitate standardized, low-cost production. The marketing division, however, is more interested in satisfying the diverse needs of consumers, requiring broad product lines and frequent product modifications adding cost to manufacturing. How have successful companies coped with this dilemma?

Recently, there has been an increasing amount of interest in the strategic linkages between product policy and manufacturing long ignored in traditional considerations of global strategy development. With aggressive competition from multinational companies emphasizing corporate product policy and concomitant manufacturing, many companies have realized that product innovations alone cannot sustain their long-term competitive position without an effective product policy linking product and manufacturing process innovations.

Four different ways of developing a global product policy are generally considered an effective means to streamline manufacturing, thus lowering manufacturing cost, without sacrificing marketing flexibility: (1) core components standardization, (2) product design families, (3) universal product with all features, and (4) universal product with different positioning.[17]

Core Components Standardization. Successful global product policy mandates the development of universal products or products that require no more than a cosmetic change for adaptation to differing local needs and use conditions. A few examples illustrate the point. Seiko, a Japanese watchmaker, offers a wide range of designs and models, but based only on a handful of different operating mechanisms. Similarly, the best-performing German machine tool making companies have a narrower range of products, use up to 50 percent fewer parts than their less successful rivals, and make continual, incremental product and design improvements, with new developments passed rapidly on to customers.

Product Design Families. This is a variant of core component standardization. For companies marketing an extremely wide range of products due to cultural differences in product-use patterns around the world, it is also possible to reap economies of scale benefits. For example, Toyota offers several car models based on a similar family design concept, ranging from Lexus models to Toyota Avalons, Camrys, and Corollas. Many of the Lexus features well received by customers have been adopted into the Toyota lines with just a few minor modifications (mostly downsizing). In the process, Toyota has been able to cut product development costs and meet the needs of different market segments. Simi-

---

[17]Hirotaka Takeuchi and Michael E. Porter, "Three Roles of International Marketing in Global Strategy," in Michael E. Porter, ed., *Competition in Global Industries* (Boston, MA: Harvard Business School Press, 1986, pp. 111–46).

larly, Electrolux, a Swedish appliance manufacturer, has adopted the concept of "design families," offering different products under four different brand names but using the same basic designs. A key to such product design standardization lies in standardization of components, including motors, pumps, and compressors. Thus, White Consolidated in the United States and Zanussi in Italy, Electrolux's subsidiaries, have the main responsibility for components production within the group for worldwide application.

Universal Product with All Features. As noted above, competitive advantage can result from standardization of core components and/or product design families. One variant of components and product standardization is to develop a universal product with all the features demanded anywhere in the world. Japan's Canon has done so successfully with its AE–1 cameras and newer models. After extensive market analyses around the world, Canon identified a set of common features customers wanted in a camera, including good picture quality, ease of operation with automatic features, technical sophistication, professional looks, and reasonable price. To develop such cameras, the company introduced a few breakthroughs in camera design and manufacturing, such as use of an electronic integrated circuitry brain to control camera operations, modularized production, and standardization and reduction of parts.

Universal Product with Different Positioning. Alternatively, a universal product can be developed with different market segments in mind. Thus, a universal product may be positioned differently in different markets. This is where marketing promotion plays a major role to accomplish such a feat. Product and/or components standardization, however, does not necessarily imply either production standardization or a narrow product line. For example, Japanese automobile manufacturers have gradually stretched out their product line offerings, while marketing them with little adaptation in many parts of the world. This strategy requires manufacturing flexibility. The crux of global product or component standardization rather calls for proactive identification of homogeneous segments around the world, and is different from the concept of marketing abroad a product originally developed for the home market. A proactive approach to product policy has gained momentum in recent years as it is made possible by intermarket segmentation. In addition to clustering of countries and identification of homogeneous segments in different countries, targeting different segments in different countries with the same products is another way to maintain a product policy of standardization

For example, Honda has marketed almost identical Accord cars around the world by positioning them differently from country to country. Accord has been promoted as a family sedan in Japan, a relatively inexpensive sports car in Germany, and a reliable commuter car in the United States. In recent years, however, Honda has begun developing some regional variations of the Accord for the United States, European, and Japanese markets. Nonetheless, Honda adheres to a policy of *core component standardization* such that at least 50 percent of the components, including the chassis and transmission, are shared across the variations of the Accord.

Marketing/R&D Interface

Both R&D and manufacturing activities are technically outside marketing managers' responsibility. However, marketing managers' knowledge of the consumers' needs is indispensable in product development. Without a good understanding of the consumers' needs, product designers and engineers are prone to impose their technical specifications on the product rather than fitting them to what consumers want. After all, consumers, not product designers or engineers, have the final say in deciding whether or not to buy the product.

Japanese companies, in particular, excel in management of the marketing/R&D interface. Indeed, their source of competitive advantage often lies in marketing and R&D divisions' willingness to coordinate their respective activities concurrently. In a traditional product development, *either* a new product was developed and pushed down from the R&D division to the manufacturing and to the marketing division for sales *or* a new product idea was pushed up from the marketing division to the R&D division for development. This top-down or bottom-up new product development takes too much time in an era of global competition in which a short product development cycle is crucial to meet constant competitive pressure from new products introduced by rival companies around the world.

R&D and marketing divisions of Japanese companies are always on the lookout for use of emerging technologies initially in existing products to satisfy customer needs better than their existing products and their competitors'. This affords them an opportunity to gain experience, debug technological glitches, reduce costs, boost performance, and adapt designs for worldwide customer use. As a result, they have been able to increase the speed of new product introductions, meet the competitive demands of a rapidly changing marketplace and capture market share.

In other words, *the marketplace becomes a virtual R&D laboratory for Japanese companies to gain production and marketing experience as well as to perfect technology.* This requires close contact with customers, whose inputs help Japanese companies improve upon their products on an ongoing basis.

In the process, they introduce new products one after another. Year after year, Japanese companies unveil not-entirely-new products that keep getting better in design, more reliable, and less expensive. For example, Philips marketed the first practical VCR in 1972, three years before Japanese competitors entered the market. However, Philips took seven years to replace the first generation VCR with the all-new V2000, while the late-coming Japanese manufacturers launched an onslaught of no fewer than three generations of improved VCRs in this five-year period.

Another recent example worth noting is the exploitation of the so-called "fuzzy" logic by Hitachi and others. Ever since fuzzy logic was conceived in the mid-1960s at the University of California at Berkeley, nobody other than several Japanese companies has paid serious heed to it for its potential application in ordinary products. The fuzzy logic allows computers to deal with shades of gray or something vague between 0 and 1—no small feat in a world of the binary computers that exist today. Today, Hitachi, Matsushita, Mitsubishi, Sony, and Nissan Motors, among others, use fuzzy logic in their products. For example, Hitachi introduced a "fuzzy" train that automatically accelerates and brakes so smoothly that no one uses the hanging straps. Matsushita, maker of Panasonic, began marketing a "fuzzy" washing machine with only one start button that automatically judges the size and dirtiness of the load and decides the optimum cycle times, amount of detergent needed, and water level. Sony introduced a palm-size computer capable of recognizing written Japanese, with a fuzzy circuit to iron out the inconsistencies in different writing styles. Now fuzzy circuits are put into the autofocus mechanisms of video cameras to get constantly clear pictures. By the beginning of 1990, fuzzy chips were appearing at a fast pace in a wide range of consumer products.

The continual introduction of *newer* and *better designed* products also brings a greater likelihood of market success. Ideal products often require a giant leap in technology and product development, and naturally are subject to a much higher risk of consumer rejection. Not only does the Japanese approach of incrementalism allow for continual improvement and a stream of new products, but it also permits quicker consumer adoption. Consumers are likely to accept improved products more quickly than very different products, since the former are more compatible with the existing patterns of product use and lifestyles.

Logistics of Sourcing Strategy

Sourcing strategy includes a number of basic choices companies make in deciding how to serve foreign markets. One choice relates to the use of imports, assembly, or production within the country to serve a foreign market. Another decision involves the use of internal or external supplies of components or finished goods. Therefore, the term "sourcing" is used to describe management by multinational companies of the flow of components and finished products in serving foreign markets.

Sourcing decision making is multifaceted and entails both contractual and locational implications. From a contractual point of view, the sourcing of major components and products by multinational companies takes place in two ways: (1) from the parents or their foreign subsidiaries on an "intrafirm" basis and (2) from independent suppliers on a "contractual" basis. The first type of sourcing is known as intrafirm sourcing. The second type of sourcing is referred to commonly as outsourcing. Similarly, from a locational point of view, multinational companies can procure components and products either (1) domestically (i.e., *domestic sourcing*) or (2) from abroad (i.e., *offshore sourcing*). Therefore, as shown in Exhibit 5–3, four possible types of sourcing strategy can be identified.

In developing viable sourcing strategies on a global scale, companies must consider not only manufacturing costs, the costs of various resources, and exchange rate fluctuations, but also availability of infrastructure (including transportation, communications, and energy), industrial and cultural environments, the ease of working with foreign host governments, and so on. Furthermore, the complex nature of sourcing strategy on a global scale spawns many barriers to its successful execution. In particular, logistics, inventory management, distance, nationalism, and lack of working knowledge about foreign business practices, among others, are major operational problems identified by multinational companies engaging in international sourcing.

Many studies have shown, however, that despite, or maybe, as a result of, those operational problems, *where* to source major components seems much less important than *how* to source them. Thus, when examining the relationship between sourcing and competitiveness of multinational companies, it is crucial to distinguish between sourcing on a "contractual" basis and sourcing on an "intrafirm" basis, for these two types of sourcing will have a different impact on their long-run competitiveness.

Intrafirm Sourcing.   Multinational companies can procure their components in-house within their corporate system around the world. They produce major components at their respective home base and/or at their affiliates overseas to be incorporated in their products

EXHIBIT 5–3   **Types of Sourcing Strategy**

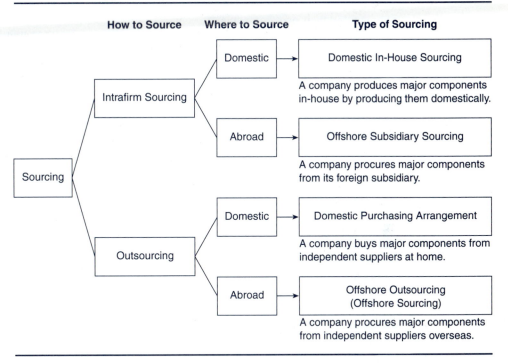

marketed in various parts of the world. Thus, trade does take place between a parent company and its subsidiaries abroad, and also between foreign subsidiaries across national boundaries. This is often referred to as *intrafirm* sourcing. If such in-house component procurement takes place at home, it is essentially *domestic in-house sourcing*. If it takes place at a company's foreign subsidiary, it is called *offshore subsidiary sourcing*. Intrafirm sourcing makes trade statistics more complex to interpret, since part of the international flow of products and components is taking place between affiliated companies within the same multinational corporate system, which transcends national boundaries.

According to a study conducted by the United Nations Center on Transnational Corporations, about 30 percent of U.S. exports is attributed to U.S. parent companies transferring products and components to their affiliates overseas, and about 40 percent of U.S. imports is accounted for by foreign affiliates exporting to their U.S. parent companies. For both Japan and Britain, intrafirm transactions account for approximately 30 percent of their total trade flows (exports and imports combined), respectively.

Outsourcing.   In the 1970s, foreign competitors gradually caught up in a productivity race with U.S. companies. This coincided with U.S. corporate strategic emphasis drifting from manufacturing to finance and marketing. As a result, manufacturing management gradually lost its organizational influence. Production managers' decision-making authority was reduced when R&D personnel prepared specifications with which production complied and marketing imposed delivery, inventory, and quality conditions. Productivity considerations were ignored. In a sense, production managers gradually took on the role of outside suppliers within their own companies.

This led to an erroneous belief that manufacturing functions could, and should, be transferred easily to independent operators and subcontractors, depending upon the cost differential between in-house and contracted-out production. A company's reliance on domestic suppliers for major components is basically a *domestic purchase arrangement.* Furthermore, in order to lower production costs under competitive pressure, U.S. companies turned increasingly to *outsourcing* of components and finished products from abroad, particularly from newly industrialized countries including Singapore, South Korea, Taiwan, Hong Kong, Brazil, and Mexico. Initially, subsidiaries were set up for production purposes (i.e., *offshore subsidiary sourcing*), but gradually, independent foreign suppliers took over component production for U.S. companies. This latter phenomenon is usually called *offshore outsourcing* (or *offshore sourcing,* for short).

Component procurement from overseas (i.e., *offshore subsidiary sourcing* and *offshore outsourcing*) has been a serious social and economic issue, as it affects domestic employment and economic structure. As stated earlier, U.S. companies using such strategy have been described pejoratively as hollow corporations. It is occasionally argued that U.S. companies are increasingly adopting a "designer role" in global competition—offering innovations in product design without investing in manufacturing process technology.

This widespread international sourcing practice could have a deleterious impact on the ability of U.S. companies to maintain their initial competitive advantage based on product innovations. Indeed, keeping abreast of emerging technology through continual improvement in R&D and manufacturing is the *sine qua non* for the company's continued competitiveness.

Long-Term Consequences

There are two opposing views of the long-term implications of offshore sourcing. One school of thought argues that many successful companies have developed a dynamic organizational network through increased use of joint ventures, subcontracting, and licensing activities across international borders. This flexible network system is broadly called *strategic alliances.* Strategic alliances allow each participant to pursue its particular competence. Therefore, each network participant can be seen as complementing rather than competing with the other participants for the common goals. Strategic alliances may even be formed by competing companies in the same industry in pursuit of complementary abilities (new technologies or skills) from each other. The other school of thought argues, however, that while the above argument may be true in the short run, there could also be negative long-term consequences resulting from a company's dependence on independent suppliers and subsequently the inherent difficulty for the company to keep abreast of constantly evolving design and engineering technologies without engaging in those developmental activities. These two opposing arguments will be elaborated below.

Strategic Alliances

The advantage of forming a strategic alliance is claimed to be its structural flexibility. Strategic alliances can accommodate a vast amount of complexity while maximizing the specialized competence of each member, and provide much more effective use of human resources that would otherwise have to be accumulated, allocated, and maintained by a single organization. In other words, a company can concentrate on performing the task at which it is most efficient. This approach is increasingly applied on a global basis with countries participating in a dynamic network as multinational companies configure and coordinate product development, manufacturing, and sourcing activities around the world.

First, due to the need for fast internationalization and related diversification, strategic alliances provide a relatively easy option to access the world markets and to combine complementary technologies. Thus, AT&T needed Olivetti's established European network to enter the European market for telephone switchboard equipment. Similarly, Toyota established a joint venture with General Motors so that the Japanese car maker could learn to work with UAW union members while General Motors could learn just-in-time inventory management from Toyota.

Second and more relevant to sourcing issues, an increasing number of companies have funneled out manufacturing functions to independent partners. In the early 1990s, for example, Apple Computer enlisted Sony to design and manufacture a new notebook-size Macintosh computer called the PowerBook 100. In this arrangement, Apple gave Sony the basic blueprint, and Sony engineers, who had little experience building personal computers, developed Apple's smallest and lightest machine from drawing board to factory floor in less than 13 months. This is a strategic alliance in which Apple's basic design ability was complemented by Sony's miniaturization technology. The result has been a spectacular success for Apple that could not have materialized without Sony's involvement.

But another result was that Apple might no longer manufacture the next generations of notebook-size computers without Sony's participation. Having mastered engineering and manufacturing of Apple's notebook computers, Sony gradually increased its role upstream to assisting Apple in product designing. Such a relationship could prove detrimental to Apple if Sony develops its own notebook computer, a possibility Apple took seriously enough to dissolve the partnership.

Dependence

Companies that rely on independent external sources of supply of major components tend to forsake part of the most important value-creating activities to, and also become dependent on, independent operators for assurance of component quality. Furthermore, those multinational companies tend to promote competition among independent suppliers, ensure continuing availability of materials in the future, and exploit full benefits of changing market conditions. However, individual suppliers are forced to operate in an uncertain business environment that inherently necessitates a shorter planning horizon. The uncertainty about the potential loss of orders to competitors often forces individual suppliers to make operating decisions that will likely increase their own long-term production and materials costs. In the process, this uncertain business environment tends to adversely affect the multinational companies sourcing components and/or finished products from independent suppliers.

The rapid decline of IBM in recent years offers the most vivid example of the problems caused by its dependence on independent suppliers for crucial components in the personal computer market. As a relatively late entrant into the burgeoning personal computer market in the early 1980s, IBM decided, contrary to its long-held policy of developing proprietary technology in-house, to rely on microprocessors from Intel and operating software from Microsoft. Given its massive size and marketing abilities, IBM was able to become a market leader in the personal computer business in a short period of time. However, Intel and Microsoft were also free to market their wares to any other companies. As a result, many small and nimble personal computer companies rushed into the personal computer market and began marketing IBM-compatible personal computers at the cost of IBM's market share position. Being slow to respond to this competition, IBM has already lost its dominant position and subsequently control of the industry that it had helped create a decade ago.

Gradual Loss of Design and Manufacturing Abilities

Those multinational companies that depend heavily on independent suppliers also tend in the long run to lose sight of emerging technologies and expertise, which could be incorporated into the development of new manufacturing processes as well as new products. Apple–Sony and IBM–Intel–Microsoft alliances may be illustrative of such possibilities. Thus, continual sourcing from independent suppliers is likely to forebode those companies' long-term loss of the ability to manufacture at competitive cost and, as a result, loss of their global competitiveness. However, if technology and expertise developed by a multinational company are exploited within its multinational corporate system (i.e., by its foreign affiliates and by the parent company itself), the company can retain its technological base to itself without unduly disseminating them to competitors. The benefit of such internalization is likely to be great, particularly when technology is highly idiosyncratic or specific with limited alternative uses, or when it is novel in the marketplace. For such a technology, the market price mechanism is known to break down as a seller and potential buyers of the technology tend to see its value very differently. Potential buyers, who do not have perfect knowledge of how useful the technology will be, tend to undervalue its true market value. As a result, the seller of the technology is not likely to get a full economic benefit of the technology by selling it in the open market.

In addition, by getting involved in design and production on its own, the multinational company can keep abreast of emerging technologies and innovations originating anywhere in the world for potential use in the future. Furthermore, management of the quality of major components is required to retain the goodwill and confidence of consumers in the products. As a result, "intrafirm" sourcing of major components and finished products between the parent company and its affiliates abroad and between its foreign affiliates themselves would more likely enable the company to retain a long-term competitive edge in the world market.

Summary

The scope of global sourcing has expanded over time. Whether or not to procure components or products from abroad was once determined strictly on price and thus strongly influenced by the fluctuating exchange rate. Thus the appreciation of the dollar prompted companies to increase offshore sourcing, while the depreciation of the dollar encouraged domestic sourcing. Today many companies consider not simply price but also quality, reliability, and technology of components and products to be procured. These companies design their sourcing decision on the basis of the interplay between their competitive advantages and the comparative advantages of various sourcing locations for long-term gains.

Trade and foreign production managed by multinational companies are very complex. In growing global competition, sourcing of components and finished products around the world within the multinational company has increased. The development of global sourcing and marketing strategies across different foreign markets has become a central issue for many multinational companies. Traditionally, a polycentric approach to organizing operations on a country-by-country basis allowed each country manager to tailor marketing strategy to the peculiarities of local markets. As such, product adaptations were considered a necessary strategy to better cater to the different needs and wants of customers in various countries. Product adaptation tends to be a reactive, rather than a proactive, strategic response to the market. A high level of product adaptation may make it difficult for multinational companies to reap economies of scale in production and marketing and to coordinate their networks of activities on a global scale.

Global sourcing strategy requires close coordination of R&D, manufacturing, and marketing activities on a global basis. Managing geographically separated R&D, manufacturing, and marketing activities, those companies face difficult coordination problems of integrating their operations and adapting them to different legal, political, and cultural environments in different countries. Furthermore, separation of manufacturing activities involves an inherent risk that manufacturing in the value chain will gradually become neglected. Such a neglect can be costly as continued involvement in manufacturing leads to pioneering product design and innovation over time. An effective global sourcing strategy calls for continual efforts to streamline manufacturing without sacrificing marketing flexibility. To accomplish this, a conscious effort to develop either core components in-house or develop product design families or universal products is called for.

A caveat should be also noted. While a company's ability to develop core components and products and market them in the world markets on its own is preferred, the enormousness of such a task should be examined in light of rapid changes in both technology and customer needs around the world. Those changes make the product life cycle extremely short, sometimes too short for many multinational companies to pursue product development, manufacturing, and marketing on a global basis without strategic alliance partners. Benefits of maintaining an independent proprietary position should always be weighed against the time cost of delayed market entry.

Supplementary Reading

Cavusgil, S. Tamer, Attila Yaprak, and Poe-lin Yeoh. "A Decision-Making Framework for Global Sourcing." *International Business Review,* Vol. 2, 1993, pp. 143–56.

Cohen, Stephen S., and John Zysman. "Why Manufacturing Matters: The Myth of the Post-Industrial Economy." *California Management Review,* Vol. 29, Spring 1987, pp. 9–26

Kotabe, Masaaki. "Efficiency vs. Effectiveness Orientation of Global Sourcing Strategy: A Comparison of U.S. and Japanese Multinational Companies." *Academy of Management Executive,* Vol. 12, November 1998, pp. 107–19.

———. *Global Sourcing Strategy: R&D, Manufacturing, and Marketing Interfaces.* New York: Quorum Books, 1992.

Markides, Constantinos, and Norman Berg. "Manufacturing Offshore Is Bad Business." *Harvard Business Review,* Vol. 66, September–October 1988, pp. 113–20.

Monczka, Robert M., and Robert J. Trent. "Global Sourcing: A Development Approach." *International Journal of Purchasing and Materials Management,* Vol. 27, Spring 1991, pp. 2–8.

Murray, Janet Y., Masaaki Kotabe, and Albert R. Wildt. "Strategic and Financial Performance Implications of Global Sourcing Strategy: A Contingency Analysis." *Journal of International Business Studies*, Vol. 26, First Quarter 1995, pp. 181–202.

Porter, Michael E., ed. *Competition in Global Industries.* Cambridge, MA: Harvard Business School Press, 1986.

6   LICENSING

Licensing is a contractual arrangement whereby the licensor (selling firm) allows its technology, patents, trademarks, designs, processes, know-how, intellectual property, or other proprietary advantages to be used for a fee by the licensee (buying firm). Licensing is a strategy for technology transfer. It is also an approach to internationalization that requires less time or depth of involvement in foreign markets, compared with export strategies, joint ventures, and foreign direct investment (FDI).

A closely related contractual arrangement to licensing is franchising. Franchising is an organizational form where the franchisor (parent company/owner) of a service, trademarked product, or brand name allows the franchisee to use the same in return for a lump sum payment and/or royalty, while conforming to required standards of quality, service, and so forth. (See the Kenny Rogers Roasters in China case for an illustration.)

Most international licensing agreements are between firms from industrialized countries. As well, licensing occurs most frequently in technology-intensive industries. It is not surprising, then, that the overall use of licensing varies greatly from country to country. For example, licensing of foreign technology by Korean firms exceeded $4 billion in 1995, with 75 percent of that going to U.S. or Japanese licensors.

A great deal of international licensing also occurs in industries that are not technology-intensive. These industries range from food to sports teams to publishing. Retail sales of all licensed merchandise, as illustrated in the Hush Puppies Chile case, was more than $100 billion in 1997. The popular press is replete with announcements regarding international licensing (see the box on page 108 for examples).

Similarly, international franchising has grown rapidly. By 1990 U.S. companies alone had more than 32,000 franchised outlets outside America. Most of this expansion occurred by selling franchises to foreign nationals.

Much of the licensing discussion that follows assumes a technology transfer. This would generally constitute a more complex form of licensing than that involving trademarks, for example.

This chapter was prepared by Paul W. Beamish.

The term "licensing" is also frequently used internationally in reference to national governments, which provide licenses for foreign banks or insurance companies to operate in their market, for resource companies to undertake exploration, and so forth. This is a different form of permission than the focus of this chapter.

When Is Licensing Employed?

The strategic advantages to be gained by licensing depend on the technology, firm size, product maturity, and extent of the firm's experience. A number of internal and external circumstances may lead a firm to employ a licensing strategy. From the perspective of the licensor these would variously include:

1. A firm lacks the capital, managerial resources, or knowledge of foreign markets required for exporting or FDI, but it wants to earn additional profits with minimal commitment.
2. Licensing is a way of testing and proactively developing a market that can later be exploited by direct investment.
3. The technology involved is not central to the licensor's core business. Not surprisingly, single—or dominant—product firms are very reluctant to license their core technology, whereas diversified firms are much more willing to license peripheral technologies.
4. Prospects of "technology feedback" are high (i.e., the licensor has been contractually ensured of access to new developments generated by the licensee and based on licensed knowledge).
5. The licensor wishes to exploit its technology in secondary markets that may be too small to justify larger investments; the required economies of scale may not be attainable.
6. Host-country governments restrict imports or FDI, or both; or the risk of nationalization or foreign control is too great.
7. The licensee is unlikely to become a future competitor.
8. The pace of technological change is sufficiently rapid that the licensor can remain technologically superior and ahead of the licensee, who is a potential competitor. As well, if the technology may become obsolete quickly, there is pressure to exploit it fully while the opportunity exists.

From the perspective of the licensee, the main advantage of licensing is that the licensee's existing products or technology can be acquired more cheaply, faster, and with less risk from third parties (licensors) than by internal R&D. Another advantage is that the licensee can gain product designs for a desired diversification, to complement other assets it possesses such as production or marketing capability.

Risks Associated with Licensing

The most important risk associated with licensing (or franchising) is that the licensor risks the dissipation of its proprietary advantage, since the licensee acquires at least a portion of the advantage via licensing. Thus, any licensor should try to ensure that its licensee will not be a future competitor or act opportunistically. Not surprisingly, many license agreements are made between firms from different countries so as to reduce the likelihood of creating a competitor in the domestic market. Other approaches include limiting the licensee's market and insisting on technology feedback or flowback clauses.

Licensed trademarks remain the licensor's property in perpetuity, whereas licenses normally have a finite lifetime. A licensor may retain considerable bargaining power in proportion to the perishability of the licensed technology and the licensor's ability to provide a continuing supply of new technology in the future.

A second risk with licensing is that the licensor jeopardizes its worldwide reputation if the licensee cannot maintain the desired product standards and quality or if it engages in questionable practices. Because the licensor will typically become aware of licensee questionable practices only after the fact, this suggests the need to devote more time during the original negotiations to understanding the character of the licensee.

Another consideration with licensing is that profits to the licensor may not be maximized. This is because (a) their involvement in the licensed markets is indirect, (b) exchange rates change, (c) some countries limit the amount of outward payments for licenses, and so forth.

Some of the standard elements of a license agreement are more difficult than others for the licensor to enforce. These would include (a) guaranteeing flowback of actual improvements, (b) sublicensing, (c) diligence that the terms are being honored, and (d) quality control. As a result, sometimes licensing may not provide even the minimum expected benefits.

Intellectual Property Rights

In many countries intellectual property legislation either does not exist or is not enforced. Not surprisingly, a major issue for many companies is infringement of their intellectual property rights as the Sicom case illustrates. With billions of dollars at stake, this issue has also become a key element in trade negotiations.

Some companies have deemed it necessary to enter into license agreements as a means of offsetting trademark piracy. The logic behind such "reluctant licensing" is that by licensing a local firm the local firm will, in turn, take the necessary steps to stop unlicensed domestic competitors from using the intellectual property.

There are numerous implications with such a scenario. For example, many organizations are feeling pressure to internationalize their operations sooner than they were expecting. As a consequence, they view licensing as a defensive solution, rather than an opportunity.

Costs of Licensing

Licensing is sometimes incorrectly viewed as a one-time transaction involving little in the way of costs for the licensor. In reality, there are costs associated with (a) the protection of industrial property, (b) establishing the license agreement, and (c) maintaining the license agreement.

Establishment costs would include expenses for searching for suitable licensees, communication, training, equipment testing, and so forth. Some products/technologies lend themselves to licensing, while others do not. The greater the cost and complexity of modifying the underlying intellectual property, the more difficult it is to effectively employ a licensing strategy.

Recent International Licensing Announcements

Licensed properties account for nearly half of the $4 billion in home decorating retail sales sold for the Halloween season, including 70 percent of costumes sales, 50 percent of decorations and greeting cards, and 10 percent of candies.

Corning takes legal action against European and U.S. companies for infringing Corning's optical fiber patent.

Texas Instrument Incorporated (TI) and Vanguard International Semiconductor Corporation (VIS) announced a 10-year worldwide semiconductor cross-license patent agreement. This is the first semiconductor patent agreement between TI and a Taiwanese company other than TI's joint venture with the Acer Group.

New York, NY, January 20, 1999—The International Licensing Industry Merchandisers' Association announced a major initiative in conjunction with a consortium of marketing experts to develop the most significant study to date on the business of licensing.

Compaq Computer Corp. is licensing high-performance XG software wavetable synthesizer technology from Yamaha Systems Technology Inc. for its Presario PC line.

Telstra, the Australian telecommunication company, announced that US West is licensing its flexible charging and business-billing system.

Warner Bros. Sports Licensing Expands Sport Athlete Roster with Philadelphia Flyers' John LeClair. LeClair is the first NHL player to join several star athletes from the NBA, NFL, and MLB. LeClair will be covered from head to toe under the licensing program, which includes: footwear, apparel and headwear; socks and sleepwear; inflatables, watches, sports bags; ties and boxers; sunglasses, toys, and games.

Excalibur Technologies of Belgium signed comprehensive licensing agreement with Sony Marketing (Japan) Inc. for knowledge-retrievable software products.

Ottawa, Canada, November 9, 1998—Corel Corporation and Trellix Corporation of Massachusetts announced a worldwide licensing and marketing agreement under which Trellix® 2.0 will be included in the next version of Corel's award-winning office suite.

Microsoft and EUnet International announced first phase of Pan-European Licensing Agreement for Microsoft Internet Explorer 3.0.

Art licensing represents $5.2 billion of the licensing industry and is growing steadily. The boom in art licensing is a direct result of the need for manufacturers to provide product offerings to the growing needs of their discriminating consumers. Cause-related licensing, catalog, business premiums, consumer premiums, and Internet marketing are emerging niche channels for art licensed images.

The International Licensing Industry Merchandisers' Association (LIMA) 1998 award for Promotion of the Year went to MGM Studios for its "James Bond: Tomorrow Never Dies" promotional campaign. The promotional program included partnerships with BMW, Ericsson, Omega, Smirnoff, Avis, L'Oreal, and TBS.

Starbucks, the U.S. coffee chain, hopes to have 500 branches in Asia by 2003. Though Starbucks prefers the control which joint ventures offer, it is not willing to pay for half of each branch it opens. Although franchising could get around this problem, Starbucks is not comfortable having a franchise partner select subfranchisers, as is usually the case. Licensing agreements allow Starbucks to maintain control over its expansion while limiting its financial exposure. The licensee funds the capital costs of expansion—and bears the risks of a downturn. Detailed licensing agreements give the local companies exclusive rights to develop and operate Starbucks retail stores. However, they also stipulate that Starbucks remains involved in every aspect of planning, operations, design, and training.

Maintenance costs might include backup services for licensees, audit, ongoing market research, and so forth. These are nontrivial expenses. For example, Seattle-based consultants from Starbucks Coffee visit each foreign store (licensee) at least once a month. Monitoring costs will directly and significantly affect the willingness of companies to license or franchise internationally.

To all of these out-of-pocket expenses must be added opportunity costs. Opportunity costs are made up of the loss of current or prospective revenues from exports or other sources.

Unattractive Markets for Licensing

A number of conditions directly impact "real" licensing returns and make a particular country an unattractive market for licensing. The first of these conditions occurs where there is a regulatory scheme governing licensing. In some countries—such as France, Ireland, and Spain—licenses are not valid until government approval or registration is completed.

A second condition occurs when licenses granting exclusive rights to certain products or territories are not allowed. In some cases, governments may prohibit them because competition will be substantially lessened. Also, some countries place limits on the allowable duration of agreements.

Another condition occurs when there are foreign exchange controls or other restrictions on royalty payments (license fees). Frequently, a withholding tax on royalty payments to nonresident licensors may be applied. In Europe, the combined withholding tax and VAT (value-added tax) can range up to about 50 percent.

Finally, some countries impose royalty and fee limits. Some use a 10 percent limit, while others employ a more stringent 3 percent limit. Any of these government-set rates can, and frequently do, change over time.

Overall, licensing tends to be more attractive when agreements formed in the country enjoy the benefit of freedom of contract. Here the parties may, for the most part, create their own legal framework by the manner in which the contract is written.

Major Elements of the License Agreement

The license agreement is the essential commercial contract between licensee and licensor, which specifies the rights to be granted, the consideration payable, and the duration of the terms. The licensed rights usually take the form of patents, registered trademarks, registered industrial designs, unpatented technology, trade secrets, know-how, or copyrights. The license agreement should make explicit reference to the product as well as to the underlying "intangible" or "intellectual" property rights.

Although no definitive standard form exists for license agreements, certain points are typically covered. In many cases, licensors will have developed standard forms for these contracts, based on their past experiences in licensing. Typically, a license agreement will include the following:

1. A clear and correct description of the parties to the agreement, identifying the corporate names of each party, its incorporating jurisdiction, and its principal place of business.

2. A preamble or recitals describing the parties, their reasons for entering into the arrangement, and their respective roles.

3. A list of defined terms for the purposes of the particular contract to simplify this complex document and to eliminate ambiguity or vagueness (e.g., definitions of the terms *licensed, product, net profit, territory,* and so forth).

4. A set of schedules, in an exhibit or appendix, where necessary, to segregate lengthy detailed descriptions of any kind.

5. The grant that is fundamental to the agreement and explicitly describes the nature of the rights being granted to the licensee. This grant may be based on promotion methods, trade secrets, list of customers, drawings and photographs, models, tools, and parts; or know-how. Know-how, in turn, may be based on invention records, laboratory records, research reports, development reports, engineering reports, pilot plant design, production plant design, production specifications, raw material specifications, quality controls, economic surveys, market surveys, etc.

6. A description of any geographical limitations to be imposed on the licensee's manufacturing, selling, or sublicensing activities.

7. A description of any exclusive rights to manufacture and sell that may be granted.

8. A discussion of any rights to sublicense.

9. The terms relating to the duration of the agreement, including the initial term and any necessary provisions for the automatic extension or review of the agreement.

10. Provisions for the granting of rights to downstream refinements or improvements made by the licensor in the future.

11. Provisions for "technological flowback" agreements where some benefit of improvements made by the licensee reverts to the licensor. The rights to the future improvements by either the licensor or licensee are often used as leverage in negotiations.

12. Details regarding the royalties or periodic payments based on the use of licensed rights. The percentage rate of the royalty may be fixed or variable (based on time, production level, sales level, and so forth), but the "royalty base" for this rate must be explicitly defined. Some methods of calculating royalties include percentage of sales, royalties based on production, percentage of net profit, lump-sum payments, or payment-free licenses in cross-licensing arrangements. Aulakh et al. found that "Licensor's monitoring of the licensee and interfirm interaction are significantly higher in a royalties-based agreement, and that licensor firms prefer lump-sum fee agreements when faced with uncertainties related to intellectual property protection and ability to repatriate earnings from foreign markets." (p. 417)

There are no hard-and-fast rules for establishing royalty rates. One arbitrary rule (see Contractor in Supplementary Reading) is the "25 percent rule of thumb," which suggests that the licensor aim for a 25 percent share of the licensee's related profits and then convert this profit level to a certain royalty rate. Others suggest that licensors will often specify a minimum or target absolute compensation. This can be derived from technology transfer cost considerations or a judgment of how much it may cost the prospective licensee to acquire the technology by other means or from an "industry norm." Royalty escalation clauses and the currency of payment should also be specified.

It is often quite difficult for the licensor to accurately estimate the market potential for its property. As a consequence, the licensee, with its greater knowledge of local conditions, is often in a stronger position when the royalty rate terms are being negotiated.

13. Specification of minimum performance requirements (e.g., minimum royalty payments, unit sales volumes, employment of personnel, minimum promotion expenditures, and so forth) to ensure the "best efforts" of the licensee so that the license potential is fully exploited. For example, most license agreements that confer exclusive selling rights in a given area to the licensee also require either a sizable down payment or a minimum annual royalty payment. Otherwise, the licensee may "sit on" the license and block the licensor from entering the market in question.

14. Other clauses common to most license agreements include those to protect the licensed rights against licensees and third parties and those regarding title retention by the licensor, confidentiality of know-how, quality control, most-favored-licensee status, the applicable language of the contract, and any provisions with respect to the assignability of rights by the licensee.

The above list of elements common to most license agreements is by no means exhaustive. For a more detailed checklist for license agreements, see Stitt and Baker in Supplementary Reading. Any potential license agreement should be reviewed by company counsel. It must be noted that every license agreement is unique in some way and, therefore, great care should be taken in its negotiation and formal documentation.

Supplementary Reading

Licensing

Atuahene-Gima, Kwaku. "International Licensing of Technology: An Empirical Study of the Differences between Licensee and Non-Licensee Firms." *Journal of International Marketing,* Vol. 1, No. 2, 1993, pp. 71–87.

Aulakh, Preet S., S. Tamer Cavusgil, and M.B. Sarkar. "Compensation in International Licensing Agreements." *Journal of International Business Studies,* Vol. 29, No. 2, 1998, pp. 409–20.

Buckley, Peter J. "New Forms of International Industrial Co-operation." In *The Economic Theory of the Multinational Enterprise.* Ed. P.J. Buckley and M. Casson. London: Macmillan, 1985.

Business International Corporation. *International Licensing Management.* New York: Business International Corporation, 1988.

Caves, Richard E. *Multinational Enterprise and Economic Analysis.* 2nd ed. Cambridge, MA: Cambridge University Press, 1996.

Caves, Richard E., Harold Crookell, and J. Peter Killing. "The Imperfect Market for Technology Licenses." *Oxford Bulletin of Economics and Statistics,* August 1983, pp. 249–67.

Clegg, Jeremy. "The Determinants of Aggregate International Licensing Behavior: Evidence from Five Countries." *Management International Review,* Vol. 30, No. 3, 1990, pp. 231–51.

Contractor, Farok J. "A Generalized Theorem for Joint-Venture and Licensing Negotiations." *Journal of International Business Studies,* Summer 1985, pp. 25–47.

Ehrbar, Thomas J. *Business International's Guide to International Licensing: Building a Licensing Strategy for 14 Key Markets around the World.* New York: McGraw-Hill, 1993.

Hill, Charles W.L. "Strategies for Exploiting Technological Innovations: When and When Not to License." *Organization Science,* Vol. 3, No. 3, 1992, pp. 428–41.

Horstmann, Ignatius, and James R. Markusen. "Licensing versus Direct Investment: A Model of Internalization by the Multinational Enterprise." *Canadian Journal of Economics,* Vol. 20, No. 3, 1987, pp. 464–81.

Pfaff, John F. "Changes in the EC Licensing Environment and Their Effect on Licensing as a Strategy for Europe 1992." *The International Executive,* Vol. 34, No. 5, 1992, pp. 415–39.

Root, Franklin, R. *Entry Strategies for International Markets.* Lexington, MA: Lexington Books, 1987.

Stitt, Hubert J., and Samuel R. Baker. *The Licensing and Joint Venture Guide.* 3rd ed. Toronto: Ontario Ministry of Industry, Trade, and Technology, 1985.

Franchising

Fladmoe-Lindquist, Karin. "International Franchising Capabilities and Development." *Journal of Business Venturing,* Vol. 11, 1996, pp. 419–38.

Fladmoe-Lindquist, Karin, and Laurent L. Jacque. "Control Modes in International Service Operations: The Propensity to Franchise." *Management Science,* Vol. 41, No. 7, 1995, pp. 1238–49.

Shane, Scott A. "Why Franchise Companies Expand Overseas." *Journal of Business Venturing,* Vol. 11, 1996, pp. 73–88.

7 THE DESIGN AND MANAGEMENT OF INTERNATIONAL JOINT VENTURES

An international joint venture is a company that is owned by two or more firms of different nationality. International joint ventures may be formed from a starting (or greenfield) basis or may be the result of several established companies deciding to merge existing divisions. However they are formed, the purpose of most international joint ventures is to allow partners to pool resources and coordinate their efforts to achieve results that neither could obtain acting alone.

International joint ventures and other forms of corporate alliances have become increasingly popular. For example, in the airline sector, virtually every major carrier has links with foreign carriers. These may be equity- or nonequity (i.e., code share, frequent flyer programs, etc.)-based and are culminating in truly global network arrangements such as Star Alliance and One World.

As Exhibit 7–1 illustrates, a broad range of strategic alliances exists. They vary widely in terms of the level of interaction and type. While many of the comments in this chapter focus on equity joint venture—the alliance form usually requiring the greatest level of interaction, cooperation, and investment—many of the issues are applicable to other forms of alliances. For example, IKEA, the giant Swedish furniture retailer, operates a series of nonequity buyer–supplier alliances around the world. IKEA provides component suppliers with product design, technical assistance, leased equipment, and even loans. IKEA's suppliers get new skills, direct access to a large and growing retailer, and steadier sales. This not only generates for IKEA low-cost and high-quality supply but a sense of partnership with, and loyalty to/from, suppliers.

Joint ventures have moved from being a way to enter foreign markets of peripheral interest to become a part of the mainstream of corporate activity. Virtually all MNEs are

This chapter was prepared by Paul W. Beamish.

Exhibit 7–1   Range of Strategic Alliances

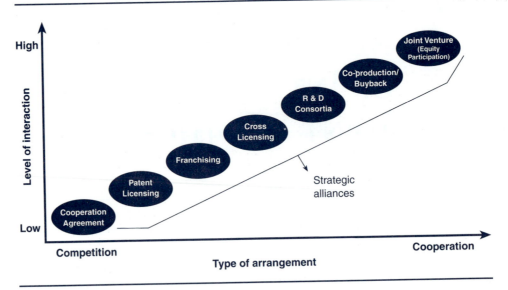

using international joint ventures, many as a key element of their corporate strategies. Merck, for example, has joint ventures with Astra (1997 JV sales of $2.3 billion), Johnson & Johnson (1997 JV sales of $.5 billion), Du Pont (1997 JV sales of $1.3 billion), Pasteur (1997 JV sales of $.6 billion), Rhône-Poulenc (1997 JV sales of $.7 billion), and so forth. Even firms that have traditionally operated independently around the world are increasingly turning to joint ventures.

The popularity and use of international joint ventures and cooperative alliances remained strong through the 1990s. The rate of joint venture use does not change much from year to year. In general, joint ventures are the mode of choice about 35 percent of the time by U.S. multinationals and in 40 to 45 percent of foreign subsidiaries formed by Japanese multinationals.

The popularity of alliances has continued despite their reputation for being difficult to manage. Failures exist and are usually widely publicized. Dow Chemical, for example, reportedly lost more than $100 million after a dispute with its Korean joint venture partners caused the firm to sell its 50 percent interest in its Korean venture at a loss, and to sell below cost its nearby wholly owned chemical plant.

While early surveys suggested that as many as half the companies with international joint ventures were dissatisfied with their ventures' performance, there is reason to believe that some of the earlier concern can now be ameliorated. This is primarily because there is far greater alliance experience and insight to draw from. There is now widespread appreciation that joint ventures are not necessarily transitional organization forms, shorter-lived, or less profitable. For many organizations they are the mode of choice.

Why do managers keep creating new joint ventures? The reasons are presented in the remainder of this chapter, as are some guidelines for international joint venture success.

Why Companies Create International Joint Ventures

International joint ventures can be used to achieve one of four basic purposes. As shown in Exhibit 7–2, these are: *to strengthen the firm's existing business, to take the firm's existing products into new markets, to obtain new products that can be sold in the firm's existing markets, and to diversify into a new business.*

Companies using joint ventures for each of these purposes will have different concerns and will be looking for partners with different characteristics. Firms wanting to strengthen their existing business, for example, will most likely be looking for partners among their current competitors, while those wanting to enter new geographic markets will be looking for overseas firms in related businesses with good local market knowledge. Although often treated as a single category of business activity, international joint ventures are remarkably diverse, as the following descriptions indicate.

Strengthening the Existing Business

International joint ventures are used in a variety of ways by firms wishing to strengthen or protect their existing businesses. Among the most important are joint ventures formed to achieve economies of scale, joint ventures that allow the firm to acquire needed technology and know-how, and ventures that reduce the financial risk of major projects. Joint ventures formed for the latter two reasons may have the added benefit of eliminating a potential competitor from a particular product or market area.

Achieving Economies of Scale.   Firms often use joint ventures to attempt to match the economies of scale achieved by their larger competitors. Joint ventures have been used to give their parents economies of scale in raw material and component supply, in research and development, and in marketing and distribution. Joint ventures have also been used as a vehicle for carrying out divisional mergers, which yield economies across the full spectrum of business activity.

Very small, entrepreneurial firms are more likely to participate in a network than an equity joint venture in order to strengthen their business through economies of scale. Small firms may form a network to reduce the costs, and increase the potential, of foreign market entry, or to meet some other focused objective. Most of these networks tend to have a relatively low ease of entry and exit and a loose structure and require a limited investment (primarily time, as they might be self-financing through fees). International equity joint ventures by very small firms are unusual because such firms must typically overcome some combination of liabilities of size, newness, foreignness, and relational orientation (often they were initially successful because of their single-minded, do-it-themselves orientation).

Raw Material and Component Supply.   In many industries the smaller firms create joint ventures to obtain raw materials or jointly manufacture components. Automakers, for instance, may develop a jointly owned engine plant to supply certain low-volume engines to each company. Producing engines for the parents provides economies of scale, with each company receiving engines at a lower cost than it could obtain if it were to produce them itself.

EXHIBIT 7–2   Motives for International Joint Venture Formation

	Existing Products	New Products
New Markets	To take existing products to foreign markets	To diversify into a new business
Existing Markets	To strengthen the existing business	To bring foreign products to local markets

The managers involved in such ventures are quick to point out that these financial savings do not come without a cost. Design changes in jointly produced engines, for example, tend to be slow because all partners have to agree on them. In fact, one joint venture that produced computer printers fell seriously behind the state of the art in printer design because the parents could not agree on the features they wanted in the jointly designed printer. Because all of the venture's output was sold to the parents, the joint venture personnel had no direct contact with end customers and could not resolve the dispute.

Transfer pricing is another headache that arises in joint ventures that supply their parents. A low transfer price on products shipped from the venture to the parents, for instance, means that whichever parent buys the most product obtains the most benefit. Many higher-volume-taking parents claim that this is fair, as it is their volume that plays an important role in making the joint venture viable. On the other hand, some parents argue for a higher transfer price, which means that the economic benefits are captured in the venture and will flow, most likely via dividends, to the parents in proportion to their share holdings in the venture. As the share holdings generally reflect the original asset contributions to the venture and not the volumes taken out every year, this means that different parents will do well under this arrangement. Clearly, the potential for transfer price disputes is significant.

Research and Development.   Shared research and development efforts are increasingly common. The rationale for such programs is that participating firms can save both time and money by collaborating and may, by combining the efforts of the participating companies' scientists, come up with results that would otherwise have been impossible.

The choice facing firms wishing to carry out collaborative research is whether to simply coordinate their efforts and share costs or to actually set up a jointly owned company.

Hundreds of multicompany research programs are not joint ventures. Typically, scientists from the participating companies agree on the research objectives and the most likely avenues of exploration to achieve those objectives. If there are, say, four promising ways to attack a particular problem, each of four participating companies would be assigned one route and told to pursue it. Meetings would be held, perhaps quarterly, to share results and approaches taken and when (hopefully) one route proved to be successful, all firms would be fully informed on the new techniques and technology.

The alternative way to carry out collaborative research is to establish a jointly owned company and to provide it with staff, budget, and a physical location. In early 1999 for example, discussions were under way for a proposed, not-for-profit consortium of major drug companies that would fund work on decoding the human genome. At a cost of $75–100 million from participants, the proposed joint venture would compete directly with the small biotech companies already working on the project. The large pharmaceutical companies share an interest in having open access to a map of genetic landmarks, as they feel this will be essential to the way new drugs will be tested and developed in the future.

In the United States, a somewhat different problem arose when the president of a joint research company established by a dozen U.S. computer firms discovered that the participating companies were not sending their best people to the new company. He ended up hiring more than 200 of the firm's 330 scientists from the outside.

A sensitive issue for firms engaging in collaborative research, whether through joint ventures or not, is how far the collaboration should extend. Because the partners are usually competitors, the often expressed ideal is that the joint effort will focus only on "precompetitive" basic research and not, for example, on product development work. This is often a difficult line to draw.

Marketing and Distribution.   Many international joint ventures involve shared research, development, and production but stop short of joint marketing. The vehicles coming out of the widely publicized joint venture between Toyota and General Motors in California, for instance, are clearly branded as GM or Toyota products and are sold competitively through each parent's distribution network. Antitrust plays a role in the decision to keep marketing activities separate, but so does the partners' intrinsic desire to maintain separate brand identities and increase their own market share. These cooperating firms have not forgotten that they are competitors.

There are, nevertheless, some ventures formed for the express purpose of achieving economies in marketing and distribution. A three-way venture formed between Bacardi International of the United States, Martini and Rossi of Italy, and Bass, Britain's largest brewer, to sell a combined portfolio of the brands of all three companies in England and Wales is a typical example of what can be done. Each firm is hoping for wider market coverage at a lower cost. The trade-off is a loss of direct control over the sales force, potentially slower decision making, and a possible loss of direct contact with the customer.

Somewhat similar in intent are cooperative marketing agreements, which are not joint ventures but agreements by two firms with related product lines to sell one another's products. Here companies end up with a more complete line to sell, without the managerial complications of a joint venture. Sometimes the cooperative marketing agreement can in fact entail joint branding, as the Neilson International in Mexico case discusses.

Divisional Mergers.   Multinational companies with subsidiaries that they have concluded are too small to be economic have sometimes chosen to create a joint venture by combining their "too small" operations with those of a competitor. Fiat and Peugeot, for example, merged their automobile operations in Argentina, where both companies were doing poorly. The new joint venture started life with a market share of 35 percent and a chance for greatly improved economies in design, production, and marketing. Faced with similar pressures, Ford and Volkswagen have done the same thing in Brazil, creating a jointly owned company called Auto Latina.

Similarly, Dresser Industries of Illinois and Komatsu of Japan combined existing businesses to create an equally owned joint venture to compete in the construction and mining equipment business in the Western Hemisphere. Komatsu's motivation for entering the venture was to establish a manufacturing source for its products in North America, as balance of trade pressures and currency values made sourcing from Japan ever more risky. Explaining Dresser's desire for the joint venture, a vice president stated that the equipment business was becoming ever more capital-intensive, and the only routes to success were to be a very narrow niche player or a major full-line producer. The Komatsu deal created the latter—a strong full-line company with first-year sales in excess of $1.5 billion, ranked number two in the Americas.

A divisional merger can also allow a firm a graceful exit from a business in which it is no longer interested. Honeywell gave up trying to continue alone in the computer industry when it folded its business into a venture with Machines Bull of France and NEC of Japan. Honeywell held a 40 percent stake in the resulting joint venture.

Acquiring Technology in the Core Business

Firms that have wanted to acquire technology in their core business area have traditionally done so through license agreements or by developing the technology themselves. Increasingly, however, companies are turning to joint ventures for this purpose, because developing technology in-house is seen as taking too long, and license agreements, while giving the firm access to patent rights and engineers' ideas, may not provide much in the way of shop floor know-how. The power of a joint venture is that a firm may be able to have its employees working shoulder to shoulder with those of its partner, trying to solve the same problems. For example, the General Motors joint venture with Toyota provided an opportunity for GM to obtain a source of low-cost small cars and to watch firsthand how Toyota managers, who were in operational control of the venture, were able to produce high-quality automobiles at low cost. Most observers have concluded that the opportunity for General Motors to learn new production techniques was more significant than the supply of cars coming from the venture.

Reducing Financial Risk

Some projects are too big or too risky for firms to tackle alone. This is why oil companies use joint ventures to split the costs of searching for new oil fields, and why the aircraft industry is increasingly using joint ventures and "risk-sharing subcontractors" to put up some of the funds required to develop new aircraft and engines.

Do such joint ventures make sense? For the oil companies the answer is a clear yes. In these ventures, one partner takes a lead role and manages the venture on a day-to-day basis. Management complexity, a major potential drawback of joint ventures, is kept to a minimum. If the venture finds oil, transfer prices are not a problem—the rewards of the venture are easy to divide between the partners. In situations like this, forming a joint venture is an efficient and sensible way of sharing risk.

It is not as obvious that some other industry ventures are a good idea, at least not for industry leaders. Their partners are not entering these ventures simply in the hopes of earning an attractive return on their investment. They are gearing up to produce, sooner or later, their own product. Why would a company be willing to train potential competitors? For many firms, it is the realization that their partner is going to hook up with someone anyway, so better to have a portion of a smaller future pie than none at all, even if it means you may be eventually competing against yourself.

Taking Products to Foreign Markets

Firms with domestic products that they believe will be successful in foreign markets face a choice. As discussed in Chapter 1, they can produce the product at home and export it, license the technology to local firms around the world, establish wholly owned subsidiaries in foreign countries, or form joint ventures with local partners. Many firms conclude that exporting is unlikely to lead to significant market penetration, building wholly owned subsidiaries is too slow and requires too many resources, and licensing does not offer an adequate financial return. The result is that an international joint venture, while seldom seen as an ideal choice, is often the most attractive compromise.

Moving into foreign markets entails a degree of risk, and most firms that decide to form a joint venture with a local firm are doing so to reduce the risk associated with their new market entry. Very often, they look for a partner that deals with a related product line and, thus, has a good feel for the local market. As a further risk-reducing measure, the joint venture may begin life as simply a sales and marketing operation, until the product begins to sell well and volumes rise. Then a "screwdriver" assembly plant may be set up to assemble components shipped from the foreign parent. Eventually, the venture may modify or redesign the product to better suit the local market and may establish complete local manufacturing, sourcing raw material and components locally. The objective is to withhold major investment until the market uncertainty is reduced.

Following Customers to Foreign Markets.   Another way to reduce the risk of a foreign market entry is to follow firms that are already customers at home. Thus, many Japanese automobile suppliers have followed Honda, Toyota, and Nissan as they set up new plants in North America and Europe. As in the Wilmor case, very often these suppliers, uncertain of their ability to operate in a foreign environment, decide to form a joint venture with a local partner. There are, for example, a great many automobile supplier joint ventures in the United States originally formed between Japanese and American auto suppliers to supply the Japanese "transplant" automobile manufacturers. For the Americans, such ventures provide a way to learn Japanese manufacturing techniques and to tap into a growing market.

Investing in "Markets of the Future."   Some of the riskiest joint ventures are those established by firms taking an early position in what they see as emerging markets. These areas offer very large untapped markets, as well as a possible source of low-cost raw materials and labor. The major problems faced by Western firms in penetrating such markets are their unfamiliarity with the local culture, establishing Western attitudes toward quality, and, in some areas, repatriating earnings in hard currency. The solution (sometimes imposed by local government) has often been the creation of joint ventures with local partners who "know the ropes" and can deal with the local bureaucracy.

Even a local partner, however, is no guarantee of success, as the rules of the game can change overnight in such regions. This can be due to a new government coming to power, a revision of existing practice in response to a financial crisis, pressure from international funding agencies, and so forth.

Bringing Foreign Products to Local Markets

For every firm that uses an international joint venture to take its product to a foreign market, a local company sees the joint venture as an attractive way to bring a foreign product to its existing market. It is, of course, this complementarity of interest that makes the joint venture possible.

Local partners enter joint ventures to get better utilization of existing plants or distribution channels, to protect themselves against threatening new technology, or simply as an impetus for new growth. Typically, the financial rewards that the local partner receives from a venture are different from those accruing to the foreign partner. For example:

- Many foreign partners make a profit shipping finished products and components to their joint ventures. These profits are particularly attractive because they are in hard currency, which may not be true of the venture's profits, and because the foreign partner captures 100 percent of them, not just a share.
- Many foreign partners receive a technology fee, which is a fixed percentage of the sales volume of the joint venture. The local partner may or may not receive a management fee of like amount.
- Foreign partners typically pay a withholding tax on dividends remitted to them from the venture. Local firms do not.

As a result of these differences, the local partner is often far more concerned with the venture's bottom line earnings and dividend payout than the foreign partner. This means the foreign partner is likely to be happier to keep the venture as simply a marketing or assembly operation, as previously described, than to develop it to the point where it buys less imported material.

Although this logic is understandable, such thinking is shortsighted. The best example of the benefits that can come back to a parent from a powerful joint venture is Fuji Xerox, a venture begun in Japan in the early 1960s between Xerox and Fuji Photo. This is among the most successful American–Japanese joint ventures in Japan.

For the first 10 years of its life, Fuji Xerox was strictly a marketing organization. It did its best to sell Xerox copiers in the Japanese market, even though it was painfully obvious that the U.S. company had done nothing to adapt the machine to the Japanese market. For example, to reach the print button on one model, Japanese secretaries had to stand on a box. After 10 years of operation, Fuji Xerox began to manufacture its own machines, and by 1975 it was redesigning U.S. equipment for the Japanese market. Soon thereafter, with the encouragement of Fuji Photo, and in spite of the resistance of Xerox engineers in the United States, the firm began to design its own copier equipment. Its goal was to design and build a copier in half the time and at half the cost of previous machines. When this was accomplished, the firm set its sights on winning the Deming award, a highly coveted Japanese prize for excellence in total quality control. Fuji Xerox won the award in 1980.

It was also in 1980 that Xerox, reeling under the impact of intense competition from Japanese copier companies, finally began to pay attention to the lessons that it could learn from Fuji Xerox. Adopting the Japanese joint venture's manufacturing techniques and quality programs, the parent company fought its way back to health in the mid-1980s. By 1991, Xerox International Partners was established as a joint venture between Fuji Xerox and Xerox Corporation to sell low-end printers in North America and Europe. In 1998, exports to the United States grew substantially with digital color copiers and OEM printer engines. Both the lessons learned from Fuji Xerox and the contributions they have made to Xerox have inevitably helped Xerox prosper as an independent company.

Using Joint Ventures for Diversification

As the previous examples illustrate, many joint ventures take products that one parent knows well into a market that the other knows well. However, some break new ground and move one or both parents into products and markets that are new to them.

Arrangements to acquire the skills necessary to compete in a new business is a long-term proposition, but one that some firms are willing to undertake. Given the fact that most acquisitions of unrelated businesses do not succeed, and that trying to enter a new business without help is extremely difficult, choosing partners who will help you learn the business may not be a bad strategy if you are already familiar with the partner. However, to enter a new market, with a new product, and a new partner—even when the probability of success for each is 80 percent—leaves one with an overall probability of success of (.8 x .8 x .8) about 50 percent!

In recent years, there has been some discussion about whether joint ventures can be viewed as vehicles for learning. Here the modes of learning go beyond knowledge transfer (i.e., existing know-how) to include transformation and harvesting. In practice, most IJV partners engage in the transfer of existing knowledge, but stop short of knowledge transformation or harvesting. Further, there is little empirical evidence that the learning activities of transfer, transformation, and harvesting relate directly to positive IJV performance.

Requirements for International Joint Venture Success

The checklist in Exhibit 7–3 presents many of the items that a manager should consider when establishing an international joint venture. Each of these is discussed in the following sections.

EXHIBIT 7–3   Joint Venture Checklist

1. Test the strategic logic.
   - Do you really need a partner? For how long? Does your partner?
   - How big is the payoff for both parties? How likely is success?
   - Is a joint venture the best option?
   - Do congruent performance measures exist?

2. Partnership and fit.
   - Does the partner share your objectives for the venture?
   - Does the partner have the necessary skills and resources? Will you get access to them?
   - Will you be compatible?
   - Can you arrange an "engagement period"?
   - Is there a comfort versus competence trade-off?

3. Shape and design.
   - Define the venture's scope of activity and its strategic freedom vis-à-vis its parents.
   - Lay out each parent's duties and payoffs to create a win-win situation. Ensure that there are comparable contributions over time.
   - Establish the managerial role of each partner.

4. Doing the deal.
   - How much paperwork is enough? Trust versus legal considerations?
   - Agree on an endgame.

5. Making the venture work.
   - Give the venture continuing top management attention.
   - Manage cultural differences.
   - Watch out for inequities.
   - Be flexible.

Testing the Strategic Logic

The decision to enter a joint venture should not be taken lightly. As mentioned earlier, joint ventures require a great deal of management attention, and, in spite of the care and attention they receive, many prove unsatisfactory to their parents.

Firms considering entering a joint venture should satisfy themselves that there is not a simpler way, such as a nonequity alliance of the type referred to in Chapter 1, to get what they need. They should also carefully consider the time period for which they are likely to need help. Joint ventures have been labeled "permanent solutions to temporary problems" by firms that entered a venture to get help on some aspect of their business; then, when they no longer needed the help, they were still stuck with the joint venture.

The same tough questions a firm may ask itself before forming a joint venture need to be asked of its partner. How long will the partner need it? Is the added potential payoff high enough to both partners to compensate for the increased coordination/communications costs which go with the formation of a joint venture?

A major issue in the discussion of strategic logic is to determine whether congruent measures of performance exist. As Exhibit 7–4 suggests, in many joint ventures, incongruity exists. In this example the foreign partner was looking for a joint venture that would generate 20

EXHIBIT 7–4   Measuring JV Performance: The Search for Congruity

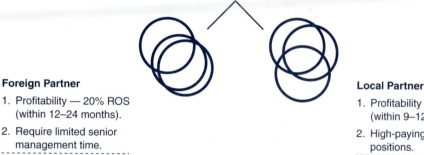

Foreign Partner

1. Profitability — 20% ROS
   (within 12–24 months).

2. Require limited senior
   management time.

3. Maximize local sales.

4. Exploit peripheral or
   mature technology.

Local Partner

1. Profitability
   (within 9–12 months).

2. High-paying salaried
   positions.

3. Opportunity to export.

4. Obtain newest
   technology.

---

percent return on sales in a 1–2 year period and require a limited amount of senior management time. The local partner in turn was seeking a JV that would be quickly profitable and be able to justify some high-paying salaried positions (for the local partner and several family members/friends). While each partner's performance objectives seem defensible, this venture would need to resolve several major problem areas in order to succeed. First, each partner did not make explicit all their primary performance objectives. Implicit measures (those below the dotted line in Exhibit 7–4), are a source of latent disagreement/misunderstanding. Second, the explicit versus implicit measures of each partner were internally inconsistent. The foreign partner wanted high profitability while using little senior management time and old technology. The local partner wanted quick profits but high-paying local salaries.

Partnership and Fit

Joint ventures are sometimes formed to satisfy complementary needs. But when one partner acquires (learns) another's capabilities, the joint venture becomes unstable. The acquisition of a partner's capabilities means that the partner is no longer needed. If capabilities are only accessed, the joint venture is more stable. It is not easy, before a venture begins, to determine many of the things a manager would most like to know about a potential partner, like the true extent of its capabilities, what its objectives are in forming the venture, and whether it will be easy to work with. A hasty answer to such questions may lead a firm into a bad relationship or cause it to pass up a good opportunity.

For these reasons, it is often best if companies begin a relationship in a small way, with a simple agreement that is important but not a matter of life and death to either parent. As confidence between the firms grows, the scope of the business activities can broaden.

A good example is provided by Corning Glass, which in 1970 made a major breakthrough in the development of optical fibers that could be used for telecommunication applications, replacing traditional copper wire or coaxial cable. The most likely customers of this fiber outside the United States were the European national telecoms, which were well known to be very nationalistic purchasers. To gain access to these customers, Corning set up development agreements in 1973 and 1974 with companies in England, France, Germany, and Italy that were already suppliers to the telecoms. These agreements called for the European firms to develop the technology necessary to combine the fibers into cables, while Corning itself continued to develop the optical fibers. Soon the partners began to import fiber from Corning and cable it locally. Then, when the partners were comfortable with each other and each market was ready, Corning and the partners set up joint ventures to produce optical fiber locally. These ventures have worked extremely well, and their continuing success became particularly important in the late 1980s, as growth in the U.S. market leveled off. Corning is widely acknowledged as one of the world's most successful users of joint ventures.

When assessing issues around partnership and fit, it is useful to consider whether the partner not only shares the same objectives for the venture but also has a similar appetite for risk. In practice this often results in joint ventures having parents of roughly comparable size. It is difficult for parent firms of very different size to establish sustainable joint ventures because of varying resource sets, payback period requirements, and corporate cultures.

Corporate culture similarity—or compatibility—can be a make-or-break issue in many joint ventures. It is not enough to find a partner with the necessary skills, you need to be able to get access to them and to be compatible. Managers are constantly told that they should choose a joint venture partner they trust. As these examples suggest, however, trust between partners is something that can only be developed over time as a result of shared experiences. You can't start with trust.

Shape and Design

In the excitement of setting up a new operation in a foreign country, or getting access to technology provided by an overseas partner, it is important not to lose sight of the basic strategic requirements that must be met if a joint venture is to be successful. The questions that must be addressed are the same when any new business is proposed: Is the market attractive? How strong is the competition? How will the new company compete? Will it have the required resources? And so on.

In addition to these concerns, three others are particularly relevant to joint venture design. One is the question of strategic freedom, which has to do with the relationship between the venture and its parents. How much freedom will the venture be given to do as it wishes with respect to choosing suppliers, a product line, and customers? In the Dow Chemical venture referred to earlier, the dispute between the partners centered on the requirement that the venture buy materials, at what the Koreans believed to be an inflated price, from Dow's new wholly owned Korean plant. Clearly the American and Korean vision of the amount of strategic freedom open to the venture was rather different.

The second issue of importance is that the joint venture be a win-win situation. This means that the payoff to each parent if the venture is successful should be a big one, because this will keep both parents working for the success of the venture when times are tough. If the strategic analysis suggests that the return to either parent over time will be marginal, the venture should be restructured or abandoned.

Finally, it is critical to decide on the management roles that each parent company will play. The venture will be easier to manage if one parent plays a dominant role and has a lot of influence over both the strategic and the day-to-day operations of the venture, or if one parent plays a lead role in the day-to-day operation of the joint venture. More difficult to manage are shared management ventures, in which both parents have a significant input into both strategic decisions and the everyday operations of the venture. A middle ground is split management decisions, where one partner has primary influence over certain functional areas, and the other partner over different functional areas. This is the most common form.

In some ventures, the partners place too much emphasis on competing with each other about which one will have management control. They lose sight of the fact that the intent of the joint venture is to capture benefits from two partners that will allow the venture (not one of the partners) to compete in the market better than would have been possible by going it alone.

The objective of most joint ventures is superior performance. Thus the fact that dominant-parent ventures are easier to manage than shared-management ventures does not mean they are the appropriate type of venture to establish. Dominant parent ventures are most likely to be effective when one partner has the knowledge and skill to make the venture a success and the other party is contributing simply money, a trademark, or perhaps a one-time transfer of technology. Such a venture, however, begs the question "What are the unique continuing contributions of the partner?" Shared-management ventures are necessary when the venture needs active consultation between members of each parent company, as when deciding how to modify a product supplied by one parent for the local market that is well known by the other, or to modify a production process designed by one parent to be suitable for a workforce and working conditions well known by the other.

A joint venture is headed for trouble when a parent tries to take a larger role in its management than makes sense. An American company with a joint venture in Japan, for instance, insisted that one of its people be the executive vice president of the venture. This was not reasonable, because the man had nothing to bring to the management of the venture. He simply served as a constant reminder to the Japanese that the American partner did not trust them. The Americans were pushing for a shared-management venture when it was more logical to allow the Japanese, who certainly had all the necessary skills, to be the dominant or at least the leading firm. The major American contribution to the venture was to allow it to use its world-famous trademarks and brand names.

A second example, also in Japan, involves the French firm referred to at the start of this chapter. This company was bringing complex technology to the venture that needed to be modified for the Japanese market. It was clear that the French firm required a significant say in the management of the venture. On the other hand, the French had no knowledge of the Japanese market and, thus, the Japanese also needed a significant role in the venture. The logical solution would have been a shared-management venture and equal influence in decisions made at the board level. Unfortunately, both companies wanted to play a dominant role, and the venture collapsed in a decision-making stalemate.

Doing the Deal

Experienced managers argue that it is the relationship between the partners that is of key importance in a joint venture, not the legal agreement that binds them together. Nevertheless, most are careful to ensure that they have a good agreement in place—one that they understand and are comfortable with.

The principal elements of a joint venture agreement are listed in Exhibit 7–5. Most of these are straightforward and relate to topics discussed in this chapter. One item on the list that has not been discussed is the termination of the venture.

Although some managers balk at discussing divorce during the prenuptial period, it is important to work out a method of terminating the venture in the event of a serious disagreement, and to do this at a time when heads are cool and goodwill abounds. The usual technique is to use a shotgun clause, which allows either party to name a price at which it will buy the other's shares in the venture. However, once this provision is activated and the first company has named a price, the second firm has the option of selling at this price or buying the first company's shares at the same price. This ensures that only fair offers are made, at least as long as both parents are large enough to be capable of buying each other out.

Making the Venture Work

Joint ventures need close and continuing attention, particularly in their early months. In addition to establishing a healthy working relationship between the parents and the venture general manager, managers should be on the lookout for the impact that cultural differences may be having on the venture and for the emergence of unforeseen inequities.

International joint ventures, like any type of international activity, require that managers of different national cultures work together. This requires the selection of capable people in key roles. Unless managers have been sensitized to the characteristics of the culture that they are dealing with, this can lead to misunderstandings and serious problems. Many Western managers, for instance, are frustrated by the slow, consensus-oriented decision-making style of the Japanese. Equally, the Japanese find American individualistic decision making to be surprising, as the decisions are made so quickly, but the implementation is often so slow. Firms that are sophisticated in the use of international joint ventures are well

---

EXHIBIT 7–5   Principal Elements of a Joint Venture Agreement

- Definitions
- Scope of operations
- Management:
    1. Shareholders and supervisory roles regarding board
    2. Executive board
    3. Arrangements in the event of deadlock
    4. Operating management
- Arbitration
- Representations and warranties of each partner
- Organization and capitalization
- Financial arrangements
- Contractual links with parents
- Rights and obligations and intellectual property
- Termination agreements
- Force majeure
- Covenants

Source: "Teaming Up for the Nineties—Can You Survive without a Partner?" Deloitte, Haskins & Sells International, undated.

aware of such problems and have taken action to minimize them. Ford, for example, has put more than 1,500 managers through courses to improve their ability to work with Japanese and Korean managers.

It is important to remember that cultural differences do not just arise from differences in nationality. For example:

- Small firms working with large partners are often surprised and dismayed by the fact that it can take months, rather than days, to get approval of a new project. In some cases the cultural differences appear to be greater between small and large firms of the same nationality than, say, between multinationals of different nationality, particularly if the multinationals are in the same industry.

- Firms working with two partners from the same country have been surprised to find how different the companies are in cultural habits. A Japanese automobile firm headquartered in rural Japan is a very different company from one run from Tokyo.

- Cultural differences between managers working in different functional areas may be greater than those between managers in the same function in different firms. European engineers, for example, discovered when discussing a potential joint venture with an American partner that they had more in common with the American engineers than with the marketing people in their own company.

A very common joint venture problem is that the objectives of the parents, which coincided when the venture was formed, diverge over time. Such divergences can be brought on by changes in the fortunes of the partners. This was the case in the breakup of the General Motors–Daewoo joint venture in Korea. Relations between the partners were already strained due to GM's unwillingness to put further equity into the venture, in spite of a debt to equity ratio of more than 8 to 1, when, faced with rapidly declining market share, the Korean parent decided that the venture should go for growth and maximize market share, whereas General Motors, itself in a poor financial position, insisted that the emphasis be on current profitability. When Daewoo, without telling General Motors, introduced a concessionary financing program for the joint venture's customers, the relationship was damaged, never to recover.

A final note concerns the unintended inequities that may arise during the life of a venture. Due to an unforeseen circumstance, one parent may be winning from the venture while the other is losing. A venture established in the late 1990s between Indonesian and American parents, for instance, was buying components from the American parent at prices based in dollars. As the rupiah declined in value, the Indonesian partner could afford fewer components in each shipment. The advice of many experienced venture managers is that, in such a situation, a change in the original agreement should be made, so the hardship is shared between the parents. That was done in this case, and the venture is surviving, although it is not as profitable as originally anticipated.

In reviewing any checklist of the things to be considered when forming a joint venture, it is important to recognize that such a list will vary somewhat depending on where the international joint venture is established. Exhibit 7–6 summarizes 12 characteristics of joint ventures according to whether they are established in developed versus developing countries.

EXHIBIT 7–6   Summary of Differences of Joint-Venture Characteristics

Characteristics	Developed Country	Developing Country	
	Market Economy	*Market Economy*	*Planned Economy (China)*
Major reason for creating venture	Skill required	Government pressure	Government pressure
Frequency of association with government partners	Low	Moderate	Very High
Overall use of JVs versus other modes of foreign involvement	Significant (20-40%)	High (but contingent on country, industry, and technology level)	Very high (regardless of country, industry, or technology level) but declining
Usual origin of foreign partner	Other developed countries	Developed countries	Ethnic Related Locales (i.e., Hong Kong, Taiwan)
Proportion of intended JVs actually implemented	High	Relatively high	Low (under 50%)
Use of JVs with a predetermined duration	Low (except in certain industries)	Low	Previously high, but declining
Most common level of ownership for foreign MNE	Equal	Minority	Minority
Number of autonomously managed ventures	Small	Negligible	Negligible
Ownership-control relationship*	Direct (dominant control with majority ownership; shared control with equal ownership)	Difficult to discern because most MNEs have a minority ownership position	Indirect
Control-performance relationship in successful JVs	Inconclusive	Shared or split	Split control
Instability rate	30%	45%	Low
MNE managerial assessment of dissatisfaction with performance	37%	61%	High

Sources: Paul W. Beamish, "The Characteristics of Joint Ventures in Developed and Developing Countries," *Columbia Journal of World Business,* Fall 1985, pp. 12-19; and Paul W. Beamish "The Characteristics of Joint Ventures in The People's Republic of China," *Journal of International Marketing,* Vol. 1 No. 2, pp. 29-48.

Most of the descriptions of the characteristics considered are self-explanatory. Yet, more fine-grained analyses are always possible. For example, the discussion in this chapter has generally assumed a traditional equity joint venture, one focused between two firms from two different countries. Yet other types of equity joint ventures exist (see Exhibit 7–7), including those between firms from two different countries that set up in a third country (i.e., trinational), those formed between subsidiaries of the same MNE (i.e., intrafirm) and those formed with companies of the same nationality but located in a different country (i.e., cross-national domestic joint ventures). Further, many joint ventures have more than two

EXHIBIT 7–7   Japanese JV Ownership Structure, Performance, and Termination Rate

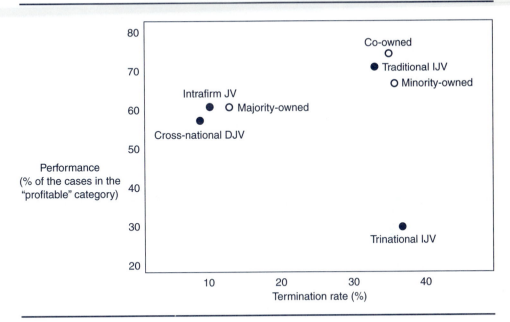

Source: Shige Makino and Paul W. Beamish, "Performance and Survival of Joint Ventures with Non-Conventional Ownerhsip Structures," *Journal of International Business Studies,* Vol. 29 (4), 1998, p. 811.

partners. Interestingly, the traditional JVs (formed by Japanese MNEs) tend to simultaneously be more profitable and to have a higher termination rate than the alternative structures available.

Summary

For the reasons outlined in this chapter, international joint ventures are an increasingly important part of the strategy of many firms. They are, however, sometime difficult to design and manage well, in part because some organizations do not treat them as "true" alliances (see Exhibit 7–8). The fact that some ventures are performing below their management's expectations should not be an excuse for firms to avoid such ventures. In many industries, the winners are going to be the companies that most quickly learn to manage international ventures effectively. The losers will be the managers who throw up their hands and say that joint ventures are too difficult, so we had better go it alone.

In the future, will we see more or fewer international joint ventures? Certainly the reduction in investment regulations in many countries, coupled with increased international

EXHIBIT 7–8   The True Alliance versus the Pseudo Alliance

	The True Alliance	The Pseudo Alliance
Planned level of parent input and involvement	Continuing	One-time
Distribution of risks/rewards	Roughly even	Uneven
Parent attitude toward the JV	A unique organization with unique needs	One more subsidiary
The formal JV agreement	Flexible guideline	Frequently referenced rulebook
Performance objectives	Clearly specified and congruent	Partially overlapping/ ambiguous

experience by many firms, suggests there may be fewer joint ventures. Yet other countervailing pressures exist. With shortening product life cycles, it is increasingly difficult to go it alone. And with the increase in the number of MNEs from emerging markets, both the supply and demand of potential partners will likely escalate.

Supplementary Reading

Beamish, Paul W., and J. Peter Killing, eds. *Cooperative Strategies: European Perspectives, Cooperative Strategies: North American Perspectives,* and *Cooperative Strategies: Asian Perspectives.* San Francisco: The New Lexington Press, 1997. (Three volumes.)

———. Special Issue on Cooperative Strategies, *Journal of International Business Studies,* Vol. 27, No.5, 1996.

Berdrow, Iris, and P. W. Beamish. "Unfolding the Myth of IJV Learning." Ivey Working Paper Series, 1999.

Datta, Deepak K. "International Joint Ventures: A Framework for Analysis." *Journal of General Management,* Vol. 14, No. 2, Winter 1988.

Doz, Yves L., and Gary Hamel. *Alliance Advantage.* Cambridge, MA: Harvard Business School Press, 1999.

Fey, Carl F. "Important Design Characteristics for Russian–Foreign Joint Ventures." *European Management Journal,* Vol. 13, 1995, pp. 405–15.

Hamel, Gary, Yves Doz, and C. K. Prahalad. "Collaborate with Your Competitors—and Win." *Harvard Business Review,* January-February 1989.

Inkpen, Andrew C., and Paul W. Beamish. "Knowledge, Bargaining Power and International Joint Venture Stability." *Academy of Management Review,* Vol. 22, No. 1, 1997.

Killing, Peter. "How to Make a Global Joint Venture Work." *Harvard Business Review,* May-June 1982, pp. 120–27.

Lane, Henry W., and Paul W. Beamish. "Cross-Cultural Cooperative Behavior in Joint Ventures in LDCs." *Management International Review,* Special Issue 1990, pp. 87–102.

Schaan, Jean-Louis. "How to Control a Joint Venture Even as a Minority Partner." *Journal of General Management* Vol. 14, No. 1, Autumn 1988.

Schaan, Jean-Louis, and Paul W. Beamish. "Joint Venture General Managers in Developing Countries." In *Cooperative Strategies in International Business.* Ed. F. Contractor and P. Lorange. Lexington, MA: Lexington Books, 1988, pp. 279–99.

8 INTERNATIONAL STRATEGY FORMULATION

This chapter focuses on the formulation of strategies to maximize the international competitiveness of the firm. Implicit in the discussion is the notion that international strategy evolves with changes in the competitive environment. As barriers to market penetration have been dismantled and as technologies have emerged that facilitate international organizational control, businesses have worked hard to expand their scope to include new international markets. Globalization, a term used somewhat loosely to describe an interdependent, borderless world, has now become a common objective for many businesses. As a result of a broad movement toward more global competition, businesses have increasingly abandoned traditional approaches to international competition in favor of new, more innovative strategies. More recently, the economic troubles of many developing countries have begun to raise questions about the merits of pursuing global strategies. Increasingly, companies are turning to ever more complex patterns of competition.

Changes in the Global Competitive Environment

During the late 1980s and early 1990s a series of dramatic events transformed the business environment. The Soviet Union, burdened by inefficient industries at home and witnessing rapid expansion of Pacific Rim economies, embraced perestroika and later, as a splintered association of quasi-independent republics, free market reform. In Moscow alone, an estimated 80,000 foreigners had set up residence by 1994. In China, market reforms unleashed by Deng Xiaoping continued to gather steam. Annual GNP growth rates hovered around 10 percent for China throughout the first half of the 1990s. In India, reforms begun in 1991 by Prime Minister P.V. Narasimha Rao pushed economic growth from only 0.6 percent in the early 1990s to an estimated 6 percent in 1995. In Europe, the move toward greater economic

This chapter was prepared by Allen J. Morrison.

integration continued despite lingering concerns over the desirability of monetary union. Eastern European countries including Poland, Hungary, and the Czech Republic have pushed for full membership in the European Union. During the early 1990s, the Canada–U.S. Free Trade Agreement was expanded to include Mexico. Although Chile was lobbying hard to be included in an expanded North American Free Trade area, resistance from the United States pushed Chile in 1995 to pursue a bilateral free trade agreement with Canada. Throughout Latin America, the replacement of military-led governments with populist regimes has led to reduced inflation, greater economic openness, reduced nationalist tendencies, and rapid economic growth. In Brazil, annual GNP growth averaged 8 percent throughout the first half of the 1990s; it was expected to stay at this level through the turn of the century.

Many of the promises of the early 1990s seemed to have slipped away by the end of the decade. By 1999, many emerging market economies were in a state of crisis. After years of poor banking sector supervision, imprudent borrowing, corruption, and speculative over-building, a wave of despair hit much of the developing world beginning in 1997. One triggering event was the floating of the Thai baht in July 1997. Almost overnight, the baht plunged 50 percent, leading to the collapse of 56 of the Thailand's 58 financial institutions in the summer of 1997. The crisis quickly spread to South Korea, Indonesia, Malaysia, and the Philippines, and then to Brazil and Russia.

Every country seemed to have a different nightmare story to tell. Rioting and political unrest exacerbated the situation in Indonesia where the GNP fell by an estimated 15 percent in 1998. In Russia, in August 1998, the government defaulted on $40 billion of ruble-denominated bonds and then allowed the ruble to float. The resulting massive capital flight, combined with corruption and inefficient distribution channels, led to reports of starvation and untold hardships for many Russians. In Brazil, the government gave up trying to defend the real in January 1999. Almost overnight, the Brazilian currency plummeted in value leading to analysts' expectations that the economy would shrink by a full 3 percent in 1999. While faring somewhat better than other countries, Japan, Hong Kong, China, and Singapore were also badly hurt. One study by the Japan Real Estate Board showed that commercial property values in six Japanese cities fell by nearly 75 percent between 1990 to 1998.[1] In Hong Kong, real estate prices fell 50 percent between mid-1997 and year-end 1998, and in 1998 the economy contracted by over 5 percent. In Hong Kong in August 1998, the government spent $15 billion buying Hong Kong stocks in an attempt to prop up shaky markets.

Faced with turmoil in many emerging markets, multinational companies are starting to re-examine their approach to international markets. Although they understand the importance of being internationally competitive, a growing number of companies were badly burned by ill-conceived globalization strategies. Not surprisingly, MNCs are now paying much closer attention to country and market analyses in formulating international strategies. The days of follow-the-leader internationalization strategies seem to be over.

Not surprisingly, it is in determining how and where to compete that most MNCs run into problems. MNCs in the late 1990s are confronted with a bewildering array of strategy options. Most MNCs conceptualize strategy as a hierarchy that includes corporate-level

---

[1]"Japan Ponders Merits of Soft, Hard Landings," *Asian Wall Street Journal,* August 21–22, 1998, p. 1.

strategies and business-unit–level initiatives. Corporate strategies typically focus on two things: (1) determining the industries in which the MNC will compete, and (2) determining how the various businesses within the MNC will coordinate activities. Business-unit strategies focus on market share battles through competitive and international positioning. Business-unit managers rather than corporate executives have become the primary drivers of international strategy.

Most MNCs have multiple international strategies. Each strategy is driven by business units striving to match their unique skills with market opportunities. For example, IBM designs and manufactures microprocessors, a globally demanded product. Competing in this industry requires IBM to construct world-scale fabrication facilities that produce globally standardized semiconductor products. IBM also competes in service industries where customers require enormous care and localized attention. A strategy based on maximizing local responsiveness seems most appropriate for much of IBM's service activities. To maximize its overall competitiveness, IBM encourages each business to approach international markets in ways that are most consistent with industry pressures. As a result, understanding MNC strategy means focusing on businesses and the industry pressures they confront.

Understanding Industry Pressures

An appropriate starting point for understanding international strategy is analyzing the industry forces confronting each business within the MNC. These forces impact every industry—whether high-tech or low-tech, service or manufacturing—and include two sets of pressures: pressures to be globally integrated, and pressures to be locally responsive. These pressures drive business strategy and cannot be overlooked in formulating an appropriate international strategy.

Pressures toward Globalization

Pressures that encourage businesses to adopt global integration strategies include both broad facilitating factors and industry-specific imperatives. Broad facilitating factors include three developments:

- Freer trade.
- Global financial services and capital markets.
- Advances in communications technology.

Together, these facilitating factors have made global competition possible but not necessarily desirable for all businesses. To determine whether global integration is advisable, businesses are encouraged to examine pressures that are specific to their particular industry. These industry-specific imperatives include:

- Universal customer needs.
- Global customers.
- Global competitors.

- High investment intensity.
- Pressures for cost reduction.

Broad Facilitating Factors

Freer Trade. For the past 50 years, declining tariffs and the emergence of regional trading blocs have had an enormous impact on world trade and investment. Successive rounds of General Agreement on Tariffs and Trade (GATT) agreements, plus multilateral cooperation under the World Trade Organization, have resulted in the adoption of new commercial liberalization policies by numerous governments. In 1996, the value of world merchandise exports topped $5.1 trillion; service exports reached $1.2 trillion in value. In 1998, U.S. exports of goods and serves reached $931 billion; imports of goods and services in 1998 were $1.1 trillion.

Regional trading blocs have strengthened business ties in North America, Europe, Southeast Asia, Africa, and Latin America. The removal of tariffs and nontariff barriers signals a weakening of the economic role of nation-states and an invitation to companies to "think globally." In Europe, 11 European Union countries agreed to adopt the euro currency unit as the basis of trade and commerce. Listed in order of their capital contributions, these countries include: Germany, France, Italy, Spain, Netherlands, Belgium, Austria, Portugal, Finland, Ireland, and Luxembourg. Companies in these countries will find it much easier to carry out business across a broad geographic base.

It should be pointed out that the objectives of the European Union and those of the free trade agreements established by ASEAN countries, as well as Canada, the United States, and Mexico, are quite different. The European Union is designed to limit national sovereignty by creating supranational political and administrative bodies. In contrast, free trade agreements attempt to achieve the economic benefits of tariff removal without so much loss of national sovereignty. While Europe is harmonizing its regulatory affairs, most of the rest of the world is not.

Global Financial Services and Capital Markets.   The globalization of financial services and capital markets has facilitated the efforts of many businesses to globally integrate their activities. Capital can now be sourced through transnational banks (for example, Citibank), overseas venture capitalists (for example, Investcorp, a Saudi-owned firm), and other sources via the Internet. Recent trends in financial technology allow the trading of financial instruments 24 hours per day, 365 days per year, irrespective of national location. In addition, the ability of MNCs to manage interest rate risk and currency exchange rates through hedging and computerized market trading have reduced the importance of placing investment capital under one national umbrella.

Advances in Communications Technology.   Managing a far-flung international business requires extensive communication in order to maintain organizational control. Advances in computer and fax technology have made such communication easier and less costly. The availability of huge, on-line data bases, in-house e-mail systems, and the Internet have greatly increased the ability of companies to manage international operations. Direct electronic links, for example, have enabled Boeing and a consortium of Japanese partners to design aircraft together. Advances in information technology have also made it possible for the financial services industry in New York to export thousands of back-room data processing jobs to lower-cost Ireland. They have also allowed Singapore Airlines to perform essentially all of its software development work in Madras, India.

Industry-Specific Pressures

Universal Customer Needs.   While advances in telecommunications have enabled companies to better control global activities, television, movies, radio, the print media, and telephones have dramatically increased the information available to consumers around the world. By seeing what other people have or enjoy doing, consumers put enormous pressure on businesses to globalize. Successful world products like watches, cameras, fast food, blue jeans, luxury writing instruments, personal computers, and cellular telephones are welcomed in more and more national markets. Many sports have also become globalized. The popularity of U.S. sports has led to sell-out crowds for American football and basketball games in Europe and Japan and a surging public interest in sports celebrities whose names are used to sell everything from perfume to pizza. Depending on the industry, people increasingly want the same products and services irrespective of home country.

Global Customers.   Many MNCs do not sell directly to consumers but focus instead on other MNCs as customers. When customers are global, they demand standardized inputs around the world. General Motors, for example, has made major progress in globalizing its purchasing activities. To GM this means that it searches the world for the best products at the lowest prices. An automotive components company must be able to meet GM's global standards for quality, features, and pricing. As GM moves into new markets, these suppliers are expected to respond. Take Prince Corp., for example. Prince is a Holland, Michigan–based manufacturer of dashboard components and interior paneling for the automotive industry. One of Prince's biggest customers is GM. In order to streamline design, keep costs low, and maximize production efficiencies, Prince and GM have developed a very close working relationship. As GM expands its presence in Latin America, it has encouraged Prince to establish a major production facility near its manufacturing complex in Brazil. Prince must respond in a positive way or risk jeopardizing its core North American partnership with GM.

Global Competitors.   No pressure is quite so strong as an international competitor taking your market share. Some industries are dominated by global businesses that establish competitive norms. Once competitive norms have been set in an industry, businesses can chose either to follow the pack and adhere to the norms or pursue much narrower niche strategies.

High Investment Intensity.   Investment intensity includes costs for developing products and gearing up for production. In general, the higher the investment intensity the greater the pressure on businesses to globally standardize output. Boeing, for example, spent just under $6 billion bringing the B-777 aircraft to market. The key for Boeing will be to maximize the number of planes sold and thereby reduce the per-unit development costs. In another example, Gillette launched its new MACH3 razor on April 14, 1998. The company spent six years and $750 million to bring the three-bladed razor to market versus only $200 million launching the simpler Sensor brand razor in 1989. In order to recoup the enormous investment costs, Gillette spent an estimated $300 million marketing the razor; of this amount, $100 million was directed at U.S. sales and $200 million was budged for international sales. Gillette estimated that by the end of 1999, the MACH3 would be sold in 100 countries, a feat that took Sensor five years to achieve. Other industries, including computer software, telecommunications equipment, and automobiles, face similar pressures to amortize often substantial development costs through rapid globalization.

Pressures for Cost Reduction.   In industries where price is the key purchase criterion, producers have a great incentive to find new ways to lower costs to maintain profits. Economies of scale and learning both have enormous impacts on operational efficiency. The greater the impact of learning and volume, the greater the incentive to maximize output. The issue in terms of globalization is a determination of the volume where minimum per unit costs can be achieved. If minimum per-unit costs can be achieved at an output of 200,000 units per year and if domestic demand is only 50,000 units per year, businesses have an incentive to standardize output and get into the export business for the remaining 75 percent of output. Whether the business actually exports or not will depend in part on the importance the customer places on price. In the petroleum industry price is critical and so producers push production volumes out as far as possible. In the newspaper industry, local content and responsiveness are far more important than production efficiencies.

Pressures toward Localization

Although during the 1990s the pendulum swung decisively in the direction of globalization, industries have been affected in different ways. The transition to globalization is not complete and may well pass some industries by. Localization pressures include both country-specific factors and MNC-specific factors. Country-specific factors include three primary pressures:

- Trade barriers.
- Cultural differences.
- Nationalism.

MNC-specific factors include four principal pressures that either limit an MNC's ability to respond to globalization pressures or facilitate its ability to be locally responsive:

- Organizational resistance to change.
- Transportation limitations.
- New production technologies.
- Just-in-time manufacturing.

Country-Specific Pressures

Trade Barriers.   Tariff barriers encourage businesses to compete internationally through foreign direct investment rather than trade. Servicing a local market through a dedicated manufacturing facility enables businesses to maximize local responsiveness, which is typically an objective of government-imposed barriers. With tariffs in place, competitors are encouraged to establish autonomous operations in a host country, thereby preserving national culture and sovereignty. When tariffs decline, the international competitiveness of a country's industries becomes more vital. Serious loss of market share to imports often triggers nontariff barriers in nations concerned over the short-term loss of jobs. Subsidies directed at domestic producers represent a common nontariff barrier.

Every country is guilty of subsidizing domestic production. One of the better-known examples of government subsidies is Sematech, a U.S.-based consortium of 14 electronics companies set up in the mid-1980s. Over a period of eight years, the U.S. government gave $800 million to these companies to offset what was at the time perceived to be an unfair advantage by Japanese semiconductor manufacturers. In response, the European Union put a 14 percent tariff on imported semiconductor chips from the United States and Japan. In addition to protecting high-tech industries, virtually every country in the world maintains some form of agricultural subsidies, including supply management schemes, import restrictions, and direct financial support to farmers. In 1998, Canadian tariffs on butter were 300 percent, Japanese tariffs on rice were 550 percent, and U.S. tariffs on sweet powdered milk were 179 percent. Other industries commonly protected include transportation, communications, steel, and entertainment. For example, in 1998 Indonesia imposed tariffs on cars of 200 percent, while Thailand's rate on cars averaged 75 percent.

Voluntary export restrictions represent another common nontariff barrier to trade. In the early 1980s, Japanese automobile manufacturers agreed to limit exports of automobiles to the United States. One study found that as a result of the export restrictions, Japanese automobile manufacturers began shifting production to the United States , creating an estimated 55,000 jobs by the middle of the decade. [2] However, the study also found that both U.S. and Japanese automobile manufacturers raised prices substantially as a result of the export restrictions. It was estimated that Japanese manufacturers captured an additional $2.2 billion in cash flow by using increases in prices to limit volume; U.S. producers captured an additional $2.6 billion by matching Japanese price increases. In all, the study estimated that the same reduction in Japanese automobile exports could have been achieved with an imposition of an 11 percent tariff. In the final analysis, export restrictions may have helped Japanese manufacturers more than they hurt.

Government regulations are a third important means of restricting trade. A clear example of the limits of globalization is the international television industry. The international television industry remains dominated by three global broadcast standards: one for North America, one for Europe, and one for Japan/Asia Pacific. While the emergence of high definition TV has promoted a convergence in broadcast standards, political pressures have put these efforts on hold. Imbedded in each of the broad regional standards are intraregional standards. In Europe, for example, technical standards for television differ across countries in seven different areas of technical design. European integration has had only a modest impact on these standards.

---

[2] See G. Hufbauer, D. Berliner, and K. Elliot. *Trade Protection in the United States: 31 Case Studies* (Washington, DC: Institute for International Economics, 1986).

Cultural Differences. While satellite television and the international media are shrinking the world and homogenizing consumer tastes, national culture continues to pull in the opposite direction. Traditions and religious beliefs run deep and often conflict with international media messages. Although individuals may display an initial interest in a product because it is "foreign," they may also shun the same product over time because of the changes in lifestyles it promotes. For example, McDonald's opened its first store in India in late October 1996 in the city of Delhi. In a country that venerates the cow, McDonald's substituted the Big Mac with the Maharaja Mac made with mutton, and offered vegetarian rice-patties flavored with vegetables and spice. Despite these moves, McDonald's was facing a nationwide protest against a multinational that was responsible for the death of perhaps millions of cows each year. To the extent different cultures lead to divergent consumer preferences, global product strategies can miss the mark, or can require major adaptation from market to market.

Nationalism. From the republics of former Yugoslavia, to the Basque region of Spain, to the Canadian province of Quebec, to the U.S. state of Hawaii, nationalism enjoyed a significant resurgence in the mid-to-late 1990s. New political freedoms and the backlash against the forces of globalization have merged to create soaring aspirations for national autonomy around the world. Nationalism is often symbolic and almost always powerfully emotional. By representing common values and attitudes, nationalism provides the basis for social cohesion and is often used to justify obstructions in the international movement of goods and services. In countries where national institutions and power systems have been fractured, tribalism has seen a renaissance. Tribal loyalties, often born of common language and history, are fast replacing national allegiances in countries torn by civil war or economic strife. By focusing attention inward, both nationalism and tribalism foster values that deter globalization.

MNC-Specific Pressures

Organizational Resistance to Change. Globalization for MNCs means imposing central control on country managers who in many cases have been functioning with substantial autonomy. This imposition of corporate control often means the redesign of an affiliate's product to meet global specifications or the rationalization of operations for the good of the overall corporation. In either case, the "not invented here" syndrome may intervene. For MNCs with histories of autonomous affiliates—companies like General Motors, Ford, IBM, Philips, and Nestlé—organizational resistance to global integration has become a major obstacle. A case in point is Warner Lambert's pharmaceutical operations in Europe. In 1970 Warner Lambert acquired Parke-Davis in an effort to expand its international position in pharmaceuticals. With decades of experience in Europe, Parke-Davis had established manufacturing operations France, the U.K., Italy, Spain, Germany, Belgium, and Ireland. Affiliates in these countries were given considerable autonomy and developed substantial competencies. Beginning in the mid-1980s, Warner Lambert began a major initiative to reduce the number of pharmaceutical manufacturing units in Europe while concurrently specializing production in the units that remained. Fearful of losing power and convinced that the parent was overestimating the impact of globalization, affiliate managers fought back. Working together, the major affiliates were able to convince the parent to proceed much more cautiously than planned. Decisions that were expected to have been made in weeks or a few months ended up being moved to committees that took over three years to process. While the parent has now made a number of rationalization decisions, the major European affiliates have been successful in retaining much of their original powers.

Other companies have experienced similar resistance to change. In Europe, powerful unions have opposed Europeanwide re-engineering. At IBM, for example, French unions filed suit in 1994 to stop the company from cutting 1,300 jobs. In September 1994, IBM Europe's chairman, Hans-Olaf Henkel, resigned after IBM Chairman Lou Gerstner forced a reorganization of the European sales force that augmented the role of corporate head office decision makers over regional chiefs.[3]

Management Shortcomings.   Despite interests in expanding overseas, companies continue to report a shortage of global leaders. Quality leaders who can manage cross-culturally are in short supply in many companies. Furthermore, managers with the requisite skills risk burnout in careers that for many involve nonstop travel and months away from home. Travelling hundreds of thousands of kilometers (or miles) per year, spending 200-plus days a year on the road, and suffering incessant jet lag are some of the prices of running far-flung operations. Some managers are increasingly saying no to globalization: not for business reasons, but for reasons of personal or family preferences.

Transportation Difficulties.   Businesses with products that are highly susceptible to spoilage or which have a high weight-to-value ratios are not typically good candidates for globalization. The dairy and bread industries, for example, tend to be some of the most locally responsive in part because of short shelf lives. Other industries such as fresh seafood and cut flowers have largely overcome spoilage problems by developing special packaging and efficient transportation procedures. However, they add substantial costs to the consumer and are only justifiable to the degree premium prices can be passed on. In industries with high weight to value, transportation costs may outweigh any benefits of global integration. Sand, gravel, coal, potted plants, diapers, and paint are examples of products whose high weight-to-value ratio discourages global integration.

New Production Technologies.   New computer-assisted design and manufacturing technologies have allowed an increasing number of industries to maximize efficiencies at relatively small production volumes. Multiple products in a single factory are more practical because machine changeover time has been reduced dramatically. In the U.S. steel industry, for example, Nucor Corporation and Chaparral Steel, through their development of minimill and micromill technologies, emerged in the mid-1980s as fast-growing, international success stories. The result of short-production-run technologies is that products can be adapted, if necessary, for different markets at a more reasonable cost than used to be possible. New technologies have also made it possible to introduce new products in record time, making speed a new source of competitive advantage. Whistler, one of the largest manufacturers

---

[3]W. Echikson, "IBM's European Travail," *Fortune,* October 3, 1994, p. 88.

of radar detectors in the United States, introduced leading-edge technology in product design and manufacturing configuration and raised its pass rate on its assembly line from 75 percent to over 99 percent. In doing so, it cut production delays and reduced overall costs, saving hundreds of U.S.-based jobs that were slated for transfer to South Korea.

Just-in-Time Manufacturing.   Heavy equipment manufacturers and automotive assemblers have led the way in pursuing just-in-time manufacturing strategies. In many cases suppliers to these industries are required to ship an agreed-upon quantity of components so that they arrive at the customer's plant within hours of assembly. By adopting just-in-time manufacturing, the assemblers are able to pass inventory costs as well as other risks on to suppliers. In many cases these saving more than offset the potential production economies that may result from global component manufacturing. Businesses that supply inputs to just-in-time customers face serious limitations insofar as globalization is concerned.

Globalization Impacts Industries

In assessing the net impact of globalization and localization pressures, it is essential to recognize that globalization pressures vary from industry to industry. For example, while a reduction in trade barriers may have a dramatic impact on the computer industry, it may be of little consequence to the cement industry. Similarly, while advances in telecommunications may make it easier to develop standardized advertising programs, the demand for a wide variety of products remains deeply imbedded in local cultures. Within industries, globalization and localization pressures vary in intensity. Relatively few industries emphasize all globalization or localization pressures to the maximum degree. For example, while many segments of the food processing industry could theoretically achieve considerable cost savings through global production, the industry's globalization potential is limited by spoilage problems and low value to weight, which make shipping prohibitively expensive.

Before further exploring MNC strategies, it is useful to determine which industries or products require local adaptation and therefore strong local responsiveness strategies and which face strong globalization pressures (i.e., major scale economies in production, R&D, or marketing) and therefore strong central control. The following two-by-two matrix attempts to do this by contrasting the pressures toward globalization with the pressures toward localization (Exhibit 8–1).

In the two right quadrants, local adaptation is important. In the two top quadrants, the pressures toward globalization are significant. The top left quadrant identifies industries where local differences are minor and the benefits to global integration are significant. The bottom right quadrant represents the opposite extreme where local differences are significant and there are few advantages to globalization. The bottom left quadrant represents industries where local differences are minor but globalization is limited by other factors (e.g., transportation in the case of cement). The types of organization strategy best suited to the key quadrants are shown in the diagram and are discussed below. It is important to repeat, however, that when we talk of globalization pressures increasing, what we mean is that more and more products and industries are moving up from the bottom quadrants to the top quadrants.

EXHIBIT 8–1   Organization Consequences of Internationalization

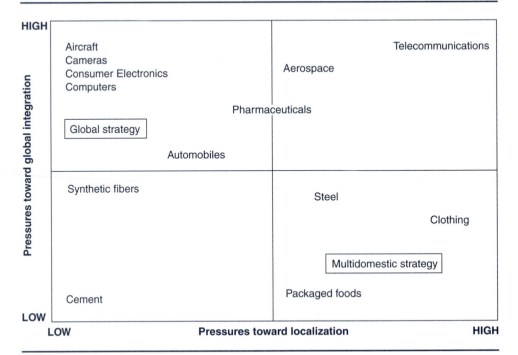

Globalization Impacts Business Strategy

Historically, U.S. and European MNCs have approached international competition by pursuing multidomestic strategies. Multidomestic strategies are designed to maximize the local responsiveness of businesses. Encouraged by historically fragmented European markets, and cultures that readily accommodated the delegation of decision making to overseas managers, U.S. and European MNCs achieved major successes in international markets in the 1960s and 1970s by emphasizing multidomestic strategies. From 1975 to 1987, FDI stocks increased by 350 percent to almost $428 billion. By 1990, U.S. MNCs employed more than two million people in Europe and produced about 85 percent of all U.S.-branded goods and services marketed in the European Union in facilities located in Europe (the remaining 15 percent were generated from exports from the United States or other countries). During the early-to-mid-1990s the pace of FDI increased. From 1995 to 1996, world FDI inflows grew by 10 percent to $349 billion.[4]

Despite the economic turmoil in much of the developing world, FDI growth continued in the late 1990s. Between 1997 and 1998, FDI grew by a further 10 percent to reach approximately $430 billion. By 1999, the United States was the world's largest source of FDI and

---

[4]*Wall Street Journal,* "Foreign Direct Investment Increased by 10% in 1996," July 1997, p. A9A.

its largest target for FDI. The outward stock of FDI from U.S. companies reached nearly $900 billion in 1997. Britain was number two with approximately $400 billion invested overseas.[5] Much of the growth in FDI was spurred by the rise in international mergers and acquisitions. In 1997, majority-owned cross-border mergers accounted for $236 billion or nearly 60 percent of all FDI, up from less than 50 percent of all FDI the year earlier.[6] Cross-border mergers accelerated in 1998. Topping the list were the mergers of British Petroleum and Amoco ($55.0 billion) and Daimler-Benz and Chrysler ($40.5 billion). In January 1999, Ford announced that it would buy Sweden's AB Volvo for $6.45 billion.

Multidomestic Strategies

The establishment of stand-alone overseas affiliates is consistent with the adoption of multidomestic strategies. Businesses pursuing multidomestic strategies first develop products for their home market and then offer them for sale or adaptation by their overseas affiliates. Affiliates are developed with the capacity to absorb parent company technology and adapt the resulting products to local conditions and tastes. Traditionally, multidomestic affiliates manufacture products for their own national markets, adapting the parent company product line as required. If specialization is at the heart of global strategies, duplication and autonomy are at the heart of multidomestic strategies. In the pure multidomestic model, it is technology and skills that cross national boundaries, not products.

During the high-tariff decades of the 1950s, 1960s, and 1970s, multidomestic strategies appeared appropriate. However, with the first emergence of globalization pressures in the 1970s, multidomestic strategies became inappropriate in many industries. As industry pressures began to take on more global dimensions, it became possible for business to gain a competitive advantage by pursuing global strategies.

Global Strategies

Under a global strategy, businesses focus on maximizing international efficiency by locating activities in low-cost countries, producing standardized products from world-scale facilities, globally integrating operations, and subsidizing intercountry market share battles. Global businesses conceive and design products for world markets from the outset. Frequently, affiliates in key markets have input into product design, but once the parent organization launches a new product the affiliate's role reverts to that of implementer.

Global products usually emphasize international similarities rather than cultural differences. Not surprisingly, marketing strategies are typically established in and by the parent organization. Products are manufactured wherever in the world the necessary quality standards can be achieved at the lowest cost including transportation to key markets. As a

---

[5]*The Economist,* "Ruling the Merger Wave," January 23, 1999, p. 53.
[6]K. Sauvant, "How to Prime the FDI Engine," *Global Finance,* Vol. 12, No. 12, 1998, p. 34.

practical matter, large markets attract production because market share is often enhanced by the presence of a production facility. Also, host country governments sometimes induce local production through nontariff barriers to trade, but the classic global strategy is conceived without artificial impediments to the movement of goods.

Globalization Impacts Host Governments

Increasing demands by governments for investment capital, for economic and trade diversification, and for increasingly sophisticated product and process technologies have shifted the bargaining power in favor of MNCs. While these needs augment the bargaining power of all MNCs, MNCs pursuing globally integrated strategies further strengthen their bargaining power vis-à-vis governments. In developing policies to respond to global MNCs, a critical issue facing governments is the degree to which MNCs have adopted truly global strategies.

MNCs pursuing global strategies gain additional bargaining power over governments as a result of their abilities to control both how and where activities are geographically positioned and how they are coordinated. These abilities are manifest in two broad areas.[7] First, globally integrated MNCs can bias the financial results of affiliates and thereby shift profits from high to low tax rate countries. The manipulation of financial results can be achieved through transfer pricing and favorable remittance policies. Exhibit 8–2 presents the hypothetical example of a company with two affiliates. Under this example, the affiliate in country A produces only 1,000 units of output per month at a unit cost of $0.12. The affiliate in country B produces 10,000 units per month at a per-unit cost of $0.07. If the affiliate in country A shuts down its factory and sources from country B, its costs will go down to just below $0.07 per unit. However, if country A's marginal tax rate is higher than that of country B, the company may want to charge the affiliate in country A the old rate of $0.12 per unit. In this way, profits are shifted from country A to country B and taxes are minimized.

A second way globally integrated MNCs exert power over host governments is through their ability to control the direction and location of technology and skills. MNCs often have the capability to rapidly reconfigure value-adding activities. By constantly focusing on shifting patterns of comparative advantage, MNCs can move operations from one country to another as factor costs shift. This mobility, combined with the ownership of technology, skills, and jobs and the ability of MNCs to generate tax revenues, results in countries competing against each other for new investment as well as the retention of existing MNC activities. Even subnational governments are getting into the bidding game. In Phoenix, Arizona, for example, the city council in 1995 voted to approve major tax breaks and infrastructure investments to encourage Sitix, a division of Japan giant Sumitomo Corporation, to invest almost $500 million in a silicon wafer manufacturing plant. The Phoenix area was already home to major microprocessor fabrication plants by Intel, Motorola, and SGS-Thomson and was concerned about maintaining its global position as a center of high-tech excellence.

---

[7]For a more complete discussion of the concerns of host countries regarding integrated MNCs, see Y. Doz, "Government Policies and Global Industries," in M. Porter, ed., *Competition in Global Industries* (Boston: Harvard Business School Press, 1986), pp. 225–66.

EXHIBIT 8–2   The Impact of Economies of Scale on Transfer Pricing

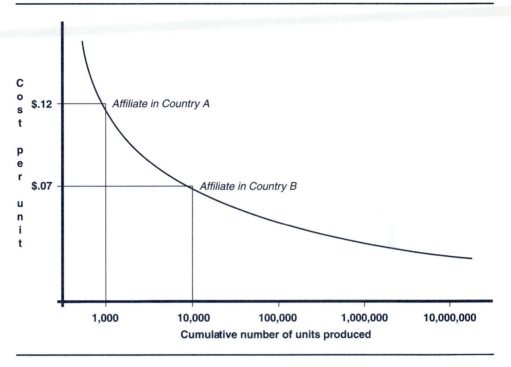

Key Considerations in Adopting an International Strategy

Although global strategy has been viewed as ideal in global industries, not all businesses compete in global industries, nor are all businesses capable of pursuing a global strategy. Resource constraints, bureaucratic obstacles, and histories of affiliate autonomy have forced a large number of businesses to pursue a variety of nonglobal options. Some have viewed country-based, multidomestic strategies as ultimately untenable in global industries. Others have argued that multidomestic strategies are appropriate as a long-term niche approach to international competition.

Although pure global strategies may not always be appropriate, heightened international competition is forcing almost every business to reconsider how and where they compete. In determining an appropriate international strategy—whether multidomestic or global—the following steps should be considered.

1. Determine Where the Critical Scale Economies and Other Benefits of Globalization Lie

Offshore production is often the first thought of North American or European firms threatened by heightened international competition. Many managers may feel that the perfect solution is to shift the labor-intensive production processes to low-wage countries and otherwise continue business as usual. A globalization strategy, however, implies much more than this. Products need to be designed for key world markets; furthermore, designs need to be sensitive to production processes and to global standards of product reliability, technology, and quality. Under globalization, the issue is not where a business can make it cheaper, but where a business can achieve the best combination of technology, quality, and cost.

On this basis, different products end up being manufactured in different countries. Some factories concentrate on component parts; others on assembly. In both cases, factories are set up to serve the business's worldwide needs, or at least a major portion of them. Many large businesses are nervous about having single sources of supply of key products or components. Although they often develop multiple sources, they normally designate one factory as the prime source and assign to it the ongoing related product development responsibility. Other competing units within the corporation may over time try to displace it as the prime source of products based on superior cost and quality performance.

While production scale economies are an important benefit of globalization, they are not the only benefit. Advertising and promotion can in some cases be globalized too. It is just as possible to advertise to global similarities as to national differences, but to do it successfully requires a lot of understanding of the mood and mind-set of different regions. There is an enormous difference between successful global advertising and the view that what's good for Iowa or Ontario is good for India or Malaysia. The same is true for global product design.

Just as the globalization benefits are not the same for all industries, they differ significantly from product to product and from activity to activity. Key questions include: How homogeneous are customer needs from one country to another? What savings are possible from designing the product for global markets and manufacturing it to global capacity? What technology does large-scale specialized production make possible? Can the company benefit by adopting a common approach to marketing the product around the world? What problems might arise in particular countries or regions from such an approach? As questions like these are answered product line by product line and activity by activity, it is possible to identify where globalization fits best and where localization is more important.

2. Rotate Country Managers More Frequently to Help Them Develop a Global Vision

Country managers with long-term appointments do not easily develop global perspectives, and it is difficult to globalize an organization successfully without those perspectives in place. One way to accelerate globalization is to move senior people from one international affiliate to another, or from the affiliate to head office and back. Of course, this means sending in nonnationals to run affiliates, but if the rotation is understood as global management training, resentment of the nonnational boss can be minimized. There are other benefits to rotation too. The corporation is able to utilize managers from all over the world in whatever positions they best fit. Furthermore, morale in the affiliates is sometimes higher because managers there see opportunities beyond their own borders.

A wide variety of corporations including Ford, 3M, ABB, Samsung, and Dow Chemical use management rotation regularly to build up a core of international managers. Not everyone likes to be moved around the world, however. Some managers like the opportunity when they are early in their careers, but not when they have to worry about their children's schooling and other family matters. It is also expensive. Expatriate managers usually get paid a premium for living abroad or get their living accommodation paid. Family trips back home and private schooling for dependent children are also often part of the package. Building a global management team leads to some expensive traditions in corporate culture. These benefits are also often very visible to host country nationals, who often view them as excessive.

3. Reassess the Performance Measurement System and Reward System

Under traditional multidomestic strategies, country managers have broad strategic autonomy over activities in their country and should therefore reasonably be evaluated on the basis of country-specific results. Broad measures of growth and return on invested capital are commonly used criteria. However, to hold a manager responsible for results after his or her autonomy is reduced under globalization is more problematic. The company, of course, is more interested in its overall global results than in the results of any one affiliate, but if results are to be used to measure a manager's performance, they must somehow fit the manager's responsibility. While normal growth and return on investment criteria might apply to products made for the domestic market only, imported products may be better evaluated with a system that measures sales growth by market segment. And products made for world markets may require a system that evaluates cost of production only. On the other hand, if the affiliate has the marketing assignment for its global products, the measurement system might include growth of export sales.

Clearly, globalization leads to more complex measurement systems. That is because responsibility is divided in different ways. This is evidenced in Figure 8–2 where the affiliate manager in country *A* may be responsible for perpetually subsidizing the profits of another affiliate. Being responsible to sell a product designed for the global market at a price set by head office is quite different from selling a domestically designed product at a price set at home. Measurement systems have to reflect these changes in responsibility. They are complicated further by transfer prices on intercorporate trade and intercorporate trade increases significantly under globalization.

The trend toward globalization is now unstoppable. In 1996, investment in foreign affiliates was an estimated $1.4 trillion, of which only $350 billion was financed through FDI.[8] Given the huge number of foreign affiliates as well as the growing number of domestic competitors in overseas markets, determining an appropriate international strategy is a complex, difficult job. Given the rate of change in the environment, even the best strategy rapidly diminishes in value. As a result, managers must be constantly on the alert for not only new market opportunities but new competitors as well. In the final analysis, no strategy is perfect. But some strategies are better than others. The better strategies of tomorrow will no doubt accommodate the need for greater complexity and flexibility. This is the focus of Chapter 9.

---

[8]*World Investment Report, 1997: Transnational Corporations, Market Structure and Competition Policy* (New York: United Nations, 1997), p. xvi.

Supplementary Reading

Birkinshaw, Julian, and Warren Richie. "Balancing the Global Portfolio." *Business Quarterly,* Summer 1993, pp. 40–49.

Hamel, Gary, and C.K. Prahalad. "Do You Really Have a Global Strategy?" *Harvard Business Review,* July-August 1985, pp. 139–48.

Hedlund, Gunnar. "The Hypermodern MNC: A Heterarchy?" *Human Resource Management,* Spring 1986.

Kanter, Rosabeth Moss, and Thomas Dretler. "Global Strategy and Its Impact on Local Operations: Lessons from Gillette Singapore." *The Academy of Management Executive,* November 1998, pp. 60–68.

Kim, W. Chan, and Renee Mauborgne. "Making Global Strategies Work." *Sloan Management Review,* Spring 1993, pp. 11–27.

Morrison, Allen. *Strategies in Global Industries: How U.S. Businesses Compete.* Westport, CT: Quorum Books, 1990.

Morrison, Allen, and Kendall Roth. "A Taxonomy of Business-Level Strategies in Global Industries." *Strategic Management Journal,* Vol. 13, 1992, pp. 399–417.

Ohmae, Kenichi. "Planting for a Global Harvest." *Harvard Business Review,* July-August 1989.

Porter, Michael. "Changing Patterns of International Competition." *California Management Review,* Vol. 28, 1986, pp. 9–40.

Prahalad, C. K., and Yves Doz. *The Multinational Mission: Balancing Local Demands and Global Vision.* New York: The Free Press, 1987.

Schutte, Hellmut. "Strategy and Organization: Challenges for European MNCs in Asia." *European Management Journal,* Vol. 15, No. 4, 1997, pp. 436–45.

Yip, George. *Total Global Strategy: Managing for Worldwide Competitive Advantage.* Englewood Cliffs, NJ: Prentice Hall, 1992.

Yip, George, Johny Johansson, and Johan Roos. "Effects of Nationality on Global Strategy." *Management International Reviewer,* Vol. 37, No. 4, 1997, pp. 365–85.

9 THE IMPACT OF GLOBALIZATION ON THE ORGANIZATION OF ACTIVITIES

This chapter focuses on the organization of business activities in the face of rising globalization. How companies organize activities—research and development, production, marketing, and service, among others—often means the difference between failure and success. Organization decisions ultimately focus on how activities are *configured* and *coordinated*.[1] Configuration pertains to the geographic positioning of activities and is driven by a company's interest in accessing markets and sources of comparative advantage. Activities range from being "concentrated" (i.e., each activity is located in a single country from which the world is served), or "dispersed" (i.e., all activities are located in each host country). In contrast, coordination pertains to the integration or interdependence of activities and is driven by a company's interest in exploiting competitive advantages across countries. Coordination ranges from very low—where each activity of a business is performed independently—to very high, where the same activities are tightly coordinated or closely integrated across countries. How a company configures and coordinates its activities directly impacts its ability to exploit country-specific comparative advantages as well as company-specific competencies.

This chapter examines how rising globalization pressures have forced managers to re-examine every aspect of the configuration and coordination of activities. More particularly, it focuses on the organization of activities and the interplay between international strategy and structure. Inasmuch as the 1990s became the decade of globalization, this chapter explores how globalization has impacted the interplay between international strategy and structure.

This chapter was prepared by Allen J. Morrison.

[1]For a more complete discussion of the concepts of configuration and coordination in international organizations, see M. Porter, "Changing Patterns of International Competition," *California Management Review,* Vol. 28, 1986, pp. 9–40.

Common International Organization Structures

International Division Structure

Much of the early work on international organization structures took the logical approach of relating it to the growth of a company's international activity. For example, a company might begin with an export department to handle the technical requirements of shipping products across national borders. With success in export markets would come a greater awareness of international opportunities, and the next organizational stage might be the establishment of an international division to look after both exports and foreign investments. The organization structure of a company with an international division might appear as shown in Exhibit 9–1.

Under an international division structure, all functional activities—with the possible exception of sales—are maintained at home. When international sales and profits are a minor percentage of a division's overall activity, it is difficult to get a busy division manager to spend time cultivating and building international activity. Time tends to get spent where the big sales and profits are. Building and cultivating business are best done by a division devoted exclusively to that task—hence the international division. One clear advantage of an international division structure is that it allows a company to give international sales much greater support and attention. As a result, the manager of the international division has to understand the product-market strategies of each product division and adapt them to international markets.

Area Division Structure

As international sales grow as a percentage of total company sales, many successful companies evolve out of an international division structure and create an area division structure (Exhibit 9–2). While an area division will often continue to report to a corporate vice president international, strategic decision making is shifted to regional and/or country managers. As a result, the position of vice president international is one of the few positions in a company where success can bring declining influence.

For many companies, area division structures capture the majority of efficiency advantages that result from globalization. Relatively few activities actually require global volumes to reach maximum levels of economic efficiency.[2] Furthermore, area organizations may be more efficient and effective than global structures because of increased responsiveness, reduced bureaucracy, communication efficiencies, and improved employee morale. In many cases area structures can also facilitate faster delivery, allow greater customization, and allow the company to maintin smaller inventories than would be necessary under more complex organization forms.

Characteristics.   Under an area division structure, regional and country managers have a high degree of autonomy in how they adapt the strategies of the home country product

---

[2]For a more complete discussion of regional organizations, see A. J. Morrison, D. Ricks, K. Roth, "Globalization versus Regionalization: Which Way for the Multinational," *Organizational Dynamics,* Winter 1991, pp. 17–29.

EXHIBIT 9–1   The International Division Structure

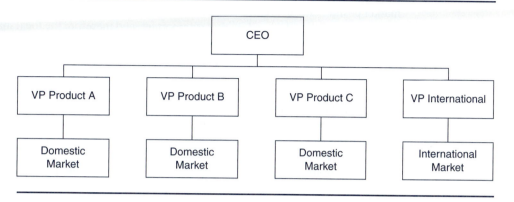

EXHIBIT 9–2   The Area Division Structure

divisions to meet the particular circumstances of their regions and countries. The Kellogg Company of Battle Creek, Michigan, has made a major commitment to its area division structure. Kellogg has 12 of the world's 15 best-selling brands of ready-to-eat cereal. However, the company decides which brands to sell, manufacture, and market on an area basis. The company's four area presidents (Europe, Asia-Pacific, North America, and Latin America) have been given wide discretionary power over marketing, production, and sourcing (they both support and help identify global brands). Ford, IBM, General Motors, and Philips Electronics are examples of other MNCs widely known for powerful area headquarters.

The more local conditions influence consumer demand, the more autonomy country managers usually get. Local responsiveness is its main achievement. As a result, an area division structure is most appropriate for companies pursuing multidomestic strategies. Take for example, the Kenny Rogers Roasters in China case. The key decision in the case centers on whether the company should make a substantial investment in time and resources to secure market access in China via the city of Beijing. Investments to secure market position are invariably based on an appraisal of the size and growth potential of the market in question. The local market is important, and therefore the local manager is going to be important. For Kenny Rogers Roasters in China, the issue of how or if local management should be controlled is an essential aspect of any investment decision.

Under an area division structure, the majority of activities are "dispersed" or located in each country where the company competes. At Shell Oil, for example, major refineries are located throughout almost all of the major markets of the world; crude oil purchasing activities are dispersed; and marketing and sales activities are also positioned around the world. Under an area division structure, these dispersed activities are loosely coordinated. This means that each activity is performed independently. For Shell Oil, purchasing decisions made in the United States are not coordinated with purchasing decisions made in France or Indonesia.

Multidomestic Affiliates.   Area structures are most often adopted by companies that pursue multidomestic strategies. Host countries have long used the term *miniature replica* to describe the traditional multidomestic affiliate. The term arises because the affiliate is like a scaled-down version of the parent, in that it produces the same products but in lower volume for a smaller "domestic" market. In many cases, trade barriers keep international markets separated and permit the affiliate to operate profitably, even though its production costs are often higher than the parent company's because of the need to produce multiple products in relatively small volume. The diagram in Exhibit 9–3 tries to capture the features of a traditional multidomestic affiliate.

Multidomestic affiliates are typically evaluated by profit center criteria keyed to results rather than obedience to head office policies. Usually, local nationals are appointed as country managers and management turnover is relatively slow. Each affiliate takes on a character and personality of its own, and formulates its own internal strategy. The role of country manager is similar to the role of the parent CEO, except for the more limited geographical sphere of activity.

Given the high levels of affiliate autonomy and the results-oriented performance measurement systems, one might suppose that host governments would be relatively pleased with multidomestic structures. Complaints against it, however, have been numerous. One of the most frequent has been that "miniature replica" affiliates do not do R&D; they simply bring in parent technology and adapt it where necessary. Most studies confirm that this complaint is fairly accurate. Many affiliates cannot afford to pay for their own R&D and still make a profit on the sales generated in the host market alone. They tend to manufacture many products for a relatively small market—a strategy that can only succeed with imported technology and tariff protection. Another complaint has been that "miniature replica" affiliates do not export—thereby bringing jobs and hard currency to developing countries. Again, this complaint has, with notable exceptions, proven fairly accurate. The reason for it has not been parent unwillingness as much as the affiliate's inability to export competitively. In many cases, that inability is due to the affiliates' lack of cost competitiveness—they are typically high-cost producers relative to their parents; and to the affiliate's lack of product differentiation—they typically use parent technology.

EXHIBIT 9–3   Multidomestic Affiliate Structure

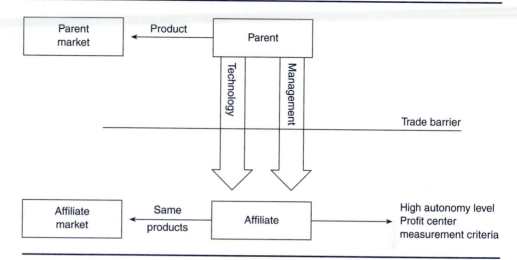

The fundamental concerns in host governments have been that tariff protection generally leads to an inefficient industrial structure. There is a growing realization among developing countries that multidomestic affiliates cannot play an effective role in the emerging globalization of business. Hence, many countries are lowering tariffs in an effort to transform their industrial structures and make them more competitive. But if host countries complained about foreign ownership under the miniature replica structure, they are likely to continue to do so under a global structure. The complaints, however, will have a different ring to them.

From a home country, head office perspective, an area-centered structure is ideal as long as it is advantageous to disperse key activities and control them with local decision makers. However, high local autonomy often results in three problems:

1. Communications between home country product divisions and distant overseas affiliates are often more complex and risk breaking down. Corporate policies and standards may not be effectively communicated to or adopted by the affiliates. In many cases important product-market information also fails to reach the field abroad. We see an example of this challenge in the Black & Decker–Eastern Hemisphere and the ADP Initiative case study. In this example, Bill Lancaster, the President of Black & Decker–Eastern Hemisphere, is left trying to decide how and when to introduce a U.S.-designed management appraisal system in Asia.

2. Affiliate autonomy is not conducive to MNC learning. Excellent practices and products can typically be found in each affiliate. To maximize learning, every affiliate must promote its products and practices within the MNC as well as embrace appropriate new practices and products generated by other affiliates. The greater the affiliate autonomy, the lower the likelihood that excellent practices and products will either be communicated or adopted.

3. As affiliates develop self-sufficiency, the power of home country managers is challenged. For products that are viewed as strategically important, home country managers may try to disrupt moves by affiliates to achieve greater autonomy. This can lead to dysfunctional behaviors and morale problems.

Global Product Divisions

As a general rule, the relative importance of product managers increases with the number of products being offered by a company. As the diversity of *foreign* products increases, many successful companies have adopted global product division structures. Du Pont became the first major U.S. company to adopt a modern divisionalized structure not long after the turn of the century. By 1970, as many as 90 percent of *Fortune 500* companies had adopted product divisional structures.

Divisions are usually organized to correspond to particular industries, or industry segments. Hong Kong–based Hutchison Whampoa Ltd., is one of the best examples of a diversified, multidivisional MNC. It has extensive interests including food processing, retailing, manufacturing, shipping, and real estate. Its real estate business includes commercial and residential development, landholding, and hotel operations. It also runs a range of telecommunications businesses including cellular phone and paging businesses. Hutchison Whampoa's shipping interests include container and other terminal facilities in Asia and Europe. The company also has energy, finance, and investment holdings. Each of these businesses is organized as a separate company, responsible to group headquarters and Chairman Li Ka-shing. Other MNCs, including ITT, Matsushita, General Electric, Grand Metropolitan, Philip Morris, and Mannesmann have highly diversified operations that lend themselves to distinct industry analyses and diverse business unit strategies.

Under a divisionalized structure, all functional activities (for example, R&D, production, marketing), are controlled by a product group. An example of a global product divisional structure is included in Exhibit 9–4.

Characteristics.   When global product divisions take over, they tend to achieve direct lines of communication into key markets and can therefore get their product and market know-how through to the field unimpeded. Because activities are tightly coordinated by divisional head office, country managers are often involved only in the local administrative, legal, and financial affairs of the company. Product decisions are made by home country managers and input from overseas affiliates is often discouraged. What is lost in terms of local responsiveness is gained in terms of global efficiencies.

Global product division structures represent a chain of vertically integrated activities. Product division managers can configure activities according to variances in costs or skills across countries. This makes the product divisions ideal for global strategies. Under a global product division structure, some activities may be dispersed—for example, component manufacturing and assembly—while others may be centrally located—for example, research and development. For U.S. and European companies, the advantages of global structural flexibility have become increasingly apparent through the growing international success of Japanese MNCs. In an attempt to drive costs down, a frequent reaction for U.S. and European companies has been to move labor-intensive upstream activities to low-wage

---

EXHIBIT 9–4   Global Product Division Structure

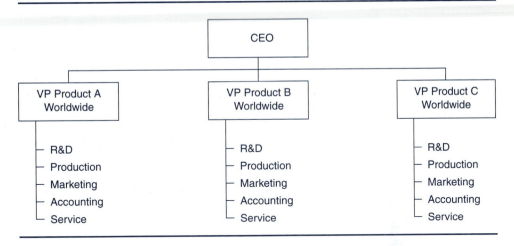

countries with highly skilled workers and duty-free zones. Many of these factories ended up in Asia, and for American companies in Mexico.

One of the reasons why many large companies have shifted to global product division structures is that it helps managers more easily focus on maximizing competitiveness. When the competitive parameters are set by the industry, competitors can be clearly identified and decisions focused on upgrading functional skills. With rising globalization, plants can be more easily focused in terms of product, robotized in terms of technology, and diversified in terms of markets served. Country managers whose chief expertise is a knowledge of their domestic markets cannot expect to survive globalization with their autonomy intact.

Global Affiliates.   Under a global product division structure, affiliates around the world do not operate with a great deal of autonomy. They become an integrated part of a global organization and often play no independent strategic role at all. If production does take place in a particular affiliate, it will often be specialized production of a single model or component for use throughout the corporation. Hence the design and specification of what is produced is seldom handled by the affiliate because it is not aimed primarily at the affiliate's market. In these conditions, coordination between parent and affiliates is critical, and is often achieved by sending parent executives to run affiliate operations for three-to-five-year terms. Because specialization is at the heart of global company strategies, affiliates are expected to be obedient and are evaluated as cost centers. The profit center concept just does not fit the strategy. Global affiliates have little strategic autonomy and take few if any initiatives.

Affiliates operating under a global product division structure are largely treated as a source of supply. Inputs—technology and components—are provided by either the parent or other affiliates within the vertically controlled structure; the inputs are further processed— components are refined or assembled—and then re-exported back to the parent or sister affiliates within the division. Examples include Matsushita, which manufacturers big-screen televisions in China, and Sharp, which makes washing machines in the Philippines. While affiliate exports may or may not return to the home country of the parent, divisional managers

EXHIBIT 9–5   Global Affiliate Structure

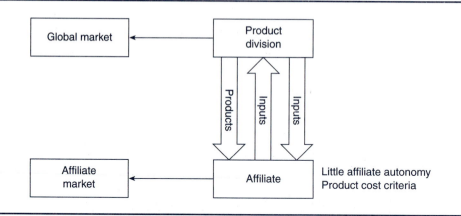

control product's destination and sales price. Once final assembly has occurred, the parent generally supervises international marketing; while affiliates may employ their own marketing staff, they are typically accountable to divisional marketing managers. The diagram in Exhibit 9–5 captures the key features of a global affiliate structure.

Contrasting Area and Global Product Division Structures

Area and global product division structures can both be appropriate depending on the objectives a company is trying to achieve. Area structures work best when international sales represent an important percentage of total sales and when the requirements for local responsiveness are high. Global product division structures work best when the number of products the company produces has proliferated and when globalization requirements are high. To establish the contrast more clearly, Exhibit 9–6 summarizes the essential differences between multidomestic area and global product division structures.

Under the global product division structure, efficient communication of product know-how is maximized. The country manager under a global structure plays administrative and legal roles rather than strategic ones. Not surprisingly, the global product structure works best in conditions where product knowledge is more vital than market knowledge. While outputs are tightly controlled, specific operations in any given country may not be well coordinated, and there may be some duplication of selling effort. However, each product line gets someone's maximum attention.

Under the area division structure, region and country managers are ultimately responsible for corporate strategy in their regions or countries. Their task is to adapt corporate strategy to local conditions. To do so, they have to become familiar with the products and markets of each division. Knowledge of local politics, markets, suppliers, and channels constitutes their distinctive competence. They may not give each product the same degree of effort, but will seek out first their strongest competitive opportunities, i.e., where market demand is highest or competition weakest.

The biggest weaknesses in the global product structure are the growing dependence over time of the affiliates on the parent and the lack of substantive ideas or initiatives arising from the affiliates. As a result, global product structures are notoriously inflexible. A case in point is Matsushita Electric Industrial, which first introduced a product division structure in 1933. Matsushita's tightly controlled structure was designed to build managerial talent, promote internal competition, and maximize international growth by treating each product division as an independent small business. Overseas marketing affiliates were established, international sales soared, and profits were consolidated on a global basis. By the mid-1980s, Matsushita had emerged as the world's largest producer of consumer electronics. Despite this success, Matsushita faced serious challenges in the 1990s. Demand for its mainstream color television and VCR products flattened and profit margins slipped substantially. Many observers blame Matsushita's once successful product division structure for much of the company's woes. By locating most R&D activities in Japan, Matsushita has missed out on a stream of critical innovations taking place in the United States and Europe. The company has also faced growing demands by host governments for local production and innovation. As technologies such as semiconductors, computers, and robots have blurred, Matsushita's reliance on strictly defined product divisions has only compounded the problems associated with product division inflexibility.

While global product structures have serious shortcomings, area structures may not be the perfect solution. The biggest weakness in the area structure is the difficulty the parent has imposing an overarching strategy on its autonomous affiliates and hence obtaining some of the benefits of specialization. As a result, area structures are notoriously inefficient. Rather than produce standardized products in worldscale production facilities, area structures rely on smaller plants that are less scale-efficient. Because research and development, purchasing, marketing, and distribution are also duplicated across geographic territories, cumulative overhead costs can be much higher than with most product structures.

In an increasingly competitive world, these added costs are often difficult to sustain. Take for example the case of General Electric Canada, which since the mid-1970s has manufactured a wide line of home appliances through its Camco affiliate. Camco has had a history of relative independence. Unfortunately, this independence combined with low-scale efficiencies resulted in refrigerators that cost 20 percent more to build in Canada than in General Electric facilities in the United States. In 1987 and 1988, General Electric invested nearly $1 billion retooling and expanding its U.S.-based refrigerator operations resulting

---

EXHIBIT 9–6   Contrasting Global Product and Multidomestic Area Structures

	Global Product Structure	Multidomestic Area Structure
Product line	Specialized	Duplicated
Market emphasis	International	National
Transfers	Product/Technology	Technology/Skills
Affiliate evaluation	Cost center	Profit center
Affiliate role	Implement strategy	Develop & implement strategy
Affiliate autonomy	Low	High
Affiliate management	Foreign, short-term	Local, long-term

in a widening of the cost differential between the Canadian affiliate and the parent. This meant that unless the Canadian market was protected (it wasn't) or customers were prepared to pay extra for unique local features or services (they weren't), Camco would have a hard time justifying its existence. Beginning in 1998, Camco fought back by spending about $60 million on new refrigerator products. This action culminated with the announcement in February 1999 of a major export initiative based on its newest "CustomStyle" refrigerator. The 22-cubic-foot-capacity refrigerator was developed by Camco and was designed to be installed flush with kitchen cabinets and included a "Smart Space" interior—the first of its kind in North America.

The weaknesses in both the area and the product structures are enhanced when a company adopts a structure inconsistent with its international strategy. In other words, if a company has a strategy that emphasizes affiliate input about local markets and yet adopts a global product structure, then lack of affiliate initiative becomes a serious impediment. On the other hand, if a company can increase its efficiency by rearranging its production and standardizing needless differences, but has adopted an area structure, then the autonomy of affiliate managers becomes a serious impediment.

The Transnational Option

What should be clear by now is that both the global product and multidomestic area structures can have serious potential problems. One gets you greater global efficiencies and the other gets you greater local responsiveness. Since perfect organizations really do not exist, one is tempted to suggest simply picking the one closest to the company's product-market thrust and learning to live with the organizational deficiencies. For many companies, that is sound advice. However, for a number of companies these deficiencies are too costly. Telecommunications is a good illustration. Telecommunications companies face powerful pressures toward globalization from high R&D costs and available scale economies, and also powerful pressures toward localization from differences in the systems in place in each country and in the politicization of the industry. Firms facing such challenges sometimes try to capture the benefits of both the global and the multidomestic structures by developing hybrid structures.

When companies ask, "Isn't there some way to have it all?" the transnational organization and the matrix system have been suggested by some as the proffered solution.[3] The key elements of the transnational structure include a two-way flow of ideas and resources, frequent movement of people between units, extensive use of local boards of directors, and a global perspective on the part of both parent and affiliate. The affiliates of transnational corporations have a good deal more autonomy than those in global corporations, but still they are an integrated part of a global strategy. In the transnational corporation, initiatives arise in affiliates as well as parents, and interaffiliate linkages are encouraged. Rather than

---

[3]For further information about transnational structures see Bartlett and Ghoshal, *Managing Across Borders—The Transnational Solution*, (Boston: Harvard Business School Press, 1989). The authors present the transnational structure as an idealized form rather than a reality in business. At the same time, they hold it out as a structure toward which many international businesses are moving because of the deficiencies of alternative approaches.

function as a hierarchy, transnational organizations function as a *network* of horizontal decision making. The trade-offs between globalization and localization are made in the field by managers committed to the corporation and its competitive objectives, and aware of local market anomalies and differences. The organizational challenge is to ensure a continuous supply of such managers over time.

A transnational structure attempts to concurrently capture all of the advantages of area and global product division structures. In order to achieve these dual sets of benefits, the configuration and coordination of activities are mixed; affiliates play leadership roles for some activities and supporting roles for others. Decisions are based on maximizing company skills and competencies, irrespective of activity location or affiliate nationality. To be both efficient and effective, linkages between the company's headquarters and affiliates as well as across affiliates are subject to rapid change.[4] As a result, a company with a transnational structure acts essentially as a network of activities with multiple headquarters spread across different countries. Affiliates are given complete control over local products, provide support roles for some global products, and control other global products. Affiliate roles shift over time and learning and sharing are emphasized. To work effectively, transnational structures emphasize extensive horizontal linkages, effective communication, and extreme flexibility so that companies are able to develop competitive responses not only at head office but in the periphery as well.[5]

A good example of a company with a transnational organization structure is DaimlerChrysler, the world's third-largest car maker in terms of sales and fifth-largest in terms of the number of cars sold. Formed in 1998 by the $40 billion acquisition of U.S.-based Chrysler by Germany's Daimler-Benz, the combined company produced about four million vehicles in 1998. Chrysler's well-known brands included Dodge, Eagle, Jeep, and Plymouth. Daimler-Benz was best known for making luxury sedans, but also commercial vehicles, sport utility vehicles, and aerospace products. With joint headquarters in Detroit and Stuttgart, the new company has provided Chrysler with new international channels of distribution for its Jeeps and minivans. It also gave Daimler Benz significant benefits by tapping into Chrysler's market savvy.

Structural fluidity, sharing of market information, purchasing, technology, and competitive intelligence, plus quick decision making based on the good of the global organization, are being stressed in the new DaimlerChrysler organization. DaimlerChysler promises the type of huge-scale efficiencies that comes through global efficiencies with local responsiveness that comes through large domestically focused operations. The first year's results seemed positive. With 1998 pro forma net profits up 29 percent to $5.75 billion, the company was looking forward to a promising 1999.

The reason so many companies are experimenting with multihub, network organizations of this kind is more than just the desire to have the coordination benefits. Other factors are at play. The rise of international alliances is more manageable for firms with strong

---

[4]A discussion of "speed" advantages of transnationals is found in C. Bartlett, "Building and Managing the Transnational: The New Organizational Challenge," in M. Porter (ed.), *Competition in Global Industries* (Boston: Harvard Business School Press, 1986).

[5]G. Hedlund, "The Hypermodern MNC: A Heterarchy?" *Human Resource Management,* Vol. 25, No. 1, 1986, pp. 9–35.

"global" affiliates. The supply of global managers is not so dependent on head office. Good people join the affiliates—because they have interesting enough mandates to attract good people—and end up in other parts of the corporation, including head office. Quality global managers are in short supply, and limiting that supply to head office, or to the "home" country, exacerbates the shortage.

Transnational Affiliates and the Development of Mandates.   Transnational organizations are designed to concurrently maximize efficiency, local responsiveness, and organizational learning. Transnational affiliates may manufacture one or two products for world markets, but also handle worldwide responsibilities for other products. In other words, the affiliate functions like a domestic product division in some areas while assuming world product mandates in others. The diagram in Exhibit 9–7 tries to capture these features of a transnational structure.

What excites many affiliate managers under the transnational structure is that it allows for direct access to world markets. Access is achieved through the development of world product mandates in the affiliate's area of specialization. World product mandates represent global strategies controlled by the affiliate as opposed to the parent. Exhibit 9–8 provides examples of affiliates that have developed global product mandates. In each of these examples, world product headquarters are located in key affiliate countries. Technically, the parent's home country is treated as a foreign market for these products.

Despite these high-profile examples, most parent companies remain reluctant to give up control of R&D and product renewal for products that they themselves developed. Sometimes the key professionals involved do not want to be transferred to an overseas location, and do not see any reason why they should be. As a result, most world product mandate arrangements that do exist come through affiliate initiative in companies whose cultures reward innovative effort. In other cases, companies acquire overseas firms with global products and then turn these firms into affiliates. Canada-based Northern Telecom's acquisition of U.S.-based Bay Networks is a good example of this.

Even in the case of hard-fought-after mandates, subsidiaries are often disappointed at their limited control over the globalization of their products and services. Take Opel, for example. Executives at Opel, the German affiliate of General Motors, have become increasingly unhappy over the parent company's raids on the subsidiary's bank accounts and talent pool. Many of these assets and the best managers are being shipped off to such countries as Brazil, China, Poland, India, and the United States. They are also upset that the parent company frequently tells them that their German-designed Opel cars must be redesigned for U.S. markets. The problem for Opel is that it has been losing market share in Europe and its executives would like to keep its money and talented managers and designers at home where they feel they are needed the most.[6]

In order for a transnational structure to work effectively, affiliates need strong managers able to function well among parent company senior executives. If an affiliate becomes a sole or major source of supply and marketing of a specified product area worldwide, its managers soon find themselves operating in the top management committees of

---

[6]For more on Opel's concerns, see "Who Pays for the Ice Cream Soda?" *Forbes,* August 11, 1997, pp. 62–63.

EXHIBIT 9–7   Transnational Affiliate Structure

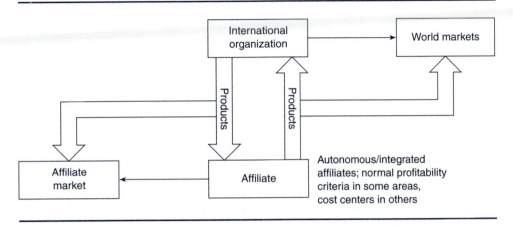

EXHIBIT 9–8   Examples of Affiliates with Global Product Responsibilities

Company	Home Country	Host Country	Product Mandate
Hyundai Electronics Industries	South Korea	U.S.A.	Microprocessors
Motorola	U.S.A.	Canada	Two-way radios
Siemens	Germany	U.K.	Air-traffic management
Du Pont	U.S.A.	Switzerland	Lycra business
Nestlé	Switzerland	U.K.	Confectionery
Wang	U.S.A.	Italy	Information technology services
Akzo	Netherlands	Germany	Fibers
Rhone Poulenc	France	Canada	Vaccines
Pechiney	France	U.S.A.	Beverage cans
Sony	Japan	U.S.A.	Motion pictures/ Television programs
Northern Telecom	Canada	U.S.A.	Computer networking
Philips	The Netherlands	U.K.	Teletexts-TV Sets
Ford	U.S.A.	Germany	Premier automobiles
Exxon	U.S.A.	U.K.	Aviation fuels

Sources: Company documents, interviews, *The Wall Street Journal,* December 9, 1991, p. B1, *The Wall Street Journal,* April 7, 1999, p. A1.

the parent organization. The parent must have confidence in the affiliate's ability to globally manage its product and to function effectively within the overall corporate system. As a rule, this means a network of affiliates interchanging sales forces and cross-linking R&D and production facilities.

Interest in affiliate mandates has increased as the number of affiliates has grown around the world. Entire sectors of many economies are dominated by foreign companies. As a result of globalization, managers may find themselves increasingly searching for international opportunities within foreign companies. The mandates they are to successfully pursue, as considered in the 3M Scotch Brite case, will depend in large part on the level of skill and competencies they display.

The Importance of Affiliate Depth and Competence.   There is always danger when recommending strategic initiatives to affiliates. If handled badly they can seriously undermine the affiliate's performance and can easily cause a quick exit for both the affiliate and the affiliate general manager. For example, affiliates are unlikely to be successful making a major acquisition without its parent's approval. The reality is that in some areas of activity, affiliate initiative is more acceptable than in others. Every company is different, of course, but if an affiliate wants to understand when to take strategic initiatives and when to wait for direction, the diagram in Exhibit 9–9 may help.

What the diagram suggests is that affiliates should be careful about taking initiatives. First, they should assess their own capability in the area in question; then they should assess the parent's capability. As a rule, the parent's competence to act in the affiliate's market will depend on whether the affiliate's market is significantly different from what the parent is used to (i.e., high localization pressures). If it is, and if the affiliate has a good depth of knowledge in the area, it should provide strategic leadership. If neither the parent nor the affiliate has the necessary competence, the company should either get out of the segment or the affiliate should try to build capability, perhaps by alliance or acquisition. In product areas where globalization potential prevails, parent company expertise will be relevant in the affiliate's market. When the affiliate's technological and market knowledge is low relative to the parent's—for example, in conditions of rationalization—the affiliate should simply follow parent company direction. However, when the affiliate's competence is also high—i.e., in conditions of product mandate—the affiliate should try to influence parent strategy.

Affiliate managers, whether taking strategic initiative or following parent instructions, absolutely have to be well plugged in at headquarters. It is not a good idea to presume the competence level of the parent in a given product area. One has to know. At the same time, it is not a good idea to make an acquisition or take a strategic initiative without prior parent approval. Taking initiative is not the same as declaring independence. It is interdependence that is needed, and interdependence requires a measure of integration and working together. Taking the initiative in an interdependent relationship means bringing ideas and plans to the

---

EXHIBIT 9–9   Affiliate Competence and Affiliate Initiative

	Low Affiliate Capability	*High Affiliate Capability*
High localization pressures	Form alliances or Make acquisitions	Take strategic initiative
High globalization pressures	Follow parent instructions	Influence parent strategies

Source: This diagram is adapted from a diagram in Bartlett and Ghoshal's "Tap Your Affiliates for Global Reach."

key management committees and championing them. Success is achieved through the quality of the ideas and through the competence with which they are expressed, but also through the preconditioning of other executives present. That is why it is essential for affiliate managers to be well plugged in at headquarters. They need to understand the mind-set of the other executives and they need opportunities to influence it.

Challenges with Developing Transnational Structures.   Managing under multiple mandates is difficult. Most managers want clarity and exactness in roles and measurements. For example, take the challenge of managing in ABB Asea Brown Boveri. ABB Asea Brown Boveri is jointly owned by ABB AB of Sweden and ABB AG of Switzerland. In 1999, ABB Asea Brown Boveri included nearly 1,000 companies and affiliates in more than 140 countries. The companies competed in the power generation, transmission, and distribution industries as well as industrial engineering and rail transportation. Each of ABB Asea Brown Boveri's business area managers acts in many ways like an air traffic controller. They know where they want the businesses to go, they can set the flight plans, but the country managers ultimately act as pilots. Some may deviate from the plan; some may not be listening. It is not a job for the fainthearted. To run smoothly, the transnational organization requires managers to work toward the benefit of the corporation as a whole. At a time when many companies are shedding employees, it is often difficult to ask employees to think first of the corporation. Transnational companies that concurrently pursue global efficiencies and local responsiveness risk crossing signals and doing neither well. Affiliates remain suspicious of each other, and many product managers, despite pleas to think globally, continue to favor home country employees and markets. As a result, the transition to a transnational organization is inherently bumpy.

Because of the difficulties of effective implementation, the transnational structure has been proposed as more of an idealized form than a widespread reality. The problem is ultimately one of definition. The transnational structure theoretically achieves the optimal blend of global efficiency and local responsiveness. But these descriptive statements do not constitute a definition of the transnational structure. How does a firm know when it has one? For some, the presence of a shared responsibility matrix structure is the best evidence. In such a structure, geographic areas and product divisions share responsibility for affiliate decisions. The idea is that by sharing the responsibility one forces a constructive dialogue through which the best decision emerges. In this sense, the best decision is one that balances the need for local adaptation with the need for global efficiency. Since the optimal balance is subjective and constantly shifting, it is difficult for a firm to know whether it has achieved it regardless of the structure it follows. Furthermore, people's egos sometimes get in the way, and the matrix structure often fails to achieve its purpose. It is entirely possible to have a transnational perspective without a matrix structure. One simply finds a way to put the matrix mentality into the heads of country managers, or of product division managers as the case may be. Figuring out how to make a transnational structure work may be one of the biggest managerial challenges of the early 21st century.

What is clear from these characteristics is that they are more about managerial attitude than about organization structure. That is why the transnational organization is an idealized form. However, what it stands for is important to companies anxious to hold on to good people throughout the world. Without good people, it is difficult for any organization to learn about critical commercial information elsewhere in the world and remain competitive. Without an interesting role or mandate for the affiliate, it is difficult to hold onto good talent there, and the company grows increasingly dependent on culturally bound head office management. When this occurs, the ability of the company to learn and adapt is impaired. In some industries this is a dangerous state of affairs given that technology generation has become a truly global phenomenon. The transnational approach is really about learning. It is about raising the awareness level of key executives worldwide about the corporate mission, and providing them an ongoing opportunity to influence it. It is much more about style, attitude, and mind-set than it is about formal organization structure.

The Seamless Organization

A driving goal of an increasing number of companies is the development of a seamless organization. Formal structures are the antithesis of seamlessness. Seamlessness is built on the notion of destroying barriers inside and outside the organization. Formal structures acknowledge and promote barriers between affiliates and headquarters, between affiliates and affiliates, and between the company and suppliers and customers. These barriers prevent learning, produce inefficiencies, and blunt responsiveness. Increasingly, companies are struggling to tear down these barriers to maximize ultimate value for the customer, while at the same time promoting an organizational context that engenders commitment and hard work among employees.[7]

Teams are the primary unit of analysis in the seamless organization. Teams involve groups of individuals who are brought together to achieve a common objective. Teams can also involve outsiders such as buyers and suppliers. For example, Boeing spent several years working with a consortium of its largest airline customers in designing its new 777 aircraft. Airline personnel became fully involved in developing the final configuration of the aircraft. At one point, United Airlines had upward of 500 people working with Boeing on 777 design issues. This involvement improved the overall quality of the final aircraft and engendered a much greater commitment of the airline companies to the 777 specifically and Boeing more generally. Other companies that have exerted enormous efforts on developing seamless interactions with customers include FedEx (through global tracking), EDS (through on-site management of computer systems), and Andersen Consulting (through its systems integration work and management consulting).

Virtually every major automobile assembler has identified a set of key suppliers that are included in design, scheduling, and quality decisions. Wal-Mart, the world's largest retailer, uses its own satellite system to provide key suppliers around the world with sales and inventory information for each Wal-Mart distribution center and store. The system has shifted inventory management (and costs) to suppliers while eliminating the need for expensive sales representatives. In China, ARCO and its joint venture partner Nan Hai West have worked closely with a huge consortium of engineering companies, steel mills, transportation and shipping companies, and marine construction companies (including 30 support boats) to lay an 880-km-long underwater natural gas pipeline from a field in the South

---

[7]The notion of ultimate value was championed by Richard D'Aveni, *Hyper-Competition: Managing the Dynamics of Strategic Maneuvering* (New York: The Free Press, 1994).

China Sea to Hong Kong. The $560 million pipeline was finished ahead of schedule (mid-1995) and on budget because the companies were able to erase barriers and work as a seamless team toward a common goal.

One of the new themes in international business strategy is the use of "clusters" of companies. Clusters are geographic concentrations of companies that include an interconnected network of suppliers, buyers, and competitors.[8] Clusters incubate new start-ups and form the basis for intense competition between companies producing similar products or supplying comparable services. For example, Italy has a powerful cluster around footwear, Venezuela has a thriving cut flower cluster, and Hong Kong has a booming cluster around apparel manufacturing. Each of these clusters includes a wide array of suppliers (with their own clusters). Geographic proximity and common purpose create webs of formal and informal alliances. Proximity facilitates relationship building, improves information gathering, and smoothes decision making. In many cases it is difficult to know where the one company ends and another company begins.

Seamless organizations are also preoccupied with erasing boundaries inside the company. Much of the re-engineering and downsizing efforts of the 1990s have been devoted to delaying management, cutting bureaucracy, and getting the people who need to talk to each other together. Teams have become a common mechanism used by companies to link people from different divisions, functions and geographies. As such, internal teams represent a type of organizational structure that may replace the more rigid boxes and lines in standard organization charts. In an era of globalization and accelerating technological change, teams can help speed organizational adaptation and improve the overall quality of decisions. Linking people with multiple backgrounds promotes an atmosphere where new ideas can emerge and where arrogance is reduced.

Technologies such as Lotus Notes, e-mail, and videoconferencing enable global teams to keep in close contract. Teams may stay intact for weeks or years. Members may come and go and the team's objectives may evolve. While the fluidity and flexibility of teams may be a great strength in terms of responsiveness, they are also troubling to some individuals who crave structure and clarity. Seamless organizations draw heavily on personal relationships and the desire and ability of individuals to work effectively together. The human element of effective teamwork is discussed in greater detail in Chapter 10.

Summary

This chapter has focused on the challenges and opportunities associated with the international organization of activities. Given the preponderance of globalization pressures, the traditional area division structure with its high autonomy and multidomestic focus is not likely to endure unscathed. MNCs will increasingly abandon country-focused structures in favor of either the global product or transnational structures. The transition is not likely to be without pain. Moving to a more global product structure means imposing corporate will on hitherto autonomous affiliates. It means changing affiliate mandates and reducing strategic independence. There are going to be a lot of organizational wrecks on the shoals of globalization.

---

[8]For a broader discussion of clusters, see M. Porter, "Clusters and the New Economics of Competition," *Harvard Business Review,* November-December 1998, pp. 77–90.

The reality is that almost every company customizes its structure in some way by using a combination of tools to organize and control activities. Few companies are identical to the structures described in this chapter. Most rely on mixed structures that are influenced by idiosyncratic histories and the personalities of key decision makers. Despite these differences, however, competitive advantage may well be achieved by those companies that can reinvent themselves by empowering those who need power and by rationalizing those who do not. Appropriate structures are ultimately determined by understanding the tasks that need to be done both today and tomorrow. As environmental change accelerates, speed and flexibility will undoubtably be more valuable over the next decade than size and past successes.

Supplementary Reading

Bartlett, Christopher A., and Sumantra Ghoshal. "Tap Your Subsidiaries for Global Reach." *Harvard Business Review,* November-December 1986.

———. "Organizing for Worldwide Effectiveness: The Transnational Solution." *California Management Review,* Fall 1988.

———. *Managing Across Borders—The Transnational Solution.* Boston: Harvard Business School Press, 1989.

Birkinshaw, Julian, and Neil Hood. "An Empirical Study of Development Processes in Foreign-Owned Subsidiaries in Canada and Scotland." *Management International Review,* Vol. 37, No. 4, 1997, pp. 339–64.

Birkinshaw, Julian, and Nick Fry. "Subsidiary Initiatives to Develop New Markets." *Sloan Management Review,* Vol. 39, No. 3, pp. 51–61.

Crookell, Harold. "Managing Canadian Affiliates in a Free Trade Environment." *Sloan Management Review,* Fall 1987.

D'Aveni, Richard. *Hyper-Competition: Managing the Dynamics of Strategic Maneuvering.* New York: The Free Press, 1994.

Egelhoff, William G. "Strategy and Structure in Multinational Corporations: A Revision of the Stopford and Wells Model." *Strategic Management Journal,* January-February 1988.

Hamel, Gary, and C. K. Prahalad. *Competing for the Future.* Boston: Harvard Business School Press, 1994.

Hedlund, Gunnar. "The Hypermodern MNC—A Heterarchy?" *Human Resource Management,* Spring 1986 (Vol. 25, No. 1).

Morrison, Allen, David Ricks and Kendall Roth. "Globalization Versus Regionalization: Which Way for the Multinational?" *Organizational Dynamics,* Winter 1991.

Porter, Michael. "Changing Patterns of International Competition." *California Management Review,* 1986 (Vol. 28, pp. 9–40).

———. "Clusters and the New Economics of Competition." *Harvard Business Review,* November-December, 1998, pp. 77–90.

Prahalad, C. K., and Yves Doz. *The Multinational Mission: Balancing Local Demands and Global Vision.* New York: The Free Press, 1987.

Roth, K., and A. J. Morrison. "Implementing Global Strategy: Global Affiliate Mandates." *Journal of International Business Studies,* 1992 (Vol. 23, No. 4).

Taggart, James. "Strategy Shifts in MNC Subsidiaries." *Strategic Management Journal,* Vol. 19, No. 7, 1998, pp. 663–81.

1997 World Investment Report: Transnational Corporations, Market Structure and Competition Policy. New York: United Nations.

10 THE EVOLVING MULTINATIONAL

Introduction

A number of chapters in this book have discussed specific forms of foreign market entry, such as managing exports and imports, licensing, and joint ventures. Each of these might be the best way to enter a specific foreign market at a particular time. Yet it is important to recognize that most multinationals do not make just *one* foreign entry, but typically make a *series* of foreign entries over the course of years. While it is important to understand the advantages and challenges of any particular entry, we should also bear in mind the overall development of the multinational firm.

The previous chapter identified some challenges of organizing and managing the MNC. The transnational model was suggested as a way for MNCs to gain global integration as well as local responsiveness. This model argued that multinational firms should be thought of as multicentered organizational forms, with subsidiaries playing different roles within a larger network structure. By adopting an internally differentiated form, rather than insisting on identical roles for each foreign subsidiary, the MNC can tap the distinctive capabilities of each subsidiary and optimize its worldwide operations. Such MNCs are also better positioned to benefit from network flexibility, as they can shift production and sourcing among subsidiaries as various external conditions—competitive, financial, or regulatory—change.

Many management experts agree on the desirability of the transnational model, but there is much less agreement about how MNCs can achieve this differentiated form. After all, very few MNCs begin as complex, internally differentiated organizations. Most begin in a single country, and establish subsidiaries in foreign countries over many years. Once established, these foreign subsidiaries usually begin operation in just one or a few lines of business, and over time take on more lines of business. Furthermore, each line of business may begin by performing a restricted set of functions, such as sales or final assembly, and

---

This chapter was prepared by Philip M. Rosenzweig.

take on added responsibilities over time. It is by evolving along each of these three dimensions—a *geographic dimension,* a *line of business dimension,* and a *functional dimension*—that MNCs achieve a complex and internally differentiated form. The result is an MNC with subsidiaries in a number of foreign markets, each of which is active in a somewhat different mix of businesses, and each of which plays a somewhat different role, ranging from a minor one to a role of worldwide strategic leadership.

This chapter focuses on the evolution of MNCs. We take a broader look at the firm's trajectory, looking not only at entry into new geographic markets but also into new lines of business and functions performed by each line of business. The first part of the chapter examines evolution along these three dimensions, offering insights into some of the factors that facilitate or impede evolution. The second part discusses the ways in which evolution along these dimensions is integrated, with knowledge leveraged so that the MNC can evolve in an efficient manner, minimizing duplication and performing activities in an optimal manner. We take the view that the ability to leverage knowledge among MNC dimensions is central to their effective management.

Dimensions of Evolution

Geographic Expansion

In recent years we have begun to see examples of firms that are "born multinational"—that from their birth have productive operations in more than one country. But these firms are a distinct minority. The great majority of MNCs begin in a home country and expand abroad. The sequence by which firms expand from their home country into foreign markets is influenced by several factors, including *geographic proximity, cultural similarity,* and *similarity in economic development.*

Geographic Proximity.   The first location for foreign direct investment is often a neighboring country. Entering a neighbor country is a natural first step, as the firm can more easily identify market opportunities and gather vital information about competitive reactions and government policies in a nearby country than in a distant one. Firms may also prefer to enter neighboring countries first, as the cost of communicating with the foreign subsidiary is lower. Once the firm has expanded into nearby countries, it may then move sequentially into countries that are farther away, minimizing the incremental distance of each move. Over time, through this process of entry based on geographic proximity, the firm can achieve a broad international position.

Cultural Similarity.   The sequence of geographic expansion may also reflect cultural similarity between the MNC's home country and the host country. Success in a foreign country requires an understanding of local customs and consumer habits: effective communication with customers, suppliers, and employees; and good relations with governmental bodies. For all these reasons, firms often prefer to enter countries that are relatively similar in culture, i.e., where the "psychic distance" is low. As they gain experience in countries that are relatively similar to their own, MNCs learn how to manage outside their home country and may subsequently enter countries that are progressively less similar. Eventually they may be able to enter countries that are at a considerable "psychic distance" from their country of origin.

Similarity in Economic Development.   The level of host country economic development also affects the choice of which markets to enter. MNCs are often attracted to foreign markets where consumer buying habits and levels of disposable income are similar to those of home market consumers. In such markets, the MNC's product formulation and its marketing approach may require only modest adaptation. As the MNC learns how to compete effectively in foreign markets of similar economic standing, it develops capabilities that allow it to enter increasingly different foreign markets.

Although they are often studied separately, *geographic proximity, cultural similarity,* and *similarity in economic development* are all examples of organizational learning and capability development. In each instance, firms first expand into countries where the capabilities developed in their home market are most likely to be successful, but defer entry into countries where success is less likely. Accumulating experience in initial foreign markets enables the firm to develop new capabilities, which allow it to expand into countries that are more distant and less similar. MNC geographic expansion is not merely the sequential exploitation of *existing* capabilities in markets that are progressively farther from home, but the development of new capabilities as well.

An example of geographic expansion through capability development is provided by Colgate-Palmolive, the American consumer products firm, which was founded in the 19th century and slowly developed into a far-flung MNC. Colgate-Palmolive's first foreign market entry was to Canada, a neighboring country that was similar to the United States both culturally and in economic development. By the 1940s, Colgate-Palmolive had established subsidiaries in 20 countries, virtually all of which were either geographically close to the United States (Canada and Mexico), shared an Anglo-Saxon culture and English language (Canada, United Kingdom, Australia, and New Zealand), or were similar to the United States in economic development (Canada, several countries in western Europe, Scandinavia, Australia, and New Zealand). By restricting itself to these countries, Colgate-Palmolive needed to make only modest adaptations in product formulation and in its marketing approach; it refrained from entering countries where it would have faced sharp differences in culture and economic development.

Based on its experiences in these initial 20 countries, Colgate-Palmolive was later able to enter more-distant markets. In the 1950s and 1960s it expanded into Central America, which was geographically close to the United States but less similar in culture or economic development. More recently, the firm expanded to several Asian and African nations, as well as to newly opened markets in eastern Europe—countries that were far from the United States, culturally dissimilar, and often sharply different in economic development. By the mid-1990s, Colgate-Palmolive managed subsidiaries in 75 countries on six continents. Its broad geographic position had not been achieved in one or even a few steps, but was the result of a gradual process of geographic expansion.

Colgate-Palmolive's pattern of incremental geographic expansion is typical of older MNCs, which evolved over the course of many years. Today's younger MNCs, including firms such as Finland's Nokia and Germany's SAP, cannot afford to evolve over decades, but must establish a presence in multiple countries in a short period of time. Even so, the *sequence* of geographic expansion is similar: from closer and more similar to farther away and less similar. Of course, there has also been a shift in the relative importance of the three factors. As the challenge of managing across long distances has declined given the enormous improvements in communication and transportation, it has become less critical for firms to follow strictly a pattern of geographic proximity. Moreover, the need to minimize "psychic distance" may also be lower than in decades past, as business practices continue to converge and as more people around the world can communicate in a common business language—English. As a consequence, firms expanding abroad in the 1990s may be less concerned with minimizing geographic distance and "psychic distance," and may more readily enter foreign markets based on economic criteria such as similar levels of economic development.

Line of Business Diversification

Some MNCs are single-business firms, but most compete in multiple lines of business. Even so, their foreign subsidiaries often begin by competing in one or a few of the parent's lines of business, over time adding more lines of business, and eventually operating in many or all of the parent's businesses. For many MNCs, *line of business diversification* represents a second dimension of evolution. Interestingly, there has been relatively little research into line of business diversification within foreign subsidiaries. It has been more common to speak of "the country subsidiary" as if it were monolithic, yet it is clear that most MNCs ramp up their activities over time, rather than entering in all lines of business at once.

How do foreign subsidiaries add lines of business? A recent study of Japanese electronics firms in the United States from 1976 to 1989 showed a sequential pattern of entry, beginning with lines of business that enjoyed the greatest advantage over local firms. By choosing their strongest line of business, these firms offset the disadvantages due to lack of familiarity with the local market and its competitive environment. As the subsidiary gained experience in doing business locally, it added lines of business that offered it a lower competitive advantage. Finally, when it learned to compete effectively in the local environment, it could add lines of business that offered little or no competitive advantage, but that sought to learn from technologically superior U.S. firms. Several subsidiaries of Japanese electronics firms added lines of business in precisely this fashion, adding new lines of business only when confident of success. This sequence is illustrated in Exhibit 10–1.

Liability of Foreignness.   A good example of sequential line of business entry is provided by Sony Corporation. Sony first entered the United States in 1972 with a television assembly plant in San Diego, California. For Sony, televisions represented a core line of business, in which it enjoyed a strong competitive advantage over U.S. firms. Two years later it entered a second line of business, audio equipment, and shortly thereafter in a third, magnetic tape. In both of these, as well, Sony had a strong advantage over local firms. Sony's diversification resumed in the mid-1980s when a shift in the yen-dollar exchange rate stimulated further foreign investment. At that time, with a strong U.S. country organization and substantial experience, Sony entered lines of business with a different motivation. Rather than exploit its existing advantages, it now entered in businesses where it sought to tap U.S.

EXHIBIT 10–1   Typical Pattern of Line of Business Diversification

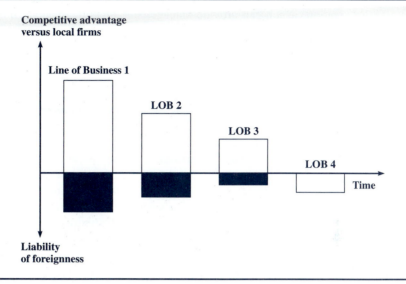

technological leadership, such as data storage systems and personal telecommunications. Related to entry by line of business is the choice of entry mode, where once again Sony's experience was consistent with existing theory. At first Sony relied on small-scale green-field investments as a way to ensure careful replication of its home country advantage; later, as it gained confidence in its ability to manage in the United States and as it sought to capture host country capabilities, it began to make acquisitions.

This pattern of incremental evolution may appear typical of Japanese firms, which are often thought to take a gradual and long-term perspective. Recent evidence, however, has shown that an evolutionary approach to the addition of lines of business describes the behavior of many MNCs, not just Japanese MNCs. Data from European electronics firms entering the United States show largely the same pattern. Some European chemicals firms also exhibit a sequential approach to line of business entry, as exemplified by the French firm Rhône-Poulenc, which first entered the United States in areas of traditional strength such as agrochemicals and basic chemicals, and later acquired positions in surfactants and pharmaceuticals to tap local expertise and leverage it around the world.

Of course, line of business diversification does not happen automatically. It's driven by a process of evaluation, action, monitoring, and further action. At each step, the firm determines if the benefits of adding new lines of business are sufficient to offset disadvantages faced in the local market. Over time, as local expertise is accumulated and the subsidiary offers a strong infrastructure for country management, the firm may become increasingly confident of its ability to add new lines of business. With each successive entry the firm adds to its resources: it develops a reputation as a good employer and as a good customer for local suppliers, it learns about local regulations, and in general it accumulates capabilities that make it possible for the firm to enter additional lines of business. Entry into these later lines of business might only be possible because of a strong country organization, which can provide management support, financial infrastructure, and technical expertise to new lines of business.

Functional Migration

A third dimension of evolution, called functional migration, takes place within each line of business. Functional migration speaks to the development of activities performed by lines of business within a country. The seminal work on internationalization by Johanson and Vahlne showed that Swedish MNCs tended first to export to foreign markets, then to set up foreign sales subsidiaries to manage these imports, and eventually to establish wholly owned subsidiaries. Once established, lines of business continued to perform functions in their home country that lent themselves to economies of scale, such as R&D, product design, and strategic leadership. They performed in the host country only those functions that called for local knowledge, typically marketing and distribution. Over time, however, the subsidiary may take on additional functions, including assembly, local design, and procurement. In some instances, when the subsidiary develops worldwide expertise in the line of business, it might take on the role of business planning and even strategic leadership. In other instances, subsidiaries establish particular functions that serve as "centers of excellence" for the MNC. This common sequence of functional migration is depicted in Exhibit 10–2.

The process of functional migration is seen most clearly in greenfield investments, where subsidiaries begin with a limited number of functions and add new ones over time. Entry through acquisition quite naturally exhibits a different pattern. If the MNC acquires a local firm that is vertically integrated, it often gains all functions in a single step. Very often, however, MNCs enter a foreign market by acquiring a local company that performs some but not all functions. For example, some MNCs acquire local firms in order to gain an established distribution network through which they can sell imported products. Initial functions are acquired rather than set up from scratch, but subsequent functions—including assembly and product design—are added over time. The subsidiary still migrates from left to right in Exhibit 10–2, but begins somewhere along the continuum rather than at the extreme left. In other instances, firms enter a foreign market with a greenfield investment, then add functions through the acquisition of local firms. Examples include the acquisition of manufacturing capacity (especially attractive when the industry has considerable excess capacity and building a new plant makes little sense) or the acquisition of a local R&D lab. Thus, acquisitions may differ from greenfield investments in that they accelerate functional migration, yet they typically do not alter the basic sequence.

As with line of business diversification, functional migration depends on an intrafirm decision process. To illustrate, consider the functional migration of Sony's television line of business in the United States. Until 1972, Sony wanted all manufacturing to take place in Japan; no functions were performed in the United States aside from sales and marketing. What triggered a change was the charge of dumping, which led Sony's CEO, Akio Morita, to consider direct investment in the United States. The combination of internal assessments and external forces led to the decision to invest in the United States initially at a low level of functionality, performing only final assembly. Technical knowledge, including both process know-how and product know-how, was transferred by expatriates from Sony's television division in Japan to San Diego, where an identical assembly process

---

Exhibit 10–2 Typical Pattern of Functional Migration

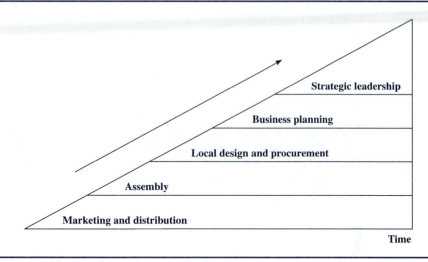

---

was built. In addition to receiving financial resources and technical and managerial know-how from its Japanese parent, the new subsidiary secured resources locally, leasing factory space, hiring local employees, and purchasing some inputs and equipment locally. By combining resources from its parent with resources secured locally, the San Diego plant began to perform its initial functions, assembling kits into working televisions. The plant was carefully monitored by managers in Japan, who wanted to know whether American workers could achieve satisfactory performance. Once Sony management was satisfied with the quality of final assembly in its U.S. plant, it began to add more functions. Soon CRT manufacturing was shifted to the United States in light of the expense and breakage associated with transpacific shipment of glass tubes. In time, additional functions were performed, including local sourcing of inputs, additional product design, and, finally, 25 years after first entry, strategic leadership for the television line of business in North America.

Migrating to higher levels of functionality is not an easy matter. In fact, the obstacles shift over time. At early steps of evolution, which usually means the location of assembly or manufacturing activities in the new subsidiary, the most important impediments involve the effective transfer of technical know-how and the ability to secure resources locally. Later stages encounter very different—and sometimes more severe—obstacles, as the objective is not merely to *replicate* existing functions in a foreign market, but to *shift* functions from the home country to a foreign subsidiary. Such a shift may trigger resistance from home country managers, making evolution to higher functions a very difficult matter.

MNC Evolution as an Integrated Process

So far we've examined three separate dimensions of evolution. We described the progression of an MNC from a home-based firm to one that is active in multiple countries, in each country active in multiple lines of business, and within each line of business moving from limited functionality to higher levels of functionality.

Of course, the hallmark of an MNC is that its dimensions are *not* separate and unrelated, but *interconnected.* As noted by Doz and Prahalad, the ability to leverage knowledge across and among dimensions is precisely what gives MNCs their most compelling advantage. Evolution along one dimension is not independent of evolution along other dimensions, but both affects and is affected by activities elsewhere. In the following sections, we identify three different ways that MNC evolution is integrated across dimensions.

Accelerated Evolution

We noted above that the accumulation of knowledge allows MNCs to evolve along each of three dimensions. Learning about doing business in foreign countries helps further geographic expansion, learning about a given host country enables a sequential line of business addition in that country, and so forth. Of course, experience gained by a line of business in one country not only leads to greater knowledge of *that* country, it can also lead to greater knowledge of the line of business, which can be leveraged *across* countries to speed up the entry of that business in other countries. In this way, leveraging knowledge across dimensions results in evolution that is faster and more extensive at any point in time than it would otherwise have been.

Again Sony provides an example. As described above, Sony first set up a television assembly plant in the United States in 1972, then entered into additional lines of business over the next few years. In 1974, Sony set up a television assembly plant in Europe, and soon entered into audio equipment. Entry in Europe in audio equipment was facilitated by two kinds of knowledge accumulation: greater expertise about Europe gained through the initial entry to Europe in televisions, and also knowledge about audio products that was transferred from the U.S. operation to the new plant in Europe. By leveraging lines of business knowledge across countries, Sony more efficiently and more successfully added a new line of business in Europe.

Functional migration can also be accelerated by knowledge of particular functions accumulated across lines of business in the same country. For instance, it may be difficult for the first line of business in a country to undertake a new function, such as local parts procurement, product design, or strategic planning. Once the first line of business has successfully added that function, its experience can be leveraged to other lines of business in the same country, helping speed up their migration to the same level of functionality. Similarly, functional knowledge can be leveraged across countries to accelerate functional migration elsewhere in the world.

Punctuated Evolution

Leveraging knowledge among dimensions of an MNC can also lead to evolution that is discontinuous, or that skips steps. We call this *punctuated evolution.* Punctuated evolution can take place along each of the three dimensions. The notion is always the same: by identifying and taking advantage of economies of scale and scope, firms may be able to share capabilities across dimensions, obviating the need to perform every step. The result is a more efficient evolution, as the firm maximizes the salutary effects of scale and scope economies.

Assume that a line of business within a subsidiary performs a variety of functions. If a new line of business is added, that line of business may perform its own functions or it may make use of functions already performed by existing lines of business. For example, if the first line of business develops an effective procurement system, or establishes a strong treasury and legal department, and if these functions offer economies of scope, lines of businesses added subsequently may avail themselves of these functions and avoid having to perform them. These lines of business may still add functions in the sequence shown in Exhibit 10–2, but may be able to skip certain ones.

MNCs may also be able to share functions across countries within a single line of business. For instance, if one line of business performs manufacturing at a sufficient capacity to serve a neighboring country as well, the line of business in the neighboring country may not need to perform any manufacturing. Similarly, the presence of a strong R&D lab in one country may obviate the need for a subsidiary in another country to perform its own R&D. In each instance, scale economies associated with the function in one country may render unnecessary the performance of that function in another country. These latter lines of business may well exhibit a sequence of functional migration similar to that shown in Exhibit 10–2, but will skip functions where they are more efficiently performed elsewhere.

If *all* functions in a given line of business offer economies of scale, it might be unnecessary to perform any functions of that line of business in a second country. In that event, there would be no need to add that line of business in a second country, since the second country could be served by the first for that line of business. If we extend this logic one step further, it could be that *all* lines of business can serve a neighboring country, making it unnecessary to establish a subsidiary in that country at all. Examples of this kind are increasingly common in the European Union, where the establishment of a subsidiary in one EU country may enable a firm to operate in other EU countries without setting up separate subsidiaries. For instance, the Turkish bank, Finansbank, needed to enter only one EU country—the Netherlands—to be able to conduct banking in all EU countries. Other examples are found in Latin America or in Asia, where a mature subsidiary in one country is considered adequate to handle all or virtually all activities in an adjacent market.

By identifying and taking advantage of economies of scale and scope, MNCs may evolve in a discontinuous manner, skipping functions in given lines of business, skipping lines of business in some countries, or even deciding not to enter particular countries at all. MNCs that evolve in a punctuated manner will exhibit a pattern of development that is irregular and asymmetrical, but that achieves a minimum of duplication and therefore secures a greater level of efficiency.

Reverse Evolution

In recent years, as global competition has intensified due to a convergence of consumer demand, increasing opportunities for economies of scale and scope, and rising levels of industrialization around the world, many MNCs have begun to restructure their worldwide operations. In some instances they have consolidated existing functions and lines of business, and in other instances have shut down entire subsidiaries. The effect has been *reverse evolution.*

When might reverse evolution be most common? Firm factors and industry factors are both likely to be important. Regarding firm factors, the potential for efficiencies through global restructuring might be most common in MNCs that expanded many years ago. Because close coordination of foreign subsidiaries was relatively difficult, older MNCs were frequently organized on a country-by-country basis and pursued a multidomestic strategy. These MNCs often performed *all* functions in each line of business, resulting in a high level of duplication among countries. Recently, because of enhanced global communications and transportation, opportunities have arisen to capture greater scale and scope economies, leading to a consolidation of functions among lines of business, as well as a consolidation of lines of business among country subsidiaries. A prime example of this consolidation is Matsushita in Europe. Matsushita had evolved in Europe on a country-by-country basis, yet by the mid-1990s it found its organization to be inefficient; it needed to adopt a pan-regional approach. The pressure for restructuring is also likely to be greater in global industries, where competition on a global scale imposes an imperative for worldwide efficiency. As firms in an industry begin to manage their activities on a worldwide basis, other firms will face an imperative to do likewise.

Taking these points together, MNCs that are most likely to restructure their activities are those that expanded abroad long ago and now find themselves in highly global industries. As an example consider IBM, the computer giant that expanded abroad long ago. When IBM set up foreign subsidiaries in many South American countries, these subsidiaries performed a full set of functions. Recently, in response to intense pressures to improve efficiency and cut costs, IBM consolidated its South American activities into three regions—Brazil; the Andean region (Venezuela, Colombia, Ecuador, Peru, and Bolivia); and southern cone (Argentina, Paraguay, Uruguay, and Chile). In the latter two regions, where several country subsidiaries were consolidated into a single entity and managed jointly, a number of functions were located in a single country and discontinued in the others. In the Andean region, for instance, human resource management was centralized in Peru; the HR function in other Andean countries was eliminated. The subsidiaries in the other Andean nations, which had performed all functions, now experienced the elimination of several functions.

Reverse evolution is difficult, as there is natural resistance within the firm to restructuring and consolidation, yet the end result is similar to that of punctuated evolution: an asymmetrical mix of functions in each line of business, a varying set of lines of business in each country, and even an irregular set of subsidiaries around the world. The exact profile of an MNC's activities will, of course, be shaped by the most efficient use of scale and scope economies. Further, as with accelerated evolution and punctuated evolution, there are clear performance implications of reverse evolution: MNCs that can identify potential economies of scale and scope, and that can restructure their activities swiftly and efficiently, will be in a better position to compete on a global basis than those that evolved in a graduated fashion but now fail to undertake such restructuring.

Summary

Multinational firms are increasingly viewed as multicentered and internally differentiated firms, yet the process by which firms achieve this complex form has not received much attention. This chapter has viewed MNC evolution as consisting of three separate dimensions: *geographic expansion, line-of-business diversification, and functional migration.* Evolution along each dimension takes place through a process of knowledge development. We have also maintained that these three dimensions are not separate and independent, but can affect each other. In fact, it is by leveraging knowledge among dimensions that MNCs avoid unnecessary duplication and achieve a profile of internal differentiation and asymmetry. By identifying opportunities for scale and scope economies, and by actively leveraging knowledge across dimensions, MNCs can evolve toward an optimal configuration. While it is important to understand the nuances of particular approaches to market entry, it is also vital that we take a holistic perspective and seek to manage the entire worldwide network, sharing functions among some lines of business, or serving some national markets from adjacent countries.

The importance of these topics is likely to grow given the ongoing globalization of economic activity. Firms that expanded abroad early in the century could afford to evolve incrementally over several decades. Competitive pressures did not compel them to accelerate their evolution; rather, they could watch the progress of overseas subsidiaries and undertake further evolution when they were ready. By contrast, firms that expanded abroad in recent decades have had to move more aggressively to build a differentiated network, seeking the benefits of scale and global integration in years rather than decades. Today the pressure is greater than ever for firms to achieve a differentiated and mature global position in a short time. It has become important for firms to think clearly about the distinct dimensions of evolution, about the impediments faced on each dimension, and about ways to leverage learning across dimensions.

Supplementary Reading

Bartlett, Christopher A., and Sumantra Ghoshal. *Managing Across Borders: The Transnational Solution.* Boston: Harvard Business School Press, 1989.

Birkinshaw, Julian. "Approaching Heterarchy: A Review of the Literature on Multinational Strategy and Structure." *Advances in International Comparative Management,* Vol. 9, 1994, pp. 111–44.

Chang, Sea-Jin. "International Expansion Strategy of Japanese Firms: Capability Building Through Sequential Entry." *Academy of Management Journal,* 1995, pp. 383–407.

Chang, Sea-Jin, and Philip M. Rosenzweig. "Functional and Line of Business Evolution Processes in MNC Subsidiaries: Sony in the USA, 1972–1995." In *Multinational Corporate Evolution and Subsidiary Development,* Julian Birkinshaw and Neil Hood (eds). London, Great Britain: Macmillan Press Ltd., 1998.

Doz, Yves L., and C. K. Prahalad. "Managing DMNCs: A Search for a New Paradigm." *Strategic Management Journal,* Vol. 12, 1991, pp. 145–64.

Johanson, Jan, and Jan-Erik Vahlne. "The Internationalization Process of the Firm: A Model of Knowledge Development and Increasing Foreign Market Commitments." *Journal of International Business Studies,* Vol. 8, 1977, pp. 23–32.

Kogut, Bruce, and Sea-Jin Chang. "Technological Capabilities and Japanese Foreign Direct Investment in the United States." *Review of Economics and Statistics,* Vol. 73, 1991, pp. 401–13.

Kogut, Bruce, and Udo Zander. "Knowledge of the Firm and the Evolutionary Theory of the Multinational Corporation." *Journal of International Business Studies,* Vol. 24, No. 4, 1993, pp. 625–45.

Malnight, Thomas W. "Globalization of an Ethnocentric Finn: An Evolutionary Perspective." *Strategic Management Journal,* Vol. 16, 1995, pp. 119–41.

Nelson, Richard R., and Sidney G. Winter. *An Evolutionary Theory of Economic Change.* Cambridge, MA: The Belknap Press of Harvard University Press, 1982.

11 THE GLOBAL MANAGER

This book is about how firms become and remain international in scope and how they come to grips with an increasingly competitive global environment. Firms often fail abroad, however, not because their strategy or structures necessarily were wrong, but because the operating plan may have been incomplete, or executives were not well prepared for their assignments. Failure may come when executives are sent overseas and are not able to understand the new culture or to function in their new environment. Someone has to implement, or oversee the implementation of, a strategy or plan. To do this means leaving headquarters and traveling to another country where it is necessary to work with people from another culture. In our experience, companies *and managers* often fail not because they had the wrong strategy, but because they were not capable of implementing it successfully. Preparation for these cross-cultural encounters is important, since the costs of failure can be high, either in terms of lost contracts and sales or in out-of-pocket costs like premature returns from long-term assignments.

International business and management are not impersonal, conceptual activities. People are required to put understanding into practice. For example, licensing agreements do not materialize from thin air and joint ventures do not spring into being unaided—managers make these arrangements happen. These agreements become reality because managers go to other countries to work out deals. The globalization phenomenon is not limited in impact to some impersonal entity called a corporation. It has an impact on managers—real people—in their daily lives. Expatriates employed in a foreign subsidiary will be working with host country nationals at many levels in the organization and, most likely, with people from government. Headquarters personnel will interact with local country managers and staff members from other cultures as headquarters and regional offices become more "international." They require new skills to cope with the demands globalization brings in order to be successful in their roles and careers.

This chapter was prepared by Henry W. Lane and Joseph J. DiStefano. It was adapted from Henry W. Lane, Joseph J. DiStefano, and Martha Maznevski, *International Management Behavior,* 3rd ed. (Cambridge, MA: Blackwell Publishers, 1996). It is published with permission of the authors. © 1997 Henry W. Lane, Joseph J. DiStefano, and Martha Maznevski. All rights reserved.

Some of the substantive issues facing managers in a diversified multinational corporation (DMNC) include:[1]

- Integrating large international acquisitions.
- Understanding the meaning of performance and accountability in a globally integrated system of product flows.
- Building and managing a worldwide logistics capability.
- Developing country-specific corporate strategies that take into account the political as well as economic imperatives.
- Forming and benefiting from collaborative arrangements around the world.
- Balancing the pressures for global integration and local demands.

Managers of the future will require knowledge of the type suggested but also an ability to take action. Although this was true in the past also, the knowledge base is now different and the skills required are dramatically different. What has changed? One of the most dramatic changes has been that now implementation takes place in many different cultures, often simultaneously. In these days of increased globalization even if one does not leave one's own country, it still will be highly likely that it will be necessary to work with someone from another culture.

The global manager will have to master more than concepts and theories; he or she will also have to command new skills. If one looks at the requirements for success in the global economy, it seems pretty clear that a global manager is going to have to have a repertoire comprising a comprehensive knowledge base and a well-developed set of relational and cross-cultural skills. It will include knowledge about business and technical matters, social, political and economic systems, and culture; an ability to define and solve problems in the face of uncertainty; implementation skills; and a keen sense of how and when previous experience is relevant in new cultural settings.

The purpose of this chapter is to identify and describe the skill set of the global manager. These include those skills necessary for possible international assignments. We realize that it is not possible to develop those skills by reading a chapter in a book, but we can challenge the readers to start thinking about where and how they will start acquiring these skills.

Skills of the Global Manager

What does the emergence of the term "global manager" really imply? In the broadest terms, it means reorganizing the way one thinks as a manager and as a student of management. As one executive put it, "To think globally really requires an alteration of our mind-set."[2] Thinking globally means *extending* concepts and models from one-to-one relationships (we to them) to holding multiple realities and relationships in one's head simultaneously, and *acting* skillfully on this more complex reality. The shift means that even if one has a regional

---

[1]C. K. Prahalad, "Globalization: The Intellectual and Managerial Challenges," *Human Resource Management,* Spring 1990, Vol. 29, No. 1, p. 29.

[2]Personal communication from Mr. Bernard Daniel, Secretary-General, Nestlé Vevey, Switzerland.

Exhibit 11–1   Executive Traits Now and in the Future[3]

Now	*The Future*
All knowing	Leader as learner
Domestic vision	Global vision
Predicts future from past	Intuits the future
Caring for individuals	Caring for institutions and individuals
Owns the vision	Facilitates vision of others
Uses power	Uses power and facilitation
Dictates goals and methods	Specifies processes
Alone at the top	Part of an executive team
Values order	Accepts paradox of order amidst chaos
Monolingual	Multicultural
Inspires the trust of boards, shareholders	Inspires the trust of owners, customers, and employees

responsibility, say, as marketing manager for Central and South America, it is likely that more will be required than an understanding of Latin cultures and a capacity to speak Spanish and Portuguese. One also may have to deal with R&D labs in Japan, Europe, and North America to provide them with customer information and to get updates on emerging new products. Similarly, the regional marketing manager may have to discuss product problems with manufacturers in Southeast Asia late at night, North American time, and then send a fax about the potential solution to an alternative supplier in eastern Europe.

Many of the requirements of a global manager were articulated at a symposium organized by the Board of Governors of the American Society for Training and Development. (See Exhibit 11–1.)

This list encompasses many of the particular skills required by global managers.[4] Reviewing a wide range of literature dealing with global strategy, global marketing, global operations management, and global human resource management, the authors identified a profile of effective global executives.[5]

1. Ability to develop and use global strategic skills.

2. Ability to manage change and transition.

3. Ability to manage cultural diversity.

4. Ability to design and function in flexible organization structures.

---

[3]Patricia A. Galagan, "Executive Development in a Changing World," *Training and Development Journal,* June 1990, pp. 23–41.

[4]Brenda McMillan, Joseph J. DiStefano, and James C. Rush, "Requisite Skills and Characteristics of Global Managers," Working Paper, National Centre for Management Research and Development, Western Business School, The University of Western Ontario, London, Canada N6A 3K7, 1991.

[5]Subsequent to our literature review and the publication of an earlier version of this chapter in *International Management Behavior,* 2nd ed. (Boston: PWS-Kent, 1992), Stephen Rhinesmith published a book, *A Manager's Guide to Globalization,* in which the chapter headings closely parallel the set of skills we elaborate below, giving further credence to their emerging importance.

5. Ability to work with others and in teams.
6. Ability to communicate.
7. Ability to learn and transfer knowledge in an organization.

To assist the reader in advancing his or her understanding of what the emerging world requires of global managers, each of these abilities is explored in the following sections. The development of these skills is a lifelong process, and it is unlikely that a single executive will master all of them.

Ability to Develop and Use Global Strategic Skills

Earlier chapters discussed the emergence of a new global economy. The result is a shift in the worldwide business base that is forcing managers and corporations to adjust and to shed their parochial views. Players in this new global environment will have a fast response capability, will be comfortable with cross-cultural influences, and will be entrepreneurial and flexible. Global managers will require a working knowledge of international relationships and foreign affairs, including global financial markets and exchange-rate movements.[6] These expanded business management skills will need to be coupled with global responsibilities to take advantage of manufacturing rationalization, "mass customization" of products, and low-cost, global sourcing.[7]

The global mind-set required by these new economic and competitive realities will be needed at all levels in the firm. Managers with this global perspective will need to strike a balance between national responsiveness and exploitation of global economies of scale. This is the vaunted ability to "think globally, but act locally."

Although the trend is toward standardization with some products and services, for others, managers must be sensitive to both local idiosyncrasies and global imperatives in reaching strategic decisions. A few examples illustrate the need to think globally, but to adapt to local conditions to avoid the pitfalls of inappropriate standardization.

- Procter and Gamble's liquid detergent failed in Europe when it was introduced in the early 1980s because European washing machines were not equipped for liquid detergent. Modifications to the detergent were made and sales subsequently improved.

- McDonald's sells beer in Germany and tropical shakes in Hong Kong, while Dunkin' Donuts sells cake donuts in the United States but yeast donuts in Brazil. Marketing strategies for global recognition were successfully implemented by adapting to local preferences.

- Kellogg's Corn Flakes were (mis)used as a snack when first introduced in Brazil. With educational advertising, corn flakes gained in acceptance as a breakfast food.

---

[6]Stephen H. Rhinesmith, John N. Williamson, David M. Ehlen, and Denise S. Maxwell, "Developing Leaders for the Global Enterprise," *Training and Development Journal,* April 1989, pp. 25–34.

[7]Masaaki Kotabe, *Global Sourcing Strtategy: R&D, Manufacturing, and Marketing Interfaces* (New York: Quorum Books, 1992).

These examples suggest that global success is contingent on striking a balance between capitalizing on resources and needs within national boundaries, and the ability to capture a vision of a world without boundaries. One aspect of managing this balance will likely include moving decision-making authority as close to the customer as possible to ensure that local requirements are satisfied. But local managers will need to know and understand the global strategy, yet enact it within the context of their local environment.

Ability to Manage Change and Transition

Managing change in the unstable environment described earlier will be an unending challenge. Constantly fine-tuning the balance between global and local pressures under changing competitive conditions will contribute to the need for frequent reorganization of resources, human networks, technology, and marketing and distribution systems. The shortening of product life cycles, driven by technological change in the products and how they are manufactured and delivered, contributes to the acceleration of change.

As difficult as these constant changes are to manage, the *overall* transition to global operations represents a formidable challenge in itself. Existing international operations, often marked by standardization of products and uniformity of procedures, may be a barrier to effective globalization. For example, a long history of mass-producing standard products may make it especially difficult to invest in and effectively operate flexible factories, one way that firms may offer differentiated products to different markets on a global scale.[8]

For a successful transition to global operations, it is also important that country managers are in agreement with the strategy. If poorly implemented, the move to globalization can pit headquarters managers against country or field managers. There is a tendency for autonomous units in a firm to protect their own turf. If global strategy is perceived as a move toward a centralization of responsibility, a local manager's role may become less strategic. Subsidiary managers who joined a company because of its commitment to local autonomy and adapting products to local environments may become disenchanted or even leave the organization.[9]

In terms of organization structure, effective global managers will need the skills to manage the transition from independence/dependence to interdependence, from control to coordination and cooperation, and from symmetry to differentiation.

Another method of making the transition to global operations is through the formation of a strategic alliance, or the formation of a network to reduce, for example, the high cost of R&D. As noted in Chapter 7, managing within international alliances or joint ventures is not the same as managing within a wholly owned subsidiary. Managing change within an alliance requires particular attention to the needs of the different partners, and an ability to enter into multiple trusting relationships.

---

[8]Sandra M. Huszagh, Richard J. Fox, and Ellen Day, "Global Marketing: An Empirical Investigation," *Columbia Journal of World Business* Vol. 20, Issue 4, 1986, pp. 31–43.

[9]John A. Quelch and Edward J. Hoff, "Customizing Global Marketing," *Harvard Business Review,* May-June 1986, pp. 59–68.

Ability to Manage Cultural Diversity[10]

As one starts to function internationally, an understanding of culture and its impact on behavior, particularly management behavior and practices, becomes essential. Very often, people experience difficulties when they have to work in another culture because peoples' world views and mental programs are different in different cultures. Culture has been called "the collective programming of the mind which distinguishes one human group from another."[11] As a result of having different mental programs, people often see situations differently and have different approaches and solutions to problems. Each tends to believe that his or her way is the right way and makes the most sense. The result can be frustration, conflict, and an inability to successfully carry out strategy or plans. Understanding has two parts: *cultural awareness* or how another person's culture affects his or her behavior; and *self-awareness* or understanding how our own culture affects our behavior. It is not sufficient to understand how others differ, if we do not understand how we also differ.

The first imperative for effectively managing cultural diversity is cultural sensitivity. The marketers of Coca-Cola, the world's most recognized brand, attribute their success to the ability of their people to hold and to understand the following perspectives simultaneously:

- Their corporate culture.
- The culture of their brand.
- The culture of the people to whom they market the brand.[12]

Sometimes cultural sensitivity leads to marketing one's products to a particular market segment *across* cultural boundaries, basically finding common subcultures within otherwise diverse cultures. In a classic study of international marketing practices of several bed linen companies headquartered in the United Kingdom, findings stressed the ability to develop a high level of cultural awareness in order to:

- Obtain high product acceptance in light of the fact that culturally rooted differences have a significant impact on a product's success in a global market.
- Understand that the older the consumption pattern, the less likely a global product will be a success.

---

[10]This is a skill set that shows the potential transfer of learning between domestic and international or global activities. The recent explosion of books on managing diversity in North America demonstrates this point. Books such as Sondra Thiederman's *Profiting in America's Multicultural Marketplace* (Lexington: Lexington Books, 1991); Roosevelt Thomas's *Beyond Race and Gender: Unleashing the Power of Your Total Workforce by Managing Diversity* (New York: AMACOM, 1991); John Fernandez's *Managing a Diverse Work Force: Regaining the Competitive Edge* (Lexington: Lexington Books, 1991); and Ann Morrison's *The New Leaders: Guidelines on Leadership Diversity in America* (San Francisco: Jossey-Bass, 1992) include concepts and approaches similar to those written about international activities.

[11]Geert Hofstede, *Culture's Consequences: International Differences in Work-Related Values* (Beverly Hills, CA: Sage Publications, 1980).

[12]Harold F. Clarke, Jr., "Consumer and Corporate Values: Yet Another View on Global Marketing," *International Journal of Advertising,* Vol. 6, 1987, pp. 29–42.

- Recognize universal themes by segmenting according to similarities instead of geographical differences.[13]

Lack of cultural awareness can be devastating to organizations competing globally. An organization not managed according to values felt by its members is likely to experience conflict. Hidden values and beliefs must be recognized and understood in order to manage effectively. In the 1970s, in the Republic of Panama, there were more than 20 serious disputes between MNCs and local labor that were related to popular culture. Also during that period, all six Central American republics imposed restrictions on expatriate managers that resulted in their replacement by nationals.[14]

Global managers must have the ability to recognize that cultural differences operate internally and externally. It is important to understand the influence of the home office's own cultural filters when dealing with foreign affiliates and to accept that the home office way of doing things will not be appropriate in all instances. In today's global environment, a firm's home culture must no longer dominate the entire organization's culture.[15] Instilling such an attitude, a global mind-set, is not as simple as sending a memo announcing the change. Attitudes are notoriously resistant to change.

There are four distinct attitude clusters that are useful in thinking about, and characterizing, corporate worldviews or mind-sets: ethnocentric, polycentric, regiocentric, and geocentric.[16] These attitudes may be reflected in a firm's structure; authority and decision-making processes; selection, development, evaluation, control, and reward systems; information flows; and geographical identification.[17] In short, these attitudes permeate the strategy and operations of a company and its managers. A brief description of these attitudes follows.

Ethnocentrism (Home Country Orientation).   This is a preference for using home country personnel in key positions around the world and rewarding them better than the locals. As with an ethnocentric attitude there is also a belief in the inherent superiority of the home country personnel, systems, and ways of operating:

> . . . This group is more intelligent, more capable, or more reliable . . . ethnocentrism is often not attributable to prejudice as much as to inexperience or lack of knowledge about foreign persons and situations.[17] (p. 17)

---

[13]Jeryl M. Whitelock, "Global Marketing and the Case for International Product Standardization," *European Journal of Marketing* (UK), Vol. 21, Issue 9, 1987, pp. 32–44.

[14]Antonio Grimaldi, "Interpreting Popular Culture: The Missing Link Between Local Labor and International Management," *Columbia Journal of World Business,* Vol. 21, Issue 4, Winter 1986, pp. 67–72.

[15]Nancy J. Adler and Fariborz Ghadar, "International Strategy from the Perspective of People and Culture: The North American Context," *Research in Global Business Management,* Vol. 1 (Greenwich, CT: JAI Press Inc., 1990).

[16]Howard V. Perlmutter, "The Tortuous Evolution of the Multinational Corporation," *The Columbia Journal of World Business,* January 1969. pp. 9–18.

[17]David A. Heenan and Howard V. Perlmutter, *Multinational Organizational Development: A Social Architectural Perspective* (Reading, MA: Addison-Wesley, 1979).

Polycentrism (Host Country Orientation).   This attitude sees and focuses on the differences among cultures and finds foreigners difficult to understand. It also tends to be a low-involvement attitude, since everything in the other country is believed to be so difficult to understand:

> In justifying a decision, headquarters executives of such a company might say: "Let the Romans do it their way. We really don't understand what's going on there, but we have to have confidence in them. As long as our foreign managers earn a profit, we want to remain in the background." Local nationals in polycentric organizations occupy virtually all the key positions in their respective local subsidiaries and appoint and develop their own people . . . Headquarters with its holding company attitude is manned by home-country nationals who try not to interfere in the territory of each local manager. This low profile approach of headquarters is justified on managerial and political grounds.[17] (p. 20)

Regiocentrism (Regional Orientation).   Corporations with this attitude see

> . . . advantages in recruiting, developing, appraising and assigning managers on a regional basis. Such a personnel policy is viewed as supportive of functional rationalization . . . Such an approach has the merit of anticipating emerging politico-economic communities. (p. 20)

Geocentrism (World Orientation).   This attitude

> . . . is evidenced in the attempt to integrate diverse regions through a global systems approach to decision-making. Headquarters and subsidiaries see themselves as parts of an organic worldwide entity. Superiority is not equated with nationality. Executives convey in their key decisions the attitude that the distinctive competence of the truly multinational firm is its capacity to optimize resource allocation on a global basis. Good ideas come from any country and go to any country within the firm.[17] (pp. 20–21)

Recent research[18] has found support for a link between a firm's mind-set or orientation and its mode of international operations. In a study of small and medium-sized Canadian companies, it was found that ethnocentric firms favored less-risky and higher control modes such as exporting and sales subsidiaries; firms with the other sets of attitudes were more likely to use a wider range of modes (with their associated risks) up to, and including, local production. A relationship was also found between international performance and attitude. Geocentric firms had the highest level of performance; poly/regiocentric were in the middle; and ethnocentric firms had the lowest performance.

Even though there may be real economic benefits to expanding the world view of executives and corporations, developing recognition of the existence and benefits of diversity in global management does not come easily to North American executives, who often have less exposure to multicultural realities in their workplace than, for instance, their European counterparts. For example, Nestlé has a long history of having many nationalities among its top 100 executives (one count had it over 40), while, in one survey, IBM had the largest number among U.S. large companies—only 11! Although these types of anecdotal reports

---

[18]Jonathan L. Calof, *The Internationalization Process: An Examination of Mode Change, Mode Choice, and Performance;* unpublished Ph.D. dissertation, The University of Western Ontario, London, Canada, 1991.

may be misleading, the limited language ability of many North American managers makes the same point another way. Language training, cross-cultural and expatriate experiences early in careers, membership on international task forces, and global content in all management training programs are among a few ways to counter the ethnocentricity of domestic managers, regardless of their country of origin. Using the case exercise presented later in this text entitled "Where Have You Been?" we have found a correlation between high mobility and exposure to other countries with a geocentric mind-set.

Learning to manage global cultural diversity effectively can start with the recognition of cultural diversity at home. The requirement to hire African Americans, Hispanics, and Native Americans in the United States is forcing many firms to come to grips with new mixes of employees. Demographic projections, which suggest that early in the next century, white males will represent only one in five of the workforce in the United States, also mean cultural diversity will be a domestic reality. There are large minorities of people newly arrived from India, Pakistan, Vietnam, Hong Kong, Central America, and eastern Europe. The opportunities to gain insight and experience in managing cultural diversity are local as well as global.

To manage diversity, domestically or globally, a modern human resource strategy requires some minimal orientations:

- An explicit recognition by headquarters that its own way of managing reflects the home culture values and assumptions.
- An explicit recognition by headquarters that foreign subsidiaries may have different ways of managing people, which may be more effective.
- A willingness to acknowledge cultural differences, and to take steps to make them discussible and, thus, usable.
- A commitment to the belief that more creative and effective ways of managing people can be developed as a result of cross-cultural learning.[19]

Ability to Design and to Function in Flexible Organizations

Given the complexities of the global economy and its attendant demands on managers, it is unlikely that any single organizational form will be adequate to the tasks. Global managers will surely need significantly increased creativity in organizational design, but limited organizational capability may represent the most critical constraint in responding to the new strategic demands.

As mentioned earlier, an individual manager cannot be expected to develop and use all the diverse skills required for successful global management. It is essential then that the organization support global managers. Global managers will, therefore, be called on to design and operate the very organizations that will help them to be more effective.

The best managers are already creating borderless organizations where the ability to learn, to be responsive, and to be efficient occurs within the firm's administrative heritage.[20]

---

[19]Andre Laurent, "The Cross-Cultural Puzzle of International Human Resource Management," *Human Resource Management,* Vol. 25, Issue 1, Spring 1986, pp. 91–102.

[20]C. A. Bartlett and S. Ghoshal, *Managing Across Borders* (Boston: Harvard Business School Press, 1989).

This suggests that a wide range of people in such firms must demonstrate the capacity for strategic thinking and action, assisted by open communication of plans, decentralization of strategic tasks, early opportunities for development of top management capabilities, and control systems measuring performance across many dimensions.[21] These new organizations will have multiple centers of influence and managers will move between jobs at these centers. This lateral movement between centers and jobs will be common and will displace hierarchy and promotion "up the ladder."

To ensure that the potential cultural diversity in such situations is taken advantage of, managers will need the ability to create an alignment of authority and responsibility between home office and field offices that moves decision making as close as possible to the customer. Balance is required though and, as noted earlier, the ability to coordinate manufacturing interdependencies to maximize economies of production will be a key task of the global manager.

To operate effectively in these radically different, global organizations will take new skills and old skills honed to a new sharpness. Some of the abilities and characteristics needed by the global manager to function in flexible organizations will be:

- High tolerance for ambiguity.
- New levels of creativity and inventiveness in organizational design.
- The ability to learn, be responsive, and be efficient, all simultaneously.
- The ability to identify and implement diverse managerial behaviors and ideas for ongoing renewal of the organization.
- The ability to coordinate complicated financial, human resource, marketing and manufacturing interdependencies, not only across functions, but also within each business activity.
- The ability to recognize different manufacturing, marketing, and organizational problems and priorities across different locations and to accommodate these with new structures and processes.[22]

Ability to Work with Others and in Teams

Even before the advent of global companies, effective teamwork was becoming essential for managerial success. As specialization of people and differentiation in organizations increased (often driven by technological improvements, fragmentation of markets, explosions in product variations, etc.), there was a concomitant increased need for integration—for putting the specialized units back together in the service of the organization's objectives. Teams, committees, and task forces were among the devices used to accomplish the desired integration.

---

[21]For an article describing these and other organizational innovations, see Gunnar Hedlund, "The Hypermodern MNC—A Heterarchy?" *Human Resource Management,* Vol. 25, No. 1, Spring 1986, pp. 9–35.

[22]K. Ferdows, J. G. Miller, J. Nakane, and T. E. Vollmann, "Evolving Global Manufacturing Strategies: Projections into the 1990s, *International Journal of Operations and Production Management,* Vol. 6, No. 4, 1986, pp. 6–16.

With the increased complexity of global operations, the ability to function in work teams—especially in culturally diverse groups—is even more important. A Conference Board Report on the experiences of 30 major MNCs in building teams to further their global interests showed the following:

- Teams used solely for communication or to provide advice and counsel still exist, but more and more firms are also using teams in different and more participative and powerful ways.
- Global teamwork can do more than provide improved market and technological intelligence. It can yield more flexible business planning, stronger commitment to achieving worldwide goals, and closer collaboration in carrying out strategic change.
- Teams that span internal organization boundaries or that span the company's outside boundary (joint venture partners, suppliers, customers) are often required.[23]

The need for transnational teamwork shows up in different ways in different functions. Consider the different assumptions about the nature and purpose of accounting and auditing in various parts of the world, for example. In one country financial statements are meant to reflect fundamental economic reality and the audit function is to ensure that this is so. In another country the audit is to check the accuracy of the statements vis-à-vis the economic records. In still another country it is only to make sure legal requirements have been met.[24] Imagine, then, the need for cross-cultural understanding and sensitivity in auditing an international subsidiary or the teamwork needed to develop international audit standards.[25]

Other functions pick up the teamwork theme differently. In operations management, the literature emphasizes the need to develop system-sensitive outlooks and processes that will develop personal relationships across subsidiaries.[26] The human resource literature emphasizes the need to develop capabilities for leading multinational teams in flexible and responsible ways. The global marketing literature discusses the ability to take advantage of a local execution strategy where "not invented here" becomes "now improved here."[27] Using this strategy, an international core team is formed to gather ideas and to pass them to local levels where the final marketing decisions are made and implemented.

The ability to work effectively with other people and in teams will be critical to the successful implementation of a global strategy. Participation in global teams should, therefore, occur early in the careers of managers in order to transform these developing people into globally effective managers.

---

[23]Ruth G. Shaeffer, "Building Global Teamwork for Growth and Survival," *The Conference Board Research Bulletin*, No. 228.

[24]Leslie G. Campbell, *International Auditing* (New York: St. Martin's Press, 1985), p. 141.

[25]William S. Albrecht, Hugh L. Marsh Jr., and Frederick H. Bentzel Jr, "Auditing an International Subsidiary," *Internal Auditor*, Vol. 45, Issue 5, October 1988, pp. 22–26; Joseph Soeters and Hein Schreuder, "The Interactions Between National and Organizational Cultures in Accounting Firms," *Accounting, Organizations and Society*, Vol. 13, No. 1, 1988, pp. 75–85; and Nicholas M. Zacchea "The Multinational Auditor: Overcoming Cultural Differences to Apply Audit Standards," *Internal Auditor*, Vol. 45, Issue 5, 1988, pp. 16–21.

[26]Briance Mascarenhas, "The Coordination of Manufacturing Interdependencies in Multinational Companies," *Journal of International Business Studies*, Winter 1984, pp. 91–106.

[27]Teresa J. Domzel and Lynette S. Unger, "Emerging Positioning Strategies in Global Marketing," *Journal of Consumer Marketing*, Vol. 4, Issue 4, Fall 1987, pp. 23–40.

Ability to Communicate

It is obvious that in a global environment managers will need to be able to communicate with diverse groups of people. To do so effectively will require multilingual skills and high levels of cross-cultural awareness and sensitivity. In addition to the positive effects of good communication skills among colleagues and with customers, there is another advantage of particular importance to geographically dispersed and culturally diverse organizations. Sensitive communications will also build trust, and a common message can help build a strong corporate culture emphasizing shared, global value systems.

In addition to the skills necessary for effective interpersonal communication, managers will need to be able to take advantage of increasingly global communications systems resulting from broadcast deregulation and growth in global media firms such as Sky Channel and Pan European Press. Data gathered in 1987 indicate that the market for Pan European advertising campaigns has been growing at a rate of more than 25 percent per year, in spite of the many technological difficulties encountered by the new satellite technology. As always, the need to be sensitive to local requirements is evidenced by several lawsuits launched against the global media by local advertisers wishing to retain advertising revenue and by regulatory bodies seeking to retain control over advertising content.[28]

The advent of global communications exposes managers to new risks as well as new advantages. Recently, CNN aired an interview with a U.S. senator from the steps of the Capitol in Washington on their European broadcasts. Apparently directing his comments to his constituents in his home state, the senator was engaging in Europe-bashing in defense of local industries. At the same time U.S. trade representatives were trying to negotiate sensitive issues with their European Community counterparts in Brussels. The senator was probably unaware that this interview would be aired the same day throughout Europe. Global communications provide as great an opportunity to offend as they do to please.

Ability to Learn and to Transfer Knowledge in an Organization

Given the diversity of market requirements and needs, the dispersion of manufacturing and sourcing, the rise of R&D leadership in Europe and Japan, and the importance of technological advances for product and process innovations, learning and transfer of knowledge are key to global success. Managers who are globally competent will be deeply curious; organizations that are successful will be able to coordinate, transfer, and use the knowledge gained by curious executives rapidly and effectively.

At the individual level, broad interests, an openness to a variety of experiences, and a willingness to experiment and to take risks are all ingredients of success. A visiting scholar from the People's Republic of China typified these characteristics for the authors. Soon after her arrival she knew more people than several others who had been at our institution for many months. Although her specialty was finance, she audited classes across all functions. She interviewed the "old-timers," secretaries, researchers, students, and seasoned teachers. Nor were her interactions confined to work. She learned humor; visited churches; traveled

---

[28]Laurel Wentz, "Global Marketing and Media: TV Nationalism Clouds Sky Gains," *Advertising Age,* Vol. 58, Issue 53, December 14, 1987, p. 56.

across the country by air, bus, train, and boat; went to country fairs; and even insisted on trying golf! By the end of her year, she understood the institution better than most who had been in it for several years; she understood the country almost as well as any native. Then, she transferred her knowledge to her colleagues in China and abroad through an extraordinary report[29] and through a series of lectures and seminars.

At an organizational level even more can be done. For example, at Citicorp, operating managers are encouraged to look for opportunities in one country that can be transferred elsewhere. These opportunities, or experiments, are the responsibility of national managers, while their transfer is the responsibility of corporate management.[30] The use of cross-national task forces for problems of corporate-level concern (or for problems that reoccur in various parts of the world) is also a feature of that company.

The transfer of technology is also important. Global MIS systems are now required and a manager must have the skills necessary to access and interpret worldwide information. One way to transfer technology is through the development of strong functional management to allow the building and transference of core competencies.

Yet there are indications that too often companies neglect the rich information made available to them by expatriates in other countries, especially when they return to their home country. These organizations not only lose out on a valuable opportunity to transfer some cross-cultural managerial knowledge, but also cause the expatriate to experience some potentially serious reentry difficulties.[31]

The ability of organizations to learn and to transfer knowledge will only increase in importance as markets continue to globalize. In a global environment, the ability of people to learn from diverse sources and to transfer knowledge within their organization is essential for success.

Summary Profile

This review might lead the reader to conclude that an effective global manager is superhuman. But keeping in mind the necessity of teamwork and the potential support to the managers through effective organizational design, systems, and processes, the prospect of developing global skills might be seen as an exciting challenge rather than an impossible task. To develop skills to the level necessary will be a lifelong process because the demands will likely expand along with the global economy. Each of us needs to continue to improve in the aforementioned areas as we move toward the new century.

---

[29]Jiping Zhang, *The Building and Operation of a North American Business School* (in Chinese), Tsinghua University Press (Beijing, 1990) (English version published March 1987 by the Western Business School, The University of Western Ontario, London, Ontario N6A 3K7.)

[30]Alan J. Zakon, "Globalization Is More than Imports and Exports," *Management Review,* Vol. 77, Issue 7, July 1988, pp. 56–57.

[31]Robert T. Moran, "Corporations Tragically Waste Overseas Experience," *International Management* (UK), Vol. 43, Issue 1, January 1988, p. 74.

Developing Global Managers

American companies went through a period of reducing the number of expatriates they sent overseas for many reasons.[32] One major reason was the expense associated with relocating them and their families. Their salaries were usually higher than those of local managers, and they usually received benefits to make an overseas move attractive. Many of these benefits were not usually provided to local employees. Benefits often included items like housing or housing allowance, moving expenses, tax equalization, home leave, overseas premiums, cost of living allowances, and schooling for children. The incremental costs to the MNE of using expatriates can be shockingly high, particularly in some locales. A high-quality apartment rental accommodation for a senior manager posted to Hong Kong can run US$100,000/year. North American managers transferred to Switzerland claim that "everything" is more expensive than what they are accustomed to paying at home for a comparable material living standard.

In addition to lowering costs, having fewer expatriates has resulted in reduced conflict between employees and groups in the local environment. As well, it has increased the development of host country managerial and technical capabilities.

Although this trend could be seen as a positive step in the globalization process of American companies, there is a question about whether the real reason for the reduction was Americans' inability to function abroad successfully. Estimates of expatriate failure rate run between 20 percent and 50 percent, and the average cost per failure to the parent company ranges from $55,000 to $150,000.[33] There are studies claiming the failure rate is between 30 and 70 percent. The accurate identification of the actual rate of failure is less important than how high the range is. The fact that this range represents a large number of managers who cannot function successfully in other cultures is disturbing. The reduction in expatriate personnel also has ramifications for strategic management and control, such as less identification with, and knowledge about, the global operations and organization, and less control by headquarters over local subsidiaries. Thus:

> . . . There is increasing value to expatriate assignment as firms become global competitors . . . A means must be found to provide this experience to as many managers as possible. That would probably involve shorter-term expatriate assignments whose purpose is avowedly developmental—for both the individual and the organization.[34]

A more recent phenomenon affecting the mobility of many (especially North American and European) managers is the dual-career reality of their family unit. As the Colgate-Palmolive case suggests, dual careers have introduced new complexities for MNEs wishing to develop global managers.

---

[32]Stephen J. Kobrin, "Expatriate Reduction and Strategic Control in American Multinational Corporations." *Human Resource Management,* Vol. 27, No. 1, 1988. See also Michael Harvey, "Empirical Evidence of Recurring International Compensation Problems," *Journal of International Business Studies,* Vol. 24, No. 4, 1993.

[33]Ibid.

[34]Ibid., p. 74.

Careful selection and preparation of expatriates—and their families—for their foreign assignments should be high-priority issues for multinationals. Unfortunately, this has not generally been the case. Now, corporations must reconsider their human resource management policies, including expatriation, in light of globalization. Cross-cultural understanding and experience are essential in today's business environment, and foreign assignments can be a critical part of a manager's development. However, experience in a job in another country does not automatically ensure a manager's increased sensitivity to cultural issues or an ability to transfer whatever has been learned to other managers. Cross-cultural training, even for experienced people, can add significantly to their understanding of their past experiences and to their skill in future assignments.

International experience is an important consideration in firms' recruiting and hiring practices. A study of 122 major Canadian corporations found a preference for hiring people with international experience for international positions.[35] The respondents to the survey also stated that expertise in international business was among the important skills that executives needed. Although corporations will have to spend more time, effort, and money in providing international experiences to their managers in order to help develop the global skills required for the future, individuals can take responsibility for their own development by seeking out international opportunities such as teaching language courses in other countries or working for agencies such as the U.S. Peace Corps or Canadian University Students Overseas (CUSO). In addition, acquiring fluency in a second or third language would be helpful.

Managing International Assignments

As was mentioned earlier, there are strategic implications to the use of expatriate personnel. MNCs must think about expatriation as a strategic tool that is used to develop managers with a global orientation, but also that is used to manage key organizational and country relationships.[36] Although organizational and management development are important, the emphasis should be:

> . . . on long-term commitment to learning about international markets. If high-potential individuals are carefully selected and trained for overseas positions, they will not only facilitate the maintenance of an international network of operations in the short term but should be allowed to continue providing informational support upon their return.[36]

Although it might sound pretty straightforward, the process of developing globally minded managers with the requisite skills is more difficult that it appears. The quote contains the conditions that most often are not met—*if high-potential individuals are carefully selected and trained*—and which are crucial to the successful use of expatriation for development and strategic purposes.

---

[35]Paul W. Beamish and Jonathan L. Calof, "International Business Education: A Corporate View," *Journal of International Business Studies,* Vol. 20, No. 3, 1989.

[36]Nakiye A. Boyacigiller, "The International Assignment Reconsidered," in *International Human Resource Management,* Mark Mendenhall and Gary Oddou, eds., Boston: PWS-Kent, 1991, p. 154.

Selection.   In 1973, published research[37] showed that people were selected for international assignments based on their proven performance in a similar job, usually domestically. The ability to work with foreign employees was at, or near, the bottom of the list of important qualifications. Unfortunately, 20 years later the situation has not changed dramatically for the better.[38] Very often technical expertise and knowledge are used as the most important selection criteria. Although these are important considerations, they should not be given undue weighting relative to a person's ability to adapt to, and function in, another culture. It does no good to send the most technically qualified engineer or finance manager to a foreign location if he or she cannot function there and has to be brought home prematurely. As noted earlier, the cost of bad selection decisions is high to the corporation as well as to the individual and to his or her family.

In a very useful model of overseas effectiveness, which focuses on adaptation, expertise, and interaction,[39] for a person to be effective, he or she:

> must adapt—both personally and with his/her family—to the overseas environment, have the expertise to carry out the assignment, and interact with the new culture and its people.[40]

Training.   The training that a person undergoes before expatriation should be a function of the degree of cultural exposure to which he or she will be subjected.[41] Two dimensions of cultural exposure are the degree of integration and the duration of stay. The integration dimension represents the intensity of the exposure. A person could be sent to a foreign country on a short-term, technical, trouble-shooting matter and experience little significant contact with the local culture. On the other hand, a person could be in Japan for only a brief visit to negotiate a contract, but the cultural interaction could be very intense and may require a great deal of cultural fluency to be successful. Similarly, an expatriate assigned abroad for a period of years is likely to experience a high degree of interaction with the local culture from living there.

One set of guidelines[42] suggests that for short stays (less than a month) and a low level of integration, an "information-giving approach" would suffice. This includes area and cultural briefings, and survival-level language training, for example. For longer stays (2–12 months) and a moderate level of integration, language training, role-plays, critical incidents, case studies, and stress reduction training are suggested. For people who will be living abroad for one to three years and/or will have to experience a high level of integration into the culture, extensive language training, sensitivity training, field experiences, and simulations are the training techniques recommended.

---

[37]E. L. Miller, "The International Selection Decision: A Study of Some Dimensions of Managerial Behavior in the Selection Decision Process," *Academy of Management Journal,* Vol. 16, No. 2, 1973, pp. 239–52.

[38]Mark E. Mendenhall, Edward Dunbar, and Gary R. Oddou, "Expatriate Selection, Training and Career Pathing: A Review and Critique," *Human Resource Management,* Vol. 26, No. 3, 1987.

[39]Daniel J. Kealey, *Cross-cultural Effectiveness: A Study of Canadian Technical Advisors Overseas,* Ottawa: Canadian International Development Agency, 1990. This study was based on a sample of over 1,300 people, including technical advisors, their spouses, and host-country counterparts.

[40]Ibid., p. 8.

[41]Mendenhall et al., op. cit.

[42]Ibid.

Effective preparation would also stress the realities and difficulties of working in another culture and the importance of establishing good working relationships with the local people.

Repatriation.   Selecting the right people, training them properly, and sending them and their families to their foreign posting is not the end of the exercise. Getting these people back and integrated into the company so that the company can continue to benefit from their experience and expertise has been shown to be a problem. Research suggests that the average repatriation failure rate—those people who return from an overseas assignment and then leave their companies within one year—is about 25 percent.[43] If companies want to retain their internationally experienced managers, they are going to have to do a better job managing the repatriation process. See the Yutaka Nakamura case for a detailed elaboration of this point.

The international assignment may be an important vehicle for developing global managers; achieving strategic management control; coordinating and integrating the global organization; and learning about international markets and competitors, as well as foreign social, political, and economic situations. However, this idealized goal of becoming a global, learning organization will be reached only if the right people are selected for foreign assignments, trained properly, repatriated with care, valued for their experience, and are used in a way that takes advantage of their unique background.

Supplementary Reading

Adler. Nancy *International Dimensions of Organization Behavior,* 2nd ed. Boston: PWS-Kent, 1991.

Beamish, Paul W., and Jonathan L. Calof. "International Business Education: A Corporate View." *Journal of International Business Studies,* Fall 1989.

Black, J. Stewart, and Hal B. Gregersen. "Serving Two Masters: Managing the Dual Allegiance of Expatriate Employees." *Sloan Management Review,* Summer 1992.

Black, J. Stewart, Hal B. Gregersen, and Mark E. Mendenhall. *Global Assignments: Successfully Expatriating and Repatriating International Managers.* San Francisco: Jossey-Bass, 1992.

Cascio, Wayne F., and Manuel G. Serapio, Jr. "Human Resources Systems in an International Alliance: The Undoing of a Done Deal." *Organizational Dynamics,* Winter 1991.

Dowling, Peter, and Randall Schuler. *International Dimensions of Human Resource Management,* Boston: PWS-Kent, 1990.

Lane, Henry W., Joseph J. DiStefano, and Martha Maznevski. *International Management Behavior,* 3rd ed., Cambridge, MA: Blackwell Publishers, 1996.

---

[43]Meg G. Birdseye and John S. Hill, "Individual, Organizational/Work and Environmental Influences on Expatriate Turnover Tendencies: An Empirical Study," *Journal of International Business Studies,* Vol. 26, No. 4, 1995. J. Stewart Black and Hal R. Gregersen, "When Yankee Comes Home: Factors Related to Expatriate and Spouse Repatriation Adjustment," *Journal of International Business Studies,* Vol. 22, No. 4, 1991; J. Stewart Black, Hal R. Gregersen, and Mark E. Mendenhall, "Toward a Theoretical Framework of Repatriation Adjustment," *Journal of International Business Studies,* Vol. 23, No. 4, 1992.

Maisonrouge, Jacques G. "The Education of a Modern International Manager." *Journal of International Business Studies,* Spring/Summer 1983.

Mendenhall, Mark, and Gary Oddou. *Readings and Cases in International Human Resource Management,* Boston: PWS-Kent, 1991.

O'Grady, Shawna, and Henry W. Lane. "The Psychic Distance Paradox." *Journal of International Business Studies,* Vol. 27, No. 2, 1996.

Pucik, Vladimir, Noel M. Tichy, and Carole K. Barnett, eds., *Globalizing Management: Creating and Leading the Competitive Organization.* New York: John Wiley & Sons, 1992.

Rhinesmith, Stephen H. *A Manager's Guide to Globalization: Six Keys to Success in a Changing World.* Burr Ridge, IL: Business One Irwin, in cooperation with The American Society for Training and Development,1992.

Rosenzweig, Philip M., and Nitin Nohria. "Influences on Human Resource Management Practices in Multinational Corporations." *Journal of International Business Studies,* Vol. 25, No.2, 1994.

12   MANAGING GOVERNMENT INTERVENTION

The purpose of this chapter is to look at how to manage under conditions of government regulation and unwanted government intervention. The first section reviews some of the major sources of trade regulation that affect both the exporter and the foreign investor. The second part focuses on the management of intervention.

Managers in multinational enterprises are concerned and frustrated by governments that force unwanted changes in their preferred method of operations. While intervention forms such as expropriation have declined, host governments intervene in subsidiaries of multinational enterprises (MNEs) by restricting foreign ownership and control; regulating financial flows, foreign management, and technical fees; and instituting requirements for local content and minimum export levels. Historically, MNEs have responded by trying to negotiate changes in either the intervention laws or their implementation, by attempting to bypass the laws; or by reducing their exposure in nations with a record of frequent interventions.

While parent companies are usually the focus of attention in such discussions, the focus here is on the subsidiary/affiliate. This is not only for the obvious reason that subsidiaries are more exposed to the policies of host governments. It is because regulatory and especially intervention policies are, sometimes, determined less by ideology, politics, and economics and more by the character of the subsidiary itself. While ideology, political stability, and the supply of hard currency reserves set the stage, the foreign subsidiary is the actor.

Given the crucial role of the subsidiary, managers should refocus their attention on subsidiary strategies. This chapter proposes a general strategy for defending the subsidiary: concentrating on a strategy that can be implemented by most multinationals without dramatic changes in their existing organization and operation.

This chapter was prepared by Paul Beamish, Donald Lecraw, and Thomas A. Poynter. Portions are adapted from T.A. Poynter "Managing Government Intervention," *Columbia Journal of World Business.* Winter 1986.

I. Trade Regulation

The GATT and the WTO.   In the middle of the last century three organizations were established to improve the performance of the world economy: the International Monetary Fund to regulate exchange rates and international capital movements, the World Bank to assist developing countries, and the General Agreement on Tariffs and Trade to deal with two aspects of international trade: tariffs and nontariff barriers to trade.

From the end of World War II through the early 1980s, trade negotiations under the auspices of the GATT succeeded in reducing barriers to trade, particularly tariff barriers, significantly. During the Tokyo round of trade negotiations in the mid-1970s, attention was turned toward reducing nontariff barriers to trade as well. By the end of negotiations in 1979, only partial success had been achieved. In part, this result was due to the number, the complexity, and the sensitivity of nontariff barriers. A study conducted by the GATT Secretariat identified over 600 nontariff barriers to trade. These ranged from quotas and antidumping and countervailing duty laws to labeling, product standards, customs inspection procedures, and government procurement regulations.

The relative lack of success was partly due to the subtle nature of the motivations for, and the administration of, many nontariff barriers to trade. For example, a country's health and safety standards could be formulated in response to legitimate concerns on these issues, or they could be designed to block trade. Requirements for periodic on-site plant inspections by nationals of the importing country could legitimately be a means of ensuring quality control to meet these standards. Alternatively, these inspections could be required to impose costs on potential exporters.

The Uruguay round of the GATT negotiations was started in 1986 and completed in December 1993. It addressed even more challenging problems. These problems were also addressed in an environment that was less hospitable to trade liberalization. A wide variety of issues were considered: standards, also known as technical barriers to trade; trade in agricultural products, a most politically charged issue; trade in services, such as banking and insurance, advertising, media, and tourism; intellectual property rights—protection of patents, trademarks, copyrights, and brand names; barriers to trade in technology, such as regulations on mandatory licensing or maximum licensing fees; and trade-related investment measures (TRIM) that link investment incentives to exports; the Multifiber Agreement (MFA), the *safeguard measures* (often called the *escape clause*) used to deal with import surges, and *voluntary export restraints* (VERs).

The number of countries involved in the negotiations had also expanded from 100 (with 70 contracting parties) in the Tokyo round to 117 (with 113 contracting countries). These negotiations took place in a more difficult environment than was the case in previous rounds. The United States was running a large and unsustainable trade deficit. Europe was struggling with the integration of the former Eastern bloc countries into a more unified trading area. At the same time, economic growth in many European countries had stagnated and unemployment was over 10 percent. The electorate in many countries was increasingly restive.

Many developing countries needed to achieve, maintain, and increase their trade surpluses if they were to have any chance of servicing their external debts. Expanding exports was also the only alternative open to them if they were to achieve even some modest economic growth. The political stability of many developing countries is directly linked to export expansion. These developing countries were not particularly interested in, and were often antagonistic to, the goals of high-income countries for liberalization of trade in services, agricultural products, protection of intellectual property rights, and technology transfer. They saw these initiatives as leading to domination by foreign financial and media firms; higher prices for imported food and loss of food self-sufficiency; higher prices for products with patents, brand names, and trademarks; and higher prices for and reduced volumes of technology transfer. Their interests lay in regaining the market access they had lost over the past decade to protectionist measures implemented by high-income countries and in enhanced access in the future. In particular, they wanted the removal of the MFA, which reduced their ability to increase exports of textiles and garments, and the "escape clause," which could be invoked to limit export growth in other products.

The Uruguay round came into full effect on January 1, 1995. By and large it was a success, although a qualified one. Many issues were agreed to in principle, but the crucial details were left for future negotiations. High-income countries agreed to reduce their tariffs over time from an average of 6.4 to 4 percent. Of special interest to developing countries, the proportion of imports from developing countries allowed duty-free access will increase from 20 to 43 percent, and tariffs on agricultural products from these countries will be reduced by 34 percent over time. The MFA will be phased out through the year 2005, and the use of VERs was further circumscribed.

High-income countries, especially the United States, also made substantial progress toward achieving their negotiating goals. Trade in services was brought within rules and disciplines of the organization with the creation of a General Agreement on Trade in Services. This agreement relates to trade in financial services, telecommunications, air transport, and the movement of labor. In agriculture, nontariff barriers to trade are to be replaced with their tariff equivalents and these tariffs reduced over time by 36 percent for high-income countries and 24 percent for developing countries. A number of export subsidy schemes were prohibited and others reduced. As well, intellectual property rights were placed within the MFN (Most Favored Nation) framework. This means that if two countries have MFN status in trade, they must also extend reciprocal protection of intellectual property rights.

Over the 12-year period from 1993 to 2005, the reduction of trade barriers under the Uruguay round is expected to lead to a 1 percent per year increase in the growth rate of trade volume (from 3 to 4 percent per year) such that trade will be $745 billion 1992 dollars higher in 2005. World income will be $230 billion higher in 2005 (in 1992 dollars), about 1 percent of world income. Of this amount, about $80 billion (about one-third) will accrue to developing countries, although the total of their GDPs is only about one-fifth world GDP.

Perhaps most important, a World Trade Organization was formed. The WTO includes the GATT, the GATS, a Dispute Settlement Board (DSB), a Trade Policy Review Board, and a Ministerial Conference, which will meet every two years. The formation of the WTO represents a major achievement for advocates of freer trade. It represents a move toward the model of an International Trade Organization, proposed after World War II, with broad powers over all forms of trade. It can also serve as an ongoing forum for further trade negotiations and dispute settlement. For example, the United States has committed to bringing its disagreements with individual countries on protection of intellectual property rights to the DSB before proceeding with invoking Section 301 of the Trade Act unilaterally against countries that it deems to be offenders.

There remains much to do on the WTO's agenda for the future. First and foremost is to finalize the details of the issues that were left unresolved at the end of the Uruguay round. The provisions on trade in services for telecommunications, finance, audiovisual products, commercial aircraft, and steel need to be extended further. The issues of trade and the environment and trade and labor standards—two contentious issues of particular interest to high-income countries—need to be addressed. On the one hand, to do this will require formulation of worldwide environmental codes and labor codes. On the other, it will require formulation of rules under which countries can block trade in products that were not produced according to these codes. This will be a formidable task. Another important area to be included within the WTO is foreign investment. Trade and foreign investment are closely linked, with about one-third of world trade undertaken by MNEs. As yet, however, country-level investment regulations are not governed by any global agreements. Finally, China and Russia will have to be brought within the WTO. At present, it is ironic that two of the five permanent members of the United Nations Security Council are not members of the WTO.

In addition to the multilateral trade agreements under the WTO, a growing number of regional trade groups have been formed. These have had a major impact on world trade and investment. For example, in 1996, General Motors announced that it would invest over one billion dollars in a manufacturing facility in Thailand. This investment was not made in relationship to the Thai market, but in relationship to the total market of the ASEAN countries—Thailand, Singapore, Indonesia, Brunei, Vietnam, and the Philippines. Under the ASEAN Free Trade Area (AFTA), tariffs among these countries have been reduced substantially and are scheduled to be reduced even further. GM was then investing to enable it to trade and sell its cars throughout the ASEAN countries.

The U.S.–Canada Free Trade Agreement.   Effective January 1988, the United States and Canada entered into a free trade agreement, thus creating the world's largest free trade area. The agreement culminated what had been an almost century-long process of formalizing and securing trade between Canada and the United States. Since the two nations enjoy the world's largest bilateral trade, with each country being the other's largest trading partner, the FTA was expected to be of considerable benefit to both nations. Of particular importance, the agreement did not set up a customs union or trading bloc. It is fully consistent with the letter and intent of the GATT; each country remains free to pursue independently its trade policy with other nations.

With a general liberalization of trade, involving reduced duties across almost every sector of the economy, the FTA is in the long-run interests of both nations. What is particularly significant, especially for the Canadians, is the dispute resolution mechanisms. In the past, whenever the United States passed a trade bill, Canadian lobbyists would have to pressure for Canadian exemption based on the "special relationship" between the United States and Canada. This moral suasion was not always successful and was understandably unreliable. The FTA established a panel of judges with an equal number of American and Canadian representatives. After a number of disputes on, among other things, forest and agricultural products, both nations appear to have been willing to abide by the panel's rulings, although individual companies and industries on both sides of the border are not happy with it.

The North American Free Trade Agreement (NAFTA).   Building on the momentum of the FTA, Canadian and American trade negotiators opened talks with Mexican representatives to establish a continentwide free trade agreement. NAFTA created the largest trading area in the world, surpassing the trade area created by the FTA. In fact, NAFTA was a logical extension of the FTA. Although the trilateral negotiations on NAFTA were set within a rhetoric of free trade, NAFTA was largely the result of uniquely U.S. and Mexican initiatives. Canada, sensing that a U.S.–Mexican agreement was virtually a certainty, became a party to the agreement in order not to be frozen out.

Concerns about the agreement generally centered on differential labor rates and working conditions and environmental issues. The claim was that companies in Mexico, especially foreign multinational enterprises, would have access to a considerably cheaper labor pool and safety standards and would not be subject to the more rigorous and expensive environmental regulations in place in the United States and Canada.

With the successful negotiation of NAFTA, other countries in Latin America, some of which with their own agreements, have approached the United States with proposals to join. Discussions and negotiations continue.

The European Union.   The integration of Europe has been a slow and at times tortuous process. However, in the more than 40 years since efforts at increased European integration were begun, what is now the European Union has grown to include 16 nations. What is most distinctive about the EU is that it is founded on the principle of supranationality (i.e., the EU councils and commissions are intended to be paramount over national laws and legislatures). For trading purposes, this means that member nations cannot enter into any trade agreements that are inconsistent with EU regulations. Within EU itself, the elimination of tariffs was achieved in 1961, as the establishment of a common external commercial policy and a common agricultural policy. With the passing of the Single Market Act in 1985, all member nations committed themselves to realizing the single market by the end of 1992. This act removed all barriers to trade in goods and services; barriers to mobility for the citizens of EU member countries; and all national regulations that might discriminate against a product, business, or individual from a member country.

The net impact on trade and investment is still uncertain. Already it has induced multinational enterprises based in countries outside Europe to invest there to have free access to this huge market. What is less certain is whether the new economic system will turn these countries into "Fortress Europe" or whether it will promote multilateral freer trade. In trade negotiations, the EU must negotiate as a unified bloc with a uniform position. Individual countries within the EU can try to influence its position on various trade issues, but they cannot "go it alone" and maintain their own position.

For managers of international trade operations, the results of all these sets of negotiations are of prime importance. Expansion of international trade operations is often a long-term investment. To make the correct decision, and to implement it effectively, will require ever increasing levels of knowledge, expertise, and sophistication in assessing the environment for international trade and in engaging in international trade operations.

II. Intervention Management: A Shift

Traditional political risk analysis no longer meets the needs of MNEs. Historically, political risk analysis focused on assessing political instability. While international banks may find this analysis still appropriate to their needs, multinational manufacturing firms know this kind of information is not particularly useful in managing their political risks. Political instability forms only a small portion of all the risks faced by multinational enterprises.[1] Instead, MNEs find that actions like forced joint ventures, unilateral contract renegotiations, and regulations calling for increased local value-added, and local ownership restrictions top their list of concerns. (See Exhibit 12–1 for an illustrative list of ownership restrictions for Asia. Note: these restrictions do vary over time.) Even when revolutions and similar shocks occur, they do not necessarily affect all firms equally.

While some nations intervene more than others, avoiding intervention by predicting a nation's intervention behavior is ineffective. "Safe" countries sometimes turn into hotbeds of intervention, while host countries led by dictators may provide profitable opportunities. It appears that almost all countries intervene in the operations of foreign-owned firms.

How then does the foreign-owned firm defend itself? One dominant characteristic of host government intervention behavior leads the way toward a solution: governments discriminate. They force some subsidiaries into unwanted joint ventures, and impose taxes and limit prices, while allowing others 100 percent foreign ownership and financially supporting them. Even when legislation calls for the equal treatment of all foreign firms, discriminatory enforcement is often the norm.

The basis of this discrimination lies in the differing characteristics of subsidiaries. Case studies, casual observation, and large-scale empirical investigations conducted by several observers lead to substantial agreement on this issue.[2] A key element is the bargaining power associated with each subsidiary. In this context, bargaining power refers to the control the *MNE parent* has over those resources necessary to operate the *subsidiary* successfully. Intervention occurs when domestic firms, entrepreneurs, or government officials feel they have sufficient resources (e.g., technology, export markets, raw material or components, and so on) to operate part or all of the activities of the subsidiary without assistance from the MNE. In other words, local groups will press the government to intervene on their behalf when continued MNE support no longer is required to keep the subsidiaries profitable. At that point, the MNE's bargaining power is low. Negotiations usually occur no matter what the bargaining power of the subsidiary, but the level of bargaining power is a good predictor of the outcome of the negotiations.

---

[1]See Theodore H. Moran, "International Political Risk Assessment, Corporate Planning and Strategies to Offset Political Risk," in *Managing International Political Risk: Strategies and Techniques,* eds. F. Ghadar, S.J. Kobrin, and T.H. Moran (Washington, D.C.: The Landegger Program in International Business Diplomacy, Georgetown University, 1983), pp. 158–66.

[2]The concept of "bargaining power" finds its roots in the work of Raymond Vernon, *Sovereignty at Bay: The Multinational Spread of U.S. Enterprises* (New York: Basic Books, 1971) and was further developed using natural resource firms by T.H. Moran, *Multinational Corporations and the Politics of Dependence: Copper in Chile* (Princeton, N.J.: Princeton University Press, 1974). The comments in this chapter are based on the substantially similar findings of four independent projects examining the causes of intervention: D.G. Bradley, "Managing Against Expropriation," *Harvard University Review,* July-August 1977; T.A. Poynter, "Government Intervention in Less Developed Countries: The Experience of Multinational Companies," *Journal of International Business Studies,* Spring-Summer 1982; N. Fagre and L.T. Wells, Jr., "The Bargaining Power of Multinationals and Host Government," *Journal of International Business Studies,* Fall 1982; Donald J. Lecraw, "Bargaining Power, Ownership and Profitability of Subsidiaries of Transnational Corporations in Developing Countries," *Journal of International Business Studies,* Spring-Summer 1984.

EXHIBIT 12–1   Summary of Local Ownership Restrictions by Country

Country	Summary of Local Ownership Restrictions (as of 1992)
Hong Kong	No distinction between local and foreign firms.
Taiwan	There is no restriction on the percentage of foreign ownership for most manufacturing companies. Foreign ownership is prohibited or restricted in some government controlled industries (e.g., armaments/munitions, tobacco and wine, public utilities). Foreign Investment Approved (F.I.A.) status is required to invest in certain industries. However, the F.I.A. is not a legal requirement, and foreign firms are technically able to invest in domestic companies.
South Korea	Foreign ownership must be less than 50 percent. Foreign ownership is prohibited or restricted in state monopoly industries (tobacco and ginseng) and other business areas including public utilities and services as well as other government-related activities, high energy consumption businesses, certain developing industries, and others.
Singapore	No distinction between local and foreign firms.
Malaysia	The level of foreign ownership will be all determined by the Malaysian Industrial Development Authority (MIDA). Foreign ownership of up to 100 percent will be allowed depending upon factors such as level of exports, level of technology, content of raw materials, types of industry, shareholders' value, employment structure.
Indonesia	Typically, local ownership is 20 percent or more, but in many cases, it may be 5 percent either when projects require large capital, when they contribute significantly to export, or when they are located in remote areas. Local partners are generally supported to attain majority ownership over a 15 to 20 year period.
Thailand	Local ownership must be 51 percent or more. A few majority-owned foreign investments in certain industries are allowed if the activities cannot be competently carried on by an entity whose majority is Thai.
Philippines	Foreign ownership of certain service industries such as retail trade, rural banks, and mass media is prohibited or restricted; foreign ownership of manufacturing sectors is basically open but needs to get the approval of the Board of Investments when it exceeds 40 percent. Foreign ownership of up to 100 percent will be allowed depending upon level of exports.

Sources: Price Waterhouse, 1990, *Corporate Taxes, Individual Taxes, Foreign Exchange Investment Regulations: An Asia Pacific Region Summary;* and The Economist, 1988, *Business Traveller's Guides: Southeast Asia.*

The bargaining power of the host nation comes from two sources. One source directly counters the power of the MNE, namely the host nation's ability to replace the business resources normally supplied by the MNE. The nation's stock of managerial, technical, and similar resources is either internally generated or is obtained through consultants, license agreements, and the like. The capabilities of host nations are growing.

The second source of host nation bargaining power comes from its control over the subsidiary's access to the host nation's market, raw materials, labor, and capital.[3] As these factors grow in importance, more MNEs compete to locate there, thus maximizing the bargaining power of the host nation. Hence, the larger and more attractive the local market becomes, the more intervention the firm will experience, all things being equal.

---

[3]For a detailed discussion of sources of a nation's bargaining power see T.A. Poynter, Multinational Enterprises and Government Intervention (New York: St. Martin's Press; and London: Croom Helm, 1985), pp. 57–68.

Summarizing the bargaining power (BP) model, intervention will not occur when the subsidiary's bargaining power is greater than the nation's business resources plus the attractiveness of the local market. In this model, bargaining power is derived from two sources: the availability of business resources needed to operate the subsidiary and, for the host nation only, the attractiveness of its market.

It is important here to reiterate the source and applicability of this model. It is based on the intervention experiences of many individual subsidiaries. The model shows what circumstances are typically found when intervention occurs. In practice, low subsidiary bargaining power sets into motion actions by domestic entrepreneurs, government officials, and the like, who actually bring about intervention. One must also note that this model does not examine why one nation would intervene on average more than another. For example, one of the reasons Nigeria intervenes more than the Ivory Coast may have to do with the latter's more open market, which is less distorted by government intervention. But this chapter is about reducing the level of intervention relative to all other firms in a nation. Given that one must choose to operate in a particular nation, defending the subsidiary against high levels of intervention is a key managerial activity.

The subsidiary's defense strategy is based on the bargaining model presented above, coupled with other subsidiary characteristics that also affect the level of intervention. Because the firm's bargaining power can usually be changed, firms can now manage intervention.

Applicability of the Strategy

Not all kinds of intervention, nor all kinds of MNEs, are covered here. The proposed strategy is only applicable to unwanted interventions and not interventions represented by such inducements as tax holidays, subsidies. and so forth. Interventions that take place before the investment is made, such as lists of businesses restricted to local ownership, are not included either.

Interventions that are the result of terrorist acts are excluded also because much international terrorism is not explicitly government sponsored. This is not to downplay the significance of terrorism, which is a very tangible risk in some countries all of the time, and all countries some of the time. Although no MNE or senior international executive can be completely protected from terrorism, strategies do exist to reduce the likelihood. None of them, however, are cost-free.

On the corporate side, the proposed strategy is restricted to manufacturing MNEs and not to those in the service sector or those involved in activities of a project nature. This chapter is also not concerned directly with organizational and integration issues within the MNE, which were considered in Chapters 8 and 9.[4]

The strategy applies to a wide selection of nations, developed and less-developed alike. Only in those select nations where discriminatory legislation against foreign firms is nonexistent, either because of judicial restraints or because the presence of overwhelming bilateral exchanges militates against intervention, does this strategy not apply.

---

[4]For a discussion of some of the implementation and integration difficulties encountered by this kind of activity, see S.J. Kobrin, *Managing Political Risk Assessment* (Berkeley: University of California Press, 1982).

Defense Strategies

Successful strategies are based on two separate activities: profitably increasing the subsidiary's bargaining power, and adapting its political behavior to its political profile. In addition, several ineffective yet popular strategies are also discussed. Finally, modifications to the basic defense strategy are described.

Maximizing Subsidiary Bargaining Power

The most frequently used method of increasing the bargaining power of the subsidiary is to stay ahead of the technical and managerial capabilities of the host nation. Over time this is operationalized by *significant technological upgrades* within the existing product line. Alternatively, if the speed of technological change is not rapid enough to outrun the domestic learning rate, or if the level of technology is not sufficiently complex, then staying ahead will require the *introduction of new products.*

The purpose of these upgrades is to keep bargaining power high by maintaining the gap between the capabilities of local entrepreneurs and businesspeople, and the capabilities needed to operate the subsidiary. While this gap is maintained, the subsidiary is still dependent on the MNE, creating a bargaining disadvantage for local interventionists.

Another means of increasing bargaining power is through *significant exports.* To be effective these must either be to a market where the MNE has a strong competitive advantage, or they must be so price-sensitive that continued MNE manufacturing support is a prerequisite. While providing rapid and visible bargaining power, the successful implementation of this strategy is also the most demanding of the defense strategies.

The final major source of bargaining power stems from MNE *sourcing or vertical integration* as discussed in Chapter 5. Obviously, there are strong disincentives for local business or government to intervene in a firm that, say, imports a proprietary one-third-completed product for further assembly, with sales locally and to other parts of the MNE. While obvious examples occur in the auto industry, manufacturers of industrial tools, of some specialized chemicals, and of electronics, can implement this strategy as well. Japanese MNEs are frequent users of this strategy, using world-scale plants and trading houses. To guarantee effectiveness, multiple sourcing of the same components or products within the MNE system is necessary to ensure that the subsidiary will not be held hostage by a government taking advantage of its role as a sole supplier within the multinational system.

Threats to the Strategy.   The effectiveness of these strategies for increasing the subsidiary's bargaining power can be reduced in two ways. The first comes from the existence of significant foreign competition either within the host nation, or outside, and wishing to enter the host nation. Such competition reduces the nation's dependence on one MNE to supply the resources needed to operate the subsidiary. In effect, such competition forces individual MNEs to build a stronger bargaining position than would otherwise be necessary.

An even greater and more recent threat to these strategies comes from the growth of alternative suppliers of complete technology. These firms supply host nation companies, eroding the role of the MNE as the exclusive supplier of such resources, and reducing the bargaining position of the foreign direct investor. These suppliers are usually small firms, from developed nations, and tend to specialize in a complex product that they sell worldwide.

Implementing the Strategy.   Successful implementation revolves around two management issues: knowing *when* to upgrade or increase the subsidiary's bargaining power, and
successfully *installing* the upgrade (new process, a profitable export market, and the like)
in both the subsidiary and the MNE's worldwide organization.

Basic to the successful management of costly intervention is the determination of the
subsidiary's bargaining position vis-à-vis any potential interventionist. In other words, to
what extent can the MNE contribution be replaced, in whole or in part, by domestic firms?
Knowing one's bargaining position helps one assess the probability of intervention and the
need for a bargaining power upgrade.

Exhibit 12–2 illustrates in a conceptual sense the subsidiary's intervention management problem. Upon entry into the host nation, the subsidiary's bargaining position is usually high ("A"). The subsidiary's level of technology and management skill is generally
higher than the capabilities resident in the host country. Over time this gap decreases, as
host nationals learn directly from the subsidiary or from other foreign firms, training, overseas education, and so forth. This learning reduces the dependence on the MNE as the supplier of these resources, which ensures the continued success of the subsidiary. In other
words, the relative bargaining power of the MNE dissipates over time as the skills are
learned by host nationals.

Conceptually, the ideal time to upgrade, or increase one's bargaining power, is just
before the host nation's bargaining power is "equal" to the firm's (point "B" in Exhibit
12–2). At this point, the host nation government or interest groups begin to believe that they
can replace the MNE contribution with domestic technology, management, sourcing, and

EXHIBIT 12–2   Relative Bargaining Power over Time

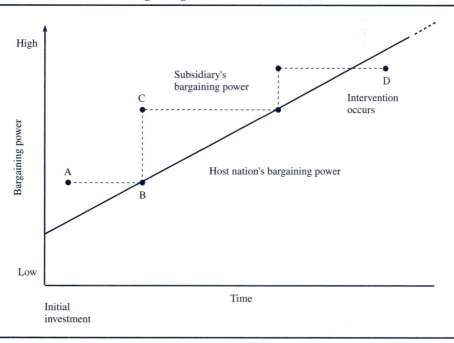

so on, without too great a loss. By this time, MNE threats to withdraw services or skills in the hope of preventing intervention are less of a deterrent to domestic entrepreneurs and others who have been pushing for government intervention.

A bargaining power upgrade at point "B" would include any of the items noted earlier in this chapter. To illustrate this point, for a subsidiary importing electronic components for assembly into a mature electromechanical device, an upgrade could involve the domestic manufacture of the more sophisticated electronic components not easily available in the host country. This tactic could raise the subsidiary's position to point "C." Failure to upgrade one's bargaining position will eventually result in some form of costly intervention (point "D"), such as a forced joint venture or a forced local-sourcing of components.

Operationally, to determine each subsidiary's bargaining power requires a measurement of the local firm's ability to provide the following resources:

- Technology (process/product).
- Management skill.
- Ability to replace MNE sourcing (inputs-outputs).

Collecting these data requires specific management resources. Executives capable of monitoring the activities, growth, and capability of existing or potential interventionists are required. Not only does this monitoring require considerable senior management time, but these executives must be familiar with and be able to obtain intelligence on local competitors. Most U.S. MNEs are particularly hard hit by the latter requirement, given their personnel strategy of frequently relocating executives.

MNEs have developed various mechanisms to collect these data. Some use staff specialized in competitor analysis, while others have the subsidiary general manager develop appropriate procedures. Generally, it appears to require a couple of years before the mechanism works well, but there are some tangible short-term benefits. The approach immediately focuses management attention—albeit without precision—on the single most important aspect of their intervention environment: existing or potential domestic competitors.

The second management issue associated with implementing the defense strategy involves the successful installation of the bargaining power upgrade. On one level, upgrading the technological and managerial complexity of the subsidiary by introducing new processes or products is strategically straightforward. Managerially, to extract a profitable return from the upgrade, the challenge is to find and train staff to handle the new activities. MNEs already accustomed to rapid technical change have a special advantage here. The container manufacturer who can progress from cork-lined to plastic-lined bottle caps, to three-seam cans, seamless cans, pressurized cans, all the way up to the sale and maintenance of complex bottling equipment, is a classic example of a firm in which one product line allows for a natural progression up the scale of technological complexity. Preparing managers and technical staff to handle those upgrades is much easier than preparing staff to handle brand new products or highly complex technologies.

Exporting as a defense mechanism is often noted by executives and observers, but very difficult to implement successfully. To be successful, production must be at world prices, with the attendant world-scale plant. While these stringent demands can be partially allayed by generous host government capital, operating subsidies, and export assistance, often the success of this strategy is mitigated by the unavailability of competitively priced inputs, uncompetitive wage and productivity rates, and managers more accustomed to operating behind tariff walls than over them.

Such an export strategy can be successful if one constructs a portfolio of different businesses with high *average* bargaining power. Multiproduct firms can establish a single export plant in a host country, providing both high bargaining power and foreign exchange. Other operations, such as the local manufacture—or even importation—of a mature product can be grouped with the export plant and, hence, be protected. Viewed in this manner, the lower intervention risk—but often lower profits—offered by the export operation when matched with the high profits obtained from imported or protected products provides an acceptable overall strategy.

The implementation problems associated with intra-MNE component and product sourcing are not unlike those associated with exporting. While the need to match the world price is slightly relaxed when sales are to associate firms, additional resources are spent ensuring that product specifications, supply, and so forth are accepted worldwide. As with exports, the ability to append products with less bargaining power, but more profit, makes this strategy more attractive.

Reducing Barriers to Successful Implementation.   Several multinationals have had problems successfully implementing some of the strategies recommended in this chapter. The difficulties appear to be of two different kinds: first, a scarcity of personnel appropriate to the new strategy; and second, the fact that this strategy runs completely counter to the MNE's traditional response to intervention.

The defense strategies call for more managerial and technical capabilities to be located in subsidiaries. Not only do export strategies, technology upgrades, and intra-MNE sourcing call for more technical skills, but—as all observers of the international scene suggest—increased numbers of politically attuned executives can be profitably used in subsidiaries, too. The high cost of the former, and the scarcity of the latter, deter some MNES.

These implementation difficulties are not found in all MNES, however. Some MNEs appear to have far fewer problems in obtaining executives willing to spend most of their careers in subsidiaries. The sources of their success include, differences in control systems, executive recruitment policies, promotion and compensation patterns, and perceived subsidiary autonomy. In addition, there is a strong suggestion that most MNEs have great difficulties managing both technologically adept executives and politically adept executives in the same organization. It appears that organizational structures, as well as promotion and reporting relationships, cannot easily adjust to dealing with such diametrically opposed executives. In a technology-driven MNE, executives with considerable political or country-based skills often find themselves in ineffectual staff positions. Such executives seem to be more active and to hold line positions in MNEs where knowledge of domestic markets, distribution channels, and so forth is the driving force behind the company, as in the consumer-packaged foods industry, for example.

While consumer-driven firms seem to be the main benefactors of the politically adept executive, the technology-driven MNEs do not automatically suffer from increased intervention as a result of their absence. The reason, of course, lies in the latter's use of changing technology as a source of bargaining power, a defense infrequently available to consumer-driven firms.

Successful MNEs are able either to accommodate both kinds of executives in the same organization, or recognize clearly their intolerance for such accommodation and behave accordingly. These latter firms decide which kind of executive their firm needs and then organize to keep a steady supply available. Consumer-driven MNEs hire, train, and promote politically skilled executives with local market knowledge who defend the subsidiary primarily through the addition of new products and adroit intervention forecasting. These executives tend to remain in particular subsidiaries for long periods. Technology-driven firms concentrate on executives who are good "transporters of technology," as one MNE called them, and who tend to treat the world as one market. These MNEs tend to develop subsidiaries with export markets, complex technologies, and proprietary sourcing.

The second problem that makes MNEs hesitate to implement the defensive strategy is the complete reversal it represents from the traditional MNE response to intervention. For much of their history most MNEs responded to threats by *reducing* their asset exposure and speeding up profit repatriation. They justified this response by referring to the highly unpredictable nature of government intervention. This response also paralleled the behavior—and won the approval—of international bankers. In contrast, new subsidiary defense strategies call for *increased* investment when intervention threatens.

Many MNEs also find the decision to increase the managerial and technical capabilities of subsidiary personnel to have a double edge. Because these capabilities can be partially acquired by potential interventionists by hiring away personnel, MNEs sometimes see the training of subsidiary personnel as a threat to their bargaining power. Some MNEs think it is best to withhold training. In reality, though, such "leakage" of capabilities and technology from the subsidiary to potential interventionists will always occur without regard to the level of capabilities. Unfortunately, the MNE does not have an option, because withholding training and new equipment only serves to reduce the MNE's bargaining power even further.

Optimum Political Strategy

The choice of political strategy is determined by the political profile the subsidiary exhibits. This political profile seems to be determined by the size of the firm and the firm's strategic importance to the host country. Action against a large employer provides greater publicity impact, allows greater opportunities for implementing political directives and, in some nations, satisfies trade unions. For similar reasons, firms in strategically important industries, such as natural resources, banking, insurance, and public utilities, also have a high political profile.

The political strategy for very high profile firms tries to affect the political as well as the economic costs of intervention. Political involvement is necessary, because raising the *economic* costs of intervention alone is frequently not sufficient to offset the high *political* benefits that accrue to interventionists. Under this strategy, some MNEs establish joint ventures involving firms from several nations, and use similarly syndicated project finance. This transnational web of MNEs and financial institutions, which raises the political as well as the economic cost of intervention, is common.[5] The object of such equity and financial participation is to involve nations that are the export markets, suppliers, bankers, political

[5]For further discussion of this role of project finance, see T.H. Moran with Debbie Havens Maddox, *Transnational Corporations in the Copper Industry* (New York: UN Center on Transnational Corporations, 1981); and Moran's outline of possible complications facing U.S. MNEs in F. Ghadar, S.J. Kobrin, and T.H. Moran, eds., *Managing International Risk* (Washington, DC: The Landegger Program, Georgetown University, 1983), p. 164.

supporters, and aid donors of the host government. This type of deterrent is subject to much criticism from host governments, but it appears to be an effective defense for firms with a high political profile.

Most subsidiaries, however, do not have a high political profile and, hence, do not automatically provide large political benefits to interventionists. Unlike the high-profile ones, these subsidiaries have a whole range of political strategies available to them. They may remain uninvolved, initiating no contacts with the host government and, when interaction is necessary, use the local board of trade instead of direct interaction. The more active alternative involves the maintenance of working relationships with several ministers and senior civil servants.

The optimum political behavior strategy is, again, determined by company characteristics. Research in several nations suggests that only small, nondescript subsidiaries should be politically noninvolved. Here the ability of the firm to remain anonymous is *enhanced* by its lack of political involvement. But all others, it is suggested, will benefit from political involvement. Politicians and civil servants can be briefed on the MNE's contribution to the subsidiary's success—its bargaining power. More importantly, such relationships can help the subsidiary identify proponents of intervention, providing the opportunity to offer arrangements satisfactory to the interventionist but less costly to the subsidiary.[6]

Ineffective Strategies

The rhetorical preoccupations of politicians, civil servants, and most critics of MNEs are not useful guides to the formulation of successful strategies. Cries for appropriate technology, for the creation of foreign exchange, for an often cited but undefined good corporate citizenship, for licensing (as discussed in Chapter 6), and for joint partnerships do not lead to a parallel reduction in the intervention experiences of MNEs that so accommodate their hosts.

While some of these recommended strategies are harmless, others have the opposite effect and cause governments to intervene at an accelerated rate. Some MNEs respond to requests for "appropriate technology" only to find that their labor-intensive, low-to-moderate technology facility has been taken over, or duplicated, by a domestic firm. Voluntary joint ventures, while providing several advantages to both partners, also provide an ideal opportunity for an active domestic partner to learn the latest technology and management skills, hence reducing the MNE's bargaining power (as discussed in Chapter 7). Some domestic partners go on to compete with their MNE partners. Italian scooter manufacturers are facing competition from their Indian ex-partners, as are U.S. petrochemical firms from South Korean ex-partners.

To offset this leakage of technology in joint ventures, the defensive strategies are usually restricted to intra-MNE sourcing, and, to a lesser extent, exporting to protected markets. However, some firms have maintained complete control over subsidiary joint ventures by continually changing the production processes—reducing the ability of local personnel to gain experience by restricting participation in local research activities to expatriates.

---

[6]For a more general discussion of the organizational issues involved when MNEs deal with host governments, see Amir Mahini, "The Management of Government Relations in U.S. Multinationals," D.B.A. dissertation, Harvard Business School, 1982.

Modifications to the Basic Strategy

While the basic defense strategy is similar for most manufacturing MNES, modifications are required, depending on the host country. The main source of the variation is the difference in bargaining power of each host nation. For many reasons, individual nations are at different positions on the bargaining power ladder. One could also postulate that nations move up the bargaining power ladder at different rates, as we have observed with the development of some of the newly industrialized countries.

Other modifications to the basic strategy are possible if MNEs have unique skills or business strategies. MNEs without access to more complex technology, export markets, or proprietary intrafirm sourcing resort to innovative techniques for increasing their bargaining power. This might include, for example, always linking up with an aggressive domestic entrepreneur.

Implications for MNE Parents

The proposed strategy for defending the subsidiary affects the MNE's allocation of human, technical, and capital resources and introduces new managerial activities to the parent's organization. The new strategy must also be institutionalized, or integrated into the MNE's organization.

The greatest implication of this strategy is that each subsidiary will require a greater amount of capital (machinery, working capital, and the like) and a larger number of better trained technicians and managers. For the majority of MNEs, such increased subsidiary needs can be so high as to be unaffordable. They face a choice of retaining either the existing number of intervention-prone subsidiaries around the world or of supporting fewer subsidiaries but with an effective defense strategy. The trade-off is difficult for many MNEs and, again, runs counter to the intuitively appealing strategy of a larger diversified portfolio of subsidiaries. The subsidiary defense strategy, on the other hand, calls for a smaller portfolio containing less risky subsidiaries.

New activities, such as intervention management, have to fit into existing organizational and decision-making structures of the MNE to be effective. While the existing organizational structures may not be optimal, organizations do not easily change structures to accommodate new activities. Those MNEs implementing this strategy find that requests for bargaining power upgrades are presented in much the same way as capital budget requests. However, the similarities end there. The staff in most MNEs have little experience in evaluating such bargaining upgrade requests; moreover, most upgrades will affect other subsidiaries as well. Export and sourcing strategics, for example, can affect the product offering of the whole MNE system.

Multinational enterprises that trade in machinery, products, processes, and managers will experience a significant increase in intracompany trade under the defense strategy. Consequently, another managerial activity is the coordination of subsidiaries that now trade with each other. Agreements must be made on product characteristics, price, and quantity, and when problems arise, they must be perceived as being equitably resolved.

EXHIBIT 12–3   Kinds of Multinational Enterprise

	Global	*Multinational*
Defense strategy	State-of-the-art technology	Introducing new products
	Exports	Better intervention forecasting
	Intra-MNE sourcing	
Political strategy	Lower priority	High local political knowledge and interaction
Staffing	Short-term, technologically oriented	Long-term, politically oriented

---

Several MNEs have centered many of the management activities in newly revived area headquarters. This is the point in the organization where there appears to be the best supply of pertinent product and country information, all of which is necessary to perform the allocation and integration activities required of the defense strategy.

While MNEs vary in how they defend their subsidiaries from intervention, some patterns are emerging. The patterns can be observed in Exhibit 12–3, which divides MNEs into those that follow a global strategy and those that follow a multidomestic strategy.

Summary

A better understanding of the changing world of government–MNE relations has prompted a shift in political risk analysis. For multinational manufacturing firms, assessing the vulnerability of each subsidiary to intervention is far more important than assessing broad political shocks. While very few nations offer a safe haven from intervention, certain kinds of subsidiaries do. This chapter suggests that MNEs should decrease their emphasis on choosing the right country and, instead, develop strategies to defend individual subsidiaries from intervention.

There are several strategies that constitute a successful defense. Strategies calling for manufacturing activities requiring continued MNE technological or managerial input, intraMNE sourcing of proprietary components and end products, and exporting are the more successful ones. The success of these strategies is facilitated as new processes and products are introduced, technological upgrades take place, and scale efficiencies allow for intraMNE sourcing and exporting. These strategies increase the cost to interventionists of unilaterally increasing their share of a foreign-owned operation.

They have their roots in a defense system, and they do not always produce short-term financial or technical benefits. One may have to say no to the engineers and the finance department, and, instead, structure the subsidiary's activities in a way that always leaves the MNE with something to offer either when the technology matures or after a coup, when vulnerability is inevitable.

Another requirement of a successful defense is to adapt the subsidiary's political behavior to its political profile. Only extremely strong or small subsidiaries without any strategic importance can afford the luxury of avoiding political interaction.

Like most strategies, implementation is a difficult phase. Capital. machinery, technicians, and managers who are well trained and politically adept, export markets, and area coordinators are the scarce resources necessary to make the defense strategy work. While the scarcity of resources poses surmountable obstacles for most MNES, the bigger obstacle is the psychological turnaround this defense mechanism represents. While traditional strategies call for asset reduction and country diversification, this new strategy usually demands an increase in the assets at stake in each country, often necessitating a commensurate decrease in the number of countries served. MNEs, for good business reasons, have difficulty accommodating dramatically different strategic responses. Change will be slow.

MNEs that compete globally will find this defense strategy relatively easy to accommodate and implement. Three popular means of defense—intra-MNE sourcing, exports, and state-of-the-art technology—are characteristic of such MNEs. MNEs that compete on a country-by-country basis tend to rely on introducing new products, building alliances with domestic firms, and better forecasting of when upgrades are necessary.

The importance of proper management of intervention is emphasized when one considers that the same qualities that make some nations attractive to MNEs also increase those nations' bargaining power and, hence, their tendency to intervene. If MNEs react to intervention by withdrawing or reducing their exposure, or by trying to confront and obstruct host government policies, they may foreclose potentially attractive investment opportunities.

The results of such a strategy for the host nation are higher average levels of technology transfer and more foreign direct investment. For the MNE, the results include lower level of intervention, stable profits, and less-frustrated executives. Upon closer examination, for MNEs accustomed to serious competition in their home market, this is a more familiar strategy than the traditional one of forecasting political stability and ideology.

Conclusion

From our introductory chapters on the global environment and internationalization, through the entire process of multinational management, our constant emphasis has been on ways of understanding and improving the practice of international management. As this chapter has demonstrated, even political risk, viewed by so many as totally beyond the control of the MNE, can, in part, be managed.

Supplementary Reading

Boddewyn, Jean J. "Political Aspects of MNE Theory." *Journal of International Business Studies,* Vol. 19, No. 3, 1988.

Brewer, Thomas L. "An Issue-Area Approach to the Analysis of MNE-Government Relations." *Journal of International Business Studies,* Vol. 23, No. 2, 1992.

Butler, Kirt C., and D.C. Joaquin. "A Note on Political Risk and the Required Return on Foreign Direct Investment." *Journal of International Business Studies,* Vol. 29, No. 3, 1998.

Doz, Y.L., and C.K. Prahalad, "How MNEs Cope with Host Government Intervention." *Harvard Business Review,* March-April 1980.

Harvey, Michael G. "A Survey of Corporate Programs for Managing Terrorist Threats." *Journal of International Business Studies,* Vol. 24, No. 3, 1993.

Makhija, Mona. "Government Intervention in the Venezuelan Petroleum Industry: An Empirical Investigation of Political Risk." *Journal of International Business Studies,* Vol. 24, No. 3, 1993.

Makino, Shige, and Paul W. Beamish. "Local Ownership Restrictions, Entry Mode Choice, and FDI Performance: Japanese Overseas Subsidiaries in Asia." *Asia Pacific Journal of Management,* Vol. 15, 1998, pp. 119–36.

Miller. Kent D. "A Framework for Integrated Risk Management in International Business." *Journal of International Business Studies,* Vol. 23, No. 2, 1992.

Minor, Michael S. "The Demise of Expropriation as an Instrument of LDC Policy, 1980-92." *Journal of International Business Studies,* Vol. 25, No. 1, 1994, pp. 177–88.

13 GLOBAL LEADERSHIP

Without doubt, the global marketplace of today is a highly risky place. It is filled with new competitors, new cultures, and huge logistical problems for managers. Despite these challenges, the global marketplace is also filled with enormous promise. The world's largest economy, the U.S. economy, represents less than one-quarter of the world's GNP. For U.S. companies, the message is clear: the biggest opportunities for sales growth are outside the United States. For non-U.S. companies, the importance of global markets is even more pronounced. As companies prepare to enter the next millennium, managers cannot afford to ignore persistent, perplexing questions that are at the heart of successfully conquering the global business frontier.

While the focus of this book has been on international management, its ultimate impact is on the practice of global leadership. Global leaders ultimately determine the map that that will guide both themselves and their companies to new heights of international competitiveness. Leadership is all about influencing the actions and beliefs of others. Global leaders are able to do this across multiple countries and markets in ways that maximize profits for their companies. Required is a combination of both knowledge and skills that will enable managers to operate effectively as leaders everywhere in the world. The requirement for more and better global leaders is vast. It has become impossible to ignore the pressures for globalization. A great need exists for global leaders. This includes not only those on international assignments, but those who work on a day-to-day basis with global business issues within their companies, and those who work for domestic companies that have international competitors or global aspirations. One study, published in 1998, reported the results of a survey of 110 Fortune 500 companies.[1] The researchers asked senior executives at participating firms whether they had enough global leaders in their companies. The results, reported in Exhibit 13–1, indicate that for the sampled companies, only 15 percent had

---

This chapter was prepared by Allen J. Morrison.

[1]H. Gregersen, A.J. Morrison, and S. Black. "Developing Leaders for the Global Frontier," *Sloan Management Review,* Fall 1998, Vol. 40, No. 1, pp. 21–32.

enough or more than enough global leaders. The same study also asked whether the existing cadre of managers had the requisite skills to be effective global leaders. These results
are reported in Exhibit 13–2. Sixty-seven percent of companies indicated that their current
managers either had no capability or less global leaderships capability than required.

Clearly, most companies lack enough high-quality global leaders. Most observers also
believe that leadership is not so much a function of position as it is a function of attitude
and competencies. Positions in an organization chart do not determine leadership. Instead,
leadership is rooted in an individual's ability to convince employees of the need to change
and to move forward with them in new and challenging ways.

EXHIBIT 13–1   The Quantity of Global Leaders

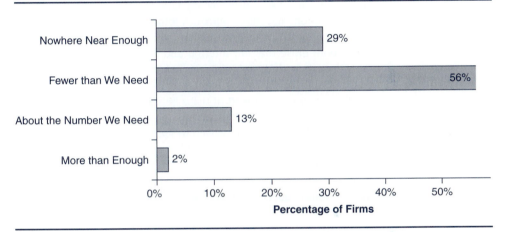

EXHIBIT 13–2   The Quality of Global Leaders

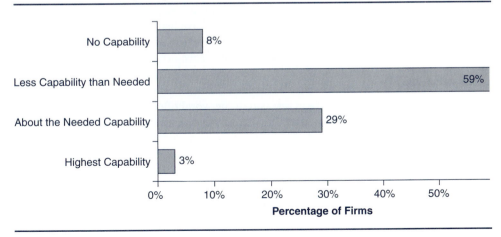

The Importance of Global Leadership

During much of the post-WWII era, international business was a topic of interest to a limited number of business professionals. These individuals typically worked in specialized international operations departments in large companies. In most companies, international business was considered secondary to domestic operations, almost an afterthought. However, beginning in the 1970s, things started to change. As trade and investment soared and as high-profile Japanese MNCs began to make inroads in U.S. and European markets, an increasing number of managers awoke to the potential of the global marketplace.

Initially, most practitioners used domestic leadership models in "going global." In the United States, leadership models have generally been grounded on several beliefs about both roles and markets. One common belief is in the importance of hierarchical command and control structures. Many U.S. models emphasize strong, decisive decision making, delegation, and tight control. Another common belief is in the power of efficient markets. Many models highlight leaders who effectively exploit short-term market inefficiencies, both those that are internal and external to the firm. External market inefficiencies primarily include opportunities in competitive markets, capital markets, and labor markets. Internal inefficiencies include matters of employee discrimination and operational redundancies. As a result of these beliefs, good leaders are portrayed as those who are resolute in performing internal audits and conducting external market research. Not surprisingly, under the U.S. approach to leadership, knowledge becomes a key determinant of success. The more you know, the more opportunities you recognize and the more your input is valued.

In most cases, individuals tend to move into leadership positions when they exemplify dominant national leadership models. Americans love leaders like Jack Welch, Andy Grove, and Lou Gerstner because their behaviors are consistent with a U.S.-centric model of leadership: they have powerful command and control skills, demonstrate strong analytical skills, and know how to make lots of money. None of this is bad, per se, but it is quintessentially American.

The U.S. leadership field has multiple foci and, without doubt, much can be learned about global leadership by studying U.S. leadership models. Unfortunately, the majority of leadership models generated in the U.S. have had problems working outside the United States.[2] What works in one country often produces less desirable outcomes in other countries. An important reason for this is the difference in cultural norms and values between countries. In matters as diverse as gift giving, compensation, job security, and the role of ethnic groups and minorities in the workplace, cultural norms vary widely.[3] As a result, leadership models that are effective in one part of the world often have problems being applied elsewhere.

European, Asian, and Latin American leadership models are often different from each other and from U.S. models. For example, in one study of 10 multinational corporations from eight different countries, researchers found that while Australians believed leaders needed to be catalysts of cultural change, Japanese and Koreans did not think this was a

---

[2]E. Jackofsky, J. Slocum, and S. McQuaid. "Cultural Values and the CEO: Alluring Companions," *Academy of Management Executive,* Vol. 2, No. 1, 1988, pp. 39–49.

[3]M. Nyaw and I. Ng. "A Comparative Analysis of Ethical Beliefs: A Four Country Study," *Journal of Business Ethics,* Vol. 13, 1994, pp. 543–55.

critical characteristic of leaders.[4] The researchers also found that a disproportionate number of Koreans and Germans valued leaders who placed a high value on integrity and trust. Meanwhile, French employees wanted leaders who demonstrated skills at managing internal and external networks. Interestingly, Americans, Germans, Australians, Italians, Koreans, and British managers placed far less emphasis on these skills. Finally, Italians were shown to value leaders who were flexible and adaptive; Australians and Americans generally cared about these competencies much less.

A number of studies have shown that leadership models differ because of cultural differences on a range of variables including interpersonal relationships, profits, bureaucracy, ethics, and risk taking.[5] A well-known expression in Japan, "the nail that stands up gets pounded back down," suggests that Japanese leaders should be good at building consensus and "fitting in." In China, maintaining and developing relationships are valued much more than maximizing company efficiency. As a result, skills associated with conducting market research and strategic thinking are valued less in China than in the United States. Also, interestingly, educational achievement and having attended elite graduate schools are far less important for being accepted as a leader in China than in the United States. Rather, in China family connections and long-term relationships are emphasized.

National leadership models generally work best when leaders deal with people from their same culture. However, as companies globalize, the leadership models that were so effective at home begin to create real problems. By their very nature, ethnocentric leadership models have a difficult time being globalized. In order for a company to operate most effectively overseas, its leaders must develop competencies that go beyond what is familiar in the home country.[6] In general, the best Japanese, German, or Canadian, or Chinese, or American leaders do not make the best global leaders.

Global leadership is ultimately about transcending national differences and embracing the most effective practices, wherever they are in the world. As a result, global companies need more than simply an American, European, or Asian approach to leadership. They require a model that can be applied everywhere they compete throughout the world. Such a model would transcend and integrate national leadership schemes and become a powerful tool for hiring, training, and retaining the leaders of tomorrow.

The Characteristics of Effective Global Leaders

Over the past decade, numerous articles and books have been published specifically on the topic of global leadership. These publications range from prescriptive books,[7] which simply address the need for more and better global leaders, to comprehensive academic articles based on systematic, multimethod research efforts. Not surprisingly, the number

---

[4]A. Yeung and D. Ready. "Developing Leadership Capabilities of Global Corporations: A Comparative Study in Eight Nations." *Human Resource Management,* Winter 1995, Vol. 34, No. 4, pp. 529–47.

[5]See, for example, N. Boyacigiller and N. Adler, "The Parochial Dinosaur: Organizational Science in a Global Context." *Academy of Management Review,* Vol. 16, No. 2, 1991, pp. 262–90; G. Hofstede, *Culture's Consequences: International Differences in Work-Related Values* (Beverly Hills: Sage Publications, 1980).

[6]T. Yamaguchi, "The Challenge of Internationalization: Japan's Kokusaika." *Academy of Management Executive.* Vol. 2, No. 1, 1988, pp. 33–36.

[7]See, for example, T. Brake, *The Global Leader: Critical Factors for Creating the World Class Organization* (Chicago: Irwin Professional Publishing, 1997).

of descriptive articles and books far outweighs the number of rigorous, systematic studies. Also, the quality of research and writing on global leadership varies widely.

One of the most comprehensive studies of global leadership was conducted over a three-year period in the late 1990s.[8] The authors interviewed more than 130 senior executives in more than 50 MNCs throughout North America, Europe, and Asia. These individuals were identified by their companies as role models or "archetypal" global leaders. One of the questions these leaders were asked was simply, "What are you good at?" Interestingly, the responses were quite similar.

The research concluded that about two-thirds of what it takes to be an effective global leader is actually generalizable. The other one-third of leadership competencies are idiosyncratic or specific to the MNC, its home country, the manager's position in the company, or the industry. For example, the leader of a French group of accountants at Renault needs a somewhat different competency base than the leader of a group of Japanese product developers at Hitachi. Because every situation is somewhat unique, global leaders need some competencies that reflect local conditions.

Despite the need for idiosyncratic competencies, the majority of global leadership competencies are highly generalizable. Every global leader needs a set of knowledge and skills that operate around the world. Three distinct sets of competencies or characteristics were identified in the research: demonstrating savvy, exhibiting character, and maintaining perspective. These are shown in Exhibit 13–3.

Demonstrating Savvy

Global leaders demonstrate two types of savvy: global business savvy and global organizational savvy. Global business savvy is ultimately based on the leader's ability to make money for the firm on a worldwide basis. As discussed in Chapter 3, making money globally comes through recognizing three different types of market opportunities: first, arbitrage opportunities, which involve differences in the cost of inputs and quality differences across countries; second, new market opportunities for the company's goods and services; and third, efficiency-maximizing opportunities that can be generated through economies of scale and the elimination of redundancies. (Global operations based on standardized products often produce huge efficiency gains for companies.) Recognizing each of these global market opportunities requires considerable insight and sensitivity. Many of the background concepts associated with global business savvy are provided in Chapters 1 through 5 and Chapter 8 of this book. In addition, an education in and knowledge of such disparate topics as international finance, marketing, and accounting are very helpful.

Global organizational savvy is required to secure the resources necessary to implement international strategies. Organizational savvy includes knowing the right people in the company, knowing where the skills and competencies are located, and knowing how things really work in the company. Many of the competencies associated with organizational savvy are described in Chapter 9. Some of the key knowledge areas include awareness of the product lines offered by key subsidiaries, familiarity with the cost structures and overall competitiveness of key subsidiaries, and insights into where managerial and employee talent are located within the global organization.

---

[8]S. Black, A. Morrison, and H. Gregersen, *Global Explorers: The Next Generation of Leaders* (New York: Routledge, 1999).

EXHIBIT 13–3   The Characteristics of Effective Global Leaders

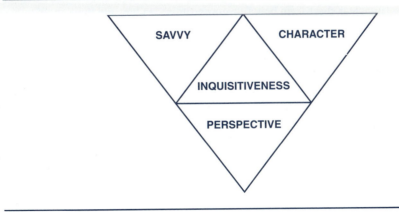

Exhibiting Character

Exhibiting character is the second characteristic of effective global leaders. Character has two different dimensions. First, it includes the ability to emotionally connect with people. Second, it involves the ability to demonstrate high personal integrity. Both of these dimensions of character are essential in developing and retaining goodwill and trust in a globally diverse workforce. Without goodwill and trust, leadership is impossible.

Emotional connections involve the establishment of close personal relationships with people. The ability to work well with others and in teams is discussed at length in Chapter 11. Emotional connections are important for three main reasons: first, they help leaders better understand local market conditions; second, they help leaders better understand conditions within the company, including what is happening in the lives of direct reports, peers, and superiors; and third, they help leaders identify and mentor future leaders within the organization. All three of these benefits assist global leaders both in formulating and implementing current and future international strategies.

Connecting emotionally enables global leaders to overcome the very real communication barriers that divide people culturally and geographically. Beyond understanding the words, emotionally connecting with people requires the interchange of feelings. As explained in Chapters 6 and 7, close personal relationships can also play an important role in the formation and stability of alliances, including licensing and equity joint ventures. In many parts of the world, personal relationships instead of legal contracts hold alliances together.

Integrity is the second dimension of character. It plays a critical role in company morale and significantly impacts the credibility of the leader. Integrity involves both external and internal activities carried out by the leader. In both types of activities, cultural differences sometimes pressure global leaders to rely on situational ethics. In some cases, the resulting activities would be frowned upon at home or might even be illegal.

The failure to embrace consistent ethical standards—whether involving external or internal activities—jeopardizes the ability of managers to lead globally. Activities that are undertaken in one part of the world are almost always heard about back at home. This applies to both companies and leaders. Lapses in ethical judgement, while not always fatal, are difficult to recover from and almost always undermine a leader's ability to engender the type of goodwill necessary to lead effectively. Situational ethics, while often providing clear short-term benefits, compromise leaders and their companies who ultimately get judged by global standards of conduct.

Maintaining Perspective

Maintaining perspective is the third characteristic of global leaders. Perspective has two dimensions: the first is the ability to manage uncertainty, and the second is the ability to balance globalization and localization pressures. Maintaining perspective is one of the most difficult tasks for global leaders, who are constantly bombarded by conflicting and often unreconcilable demands.

Uncertainty is an inescapable aspect of global business in general and leadership more specifically. Leaders ultimately arbitrate on matters involving the company's strategy, structure, and systems. Because competitive norms, markets, values, and governments differ so widely, the level of uncertainty faced by global leaders is of an order of magnitude higher than that which is confronted by domestic managers. Another challenge for global leaders occurs when they deal with emerging markets. In emerging markets, the quality and quantity of available competitive, economic, social, and political data are often severely lacking or are of dubious quality. Global leaders routinely confront either a flood of data or a dearth of data. Deciding what is believable and what is not is a huge challenge.

Many Western managers are uncomfortable acting with little of no quality data. Their normal approach is to research issues until the risk of decision making is minimized to the lowest level possible. If data cannot be collected or if the data are unreliable, decisions are delayed. In contrast, global leaders are superb at deciding when to act and when to keep researching. This ability to get the timing of decision making right, while uncommon, is a critical characteristic of effective global leaders.

Balancing tensions between globalization and localization is the second dimension of perspective. As discussed in Chapter 9, notwithstanding the general movement toward globalization, many activities and company policies can and should remain local. Global-local tensions are common across a range of issues, including:

- Whether products should be globally standardized or locally designed.
- Whether employment policies should be set by corporate headquarters to apply worldwide or should be determined on a country-by-country basis.
- Whether fund-raising should be centrally controlled or left to the discretion of affiliate managers.
- Whether affiliates have the right to export products and compete with other affiliates.
- Whether the company's brands should be globally maintained or revised and maintained by local affiliates.

Enormous judgment is required in effectively addressing these questions. Often the answers are not readily apparent. In many cases, a particular course of action creates winners and losers within the organization and, with this, negative feelings for the decision maker. As a result, balancing tensions not only presents personal challenges, but requires intellectual stretch as well. The stress associated with balancing global tensions is unique to global leadership. Global leaders do not just put up with these tensions, they actually enjoy the challenge of figuring out solutions to the very real conflicts they face.

Inquisitiveness

A fourth component of global leadership is inquisitiveness. Inquisitiveness acts like a glue that holds global leaders together and keeps them relevant. Inquisitiveness is not a competency, but rather a state of mind. Someone who is inquisitive is eager to learn and goes out of his or her way to stay current with a range of relevant issues. Without inquisitiveness, it is impossible to develop a clear understanding of global markets or organizational resources. Without inquisitiveness, a manager never learns about changing local conditions and local values, or gets close to employees and customers. Without inquisitiveness, effective and timely decision making about which activities to globalize and which activities to localize is impossible.

The reality is that as companies globalize, some managers pay a lot of attention to global issues while others essentially ignore them. Some managers seem to be genuinely interested in what is happening in far-flung parts of the world. They watch global competitors, keep track of political events around the world, assess customers in other countries, and actually think about the competitive positions of the far-flung activities over which they have responsibility. In contrast, other managers seem genuinely disinterested in events outside their home country and even if they have responsibility for international activities, rarely spend time actually thinking about what is going on overseas. Despite the potential of global markets, they prefer the familiarity of domestic customers and the security of focusing on a limited number of competitors.

In many companies, the global inquisitiveness of leaders has lagged their ability to manage the processes around the initial decision to globalize. For the most part, these managers acknowledge the benefits of going global—after all, everyone else is doing it—and may even support an initial decision to globalize a certain process or function. But after the decision to globalize is made, their attention wanes. Globalization gets their attention, but because of a lack of inquisitiveness, does not keep their attention.

In assessing your own level of global inquisitiveness, some of the following questions might be helpful:

- Do you pay the most attention to domestic competitors or do you pay equal attention to all competitors, irrespective of their home countries?
- When travelling to a new country, do you go out of your way to learn about the culture, political systems, and history of the country you are visiting?
- When travelling in a foreign city, do you spend most of your spare time in your hotel room, or do you enjoy venturing out into the streets, museums, and markets?
- When travelling overseas, do you insist on using familiar hotel chains (Marriott, Hilton, Sheraton, etc.)?
- Do you enjoy reading the latest books on business, history, culture, international relations, etc.?

- Do you go out of your way to get to know the people you work with—their family situations, educational background, personal experiences?
- When faced with a troubling business issue involving a foreign affiliate, do you ask for input from people at head office or people who work in the affiliate?
- Do you spend a lot of time thinking about how your company's products and services could be better sold overseas?

Inquisitiveness and Personal Change

Inquisitiveness is a complex topic. It is ultimately tied to personal change and a commitment to continual self-improvement. Personal change is always a challenge. Smart and successful people are often the most threatened by change. In part, this stems from their lack of experience with failure. Years of personal success can lead to complacency and arrogance. Both are inconsistent with inquisitiveness and effectiveness as a global leader.

When faced with a new challenge, most people have a tendency to rely on what has worked well in the past. They work harder, they try more earnestly, perhaps they even try to think more intensely. But in the end, most people come back to doing what they have always done. Because of this, American leaders have a tendency to exaggerate their American features when faced with the challenges of globalizing their businesses. They want more hierarchy, more process controls, more market research, more short-term performance evaluations, and so on. They try to be better at doing what they know how to do. In their own ways, the Japanese act the same way; so do the British, the French, the Germans, and everyone else.

Those who are inquisitive focus much more on doing the right thing than they do on perfecting what they are currently doing. This takes courage. It also takes great insights and enormous self-confidence. For these reasons, there are far more followers of global leaders than there are global leaders. Perhaps this is why the surveys indicate that companies want more and better global leaders. If becoming a global company means downplaying nationality, then becoming a global leader means the same thing. Downplaying nationality is never easy, particularly when it comes to changing individual interests.

The Paradox of Global Leadership

The great paradox of global leadership is that despite the desire of companies for more and better global leaders, relatively few companies are doing much about it. In the earlier cited study of global leadership, only 8 percent of Fortune 500 companies reported having a comprehensive system in place to identify, develop, and retain global leaders.[9] Another 16 percent reported having some established global leadership development system in place, and 76 percent reported having either an ad hoc approach in place or were just starting to think about global leadership development. Seemingly, while the vast majority of companies want more and better global leaders, relatively few are doing much about it.

---

[9]H. Gregersen, A. Morrison, and S. Black, "Developing Leaders for the Global Frontier," *Sloan Management Review,* Vol. 40, No. 1, 1998, pp. 21–32.

The implications for future global leaders are significant. First, because of the perceived shortage of effective global leaders, those who have the requisite competencies will be in high demand. They can expect premium salaries and lots of career opportunities. Second, the global leaders of the future will take charge of their personal development today. Because the big majority of companies lack comprehensive global leadership development programs, every opportunity for self-development must be sought. Smart managers will assume that their companies will do little to manage their careers or development. And third, those with global leadership aspirations will aggressively pursue a range of developmental opportunities. These activities should include overseas travel, participation in cross-cultural teams, involvement in formal training programs at universities and institutes, and international assignments. Each one of these developmental activities has advantages and disadvantages depending on an individual's personal situation.

The developmental needs of every individual are different. Some lack global business acumen; others lack the ability to connect with people from other cultures; still others have a difficult time dealing with the complexity of global business. This book plays an important role in assisting individuals as they strive to become more effective global leaders. Each of the case studies that follows centers on a decision maker as he or she struggles with a wide range of tough issues. Mastering these issues will provide an important contribution to the development of the global leaders of tomorrow.

Supplementary Reading

Adler, N., and S. Bartholomew. "Managing Globally Competent People." *Academy of Management Executive,* Vol. 6, No. 3, 1992, pp. 52–65.

Bartlett, C., and S. Ghoshal. "What Is a Global Manager?" *Harvard Business Review,* September–October 1992, pp. 124–32.

Black, S., A. Morrison, and H. Gregersen. *Global Explorers: The Next Generation of Leaders.* New York: Routledge, 1999.

Brake, T. *The Global Leader: Critical Factors for Creating the World Class Organization.* Chicago: Irwin Professional Publishing, 1997.

Dorfman, P. "International and Cross-Cultural Leadership." In B.J. Punnett and O. Shenkar, eds., *Handbook for International Management Research.* Cambridge, MA: Blackwell, 1996, pp. 267–349.

Gregersen, H., A. Morrison, and S. Black. "Developing Leaders for the Global Frontier." *Sloan Management Review,* Vol. 40, No. 1, 1998, pp. 21–32.

House, R.J., P. Hanges, M. Agar, and A. Ruiz-Quintanilla. Conference on Global Leadership and Organizational Behavior (GLOBE). Calgary, Canada, 1994.

Jackofsky, E., J. Slocum, and S. McQuaid. "Cultural Values and the CEO: Alluring Companions." *Academy of Management Executive,* Vol. 2, No. 1, 1988, pp. 39–49.

Jago, A., and V. Vroom. "Hierarchical Level and Leadership Style." *Organizational Behavior and Human Performance,* Vol. 18, 1977, pp. 131–45.

Laurent, A. "The Cultural Diversity of Western Conceptions of Management." *International Studies of Management and Organization,* Vol. 8, No. 2, 1983, pp. 75–96.

Misumi, J. *The Behavioral Science of Leadership: An Interdisciplinary Japanese Research Program.* Ann Arbor, MI: University of Michigan Press, 1985.

Pfeffer, J. "Competitive Advantage through People." *California Management Review,* Winter 1994, pp. 9–28.

Schriesheim, C.A., and S. Kerr. "Theories and Measures of Leadership: A Critical Appraisal." *Leadership: The Cutting Edge.* Carbondale, IL: Southern Illinois University Press, 1977, pp. 9–45.

Tung, R., and E. Miller. "Managing in the Twenty-First Century: The Need for Global Orientation." *Management International Review,* Vol. 30, 1990, pp. 5–18.

Yeung, A. and Ready, D. "Developing Leadership Capabilities of Global Corporations: A Comparative Study in Eight Nations." *Human Resource Management,* Vol. 34, No. 4, 1995, pp. 529–47.

Yukl, G.A., and D. Van Fleet. "Theory and Research on Leadership in Organizations." *Handbook of Industrial and Organizational Psychology.* Palo Alto, CA: Consulting Psychology Press, 1992, pp. 147–97.

II CASES ON INTERNATIONALIZATION

14 LEO Electron Microscopy Ltd

A Zeiss-Leica Cooperation

In the spring of 1996, the leadership team of LEO, a 50–50 joint venture owned by Leica AG of Switzerland and Carl Zeiss of Germany, was discussing the proposed production site of the LEO P1, the high end scanning electron microscope (SEM) they were developing. The P1 would be the first product developed by the LEO research and development group, and it would combine the electronics know how of the former Carl Zeiss technologists with the software expertise of the Cambridge-based scientists who had formerly worked for Leica.

The original plan had been to produce all SEMs, including the P1, in Cambridge, but several developments had led the management team to reconsider. Jan Ludwig, the head of LEO's German operations, and a former employee of Carl Zeiss, explained:

> The assembly and test of electron microscopes is not something that you can just hire someone off the street to do. Our workers in Oberkochen have what we refer to as "golden hands". It takes years to learn the skills. If we were to assemble the P1 in England, we would have to add unskilled workers to the Cambridge workforce and train them. In Germany, we have the capacity. We should do this work in Germany.

Dick Manley, who was in charge of Human Resources for LEO on an interim basis (until a German speaking HR manager could be hired) added:

> Morale in our Oberkochen plant is not high. It might be the result of cross cultural issues and communication problems, but it could be just plain insecurity about the future. If we assemble the P1 here in Cambridge, we will probably have to lay off German workers, which would only make matters worse. On the other hand, giving the work to them will be a clear vote of confidence, a real morale booster.

Joint Venture Background

The Market

After continuous growth between 1970 and 1989, the world market for electron microscopes declined between 1989 and 1994, dropping by about 20 percent in unit volume. By
1994, the market appeared to have stabilized at about $145 million and 320 units per year
for Transmission Electron Microscopes (TEMs) and $300 million and 1650 units for
SEMs[1]. However, approximately 45 percent of the SEM market consisted of microscopes
used in the manufacture of semiconductors, an application demanding extremely sophisticated equipment that neither Carl Zeiss nor Leica manufactured. Both SEM and TEM
markets were dominated by the Japanese companies Hitachi and Japan Electron Optical
Ltd (JEOL).

Leica and Carl Zeiss, who had a combined market share of approximately 14 percent
of the SEM market and 11 percent of the TEM market, were not achieving satisfactory
financial results. Carl Zeiss had reportedly been losing money in its electron microscope
business for many years, and Leica was earning a small amount, primarily because of its
after sales service activities.

Further market information is provided in Exhibit 1.

The Rationale

The impetus for the creation of the LEO joint venture had come from Dr. Peter Grassmann,
a Siemens executive who had been brought in to turn around the faltering Zeiss organization in late 1994. Originally formed by Carl Zeiss in 1846 in Jena (later part of East Germany), the Carl Zeiss organization (a German trust) comprised approximately 15,800
employees in the mid 1990s. Plans to reduce this number to 12,000 had led to worker
demonstrations on the Oberkochen site immediately prior to Peter Grassmann's arrival.
Grassmann's publicly declared objective was to create a "more professional, cost-aware,
performance-oriented and customer-oriented company". At the time of LEO's formation,
Dr. Grassmann commented that it would be at least two years before the joint venture was
operating at a profit.

Eugen Wild, a former Carl Zeiss manager, now LEO's Vice President of Marketing,
commented on the decision to form LEO:

> It was difficult for us in Zeiss to accept the need to create LEO, as we have some truly unique
> technology—in fact technology which Leica unsuccessfully tried to duplicate. But if the alter-
> natives were to sell the business or shut it down, then a joint venture looked okay.
>
> It was my idea that we consider Leica as a partner. They were small enough that they would
> not dominate us. It was vital that the venture be 50–50 in its management as well as its owner-
> ship. We would never have achieved that with someone like Phillips as a partner.

Leica's electron microscope business was based in Cambridge, England, and had originally been part of Cambridge Instruments, a company that had been merged with Wild

---

[1]SEMs were used for examining the surface of the specimen under study, whereas TEMs were used to look
inside the specimen.

EXHIBIT 1A   Electron Microscopy—Market Share 1995

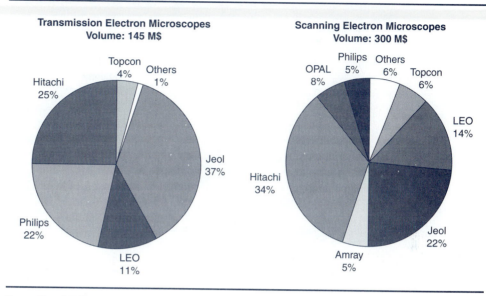

Source: Frost & Sullivan, Dataquest, Info Science.

EXHIBIT 1B   Electron Microscopy—Market Segmentation 1995

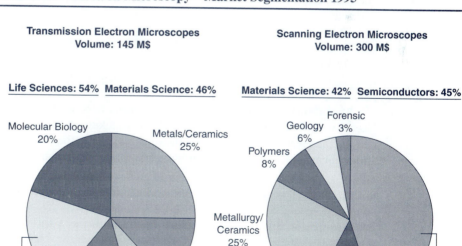

Source: Dataquest—Various 95-260/30.11.1995.

EXHIBIT 1C   Electron Microscopy—Regional Market Segments 1995

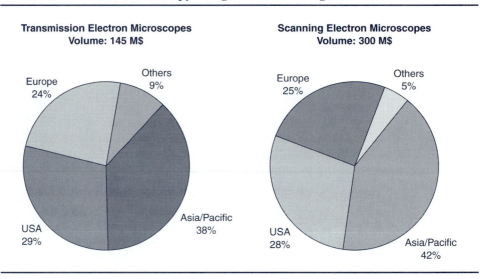

Transmission Electron Microscopes
Volume: 145 M$

- Europe 24%
- Others 9%
- Asia/Pacific 38%
- USA 29%

Scanning Electron Microscopes
Volume: 300 M$

- Europe 25%
- Others 5%
- Asia/Pacific 42%
- USA 28%

Source: Info Science, Frost & Sullivan.

Leitz of Switzerland in 1990 to form Leica. Markus Rauh, the CEO of Leica, was interested in Grassmann's proposal to improve the performance of both companies' electron microscope businesses by forming a joint venture, although his preference would have been to create a venture in which Leica had a share greater than 50 percent.

The new company was expected to begin life with annual revenues of more than DM100 million, and its products would be sold exclusively under the LEO name. Approximately 35 percent of revenues would come from Germany, 30 percent from North America, 15 percent from France, between 5 and 10 percent from Asia Pacific, and less that 5 percent from the UK.

The original venture plan called for a manager from neither parent to be hired as Chief Executive Officer. However, as he saw the plans taking shape, Karl Kalbag, a British citizen who had worked for Cambridge Instruments prior to the 1990 merger and was now the Chief Financial Officer of Leica in Switzerland, liked what he saw. He commented:

> From the outset, I thought that the venture was a good idea. At one point, one of the Zeiss mangers said, "why not you as CEO?" Why not? I thought it over and discussed it with Markus Rauh—he was reluctant to lose me, but he said that he could see it in my eyes. And I could feel it in my heart. This was what I wanted to do! I later met with Peter Grassmann and he said that he was comfortable, and we went from there.

In May 1995, Karl prepared a set of financial projections for the new company which indicated that he expected to grow the company's sales volume by about 20 percent over a three year period, primarily through increasing the average price per unit sold. In addition, he expected to improve the bottom line by reducing costs—particularly in research and development and sales and marketing. Karl also presented his personal view of how the venture should be managed.

EXHIBIT 2   LEO Electron Microscopy Ltd "Ideal" Organization Chart

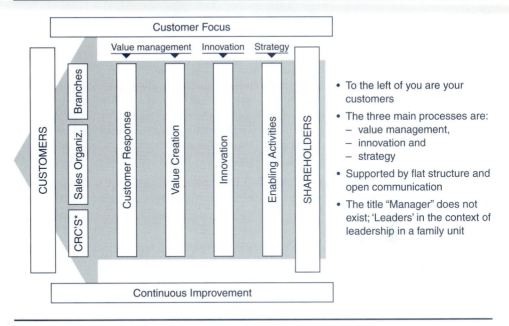

*CRC's = Customer Response Centres

1. There would be one single management team—no "castles" or "forts".
2. There would be a business process orientation. There would be no functions, only activities, and each activity would be included only if its value added to the business exceeded its cost.
3. There would be three key processes between customer and shareholder: Value management, innovation, and strategy. Karl's "ideal" organization chart is shown in Exhibit 2.
4. Ideally, all senior management would be based in Cambridge.

The board of directors would contain an equal number of directors from each parent, with Peter Grassmann as Chairman for the first two years. It was also established that neither parent could sell their shares for the venture for at least two years. Karl's contract was for three years, but he could be replaced after two years if it was judged that his actions in the job were biased toward Leica.

The New Company

LEO was formed on October 2, 1995, with 350 employees. Forty were in R&D, 120 were in the assembly and test area, 80 were service engineers, 33 were in sales, and 25 in logistics. No employee had an automatic right to return to his or her parent company, but in the words of Karl Kalbag, "no one would be fired for economic reasons, only for poor performance". The official language of the company was English. The company was given enough initial funding (the initial share capital was reported to be £5 million) that it was not expected to have to return to its parents for further funds, and it was agreed that Karl was to operate the company as he saw fit.

LEO's organization chart is shown in Exhibit 3. This chart reflected Karl's belief that processes, not functions, were key. He wanted to do away with the usual hierarchical organization and build a company based on horizontal team work. Dick Manley commented:

> Karl has a strongly held view that participative management is the key to success. In Cambridge, this philosophy fits very well, because this is an organization full of very competent technically oriented people who are used to working across functions. You might say that Karl is preaching to the converted. However, in Oberkochen hierarchy is an established way of life—and to add new management philosophies to the turmoil that our people there are already going through…well I don't think that they really understand what Karl is on about.

Prior to the creation of LEO, both parent companies manufactured many of the components needed to make electron microscopes, as well as performing the final assembly

---

EXHIBIT 3   LEO Organization chart

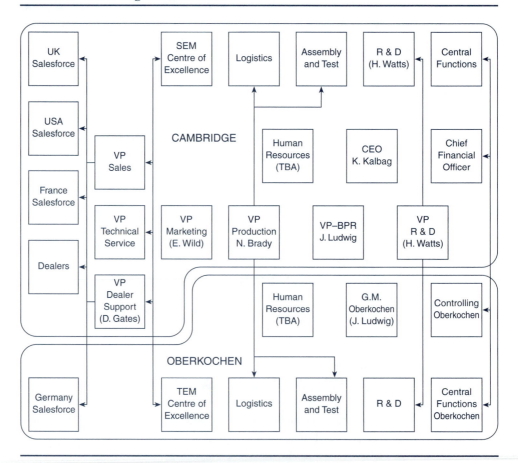

and test of the finished products. When LEO was created, the component manufacturing activities were retained by the parent companies. As a result, LEO sourced components from parents (approximately 70 percent of the cost of goods sold was bought in from the outside—most of it from the parents), and less than 10 percent of LEO's total costs were its own direct assembly and test labour.

One of the advantages of forming LEO, according to Karl Kalbag, was the degree of focus that it put on the electron microscope business, not least in the areas of sales and marketing. Prior to the creation of LEO in the United States, for example, the salesforce of each company had sold a portfolio of products, including both optical and electron microscopes. Most sales people were instinctively more comfortable with one product than the other, however, and many preferred to focus on optical microscopes as the sales cycle was not as lengthy, which meant that commission cheques were more frequent. With the creation of the joint venture, LEO was able to build a focused sales force of people highly interested in electron microscopes, and used to the long sales cycle.

LEO sold its products throughout the world via 50 dealers, who were serviced by the 80 sales engineers referred to earlier. These people also had "golden hands" and were frequently called on to disassemble and reassemble operating units in the field. In any given period, one quarter to one third of LEO's revenues came from service work.

Integration

One of Karl's early priorities was to meld the two organizations into one smoothly functioning unit. He wanted to establish strong horizontal links that cut across geographical boundaries. However, his objective of locating the senior management team in Cambridge was proving difficult, as Eugen Wild explained:

> It might be more efficient if Jan and I were located in Cambridge, but it is very important to our workforce in Germany that we are located there. Many foreign companies have made acquisitions in Germany and then closed plants. We want to make sure that it does not happen to us. Our Oberkochen workforce already feels somewhat abandoned by the Carl Zeiss "family"—we cannot abandon them further by moving to England. I know that Jan feels the same.

The area in which British-German coordination was most advanced was Research and Development. There were approximately 20 researchers in Oberkochen and 20 in Cambridge. Henry Watts, LEO's Cambridge based, Vice President of R&D, commented:

> There has not been a week go by that we have not had German research people here or Cambridge people in Oberkochen. Their strength is electronics, ours is software development. It's a good match. The English language skills of the German research people are excellent.
>
> The biggest challenge that we face is in the TEM business, which in Europe is dominated by Philips. When we started LEO, we had 5 TEM products, all produced in Oberkochen. We have discontinued two old machines, and a third is not competitive. We have no new TEM products in the pipeline.
>
> Four of my people in Germany are not doing very much—and cannot do very much—until we decide how to move forward in the TEM business. We have to make up our minds quickly, because in this business the performance of the equipment keeps going up, while prices come down. You cannot stand still. But we do not know enough about what is going on in the TEM market.

On the subject of the TEM business, Karl Kalbag added:

> One of the major reasons for Leica to enter this joint venture was to get into the TEM business. It is the high end part of the microscopy business, and we can see that eventually the semi-conductor manufacturers might move to TEMs. Carl Zeiss has some unique technology in this area.

Close coordination in the assembly and test areas was proving more difficult to achieve. The assembly and test employees in Germany did not speak English, and Nick Brady, LEO's Cambridge based Vice President of Manufacturing, had a difficult time impacting the work practices in the Oberkochen plant. He explained:

> Costs in both plants are too high—but the problem is particularly acute in Germany, where cost levels are 60 percent above those in the UK. In the UK we have created 6 measures (refer to Exhibit 4) which we are tracking as a way to improve our performance. I have translated those into German and been trying for months to get Oberkochen to adopt them. But they will not. There is always some excuse or other. I travel there once or twice a month for two or three days, but it is very frustrating as I have to do everything through an interpreter (the local financial manager).
>
> When I ask questions from Cambridge, I get the clear impression that there is a discussion up and down the German hierarchy before they decide what answer to give me. I am starting to give up. It makes more sense to expend my energy here in Cambridge, where I can make a difference. No one in Germany is listening.

Jan Ludwig was LEO's Vice President for Business Process Re-engineering and responsible for the German plant. He commented:

> We face a totally different set of issues in Germany than they do in England. In Cambridge, the microscope business was already a separate business unit, but in Germany we were an integrated part of a much larger operation, which means that we have to disentangle ourselves from the Carl Zeiss organization. We are moving into our own building, which will help. We need to set up our own systems, get our own Human Resource manager, and so on. At the moment, our information is buried in the Zeiss system and it's hard to get anything usable. We are not ready to give Nick the kind of measures that he wants. My priorities are to get the Zeiss organization to start treating us like a customer, and to build our people in Oberkochen into a team. There are 127 of us, and everyone is feeling a little insecure.
>
> Karl and I disagree about the horizontal process-based organization he wants to create. I agree that integrating R&D and sales and marketing makes sense—which means having one boss in each area—but in assembly and test, we should build a centre of competence in TEM in Germany, and SEM in Cambridge. I will manage the German operation and have responsibility for the whole TEM business, which needs a lot of attention. It makes no sense to have Nick try and be responsible for German assembly and test from Cambridge. We can't build teams of German and British workers when they don't speak the same language. But we can build a strong team here in Oberkochen.

David Gates, the vice president of dealer support, completely supported Nick Brady's assessment that LEO's costs were too high. David commented:

> Three years ago, Philips went through a major cost reduction exercise, and they now have supply sources in the Czech Republic which give them very low costs. As a result, they are pricing low when they have to, and they are growing, particularly in the TEM business. In our first three months of operation, we did not get a single order in France, because Philips under priced us in every case. There is no doubt that they are trying to put us out of the TEM business. However, they seem to have realized that we are here to stay, as we recently did win a couple of orders in France.

EXHIBIT 4   Leo Manufacturing Measures

The following were agreed in Oberkochen on the 27 September 1995. Initially there are six; however, these will be added to during October 1995.

Manufacturing Measures

M1. Customer Deliver Performance **(CDP)**
Measures the percentage of orders delivered on or before the customers order acknowledgement delivery date, by line item.
Target is 99% clean installations.

M2. Customer Clean Installation **(CCI)**
Measures the percentage of customer orders installed first time without problems.
Target is 99% on-time delivery.

Logistics Measures

L1. Order receipt to acknowledgement performance **(ORAP)**
Measures the elapsed time between receipt and acknowledgement of a customer order.
Target is 99% of orders acknowledged in less than 72 hours.

L2. Line item shortages at kitting **(LISK)**
Measures the percentage of line items short in all kits at the point of kitting.
Target is 99% of all kits are clean (i.e., 99% of all kits have no shortages).

Assembly & Test Measures

A1. Production Process Deviations **(PPD)**
Measures the deviations (variances from standard time in the areas of job cost, scrap, rework, modifications and loss).
Target is zero deviations (variances).

A2. Value creation lead-time performance **(VCLP)**
Measures the Assembly and Test lead-time by customer order from commencement of build to delivery.
Target is to establish current lead-times by product and reduce by 25% in first year.

Nick Brady
4 October 1995

Although 85 percent of our sales force is located in our traditional markets of Europe and USA, there is no growth there. The market of the future is Asia Pacific, but we are weak there. Our company owned dealers, for example, are in Europe and the United States.

The Way Forward

LEO's leadership team offered a variety of views on the best way for the young company to move forward.

Jan Ludwig:

If we decide to give the P1 project to Oberkochen, we will have made a great step forward in the building of this company. With this decision behind us, we can turn our attention to the opportunities in the TEM business.

Henry Watts:

The P1 project is important, because it is creating momentum and energy in the company, and will show our competitors that we are alive. But the product is not going to earn us a lot of money, because it is going to be expensive to produce. The German researchers are designing us a gold plated product. They just do not have much concept of cost and its relation to price. If I insisted that they get the cost out, however, it would take another year to develop. As it is, I have a British team developing a less expensive version of the product that will appear at a later date as a different model. The German team is well aware of this.

Eugen Wild:

I have the responsibility for sorting out what we do about the TEM business. We need to collect all our sales prospects and sort them out, develop a strategy for this product line, and possibly improve our dealers in this area. Henry also has to develop us a new product.

In general, I would say that we are being too conservative. We have to grow to survive. Let's compete with Philips on price when we have to; we need to generate cash, not percentage gross margins. The good news about Karl is that he has clearly demonstrated that he is no slave to Leica's interests; he clearly cares about LEO first and foremost. Also, he is soon going to start taking German lessons. The bad news is that he wants to produce good financial results too soon, and he controls pricing too closely. Let's spend on R&D so that we can develop high end microscopes for the semiconductor fabrication business. The P1 will not do this for us. Sure it's a risk, but that's where the growth is.

Karl Kalbag:

We recently had a series of meetings to think through our strategy. One question was "what do we want to be best at?" We discussed innovation, cost leadership, and customer intimacy. We decided that we would be the best company in our business in the area of customer intimacy. This makes a lot of sense for us, as about 180 of our 350 employees talk to customers on a *daily* basis. At that same meeting, we identified 12 internal constraints to success. The top three were cost, communication and lack of market knowledge. We set up three teams to work on these issues.

Jan and I disagree about how the company should be run. He wants his own operation in Germany, but that will not happen. To him, geography and nationality are very important. I want to get rid of them.

Financially, my focus is on managing cash. We are doing fine; in fact, we are ahead of budget, even though our first year losses are going to be slightly greater than planned. We are on track.

Excerpts from Karl's diary in early 1996 are represented in Exhibit 5.

EXHIBIT 5   Annotated Excerpts from Karl Kalbag's Diary

Week of January 8 1996

Tuesday and Wednesday—First ever review meetings. These will be monthly in Cambridge. One with sales people, one with manufacturing people, one with R&D*. These turned out to be training sessions (by me) for the managers involved on how to set objectives for such meetings, how to set up the agenda, and so on.

Wednesday—Meeting with Japanese dealers with respect to three pending sales in Japan on which price expectations varied greatly between us and them. I explained that there would be no special deals—we would not reduce our margin, regardless of the expectations of their major customers.   *(continued)*

---

*These labels were created by the casewriter. Inside the company these teams were known as "Value Creating", "Value Delivery" and "Innovation".

EXHIBIT 5   (concluded)

Thursday and Friday—TEM Product Strategy Meeting. This meeting of 28 people from all parts of the LEO world (who were in Cambridge for the Management Development weekend) was run by Henry Watt. It was a no holds barred brainstorming session at which we focused on development priorities for the TEM business. We came out with three main conclusions. We should consider the development of a low end TEM machine, to be manufactured in Eastern Europe. We need to find a way to focus more attention on TEM sales. These machines are expensive, and the customers' decision-making period may be 2 or 3 years. Salesmen, thinking of immediate commissions, are likely to focus on SEMs, which are easier to sell. We should develop an all-new TEM product.

Friday noon to Sunday noon—Management Development Weekend. There will be a weekend like this every seven months or so, with a group of approximately 35 LEO people from all over the world. This one focused on marketing, as we need to develop our marketing strengths. We brought in outside lecturers to talk to us about pricing, the development of marketing strategies, and so on.

It was a result of this weekend that we decided to focus on customer intimacy.

Week of January 15
Monday—Meeting of our people in charge of dealer relations who were here for the management development weekend. Brought in dealer from Italy who is highly successful, asked him to explain to all of us how he runs his business so well. This was extremely valuable.

Friday—Off-site confidential lunch – potential strategic alliance.

Week of January 22
Monday—Travel to Germany—seal the three Japanese deals (referred to earlier) with Japanese representative who was visiting Oberkochen.

Tuesday—Meet with South American dealer (in Germany) to sort out difficulties between local dealers in that region.

Wednesday—Brief the Oberkochen personnel (perhaps 100 people) on recent events. Doing this through an interpreter but must take German lessons so can do it myself. I will do these presentations monthly, and the same on the Cambridge site.

Week of January 29
Spent week in Germany, mainly listening.

Week of February 5
In Cambridge.

Monday—Cambridge briefing meeting.

Rest of Week – second round of management meetings with manufacturing, sales, research and development.

Week of February 12
In USA—Went to three sites: East coast, mid West and West coast to meet with sales and service people. First time that many of them had met—as some were former Leica, others former Carl Zeiss. Ten or eleven people in each group. Included customers in some of these meetings to tell us what they expect from us. Extremely valuable. My major purpose was to get their buy-in to the focus on customer intimacy.

Week of February 19
In France, Germany and UK. Reviewed business and budgets for fiscal year 1997.

15 Kenny Rogers Roasters in China

It was mid-October 1995 and Tony Wang, President of Franchise Investment Corporation of Asia (FICA), had just returned to Hong Kong from a one week visit to Beijing. FICA had earlier in the year been granted the franchise rights for Kenny Rogers Roasters (KRR), a rotisserie chicken restaurant concept, for both Beijing and Shanghai. While Wang was eager to move forward, serious concerns had emerged over the challenges of doing business in China. Just as most foreign companies had looked to local partners to help ameliorate some of these concerns, Wang had begun joint venture discussions with three companies. Although each potential partner appeared eager to work with FICA, Wang was wondering whether the time was right to proceed and if so, with which company.

KRR Overview

The driving force behind KRR was John Y. Brown, an entrepreneur with a long history in the food service industry. In 1964, Brown, who at the time was a 29-year-old Kentucky lawyer, and his partner, 60-year-old Jack Massey, purchased Kentucky Fried Chicken from 74-year-old Harland Sanders for $U.S. 2 million. Over the next 5 years the partners added 1,000 new stores and grew sales by an average of 96 percent per year. Observers attributed this growth to two main factors: (1) the company's reliance on less costly franchise expansion over company-owned stores, and (2) Brown's ability to select hard charging and entrepreneurial franchisees. KFC was sold to Heublen Inc. in 1971 for $U.S. 275 million, making both partners wealthy men.

THUNDERBIRD
THE AMERICAN GRADUATE SCHOOL
OF INTERNATIONAL MANAGEMENT

Copyright © 1996 Thunderbird, The American Graduate School of International Management. All rights reserved. This case was prepared by Professor Allen J. Morrison in collaboration with Professor J. Stewart Black and Tanya Spyridakis, with additional assistance provided by Jan Visser, for the purpose of classroom discussion only, and not to indicate either effective or ineffective management.

During the 1970s Brown went on to become Governor of the State of Kentucky and owner of three professional basketball teams including the Boston Celtics. In 1979 he married 1971 Miss America, Phyllis George. During the early 1980s Brown helped launch Miami Subs and Roadhouse Grill franchises and bankrolled his wife's Chicken by George line of prepared chicken sold in grocery stores.

By the late 1980s, Brown was becoming increasingly convinced of the enormous market potential for roasted chicken. The health craze that swept the United States in the 1980s significantly increased the demand for lighter, nonfried food options. This affected many segments of the food industry, and the poultry industry was no exception. Many restaurant owners began investing in rotisserie ovens and introducing more healthy menus.

In looking for a new way to grab the customer's attention, Brown thought it a natural to team with long-time friend Kenny Rogers. Kenny Rogers, once described as "the most popular singer in America," had a career that spanned more than three decades, half of which as a solo artist. Rogers's popularity manifested itself in the many awards and honors that he had received over the years: three Grammies, 11 People's Choice Awards, 18 American Music Awards, five Country Music Association Awards, eight Academy of Country Music Awards, four platinum albums, five multi-platinum albums, one platinum single, and numerous gold albums and singles. Rogers also dabbled in several businesses including a partnership in Silver Dollar City, in Branson, Missouri, considered country music's capital. When Brown came up with the concept of a rotisserie chicken restaurant chain, Rogers was very enthusiastic.

> When I saw this concept, I thought it was so outstanding I was willing to put my reputation on the line, not just as an endorser, but as an owner and partner. . . I believe nonfried chicken is the wave of the 90s, and working with folks who made fried chicken a billion dollar business gives me the confidence we are doing it right.

Kenny Rogers Roasters (KRR) began operations on January 17, 1991, in Louisville, Kentucky, and opened its first restaurant in August of that year in Coral Gables, Florida. The menu: citrus and herb-marinated wood roasted chicken and about a dozen side dishes such as mashed potatoes and gravy, corn-on-the-cob, baked beans, and pasta salad. Growth was rapid. From an original group of five people, the company grew to include a corporate staff of more than 100. By late 1995, the company had moved headquarters to Ft. Lauderdale, Florida, and had over 310 stores. KRR operated in approximately 35 U.S. states, had more than a dozen stores in Canada and had at least one store in Greece, Cyprus, Israel, Malaysia, Korea, the Philippines, Japan, Jordan, and Singapore. Company plans called for the addition of almost 1,200 new stores in the United States and 240 stores internationally by 2002.

The Rotisserie Chicken Business

The market's switch to rotisserie chicken did not escape the competition. In 1993, KFC spent $100 million to roll out its Colonel's Rotisserie Gold in all 5,100 of its stores in the United States. Rotisserie chicken constituted about 25 percent of KFC sales in company-owned stores by the end of 1995. In all, KFC enjoyed a 58 percent share of the retail chicken industry, and gross sales of over $3.5 billion. Other fast-food restaurants, noting the trend, also attempted to expand into the nonfried market. For example, Popeye's Famous Chicken entered the nonfried market despite its lack of capital; it featured a roasted chicken that could be cooked in the same ovens as its biscuits. Boston Market (formerly known as Boston Chicken) was another up-and-coming competitor in the rotisserie chicken segment. Opening its first store in 1985, by 1993 the company had 166 stores in approximately 25 states, and sales of $154 million (more than triple its 1992 sales). By the end of 1995, Boston Market had become a public company with over 825 stores operating (none outside the U.S.) and was opening a new store each business day.

While sales of rotisserie chicken were still considerably smaller ($700 million vs. $6 billion for fried chicken in 1993), advocates of nonfried chicken firmly believed that the gap would close within 10 years. Statistics confirmed the growing popularity of nonfried chicken in the United States: sales of fried chicken consumed outside the home grew an average of 3.5 percent from 1989 to 1995, while sales of nonfried chicken grew an average of 10.75 percent in the same period. Annual growth in per capita chicken consumption between 1984 and 1994 was 38.5 percent.

Despite its rapid growth, rotisserie chicken had several drawbacks. Uncooked rotisserie chicken had a shorter shelf life than fried chicken. Rotisserie chicken took 75 to 90 minutes to cook compared to 30 minutes for fried chicken. Additionally, a cooked rotisserie chicken needed moisture and would spoil if kept under a heat lamp for too long; this, however, posed no problem for fried chicken. Finally, customer demand would often be greater than supply in peak hours, which was difficult for rotisserie chicken vendors due to the longer cooking times.

Kenny Rogers Roasters

By 1995 KRR was still a privately held company, with no immediate plans to go public. The equity breakdown was approximately John Y. Brown, Jr. 28 percent; Kenny Rogers 14.5 percent; and a group of Malaysian investors 35 percent; various friends of Brown and Rogers held the remaining 22.5 percent. Brown served as the company's CEO and Chairman of the Board. Rogers sat on the board of directors and, though he was not directly involved in running the company, attended many meetings and assisted in promoting the company. In building his management team, Brown recruited several people with whom he had worked in his days at KFC. Other management talent was recruited from fast-food chains such as Wendy's, Burger King, Pizza Hut, Arby's, and McDonald's.

In the United States, KRR's restaurants averaged 2800 square feet in size, with seating capacity for 80 to 100 people. The stores had a country-western motif and were decorated with memorabilia from Rogers's career. Television monitors were also located throughout the restaurant showing customized music videos featuring performances by Rogers and other country and western entertainers. Advertising and promotional messages were interspersed with the music videos. A signature wood-fire rotisserie with surrounding wood piles were placed in full view of the customer. The serving counter was buffet-like in style, with a wide range of side dishes kept warm in a glass display case. Servers on the other side of the counter put together plates for customers based on their choice of entree and side dishes.

All menu items at KRR restaurants were prepared on-site. The chicken was marinated overnight and roasted the next day over a hard-wood fire to an internal temperature of about

180°. Most side dishes were made from scratch, though a few items were prepared from mixes developed at the company's training and development center near the corporate headquarters. The labor-intensive nature of KRR was not without its downside; labor costs averaged between 26 and 27 percent of sales, food costs ran just under 30 percent.

A free-standing Kenny Rogers restaurant with a drive-through window generally went through 1,800 chickens a week and generated approximately $1 million in annual sales. By 1995, take-out orders comprised about 45 to 50 percent of sales; the company's goal was to increase this to around 60 percent. Total KRR revenues in 1995 were estimated at $321 million, up from $68.7 million in 1993 and $150 million in 1994.

KRR Franchises

From the very beginning, franchising played a big part of the company's expansion. By 1995, franchise stores accounted for about 85 percent of KRR's 310 stores. All of KRR's international stores were owned by franchisees. Though the company had solicited a few of its franchisees, most franchisees had approached KRR. The company carefully screened all franchisees for previous restaurant experience, especially multi-unit operations experience, references, credit rating, and net worth. KRR wanted franchisees who knew and liked the restaurant business, who were or had been in it, and who appreciated the difference the company was trying to make with customer service and product quality.

KRR set up *franchise* and *development* contracts. Both typically had a duration of 20 years. A franchise agreement was for a single store; a development agreement was for a specified number of restaurants, within a set time frame, in a designated area. When signing development agreements, KRR typically awarded territories in small clusters of five to 50 restaurants. The boundaries of the territory varied depending on the size and experience of the group or individual involved, as well as availability within the region requested.[1]

The costs involved in a franchise agreement included the initial franchise payment of $29,500; a royalty fee of 4.5 percent of gross sales; and contributions to the company advertising production fund, the national advertising fund, as well as a local or regional advertising fund of 0.75 percent, 2 percent, and (a minimum of) 3 percent of gross sales, respectively. The initial franchise fee was due upon signing the franchise agreement; all other fees were due monthly once the store was in operation. Fees related to a development agreement were similar to those of a franchise agreement. In addition to normal franchise fees, a developer was typically required to pay a development fee of $10,000 for each restaurant covered under the agreement. This fee was nonrefundable and was due (along with the full $29,500 for the first store to be built) upon signing the development agreement. The development fee was to be applied in equal portions as a credit against the initial franchise fee for each restaurant to be developed under the development agreement. The balance of each additional store's (within a development area) franchise fee was due as each store went into construction, according to the development schedule.

---

[1]The franchising scheme of KRR's principal rival, Boston Market, differed considerably. Boston Market sold whole regions and provided up to 75 percent of its franchisees' financing. Boston Market did have an unusual caveat that accompanied the financing plan: After two years, Boston Market had the right to convert the unpaid debt into an ownership share in the franchise.

Company research showed that the average costs to build a new restaurant in the United States ranged from $560,000 to $672,000; the costs to convert an existing site ranged from $405,000 to $545,000. These costs included such expenses as property rental or payments, architectural and engineering fees, insurance, business licenses, equipment, furniture, signs, office supplies, opening inventory, and so forth.

Training and Development

KRR put great emphasis on training and provided franchisees and operators with three training courses. These courses took place at the company's training and development center located near corporate headquarters in Ft. Lauderdale, Florida. All expenses (travel, living, etc.) incurred in the training process were the responsibility of the franchisee. The first course was an optional three-day executive orientation program for all first-time franchisees and partners. The remaining two courses were not optional. All franchisees were required to certify and maintain a minimum of two managers for each store. The company's level one course for all managers was an intense four-week program held four to six weeks prior to the store's opening. Dubbed as KRR's version of boot camp, management trainees essentially lived with their trainer, learning all aspects of daily operations. Once a developer had opened a substantial number of stores within the designated territory, it was possible to apply for accreditation, that is, to set up its own level-one management training program. The second level of management training was required for any manager before being promoted to a general store manager. Held either before or after a store opening, this six-day program focused not so much on operational procedures, but rather on how to deal with the more sensitive issues of management, i.e., how to deal with staff members and customers, especially when there were problems.

In addition, for each new store opening, franchisees were provided an opening team to assist in the initial training of hourly employees. The size of the team and the duration of its stay depended on the number of stores the franchisee already had in operation. The opening team would be sent once KRR had received a "Certificate of Occupancy" and a completed "Pre-Opening Checklist" from the franchisee. The franchisee was responsible for making sure that the store was ready for pre-opening training, though the opening date of the store could be pushed back if the store was not ready.

In the United States, typically 60 to 65 hourly employees were hired for each new store. Of those initially hired, approximately 60 percent would quit within the first few months. KRR's training and development center designed a 12-part video training program which demonstrated proper operating procedures for equipment and preparation of food items. These videos were used to train new employees in all stores, both domestic and international.

Control Issues

Menu adjustments were a particular concern for international stores. Some side dishes did not go over well in various parts of the world. For example, baked beans with bacon was not served in Jordan and other Muslim countries. Franchisees were encouraged to offer alternative side dishes that would be better received in their country or region of the world, while still meeting the company's quality standards. Sometimes recipes of existing dishes had to be altered for regional tastes. Most notably sugar content had to be reduced for dishes served in the Asia–Pacific region where people had less of a "sweet tooth" than Americans. All new menu items or variations in recipes had to pre-approved by corporate headquarters.

In addition to approving menus, KRR developed standards and specifications for most of its food products and equipment. To ensure consistency, KRR approved suppliers of chickens, breads, spices, mixes, marinades, plastic products, packaging, and so forth, in each territory or country where the company operated. Generally, finding approved local suppliers for chickens and other major food products was not a problem. However, many overseas franchisees ordered such specialized products as marinades and packaging materials from KRR's contracted U.S. distributor.

In order to maintain constant communication between KRR's corporate office and any given store, franchisees were required to install computer systems in each store. This system allowed KRR to instantly receive information concerning sales of each restaurant, and, in turn, to provide franchisees with information necessary to prepare financial statements and better manage the restaurant. Also, the company had standard forms for use in such areas as inventory control, profit-and-loss control, and monitoring daily and weekly sales.

Tony Wang and KRR in China

KRR's efforts in China were spearheaded by Ta-Tung (Tony) Wang, a former KFC executive with considerable experience in the Far East. Wang was born in Sichuan province in the People's Republic of China in 1944 and raised in Taiwan. In the late 1960s he moved to the United States to complete graduate work. Upon graduation he took a management position with KFC in Louisville, Kentucky. A series of promotions culminated with Wang's appointment as KFC Vice President for Southeast Asia in 1986. The position, based in Singapore, charged Wang with aggressively expanding KFC throughout the Asia Pacific region. Wang focused his efforts primarily on China, a country of 1.2 billion people with an undeveloped food service industry. In 1987, he gained considerable international notoriety by operating the first Western style fast food restaurant in China. The store was KFC's largest in the world and was located just opposite Mao's mausoleum off Tiananmen Square.

Wang credited the careful selection of joint venture partners as key in securing the store's prime location and in expediting the opening of the store. Three Chinese partners were selected and each played a different role in the start-up and ongoing operation of the store: Beijing Animal Production Bureau (which owned 10 percent of the joint venture) accessed locally grown chickens; Beijing Tourist Bureau (which had a 14 percent ownership position) helped with site selection, permits, lease issues and hiring; and the Bank of China (which had a 25 percent ownership position) assisted in converting soft currency renmimbi profits to hard currency. Despite high chicken prices (KFC-approved chicken in China cost over $1 per pound, well over twice U.S. levels), the operation was a major success. In reflecting back on that time Wang noted: "We were the first Western quick service restaurant in any communist country. It was very exciting. There were crowds lining up outside the store in the morning even before we opened. It was not unusual for us to have to call the police to control the crowds."

After opening additional restaurants in China, in September 1989, Tony Wang left KFC to become president of CP Food Services Co., a subsidiary of the Charoen Pokphand Group, the largest agri-business company in Asia. In September 1991, Wang moved back to the United States to become president of Grace Food Services, a subsidiary of W.R. Grace & Co. A year later Tony Wang left Grace to become president of Foodmaker International, the $1.2 billion parent company of Jack-in-the-Box and Chi-Chi's restaurants. Wang had a mandate to open 800 new restaurants over an 8-year period, primarily in the Pacific Rim. In January 1993, catastrophe struck when contaminated hamburgers were served at a Seattle Jack-in-the-Box restaurant. Although the tainted hamburger was traced to a California-based supplier, Foodmaker was hit with a series of costly lawsuits and devastating publicity. Sales nose-dived and, in order to conserve finances, the company's international expansion plan was shelved.

Wang sensed an important win-win opportunity for all and offered to continue the company's expansion using his own money. An agreement was struck whereby Wang's own company, QSR (Quick Service Restaurant), became a Jack-in-the-Box Master Licensee with franchise and development rights for 20 countries in the Middle East and Asia (including China but not Japan). The agreement with Foodmaker, which came into effect on January 1, 1994, and lasted 10 years, gave QSR complete control over the selection and development of all franchises within these 20 countries. QSR had the right to select stand alone franchisees, establish joint ventures with franchisees, or set itself up as a franchisee within any or all of the designated countries. Under the Master License agreement, Foodmaker and QSR split all franchise fees for Jack-in-the-Box restaurants. In assessing Foodmaker's rationale in setting up the Master License agreement, Wang commented: "this is a mutually beneficial concept for both parties. If they have the know-how but not the money, what have they got? They have a great concept but are not able to implement it internationally."

FICA (Franchise Investment Corporation of Asia)

Once Wang left Foodmaker, he began to explore other franchise investment opportunities in Asia. For assistance, Wang turned to American International Group, Inc. (AIG), one of the largest U.S.-based insurance companies.[2] Wang had been discussing franchise investment concepts with several senior AIG (Asia) managers since the late 1980s. In 1990, AIG (Asia) formed FICA as a subsidiary company designed to pursue multiple franchise options and invited Wang to serve as its first president. Wang declined, saying that he thought it was premature at the time. Consequently, FICA was put on hold.

In early 1994, Wang reopened discussions with AIG and in January 1995 joined FICA as its president and co-owner. FICA's ownership was split between AIG (60 percent) and QSR (40 percent). Wang served as president and primary decision maker in an office which was established by FICA in Hong Kong. Wang commented on the ownership structure: "as president of FICA, I am also an employee of FICA. I am president because of my skills and contacts. But my 40 percent ownership is based on financial contribution."

---

[2]In 1994, AIG had net profits in excess of $4 billion on revenues in excess of $24 billion and assets of approximately $130 billion.

FICA had a threefold mandate: (1) to develop and invest in franchise concepts in Asia, (2) to act as a consultant to franchisees in the region, and (3) to establish food processing and other franchise support/commissary functions. Primary emphasis focused on investing in established franchise concepts. The philosophy was explained by Wang:

> Every franchiser has a very strict non-compete clause for products in the same category. Our strategic plan was for FICA to become a multi-concept regional franchise investment and development company. We began to look at categories of products that did not compete.

After considerable effort, FICA signed far-reaching franchise agreements with Circle-K for both the Philippines and Thailand and with Carvel Ice Cream for China. By the fall of 1995, the company was continuing negotiations with these companies for additional franchise territories within Asia Pacific. In 1994, FICA also began investigating KRR in the context of a broader China strategy. (Economic and social trends for China are shown in Exhibit 1.) Wang explained why KRR seemed natural for China:

> We identified various franchise categories and one of those was chicken. I knew a lot of people at KRR who used to work for KFC. I knew John Brown and Loy Weston [former General Manager of KFC in Japan and for 18 months President of KRR Pacific]. Some of the best people who worked for KFC now work for KRR. I also knew Lenny Abelman, [KRR's newly appointed vice-president in charge of International Development] who I had used as a consultant while I was at Foodmaker. But beyond having a lot of contacts, KRR made good business sense for China. It represents American life style. It is not fast food like KFC or McDonald's. It is an entirely new category. Also, young people in China really like Kenny Rogers as a singer.

Wang's negotiations focused on gaining the franchise rights for KRR for both Shanghai and Beijing.

> I didn't need the rights to the whole country. Beijing and Shanghai are on the leading edge of China. I am sure that KRR will not partner with anyone else until they see what happens in Beijing and Shanghai. If they can get someone else to do it better, fine. But if I do a good job, why would John Brown want someone else to do it? In any case, Beijing and Shanghai are both huge.

In the spring of 1995, FICA was granted the KRR rights for both Beijing and Shanghai. While FICA did not pay a fee for the KRR rights to these two cities, it did agree to pay an upfront franchise fee for each store based on opening 15 stores in total. According to Wang, the upfront franchise fees "were consistent with U.S. per-store fees discounted by an allowance for new market development." FICA's 1995 structure is presented in Exhibit 2.

Beyond franchise fees, Wang recognized that considerable money would be required to build the first KRR store. Costs were not directly comparable with U.S. levels. The location of the store, terms and conditions of the lease and size of the store all affected costs. To Wang, "I didn't even ask what a U.S. store cost. I knew it would be irrelevant. U.S. stores are 90 percent free standing. They also involve a lot of real estate. None in China are or will be free standing. Also you can't buy real estate in China."

In deciding on a Beijing or Shanghai location for the first store, Wang commented:

> I didn't make the decision of predetermining where the first store would be located. I looked at the opportunities and at supporting functions. The first concern was where we could get good employees and managers. We settled on Beijing.

EXHIBIT 1   Economic and Social Trends in China

Economic Indicators	1989	1990	1991	1992	1993	1994	1995*	1996*	1997*	1998*	1999*
GNP at current market prices ($ bn)	424.8	369.9	380.1	435.9	544.6	477.2	525.9	569.6	616.7	670.4	730.2
Real GNP growth (%)	4.4	4.1	8.2	13.0	13.4	11.8	9.8	8.6	8.3	8.4	8.5
GNP, per capita ($)	380.0	324.0	330.0	374.0	462.0	399.0	434.0	463.0	494.0	530.0	569.0
Consumer price inflation (%)	17.5	1.6	3.0	5.4	13.0	25.0	18.0	12.0	11.5	11.5	11.0
Exchange rate (av.) Rmb: $ (official rate)	3.8	4.8	5.3	5.5	5.8	8.6	8.6	9.5	10.0	10.5	11.0
Av. growth rate in wages; urban workers (%)[a]	10.8	10.5	9.4	15.8	19.6	18.0	15.0	13.0	12.5	13.0	12.5

Demographics	1989	1990	1991	1992	1993	1994[b]
Urban population (billion)	295.4	301.9	305.4	323.7	333.5	
Rural population (billion)	831.6	841.4	852.8	848.0	851.7	
Total population (billion)	1,127.0	1,143.3	1,158.2	1,171.7	1,185.2	

Demographic and Social Trends	1991	1996*	2001*	Annual Average % change 1991–2001*
Total population (billion)	1.15	1.13	1.31	1.3
Population growth rate (% per year)				1.3
Age profile (% of population)				
0–14	27.5	26.9	26.4	0.9
15–64	66.5	66.9	67.2	1.4
65+	6.2	6.4	6.4	2.0
Life expectancy (years)				
Male	66	67	68	N/A
Female	69			N/A
Literacy rate (% of population)				
10 years and over	80	82	84	N/A
Labor force (million)	584	645	712	2.0

*EIU estimates.
[a]State enterprises only.
[b]Data not yet available.
Source: These tables were compiled from China: *Country Report* and *Country Forecast. Economist Intelligence Unit*, 1995.

EXHIBIT 2   FICA (Franchise Investment Corporation of Asia), 1995

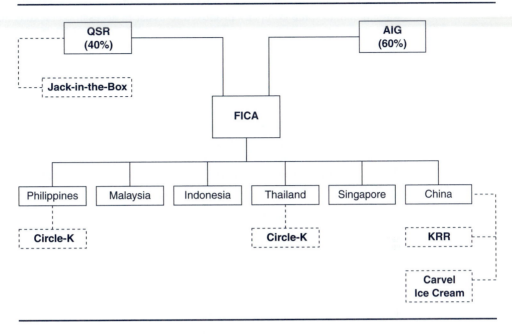

Finding a Partner

Once the decision had been made to focus on Beijing, Wang began the process of finding an appropriate local partner. Despite years of open door economic policies, Chinese investment regulations remained complex and cumbersome. There were also legal issues to be considered. Wang explained:

> The law in China is both clear and uncertain in the area of ownership. The regulations state that you cannot have 100 percent foreign ownership in food services. Beyond that it is not clear. So we had to think about a partner or several partners. . . I wanted to find a partner who could bring me some skills and organizational strength. The organizational strength might be an understanding of retailing in Beijing or an understanding of real estate or something else valuable.

Wang initially thought of contacting his old KFC partners. However, this was ruled out because of strict noncompete agreements that Wang had forced upon each partner when the original KFC joint venture was established in 1987. Wang then turned to East City Food Services and Distribution Co., a firm with which he had some familiarity. East City was a city-government-owned enterprise with 30 different Chinese style sit-down restaurants and over 100 retail food outlets in the greater Beijing area. Preliminary discussions with East City's management indicated considerable excitement at partnering with KRR. East City promised access to its extensive labor pool that could either be transferred to KRR or hired through the company's normal channels. East City also had extensive local market knowledge and could be useful in marketing efforts and pricing issues. Finally, through their upstream contacts, the company promised to assist in accessing chickens and various food ingredients that would be essential in the smooth running of KRR restaurants. In assessing their potential contributions, Wang commented:

> We would save some starting legwork by partnering with them. They could represent a smart option given my other FICA commitments. I think they are seriously worth considering. One drawback, however, is that they couldn't provide much in the way of finances.

A second option Wang was considering was the Beijing Branch of the China Great Wall Trading Co., a major investor-owned international trading company. China Great Wall had extensive international contacts and was very familiar with Western business practices. They were also very entrepreneurial and were seeking new investment opportunities with multinational corporations in Beijing. Wang sized up this option:

> China Great Wall has a lot of appeal because it can provide a bridge between the Chinese and American ways of doing business. Mr. Lu Hong Jun, the General Manager, is someone I have known for some time. He seems quite easy to work with. I admire his entrepreneurial spirit. China Great Wall also seems to have plenty of money, including access to hard currency.

As a third option, Wang considered D&D Realty Co. D&D was a Hong Kong–based real estate development and leasing company with revenues in excess of $U.S. 1.8 billion. In 1993 it began a major push into China and in 1994 opened its first office in Beijing. In early 1995 it signed a contract as leasing agent for a new 14-story office complex being built by Hong Kong investors in a commercial area in central Beijing. It was interested in filling ground floor space with a signature store and in September 1995 approached FICA with an offer to form a partnership with KRR. D&D communicated its plans for aggressive expansion in Beijing and promised Wang that as a partner it could provide relatively easy access to prime retail space within the city. Wang was clearly intrigued by the potential. "It is a very interesting concept. My worry is that they are still new and don't have mature contacts. Still, they deserve careful consideration."

Future Direction

Wang was clearly committed to moving KRR forward in Beijing in as expeditious a manner as possible. While he clearly had other responsibilities as President of FICA, Wang realized KRR's approach to the Beijing market would set a clear precedent for the expansion of other FICA retailing concepts in China. He was also aware that the competition was not standing still. By the fall of 1995, McDonald's had 17 restaurants running in Beijing; KFC was operating 10. Other restaurant companies including Hard Rock Café, Pizza Hut, and TGI Friday's, had either established operations or had broken ground for new stores in the Beijing area.

Despite the obvious popularity of Western food and the enormous potential of the Chinese market, the Chinese food service industry remained poorly developed and at risk. McDonald's and KFC were both involved in difficult lease negotiations. In February 1995,

McDonald's managers were informed that its flagship restaurant in Beijing (and McDonald's largest in the world) would be razed to accommodate the construction of an enormous shopping, office, and residential complex being developed by Hong Kong billionaire Li Ka-Shing. McDonald's refused to vacate its building arguing that it had a valid long-term lease. Demolition of the surrounding area continued and by October 1995 the restaurant was still operating, but in what appeared to be a war zone. A spokesperson for the developer asserted that McDonald's never had a clean lease on the property. Rumors that McDonald's had cut a special deal with Li Ka-Shing's group were circulating among Western business people in Beijing. One other rumor circulating was that KFC would not renew its 10-year lease on its flagship Tiananmen Square store because of soaring rent costs.

The problems of doing business in China did not stop with leasing issues. Wang learned that import duties for equipment and materials would average 50 to 100 percent. It was estimated that each KRR store would require a minimum of $U.S. 150,000 in imported equipment (not including lease-hold improvements). While import permits were relatively straightforward, Wang lacked the staff to manage the development of 15 new stores in a short period of time. Another concern was hiring and training the new workers. With 15 restaurants, over 1,000 new employees would be required over the next few years. Who would interview them, hire them and train them? No one in KRR's training group spoke Mandarin nor were Chinese language training materials available.

Wang also learned that wage rates had climbed substantially over the past decade. Multinational companies were paying from a low 1,500 RMB per month for office clerks who spoke some English to as high as 10,000 RMB per month for senior managers who spoke fluent English.[3] Over 95 percent of employees in Beijing worked for state-owned enterprises where salaries averaged between 500 to 700 RMB per month. In Beijing, anyone—including those who worked for multinational companies—making less than 2,000 RMB per month was entitled to subsidized housing. Government subsidies reduced rent costs to less than 80 RMB per month. The cheapest unsubsidized apartments started at over 1,000 RMB per month and increased sharply according to location, size, and quality.

Wang was also acutely aware that by October 1995 none of the local food suppliers had been either identified or approved by KRR's head office. Related to this was a real concern over the menu. KRR's menu had never been tested in Beijing. While chicken was commonly eaten in China, would the Chinese be attracted to a premium product that was promoted in the U.S. as a healthy alternative to fried chicken? Furthermore, should KRR develop new menu items for China and if so, who would actually develop the concepts? Even if tasty new concepts could be developed, how long would they take to get corporate approval and could they be produced economically without costly new equipment?

These were all questions that were weighing heavily on Wang's mind. One thing that was clear was that whoever was selected as FICA's local partner would have a major impact on the success or failure of KRR in China. With so many unresolved issues, Wang was wondering whether the time was right to formalize a partnership.

---

[3]In October 1995, the Chinese renminbi (RMB) had an exchange rate of 1 $U.S. = 8.11 RMB.

16 PALLISER FURNITURE LTD.

In mid-December 1997, Arthur DeFehr, President of Palliser Furniture Ltd. of Winnipeg, Manitoba, prepared for the following week's senior management committee meeting (see Exhibit 1 for an organizational chart) during which the company's strategy for expansion would be discussed and finalized. While a number of factors appeared to recommend expansion into Latin America, there had been a recent dramatic increase in competition from Asia that had to be taken into account in their plans. As a result, it was unclear how and when Palliser should respond and what form this investment, if any, should take.

A Brief History of Palliser Furniture Ltd.

With the proceeds from the sale of his car, A. A. DeFehr set up a woodworking shop in his basement in 1944 to produce various household items (i.e., laundry hangers, ironing boards). A major turning point was reached in 1949 when he brought his latest innovation, a three-legged end table, to T. Eaton & Co., one of Canada's largest retailers, and found a very receptive buyer. In particular the retailer appeared to be less sensitive to the price of the end table compared to his other products; as a result, the woodworking shop's focus was promptly redirected towards the production of residential furniture. By 1964, DeFehr Manufacturing Ltd. (DML) was operating in a 45,000 square foot building with 50

IVEY   Anthony Goerzen prepared this case under the supervision of Professor Paul Beamish solely to provide material for class discussion. The authors do not intend to illustrate either effectve or ineffective handling of a managerial situation. The authors may have disguised certain names and other identifying information to protect confidentiality. Ivey Management Services prohibits any form of reproduction, storage or transmittal without its written permission. This material is not covered under authorization from CanCopy or any reproduction rights organization. Copyright © 1995, Ivey Management Services.

EXHIBIT 1   Palliser Furniture Ltd. Senior Management

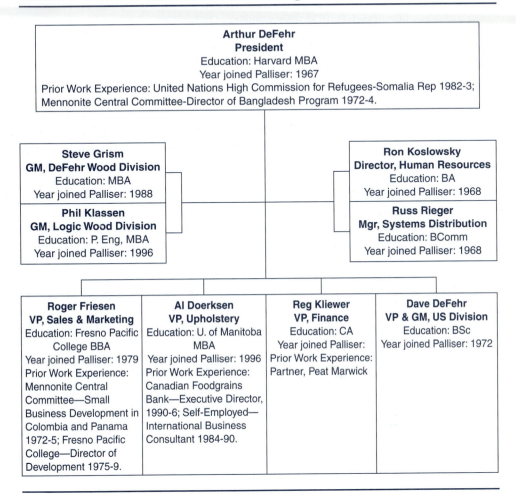

Arthur DeFehr
President
Education: Harvard MBA
Year joined Palliser: 1967
Prior Work Experience: United Nations High Commission for Refugees-Somalia Rep 1982-3;
Mennonite Central Committee-Director of Bangladesh Program 1972-4.

Steve Grism
GM, DeFehr Wood Division
Education: MBA
Year joined Palliser: 1988

Phil Klassen
GM, Logic Wood Division
Education: P. Eng, MBA
Year joined Palliser: 1996

Ron Koslowsky
Director, Human Resources
Education: BA
Year joined Palliser: 1968

Russ Rieger
Mgr, Systems Distribution
Education: BComm
Year joined Palliser: 1968

Roger Friesen
VP, Sales & Marketing
Education: Fresno Pacific
College BBA
Year joined Palliser: 1979
Prior Work Experience:
Mennonite Central
Committee—Small
Business Development in
Colombia and Panama
1972-5; Fresno Pacific
College—Director of
Development 1975-9.

Al Doerksen
VP, Upholstery
Education: U. of Manitoba
MBA
Year joined Palliser: 1996
Prior Work Experience:
Canadian Foodgrains
Bank—Executive Director,
1990-6; Self-Employed—
International Business
Consultant 1984-90.

Reg Kliewer
VP, Finance
Education: CA
Year joined Palliser:
Prior Work Experience:
Partner, Peat Marwick

Dave DeFehr
VP & GM, US Division
Education: BSc
Year joined Palliser: 1972

---

employees and annual sales of CDN$1 million. Four years later, DML entered the uphol-
stered furniture market when it made its first investment outside of Winnipeg, purchasing
a bankrupt upholstery plant in Calgary, Alberta.

Throughout 1960–70, the firm's sales grew at an annual compounded rate of 25 percent as A. A. DeFehr's three sons, Frank, Arthur, and Dave, joined the family business. Art
recalled when

> Frank and I made our first effort at selling in the United States. We loaded up the wagon and
> made our first stop in the parking lot of a store in Grand Forks. The store manager came out and
> said, "The colour is wrong, the style is wrong, and the price is wrong."

Nonetheless, by 1973, exports to the U.S. accounted for 20 percent of the firm's total sales. As the CDN$:US$ ratio continued to rise, however, exports became increasingly difficult and, in 1975, the company withdrew entirely from the export market.

In 1979, the company's founder took on the position of Chairman of the Board and Frank, the eldest son, became President. All the company's operations were amalgamated in 1980 under the name of Palliser Furniture Ltd. In order to maintain a presence in the U.S. market that would not be subject to the whims of currency exchange, Palliser established a small plant in Fargo, North Dakota, in 1981. This plant became a beachhead in the U.S., allowing Palliser to secure market access, as well as creating a window into the world's largest market. In 1984, Frank stepped down and Art became President. In response to increased competition from Taiwan, Palliser established a trading company in Taipei in 1986 to develop brokerage revenues by importing finished furniture from various offshore producers as well as furniture components (i.e., knobs and handles) for Palliser's own production. By 1987, U.S. sales through the Fargo plant accounted for about 15 percent of the company's CDN$100 million sales. In 1989, to support the firm's growing U.S. sales, a showroom was opened in High Point, North Carolina. The 1980s were good years for Palliser as it grew at 18 percent per year reaching total annual sales of over CDN$135 million by the end of the decade. During this time, A. A. DeFehr gradually became less involved in the firm, leaving day-to-day management decisions to his three sons.

In order to establish a stronger U.S.-based presence, Palliser purchased an idled 400,000 square foot furniture production facility in Troutman, North Carolina, for US$6 million in 1991. Dave spearheaded this initiative, moving to Troutman and taking on U.S. citizenship to manage the growth of Palliser's U.S. investments. Rising pressure for efficiency, however, led the company to close the small Fargo plant and lay off its workforce of 285 in 1994, and this production responsibility was transferred to the Canadian operations.

Between 1990 and 1995, revenue grew at 8 percent to 10 percent per year with total annual sales surpassing CDN$200 million by 1992. During this period, however, philosophical differences within the DeFehr family arose pertaining to issues of growth, size, and the role of the third generation. While A. A. DeFehr would have preferred that all three sons take turns leading the firm over time, there was a meeting in 1995 to resolve long-term ownership and family issues. Art decided to purchase the Leather Division and Frank again became President of Palliser. However, after 18 months it was agreed that Art would purchase majority control (53 percent) of Palliser, merge the Leather Division back into the parent company and resume the role of President. Frank purchased two supply subsidiaries and retained a 5 percent ownership in Palliser. Dave retained his 34 percent share of the company and became Chairman of the Board although he remained only partially involved in regular operations, focusing instead on the U.S. Division and two retail outlets which he purchased in North Carolina. The 8 percent balance of the firm was owned by their sister, Irene Loewen.

With an overall total of 1.8 million square feet of production space, total annual sales reached CDN$325 million by 1997 (see Exhibits 2 and 3) with CDN$25 million of that amount contributed by the U.S. Division. Sales growth was again very strong, rising to 18 percent per year. Although this growth came exclusively from U.S. exports, domestic sales still accounted for almost 50 percent of the total revenue.

EXHIBIT 2

CONDENSED BALANCE SHEET
(As at December 31, 1997)

	1997 ($000's)	1996 ($000's)
ASSETS		
Current		
Accounts Receivable	53,758	44,122
Income Taxes Recoverable	0	448
Inventories	60,576	52,016
Prepaid Expenses	2,693	2,200
Total Current Assets	117,027	98,786
Property, Plant, and Equipment	67,423	58,811
Other Assets	1,605	1,193
	186,055	158,790
LIABILITIES AND SHAREHOLDERS' EQUITY		
Current		
Bank Indebtedness, with a Majority of the Assets		
Pledged as Collateral Security	43,398	41,109
Accounts Payable and Accrued Liabilities	29,846	23,994
Income Taxes Payable	4,333	0
Loans Payable	6,229	5,797
Current Portion of Long-term Debt	360	952
Total Current Liabilities	84,166	71,852
Long-term Debt, with a Majority of the Assets		
Pledged as Collateral Security	40,757	32,412
Deferred Income Taxes	2,858	2,535
	127,781	106,799
Shareholders' Equity		
Share Capital	40,264	
Contributed Surplus	1,250	1,270
Retained Earnings	16,760	5,957
Total Shareholders' Equity	186,055	158,790

The Canadian Furniture Industry

The furniture industry in Canada had a long history as part of the country's industrial base. In 1996, there was a total of 1,406 firms in the furniture and fixture industry employing over 49,000 employees and shipping product valued at more than CDN$5.6 billion at wholesale prices. More specifically, in the household furniture segment, there were 676 firms with sales of CDN$2.3 billion annually.

EXHIBIT 3

CONDENSED INCOME STATEMENT
(As at December 31, 1997)

	1997 ($000's)	1996 ($000's)
Sales	324,061	277,210
Deduct Freight	22,118	18,789
Net Sales	301,943	258,421
Cost of Sales	208,532	182,091
Gross Margin	93,411	76,330
Expenses		
Manufacturing, Selling and Administration	55,718	48,232
Depreciation and Amortization	6,868	6,787
Interest	4,638	4,606
	67,224	59,625
Income Before Income Allocations, Loss on Partnership Investment and Income Taxes	26,187	16,705
Income Allocations		
Employee Profit-Sharing Incentive Plans	6,379	3,509
Income Before Loss on Partnership Investment and Income Taxes	19,808	13,196
Loss on Partnership Investment	668	2,522
Income Before Income Taxes	19,140	10,674
Provision for Income Taxes	7,622	4,714
Net Income for the Year	11,478	5,960

The Canadian market for household furniture was estimated at CDN$2.1 billion at wholesale prices in 1997. Demand was forecast to grow at a real annual rate of 1 percent into the next century, compared to a projected rate of 1.5 percent for total consumer expenditures. The U.S. furniture market, in contrast, was expected to grow at a rate of almost 3 percent. Niche markets were expected to grow at significantly higher rates, especially furniture for the elderly and for home entertainment applications. Key consumer niches were expected to include high-income earners and new immigrants. All furniture was sold through retail outlets, and trade shows were an important venue for sales to retailers. One of the largest international trade shows was held annually in High Point, North Carolina.

While Canada was a relatively small player on the world scene, making up only 2 percent of the world market for household furniture, it was located next to the world's largest market that consumed 28 percent of global production. Other major markets were Japan with 15 percent of total international consumption and Germany with 10 percent. Canadian manufacturers exported over CDN$1 billion of furniture, 95 percent of which was destined for the U.S. In total, Canadian shipments to the U.S. accounted for less than 15 percent of total U.S. imports. Canada also imported CDN$816 million of furniture, 60 percent of which originated in the U.S. Other important sources of imports into Canada were made up of lower quality products from China and Taiwan (16 percent of total imports) and high quality products from Italy (7 percent).

The Canadian furniture industry, located primarily in Ontario and Quebec, was characterized by a few large operations and many small ones. By comparison, the U.S. industry had seven times as many plants, 12 times the number of employees, and 15 times the shipments of the Canadian industry. Further, the average U.S. plant was twice the size of its Canadian counterpart; in fact, the largest U.S. furniture producer was equal in size to the entire Canadian market. The two largest firms in the Canadian furniture industry in 1997 were Dorel Industries Inc. and Palliser Furniture Ltd. While both companies had become international producers, Palliser generated over 85 percent of its revenue from Canadian operations whereas Dorel derived less than 20 percent of its revenue from Canada with the balance from plants in Europe, Asia, and the U.S.

In response to favorable market conditions, the Canadian furniture industry achieved a record of solid growth behind high tariff walls until 1987. The industry then underwent extensive restructuring as a result of both growing import pressure and an economic downturn in the late 1980s and early 1990s. Competitive pressure increased following the liberalization of trade as a result of the 1987 Canada-U.S. Free Trade Agreement (FTA), later replaced by the 1994 North American Free Trade Agreement (NAFTA). Further, in the 1995 accord made during the Uruguay Round negotiations under the General Agreement on Tariffs and Trade (GATT), Canada agreed to reduce its Most Favoured Nation (MFN) tariffs on furniture, furniture parts, and raw materials. Canada's tariffs on MFN furniture ranged from 6 percent to 24 percent and were scheduled to be reduced by one-third between 1995 and 2000. The GATT agreement was favorable to producers in both Europe and Asia since both were subject to Canada's MFN tariff regime.

Restructuring in the Canadian furniture industry following trade liberalization resulted in a dramatic decline of manufacturers, more rationalized, specialized, and productive operational structures, and a reorientation of marketing efforts toward the U.S. Between 1988 and 1996 in the household furniture segment, for example, the number of manufacturers fell by 42 percent, the number of employees decreased by 29 percent, and yet (after several years of adjustment) the total value of shipments remained unchanged. Throughout this period of adjustment, exports increased each year reaching levels in 1997 that were 330 percent over 1988 figures and productivity in terms of value-added per employee increased from CDN$33,000 to CDN$49,000 over the same period.

The furniture industry was labor-intensive, employing primarily unskilled and semi-skilled workers, especially immigrants. In 1996, wage rates in the industry were CDN$10.66/hour, well below the overall average of CDN$16.83 for the manufacturing sector in Canada. Yet, Canadian manufacturers had slightly higher wage costs than their U.S. counterparts; this was an important factor since the cost of labor relative to the final cost of product for leather and wooden furniture, was 20 percent and 25 percent, respectively. Labor supply had not been a critical problem for the Canadian industry, although there was an ongoing shortage of people with specialized skills. With the introduction of more computerized equipment, the demand for better-educated workers increased although approximately 40 percent of the existing work force had not completed secondary school.

Barriers to entry were fairly low although this had begun to change with the arrival of productivity-improving technologies such as computer-aided design and computer-numeric-controlled machinery. State-of-the-art machinery tended to be adopted most quickly by larger firms that had the necessary managerial and financial resources. In addition to these computer technologies, a variety of management techniques had become more widely used among Canadian manufacturers. For example, in response to retailers' demands for quicker and more efficient responses to orders and also to alleviate pressure on working capital, just-in-time manufacturing systems were adopted by many firms. In addition, various quality control techniques were implemented including material inspection processes and more sophisticated production procedures to prevent, rather than correct, error.

Due to the entrepreneurial nature of most furniture manufacturers, many operations lacked professional management, although management sophistication tended to increase with company size. In particular, there appeared to be a widespread belief that Canadian manufacturers lacked marketing skills and were generally oriented towards the production aspect of the business. The U.S. industry, in contrast, was generally credited with having a much greater marketing orientation than its Canadian counterpart. Canadian manufacturers and retailers generally agreed that the key success factors in the furniture business were (in order of importance) overall product quality, quick delivery, innovative design, customer service, and price. In contrast, U.S. manufacturers perceived their key competitive success factors to be quality of raw materials, product design, location and quality of showrooms, extent of marketing activity, and price.

Palliser's Strategy

Palliser was profoundly affected by the FTA and the NAFTA. Beginning in 1989 with the reduction of tariff barriers, there began an intense downward pressure on prices in Palliser's base domestic market. Retailers attempted to appropriate in two years the anticipated savings resulting from the reduction of import duties that were actually phased in over four. Palliser's management then realized that neither the main Winnipeg facility nor the Fargo plant was strong enough to compete head-to-head with U.S. producers. As a result, there began an intensive effort to revamp the firm's strategy in line with the internationalization of the industry. Implementation of this strategic shift took place between 1989 and 1994, when the company redefined its markets, rationalized its distribution channels, and shifted manufacturing locations.

Palliser's first priority was to protect its Canadian sales base and then to grow through exports to the U.S. The company dropped its prices as necessary in important markets and began to modify its product line in a number of ways to maximize the production efficiency of the product mix. For example, Palliser reduced the number of wood species from three to one, thus reducing the cost of raw materials inventory. In addition, Palliser decided to retain only those product lines that were the retailers' first or, at worst, second choice. As a result, the dining room line was completely eliminated, with concentration instead on bedroom and living room markets. Thus, Palliser's product line was narrowed, and was made up of products in contemporary styles that competed on value, quality, and delivery in the medium price categories. At the same time, Palliser World Trade's Taipei office was, in the view of Roger Friesen, established to encourage

> the people in Palliser to think outside of Winnipeg. Aside from developing a stream of new revenues, the trading company was intended to act as a window on new ideas and potential competitors in foreign markets.

To reduce the sensitivity to cost of Canadian labor, Palliser then introduced a line of leather furniture since the retail prices of these products were substantially higher than wooden products as was the cost of production materials (typically 54 percent of the sales prices versus 36 percent for wood). Further, Palliser's senior management perceived that the market for leather furniture was increasing more rapidly than other lines and there appeared to be excellent opportunities for growth, particularly for those manufacturers that were early movers. In fact, between 1994 and 1997 the North American leather furniture market grew between 15 percent and 18 percent annually compared to 3 percent to 4 percent for the industry as a whole. American leather furniture producers (i.e., Klausner, Viewpoint, etc.) were noted for traditional designs, whereas Italian companies (i.e., Natuzzi, Softline, Flep, etc.) captured over 50 percent of the North American leather furniture market with contemporary designs and colors. Since the furniture market appeared to be heading away from traditional designs into lighter "life style" fashions, Palliser's intention was to displace Italian imports with good quality, innovative, contemporary designs in the broad middle range of the market (i.e., leather couch retail price of US$800–1,299). Among Palliser's selling points was that it could guarantee quick delivery, a factor that had become increasingly important because retailers were becoming more resistant to holding inventory. Palliser also had a related cost advantage in that the Italian producers had to maintain a long and expensive inventory pipeline. While Palliser was able to make significant inroads into the leather market, the Italians proved to be very aggressive in maintaining their share of the lower price market.

Motivated by the conventional wisdom that wage rates were lower and that productivity was higher in the U.S., a 400,000 square foot facility that had ceased production in Troutman, North Carolina, was purchased in 1991 for US$6 million. The initial intention was that this plant would produce wooden furniture, enabling Palliser to compete on equal terms with U.S. producers in the major markets along the Eastern Seaboard. However, Palliser was not able to achieve acceptable quality of output or productivity per worker with its 256 employees at this plant. In an effort to improve the situation, the plant's product line was converted to leather furniture, given the firm's success in capturing a share of this lucrative market. A short while later, Palliser's increasing focus on cost minimization through large production runs led management to consider redundant the relatively small Fargo operation and the facility was closed in 1994.

Prior to the FTA, Palliser attempted to maximize Canadian market share by maintaining a wide distribution base, often with several distributors competing with each other for the same sales. In an effort to strengthen relationships with its top distributors before they were lured away by new U.S. competitors, Palliser decided to rationalize its Canadian distribution system by eliminating almost half of its 800 distributors. This show of commitment to the remaining distributors reinforced Palliser's strong Canadian position, although the move immediately wiped out 10 percent to 12 percent of its Canadian sales. In the U.S. market, on the other hand, Palliser began to offer its distributors the convenience of delivered prices rather than cost plus freight which was the industry standard. Within a unified production and distribution system, Palliser hoped to capture the freight savings on shipments to U.S. customers when made from Troutman versus Winnipeg.

As the organization continued to prosper, management began to feel increasingly vulnerable given that the vast majority of the firm's investments were in Canada and the majority of the costs were denominated in Canadian dollars whereas its growing markets were abroad. In addition, since Palliser had become one of the largest furniture manufacturers in Canada and the second-largest employer in Manitoba with almost 2,900 employees in Winnipeg, the firm's rising profile made it a recurring target for union recruitment drives. The possibility that unionization could lead to higher labor rates was an important consideration since the cost of labor in the production of furniture was a significant component of the final cost of products.

Palliser's Latin American Vision

Palliser's initial interest in Mexico came about in an indirect way in the early 1990s. Once their children had left home, Leona and Arthur DeFehr were interested in finding a spot to get away for a few months from the cold Winnipeg winter. They gravitated towards Mexico, rather than the more popular destination of Florida, primarily because of their interest in foreign cultures. When they were in Mexico, Art often filled his free time with visits to local manufacturers and furniture retailers. As he became more familiar with the furniture industry in Mexico, he decided that a more careful review of the opportunities for Palliser was in order.

Palliser's initial effort in Mexico in the early 1990s was to prospect for export sales. After the "Tequila Crisis," the near collapse of Mexico's banks in 1994, Palliser effectively withdrew from the Mexican market, although Palliser World Trade began importing a few items (i.e., occasional tables) into the U.S. and Canada. In addition, Palliser had established a CDN$2 million per year foothold in Latin America with shipments to Guatemala, Honduras, Costa Rica, and Ecuador. Once the financial problem subsided, Palliser attempted to reinstate its exporting program to Mexico but early success was modest.

Palliser continued to look very seriously at upgrading its involvement in Mexico as various opportunities became apparent. It was known, for example, that several major companies like Reebok, Nike, Florsheim, Rockport, and L.A. Gear had engaged in the cutting and sewing of leather products in Mexico. Palliser also knew that Arkea Salotti S.A., the leading Mexican upholstered furniture producer, who marketed the "Zarkin Leather" brand, had an annual turnover of only US$8 million. Although there were other major producers of upholstered furniture (i.e., Muebles Boal, Sabone, Mueblicentro, Monaco, Industria Mueblera Fenig, Dimher, Gestalt, Muebles Drexel, etc.), all had sales of less than US$5 million annually. While there was a clear preference on the part of retailers to buy from Mexican plants, supply was often outstripped by demand, and most retailers, frustrated with delivery delays, were looking for alternatives.

Another opportunity for Palliser was in the "Rustic" furniture segment, a line of products that looked like "antique Mexican" furniture based on Spanish colonial designs. Total production of Rustic furniture in Mexico was over US$100 million in 1997, 60 percent of which was exported to the U.S. with sales increasing at 15 percent annually. The undisputed leader of the Rustic furniture segment was Segusino S.A. Founded in 1985, Segusino employed over 1,400 people in its factory and another 2,300 in various surrounding artisans' workshops. Segusino's sales by 1997 were more than US$35 million with shipments spread throughout North America and Europe. A junior-level team began to investigate the prospect of establishing an operation that would send finished leather covers back to Winnipeg or Troutman for final assembly into furniture. Although the resulting report made a very positive recommendation (see Exhibit 4), senior management decided to pause to look more deeply into the matter. Given the various possibilities, Art believed that whatever decision Palliser made in Mexico, it would become the platform for business growth into Latin America, a long-term and complex investment.

The Mexican Furniture Industry

Total furniture production in Mexico amounted to US$2.9 billion at wholesale prices in 1997, an increase of 17 percent over 1996 levels. Over 60 percent of the Mexican industry produced residential furniture valued at a total of US$1.74 billion in 1997. Wooden furniture was produced by 80 percent of manufacturers with others working in metal and, to a lesser extent, plastic. The production of metal furniture had remained fairly static over the previous five years while the production of wooden furniture increased by 17 percent. Around 13 percent of the firms produced upholstered furniture with total annual sales of US$226 million at wholesale prices. Only 7 percent of producers made kitchen furniture with an annual value of US$122 million.

The Mexican market had an apparent domestic consumption of around US$4.35 billion at retail prices, of which US$3.35 billion was made up of home furniture in 1997. Bedroom and living room retail sales accounted for US$2.51 billion. There were about 16,000 retail outlets with an average annual turnover of US$270,000. Small and medium-sized outlets (fewer than five employees) served almost half of the market, and 600 large outlets controlled another 25 percent. Large-scale non-specialist distribution, direct sales, and marginal outlets shared the remainder.

Between 1991 and 1997, exports from Mexico quadrupled reaching US$1.7 billion, with 96 percent of these exports destined for the U.S. The dramatic increase in exports was linked directly to the NAFTA agreement. It encouraged exports to the U.S. primarily from maquiladoras that were responsible for over 60 percent of furniture exports in 1996. Residential furniture accounted for 70 percent of total exports of which 18 percent was upholstered and 2 percent was kitchen furniture. Imports, on the other hand, totalled US$250 million by 1996, after having dropped by 50 percent following the 1994 Mexican financial crisis. By 1997, domestic demand was still only 80 percent of what it had been a decade earlier. The majority of imports (74 percent) were made up of household furniture.

There were 200,000 people employed in the Mexican furniture industry creating an average annual production of US$20,000 per employee. In total, there were around 20,000

EXHIBIT 4

ESTIMATED COSTS AND REVENUES OF
ESTABLISHING A PLANT IN NORTHERN MEXICO
(all figures in $CDN)

Production Facility:

Refurbished Factory Space & Land	$7,000,000–9,000,000
Machinery & Equipment	$3,000,000–5,000,000
Office Equipment & Computers	$ 200,000– 300,000

Annual Expenses:

Travel & Entertainment	$23,000 ($750/month + $15,000 car)
Factory Operation (i.e., power)	10–15% of sales
Inventory	10% of sales
Accounts Receivable	15% of sales

Projected Annual Revenues:	*Year 1*	*Year 2*	*Year 3*
Leather Cut-and-Sew	$ 2,500,000	$ 4,800,000	$ 8,400,000
Finished Furniture			
Latin America	$ 2,300,000	$ 5,400,000	$ 9,000,000
North America	$ 6,000,000	$ 8,500,000	$14,000,000
Total	$10,800,000	$18,700,000	$31,400,000

Key Personnel Annual Wages:	*Base Salary*	*Typical Benefits*	*Profitability Bonus*
General Manager	$50,000	$17,500	$50,000–300,000
Sales Manager	$55,000	$19,250	$10,000–15,000
Financial Manager	$45,000	$15,750	$ 4,500–6,000
Plant Supervisor	$25,000	$ 8,750	$ 2,500–3,000
Sales Representative	$16,000	$ 5,500	1% of sales
Clerical & Hourly Employees	$ 4,800	$ 1,700	$ 500

Projected Number of Workers:	*Year 1*	*Year 2*	*Year 3*
Leather Cut-and-Sew	21	40	70
Finished Furniture			
Latin America	23	54	90
North America	60	85	140
Total	104	179	300

---

companies making both wooden and metal furniture of which 321 were maquiladoras employing 44,000 people. In 1997, around 40 percent of the industry was located in the northern third of Mexico. Over 95 percent of Mexican wooden furniture manufacturers were small firms, employing fewer than 15 people. Around 800 firms employed between 16 and 250 workers, and fewer than 20 firms were relatively large with over 250 employees. These factories typically paid their workers US$1.00-1.50/hour payable in cash on a weekly basis according to Mexican law.

The Mexico Decision

In October 1997, a senior-level team made an extended trip to Mexico to become more familiar with the wide range of regions and to investigate other products and supply options. The trip led through seven Mexican states and countless factories that were potential suppliers, buyers, partners, or acquisition targets. The team's overall impression was that the opportunities were very good, although much of the potential lay in shipping product back to the U.S., at least initially. This suggested a location that had a good labor climate as well as availability and was also well located in terms of both suppliers and northern transportation routes. An obvious possibility was to locate in one of the maquiladora districts along the northern border; this location was never considered seriously, however, because Palliser did not want to become involved in these socially unstable zones. The result of this research was that Saltillo, Coahuila, emerged as the strongest candidate.

Coahuila was a province located adjacent to the Texas border. It was equidistant from California and the Mid-Atlantic States and was directly south of Winnipeg. Silver mining and ranching were not part of the heritage of this region, unlike most other parts of Mexico; success had come through industrial development. There was a strong entrepreneurial and industrial mentality in this area and, as a result, an excellent infrastructure had encouraged a number of large industrial groups to locate there.

Saltillo was a city of 700,000 people about 80 km from Monterey, a major center of three million inhabitants in the neighbouring state of Nuevo Leon. Established about 400 years ago, Saltillo had an historic city centre with a number of newer areas that included gated communities, a golf course, a tennis club, good shopping, etc. Lying at an altitude of 6,000 feet, Saltillo enjoyed a dry, temperate climate. The cost of living in Saltillo was modest compared to most other international cities and, overall, it was considered an excellent location for expatriates.

Since Saltillo had an established agricultural equipment-manufacturing sector, the city was attractive to various industries including the automobile sector. Chrysler and GM both had assembly plants in Saltillo and a great number of operations had also been set up nearby to supply the automotive industry, paying workers around US$1.75-2.00/hour. It was rumored that GM had made the decision to add to its production capability in Saltillo, thus assuring the continued economic development of the region.

Saltillo had also become home to a number of manufacturers whose experience was relevant to Palliser. Garden State Tanning Ltd., for example, had a leather-cutting operation to supply BMW and GM, with plans to significantly increase their throughput. Lear Seating Inc. also had two seating plants dedicated to supplying seats to the car industry. There were also a few other firms located in the Saltillo area that were potential suppliers of furniture components (i.e., the foam producers, Woodbridge Ltd. and Foamex Ltd.). Fruit of the Loom Inc., the garment company, had also decided to locate in Saltillo, constructing five plants in a very short time that employed 3,000 people. Techno Trim, a division of Johnson Controls Inc., also had plans to set up a new fabric cutting and sewing installation with 800 employees. During their trip, the Palliser team was able to tour many of these facilities. They found that since the auto industry was very male-oriented, the industrial job opportunities for females were limited. As a result, Fruit of the Loom's employees were over 80 percent female who were willing to accept lower wages than the autoworkers—probably US$1.00–1.25/hour.

In summary, Arthur concluded that

the Mexican leather furniture industry is made up of small manufacturers with low sales volumes who do not have the capability of Palliser given our experience and financial strength. If we act now, Palliser could be the controlling force in the Mexican leather industry in 10 years, precluding our competition from making a similar move.

China—The Giant Begins to Rise

Early in the 1990s, an important trend emerged in the furniture industry as China opened itself up to the world economy. Given that wage rates in Taiwan had risen steadily in step with its growing economy, large Taiwanese furniture producers increasingly looked to China's vast and inexpensive supply of workers to reinstate their competitive cost advantage. The resulting newly established Taiwanese-owned factories in China were not truly start-up companies; rather, Taiwanese management brought their 20+ years of experience to bear on these new operations, which emerged as sophisticated competitors from the beginning.

Given the generally bulky nature of furniture, transportation costs were a significant component of the delivered cost structure. As a result, it was challenging for offshore firms to compete for North American sales. Nonetheless, Asian firms had begun to make clear inroads into the U.S. residential furniture market. By the early 1990s, imported product from China began to make a noticeable impact in the North American market. In 1992, U.S. imports of wooden residential furnishings amounted to US$970 million from Taiwan (12.3 percent of the total market) and US$528 million (6.7 percent) from other East Asian countries.

The Taiwanese-owned furniture producers in China were typically very large and highly focused operations, making a small number of products targeted for Western European and North American markets. These operations had, however, a number of important disadvantages that had to be overcome to enable them to be viable competitors outside of Asia. First, given that the Chinese had very limited sources of high quality raw wood, they were forced to source their hardwood requirements from the Northeastern U.S. The Chinese had, however, devised various ways of making due with inferior grades of wood mostly by using people, who were more adept than machines, to do the work. While the first arrivals of furniture from China were clearly of inferior quality, output improved dramatically in the ensuing years. By 1997, quality had risen to such an extent that, on certain pieces, it was difficult to find a difference between furniture produced in China and Canada. Second, transportation on a container of furniture from China to North America or Europe added at least 45 days onto the delivery time and about 15 percent onto the delivered cost of product. As a result, factory designs were based on the principle of economies of scale and on the availability of cheap labor enabling them to offset these distance-related disadvantages. However, rising ocean freight costs (three rate hikes in the summer of 1997 alone), port congestion, and the inadequacy of inland infrastructure began to make business more difficult for those involved in Chinese exports.

The first Taiwanese firm to build a factory in China was Lacquer Craft Mfg, which set up an operation in the southern Chinese city of Dong Guang in 1992. By 1997, the monthly production of this factory's 3,000 employees included 8,000 sets of dining room tables and chairs, 4,500 sets of buffets and hutches, and 35,000 occasional tables. Construction had already begun in 1997 on a one million square foot building in the northern Chinese city of Tianjin, as the company projected a sales increase of US$30 million to a total of over US$100 million by 1998. Palliser World Trade had developed a solid import business in Chinese furniture and maintained good relationships with well over 25 large Chinese furniture manufacturers, all of whom seemed to be expanding their operations and looking for western markets. Opportunities appeared for Palliser to become more involved in the Chinese furniture industry. Lacquer Craft's President, for example, indicated in 1997 that he "would love to put Palliser's name on one of [his] factories."

Since its establishment, Palliser World Trade had been active in the Far East with 60 percent of its CDN$14 million annual revenues in 1997 derived from products purchased in Asia. In a meeting with a major North American retailer, however, Palliser was told that its assistance in dealing with the Chinese was no longer needed. The best Chinese producers were increasingly able to market without an intermediary, and the largest North American buyers were capable of making the direct connections that would save them the 25 percent margin charged by a broker. Of the top 100 retailers that Palliser counted as customers, perhaps 30 had the resources to develop the capability to buy directly from the Chinese. The balance of 70 companies would still be interested in working with Palliser as an intermediary, but it was known that once a certain number of retailers purchased direct, wholesale price points would be established making it difficult for brokers to set their own pricing. In addition, Palliser found that one of its largest North American retailer customers had taken drawings of a Palliser table to Asia and was successful in finding a Chinese manufacturer who would make it more cheaply resulting in a loss of CDN$500,000 in annual revenue for Palliser. It appeared that not only would it become increasingly difficult for Palliser to maintain a pure trading business in China, but that Asian manufacturers were a force that had to be reckoned with. According to Roger Friesen,

> competition from China is highlighting the fact that we do not know the details of our costs of production on specific pieces of furniture. There are some types of furniture that we will be able to do better here and others where we will not be able to match the Chinese. Our knowledge of our precise costs needs to be improved and we need to focus on those products that we can do better than anyone else.

The December 1997 Senior Management Committee Meeting

During recent trips to Mexico, Palliser management had heard many rumors about other furniture companies that were actively considering the possibility of locating in Mexico; therefore, time was of the essence. The decision to go ahead in Mexico was, according to Art,

> a complex one that would have an obvious immediate impact on the company and, more significantly, it would probably have an impact on Palliser 20 years down the road.

At the same time, although it had been "many years since Palliser's senior management had travelled to Asia," the threats and opportunities in China had to be evaluated prior to any move.

17 NEILSON INTERNATIONAL IN MEXICO

In January 1993, Howard Bateman, Vice President of International Operations for Neilson International, a division of William Neilson Limited, was assessing a recent proposal from Sabritas, a division of Pepsico Foods in Mexico, to launch Neilson's brands in the Mexican market. Neilson, a leading producer of high quality confectionery products, had grown to achieve a leadership position in the Canadian market and was currently producing Canada's top selling chocolate bar, "Crispy Crunch". In the world chocolate bar market, however, Neilson was dwarfed by major players such as M&M/Mars, Hershey/Lowney and Nestlé-Rowntree. Recognizing their position as a smaller player with fewer resources, in a stagnant domestic market, Neilson in 1990 formed its International Division to develop competitive strategies for their exporting efforts.

Recent attempts to expand into several foreign markets, including the United States, had taught them some valuable lessons. Although it was now evident that they had world class products to offer to global markets, their competitive performance was being constrained by limited resources. Pepsico's joint branding proposal would allow greater market penetration than Neilson could afford. But, at what cost?

Given the decision to pursue international opportunities more aggressively, Bateman's biggest challenge was to determine the distributor relationships Neilson should pursue in order to become a global competitor.

IVEY Gayle Duncan and Shari Ann Wortel prepared this case under the supervision of Professors P.W. Beamish and C.B. Johnston solely to provide material for class discussion. The authors do not intend to illustrate either effective or ineffective handling of a managerial situation. The authors may have disguised certain names and other identifying information to protect confidentiality. Ivey Management Services prohibits any form of reproduction, storage or transmittal without its written permission. This material is not covered under authorization from CanCopy or any reproduction rights organization. Copyright © 1995, Ivey Management Services.

EXHIBIT 1   **World Chocolate Exports (Value as % of Total)–1990**

	1987	*1988*	*1989*	*1990*
Africa	x1.5	x1.0	x1.1	x0.7
Americas	8.1	9.1	9.2	x9.1
LAIC[1]	2.1	1.9	1.4	x1.4
CACM[2]	0.1	x0.1	x0.1	x0.1
Asia	2.5	3.2	3.4	2.9
Middle East	x0.5	x0.5	x0.7	x0.4
Europe	86.4	85.0	84.2	85.4
EEC (12)[3]	73.3	71.8	71.3	73.5
EFTA[4]	12.5	12.7	12.1	11.5
Oceania	x1.5	1.8	x2.1	x1.8

Figures denoted with an "x" are provisional or estimated.

[1]LAIC = Latin American Industrialists Association.

[2]CACM = Central American Common Market.

[3]EEC (12) = The twelve nations of the European Economic Community.

[4]EFTA = European Free Trade Association.

Source: Adapted from The United Nations, "International Trade Statistics Yearbook," Vol. II, 1990.

The Chocolate Confectionery Industry[1]

The "confectionery" industry consisted of the "sugar" segment, including all types of sugar confectionery, chewing gum, and the "chocolate" segment, which included chocolates and other cocoa based products. Most large chocolate operations were dedicated to two major products: boxed chocolates and bar chocolates, which represented nearly 50 percent of the confectionery industry by volume.

Competition from imports was significant, with the majority of products coming from the United States (39 percent). European countries such as Switzerland, Germany, the United Kingdom, and Belgium were also major sources of confectionery, especially for premium products such as boxed chocolates. (See Exhibit 1 for a profile of chocolate exporting countries.) In order to maintain production volumes and to relieve the burden of fixed costs on operations, Canadian manufacturers used excess capacity to produce goods for exporting. Although nearly all of these products were traditionally exported to the United States, in the early nineties, the world market had become increasingly more attractive.

Firms in the confectionery industry competed on the basis of brand name products, product quality and cost of production. Although Canadian producers had the advantage of being able to purchase sugar at the usually lower world price, savings were offset by the

---

[1]Some information in this section was derived from: J. C. Ellert, J. Peter Killing and Dana Hyde, "Nestlé-Rowntree (A)", in *Business Policy, A Canadian Casebook,* Joseph N. Fry et al. (Eds.), Prentice Hall Canada Inc., 1992, pp. 655–667.

higher prices for dairy ingredients used in products manufactured for domestic consumption. Other commodity ingredients, often experiencing widely fluctuating prices, caused significant variations in manufacturing costs. Producers were reluctant to raise their prices due to the highly elastic demand for chocolate. Consequently, they sometimes reformatted or reformulated their products through size or ingredient changes to sustain margins. Three major product types were manufactured for domestic and export sales:

Blocks
These products are molded blocks of chocolate that are sold by weight and manufactured in a variety of flavours, with or without additional ingredients such as fruit or nuts. Block chocolate was sold primarily in grocery outlets or directly to confectionery manufacturers. (Examples: baking chocolate, Hershey's Chocolate Bar, Suchard's Toblerone.)

Boxed Chocolates
These products included a variety of bite-sized sweets and were generally regarded as "gift" or "occasion" purchases. Sales in grocery outlets tended to be more seasonal than for other chocolate products, with 80 percent sold at Christmas and Easter. Sales in other outlets remained steady year round. (Examples: Cadbury's Milk Tray, Rowntree's Black Magic, and After Eights.)

Countlines
These were chocolate covered products sold by count rather than by weight, and were generally referred to by consumers as "chocolate bars". The products varied widely in size, shape, weight, and composition, and had a wider distribution than the other two product types. Most countlines were sold through nongrocery outlets such as convenience and drug stores. (Examples: Neilson's Crispy Crunch, Nestlé-Rowntree's Coffee Crisp, M&M/Mars' Snickers, and Hershey/Lowney's Oh Henry!)

Sweet chocolate was the basic semi-finished product used in the manufacture of block, countline, and boxed chocolate products. Average costs of sweet chocolate for a representative portfolio of all three product types could be broken down as follows:

Raw material	35%
Packaging	10
Production	20
Distribution	5
Marketing/sales	20
Trading profit	10
Total	100% (of manufacturer's selling price)

For countline products, raw material costs were proportionately lower because a smaller amount of cocoa was used.

In value terms, more chocolate was consumed than any other manufactured food product in the world. In the late eighties, the world's eight major markets (representing over 60 percent of the total world chocolate market) consumed nearly three million tonnes with a retail value close to $20 billion. During the 1980s countline was the fastest growing segment with close to 50 percent of the world chocolate market by volume and an average annual rate of growth of 7 percent. An increasing trend towards indulgence in snack and "comfort" foods strongly suggested that future growth would remain strong.

Competitive Environment

In 1993, chocolate producers in the world included: M&M/Mars, Hershey Foods, Cadbury-Schweppes, Jacobs Suchard, Nestlé-Rowntree, United Biscuits, Ferrero, Nabisco and George Weston Ltd. (Neilson). Chocolate represented varying proportions of these manufacturers' total sales.

For the most part, it was difficult to sustain competitive advantages in manufacturing or product features due to a lack of proprietary technology. There was also limited potential for new product development since the basic ingredients in countline product manufacturing could only be blended in a limited variety of combinations. This forced an emphasis on competition through distribution and advertising.

Product promotion played a critical role in establishing brand name recognition. Demand was typified by high-impulse and discretionary purchasing behaviour. Since consumers, generally, had a selection of at least three or four favourite brands from which to choose, the biggest challenge facing producers was to create the brand awareness necessary to break into these menus. In recognition of the wide selection of competing brands and the broad range of snack food substitutes available, expenditures for media and trade promotions were considerable. For example, Canadian chocolate bar makers spent more than $30 million for advertising in Canada in 1992, mostly on television. This was often a barrier to entry for smaller producers.

Major Competitors

M&M/Mars

As the world leader in chocolate confectionery M&M/Mars dominated the countline sector, particularly in North America and Europe, with such famous global brands as Snickers, M&Ms, and Milky Way. However, in Canada, in 1992, M&M/Mars held fourth place with an 18.7 percent market share of single bars. (Exhibits 2 and 3 compare Canadian market positions for major competitors.)

M&M/Mars' strategy was to produce high quality products which were simple to manufacture and which allowed for high volume and automated production processes. They supported their products with heavy advertising and aggressive sales, focusing marketing efforts on strengthening their global brands.

Hershey/Lowney

Hershey's strength in North America was in the block chocolate category in which it held the leading market position. Hershey also supplied export markets in Asia, Australia, Sweden,

EXHIBIT 2   Single Bars Canadian Market Share: 1991–1992

Manufacturer	1992	1991
Neilson	28.1%	29.4%
Nestlé/Rowntree	26.9	26.2
Hershey/Lowney	21.6	21.9
M&M/Mars	18.7	19.0
Others	4.7	3.5

Source: Neilson News—Issue #1, 1993.

EXHIBIT 3   Top Single Candy Bars in Canada: 1991–1992

Top Single Bars	Manufacturer	1992	1991
Crispy Crunch	Neilson	1	1
Coffee Crisp	Nestlé/Rowntree	2	3
Kit Kat	Nestlé/Rowntree	3	2
Mars Bar	M&M/Mars	4	4
Caramilk	Cadbury Schweppes	5	6
Oh Henry!	Hershey/Lowney	6	5
Smarties	Nestlé/Rowntree	7	7
Peanut Butter Cups	Hershey/Lowney	8	8
Mr. Big	Neilson	9	11
Aero	Hershey/Lowney	10	10
Snickers	M&M/Mars	11	9
Crunchie	Cadbury Schweppes	12	12

Source: Neilson News—Issue #1, 1993.

and Mexico from their chocolate production facilities in Pennsylvania. In Canada, in 1992, Hershey held third place in the countline segment with a 21.6 percent share of the market.

Hershey's strategy was to reduce exposure to volatile cocoa prices by diversifying within the confectionery and snack businesses. By 1987, only 45 percent of Hershey's sales came from products with 70 percent or more chocolate content. This was down from 80 percent in 1963.

Cadbury Schweppes

Cadbury was a major world name in chocolate, with a portfolio of brands such as Dairy Milk, Creme Eggs, and Crunchie. Although its main business was in the United Kingdom, it was also a strong competitor in major markets such as Australia and South Africa.

Cadbury Schweppes diversified its product line and expanded into new geographic markets throughout the 1980s. In 1987, Cadbury International sold the Canadian distribution rights for their chocolate products to William Neilson Ltd. Only in Canada were the Cadbury brands incorporated into the Neilson confectionery division under the name Neilson/Cadbury. In 1988, Cadbury sold its U.S. operations to Hershey.

Nestlé-Rowntree

In 1991, chocolate and confectionery comprised 16 percent of Nestlé's SFr 50.5 billion revenue, up sharply from only 8 percent in 1987. (In January 1993, 1SFr = $0.88 CAD = .69 U.S.) This was largely a result of their move into the countline sector through the acquisition in 1988 of Rowntree PLC, a leading British manufacturer with strong global brands such as Kit Kat, After Eights and Smarties. In 1990, they also added Baby Ruth and Butterfinger to their portfolio, both "Top 20" brands in the U.S. Considering these recent heavy investments to acquire global brands and expertise, it was clear that Nestlé-Rowntree intended to remain a significant player in growing global markets.

Neilson

Company History

William Neilson Ltd. was founded in 1893, when the Neilson family began selling milk and homemade ice cream to the Toronto market. By 1905 they had erected a house and factory at 277 Gladstone Ave., from which they shipped ice cream as far west as Winnipeg and as far east as Quebec City. Chocolate bar production was initiated to offset the decreased demand for ice cream during the colder winter months and as a way of retaining the skilled labour pool. By 1914, the company was producing one million pounds of ice cream and 500,000 pounds of chocolate per year.

William Neilson died in 1915, and the business was handed down to his son Morden, who had been involved since its inception. Between 1924 and 1934, the "Jersey Milk", "Crispy Crunch" and "Malted Milk" bars were introduced. Upon the death of Morden Neilson in 1947, the company was sold to George Weston Foods for $4.5 million.

By 1974, "Crispy Crunch" was the number one selling bar in Canada. In 1977, "Mr. Big" was introduced and became the number one teen bar by 1986. By 1991, the Neilson dairy operations had been moved to a separate location and the ice cream division had been sold to Ault Foods. The Gladstone location continued to be used to manufacture Neilson chocolate and confectionery.

Bateman explained that Neilson's efforts under the direction of the new president, Arthur Soler, had become more competitive in the domestic market over the past three years, through improved customer service and retail merchandising. Significant improvements had already been made in Administration and Operations. All of these initiatives had assisted in reversing decades of consumer share erosion. As a result, Neilson was now in a position to defend its share of the domestic market and to develop an international business that would enhance shareholder value. (Exhibit 4 outlines the Canadian chocolate confectionery market.)

EXHIBIT 4   Canadian Confectionery Market–1993

	Dollars (millions)	%
Total Confectionery Category	**$1,301.4**	**100.0**
Gum	296.5	22.8
Boxed Chocolates	159.7	12.3
Cough Drops	77.0	5.9
Rolled Candy	61.3	4.7
Bagged Chocolates	30.3	2.3
Easter Eggs	22.0	1.7
Valentines	9.4	0.7
Lunch Pack	3.6	0.3
Countline Chocolate Bars	641.6	49.3
Total Chocolate Bar Market Growth		**+8%**

Source: Neilson Marketing Department Estimates.

Neilson's Exporting Efforts

Initial export efforts prior to 1990 were contracted to a local export broker—Grenadier International. The original company objective was to determine "what could be done in foreign markets" using only working capital resources and avoiding capital investments in equipment or new markets.

Through careful selection of markets on the basis of distributor interest, Grenadier's export manager, Scott Begg, had begun the slow process of introducing Neilson brands into the Far East. The results were impressive. Orders were secured for containers of "Mr. Big" and "Crispy Crunch" countlines from local distributors in Korea, Taiwan, and Japan. "Canadian Classics" boxed chocolates were developed for the vast Japanese gift ("Omiyagi") market. Total 1993 sales to these markets were projected to be $1.6 million.

For each of these markets, Neilson retained the responsibility for packaging design and product formulation. While distributors offered suggestions as to how products could be improved to suit local tastes, they were not formally obliged to do so. To secure distribution in Taiwan, Neilson had agreed to launch the "Mr. Big" bar under the distributor's private brand name "Bang Bang," which was expected to generate a favourable impression with consumers. Although sales were strong, Bateman realized that since consumer loyalty was linked to brand names, the brand equity being generated for "Bang Bang", ultimately, would belong to the distributor. This put the distributor in a powerful position from which they were able to place significant downward pressure on operating margins.

Market Evaluation Study

In response to these successful early exporting efforts Bateman began exploring the possible launch of Neilson brands into the United States (discussed later). With limited working capital and numerous export opportunities, it became obvious to the International

EXHIBIT 5   World Chocolate Imports (Value as % of Total)–1990

	1987	1988	1989	1990
Africa	x0.7	x0.7	x0.7	x0.7
Americas	x15.6	x15.0	x13.9	x13.2
LAIC[1]	0.2	0.4	1.1	x1.3
CACM[2]	x0.1	x0.1	x0.1	x0.1
Asia	11.7	x13.9	x15.6	x12.9
Middle East	x3.5	x3.3	x3.9	x2.8
Europe	70.8	68.9	67.7	71.4
EEC (12)[3]	61.1	59.5	57.7	59.3
EFTA[4]	9.3	9.0	8.9	8.4
Oceania	x1.3	x1.7	x2.1	x1.8

Figures denoted with an "x" are provisional or estimated.

[1]LAIC = Latin American Industrialists Association.
[2]CACM = Central American Common Market.
[3]EEC (12) = The twelve nations of the European Economic Community.
[4]EFTA = European Free Trade Association.
Source: Adapted from the United Nations, "International Trade Statistics Yearbook," Vol. II, 1990.

Division that some kind of formal strategy was required to evaluate and to compare these new markets.

Accordingly, a set of weighted criteria was developed during the summer of 1992 to evaluate countries that were being considered by the International Division. (See Exhibit 5 for a profile of the world's major chocolate importers.) The study was intended to provide a standard means of evaluating potential markets. Resources could then be allocated among those markets that promised long term incremental growth and those which were strictly opportunistic. While the revenues from opportunistic markets would contribute to the fixed costs of domestic production, the long term efforts could be pursued for more strategic reasons. By the end of the summer, the study had been applied to thirteen international markets, including the United States. (See Exhibit 6 for a summary of this study.)

Meanwhile, Grenadier had added Hong Kong/China, Singapore, and New Zealand to Neilson's portfolio of export markets, and Bateman had contracted a second local broker, CANCON Corp. Ltd, to initiate sales to the Middle East. By the end of 1992, the International Division comprised 9 people who had achieved penetration of 11 countries for export sales (see Exhibit 7 for a description of these markets). As of January 1993, market shares in these countries were very small.

The U.S. Experience

In 1991, the American chocolate confectionery market was worth US$5.1 billion wholesale. Neilson had wanted to sneak into this vast market with the intention of quietly selling off excess capacity. However, as Bateman explained, the quiet U.S. launch became a Canadian celebration:

EXHIBIT 6   Summary of Criteria for Market Study—1992

Criteria	Weight	Australia	China	Hong Kong	Indonesia	Japan	Korea	Malaysia	New Zealand	Singapore	Taiwan	Mexico	EEC	USA
* U.S. countline	—	4	4	4	4	4	4	4	4	4	4	4	4	4
1 Candy bar economics	30	20	20	30	20	20	28	20	15	25	15	20	10	10
2 Target market	22	12.5	14	13	15.5	19	15	10	7	9.5	12.5	21	22	22
3 Competitor dynamics	20	12	15	8	7.5	11	13.5	10	12	14.5	12	**11**	20	6.5
4 Distribution access	10	9	4	4	3.5	5	6	6.5	9	3.5	7.5	9.5	9	9
5 Industry economics	9	2.5	3.5	6	5.5	2	5	2.5	7	4.5	3	3.5	3.5	4.5
6 Product fit	8	7	6	6	6	3	7.5	7.5	7.5	8	4	8	5	8
7 Payback	5	4	4	1	2.5	4	5	2.5	4	2	2	5	2	1
8 Country dynamics	5	5	1	4	3	5	3.5	4.5	4.5	5	4	3	2	4
Total	109	72	67.5	72	63.5	69	83.5	63.5	66	72	60	81	73.5	65

Competitor Dynamics	Score	Mexico
Financial success of other exporters	0-8	5
Nature (passivity) of competition	0-6	2.5
Brand image (vs price) positioning	0-6	3.5
Score/20	/20	11

Due to Neilson/Cadbury's limited resources, it was not feasible to launch the first western-style brands into new markets. The basic minimum criteria for a given market, therefore, was the presence of major western industry players (ie: Mars or Hershey). Countries were then measured on the basis of 8 criteria which were weighted by the International Group according to their perceived importance as determinants of a successful market entry. (See upper table.) Each criterion was then subdivided into several elements as defined by the International Group, which allocated the total weighted score accordingly. (See lower table.)

This illustration depicts a single criteria, subdivided and scored for Mexico.

Source: Company records.

Next thing we knew, there were bands in the streets, Neilson t-shirts and baseball caps, and newspaper articles and T.V. specials describing our big U.S. launch!

The publicity greatly increased the pressure to succeed. After careful consideration, Pro Set, a collectible trading card manufacturer and marketer, was selected as a distributor. This relationship developed into a joint venture by which the Neilson Import Division was later appointed distributor of the Pro Set cards in Canada. With an internal sales management team, full distribution and invoicing infrastructures, and a 45-broker national sales network, Pro Set seemed ideally suited to diversify into confectionery products.

Unfortunately, Pro Set quickly proved to be an inadequate partner in this venture. Although they had access to the right outlets, the confectionery selling task differed significantly from card sales. Confectionery items demanded more sensitive product handling

EXHIBIT 7   **Neilson Export Markets–1993**

Agent (Commission)	Country	Brands
Grenadier International	Taiwan	Bang Bang
	Japan	Mr. Big, Crispy Crunch, Canadian Classics
	Korea	Mr. Big, Crispy Crunch
	Hong Kong/China	Mr. Big, Crispy Crunch, Canadian Classics
	Singapore	Mr. Big, Crispy Crunch
CANCON Corp. Ltd.	Saudi Arabia	Mr. Big, Crispy Crunch, Malted Milk
	Bahrain	Mr. Big, Crispy Crunch, Malted Milk
	United Arab Emirates	Mr. Big, Crispy Crunch, Malted Milk
	Kuwait	Mr. Big, Crispy Crunch, Malted Milk
Neilson International	Mexico	Mr. Big, Crispy Crunch, Malted Milk
	United States	Mr. Big, Crispy Crunch, Malted Milk

Source: Company records.

and a greater amount of sales effort by the Pro Set representatives who were used to carrying a self-promoting line.

To compound these difficulties, Pro Set sales plummeted as the trading-card market became over-saturated. Trapped by intense cashflow problems and increasing fixed costs, Pro Set filed for Chapter 11 bankruptcy, leaving Neilson with huge inventory losses and a customer base that associated them with their defunct distributor. Although it was tempting to attribute the U.S. failure to inappropriate partner selection, the U.S. had also ranked poorly relative to other markets in the criteria study that had just been completed that summer. In addition to their distribution problems, Neilson was at a serious disadvantage due to intense competition from the major industry players in the form of advertising expenditures, trade promotions, and brand proliferation. Faced with duties and a higher cost of production, Neilson was unable to maintain price competitiveness.

The International Division was now faced with the task of internalizing distribution in the U.S., including sales management, broker contact, warehousing, shipping, and collections. Neilson managed to reestablish a limited presence in the American market using several local brokers to target profitable niches. For example, they placed strong emphasis on vending-machine sales to increase product trial with minimal advertising. Since consumer purchasing patterns demanded product variety in vending-machines, Neilson's presence in this segment was not considered threatening by major competitors.

In the autumn of 1992, as the International Division made the changes necessary to salvage past efforts in the U.S., several options for entering the Mexican confectionery market were also being considered.

Mexico

Neilson made the decision to enter the Mexican market late in 1992, prompted by its parent company's, Weston Foods Ltd., own investigations into possible market opportunities which would emerge as a result of the North American Free Trade Agreement (NAFTA). Mexico was an attractive market which scored very highly in the market evaluation study. Due to their favourable demographics (50 percent of the population was within the target age group), Mexico offered huge potential for countline sales. The rapid adoption of American tastes resulted in an increasing demand for U.S. snack foods. With only a limited number of competitors, the untapped demand afforded a window of opportunity for smaller players to enter the market.

Working through the Ontario Ministry of Agriculture and Food (OMAF), Neilson found two potential independent distributors:

> Grupo Corvi—a Mexican food manufacturer, operated seven plants and had an extensive sales force reaching local wholesalers. They also had access to a convoluted infrastructure which indirectly supplied an estimated 100,000 street vendor stands or kiosks (known as "tiendas") representing nearly 70 percent of the Mexican confectionery market. (This informal segment was usually overlooked by marketing research services and competitors alike.) Grupo Corvi currently had no American or European style countline products.

> Grupo Hajj—a Mexican distributor with some experience in confectionery, offered access to only a small number of retail stores. This limited network made Grupo Hajj relatively unattractive when compared to other distributors. Like Grupo Corvi, this local firm dealt exclusively in Mexican pesos, historically, a volatile currency. (In January 1993, 1 peso = $0.41 CAD.)

While considering these distributors, Neilson was approached by Sabritas, the snack food division of Pepsico Foods in Mexico, who felt that there was a strategic fit between their organizations. Although Sabritas had no previous experience handling chocolate confectionery, they had for six years been seeking a product line to round out their portfolio. They were currently each week supplying Frito-Lay type snacks directly to 450,000 retail stores and tiendas. (The trade referred to such extensive customer networks as "numeric distribution.") After listening to the initial proposal, Neilson agreed to give Sabritas three months to conduct research into the Mexican market.

Although the research revealed strong market potential for the Neilson products, Bateman felt that pricing at 2 pesos (at parity with other American style brands) would not provide any competitive advantage. Sabritas agreed that a one peso product, downsized to 40 grams (from a Canadian-US standard of 43–65 grams), would provide an attractive strategy to offer "imported chocolate at Mexican prices".

Proposing a deal significantly different from the relationships offered by the two Mexican distributors, Sabritas intended to market the "Mr. Big", "Crispy Crunch," and "Malted Milk" bars as the first brands in the "Milch" product line. "Milch" was a fictitious word in Spanish, created and owned by Sabritas, and thought to denote goodness and health due to its similarity to the word "milk". Sabritas would offer Neilson 50 percent ownership of the Milch name, in exchange for 50 percent of Neilson's brand names, both of which would appear on each bar. As part of the joint branding agreement, Sabritas would assume all responsibility for advertising, promotion, distribution and merchandising. The joint ownership of the brand names would provide Sabritas with brand equity in exchange for building brand awareness through heavy investments in marketing. By delegating responsibility for all marketing efforts to Sabritas, Neilson would be able to compete on a scale not affordable by Canadian standards.

Under the proposal, all "Milch" chocolate bars would be produced in Canada by Neilson. Neilson would be the exclusive supplier. Ownership of the bars would pass to Sabritas once the finished goods had been shipped. Sabritas in turn would be responsible for all sales to final consumers. Sabritas would be the exclusive distributor. Consumer prices could not be changed without the mutual agreement of Neilson and Sabritas.

Issues

Bateman reflected upon the decision he now faced for the Mexican market. The speed with which Sabritas could help them gain market penetration, their competitive advertising budget, and their "store door access" to nearly a half million retailers were attractive advantages offered by this joint venture proposal. But what were the implications of omitting the Neilson name from their popular chocolate bars? Would they be exposed to problems like those encountered in Taiwan with the "Bang Bang" launch, especially considering the strength and size of Pepsico Foods?

The alternative was to keep the Neilson name and to launch their brands independently, using one of the national distributors. Unfortunately, limited resources meant that Neilson would develop its presence much more slowly. With countline demand in Mexico growing at 30 percent per year, could they afford to delay? Scott Begg had indicated that early entry was critical in burgeoning markets, since establishing market presence and gaining share were less difficult when undertaken before the major players had dominated the market and "defined the rules of play."

Bateman also questioned their traditional means of evaluating potential markets. Were the criteria considered in the market evaluation study really the key success factors, or were the competitive advantages offered through ventures with distributors more important? If partnerships were necessary, should Neilson continue to rely on independent, national distributors who were interested in adding Neilson brands to their portfolio, or should they pursue strategic partnerships similar to the Sabritas opportunity instead? No matter which distributor was chosen, product quality and handling were of paramount importance. Every chocolate bar reaching consumers, especially first time buyers, must be of the same freshness and quality as those distributed to Canadian consumers. How could this type of control best be achieved?

18 SELKIRK GROUP IN ASIA

From their modern brick building in Victoria, Australia, it seemed a long way from the economic crisis that had engulfed Asia in the past 18 months. At one side of the board table sat Bernie Segrave, the Managing Director of the Selkirk Group of Companies and the person who had taken direct charge of the group's export marketing strategy across Asia. On the other side, and with a view of the large brick chimney that announced Selkirk Brick's presence in the local community, sat Peter Blackburn, Export Manager and the person being groomed to progressively take over the exporting responsibilities. Both were looking at the export performance graphs of the group over the past five years as background preparation for their forthcoming trip.

Ahead of them (in late October 1998) was an overseas tour to meet their existing network of agents and potential customers in Singapore, Thailand, Hong Kong, and Taiwan. Their largest market, Japan, was not included in this tour. The reasons for the tour were quite straightforward in Segrave's mind:

> We have made a strategic decision to continue developing and building relationships in Asia in these bad times. We went to Japan earlier this year. In this downturn, we are very lucky we have good agents in Japan. If Japan goes, we don't want to think about it—but I guess the rest of the world goes as well.
>
> Asia is very important in the long term because we continue to develop products of excellent technical quality which are appreciated by Asians. It's very important to us in terms of sales and output. Within five years we expect to have either a subsidiary or a selling arm in an Asian destination.

At issue was how to continue developing their business in Asia. Both Segrave and Blackburn were wondering about the business opportunities they would uncover and whether it was time to review their export strategy and organisation for the region.

Selkirk Brick—A Family Business for Over 100 Years

Selkirk Brick was established in 1883, when the gold rush in colonial Victoria brought together fortune seekers and entrepreneurs from across the world. Chinese, Scots, Irish, and even Californians were among the immigrants who saw the opportunity to prosper in the colony. Among them was Robert Selkirk, a Scottish stonemason, who sought to capitalise on the building boom accompanying the wealth generated from gold and wool. He started making bricks using a local clay deposit in Allendale but moved to nearby Ballarat in 1900 where suitable clay deposits had been identified on 10 hectares of land in Howitt Street, the present-day site of the works and head office.

Though clay bricks and pavers were often seen as a low-tech product, there was, in fact, considerable technical expertise required to produce a high quality product. Apart from selecting the right clays as the raw material for firing into bricks and pavers, a number of other factors needed to be managed carefully. The moisture content in the clay was critical to both moulding and firing outcomes achieved. Various oxides and other additives were used to achieve specific colors and finishes. Kiln temperature, length of time in the kiln, and airflows also needed to be carefully controlled to achieve consistency in strength and color characteristics.

The high quality of Australian clay bricks and pavers has led to their extensive use as a building material for external cladding. Many houses had been traditionally built with double brick walls, particularly in the more temperate climate zones in Australia ranging from New South Wales, through Victoria, South Australia, and Tasmania (refer to Exhibit 1 for geographic locations in Australia). In recent years, the use of brick had declined as brick veneer, steel frames, timber, concrete, and even mud-brick homes gained popularity with the home buyer. Increasingly, clay bricks and pavers were being used as architectural features rather than simply as a construction material.

From a study of the company's history (see Appendix 1), Selkirk Brick could be characterised as a company which was managed in a financially conservative manner but which embraced (world-class at the time) technological innovation to maintain technical superiority and cost efficiency in the marketplace. It was a company which had resisted buyouts and generational fragmentation in the process.

The shareholders were well aware that by the time a family company reached the fifth generation, it was unlikely to accommodate the needs of all who might expect to work there. Robert Selkirk, who became Chairman in 1985 and was in charge of marketing, commented on the roles of the working shareholders:

> It's something that you have to work at every day of your life. There are conflicts; we all see things differently. The challenge is to try to put personal and family disagreements to one side when in the office.

EXHIBIT 1   **Geographic Locations**

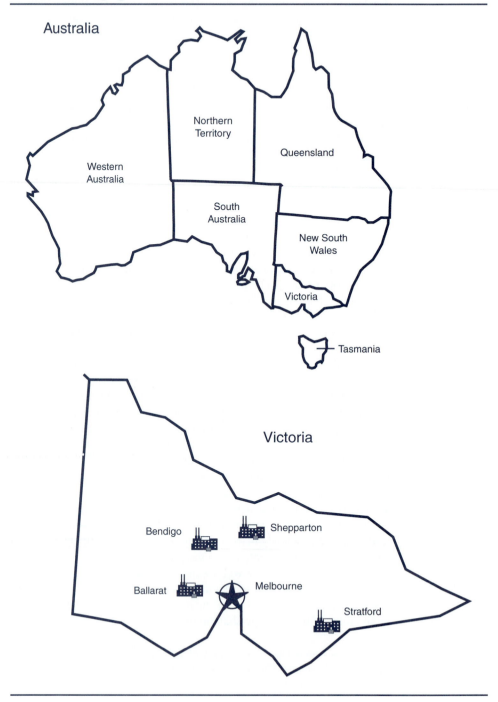

Jim Selkirk, Finance Director since 1986, suggested a few basic requirements for a family company: no gamblers, squanderers, or alcoholics; no tendency to over-borrow or be over-acquisitive; be prepared to spend most of your time with the company; and no expensive or messy divorces.

Overall, the Selkirk family believed their success stemmed from a number of features: a mix of family and non-family directors, conservative finance, market leadership through technology, maintaining a good reputation in the market and a belief that nothing happens until you make a sale. They saw themselves as adaptable, able to make decisions quickly, having a close rapport with repeat customers, and constantly examining their strategies to produce long-term success.

The Selkirk Group—Diversification in the 1980s and 1990s

Between 1982 and 1992, the company made three major acquisitions, none of which were cheap but all of which were easily absorbed into the balance sheet:

- Phillips Bricks and Pottery Pty Ltd was acquired in 1982. This Bendigo-based company had a strong market-presence in northwestern Victoria and was converted from the traditional extruded to the higher-priced pressed brick production in 1986. (Segrave became Managing Director of Phillips in 1983.)

- In 1987, Selkirk purchased Hick Timbers in Altona (a suburb of Melbourne) in a move that took it outside bricks but still serving the needs of the building industry. Hick was a specialised supplier of structural timber importing softwoods from the USA, Canada, New Zealand and Finland and supplying engineered timber beams.

- Shepparton Bricks and Pavers, one of Victoria's largest concrete building and landscaping products manufacturers, was acquired in 1992. While Selkirk had been supplying clay pavers since 1983, this acquisition took the company into the less expensive concrete paver business in a booming market for pavers.

At a time when Australian entrepreneurs like (the subsequently convicted) Alan Bond and (the fugitive) Christopher Skase had created conglomerates through leveraged acquisitions, Selkirk Brick had been tempted to the brink of over-expansion, according to Jim Selkirk, but was saved at the eleventh hour by a bidder with deeper pockets. To date, its diversification had been within the confines of its perceived area of expertise, the building industry. Each of the acquisitions was valuable for adding manufacturing capacity and for providing additional sales outlets. Each office and outlet sold the complete range of Selkirk products.

Hick Timbers was closed down in 1997 though the company name was retained. Margins in the timber business were falling for players, and the company was being outmuscled in the marketplace by large integrated timber and hardware groups such as Bunnings (which had established a series of home/trade superstores across the Melbourne metropolitan area). The Board of Selkirk had taken a common-sense but courageous strategic decision to quit while they were ahead.

While diversifying through acquisition, Selkirk Brick also embarked on a three-stage, $5 million program of modernisation between 1982 and 1986, which resulted in world-class product quality outcomes. This investment program involved modernising the processes for extrusion and material preparation in the first stage, improving the productivity and energy efficiency of the drying tunnel in the second stage, and replacing the 25-year-old tunnel kiln with an energy-efficient one in the final stage.

By 1988, pavers had come to represent 20 percent of the company's production volume and Selkirk Brick was recognised as the only brick company supplying products compliant with Australian Products Standard AS1225. While most of the product sales were in Victoria, the sales region was progressively being extended into the South Australian and New South Wales marketplace, where product quality and service were being used to overcome price and transport barriers to competition. Selkirk was reputed to have a 15 percent share in the Victorian clay building products market and was the largest privately owned brick company in Australia.

Selkirk Brick survived the severe economic recession that hit Victoria in the early 1990s by halving production at one stage and closing one plant for 10 months in 1991. By late 1993, utilisation had recovered to 75 percent and by 1998 the plants were operating again at full capacity. Selkirk Brick acquired Stratblox, a manufacturer of quality concrete building products located in the Gippsland region of Victoria, in 1998. This acquisition meant that Selkirk had geographically encircled the Melbourne metropolitan area through a series of country acquisitions and had established itself as the dominant player in rural Victoria.

The capacity of the Selkirk Group of Companies exceeded 70 million bricks and pavers prior to that acquisition. Production capacity at Bendigo was 10 million units (bricks and pavers) per annum while Shepparton capacity was 23,000 tonnes per annum. The Gippsland acquisition added 27,000 tonnes per annum of capacity. Total Victorian sales were in the range of $25 and $30 million per annum (refer to Exhibit 2 for external estimates of group revenue). The company employed 170 people, 100 people at the Ballarat head-office and operations alone. With the acquisition of Stratblox, Selkirk Brick could no longer be seen as a specialist clay brick and paver company (refer to Appendix 2 for additional information on the Australian Brick and Paver Industry) but as a more broadly diversified company in the clay and concrete brick and paver business.

Company documents indicate that each of the acquisitions was a wholly owned subsidiary of Selkirk Brick Pty Ltd but they were managed autonomously, each with its own Board of Management and Board of Directors. In 1998, Robert Selkirk was Non-Executive Chairman of the Board, Bernie Segrave was the Managing Director, Jim Selkirk was the Finance Director, and Iain Selkirk was the Works Director. In 1994, Jamie Selkirk (son of the Chairman) became the first of the fifth-generation to join the family company.

Asia—A Selkirk Success Story of the 1990s

The export trading activities of Selkirk Brick began in earnest in 1992 when Robert Selkirk attended a Global Business Opportunities Convention in Osaka, Japan. A Japanese company had been looking at securing a supply of sandstone from Australia and had seen Selkirk pavers extensively used at Bond University in Queensland. (A major Japanese construction

---

EXHIBIT 2   **Group Sales Estimates**

Year	Sales Revenue ($A millions)
1987/88	$19.9
1988/89	$24.8
1989/90	$25.5
1990/91	$20.7
1991/92	$19.0
1992/93	$23.5
1993/94	$24.9
1994/95	$25.8
1995/96	$23.2
1996/97	$22.2
1997/98	$27.8

Note: Estimates derived from industry data.

and development company was a joint-venture partner in the university at the time.) Selkirk pavers had been selected for their ability to withstand the high traffic and high humidity requirements of Australia's first private university in 1988. Following a visit of Japanese personnel to the plant in Ballarat, a trading alliance was formed and Selkirk began to export to Japan. As Robert Selkirk reminded people within the company, not everybody had approved of the move at the time:

> Six years ago, we wouldn't have believed where we are now. It was all done on an exploratory "try it and see" basis. We had (Prime Minister) Paul Keating telling us that Australian companies had to be in Asia. There was considerable criticism at the time on the expense and management attention being directed to the export efforts. We were advised that we had to be patient. Then we got the first order within 12 months and it was done on a handshake.

Total exports had grown strongly from the first export order to Japan of 49,000 paving units (approximately six containers) in 1992. Exports to all destinations increased by 735 percent in 1993, followed by a 69 percent increase in 1994 and a 150 percent increase in 1995. Flat sales in 1996 and 1997 were followed by a massive increase in 1998 to approximately four million units. While initial sales were to Japan, by 1998 Selkirk Brick was exporting pavers and some bricks across Asia to countries such as Hong Kong ('94) and Taiwan ('96) as well as Singapore, Indonesia, New Zealand, and Malaysia. Japan was the largest export destination, but healthy sales were beginning to be experienced in Taiwan where product quality and service were considered to be key selling features.

By 1998, Asian exports had become a small but increasingly important part of Selkirk Brick's business. Exports accounted for just under 10 percent of total sales volume (slightly higher in terms of sales value) in the 1997/98 financial year and that figure was expected to increase. Well over 25 percent of paver manufacturing volume was now being exported. The clay paver market had been facing low growth and market share losses in the highly competitive Australian market to cheaper pavers made from concrete and other composite materials. Exports were an important sales outlet for the company.

Selkirk had a policy of appointing non-exclusive distributor agents in the marketplace and currently had 18 distributors across Asia: five in Japan, four in Hong Kong, three in Taiwan, two in Singapore, and one each in Malaysia, Indonesia, Thailand, and New Zealand. Letters from overseas parties interested in purchasing directly and offering their local services were inevitably referred back to the nearest agent. Product was usually sold C.I.F. (Cost, Insurance, and Freight to Destination Port). Prices ex-factory and loaded into containers were generally 70 percent of the C.I.F. price. Anecdotal data suggested that a unit price of A$0.47 F.O.B. (Free on Board at Shipping Port) for shipped products could be sold for as high as A$2.00 per unit in Japan to end-users (refer to Exhibit 3 for Export Pricing Nomenclature and Value-Added). The use of agents did mean, however, that there was a lack of information on who was the ultimate user of products and what margins were being charged locally.

Information on the clay brick and paver market across Asia was otherwise limited and generally anecdotal in nature. Housing construction materials varied considerably across the region, and clay bricks were not traditionally used. Local brick manufacturers in countries such as Malaysia ran "cottage-industry" facilities using kilns with inadequate temperature controls and with a poor understanding of quality control mechanisms. Brick walls were often rendered and thus considered a "filler" material which did not require high quality standards. Clay brick and pavers were being increasingly seen in large "upper middle class" housing estates across the region where developers were taking the lead in developing suburban housing and shopping communities.

Exports to the region came from a number of countries, with Canada, the United States, the United Kingdom, South Africa, and Australia mentioned frequently. Export data often lumped clay bricks and pavers with other construction materials such as timber and composite materials. The Australian data on exports were derived from shipping data collected at ports of origin, but some ports used different classification methods, making accurate information difficult to ascertain. Australian brick and paver products were reputed to have more durability, better water repelling capability and more vibrant color attributes than the cheaper product sourced from local or imported Asian producers.

EXHIBIT 3   Export Pricing Nomenclature and Value-Added

ex-Factory Gate Goods in vehicle at factory gate.	**A$3500/container**
Free Alongside Ship (F.A.S.) Goods unloaded off vehicle on wharf at port of origin.	**A$3800/container**
Free on-Board (F.O.B.) Goods loaded on vessel at port of origin.	**A$4000/container**
Cost, Insurance and Freight (C.I.F.) Goods on vessel at port of destination with insurance premiums included.	**A$5000/container**
Market Price Price of goods at final consumer market.	**A$12000 to $17500/container**

Sales Distribution Agreement in Japan

Exports to Japan had grown steadily from 900,000 units in 1995/96 to 1.8 million units in 1996/97 and 3.5 million units in 1997/98. One reason for the growth was a five-year distribution agreement that had been signed in 1997 with a leading Japanese building products company, and that agreement was expected to triple current export figures within two years. Segrave commented on his experiences in doing business with their Japanese agents:

> We find the Japanese are very tough negotiators—but also very fair. We are thrilled they fully appreciate the technical qualities of our products. So often here in Australia, aesthetic requirements dominate a specifier's consideration. Mind you, we have been developing a clay brick with smaller width dimensions and new colors to suit the Japanese market (in conjunction with the Stonehenge Group, a major builder in urban Victoria). Our wide variety of pavers and special shapes also meets their needs.
>
> Understand that the Japanese do not tolerate mediocrity, which means you must send your most senior people to negotiate with them. In 1992 we had employed a retired General Manager of a large clay brick and paver company in Western Australia who had the requisite seniority, technical knowledge, and excellent sales skills to become our first Export Manager.
>
> One must also be courteous, pleasant, and respectful with the Japanese and become practised in Nemawashi: the art of building relationships and personal trust over time. Our success can be measured by the fact that the 1997 distributor agreement had everybody from the Managing Director down to the most senior functional managers attending the Agreement Signing ceremony. What may look like a simple commercial arrangement to us was a symbol of strategic intent and business partnering in their eyes.

While exact details of the 1997 Sales License Agreement were confidential, certain aspects of the Agreement have been disclosed (refer to Appendix 3).

Selkirk retained the brand and trademark for its range of products in Japan, prohibited the transfer of distribution rights to other companies without its approval, had the ability to terminate the agreement with 90 days' notice, and ensured any arbitration was done through "officially approved" channels. The term of the agreement was for five years and required 90 days' written notice on either side to terminate. Advertising and sales promotions in Japan were at the expense of the agent.

The Japanese agent had secured a number of conditions in the agreement as well. No new agents were to be appointed without their prior agreement. The primary language of the agreement was English, but it was to be interpreted under Japanese commercial law. The bricks and pavers were to carry a Japanese logo and meet the requirements of the Japanese Industrial Standard but to be labelled as "Made in Australia". All products were to be inspected and certified by Selkirk Brick as meeting the product and shipping standards specified in the agreement, with the agent being able to reject shipments in Japan if these conditions were not met.

The Export Function in Selkirk Brick

The Group Managing Director, Bernie Segrave, was directly responsible for overseeing all export matters including communication with the main agents, creating new relationships across Asia and being one-half of the trade show that travelled to Asia every four to five months. He spent approximately 15 percent of his time on export-related matters across a year but this time allocation varied between 100 percent and zero percent on a weekly basis. Having started in sales and marketing with Selkirk Brick in 1968, Segrave brought significant experience and credibility to the role. He reported directly to the Board of Directors (see Exhibit 4: Organisation Chart).

The Export Manager, Peter Blackburn, spent between five and 20 percent of his time on export matters during the course of a week. He reported directly to the Group Managing Director on these export matters. The rest of the time, Blackburn was officially the Regional Sales Manager for Western Victoria. In addition to maintaining relationships with agents across Asia, Blackburn was involved in developing products for export markets and

EXHIBIT 4   Organisation Chart

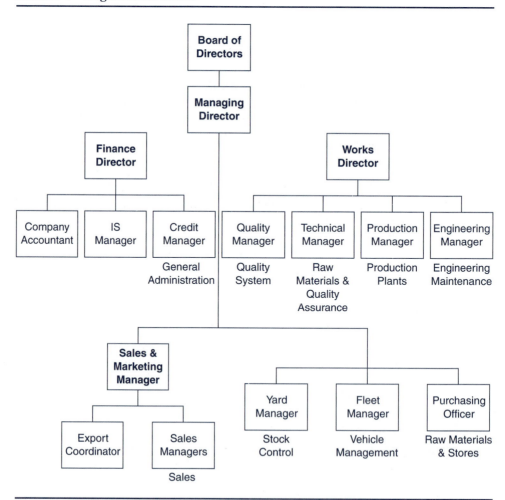

ensuring that products exported met the highest technical standards. One of his current projects was working with an Australian residential building group to develop smaller, thinner bricks for the Japanese market.

Blackburn had joined Selkirk Brick four years ago, though he had extensive industry experience with NuBrik. He was in the process of gradually assuming responsibility for all export business matters and had accompanied Segrave on all the recent overseas export development tours. In his view, Selkirk had been successful in Asia because it spent time building relationships with its agents, delivered products required in the marketplace on the basis of technical excellence and service rather than price alone, was committed to helping agents secure orders, and maintained face-to-face relationships in order to avoid "long-distance communications and language" barriers.

Assisting the senior export marketing duo was Clare McGuinness, Export and Agency Sales Coordinator, who spent some 80 percent of her time specifically on export matters. Among her responsibilities were receiving export orders, arranging all aspects of an export order (stock, shipping, letters of credit, and export documents) and preparing all correspondence for Segrave on export related matters. All product for export markets was palletised and containerised at the brick yard adjacent to the head office in Ballarat. Selecting the appropriate bricks and pavers to ensure that they met required quality and aesthetic standards was considered to be critical in meeting customer needs. The Yard Stock Controller, Steve Banks, played an important role in this.

Overseas trips to visit agents and develop new business opportunities were generally scheduled every four to five months with Segrave and Blackburn travelling together to visit two to three countries over a two- or three-week period. Accompanying them on these trips was a technical reference manual, "The Selkirk Technical Advantage", that contained over 400 pages of technical specifications, photos of significant building projects where Selkirk bricks and pavers had been used across Asia, and a whole range of information on Frequently Asked Questions. This manual was provided for the exclusive use of agents in each country as a selling tool but was not to be distributed further.

The cost of these overseas trips was substantial for a small family-owned company, each in the range of A$15, 000 to $25,000, depending upon the countries visited and the length of the trip. Typically, these trips involved more than meeting with existing agents. They included talking to customers, meeting with architects, and providing technical information on products and services offered. Often these visits coincided with local trade fairs and with Austrade government missions to specific countries. The company tried to see each overseas agent at least once per annum. Most of the agents had visited Selkirk Brick's operations at head-office at least once, and some of the Japanese agents had visited three or four times each.

Looking to the Future of Asia

The future of the Australian export business to Asia was in some doubt in early October 1998. According to the internationally respected newsmagazine *Business Week,* Asia was experiencing a widespread social backlash to the collapsing economic situation and stringent conditions imposed by the IMF (International Monetary Fund). The headlines of one issue (August 17th, 1998) were quite pointed:

- Joblessness is soaring in Japan.
- Bitterness is growing in Korea.
- Political opposition is rallying in Thailand.
- Will the repercussions of recession scuttle Asia's economic reforms?

The Asian crisis had, in fact, spread to create global financial risk from collapsing economies and the flight of capital needed to underpin economic growth. Malaysia had already imposed currency controls on the Ringgit, and in China there was strong evidence that Beijing was resorting to import controls and other measures to keep the Asian crisis at bay. Indonesia was still an open currency economy (despite moves earlier that year to establish a Currency Board), but the value of the Rupiah (R12,000 to the US$1.00) meant that imports were effectively priced out of the market.

During the months of August and September, the Australian dollar had suffered a significant decline against the U.S. dollar, dropping to a low of US$0.56 per A$1.00 before recovering to US$0.63. In 1997 the Australian dollar had traded at US$0.73. Though not suffering as high a devaluation as the Thai Baht or the Indonesian Rupiah, the Australian dollar had devalued in line with the decline in the Japanese Yen and Korean Won against the U.S. dollar because Japan and South Korea were the major export market destinations for Australian products. The Australian balance-of-trade data suggested that a falling Australian dollar rate and an aggressive shift to European and North American markets had reduced the (potentially negative) impact of the Asian crisis on the Australian economy.

In this global economic context, the prospects for future export business were difficult to predict. Segrave was expecting a large export order from the Greater China triangle (China, Hong Kong, and Taiwan), but the strength of home startups in the local building industry in Victoria meant that export orders would be competing with local orders in the short term. The forthcoming trip would be useful in providing first-hand evidence on the future prospects for their export business across Asia. This would be another factor to consider in developing a strategy and organisational structure for their Asian export business.

At this stage, Selkirk did not have any licensing agreements, joint-venture operations, or subsidiaries overseas. Segrave thought it was an interesting question:

> These types of strategic alliances are all useful. In fact, we have a new product right now which we are considering licensing to Asian companies.
>
> We would consider a licensing agreement (for bricks and pavers) if someone wanted to do it on their own in Asia. We would joint-venture if that was more appropriate (and it was commercially viable). These both have great benefits as we don't really know much about the Asian marketplace. Establishing an Asian subsidiary would depend upon the state of our core business in Australia.
>
> It also depends upon the state of Asia and the business opportunities that arise. We have thought of dedicating one plant here in Ballarat to meeting (the higher standard) needs of the Asian marketplace. This would allow us to ensure product quality and still take advantage of our unique clay deposits.

Thus far Selkirk Brick had concentrated on exporting product to Asia and using existing production capacity to meet market needs. The current strategy of appointing export agents made sense in that context.

Nevertheless, there was some concern that increasing exports to the region and a future recovery of the Asian marketplace would change the economics of competing locally as brick and paver utilisation increased. In that case, product and brand licensing would become attractive alternatives and technical support agreements would become viable. Segrave was also concerned that new technologies could make "mini-kilns" economically viable and change the economic attractiveness of local production. This would require a change not only in their international export strategy but also to their whole way of doing business in Asia.

APPENDIX 1

HISTORICAL HIGHLIGHTS OF SELKIRK BRICK

Extracted from a profile of Selkirk Brick, one of eight companies examined by Edna Carew and published in "Family Business: The Story of Successful Family Companies in Australia".

- In 1883, Robert Selkirk began making bricks using a clay deposit in Allendale, Victoria. Bricks were hand-made using moulds. A brick press and engine purchased in 1892 signalled the beginning of mechanised production.
- In 1905, Selkirk was using coal-fired kilns to produce five brick types in batches. During that year, they began continuous firing of bricks on a three-shift, 24-hour, seven-day-a-week basis.
- In 1921, James Selkirk assumed control of Selkirk Brick (upon the death of his father) and was assisted by Bill Gillman, his brother-in-law, as company secretary.
- In 1935, James Selkirk suffered a heart attack and was ultimately succeeded by his two sons, Bill and Ron Selkirk. They managed the business until they enlisted and handed over control to Bill Gillman (Uncle Willy) during the war years.
- The post-WWII years saw Bill and Ron return to the family business, with Bill managing operations and staffing while Ron handled management and accounting.
- The late '40s and '50s were years of a great (re)building boom for Australia, and Selkirk often needed to resort to a lottery to allocate bricks to customers. Innovation was central to its continued success; mechanised claypit in 1952, forklifts in 1953, its own transport company in 1954, "packaged" bricks in 1955, and the appointment of its first Sales Rep in 1959.
- By 1962, the brick works was completely redeveloped and a tunnel-kiln was built that allowed a clean-burning butane gas and an automated plant, both of which substantially enhanced the quality of bricks produced but also left the company with debt that stretched it financially for the next decade.
- During the '60s, the boom market evaporated and Selkirk Brick began to market its bricks across state boundaries into New South Wales and Canberra (the national capital). In 1969, Bill and Ron Selkirk became joint chairmen of the company.
- In 1974, production capacity was doubled to 50 million bricks a year with Plant No. 2 commissioned in Ballarat and in 1978 the fourth generation of Selkirks (Robert, Iain and Jim) was appointed to the Board.
- Bill and Ron Selkirk retired from day-to-day management in 1981; Ian McCoy (who had joined the company in 1951) became Chairman and several other long-term employees, who had joined the Board in 1969, were also promoted.

APPENDIX 2

THE AUSTRALIAN CLAY BRICK MANUFACTURING INDUSTRY IN 1998

The Australian clay brick industry was small, accounting for 0.09 percent of GDP in 1997/98. Products included clay bricks and pavers used in new housing construction (70 percent), housing renovations (15 percent), and commercial construction (15 percent). The state of New South Wales had the largest market share (36.3 percent) followed by Queensland (18.9 percent), Western Australia (17 percent) and Victoria (16.9 percent). Exports were low at 2.3 percent of turnover in 1997/98 and imports were negligible.

Market Demand and Prices

Industry turnover reached $906 million in 1992/93 but then declined to $728 million in 1996/97 before climbing to $780 million in 1997/98. Clay brick production was estimated to be 1,532 million bricks in 1997/98. Approximately 87 percent of housing was constructed using clay brick (typically as brick veneer, with the external walls using brick and interior walls using plaster or fibre board). Premium bricks (used in exterior walls) cost approximately $500 per 1,000 bricks while seconds (used as fill-in) cost in the order of $300 per 1,000. Pavers represented 15 percent of production but less than 10 percent of sales revenue.

The outlook for 1998/99 was for a solid increase in sales to $880 million due to a strong residential housing construction demand fuelled by low mortgage interest rates, a strong domestic economy (despite the Asian crisis) and widespread concerns that the proposed 10 percent value-added tax in July 2000 would increase housing costs. (Clay bricks and pavers were currently exempt from wholesale sales tax.) The long-term market demand was expected to decline as new materials (concrete bricks, steel panels, and prestressed concrete) and new construction techniques (steel frames in particular) acted as substitutes. Steel-framed buildings using steel or corrugated iron cladding were reputed to cost about two-thirds the cost of brick-veneer.

Prices across markets were believed to be stable with competition based on product differentiation and distribution networks. High transportation costs and fear of price wars in a concentrated marketplace led to careful geographic competition. The industry cost structure had been estimated as follows:

- Material Purchases   9%
- Electricity and Fuel   12%
- Freight and Cartage   8%
- Repairs and Maintenance   7%
- Wages and Salaries   22%
- Other (Overheads/Profits)   42%

Industry Competition

Industry concentration was considered to be relatively high with the top five competitors accounting for 85 percent of sales: the top four competitors also accounted for 35 of the 75 enterprise units in the Australian market.

Company	Market Share	Industry Revenue
Boral Limited	33%	$235 million
CSR Limited	21%	$150 million
Pioneer International	13%	$95 million
Futuris Limited	10%	$72 million
Brickworks Limited	8%	$56 million

The industry could be divided into three strategic groups:

National Competitors Boral, Pioneer and CSR were competitors nationally with operations in a number of states. They were all diversified building products companies with manufacturing interests in related markets and with significant overseas manufacturing interests. Boral and CSR were each reported to have brick manufacturing capacity of 500 to 550 million bricks across Australia. Boral, Pioneer and CSR had recently been penalised by the Australian Consumer and Competition Commission for collusive pricing in the Queensland cement market.

Regional Competitors Futuris (Western Australia), Brickworks (NSW/Queensland) and Selkirk (Victoria) were considered to be regional players. They were specialist clay brick and paver companies, with a number of plants and brands under their umbrella. Futuris had a manufacturing capacity of 200 million bricks.

Local Competitors A number of small companies with local distribution and very small production capacities. Pioneer was the dominant player in Victoria with a 50 percent market share followed by Boral with 25 percent. Victoria's share of national production had fallen from 21 percent in 1990/91 to less than 17 percent in 1993/94. Overcapacity was considered to be high. Production in 1997/98 had reached 2177 million bricks.

International Business

Australian bricks were gaining export markets across Asia due to their natural colors and strength. Boral was successfully exporting through its Western Australian subsidiary, Midland Bricks. Exports had risen to $14.9 million in 1993/94 but had fallen subsequently to $14.0 million in 1994/95 and remained at that level in the two years that followed. The three largest companies all had overseas brick-making operations though the scale and importance of these varied considerably.

APPENDIX 3

OUTLINE OF DISTRIBUTOR SALES AGREEMENT

1.1 Definitions.

1.2 Appointment Period.

1.3 Terms and Conditions of Sale.

1.4 Trademarks.

1.5 Advertising and Sales Promotions.

1.6 Management Reports.

1.7 Product Specifications.

1.8 Acceptance Test and Inspections.

1.9 Termination, Extensions and Revisions.

1.10 Transfer of Rights.

1.11 Business Secrecy.

1.12 Force Majeure.

1.13 Arbitration.

1.14 Notice Addresses.

1.15 Governing Laws.

19 RUSSKI ADVENTURES

On July 15, 1991, Guy Crevasse and Andrei Kakov, the two major partners in Russki Adventures (Russki), contemplated their next move. They had spent the last year and a half exploring the possibility of starting a helicopter skiing operation in the USSR. Their plan was to bring clients from Europe, North America, and Japan to a remote location in the USSR to ski the vast areas of secluded mountain terrain made accessible by the use of helicopters and the recent business opportunities offered by "glasnost".

During the exploration process, Crevasse and Kakov had visited a number of potential locations in the USSR, including the Caucasus Mountains near the Black Sea and the Tien Shen and Pamir ranges north of Pakistan in the republics of Kazakistan and Tadzhikistan, respectively. After close inspection of the three areas, and consideration of many issues, the partners had decided upon the Caucasus region.

After almost two years of planning and research, the thought of making a solid commitment weighed heavily on their minds. Their first option was to accept the partnership offer with Extreme Dreams, a French company that had started a small ski operation in the Caucasus Mountains during the 1991 season. Their second option was to enter a partnership with the USSR's Trade Union DFSO and a Russian mountaineer, and establish their own venture in a Caucasus Mountains area made available to them by a Soviet government agency. Their final option was to wait, save their money, and not proceed with the venture at this time.

IVEY　Ian Sullivan prepared this case under the supervision of Professor Paul Beamish solely to provide material for class discussion. The authors do not intend to illustrate either effective or ineffective handling of a managerial situation. The authors may have disguised certain names and other identifying information to protect confidentiality. Ivey Management Services prohibits any form of reproduction, storage or transmittal without its written permission. This material is not covered under authorization from CanCopy or any reproduction rights organization. Copyright © 1992, Ivey Management Services.

The Partners

Andrei Kakov, 27, was born in Russia. His family emigrated to Italy, and then to Canada when he was 17 years old. After completing an undergraduate degree in economics at the University of Toronto, he worked with Sebaco for two years before enroling in 1989 in the Masters of Business Administration (MBA) program at the University of Western Ontario (Western). Sebaco was a Canadian-Soviet joint venture that, since 1980, had been facilitating business ventures in the Soviet Union by acting as a liaison between the foreign firms and the different levels of Soviet government and industry. This job gave Kakov extensive contacts in the Soviet Union and in many of the firms, such as McDonald's and Pepsico, which were doing business in the Soviet Union. Kakov was fluent in Russian, Italian, English, and Japanese.

Guy Crevasse, 28, had an extensive ski racing career which began at a young age and culminated in the World Cup with the Canadian National Ski Team. His skiing career took him to many countries in Europe, North America, and South America. During his travels he learned to speak French, Italian, and some German. After retiring from competitive ski racing in 1984, Crevasse remained active in the ski industry as a member of the Canadian Ski Coaches Federation. He led the University of Western Ontario Varsity Ski Team to four consecutive Can-Am titles as a racer/coach while pursuing an undergraduate degree at Western. Before returning to Western to complete an MBA, Crevasse worked for Motorola Inc. in its sales and marketing departments, where he worked on key accounts, set up product distribution channels, and developed product programs with original equipment manufacturers in the automobile industry. Crevasse had also worked with a ski resort planning and development firm on a number of different projects.

Overview of the Skiing and Helicopter Skiing Industries

Development of the Ski Resort Industry

In 1990, the worldwide ski market was estimated at 40 million skiers. The great boom period was in the 1960s and 1970s when growth ran between 10 and 20 percent annually. However, the growth stagnation which began during the 1980s was expected to continue during the 1990s. Some of this decline was attributable to increased competition for vacationers' time, the rapidly rising real costs of skiing, and baby boom effects. The only growth segment was female skiers, who represented 65 percent of all new skiers. The total revenue generated by ski resorts in the United States for 1990 was estimated at $1.5 billion. This figure did not include any hotel or accommodation figures.

Prior to World War II, most skiing took place in Europe. Since there were no ski lifts, most skiing was essentially unmarked wilderness skiing, requiring participants who enjoyed the thrill of a downhill run to spend most of their time climbing. There were no slope grooming machines and few slopes cut especially for skiing.

The development of ski lifts revolutionized the sport, increased the accessibility to many previously unaccessible areas, and led to the development of ski resorts. After the skiing market matured, competition for skiers intensified and resort operators shifted their efforts away from the risk sport focus towards vacation and entertainment. In order to service this new market and to recover their large capital investments, the large resorts had developed mass market strategies, and modified the runs and the facilities to make them safer and easier to ski in order to serve a greater number of customers.

Introduction of Helicopter Skiing

This change in focus left the more adventurous skiing segments unsatisfied. For many, the search for new slopes and virgin snow was always a goal. The rapid rise in the popularity of skiing after World War II increased demand on existing ski facilities and thus competition for the best snow and hills became more intense. Those who wanted to experience the joys of powder skiing in virgin areas were forced to either get up earlier to ski the good snow before the masses got to it, or hike for hours from the top of ski areas to find new areas close to existing cut ski runs. Hiking to unmarked areas was tiring, time consuming, and more dangerous because of the exposure to crevasses and avalanches.

This desire to ski in unlimited powder snow and new terrain away from the crowds eventually led to the development of the helicopter skiing industry. The commonly held conception was that powder skiing was the champagne of all skiing, and helicopter skiing was the Dom Perignon. The first helicopter operations began in Canada. From the beginning of the industry in 1961, Canadian operations have been typically regarded as the premium product in the helicopter skiing industry for many reasons, including the wild, untamed mountains in the western regions. For many skiers worldwide, a trip to a Western Canadian heli-ski operation is their "mecca."

Operators used helicopters as a means of accessing vast tracts of wilderness areas which were used solely by one operator through a lease arrangement with the governments, forest services, or regional authorities. The average area leased for skiing was 2,000 to 3,000 square thousand kilometres in size, with 100 to 150 runs. Due to the high costs in buying, operating, maintaining, and insuring a helicopter, the vast majority of operators leased their machines on an as-needed basis with rates based on hours of flight time.

In the 1970s and early 1980s, the helicopter skiing industry was concentrated among a few players. During 1990 and 1991, the number of adventure/wilderness skiing operators increased from 41 to over 77. The industry could be divided between those operations that provided day trips from existing alpine resorts (day-trippers) and those operations that offered week long trips (destination-location).

By 1991, the entire global market for both day-trippers and destination-location was estimated to be just over 23,000 skiers per year, with the latter group representing roughly 12,000 to 15,000 skiers. Wilderness skiing represented the largest area of growth within the ski industry in the 1970s and 1980s. Market growth in the 1980s was 15 percent per year. Only capacity limitations had restrained growth. The addictive nature of helicopter skiing was illustrated by the fact that repeat customers accounted for over 75 percent of clients annually. The conservative estimate of total margin available to the destination-location skiing industry (before selling and administration costs) was US$12.4 million in 1990. Exhibit 1 gives typical industry margin figures per skier for heli-skiing.

From a cost standpoint, efficient management of the helicopter operations was essential. Exhibit 2 provides a larger list of industry key success factors.

EXHIBIT 1   Helicopter Skiing Margin per Skier Week (North America)

Price	$3,500	100%
Costs:		
Helicopter*	1,260	36
Food and lodging	900	26
Guides	100	3
Total operating costs	2,260	65
Total margin	$1,240	35%

*Note: Helicopter costs were semivariable, but were based largely on a variable basis (in-flight hours). The fixed nature of helicopter costs arose through minimum flying hours requirements and the rate negotiation (better rates were charged to customers with higher usage). On average, a helicopter skier used seven hours of helicopter time during a one-week trip. A typical all-in rate for a 12-person helicopter was $1,800 per flying hour. Hence, the above figure of $1,260 was calculated assuming full capacity of the helicopter using the following: $1,800 per hour for seven hours for 10 skiers + pilot + guide.

EXHIBIT 2   Helicopter Skiing Industry Key Success Factors

Factors within management control:

• Establishing a safe operation and a reliable reputation.
• Developing great skiing operations.
• Attracting and keeping customers with minimal marketing costs.
• Obtaining repeat business through operation's excellence.
• Providing professional and sociable guides.
• Obtaining operating permits from government.
• Managing relationships with environmentalists.

Location factors:

• Accessible destinations by air travel.
• Available emergency and medical support.
• Favorable weather conditions, i.e., annual snowfall, humidity, altitude.
• Appropriate daily temperature, sunshine, daylight time.
• Suitable terrain.
• Quality food and lodging.

Combination of Resort and Helicopter Skiing

The number of resorts operating day facilities doubled in 1990. Competition in the industry increased for a number of reasons. Many new competitors entered because of the low cost of entry (about $250,000), low exit barriers, the significant market growth, and the rewarding margin in the industry. The major growth worldwide came mainly from the day operations at existing areas, as they attempted to meet the needs for adventure and skiing from their clientele. The major concentration of helicopter operators was in Canada; however, competition was increasing internationally. Industry representatives thought that such growth was good because it would help increase the popularity of helicopter skiing and introduce more people to the sport.

In Canada, where helicopter skiing originated, the situation was somewhat different. Out of the 20 wilderness skiing operations in Canada in 1991, only two were tied to resorts. However, for the rest of the world, roughly 80 percent of all the operations were located and tied closely to existing ski operations. Both Crevasse and Kakov realized that there were opportunities to create partnerships or agreements with existing resorts to serve as an outlet for their helicopter skiing demand.

Russki's Research of the Heli-Ski Industry

Profile of the Skier

The research that the Russki group had completed revealed some important facts. Most helicopter skiers were wealthy, independent, professional males of North American or European origin. Increasingly, the Japanese skiers were joining the ranks. The vast majority of the skiers were in their late 30s to mid 60s in age. For them, helicopter skiing provided an escape from the high pace of their professional lives. These people, who were financially secure with lots of disposable income, were well educated and had done a great many things. Helicopter skiing was a good fit with their calculated risk taker image. Exhibit 3 describes a typical customer. It was not unusual for the skiing "addict" to exceed 100,000 vertical feet of skiing in a week. A premium was then charged to the skier.

Buyers tended to buy in groups rather than as individuals. They typically had some form of close association, such as membership in a common profession or club. In most cases, trips were planned a year in advance.

Geographically, helicopter skiers could be grouped into three segments: Japan, North America (USA and Canada), and Europe. In 1991, they represented 10 percent, 40 percent (30 percent and 10 percent), and 50 percent of the market respectively. There were unique features associated with each segment and Crevasse and Kakov knew that all marketing plans would need to be tailored specifically to each segment. In general, they felt that the European and North American customers placed more emphasis on the adventure, were less risk adverse, and had a propensity to try new things.

Analysis of the Competition

Crevasse and Kakov had thought that more detailed information on their competitors would help answer some of their questions. During the winter of 1991, they conducted a complete physical inspection of skiing and business facilities of many helicopter skiing operations. As a result of the research, Russki determined that the following companies were very significant: Rocky Mountain Helisports (RMH), Cariboo Snowtours, and Heliski India. RMH and Cariboo Snowtours were industry leaders and Heliski India was another new entrant trying to establish itself in the market. A close analysis had provided Crevasse and Kakov with some encouraging information.

Rocky Mountain Helisports, the first operation to offer helicopter skiing, was started in 1965 in Canada by Gunther Pistler, a German immigrant and the "inventor" of helicopter skiing. In 1991 his operation, servicing 6,000 skiers, represented roughly 40–50 percent

EXHIBIT 3   Description of a Typical Helicopter Skiing Addict

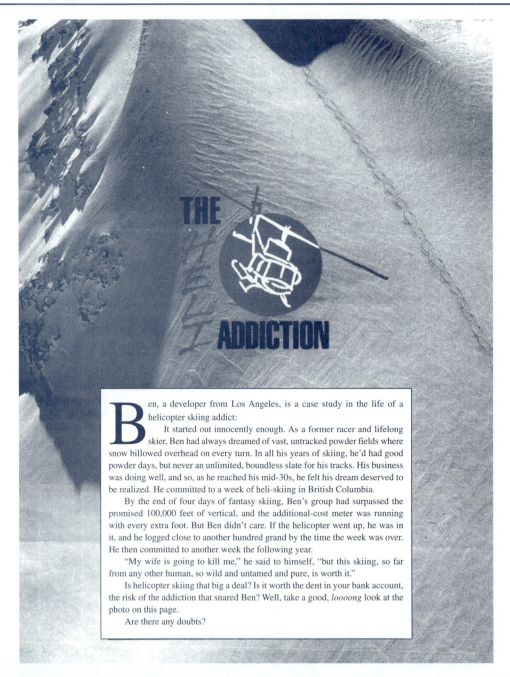

en, a developer from Los Angeles, is a case study in the life of a
helicopter skiing addict:

It started out innocently enough. As a former racer and lifelong
skier, Ben had always dreamed of vast, untracked powder fields where
snow billowed overhead on every turn. In all his years of skiing, he'd had good
powder days, but never an unlimited, boundless slate for his tracks. His business
was doing well, and so, as he reached his mid-30s, he felt his dream deserved to
be realized. He committed to a week of heli-skiing in British Columbia.

By the end of four days of fantasy skiing, Ben's group had surpassed the
promised 100,000 feet of vertical, and the additional-cost meter was running
with every extra foot. But Ben didn't care. If the helicopter went up, he was in
it, and he logged close to another hundred grand by the time the week was over.
He then committed to another week the following year.

"My wife is going to kill me," he said to himself, "but this skiing, so far
from any other human, so wild and untamed and pure, is worth it."

Is helicopter skiing that big a deal? Is it worth the dent in your bank account,
the risk of the addiction that snared Ben? Well, take a good, *loooong* look at the
photo on this page.

Are there any doubts?

Source: *Powder: The Skier's Magazine,* November 1990.

of the worldwide destination-location market. He followed a strategy which cloned small operating units at seven different sites in the interior of British Columbia. RMH's strategy was designed to offer a product that catered to a variety of different skier abilities and skiing experiences. The company serviced all segments that could afford the $4,000 price of admission, including introducing less able skiers to the experience of helicopter skiing. Compared with the revenue of traditional Canadian ski resorts, such as Whistler Resorts in British Columbia, RMH's gross revenue for the 1990 season was larger than any resort in Canada at over $21 million. RMH, which had developed a loyal following of customers in North America and Europe, enjoyed significant competitive advantage because of proprietary client lists, a loyal consumer base, and economies of scale due to its large size.

Cariboo Snowtours, the second-largest operation in the world, was established by another German immigrant, Fritz Mogler, at Blue River, British Columbia. In 1991, Cariboo Snowtours served over 2,000 skiers, a number which represented roughly 18 percent of the market. Mogler developed a strategy of one mega-operation and enjoyed economies of scale in the operations area. Similar to RMH, Cariboo Snowtours had a loyal following from North America and Europe, and catered to a variety of skiing abilities and price levels.

Heliski India was a new entrant to the helicopter skiing business. In 1990, the first year of operation, the company serviced 30 skiers in a three week period, increasing to 120 skiers during the 1991 season. Heliski India followed a more exclusive and adventurous strategy aimed at the experienced helicopter skiing enthusiast. To cover the high costs and low volume, the operation charged $5,500.

Russski estimated margins and profit dynamics for these three operations. Exhibit 4 contains the projection for RMH. These projected statements were best-guess estimates based on discussions with a wide range of industry experts, managers, and investors. Cariboo Snowtour's total profit was estimated as slightly over $2 million, while Heliski India was projected to turn a small profit. Crevasse and Kakov found these figures very encouraging.

Land Usage and Environmental Concerns in the Industry

The helicopter skiing industry was facing some land use issues which were tough on many operators, but which also created new opportunities on which Russski wanted to capitalize. Of particular concern to many helicopter skiing operations, especially European, were pressures from environmentalists who were concerned that noise from helicopters could adversely affect wildlife habitat, and start avalanches.

As a result, severe downsizing or complete shutdown of existing European operations had recently occurred, leaving only eight helicopter skiing operations in continental Europe in 1991. The one Swiss and one Austrian operation were under pressure to close, and a 1992 season for the latter was already doubtful. The six small operations in Italy, which worked in conjunction with existing ski areas, were basically the only helicopter skiing available in Western Europe. Flying for skiing in France was illegal due to environmentalists' concerns about a negative impact on the limited areas in the Alps. In Sweden, a few companies operated with a shorter season due to the high latitude, and provided less expensive daily services for visitors who skied within the existing lift systems, but weeklong packages were not part of their program.

EXHIBIT 4

RUSSKI'S 1991 PROJECTIONS:*
Profit Dynamics of Typical RMH Operation

REVENUES

Ski season duration—peak	20 wks		
—regular	0 wks		
Total season duration	20 wks		
Revenue per skier—peak		$3,500	
Weekly group size: (10 skiers + 1 guide × 4) 44 people			
Total season regular revenue (3,500 × 40 skiers × 20 wks)			$2,800,000
Revenue from skiers exceeding 100,000 vertical feet (10%)			280,000

TOTAL REVENUE $3,080,000

Expenses

Variable:

9 nights lodging/person/night		$80	$ 720
9 days meals/person/day		50	450
Total variable cost/person/week			$ 1,170
Total annual variable costs (20 wks × 44 × $1,170)			$1,029,600
Contribution margin			$2,050,400

Fixed:

Helicopter cost/weekly basis (20 week season)		$50,000	$1,000,000
Guides—1 guide per 10 skiers @ $50,000 per guide/year	4 guides		$200,000
Support staff—5 employees @ $20,000 per employee			$100,000
Promotional			$250,000

TOTAL DIRECT FIXED COSTS $1,550,000

TOTAL MARGIN (Revenue – Dir. variable costs – Dir. fixed costs) $500,400

Annual overhead—communication	$20,000	
—staff travel	50,000	
—office branch	20,000	
—office North America	100,000	
—insurance @ $5/day/person	50,000	

TOTAL OVERHEAD .... $ 240,000

Operating profit		$249,600
Number of operations	7	
Total operating profit		$1,747,200

*These projected statements were best-guess estimates based on discussions with a wide range of industry experts, managers, and investors.

The North American industry had not been exposed to the same environmental and limited area constraints as the European, mainly because of the vast size of the mountain ranges and good relationships with all interested parties. The American operators, who were associated mostly with the large ski areas, had good working relationships with the forest services, which controlled the areas and issued the working permits.

Canadian operators received their permits from the Ministry of Lands and Forests and the provincial governments. Helicopter skiing had been encouraged because of its ability to bring money into the regions. Due to the vast size of the Canadian mountain ranges and the limited competition for the land use, pressure on the operators in any form had been minimal or nonexistent.

Crevasse and Kakov realized that the environmental and capacity constraints in Europe provided helicopter skiing operators worldwide with significant opportunities. Thus far, it had been mainly the North American operators who had capitalized on this situation, and Russki wanted to find a way to capture unsatisfied demand.

Russian Environment

The Political Environment

Crevasse and Kakov knew that starting a venture in the Soviet Union at this time would be complex. The political situation was very unstable in July 1991, and most expert predictions were not encouraging, including the possibility that the Soviet Union might not exist in the near future. There was a major power struggle going on: the hardliners, most of whom were from the old guard of the Communist Party, were trying to hang onto power; and others, such as Russian President Boris Yeltsin, wanted sweeping democratic changes. The new buzz word on the streets was not "glasnost" or "perestroika" but "razgosudarstvo", which refers to the breakup of the Soviet state. Secession pressures from many of the republics, such as the Baltics, tested the mettle of the political leaders, perestroika, and the strength of the union itself.

On a regional basis, the future status of some of the regions and republics where the physical conditions met the requirements for helicopter skiing, such as Georgia and Kazakhistan, was unknown. However, Crevasse and Kakov were encouraged by the fact that experts predicted that no matter what the state of the whole union, Russia would remain intact and continue to function as a unit. This was one of the many reasons why the Russian Republic was selected for the potential initial location.

The Economic Environment

The economy of the Soviet Union was in dire straits. Confusion, lack of focus, and compromise, were crippling the process of change from a government controlled economy to a market based one. Real Gross Domestic Product was projected to drop anywhere from 3 to 11 percent or more in 1991. Soviet President Mikhail Gorbachev had been given authority to overhaul the economy. However, what changes he would initiate, and whether he still had the support and power to see the process through to completion, were questionable.

Therefore, developing a helicopter skiing operation in the Soviet Union presented Russki with a difficult business environment. Marshall Goldman, Director of Harvard's Russian Research Centre, summed up part of the dilemma facing any new venture in the Soviet Union at this time:

> for those entrepreneurs who think chaos is an ideal environment, this is a perfect time, but for others it is a scary time. The society is collapsing. The economy—both the marketing portion and the planning and administrative sector—is a shambles.

Russki's research indicated that only 20 percent of the 1,300 joint ventures signed since 1987 were operational because of currency exchange problems, bureaucratic delays, and lack of legal framework to make agreements. Also, it had been very hard for the few operational ventures to realize a return on their investment. In 1991, any business in the Soviet Union had to be viewed with a long term bias in mind. The big question for many businesses was getting hard currency out of Soviet ventures because there was no international market for the Soviet currency, the ruble. Those who were operating business ventures in the Soviet Union suggested to Russki that it was not an area for the faint hearted to tread. PlanEcon's Keith Crane advised that "even after the agreement has been signed it can be very difficult to get down to specifics and venture into working entities. It took McDonald's 14 years to do it". Due to the political and economic realities of the Soviet environment, firms were making deals with republics, with city agencies, directly with Soviet firms or factories, and sometimes with all of them. More and more frequently, firms had to go to the enterprise level to find the right people and partners. Additionally, foreign firms found the business environment difficult because the concept of business that Westerners had was very different from the one that the Soviets had after 70 years of a controlled Marxist economy. The addition of cultural differences made for a demanding business climate. Russki thought long and hard about the fact that doing business in the Soviet Union had never been easy. In 1991, as the nation wrestled with the gargantuan task of restructuring the country, most firms were finding it more confusing than ever. No road map or blueprint for business development existed.

In addition, without the significant financial resources of a highly capitalized firm that could overlook short term profits for long term gains, Crevasse and Kakov realized they would be in a more exposed position if they decided to go ahead with the venture. Political unrest or civil war in the Soviet Union, especially in Russia, could destroy their business and investment. Without a steady supply of repeat and new customers, the venture would be finished as an on-going concern. They knew that credibility from an existing operation or established name would make the task of attracting customers to an uncertain environment easier but, in a time of crisis, would guarantee nothing.

The Opportunities

Despite all the negatives, Crevasse and Kakov thought that helicopter skiing in the Soviet Union would be developed on a large scale in the next few years for a number of reasons. The sport was experiencing tremendous growth, environmental pressures were great in Europe, and capacity at all of the good locations was already stretched.

Therefore, a current opportunity existed in the industry. The partners speculated about how fast they could proceed with their business plan and whether they were exposing themselves to too much risk for the return. Would the opportunity still exist in a couple of years? Could a business of this nature function with the future of the Soviet Union being so unstable? The complete answer to these questions was unknown. Crevasse and Kakov felt as if they were doing a case back at business school where someone had left out half the case facts. Regardless, this was a real life situation, and a decision had to be made on the knowledge available.

After looking closely at their competition and the general environment, they concluded that despite the instability in the Soviet environment, there were a number of strong points that suggested that they might be able to make a venture of this nature work. On a positive note, the Canadian Prime Minister, Brian Mulroney, had recently signed the Foreign

Investment Protection agreement to ensure stability of Canadian ventures in the USSR. Also encouraging to entrepreneurs wanting to enter the Soviet Union was the new law that allowed for full ownership of Soviet subsidiaries by foreign firms. Experts suggested that these agreements would be honoured by whatever form of government was in place.

The critical factor in the minds of the Russki partners was the fact that they would be taking in all revenue in hard currency. Thus, the absence of profit repatriation risk decreased this business exposure dramatically. Russki would operate all of the sales and administrative tasks outside of the Soviet Union and, as a result, all of its revenues would be collected in the West in hard currency, thereby eliminating the currency risk completely. This was a position that would be envied by any firm attempting to do business in the Soviet Union. Also, Russki was attractive to all levels of government because the venture would bring desperately needed hard currency into the country.

Mt. Elbrus, the highest peak in Europe and the Caucasus mountain region, was where Russki had options to locate. It was well known throughout Europe and its high altitudes and warm climate offered ideal skiing conditions. Because a strong allegiance already existed between the European customers and the Canadian operators, Russki's Canadian background would sit well with customers. In addition, Russki would deliver comparative cost advantage for the Europeans in a Soviet operation, as shown in Exhibit 5, even if Russki charged similar costs for a week of skiing.

The uniqueness of the region and mystique of Russia offered an interesting alternative for tourism. Russia had a 2,000 year history and a rich culture, which was reflected in the traditions of the local people and the architecture. Furthermore, the Black Sea area which was close to the Caucasus Mountains had been used as a resort area for centuries. The dramatic changes during the early 1990s in the Soviet Union and Eastern Europe had resulted in tremendous interest in these areas.

EXHIBIT 5   Cost Comparison by Geographic Location

North America:
Costs for customer to go Heliskiing in North America from different geographic locations.

Origin of Skier	Trip	Transportation	Total
Japan	$4,000	$2,500	$6,500
Europe	$4,000	$2,000	$6,000
North America	$4,000	$ 750	$4,750

Russia:
Cost for customer to go Heliskiing in Russia from different geographic locations.

Origin of Skier	Trip	Transportation	Total
Japan	$4,000	$2,000	$6,000
Europe	$4,000	$1,000	$5,000
North America	$4,000	$2,500	$6,500

Conclusion: This comparative analysis of all-in costs to the consumer shows that the Russian operation offers a 20 percent cost advantage to the European and Japanese customers.

Since Russki already had the money required for startup, the company could move quickly without having to take time to raise the capital. The low cost of leasing Soviet helicopters, pilot salaries, service, and fuel as compared with North America was a distinct advantage, and one of the original attractions of Russia. Negotiations with the Russians had shown that this cost advantage was obtainable. The high costs of helicopter operations represented the largest part of the operating costs in helicopter skiing. Lower helicopter costs in Russia would result in cost savings in the range of 50 percent or more in this expense relative to North American competitors.

The Russki management team was strong. Both men were business school trained individuals with international work experience, language skills, and ski industry background. Additional hard-to-copy assets, including access to the "Crazy Canucks" (a World Cup ski team) and European ski stars as Guest Guides, and Soviet knowledge, would be tough for anyone to match in the short term.

Positioning and Marketing of Russki Adventures

Positioning and Pricing

The Russki team had considered two positioning strategies, a high and low pricing strategy. A premium pricing and service strategy like that of Heliski India at around US $6,000 would require superior service in every aspect of the operation. The lower priced strategy at $3,500 to $4,000 was $500 below the US$4,000 to US$4,500 pricing of Canadian operators like RMH for the initial season. The second positioning strategy would be designed to target a larger market and concentrate on building market share during the first few years, allowing more time and flexibility to move down the learning curve.

Even with parallel pricing of US$4,000, the "all in" (as shown in Exhibit 5) would give a cost advantage to the European and Japanese customers. Crevasse and Kakov knew that this situation would help challenge customers' traditional allegiance to the Canadian operators.

Based on a "best guess scenario," profit models for the two pricing strategies using conservative sales levels are shown in Exhibits 6 and 7. Though the higher priced strategy was more lucrative, Crevasse and Kakov felt that they had a higher capacity to execute the lower priced strategy during the first few years of operations regardless of which partner they chose. They were not sure that they could meet the sales volume for the premium strategy as shown in Exhibit 7, regardless of the realization of savings from use of Russian helicopters. (In the unlikely event that the projected helicopter saving could not be realized, the discounted cash flow in Exhibit 6 dropped from $526,613 to $293, and in Exhibit 7 from $597,926 to $194,484.)

These estimates were extremely conservative. One helicopter could service 44 people per week (four groups of 10 skiers and one guide). All projections for the profit dynamics were made with the number of skiers per week below capacity. In addition, the first two years were estimated using 10 and 15 skiers respectively. In subsequent years, the number of skiers was increased, but never to full capacity, in order to keep estimates conservative. Russki realized that operating at or close to capacity on a weekly basis would increase its efficiency and returns dramatically.

EXHIBIT 6   Profit Dynamics Low Price Strategy with Low Helicopter Costs

	Year 1	Year 2	Year 3	Year 4	Year 5
REVENUES					
Total season duration:	10 weeks	15 weeks	15 weeks	20 weeks	20 weeks
Revenue per skier—peak	$4,000	$4,000	$4,000	$4,000	$4,000
Weekly group size:	10	15	20	25	25
Total season revenue	$400,000	$900,000	$1,200,000	$2,000,000	$2,000,000
EXPENSES					
Total variable cost: (variable cost/skiers @ $1,000)	$100,000	$225,000	$300,000	$500,000	$500,000
CONTRIBUTION MARGIN	$300,000	$675,000	$900,000	$1,500,000	$1,500,000
FIXED					
Helicopter cost: (assumes Soviet costs of $10,000/week)	$100,000	$150,000	$150,000	$200,000	$200,000
Guides—1 guide per 10 skiers @ $50,000 per guide/year	$50,000	$75,000	$100,000	$125,000	$125,000
Soviet staff—3 employees @ $5,000 per employee	$15,000	$15,000	$15,000	$15,000	$15,000
Promotional	$100,000	$100,000	$100,000	$100,000	$100,000
TOTAL DIRECT FIXED COSTS	$265,000	$340,000	$365,000	$440,000	$440,000
TOTAL MARGIN					
(Revenues—Direct variable costs—Direct fixed costs)	$35,000	$335,000	$535,000	$1,060,000	$1,060,000
TOTAL OVERHEAD	$35,000	$115,000	$115,000	$115,000	$115,000
OPERATING PROFIT	0	$220,000	$420,000	$945,000	$945,000

	Year 0	Year 1	Year 2	Year 3	Year 4	Year 5
INVESTMENT	−$230,000					
Operating profit		0	$220,000	$420,000	$945,000	$945,000
N.A. Partner's Share: 100%		0	$220,000	$420,000	$945,000	$945,000
Taxes @ 30%						
Profit	−$230,000	0	$154,000	$294,000	$661,500	$661,500
DCF year 1–5 PV @ 20.00%		$526,613				
IRR	71.86%					

Russki also built in an additional $250 in the variable costs per skier per week for contingent expenses such as the cost of importing all food stuffs.

If Russki proceeded with the lower priced approach, it would position its product just below the industry standard at $4,000 initially. The intent would be to attack the market as the Japanese automobile manufactures had done when entering into the North American luxury car market.

Crevasse and Kakov were encouraged by the numbers because the conservative sales estimates using the low price positioning strategy would allow them to generate a profit in the second year of operations if they could realize the projected savings with Russian helicopters. However, if they didn't, the strategy would still show a profit in the third year. They thought that the return on their investment would be sufficient as far as the internal rate of return was concerned, but they wondered whether the risk of the Soviet environment should increase their demands even more.

EXHIBIT 7   Profit Dynamics Premium Price Strategy with Low Helicopter Costs

	Year 1	Year 2	Year 3	Year 4	Year 5
REVENUES					
Total season duration	5 weeks	10 weeks	10 weeks	20 weeks	20 weeks
Revenue per skier—peak	$6,000	$6,000	$6,000	$6,000	$6,000
Weekly group size	10	10	15	15	20
Total season revenue	$300,000	$600,000	$900,000	$1,800,000	$2,400,000
EXPENSES					
Total variable cost: (variable cost/skier @ $1,000)	50,000	$100,000	$150,000	$300,000	$400,000
Contribution margin	$250,000	$500,000	$750,000	$1,500,000	$2,000,000
FIXED					
Helicopter cost: (assumes Soviet costs of $10,000/week)	$50,000	$100,000	$100,000	$200,000	$200,000
Guides—1 guide per 10 skiers @ $50,000 per guide/year	$50,000	$50,000	$75,000	$75,000	$100,000
Soviet staff—3 employees @ $5,000 per employee	$15,000	$15,000	$15,000	$15,000	$15,000
Promotional	$100,000	$100,000	$100,000	$100,000	$100,000
TOTAL DIRECT FIXED COSTS	$215,000	$265,000	$290,000	$390,000	$415,000
TOTAL MARGIN					
(Revenues—Direct variable costs—Direct fixed costs)	$35,000	$235,000	$460,000	$1,110,000	$1,585,000
TOTAL OVERHEAD	$35,000	$115,000	$115,000	$115,000	$115,000
OPERATING PROFIT	0	$120,000	$345,000	$995,000	$1,470,000

	Year 0	Year 1	Year 2	Year 3	Year 4	Year 5
INVESTMENT	−$230,000					
Operating profit		0	$120,000	$345,000	$995,000	$1,470,000
N.A. partner's share: 100%		0	$120,000	$345,000	$995,000	$1,470,000
Taxes @ 30%			0			
Profit	−$230,000	0	$ 84,000	$241,000	$696,500	$1,029,500
DCF year 1–5 PV @ 20.00%		$597,926				
IRR	70.78%					

Product

Crevasse and Kakov planned to model the Russki product after the RMH operation, which was the best in the industry, by evaluating what RMH had built and improving on its processes. Although Russki wanted very much to differentiate itself from the rest of the industry, the partners were not sure how far they could go within the constraints of the Soviet environment.

Geographical Distribution

Although Russki would focus on the European and North American markets, the former segment was most important. Both Crevasse and Kakov realized that they would need a strong European operation in marketing and sales if they were going to capitalize on the

---

EXHIBIT 8   Marketing Promotion Budget—Year 1

Information nights with cocktails @ $1,000/night @ 20 cities	$20,000
Travel Expenses	10,000
Trip Discounts (1 free trip in 10 to groups)	25,000
Direct Mail	5,000
Brochures	5,000
Commissions	15,000
Celebrity	20,000
Total	$100,000

---

opportunity available. Developing these functions quickly, especially in Europe, which was not their home turf, was a major concern. They had to decide on the best sales and marketing channels immediately and set them up as soon as possible if they decided to go ahead with the venture.

Promotion

Due to the small size of the target market and promotion budgets, the new company would have to make sure that the promotional dollars spent were directed effectively. Russki would do this by direct mail, personal selling by the owners, travel agents, and free tour incentives to trip organizers and guides. Long term word of mouth would be the best promotional tool, but it had to be supplemented especially in the start-up phase of the business.

Additionally, Crevasse and Kakov planned to increase the value to customers by inviting business and political speakers to participate in the skiing activities with the groups in return for their speaking services. Celebrity skiers such as Canadian Olympic bronze medallist and World Cup champion, Steve Podborski, would be used as customer attractions. As outlined in Exhibit 8, they budgeted $100,000 for promotional expenses.

Labour

Where possible, Russki planned to employ Russians and make sure that they received excellent training and compensation, thereby adding authenticity to the customers' experience. Providing local employment would also ensure the Canadian company's existence and create positive relations with the authorities.

Currency

Through Kakov's contacts, Russki had worked out a deal to purchase excess rubles from a couple of foreign firms which were already operating in the Soviet Union but which were experiencing profit repatriation problems. Russki would pay for as many things as possible with soft currency.

The Partnership Dilemma

During the exploration period, Crevasse and Kakov had well over a dozen offers from groups and individuals to either form partnerships or provide services and access to facilities and natural resources. They even had offers from people who wanted them to invest millions to build full scale Alpine Resorts. Many of the offers were easy to dismiss because these groups did not have the ability to deliver what they promised or their skill sets did not meet the needs of Russki. Crevasse and Kakov's inspection and site evaluation helped them to determine further the best opportunities and to evaluate first hand whether the site and potential partner were realistic. This research gave Russki a couple of excellent but very distinct partnership possibilities. They knew that both options had trade-offs.

Extreme Dreams

A partnership with the Extreme Dream group had some definite strengths. This French company, located in Chamonix, an alpine town in the French Alps, had been running the premier guiding service in and around Mont Blanc, the highest peak in the Alps, for 11 years. Chamonix was the "avant garde" for alpinists in Europe and one of the top alpine centres in the world. Extreme Dreams had a 5,000 person client list, mostly European but with some North American names.

What Extreme Dreams had was the operational expertise Russki needed to acquire in order to run the helicopter skiing and guiding side of the business. However, they lacked experience in the key functional areas of business. During the 1991 winter season, it had run a three-week operation servicing 50 skiers in the Elbrus region in the Caucasus Mountains. The Soviet partner facilitated an arrangement with a small resort villa in the area. The facilities, which had just been upgraded during the summer, now met Western standards.

The French company had invested roughly US$100,000, and although it did not have a capital shortage, the partnership agreement that was outlined would require Russki to inject the same amount of capital into the business. The firm would be incorporated in the United States and the share split would be equal amounts of 45 percent of the stock with 10 percent left over for future employee purchase. The Soviet partner, a government organization that helped facilitate the land use agreements and permits, would be paid a set fee for yearly exclusive use of the land.

However, Extreme Dreams lacked experience in the key functional areas of business. Possibly, this situation could be rectified by the partnership agreement whereby the management team would consist of three members. Marc Testut, president of Extreme Dreams, would be in charge of all operations. Guy Crevasse would act as president for the first two years and his areas of expertise would be sales and marketing. Andrei Kakov would be Chief Financial Officer and responsible for Soviet relations.

Extreme Dreams had overcome the lack of some food stuffs by importing, on a weekly basis, products not securely attainable in Russia. These additional costs were built into the variable cost in projected financial statements. Russki would do the same if it did not choose Extreme Dreams as a partner.

Trade Union DFSO

The other potential partnership had its strengths as well. The partnership would be with the All-Union Council of Trade Union DFSO, and with a mountaineer named Yuri Golodov, one of the USSR's best known mountaineers, who had agreed to be part of the management team. Golodov, who had been bringing mountaineers from all over the world to parts of the Soviet Union for many years, possessed valuable expertise and knowledge of the Caucasus area. One of his tasks would be coordination of travel logistics for Soviet clientele. Sergei Oganezovich, chief of the mountaineering department, had made available to Russki the exclusive rights to over 4,000 square kilometres in the Caucasus Mountain Range about 50 kilometres from the area awarded to Extreme Dreams. A small user fee per skier would be paid to the trade organization in return for exclusive helicopter access to the area.

A profit sharing agreement with Golodov, which would allow him to purchase shares in Russki and share in the profits, was agreed to in principle by Russki, the Trade Union DFSO, and Golodov. Under this agreement, Crevasse and Kakov would remain in control of the major portion of the shares. Capital requirements for this option would be in the $230,000 range over the first two years. The two Canadians would perform essentially the same roles as those proposed in the Extreme Dreams agreement. If Crevasse and Kakov selected this option, they would need to bring in a head guide, preferably European, to run the skiing operations. On a positive note, a small resort centre that met the standards required by Western travellers had been selected for accommodations in the area.

As far as medical care in case of accidents, both locations were within an hour of a major city and hospital. Less than an hour was well under the industry norm. In addition, all staff were required to take a comprehensive first aid course.

After discussions with many business ventures in the Soviet Union and with Extreme Dreams, Russki concluded that having the ability to pay for goods and services with hard currency would be a real asset if the situation were critical. Russki would use hard currency, where necessary, to ensure that the level of service was up to the standard required by an operation of this nature.

Crevasse and Kakov knew that selecting a compatible and productive partner would be a great benefit in this tough environment. Yet, they had to remember that a partnership would not guarantee customer support for this venture in the Soviet environment or that the USSR would remain stable enough to function as an on-going concern.

The Decision

Crevasse and Kakov knew that it would take some time for the business to grow to the level of full capacity. They were willing to do whatever it took to make ends meet during the early years of the business. Because helicopter skiing was a seasonal business, they realized that they would need to find a supplementary source of income during the off-season, especially in the start-up phase.

However, they also were confident that if they could find a way to make their plan work, they could be the ones to capitalize on the growing market. The Soviet Union had the right physical conditions for helicopter skiing, but the business environment would present difficulties. Moreover, the two partners were aware that starting a venture of this nature at any time was not an easy task. Starting it in the present state of the Soviet Union during a recession would only complicate their task further. Yet the timing was right for a new venture in the industry and, in general, they were encouraged by the potential of the business.

Crevasse and Kakov had to let all parties involved know of their decision by the end of the week. If they decided to go ahead with the venture, they had to move quickly if they wanted to be operational in the 1992 season. That night they had to decide if they would proceed, who they would select as partners if they went ahead, and how they would go. It was going to be a late night.

20 SAMSUNG CHINA

THE INTRODUCTION
OF COLOR TV

In October 1995, Mr. Chung Yong[1], President of Samsung China Headquarters (SCH), was spearheading a major drive to integrate various business units in China into a single Samsung. Prior to the establishment of SCH in 1995, business activities in China had been conducted separately by each of Samsung's business units, based on its own business strategies. Mr. Chung was considering a recent meeting with the SCH marketing director, Hyun Young-Koo, who was responsible for developing a marketing strategy for the entire China market. The topic at the meeting was the marketing strategy for color TVs, which had been chosen as the flagship product for the China market. However, they had not yet agreed on a basic market strategy for China. The immediate decision was on the market segment and product line that SCH should target. Should SCH cover all the market segments and product lines? Or should SCH focus on the low-end market segment with a limited line of products, just as Samsung Electronics had done when it entered the U.S. market? Or should SCH target the high-end market segment, as most Japanese electronics companies had done in the U.S. and China markets?

IVEY   Chang-Bum Choi prepared this case under the supervision of Professors Paul Beamish and David Sharp solely to provide material for class discussion. The authors do not intend to illustrate either effective or ineffective handling of a managerial situation. The authors may have disguised certain names and other identifying information to protect confidentiality. Ivey Management Services prohibits any form of reproduction, storage or transmittal without its written permission. This material is not covered under authorization from CanCopy or any reproduction rights organization. Copyright © 1998, Ivey Management Services.

[1]The name is written as it would be in Korean: family name first and first name last.

The Chinese Economic Environment in 1995

The Macro Environment

Although China had introduced many market-driven economic reforms, it was still primarily a centrally planned socialist economy. The most important lesson learned by foreign firms in China was that there was a huge gap between the stated plans and the actual ability of the government to manage and control the economy. Therefore, a tremendous amount of economic interaction took place outside the government's formal economic plan. In China's computer industry, for example, factories stood idle when printed circuit boards failed to be delivered as promised. The reason was either that circuit boards were diverted to another facility through the so-called "back door" or that the circuit board factory received the wrong order. Furthermore, smuggling and piracy were major issues in China as well as the USSR and other former Eastern Bloc nations.

Competition among Governments: Self-Interest versus National Interest.   There existed a high degree of competition among governments at both the central and local levels. This was due to a scarcity problem as well as the incomplete planning system. Governments tended to vie with one another to protect their already scarce resources. The self-interested competition among local governments caused another form of competition— "regional blockades". For example, one province or city might make an effort to utilize a foreign joint venture project as a means of expanding national market share. To counter what it called "market trespassing," government authorities in certain localities created various obstacles to block such competition. It was only after high level intervention from Beijing that the distribution channel would be opened up. Therefore, some MNEs targeting both the domestic market and the export market set up production bases in at least two places: typically, one in the south and the other in the north.

Difference in Emphasis on Economic Profitability versus Social Profitability.   The Chinese government emphasized social profitability more than economic profitability when it evaluated the worthiness of a proposed project or the success of an existing project. The Chinese concept of social profitability referred to the benefits of a particular project in terms of "social factors" such as employment, the construction of a new building, the training of workers, the prestige or recognition that came from having a big, foreign-invested project located in one's province or city. These "soft" criteria could be a major source of confusion for foreign firms when determining whether or not a project would be attractive to their Chinese partner, because their socialist counterpart might be interested in something other than the basic ROI.

The Over-Employment Problem.   Underlying the issue of social profitability was the fact that many socialist enterprises suffered from the problem of over-employment. Foreign managers visiting Chinese factories often commented on the huge number of workers that seemed to be present, but not engaged in any real productive activities. Many foreign firms entering into joint venture agreements with socialist firms had found themselves in the position of having to inherit a large number of workers and staff, of which perhaps only 50 percent were needed to complete the production tasks at hand. While changes had been introduced to allow the streamlining of the work force, it was often politically difficult to release workers. Besides, China made it a compulsory rule to work only five days a week. The idea was that a five-day work week would make the company employ more workers.

The Micro Environment

The Chinese Color TV Industry.   China was estimated to have an annual production capacity of 18 million color TV sets, with total output for 1995 hitting 16 million sets, including two million units exported to Europe, North America, Africa, and Australia. The Chinese government judged that its current TV production capacity was sufficient to fulfill demand in both domestic and export markets. On the demand side, the Chinese color TV market was the second-largest after the U.S. and the third-largest after NAFTA and EU in unit sales. As such, it had been the principal battleground for the major international color TV manufacturers. Therefore, the Chinese color TV industry was quite heterogeneous in terms of the composition of its supplying firms which came from many different nations, notably Japan, the Netherlands, France, and Germany. Exhibit 1 shows the market size of China, together with the other major markets.

Competition.   Since the Chinese market was strategically important, competition in the color TV market was intense. In particular, Japanese firms stood out in the high-end market segment. Sony and Matsushita, with excellent brand recognition from high-income

---

EXHIBIT 1   **The Demand for Color TVs in Selected Markets (in millions)**

1990		1995		2000	
USA	20.8	NAFTA	29.4	NAFTA	28.7
Canada	1.6				
Mexico	1.2				
Germany	5.6	EU	20.5	EEA	22.9
UK	3.3				
Italy	2.8				
France	2.7	China	14.0	China	21.0
Netherlands	0.8	Japan	10.1	Japan	10.3
Spain	2.0	CIS	4.8	MERCOSUR*	7.6
China	7.7	Brazil	3.8		
Japan	9.6	Korea	2.1		
CIS	6.5	India	1.4	CIS	6.0
Brazil	2.3	Indonesia	1.2	ASEAN	4.7
Korea	2.0	Thailand	1.2		
India	0.7	Argentina	1.1	Korea	2.5
Thailand	0.9			India	2.0
Australia	0.9			Australia	0.8
Taiwan	0.8				
Poland	1.0				

*MERCOSUR is common market in South America. Member countries are Brazil, Argentina, Paraguay, and Uruguay.
Source: JETRO, 1994.

consumers, had a combined market share of about 75 percent in the high-end market segment. Their combined sales in 1994 were estimated to be around 1.5 million units. The next group of firms, including Sharp, Sanyo, Toshiba, Mitsubishi, JVC, and Hitachi, had also established significant market share. On the production side, Japanese firms had already set up 19 production bases all over China. As part of their strategy to increase sales in China, they were said to have plans to increase the production bases from 19 to 30. On average, Japanese color TV manufacturers produced 69 percent of their production outside Japan. In the case of Sony, the overseas production ratio approached 90 percent.

China had more than 20 indigenous firms which focused on the low-end market segment. Some of them were competitive enough to attack the medium-end market segment. Changhong, Konka, and Panda were the three major local TV manufacturers in the country, with a combined domestic market share of nearly 35 percent. While Chinese firms were capable of competing with foreign firms in producing small and medium-sized sets, they were less competitive in large screen color TVs because of their low technology, insufficient capital, and lack of promotion. Furthermore, unlike the foreign firms, which were notable for their global strategies, Chinese firms remained mostly national in the scope of their operations. Exhibit 2 shows the major Chinese firms and their product lines.

Market Size by Product Line.   In the Chinese market, the small color TV (less than 17") market was shrinking rapidly while the medium and large screen color TV markets were growing fast. As of 1995, the 18", 20," and 21" sets made up the largest segments of the

---

EXHIBIT 2   Major Chinese Color TV Manufacturers

Brand Name	Product Size (in inches)
1. Changhong	18, 20, 21, 25, 29
2. Xiongmao (Panda)	18, 20, 21, 25, 29
3. Konka	18, 21, 25
4. Haiyan (Petrel)	18, 20
5. Hongmei	18, 20
6. Kongque (Peacock)	18, 20
7. Jingfeng	18, 20
8. Kaige	18, 20
9. Feiyao	18, 21
10. Changcheng (Great Wall)	18, 21
11. Xihu	18
12. Jingxing	18, 21
13. Xinghai	18
14. Shanyuan	18
15. Huanghe (Yellow River)	18
16. Beijing	20, 21
17. Shangahi	20, 21
18. Mudan (Peony)	18, 20

Source: KORTA, 1995.

color TV market. Together the 20" and 21" screen sizes represented 60 percent of the total in 1994. The second-largest screen-size category was 18" which represented 23 percent of sales. Most Chinese firms marketed only a few of the most popular sizes of television sets, such as 18", 20," and 21", because the large market size of these product lines facilitated the fast achievement of cost reduction not only through the experience curve but also through economies of scale. China's market size by product line was 29"—2 percent; 25"—11 percent; 21"—36 percent; 20"—24 percent; 18"—23 percent; 17" or less—4 percent.

Market Penetration Level.   In 1994, China had 300 million households. The percentage of households with a color TV set was just 41 percent. However, unlike the rural market, the urban market for color TV sets was nearing saturation. It was estimated that about 80 percent of China's 80 million urban households already owned a color TV, whereas only 28 percent of 220 million rural households owned color TV sets. Though replacement demand in urban markets still remained, it did not offset the decreasing market potential for these products. This situation implied that the market strategy of depending on a low- and medium-end urban market segment was not a viable long-term option. However, the overall market was still expanding at a rate of 10 percent per year. The color TV market in China expanded rapidly from 12.6 million units in 1994 to 14 million units in 1995. In terms of unit sales, China's market size was one and half times as large as Japan's.

Consumer's Buying Power.   McKinsey, the management consulting firm, determined that 60 million Chinese had per capita purchasing power exceeding US$1,000, an income level above which Chinese could start buying color TVs, washing machines, and imported clothing. By 1992, average per capita income levels in five urban areas had already topped the US$1,000 threshold. These were Shenzhen with US$2,000, Shanghai with US$1,700, Guangzhou with US$1,500, Beijing with US$1,400, and Tianjin with US$1,100. Exhibit 3 shows the cities where per capita income in 1995 exceeded Guangzhou's. Experts predicted that the list would grow to between 30 and 40 cities by the year 2000, and the number of Chinese above the US$ 1,000 threshold would hit 200 million.

Where were the Chinese getting all this money? First, many Chinese did not report all their income—they had more than the government knew about, thanks to a booming black market in labor, goods, services, and foreign exchange. Second, government housing subsidies meant that there were no mortgages in China. Hence, the amount of household income the Chinese spent on housing and utilities was between 5 and 10 percent, compared with 20 to 40 percent in other East and Southeast Asian countries. All this implies that the Chinese market had started to expand quickly in terms of high-end as well as low-end market segments.

First Mover Advantage.   China was a market where the first mover enjoyed advantages over late comers. Consumers had a tendency to be loyal to a first mover's products. This meant that the first image of a product lasted long in the eyes of the consumer and that the first to enter the market could gain the largest market share. In China, there was a saying that "old friends are welcome," meaning that firms that came into the market early could be guaranteed that their initial "good will" would not be forgotten when other firms entered the market. The first mover advantage effect can be evidenced by the market competition

EXHIBIT 3   Cities above 1995 Guangzhou Level in Per Capita Income

Estimated.
Source: *China Statistical Yearbook,* 1995; McKinsey analysis.

between Pepsi and Coca-Cola in China; whichever firm had entered a city/province first, continued to have the dominant market share. In the color TV market, Japanese manufacturers that entered the China market first received the highest brand recognition from Chinese consumers. In particular, the Sony and Panasonic brands made up the largest market share in the high-end market segment.

Consumer Preferences.   Consumers' color TV preferences in urban areas were different from those in rural areas. City dwellers were more concerned about brand names and the functionality of the products, while consumers in rural markets preferred color TVs with reasonable quality and lower prices. Consumers in rural areas preferred TVs with 21" and

19" screens, which cost less than RMB 3,000 (US$361). Local manufacturers with the brand name of Panda shipped 21" TVs at a price of RMB 3,000, whereas Japanese brand TVs cost well over RMB 4,000.

Protectionism.   China was a highly protected market. Although the tariff for color TVs had decreased from 100 percent to 60 percent on average in 1995, it was still high. The tariffs for smaller than 15", 17", or 18", and more than 19" screen color TVs were 50 percent, 60 percent, and 65 percent respectively. In late 1995, the Ministry of Foreign Trade and Economic Cooperation (MOFTEC) announced that the tariff rates were scheduled to be lowered to 36 percent on average in 1997 and that it would make continuous efforts to lower its import tariffs to 15 percent, a level equal to that in most developing economies. Industry observers said that China strongly hoped to enter the World Trade Organization (WTO), which encouraged free trade among nations.

The TV Industry

Product Differentiation

The importance of product differentiation through brand name recognition posed another barrier against firms relying on low prices for their unknown branded products. In the TV set industry, a few established firms such as Sony, Matsushita, and Philips had succeeded in making their brand names (Sony, Panasonic, and Philips, respectively) well entrenched in many national markets through their global coverage. They had made significant up-front investments not only in advertising, but also in after-sales service facilities and dealer networks to support the brand image and to move from the low-end to the high-end market segment.

Economies of Scale and Learning Effects

Cost competitiveness obtained through economies of scale and the learning effect was a critical competitive weapon. Given that economies of scale always led to cost advantages for large scale firms over small scale firms and that the learning effect did the same thing unless the smaller firms came up with advanced production technologies, economies of scale and the learning curve effect functioned as other entry barriers in the TV set industry. In particular, Japanese giants in the consumer electronics industry were famous for exploiting these advantages on a large scale.

Home Country (South Korea)

Realities of the 1990s

One of the most significant threats Korean firms were facing by the mid-1990s was that Korea's major advantages in labor costs had been deteriorating not only in relation to advanced countries, but more importantly, in relation to its immediate competitors such as the Southeast Asian countries. Wages, averaging $1,144 a month, were now among the highest in Asia outside Japan. Considering the entry into the color TV industry of firms from the Peoples' Republic of China, the relative position of Korean firms as low cost suppliers would be increasingly endangered. Furthermore, The World Competitiveness Report of 1994, an annual assessment of relative economic prowess by Swiss business school IMD and the World Economic Forum, ranked South Korea sixth among 15 newly industrializing economies—behind even Malaysia and Chile. The South Korean economy was undergoing a fundamental restructuring. Moreover, the government, once so supportive of big business, had cut back on subsidies and export credits.

In short, Korean industries were no longer competitive in the low-end products. As an example, the market performance of Korean goods in the US market, a representative global market, was poor. In particular, Korean goods were losing market share to Chinese goods. Korean share in the US market declined from 3.7 percent in 1990 to 2.6 percent in 1996, whereas that of China went up from 2.0 percent to 6.4 percent in the same period. In order to make up for lost market share in low-end products and traditional industries, Korea had to catch up to developed countries in high-end products and in high-tech industries.

Market Liberalization

Another change in the home market was that the Korean domestic market witnessed new entries as it became more competitive. Thanks to deregulation of distribution channels in Korean markets, foreign firms were allowed to sell their products directly to consumers as of July 1993. Market entry barriers were supposed to be fully deregulated by 1996. By October 1995, foreign firms such as Sony, Matsushita, Sanyo, Sharp, Philips, GE, Siemens, Whirlpool, and Laox were busy building their market competitiveness by developing distribution networks, professional sales forces, and after-sales services.

Existing firms would have to rely more on foreign business to compensate for potential losses in the domestic market. Samsung was facing increased competition in the home market as well as the global market.

Samsung's Experience in the U.S.

Samsung Electronics Co. actively started to penetrate the U.S. market when it first set up its overseas marketing subsidiary there in 1979. The market strategy for the U.S. was to focus on the low-end market segment, based on its home country-specific comparative advantage in low labor costs. The low-end segment had two merits. One was that it had a large demand base and the other was that the market entry barriers were low.

Samsung particularly selected only a few of the most popular sizes of television sets, such as 13" and 19" sets, because the large market size of these two products enabled it to achieve cost reduction through economies of scale and the experience curve. In the market, traditionally the 13" and 19" sets had constituted the largest segments of the color TV market. The 19" screen size represented 52 percent of total sales in 1983. The second-largest screen-size category was 13" which represented 19 percent of sales.

Furthermore, the competition in the low-end market segment was low because Japanese firms were changing their focus from the low-end to the medium- and high-end market segment. Investing heavily in advertising, Japanese firms were emphasizing color TV sets with innovative features suited to high-income markets.

At the beginning of U.S. market penetration, Samsung adopted mostly a "buyer brand name" product policy. It was understandable that given its unknown brand names, the only way to create a volume large enough to achieve economies of scale was to adopt a "buyer brand name" policy, especially for large retailers or O.E.M.'s. By doing so, Samsung could rely on foreign buyers for marketing and physical distribution functions through the latter's established marketing networks.

However, Samsung tried to build its own brand image at the same time as it adopted a "buyer brand name" policy. Samsung retained its own brands mostly for small to medium-size buyers, and used buyers' brands for mass retailers and O.E.M. buyers. This dual branded-product policy was intended to reconcile both the short-term and long-term objectives of the firm. The short-term objective was high volume business initially to achieve the experience curve and economies of scale, and the long-term one was stable volume business with differentiated products through the establishment of its brand name.

In terms of production, it served the U.S. market by establishing a production subsidiary in 1984. According to the firm, the major reason was that the U.S. trade barrier, which it had thought to be temporary, turned out to be a more or less long-standing one, though not permanent. The clincher was the antidumping suit filed by a few U.S. domestic firms and labor unions in 1983. This charge, which would add extra costs in the form of antidumping duties if Korean firms were found guilty, would easily wipe out the already low margins of the export business. However, in anticipation of NAFTA, the assembly plant in New Jersey was moved to Tijuana, Mexico, in 1988. Samsung Electronics Mexicana (SAMEX), which had been expanded in 1992, produced 1.17 million color TVs in 1994. Exhibit 4 shows SEC's color TV production network in 1994.

EXHIBIT 4   Samsung Electronics' 1994 Color TV Production
(1000s of units)

	Suwon (Korea)	SAMEX (Mexico)	SEH (Hungry)	SEMUK (UK)	SETAS (Turkey)	TSE (Thai)	TTSEC (China)	Total
13"	1	219				264	15	499
14"	1,188	43	71	97	9	109	55	1,572
16"	96					8		104
19"	12	610						623
20"	1,480	48	80	398	32	46		2,083
21"	454	62	12	160	12	25		725
25"	53	99	2	36		1		190
26"	23	5						29
27'		70						70
28"	6			51				57
29"	69	8	1					78
31"		3						3
33"	2	3						5
Others	14							14
Total	**3,397**	**1,172**	**165**	**742**	**53**	**453**	**70**	**6,051**

Source: Company data.

In the U.S. market, Samsung Electronics grew to be one of the top 12 companies with approximately 3 percent of market share in 1995 (see Exhibit 5). However, Samsung Electronics' operating profit was much smaller than that of Matsushita (Panasonic) with 4 percent market share. The reason was that Samsung could not avoid intense competition in the low-end segment because products in that segment were not differentiated. However, Matsushita in the high-end market could avoid intense competition and so commanded a much higher price than Samsung, based on differentiating its products through brand name recognition (see Exhibit 6). Exhibit 7 shows Samsung's quality score in 1995 according to *Consumer Reports*. Samsung still seemed to pursue an aggressive pricing strategy.

In 1995, Samsung Electronics' total color TV production volume was 6 million units, 44 percent of which were produced overseas. It had six overseas production bases: SAMEX (Mexico), SEH (Hungry), SEMUK (UK), SETAS (Turkey), TSE (Thailand), TTSEC (China). The largest production base was SAMEX in Mexico which produced 19 percent of overseas production. TTSEC of China produced 70,000 units, most of which were 14" TV sets. TTSEC was originally intended as an export base. Besides six overseas production bases, four more production bases—SEDA (Brazil), SVEC (Vietnam), SEIL (India), and SESA (Spain)—were under construction.

Samsung Electronics, ranked 221st in Fortune's Global 500 in 1995, was the largest consumer electronics firm in Korea. It recorded US$21 billion in total sales in 1995, up 40 percent from the 1994 figure of $14.6 billion. Net income grew to $3.2 billion in 1995 from $1.2 billion in 1994.

Samsung Electronics was organized into four divisions—semiconductors, telecommunication systems, multimedia, and home appliances. In terms of sales contribution, the largest division was the semiconductor division, which accounted for 47.9 percent of total sales in 1995, a big jump from 39.8 percent in 1994. The semiconductor division made Samsung the second-largest DRAM chip producer in the world. Home appliances was Samsung Electronics' second-largest division. In 1996, the sales of the home appliances division grew by 13.3 percent to 5,127 billion Korean won, thanks to a 31 percent increase in TV sales in emerging markets.

Samsung's Market Participation in China

In 1985, when Chung first moved to Beijing to pioneer new businesses for the Samsung Group, his phone rarely rang. These days, he sits in a suite on the fifteenth-floor of the Beijing Bright China Chang An Building and his phone rings constantly. "Now we have more than 13 projects all over China and the list is getting longer all the time," he said, motioning towards the maps on his wall (see Exhibit 8). More than 16 projects throughout China projected Samsung both as a major investor in China and as a multinational company with a global vision.

However, Samsung's active move into the Chinese market had really started only after Beijing and Seoul established diplomatic relations in 1992. Before 1992, the Chinese market was indirectly penetrated through Hong Kong because the Korean government strictly regulated business investment in China. As a result, Samsung's market presence was far behind that of the Japanese electronics companies. Furthermore, prior to the establishment

---

EXHIBIT 5   Color TV Market Share and Price Position in the U.S.

Company (Brand Name)	Market Share (1) (%)	Overall Price Position (2)
Thomson (RCA / GE)	21	72/65
North America Philips (Magnavox)	14	70
Zenith (Zenith)	13	75
Sony (Sony)	7	80
Sharp (Sharp)	6	69
Emerson (Emerson)	5	64
Sanyo Fisher (Sanyo)	5	69
Toshiba (Toshiba)	5	73
Matsushita (Panasonic / JVC)	4	72/73
Mitsubishi (Mitsubishi)	3	75
Samsung (Samsung)	3	67
LG (LG)	2	61
Others	12	

Note: 1. Market shares shown are based on 25.2 million units shipped in 1995.

2. Ratings are based on a scale of 0 to 100.

3. According to 1996 report of US Bureau of Census, population and households are 265 and 98 million, respectively.

Source: Robert Lanich, Market Share Reporter—1997, Gale, New York, 1997. Gale Research Inc., *Consumer Product and Manufacturer Ratings,* Detroit, 1994.

EXHIBIT 6   Comparison of Advertising Expenses among Major Electronics Firms in the U.S. Market (1968–94)

Brand	Cumulative Advertising Expenses (US$ million)
Sony	522
Matsushita (Panasonic)	413
Sharp	278
Samsung	27

Source: Media Watch.

---

of SCH in 1995, Samsung's focus was on investment in production facilities all over China rather than marketing its own products in China. That was because the Chinese government strongly encouraged foreign companies in China to focus on exports rather than the domestic market.

In 1995, Samsung established SCH in Beijing to coordinate the more than 16 operations, each of which had been separately managed by the various business units of the Samsung Group. SCH would be responsible for coordinating all development, production, logistics, and marketing in China, most of which had previously been done in Seoul. SCH would also formulate the overall marketing strategy for China, in place of separate plans from each

EXHIBIT 7   **The Comparison between Quality and Price**

20" Color TV - 1995

Brand Name	Quality Index	Average Retail Price (US$)
Sharp20-FM100	86	235
ZenithSMS2049S	83	235
RCAF20602SE	82	235
ZenithSMS1935S	82	225
GE20GT324	81	215
SamsungTTB-2012	**80**	**210**
SonyKV-20M10	79	290
SanyoAVM-2004	75	210
ZenithSMS1917GS	70	210
PanasonicCT-20R11	68	260
EmersonTC1972A	59	185

27" Color TV - 1995

Brand Name	Quality Index	Average Retail Price (US$)
PanasonicCT-27SF11	95	650
SamsungTXB2735	**94**	**430**
SonyKV-2756	93	740
ToshibaCF27D50	93	555
JVCAV-27BP5	90	615
MitsubishiCS-27303	89	635
ToshibaCX27D60	89	630
RCAF27701BK	87	605
MagnavoxTP2790 B101	86	565
RCAF27701BK	86	535
ZenithSM2789BT	85	620
GoldstarGCT2754S	83	405
SonyKV-27V10	82	615
PanasonicCT-27S18	79	590
SanyoAVM-2754	79	380
GE27GTR618	78	400
ZenithS2773BT	75	520

Source: *Consumer Reports*, 1995.

business unit headquarters in Seoul. The establishment of SCH would enhance Samsung's insider image in China because it showed Samsung's commitment to the Chinese market. The SCH would also speed up the accumulation of local knowledge of the market which had been acquired by each business unit. In April 1995 when Lee Kun-Hee, chairman of Samsung (the largest non-Japanese conglomerate in Asia with US$ 54 billion in sales), visited Beijing, he announced that the Samsung Group would invest an additional US$ 4 billion in China by the year 2000. Exhibit 9 shows the relationship of SCH to other business units in the Samsung Group and Exhibit 10 shows the organization chart of SCH.

EXHIBIT 8   Samsung Business Group's Production Facilities in China

Business Unit of Samsung Group	Location	Equity Position	Products	Investment Startup	Operation Startup
Samsung Electronics Co., Ltd.	Huizhou	90 %	Audio system	Aug. 1992	Jul. 1993
	Tianjin	50 %	VCR	Feb. 1993	Jun. 1993
	Standing, Weihai	62 %	Telecommunication switching system	Aug. 1993	Sep. 1993
	Guangdong	90 %	Compact disk player	Sep. 1993	
	Tianjin	50 %	CTV	Jun. 1994	Jan. 1995
	Suzhou	100 %	Semiconductor assembly	Dec. 1994	Jul. 1996
	Suzhou complex	80 %	Refrigerator Microwave oven Washing machine Air conditioner	Jul. 1995	Sep. 1996
Samsung Aerospace Industries Co., Ltd.	Tianjin	55 %	Camera	Feb. 1994	
Samsung Corning Co., Ltd.	Tianjin	100 %	Head drum for VTR	Apr. 1992	
Samsung Electro-Mechanics Co., Ltd.	Tianjin	91 %	Electronic components for TV	Dec. 1993	
	Tianjin	91 %	Assembly metal	Dec. 1995	
	Guangdong	100 %	Speaker, Deck, Keyboard.	Jul. 1992	
	Guangdong	100 %	Assembly metal	Dec. 1995	

Source: Company data.

Options and Controversies

Mr. Chung, who was responsible for coordinating Samsung's business units in China, had proposed that Samsung introduce the high-end color TV first in order to position Samsung as a premium product producer. His argument for prioritizing a premium brand image was aligned with Samsung Group's recent commitment to its higher quality image. However, the idea had been met with skepticism from Samsung's Seoul headquarters. Many in Seoul questioned the idea of introducing a high-end product in a market with annual per capita income levels of US\$ 353. China was stereotyped in Seoul as the land of "subsistence-level peasants, mystic sages on mountaintops, Chairman Mao's "Little Red Book", 89-year-old Deng Xiaoping and the events in Tiananmen Square."

Many in Samsung Electronics supported the low-end market strategy. It emphasized that the low-end market segment was still the largest market segment in China. It also pointed to the relatively faster growth in sales of small and medium-sized product lines. Moreover, it was argued that the Samsung brand could compete effectively with local TV manufacturers better than Japanese TV manufacturers. They asserted that these markets, where the largest demand existed, should be targeted.

EXHIBIT 9   Organization Chart of Samsung Business Group

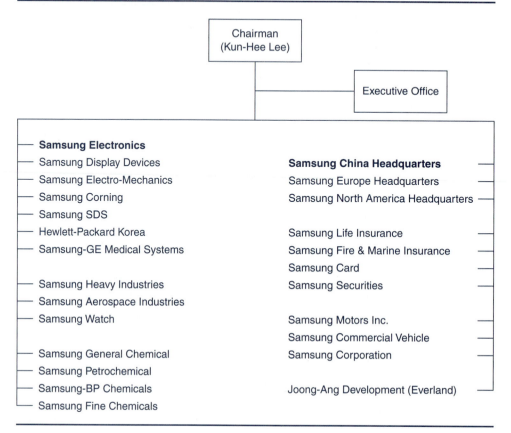

Source: Company data.

Moreover, a premium-priced product would not sell in large volumes in the Chinese market, it was argued. Some of the Seoul-based people in Samsung Electronics, which was supposed to supply SCH with color TVs, were more interested in sales volume. Because Korean consumer electronics firms had invested in production capacities which far exceeded the domestic market size to realize scale economies, they had a high fixed cost. This led to a volume business-oriented strategy necessary to achieve break-even. In fact, the consumer electronics industry, including color TVs, was recognized as a global industry where scale economies in product development and manufacturing, rather than responsiveness to national market demands, were considered key success factors.

However, Mr. Chung thought that if Samsung did not establish a strong brand image in China, it would have to lower prices to offset the Japanese high brand image. In fact, Japanese firms that had a high quality brand reputation commanded a high price in both China and North America. Moreover, Japanese consumer electronics products which were produced in Southeast Asia were as competitive in terms of price as Korean consumer

EXHIBIT 10   Organization Chart of Samsung China Headquarters

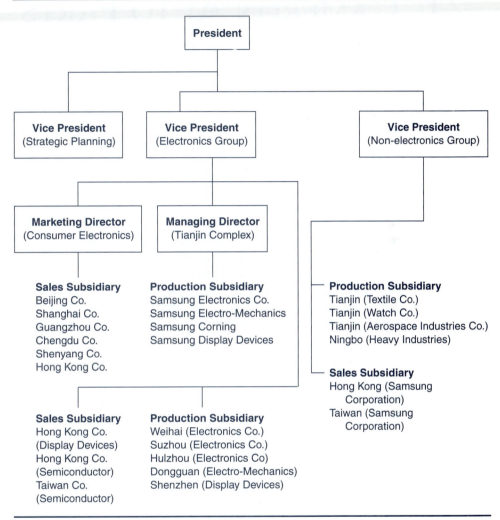

Source: Company data.

electronics products which were produced in Korea and Southeast Asia. Therefore, Mr. Chung thought, " if we do not build up a brand image equivalent to that of Japanese firms, we could not compete in China as well as in North America in the near future". Mr. Chung also thought that China was not going to stay in the low-end market even though the low-end market was currently the largest one. The product line Mr. Chung wanted to introduce to China was the latest 29" model which had recent success in Korea. Mr. Chung wanted to present to the people in Seoul a clear reason why Samsung China should start with high-end products rather than low-end products.

21   CAMERON AUTO PARTS (A)—REVISED

Alex Cameron's first years in business were unusually harsh and turbulent. He graduated from a leading Michigan business school in 1991 when the American economy was just edging out of recession. It was not that Alex had difficulty finding a job, however; it was that he took over the reins of the family business. His father timed his retirement to coincide with Alex's graduation and left him with the unenviable task of cutting back the workforce to match the severe sales declines the company was experiencing.

History

Cameron Auto Parts was founded in 1965 by Alex's father to seize opportunities created by the signing of the Auto Pact between Canada and the United States. The Auto Pact permitted the Big Three automotive manufacturers to ship cars, trucks, and original equipment (OEM) parts between Canada and the United States tariff free, as long as they maintained auto assembly facilities on both sides of the border. The Pact had been very successful with the result that a lot of auto parts firms sprang up in Canada to supply the Big Three. Cameron Auto Parts prospered in this environment until, by 1989, sales had reached $60 million with profits of $1.75 million. The product focus was largely on small engine parts and auto accessories such as oil and air filters, fan belts, and wiper blades, all sold as original equipment under the Auto Pact.

IVEY   Professor Harold Crookell prepared this case solely to provide material for class discussion. Revised by Professor Paul Beamish. The author does not intend to illustrate either effective or ineffective handling of a managerial situation. The author may have disguised certain names and other identifying information to protect confidentiality. Ivey Management Services prohibits any form of reproduction, storage or transmittal without its written permission. This material is not covered under authorization from CanCopy or any reproduction rights organization. Copyright © 1996, Ivey Management Services.

When Alex took over in 1991, the company's financial position was precarious. Sales in 1990 dropped to $48 million and for the first six months of 1991 to $18 million. Not only were car sales declining in North America, but the Japanese were taking an increasing share of the market. As a result, the major North American auto producers were frantically trying to advance their technology and to lower their prices at the same time. It was not a good year to be one of their suppliers. In 1990, Cameron Auto Parts lost $2.5 million, and had lost the same amount again in the first six months of 1991. Pressure for modernization and cost reduction had required close to $4 million in new investment in equipment and computer-assisted design and manufacturing systems. As a result, the company had taken up over $10 million of its $12 million line of bank credit at an interest rate which stood at 9.5 percent in 1991.

Alex's first six months in the business were spent in what he later referred to as "operation survival". There was not much he could do about working capital management, as both inventory and receivables were kept relatively low via contract arrangements with the Big Three. Marketing costs were negligible. Where costs had to be cut were in production and, specifically, in people, many of whom had been with the company for over 15 years and were personal friends of Alex's father. Nevertheless, by the end of 1991, the workforce had been cut from 720 to 470, the losses had been stemmed and the company saved from almost certain bankruptcy. Having to be the hatchet man, however, left an indelible impression on Alex. As things began to pick up during 1992 and 1993, he added as few permanent workers as possible, relying instead on overtime, part-timers or subcontracting.

Recovery and Diversification

For Cameron Auto Parts, the year 1991 ended with sales of $38 million and losses of $3.5 million (see Exhibit 1). Sales began to pick up in 1992 reaching $45 million by year-end with a small profit. By mid-1993, it was clear that the recovery was well under way. Alex, however, while welcoming the turnaround, was suspicious of the basis for it. Cameron's own sales hit $27 million in the first six months of 1993 and company profits were over $2 million. The Canadian dollar had dropped as low as 73 cents in terms of U.S. currency, and Cameron was faced with more aggressive competition from Canadian parts manufacturers. While the short-term future for Cameron seemed distinctly positive, the popularity of Japanese cars left Alex feeling vulnerable to continued total dependence on the volatile automotive industry. Diversification was on his mind as early as 1991. He had an ambition to take the company public by 1997, and diversification was an important part of that ambition.

Unfortunately, working as an OEM parts supplier to the automotive industry did little to prepare Cameron to become more innovative. The auto industry tended to standardize its parts requirements to the point that Cameron's products were made to precise industry specifications and consequently did not find a ready market outside the industry. Without a major product innovation it appeared that Cameron's dependence on the Big Three was likely to continue. Furthermore, the company had developed no "in-house" design and engineering strength from which to launch an attempt at new product development.

EXHIBIT 1

INCOME STATEMENTS
FOR YEARS ENDED DECEMBER 31, 1991, 1992, 1993
($000's)

	1991	*1992*	*1993*
Net Sales	$38,150	$45,200	$67,875
Cost of goods sold:			
Direct materials	6,750	8,050	12,400
Direct labor	12,900	10,550	12,875
Overheads (including depreciation)	16,450	19,650	27,600
Total	36,100	38,250	52,875
Gross Profit	2,050	6,950	15,000
Expenses			
Selling and administration			
(includes design team)	3,150	3,800	6,200
Other (includes interest)	2,400	2,900	3,000
Total	5,500	6,700	9,200
Net Profit before Tax	(3,500)	250	5,800
Income Tax	(500)	0	200
Net Profit after Tax	$(3,000)	$ 250	$5,600

Note: Alex expected total sales to reach $85 million in 1994 with profits before tax of $10 million. Flexible couplings were expected to contribute sales of $30 million and profits of $5 million on assets of $12 million.

Because product specifications had always come down in detail from the Big Three, Cameron had never needed to design and develop its own products and had never hired any design engineers.

In the midst of "operation survival" in mid-1991, Alex boldly decided to do something about diversification. He personally brought in a team of four design engineers and instructed them to concentrate on developing products related to the existing line but with a wider "non-automotive" market appeal. Their first year together showed little positive progress, and the question of whether to fund the team for another year (estimated budget $425,000) came to the management group:

> *Alex:* Maybe we just expected too much in the first year. They did come up with the flexible coupling idea, but you didn't seem to encourage them, Andy (production manager).
>
> *Andy McIntyre:* That's right! They had no idea at all how to produce such a thing in our facilities. Just a lot of ideas about how it could be used. When I told them a Canadian outfit was already producing them, the team sort of lost interest.
>
> *John Ellis (Finance):* We might as well face the fact that we made a mistake, and cut it off before we sink any more money into it. This is hardly the time for unnecessary risks.

Alex: Why don't we shorten the whole process by getting a production licence from the Canadian firm? We could start out that way and then build up our own technology over time.

Andy: The team looked into that, but it turned out the Canadians already have a subsidiary operating in United States—not too well from what I can gather—and they are not anxious to licence anyone to compete with it.

Alex: Is the product patented?

Andy: Yes, but apparently it doesn't have long to run.

At this point a set of ideas began to form in Alex's mind, and in a matter of months he had lured away a key engineer from the Canadian firm with an $110,000 salary offer and put him in charge of the product development team. By mid-1993, the company had developed its own line of flexible couplings with an advanced design and an efficient production process using the latest in production equipment. Looking back, in retrospect, Alex commented:

> We were very fortunate in the speed with which we got things done. Even then the project as a whole had cost us close to $1 million in salaries and related costs.

Marketing the New Product

Alex continued:

> We then faced a very difficult set of problems, because of uncertainties in the market place. We knew there was a good market for the flexible type of coupling because of its wide application across so many different industries. But, we didn't know how big the market was nor how much of it we could secure. This meant we weren't sure what volume to tool up for, what kind or size of equipment to purchase, or how to go about the marketing job. We were tempted to start small and grow as our share of market grew, but this could be costly too and could allow too much time for competitive response. Our Canadian engineer was very helpful here. He had a lot of confidence in our product and had seen it marketed in both Canada and the United States. At his suggestion we tooled up for a sales estimate of $30 million—which was pretty daring. In addition, we hired eight field sales representatives to back up the nationwide distributor and soon afterwards hired several Canadian-based sales representatives to cover major markets. We found that our key Canadian competitor was pricing rather high and had not cultivated very friendly customer relations. We were able to pay the modest (and declining) Canadian tariffs and still come in at, or slightly below, his prices. We were surprised how quickly we were able to secure significant penetration into the Canadian market. It just wasn't being well-serviced.

During 1993, the company actually spent a total of $2.5 million on equipment for flexible coupling production. In addition, a fixed commitment of $1.5 million a year in marketing expenditures on flexible couplings arose from the hiring of sales representatives. A small amount of trade advertising was included in this sum. The total commitment represented a significant part of the company's resources and threatened serious damage to the company's financial position if the sales failed to materialize. "It was quite a gamble at the time," Alex added. " By the end of 1993, it was clear that the gamble was going to pay off."

Sales by Market Sector ($millions)

	OEM Parts Sales	Flexible Couplings Sales	Total Sales	After Tax Profits
1989	60	Nil	60	1.75
1990	48	Nil	48	(2.50)
1991	38	Nil	38	(3.50)
1992	45	Nil	45	.25
1993	58	10 (six months)	68	5.80

Cameron's approach to competition in flexible couplings was to stress product quality, service, and speed of delivery, but not price. Certain sizes of couplings were priced slightly below the competition but others were not. In the words of one Cameron sales representative:

> Our job is really a technical function. Certainly, we help predispose the customer to buy and we'll even take orders, but we put them through our distributors. Flexible couplings can be used in almost all areas of secondary industry, by both large and small firms. This is why we need a large distributor with wide reach in the market. What we do is give our product the kind of emphasis a distributor can't give. We develop relationships with key buyers in most major industries, and we work with them to keep abreast of new potential uses for our product, or of changes in size requirements or other performance characteristics. Then we feed this kind of information back to our design group. We meet with the design group quite often to find out what new types of couplings are being developed and what the intended uses are, etc. Sometimes they help us solve a customer's problem. Of course, these "solutions" are usually built around the use of one of our products.

Financing Plant Capacity

When Alex first set his diversification plans in motion in 1991, the company's plant in suburban Detroit was operating at 50 percent capacity. However, by early 1994, sales of auto parts had recovered almost to 1989 levels and the flexible coupling line was squeezed for space. Andy McIntyre put the problem this way:

> I don't see how we can get sales of more than $85 million out of this plant without going to a permanent two-shift system, which Alex doesn't want to do. With two full shifts we could probably reach sales of $125 million. The problem is that both our product lines are growing very quickly. Auto parts could easily hit $80 million on their own this year, and flexible couplings! Well, who would have thought we'd sell $10 million in the first six months? Our salespeople are looking for $35–40 million during 1994. It's wild! We just have to have more capacity.
>
> There are two problems pressing us to consider putting flexible couplings under a different roof. The first is internal: we are making more and more types and sizes, and sales are growing to such a point that we may be able to produce more efficiently in a separate facility. The second is external: The Big Three like to tour our plant regularly and tell us how to make auto parts cheaper. Having these flexible couplings all over the place seems to upset them, because they

have trouble determining how much of our costs belong to Auto Parts. If it were left to me I'd just let them be upset, but Alex feels differently. He's afraid of losing orders. Sometimes I wonder if he's right. Maybe we should lose a few orders to the Big Three and fill up the plant with our own product instead of expanding.

Flexible couplings were produced on a batch basis and there were considerable savings involved as batches got larger. Thus as sales grew, and inventory requirements made large batches possible, unit production costs decreased, sometimes substantially. Mr. McIntyre estimated that unit production costs would decline by some 20 percent as annual sales climbed from $20 million to $100 million, and by a further 10 percent at $250 million. Scale economies beyond sales of $250 million were not expected to be significant.

John Ellis, the company's financial manager, expressed his own reservations about new plant expansion from a cash flow perspective:

> We really don't have the balance sheet (Exhibit 2) ready for major plant expansion yet. I think we should grow more slowly and safely for two more years and pay off our debts. If we could hold sales at $75 million for 1994 and $85 million for 1995, we would be able to put ourselves in a much stronger financial position. The problem is that people only look at the profits. They don't realize that every dollar of flexible coupling sales requires an investment in inventory and receivables of about 30 cents. It's not like selling to the Big Three. You have to manufacture to inventory and then wait for payment from a variety of sources.
>
> As it is, Alex wants to invest $10 million in new plant and equipment right away to allow flexible coupling sales to grow as fast as the market will allow. We have the space on our existing site to add a separate plant for flexible couplings. It's the money I worry about.

Foreign Markets

As the company's market position in North America began to improve, Alex began to wonder about foreign markets. The company had always been a major exporter to Canada, but it had never had to market there. The Big Three placed their orders often a year or two in advance, and Cameron just supplied them. As Alex put it:

> It was different with the flexible coupling. We had to find our own way into the market. We did, however, start getting orders from Europe and South America, at first from the subsidiaries of our U.S. customers and then from a few other firms as word got around. We got $40,000 in orders during 1993 and the same amount during the first four months of 1994. This was a time when we were frantically busy and hopelessly understaffed in the management area, so all we did was fill the orders on an FOB, Detroit, basis. The customers had to pay import duties of 5 percent into most European countries (and a value added tax of about 20 percent) and 20–50 percent into South America, on top of the freight and insurance, and still orders came in.

Seeing the potential in Europe, Alex promptly took an European patent from the European Patent Office in the U.K. The cost of the whole process was $30,000. The European Patent Office (EPO) headquartered in Munich, Germany, received more than 50,000 patent applications each year. Since the EPO opened in 1978, additional countries had joined the EPO, often in step with joining the European Economic Community, now known as the European Union (EU). However, the EPO was not part of the EU; rather it was an autonomous

EXHIBIT 2

BALANCE SHEETS
FOR YEARS ENDED DECEMBER 31, 1991, 1992, 1993
($000's)

	1991	1992	1993
Assets			
Cash	$ 615	$ 430	$ 400
Accounts Receivable	5,850	6,850	10,400
Inventories	4,995	4,920	7,500
Total Current Assets	11,460	12,200	18,300
Property, Plant and Equipment (net)	10,790	11,800	13,000
Total Assets	22,250	24,000	31,300
Liabilities			
Accounts Payable	4,850	5,900	9,500
Bank Loan	11,500	12,000	10,000
Accrued Items (including taxes)	450	400	500
Total Current Liabilities	16,800	18,300	20,000
Common Stock (Held by Cameron family)	500	500	500
Retained Earnings	4,950	5,200	10,800
Total Equity	5,450	5,700	11,300
Total Liabilities	$22,250	$24,000	$31,300

organization. The current 17 member states of the EPO are Austria, Belgium, Denmark, Finland, France, Germany, Greece, Ireland, Italy, Luxembourg, Monaco, Netherlands, Portugal, Spain, Sweden, Switzerland (including Liechtenstein), and United Kingdom. The official filing fees, although high, were much less than the fees which would be encountered by filing separate patent applications before the individual national patent offices.

A Licensing Opportunity

In the spring of 1994, Alex made a vacation trip to Scotland and decided while he was there to drop in on one of the company's new foreign customers, McTaggart Supplies Ltd. Cameron Auto Parts had received unsolicited orders from overseas amounting to $40,000 in the first four months of 1994, and over 10 percent of these had come from McTaggart. Alex was pleasantly surprised at the reception given to him by Sandy McTaggart, the 60-year-old head of the company.

> *Sandy:* Come in! Talk of the devil. We were just saying what a shame it is you don't make those flexible couplings in this part of the world. There's a very good market for them. Why my men can even sell them to the English!
>
> *Alex:* Well, we're delighted to supply your needs. I think we've always shipped your orders promptly, and I don't see why we can't continue . . .

Sandy: That's not the point, laddie! That's not the point! Those orders are already sold before we place them. The point is we can't really build the market here on the basis of shipments from America. There's a 5 percent tariff coming in, freight and insurance cost us another 10 percent on top of your price, then there's the matter of currency values. I get my orders in pounds (£)[1] but I have to pay you in dollars. And on top of all that, I never know how long the goods will take to get here, especially with all the dock strikes we have to put up with. Listen, why don't you license us to produce flexible couplings here?

After a lengthy bargaining session, during which Alex secured the information shown in Exhibit 3, he came round to the view that a license agreement with McTaggart might be a good way of achieving swift penetration of the U.K. market via McTaggart's sales force. McTaggart's production skills were not as up-to-date as Cameron's, but his plant showed evidence of a lot of original ideas to keep manufacturing costs down. Furthermore, the firm seemed committed enough to invest in some new equipment and to put a major effort into developing the U.K. market. At this point the two executives began to discuss specific terms of the license arrangements:

Alex: Let's talk about price. I think a figure around 3 percent of your sales of flexible couplings would be about right.
Sandy: That's a bit high for an industrial license of this kind. I think 1½ percent is more normal.
Alex: That may be, but we're going to be providing more than just blueprints. We'll have to help you choose equipment and train your operators as well.
Sandy: Aye, so you will. But we'll pay you for that separately. It's going to cost us £500,000 in special equipment as it is, plus, let's say, a $100,000 fee to you to help set things up. Now you have to give us a chance to price competitively in the market, or neither of us will benefit. With a royalty of 1½ percent I reckon we could reach sales of £500,000 in our first year and £1 million in our second.
Alex: The equipment will let you produce up to £4 million of annual output. Surely you can sell more than a million. We're getting unsolicited orders without even trying.
Sandy: With the right kind of incentive, we might do a lot better. Why don't we agree to a royalty of 2½ percent on the first million in sales and 1½ percent after that. Now mind you, we're to become exclusive agents for the U.K. market. We'll supply your present customers from our own plant.
Alex: But just in the U.K.! Now 2 percent is as low as I'm prepared to go. You make those figures 3 percent and 2 percent and you have a deal. But it has to include a free technology flow-back clause in the event you make any improvements or adaptations to our manufacturing process.
Sandy: You drive a hard bargain! But it's your product, and we do want it. I'll have our lawyers draw up a contract accordingly. What do you say to a five year deal, renewable for another five if we are both happy?
Alex: Sounds good. Let's do it.

---

[1]One pound was equivalent to US $1.50 in 1994.

EXHIBIT 3   Data on McTaggart Supplies Ltd.

1993 sales   £35 million (down from £44 million in 1991).

Total assets   £11 million: Equity £6.5 million.

Net profit after tax   ±£1.5 million.

Control   McTaggart Family.

Market coverage   15 sales representatives in U.K., 2 in Europe, 1 in Australia, 1 in New Zealand, 1 in India.

Average factory   £5.00 per hour (which is below the UK mean of £6.70 due to the factory being
wage rate   located in a depressed area (versus $11.70 in America).

Factory   Old and larger than necessary. Some very imaginative manufacturing know-how in evidence.

Reputation   Excellent credit record, business now 130 years old, good market contacts (high calibre sales force).

Other   Company sales took a beating during 1991–92 as one of the company's staple products was badly hurt by a U.S. product of superior technology. Company filled out its line by distributing products obtained from other manufacturers. Currently about one-half of company sales are purchased from others. Company has capacity to increase production substantially.

Pricing	*Index*
Cameron's price to McTaggart	100
(same as net price to distributor in America)	
+ Import duty	4
+ Freight and insurance	11
Importer's Cost	115
+ Distributor's (McTaggart's) margin (30%)	35
+ Value-added tax (17.5% on cost plus margin)	26
= Price charged by McTaggart	176
vs. Price charged by American distributor in U.S.	120

Note: Under the European Union agreement, all imports from non-EU countries were subject to common external tariffs (CET). In 1994, the CET for the flexible coupling had an import duty of 4 percent. (It was expected that with the GATT agreement, CET would be totally abolished by 2000 AD.) In addition to the import duty, all imported items were subjected to the value-added tax (VAT) which was applied on all manufactured goods—for both imported as well as locally made. The VAT was going through a harmonization process but it was expected to take some years before a common VAT system was in place. As of 1994, the VAT for United Kingdom was 17.5 percent, and France 20.6 percent. Sweden had the highest VAT at 25 percent.

Alex signed the contract the same week and then headed back to America to break the news. He travelled with mixed feelings, however. On the one hand, he felt he had got the better of Sandy McTaggart in the bargaining, while on the other, he felt he had no objective yardstick against which to evaluate the royalty rate he had agreed on. This was pretty much the way he presented the situation to his executive group when he got home.

Alex: . . . so I think it's a good contract, and I have a cheque here for $100,000 to cover our costs in helping McTaggart get set up.

John: We can certainly use the cash right now. And there doesn't seem to be any risk (finance) involved. I like the idea, Alex.

Andy: Well, I don't. And Chuck (head of the Cameron design team) won't either when (production) he hears about it. I think you've sold out the whole U.K. market for a pittance. I thought you wanted to capture foreign markets directly.

Alex: But Andy, we just don't have the resources to capture foreign markets ourselves. We might as well get what we can through licensing, now that we've patented our process.

Andy: Well, maybe. But I don't like it. It's the thin edge of the wedge if you ask me. Our know-how on the production of this product is pretty special, and it's getting better all the time. I hate to hand it over to old McTaggart on a silver platter. I reckon we're going to sell over $20 million in flexible couplings in the United States alone during 1994.

22 HUSH PUPPIES CHILE

In July 1992, Ricardo Swett, age 50, could look back on a decade of exceptional growth of his family-owned Hush Puppies line of casual shoes and retail outlets in Chile. Unlike the parent company, which had experienced serious difficulties in the 1980s, Hush Puppies in Chile had seen profits climb and sales explode by an average of 30 percent per year since 1985. By emphasizing excellence in design and by developing a chain of upscale retail shoe stores as well as an efficient factory, Hush Puppies had become the favorite brand of upper-class Chilean men. Expansion into women's and children's shoes during the last three years had also been successfully implemented.

As the company's market position in Chile soared, Ricardo Swett, who served as general manager of Hush Puppies in Chile, began to contemplate further expansion in other Latin American markets. The company had recently established a limited presence in Uruguay, Bolivia and Paraguay and was beginning to enter Argentina with its line of Brooks athletic shoes. Ricardo was uncertain how fast the company should expand in these countries or whether efforts should be focused instead on promoting exports to North America or on consolidating the company's market position in Chile. Ricardo was also wondering about expanding into other retailing concepts in Chile including athletic and outdoor clothing stores as well as children's shoes and apparel. In contemplating how and when to proceed, Ricardo recognized that key family members were waiting for a recommendation.

Company Background

Hush Puppies Chile began operations in 1980 through the concerted efforts of three brothers, Alfonso, Ricardo, and Juan Pablo Swett. In the early 1960s, the three brothers formed NORSEG, a start-up company that supplied safety equipment to industrial and mining sites throughout Chile. With rising sales and a healthy cash flow, the brothers gradually expanded operations to include real estate development, several agricultural projects and a 10 percent equity position in Elecmetal S.A., one of the largest industrial companies in Chile. Over time, these operations were organized as separate companies under the family-owned Costanera S.A.C.I. Holding Co.

Wolverine World Wide

In the spring of 1979, the three Swett brothers were informed by their advertising agency, Veritas Ltd., that Wolverine World Wide was interested in expanding into Chile. Wolverine, based in Rockford, Michigan, controlled a portfolio of footwear brands including Hush Puppies casual shoes, Wolverine work and outdoor boots, Bates uniform shoes, and Brooks athletic shoes. Incorporated in 1954, Wolverine traced much of its initial success in footwear markets to its reliance on the production of casual pigskin shoes. In the mid-1950s, Wolverine developed a new elaborate pigskin tannage technology to take advantage of the characteristics of fine grain pigskin and in 1958 introduced Hush Puppies casual pigskin shoes.

During the 1960s and 1970s, Hush Puppies emerged as a major brand with particular strength in the men's segment. The infamous basset hound became a widely recognized symbol for quality and comfort. Success in the U.S. was followed by international expansion, initially in Canada and Europe. In the early 1980s, spurred by fears that the U.S. government might lift import quotas on low cost shoes from the Far East and Latin America, Wolverine moved to accelerate its international expansion. By 1992, Wolverine World Wide had established joint ventures or licensing agreements in over 40 countries including most of Europe, Japan, and South America.

In Chile, Wolverine was looking for an agent to import or manufacture Hush Puppies brand shoes under license. In response to Wolverine's initiatives, the Swett brothers commissioned market research studies which revealed that the Chilean shoe market was dominated by formal, dressy products and that no companies effectively met the demand for casual shoes. The market research also indicated that Bata, a large Canadian-owned shoe company with worldwide operations, controlled an estimated 60 percent market share in Chile. Bata Chile operated primarily as a manufacturing company which sold the bulk of its output to small independent stores throughout the country. Independent retailers had considerable power over manufacturers in controlling which brands to promote and which styles to display. Bata also operated several dozen of its own retail stores throughout Chile and was rumored to be considering further expansion.

Like most Chileans, Ricardo, Alfonso and Juan Pablo believed that the open market of 1980 provided an ideal opportunity to start a new business. The brothers were particularly interested in the upper class market in Chile which, by exposure through international travel, was familiar with the Hush Puppies brand, quality and unique designs. Wolverine World Wide also appeared to be an open company; its managers were supportive and personable. The brothers agreed that any venture with Wolverine would succeed.

A Move to Retailing

In working with Wolverine, the brothers decided early on that retailing provided the best option for getting Hush Puppies into Chile. According to Renato Figueroa, Commercial Manager of Hush Puppies Chile in 1980.

> Manufacturers risked their efforts, their capital and their futures, while the retailers had control of the market. . . . Retailers treated all brands alike, not giving special treatment to any brand in particular. [We came to the conclusion that] the best way was to build our own store chain. . . . Our decision was based on the notion that we would be able to influence and handle the market. We would know our consumers. This would enable us to place Hush Puppies in a different position from the rest of the competition in Chile.

After negotiations with Wolverine, Hush Puppies Chile was given exclusive rights to import Hush Puppies shoes and develop retail outlets in Chile. Although no up-front fees were paid to Wolverine, the brothers committed to opening as many as 25 retail stores within three years. Expectations were that the costs for the first five stores, including leasehold improvements, training, inventories, and so on, would total about $2.0 million. Of this amount, about $1.0 million would be borrowed. The remaining $1.0 million represented a substantial risk to the brothers.

As agreed, stores were designed as family concept outlets in which both parents and children could find comfortable, casual shoes. The best Hush Puppies shoes would be imported from around the world with about 80 percent coming from the U.S. The target market was identified as high income consumers representing the ABC_1 market (top 10 percent of wage earners) in Chile. Given the stratification of wealth in Chile, these consumers compared favorably with upper-middle and upper class U.S. consumers. However, a major difference was that wealthy American consumers were generally not targeted by Hush Puppies in the United States.

Stores were situated in large, convenient locations primarily in the Santiago metropolitan area. The sales staff was extensively trained to better relate to the upscale customers and were well compensated, reflecting the desire for continuity and professionalism. Shoe prices were set at a 10 percent premium over average shoe prices and were the same in every store. In distant locations in Chile, the plan was for Hush Puppies Chile to grant franchises to independent retailers. As agreed upon by the brothers, Ricardo assumed responsibility as the general manager of Hush Puppies Chile. Juan Pablo Swett assumed responsibility as the general manager of NORSEG Chile. Alfonso was involved in major investment decisions and strategic planning for all family owned businesses as well as some day-to-day decision making at Hush Puppies Chile. By early 1982, Hush Puppies Chile had established seven shoe stores in the greater Santiago area.

A Move into Manufacturing

After several years of promising economic growth, the bottom fell out of Latin American economies in 1982. Hit by slumping commodity prices, massive national debt, soaring interest rates, and worldwide recession, the Chilean economy, like every other in Latin America, plunged into a state of depression. In Chile, the GNP fell by 14 percent in 1982 alone. Between 1982 and 1985, unemployment officially hovered around 14 percent; unofficially, it surpassed 30 percent. During the same period, the Chilean Peso dropped by 300 percent, leading to a commensurate rise in import costs.

With Hush Puppies Chile totally reliant on imported shoes, the company was devastated by the economic downturn. Only two options appeared possible: shut down in the face of massive losses or move into manufacturing. According to Alfonso and Ricardo,

> We believed in the brand. The consumer liked it. As a result, we had no choice but to get into manufacturing. All our businesses have always been very conservative with low debt load. So we weren't at real risk in the downturn. We saw the business in the long term. Besides, we could get into manufacturing inexpensively as everyone else was getting out, so real estate was cheap.

In April 1982, the decision was made to move Hush Puppies Chile into shoe manufacturing. In November 1982, a partnership was formed between Wolverine World Wide and Hush Puppies Chile with 70 percent of the manufacturing joint venture owned by Hush Puppies Chile and 30 percent owned by Wolverine. Both partners agreed to contribute representative amounts of capital to ensure that manufacturing output met growth targets.

From Wolverine's perspective, a manufacturing facility in Chile made sense for a number of reasons. In 1981, import quotas ended in the U.S. and Wolverine moved aggressively to shift production overseas. Under the joint venture agreement with Hush Puppies Chile, Wolverine would have access to a new source of shoes made with low cost Chilean labor. The U.S. company would also receive royalties on Hush Puppies sales as well as benefit from profit sharing from the Chilean production facility. Finally, Wolverine's wholly-owned Puerto Rican affiliate would become an ongoing supplier of some selected components for the Chilean operation.

In February 1983, a small new manufacturing facility was opened in suburban Santiago which included approximately 10,000 square meters of manufacturing capacity, a two story executive office complex and factory retail outlet. Manufacturing, import and export sales were handled by Hush Puppies Chile, Ltd. Retail operations were organized under the separate company name of Commercial Puppies, Ltd.

Hush Puppies Chile and Commercial Puppies were both organized with their own board of directors, which included the three Swett brothers, as well as a small group of trusted, Western-educated managers from the operating companies. Most directors served on two or three boards. Strategic decisions were made at the board level and passed down to the operating company general managers. While both Hush Puppies Chile and Commercial Puppies were recognized as separate companies with their own functional structures, managers worked closely together to coordinate activities.

Rapid Growth

By 1985, the Chilean economy started to turn around and from 1985 to 1990 the company enjoyed rapid growth. In 1985, Hush Puppies added Brooks athletic shoes to fill out its product line. Brooks Athletic Shoes was owned by Wolverine and had benefited in the U.S. by the upsurge in interest in physical fitness. While some of the Brooks shoes were to be manufactured in the Santiago area, most were to be imported from the Far East. It was anticipated that about 70 percent of the Brooks shoes distributed in Chile would be sold to outside retailers; the remaining 30 percent would be sold in Hush Puppies shoe stores.

As overall sales picked up, Hush Puppies Chile and Commercial Puppies focused more on building and maintaining key brands. The objective was to develop a reputation for excellence in marketing by emphasizing advertising, service and style. Feedback from retail stores proved a major strength in focusing design and manufacturing on consumer needs. Hush Puppies Chile managers regarded the company as market oriented as opposed to manufacturing oriented, thus differentiating the company from many Far East suppliers. By the end of 1985, Commercial Puppies was managing 22 company-owned stores and Hush Puppies Chile was supervising four franchise stores.

To strengthen marketing efforts, advertising budgets were expanded, reaching 5 percent of sales in 1987. In 1987, the company started a major advertising program titled "the pleasure of walking" which was particularly appealing to increasingly health conscious upper and upper-middle class Chileans. Follow-up multicolor ads promoting Hush Puppies' line of outdoor casual and hiking boots were placed in major newspapers and top magazines throughout the country (see Exhibit 1). Television advertisements were also developed which focused on Hush Puppies as statements of quality and style. During the late 1980s and early 1990s, Hush Puppies Chile won three annual Wolverine World Wide awards for the quality of its advertising campaign and marketing strategy.

The company's strategy to strengthen the Hush Puppies brand succeeded. By the end of 1987, the production of shoes reached 265,000 pairs, an increase of 18 percent over 1986. In 1988, production increased an additional 15 percent to 305,000 pairs; in 1989, shoe production was up 29 percent to 392,000 pairs. Despite these impressive gains, the company remained relatively weak in two important categories: women's shoes and children's shoes. In an effort to reposition itself in these fast-growing segments, several bold initiatives were undertaken in the late 1980s.

A Move into Women's and Children's Shoes

To strengthen the company's position in the women's shoe market, more effort was devoted to product design and marketing. The women's product manager, Cardina Schmidt, believed that prior to 1990 the women's product line had not adequately satisfied the style and fashion demands of Chilean women. Good design was particularly important in the women's segment in which styles changed nearly every six months. Women in the target segment were particularly fashion conscious and were generally familiar with the newest fashions in Europe and North America.

In order to make Hush Puppies more appealing to women, high fashion shoes were imported from Italy, France, and Argentina. Hush Puppies Chile also hired exclusive

---

**EXHIBIT 1   Sample Advertisement Placed by Hush Puppies Chile in
Major National Magazines**

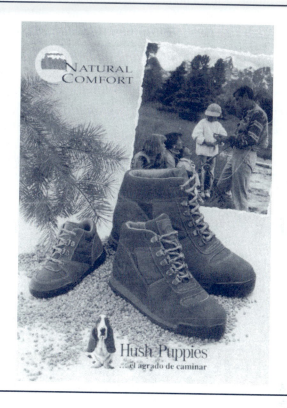

---

designers to develop its own collection of women's shoes. Designers and managers regularly visited Hush Puppies stores to question women on desired design features like colors and styles. New window displays were designed to establish a more stylish image and a major television advertising campaign was launched. As a result of these efforts, sales growth in the women's segment increased dramatically.

During this same period, the company also undertook a major initiative in children's shoes. The history of the company's efforts with children's shoes was reported by Sebastian Swett, a second generation family member and Product Manager for children's shoes,

> Surveys detected great opportunities for us in the children's market. The market was very traditional. It offered old models in brown or white. . . . The market seemed willing to pay a higher price for shoes with aggressive colors and concepts such as comfort and security. . . . We had a few advantages such as the excellent Hush Puppies' image which was attractive for children and easily identified. . . . We also had several disadvantages. Our stores were not appropriate for selling kid's shoes; other competitors had years in the market; [and finally] we didn't have the machinery to develop a great collection for kids up until 12 years in age.

In early 1990, Hush Puppies for Kids was launched, consisting of four different categories which varied according to the age of the child. Soft Puppies shoes were introduced for infants; Little Puppies were designed for children age one to three years; Young Puppies were introduced for children age four to eight years; and finally, Junior Puppies were designed for children age nine to fourteen years. The introduction was accompanied by extensive television advertising. Hush Puppies for Kids was an immediate success.

Strengthening the Athletic Position

By the summer of 1989, Brooks was positioned as the number three brand in the Chilean athletic shoe market after Diadora and Adidas. In the U.S., however, Brooks was a relatively weak brand, a fact not altogether lost on fashion-conscious Chilean adolescents, and L.A. Gear was emerging as the top brand for adolescents. L.A. Gear was a relative new comer in the athletic shoe industry and, to capitalize on its increasing popularity, had begun to search for international distributors. The opportunity to market a more fashionable brand in L.A. Gear was clear and Alfonso approached the company in the summer of 1990.

After considerable discussion, L.A. Gear agreed in the Fall of 1990 to work with Hush Puppies Chile to bring the L.A. Gear brand to Chile. L.A. Gear shoes would be imported from U.S. inventories or directly from the shoes' manufacturers in Korea and China, thus sparing Hush Puppies any manufacturing risks. Hush Puppies Chile's intention was to consolidate the L.A. Gear operations with those of Brooks; however, L.A. Gear insisted that Hush Puppies Chile create a distinct sales company to maximize the brand's potential. Wolverine World Wide was also very concerned about the impact that the L.A. Gear initiative would have on Brooks in Chile. In response, Costanera created Topsport to manage the sale of L.A. Gear. A separate company, Coast Sport, was organized to manage all Brooks sales. It was hoped that creating separate companies for athletic shoes would allow greater focus on Hush Puppies brands as well as encourage new sales initiatives for athletic shoes.

Wolverine's Manufacturing Position is Purchased

In December of 1991, Costanera acquired the 30 percent of Hush Puppies Chile operations owned by Wolverine World Wide. The buyout was prompted by Wolverine's failure to support Hush Puppies Chile's ambitious expansion plans. During late 1989 and 1990, manufacturing facilities were increased over 30 percent in Chile in order to keep pace with booming demand. Plans called for production capacity to be increased by another 20 percent in 1991. New investment requirements in Chile as well as other countries, combined with the need to reinvest profits, translated into a negative cash flow for Wolverine. At the same time, Wolverine was facing changes in the business in the U.S. and was struggling to conserve capital. As a result, a buyout became an attractive option for both parties. The purchase of Wolverine's 30 percent share of manufacturing was estimated to have cost Costanera approximately $3.6 million. With the buyout complete, Hush Puppies Chile changed its name to Forus, S.A. In January 1992, the name of Commercial Puppies was changed to For-Shop, Ltd. Exhibit 2 provides a full organization chart for Costanera Holding.

EXHIBIT 2   Costanera Holding: Organization Chart

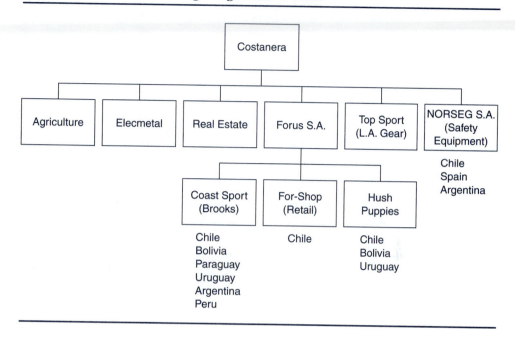

Under the terms of the acquisition, Wolverine extended its licensing agreement to Forus for 20 years. In addition, Forus pushed for and received the rights to manufacture and sell Hush Puppies brands in Bolivia, Paraguay, and Uruguay. Forus was also licensed to sell—but not manufacture—Brooks athletic shoes in Bolivia, Paraguay, Uruguay, Chile, Argentina, and Peru. Outside these countries, sales of Hush Puppies or Brooks brand products could only be made to other Wolverine licensees. For Wolverine, Costanera's program for growth, endorsed by the success obtained in Chile, made it the best company to build sales in Latin America. Increased sales in the region would mean higher royalties to Wolverine as well as an increase in the export of raw materials.

After the buyout, the relationship between Costanera and Wolverine remained strong. Both companies continued to share designs and coordinate product introductions. Forus also remained a major purchaser of leather and leather products as well as Brooks shoes. Exhibit 3 reports the extent of business relations between Forus and Wolverine World Wide over a six-year period.

Broad Market Appeal

By the end of 1991, Forus had succeeded in significantly broadening the market appeal of its Hush Puppies brands. In the ABC_1 men's market, Hush Puppies was number one in market share; in the ABC_1 women's market, Hush Puppies was number five in market share;

EXHIBIT 3   **Business Relations with Wolverine World Wide (thousands of U.S. dollars)**

	Total 1987–91	Projected 1992
Purchases		
Leather and raw material	$ 6,302	$2,000
Hush Puppies finished shoes	557	640
Brooks shoes	3,960	1,400
Total	**$10,819**	**$4,040**
Royalties		
Hush Puppies	$ 1,032	$ 500
Brooks	441	120
Total	**$ 1,473**	**$ 783**

and in the ABC_1's children's market, Hush Puppies was number four in market share. Market mix for the ABC_1 segment and Hush Puppies brand sales ratios on a unit volume basis are included in Exhibit 4.

Growth in Retail Operations

By the end of 1991, total retail sales of Hush Puppies, Brooks and L.A. Gear shoes amounted to 328,000 pairs. About 74 percent of these shoes were sold in 25 company-owned stores. An additional 9 percent of sales was generated through "Hush Puppies Corners" which had been established in shoe departments of 14 major retail department stores. In promoting Hush Puppies Corners, For-Shop agreed to train sales employees and assist in designing and setting up displays. About 10 percent of the company's sales was also generated through small independent retail outlets. Franchise sales represented approximately 7 percent of total retail sales. In 1991, the company had five franchise stores located in isolated cities in Chile. By the summer of 1992, the number of company-owned retail stores in Chile had increased to 26 with four more planned by year-end. Exhibit 5 presents retail sales data for 1990 and 1991, as well as projections for 1992.

International Expansion

Although the Swett brothers were pleased with Hush Puppies' overall growth in Chile, they were constantly reminded of their sense of vulnerability in the early 1980s. Certainly Costanera was a much more balanced company by mid-1992 than it had been 10 years earlier. It had a healthy balance sheet, a portfolio of popular American brand names, improving manufacturing capabilities, world class design skills and substantial marketing expertise.

EXHIBIT 4   ABC$_1$ Segment Mix and Hush Puppy Sales Mix (year end, 1991)

ABC$_1$ Market Mix (%)		Hush Puppies Sales Mix (%)		Hush Puppies Market Share (%)	
Men	24%	Men	46%	Men	30%
Women	47	Women	30	Women	8
Children	29	Children	24	Children	11

EXHIBIT 5   For-Shop: Retail Sales, 1990–1992

	1990	1991	1992[1]
Number of stores	25	25	26
Sales (pairs in 000s):			
H.P. men's	164	188	
H.P. women's	69	74	125
H.P. children's	37	49	61
Sports shoes	31	41	44
Total pairs	289	328	418
Sales (US$000s):			
Total shoes	$8,575	$12,163	$17,260
Total accessories	519	841	1,226
Total	$9,094	$13,004	$18,486
Avg. US$ retail price (pair)	$29.67	$37.08	$41.29
Avg. monthly inventory (pairs 000s)	122	129	158
Annual inventory turnover	2.4	2.5	2.7
Number of employees	154	177	203

[1]1992 sales are estimates.

Note: These figures do not include franchises, department stores, or export sales.

Despite these advantages, Ricardo and several managers began to realize that the depth of Hush Puppies Chile's market penetration, particularly in the ABC$_1$ men's casuals, would lead to increased competition from new European and American brands.

    With these concerns in mind, Ricardo began considering other alternatives for growth. A move into men's dress shoes was rejected because the segment was already highly competitive and because managers at Hush Puppies Chile did not believe that their skill base would provide the company with a significant competitive advantage. However, other opportunities for growth were being seriously studied. These included growth by expanding exports to North America and Europe and growth through product and market diversification in South America.

Export Opportunities—North America

Since it began manufacturing almost 10 years earlier, Hush Puppies Chile had always hoped to develop a strong export business, particularly to North America and Europe. Success in exports seemed likely given Chile's comparative advantage of low-cost labor and Hush Puppies Chile's excellent styling and product-development skills. Hush Puppies Chile's manufacturing labor costs in 1991 averaged $2.00/hr. including all benefits; in neighboring Argentina, wages in the shoe industry averaged from between $2.25 and $2.50 per hour. In addition to being at least comparable in terms of costs, the quality and consistency of Chilean labor was generally regarded as superior to that available in neighboring countries.

From a company perspective, an emphasis on exporting seemed to make sense for two reasons. First, sales to the Northern Hemisphere could potentially offset cyclical sales in the Southern Hemisphere. Forus was typically over capacity in the period leading up to Fall/Winter (February through July) and under capacity in Spring/Summer (August through January). Any additional export sales during the off-season would provide a better utilization of plant and equipment while minimizing fluctuations in employment levels. Second, the additional export sales volume would contribute to ever-increasing manufacturing and new product development overheads, thereby boosting overall profits.

Despite the appeal, exports to North America and Europe remained relatively modest. One problem was that exports from Chile were expected to compete with much lower cost footwear from China, India, and the Philippines. Hush Puppies' domestic target market was also the high-end segment which added design and service costs that negated many of Chile's labor cost advantages. Also, Hush Puppies Chile's very diversified product line increased per-unit production costs through short production runs while at the same time removing opportunities for high volume exports. A final problem was that direct and indirect labor costs represented only about 25 percent of total manufacturing costs, thus limiting the company's ability to pursue a low cost exporting strategy. Because of these difficulties, several managers in the company believed that an export strategy built on superior design and marketing had the most chance to succeed. Others disagreed, arguing that if Hush Puppies Chile was serious about substantially increasing exports to North America and Europe it would have to develop lower priced shoes. Such a move would also open additional mass market opportunities for the company in Chile.

The company had never seriously considered shifting manufacturing to lower cost Asian countries. Difficulties in controlling overseas production and the need to respond to rather fickle customer needs undermined the potential savings of overseas manufacturing. Managers at Hush Puppies Chile also believed the company had no competitive advantage in importing. Estimates for 1992 were that the company would import about $US 3.0 million in raw materials (mostly soles and leathers) and about $US 1.7 million in finished shoes. The U.S. would supply approximately 25 percent of these imports with the rest coming from the Far East, Argentina, Brazil, Italy, Spain, Germany, Mexico, and the U.K.

Opportunities in Latin America

From 1987 to 1991, the average annual sales growth for Forus, For-Shop, and Coast Sport was 20 percent per year. From 1990 to 1991, sales growth accelerated to a staggering 35 percent, encouraged in part by the rapid growth of the Chilean economy. Strict adherence to free markets and free trade had led to booming economic growth in Chile with the economy expanding an average of 6 percent per year from 1987 to 1992. Many economists were predicting GDP growth of 10 percent per annum throughout the remainder of 1992, making Chile one of the fastest growing economies in the world and an engine of economic growth in the region. (For a brief overview of Chile's economic development over the last two decades, see Exhibit 6.)

The company's initiative in Latin America began in earnest in May of 1989 when Hush Puppies Chile began exporting Hush Puppies shoes to Uruguay. With air freight to Uruguay averaging about $US 0.55 per kg., transportation costs appeared favorable for exports. By the end of 1989, the company had sold just over 19,000 pairs of shoes in a country with a population of more than 3 million. In 1990, Hush Puppies Chile granted exclusive franchise rights to the Moliterno family, a diversified industrial company based in the capital city of Montevideo. Moliterno quickly established Hush Puppies Uruguay as a

---

EXHIBIT 6   The Chilean Economy: A Brief Overview

Political polarization under the left wing government of President Salvador Allende (1970–73) brought the country close to a civil war, and ended in September 1973 with a *coup d'état* led by General Augusto Pinochet. During his 17-year rule, Pinochet turned to the writings of free market advocate and Nobel Prize winning economist Milton Friedman to guide national industrial policy. Immediately after seizing power, martial law was imposed, the economy was liberalized and foreign corporations were invited to return to Chile. Pinochet's 1980 blueprint for political democratization was completed on December 14, 1989, when a national plebescite was held and Patricio Alwin, the Christian Democratic leader of a center-left coalition was elected president. He took office on March 11, 1990. While Augusto Pinochet remained commander of the nation's armed forces in mid-1992, the emerging democracy seemed stable and strong to most observers.

The success of Chile's free market reforms after a decade of stagflation and debt crisis amazed many observers. Most economists attributed Chile's enviable economic growth to its unrelenting dedication to free markets. By mid-1992, the bulk of the Chilean left was no longer anti-capitalist, and a remarkable degree of consensus existed in the country about the need to maintain a liberal market economy and prudent fiscal policies. The main dividing issues related to a new labor code granting more rights to unions, and the question of what to do about serious human rights violations that occurred under the Pinochet regime.

Economic Data for Chile, 1983–1991

	1983	1985	1987	1989	1991
GDP ($ billions)	19.8	15.6	18.9	25.4	30.0
Population (millions)	11.7	12.1	12.5	13.0	13.1
GDP per head ($'000)	1,692	1,289	1,512	1,954	2,239
Inflation (%)	23.1	26.4	21.5	21.4	18.7
Unemployment	17.4	10.9	8.0	4.8	5.2
Total debt/GDP (%)	91.9	130.7	109.3	68.4	63.1

Despite its interest in open markets, Chile has shunned involvement in Mercosur, or the free trade zone that neighboring Paraguay, Uruguay, Argentina, and Brazil hoped to have running by 1994. Confident after nine years of stability and growth, Chile in 1992 was aspiring to become the first Latin American country to join the NAFTA. If NAFTA membership were to prove elusive, the government intended to pursue a free trade agreement with Japan, Chile's top export market after the United States.

wholly-owned subsidiary. During 1990, three Hush Puppies retail outlets were opened, two in Montevideo and one in Maldonado.

Despite high ambitions, sales remained weak. Ricardo was convinced that Moliterno, with little experience in retailing, had chosen less than optimal retail locations. Stores were poorly maintained and Moliterno spent essentially nothing on Hush Puppies advertising and promotion. Sales were also hurt by competition from low priced footwear exported by financially strapped manufacturers in Argentina and Brazil.

In the Spring of 1991, Forus purchased 55 percent of Hush Puppies Uruguay. According to Ricardo, Hush Puppies Chile had always wanted to be a partner with Moliterno. The original agreement included an option to buy a majority stake in Hush Puppies Uruguay that Forus decided to exercise. Under the terms of the investment, Forus and Moliterno contributed $US 400,000 to create a new company called Hush Puppies Uruguay S.A., which in turn purchased the Hush Puppies related assets of Moliterno. After gaining effective control over retailing, Hush Puppies Chile moved to strengthen operations. Sales employees received additional training and new store locations were sought out. By the end of 1991, three more Hush Puppies Uruguay stores were opened, bringing to six the total number of Hush Puppies locations in that country.

Essentially no Hush Puppies shoes were exported to Paraguay in 1991 and no changes were planned for 1992. Customs duties on shoes averaged 70 percent in Paraguay but were being slowly cut under pressure from the General Agreement on Tariffs and Trade (GATT) as well as broader initiatives undertaken in creating the Southern Cone Economic Market. Ricardo believed that as the economy opened up in 1993, Forus would begin some modest exports.

In Bolivia, a country of seven million, Forus established a licensing agreement with Global Trading Company of La Paz. Although the agreement had been in place for less than a year, two stores had been opened and Hush Puppies Corners had been set up in two department stores. Ricardo estimated that exports for 1992 would amount to about 15,000 pairs or about $U.S. 525,000. Because of prevailing import tariffs, retail prices in Bolivia were set at a 10 percent premium over Chilean net prices. Although it was too early for managers at Forus to evaluate the long term effectiveness of Global Trading Company in Bolivia, Forus had an option to buy up to a 50 percent equity position in the company at a time of its choosing.

In 1992, the company's efforts in Argentina were focused exclusively on promoting its Brooks line of athletic shoes. Coast Sport Argentina was established in 1991 and acted exclusively as a wholesaler for a variety of independent retail outlets in the country. Coast Sport Chile owned 80 percent of the new company, with the remaining 20 percent owned by NORSEG Argentina, which had NORSEG Chile as a majority owner. Brooks shoes were imported directly from factories in the Far East or from Coast Sport inventories in Chile. Ricardo estimated that in 1992 in Argentina the company would sell about 32,500 pairs of Brooks shoes, worth approximately $US 1.0 million.

Recent Developments

After witnessing almost a decade of accelerating growth and profits, Ricardo was reflective. Projections indicated that 1992 would be the best year for the company with after-tax profits at over 15 percent of sales and return on equity surpassing 35 percent. (Financial statements for 1990 and 1991 are reported in Exhibit 7.) With such growth and profitability, it was easy to feel confident.

By the summer of 1992, Ricardo was weighing a number of options to recommend to Alfonso and Juan Pablo for consideration. One major thrust under consideration was to move aggressively into the retailing of apparel. Although Costanera had little experience with clothing, apparel seemed to fit well with the company's other retail operations. It was thought that the best way to proceed would be to open a chain of stores combining both Brooks and L.A. Gear athletic shoes with brand sports clothing. While the combination of

EXHIBIT 7

FINANCIAL STATEMENTS FOR FORUS, S.A.
(for the years ended December 31, 1990 and 1991)

	Income Statements	
	1990 (Ch. $)	*1991 (Ch. $)*
Operating revenues	$3,917,656,542	$5,092,329,385
Operating costs	(2,874,204,603)	(3,507,627,947)
Gross margin	1,043,451,939	1,584,701,438
Administrative and sales expenses	(534,015,090)	(666,112,679)
Operating results	509,436,849	918,588,759
Nonoperating expenses	(113,686,107)	110,645,279
Income before tax	395,750,742	1,029,234,038
Income tax	16,273,224	49,547,770
Net income	$ 379,477,518	$ 979,686,268
Chilean$/US$	337.09	374.09

	Balance Sheet	
	1990(Ch. $)	*1991 (Ch. $)*
Assets		
Total current assets	$1,678,518,025	$2,561,279,678
Total fixed assets	2,084,031,742	2,387,101,951
Less accumulated depreciation	(544,166,086)	(699,091,557)
Net fixed assets	1,539,865,656	1,688,010,394
Investment in related companies		
plus other assets	1,632,891,422	1,966,126,263
Total assets	$4,851,275,163	$6,215,416,335
Liabilities and Shareholders' Equity		
Total current liabilities	$1,530,707,772	$1,756,973,367
Long-term liabilities:		
Bank debt	377,752,696	608,837,630
Other accounts payable	130,702,501	152,427,111
Total long-term liabilities	508,455,197	761,264,741
Total stockholders' equity	2,812,112,194	3,697,178,227
Total liabilities and equity	$4,851,275,163	$6,215,416,335

athletic shoe and clothing stores had proved a major hit in Europe, Japan, and North America, it had yet to be effectively pursued in Chile. A combination outlet would have the advantage of allowing the company to move incrementally into apparel while concurrently expanding athletic shoe sales. Costs for retail space in a typical upscale Santiago shopping mall were estimated at 7 percent of net sales with leasehold improvements averaging about $US 30,000. Unfortunately, the company did not have a brand under consideration and was wondering how to aggressively proceed.

A second option being considered was to open a chain of outdoor clothing stores. The outdoor clothing and accessory market was particularly attractive because it was a segment that appeared to have been neglected in Chile. Through visits to the U.S., all three Swett brothers had become familiar with a variety of fast growing outdoor clothing stores such as Timberland, Eddie Bauer, and North-by-Northwest. Market research in Chile indicated that outdoor clothing sales could grow rapidly and Ricardo wondered if he should recommend a major move into this segment. What was uncertain was the extent to which the skills learned in marketing shoes could be transferred to outdoor clothing.

A third option for the company was the introduction of a new retailing concept for children's shoes and apparel. While first Hush Puppies Chile and then Forus had been selling children's shoes for the past 10 years, the introduction of Hush Puppies for Kids had been a major hit in the marketplace. In July 1992, managers at Hush Puppies Chile were debating whether to extend the Kids line to include brand children's clothing and accessories. A full line of merchandise would accompany a full move into children's retailing by filling out stores and providing an added draw for consumers. Wolverine had been trying for years to introduce Hush Puppies brand clothes for children in the U.S. but the efforts had not gone well. To better develop a recognizable brand in the U.S., Wolverine had just recently adopted the Hush Puppies for Kids logo which had been developed in Chile. While Ricardo realized the potential for new retail concepts, he was also fully aware that a movement into retailing would have serious consequences for the company.

Behind the increasing interest in diversifying the retail base of the company was the recognition that retailing was becoming more specialized. The need for even greater specialization was articulated by Renato Figueroa, General Manager of For-Shop's retail operations: "As the market becomes more globalized, our next move must be to specialize in our stores. Where we have family stores, we must in the future have men's stores, kid's stores, women's stores, and lifestyle stores."

Ricardo was also faced with the decision of focusing management efforts on either increasing sales in Chile or on expanding sales in other Latin American countries. Some in the company argued that Costanera could do both at the same time. Others disagreed by highlighting the risk that foreign operations would siphon critical resources away from core Chilean operations. For Ricardo Swett, the critical issue was management.

> Our big problem with growth is people. How can the management of the company keep up with such rapid growth? We need good middle managers. . . . On average, about 60 percent of our senior managers have had formal university training in management. When we exclude manufacturing managers, this number climbs to about 80 percent. Still, we spend a lot of effort training our managers. On average, each of our managers receives about 2½ weeks of training per year.

Sometimes I feel that we are moving too slowly. The world is changing so fast that it is increasingly difficult to stay abreast of what is going on internationally. What worries me is that our managers might not be reacting fast enough. There needs to be a daily commitment to learning.

Clearly, Ricardo had much to consider. While any major decision would require the support of both Alfonso and Juan Pablo, Ricardo realized that they would be relying on him for direction. Ricardo seemed to have more questions than answers. How fast should they move and where should they target expansion? Despite enormous success in the past, it was uncertain which direction to turn.

23 TECHNOPHAR IN VIET NAM

As Gary Dube, vice-president of Technophar Equipment & Service Ltd. (Technophar), a leading manufacturer of hard and soft gelatin capsule machines, proceeded to his meeting with Mark Habuda, vice-president of marketing, and Herman Victorov, president, he reviewed the history of their recent venture in Viet Nam. Negotiations had proceeded smoothly since the initial contact 18 months ago, and an agreement had been reached with the Vietnamese partner, Cuulong Pharmaceutical Import and Export Company (Cuulong). However, the initial deposit, due on December 15, 1994, had not arrived, and now, on January 15, 1995, concern about the Viet Nam contract had intensified. Dube wondered if Technophar should re-negotiate the contract, cancel the contract, or continue to wait patiently for a payment that might not ever arrive. In the back of his mind, Dube re-evaluated their approach to securing foreign contracts.

The Gelatin Capsule Industry

Hard gelatin capsules were invented in 1833 by the French pharmacist A. Mathes. Originally produced in a hand process by Parke Davis (Capsugel), they were first machine-processed by Eli-Lilly (Elanco) in the late 19th century. The first semi-automatic machine

IVEY   Andrew Delios prepared this case under the supervision of Professor Paul Beamish solely to provide material for class discussion. The authors do not intend to illustrate either effective or ineffective handling of a managerial situation. The authors may have disguised certain names and other identifying information to protect confidentiality. Ivey Management Services prohibits any form of reproduction, storage or transmittal without its written permission. This material is not covered under authorization from CanCopy or any reproduction rights organization. Copyright © 1995, Ivey Management Services.

was developed in 1909 by Arthur Colton, who continued to innovate and improve the capsule manufacture process through the first half of the 20th century. He introduced the first fully automatic machine in the 1930s and eventually sold his company and machine design patents to Snyder Co. of Detroit, Michigan. In 1963, Snyder Co. was purchased by Cherry-Burrell Corporation, the company from which Technophar was spun off.

Technophar's position in the gelatin capsule industry was that of a supplier of machines and turn-key plants for the manufacture of hard and soft gelatin capsules (see Exhibit 1). Two other firms, one in Canada and the other in the United States, competed directly with Technophar. Technophar manufactured machines that were widely considered technologically superior in design and operating performance. In 1995 it was the industry leader with an 80 percent share of the growing worldwide market for capsule machines. However, high price sensitivity among machine purchasers required Technophar to price their machines on par with competitors' machines.

Capsule machine manufacture and gelatin capsule production existed as niche businesses within the larger pharmaceutical industry. Large pharmaceutical firms, with the exception of Shinogi and Capsugel, were not involved in gelatin capsule production. Pharmaceutical firms were reluctant to integrate backwards for three reasons: (1) pharmaceutical firms preferred to concentrate on the production of fine chemicals used in pharmacological products, (2) a small capsule factory produced 1.5 billion capsules per year, and most pharmaceutical firms filled fewer than a billion capsules annually, and (3) gelatin capsule production was a notoriously difficult and finicky process. Capsules were easier to buy than produce; as a result, the gelatin capsule industry was initially a duopoly.

In the early 1970s, the U.S. based R. P. Scherer Co. (Scherer) entered into capsule production, joining the first two producers of hard gelatin capsules: Capsugel and Elanco. By

EXHIBIT 1   The Gelatin Capsule Industry

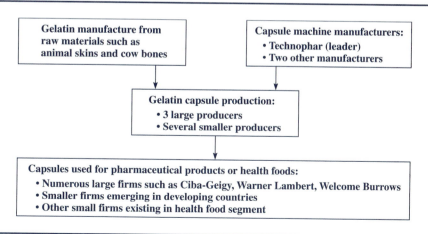

the 1990s, these three producers had secured an 80–85 percent share of the worldwide gelatin capsule market and were protective of their processes and technology. Dube commented on the impression these capsule producers had created:

> For many years Capsugel and Elanco portrayed the technology of making capsules as an exclusive, painstaking craft which few people had the God-given ability to do well, and these few were employed by Capsugel and Elanco. Consequently these two companies put factories in a few key countries around the world, and really controlled the market until the early 1970s. Then R. P. Scherer came in and took a little bite out of it. Finally we started to sell the technology which opened up the industry.

Capsugel was the largest producer of hard capsules with 140 hard capsule machines located in eight countries around the world (see Exhibit 2). Shinogi, a Japanese pharmaceutical firm and previously Elanco's joint venture partner in Japan, purchased Elanco's capsule production business in the 1990s. Shinogi operated 80 hard capsule machines and had centralized capsule production to facilities in the U.S., Spain and Japan. Scherer, the third-largest producer of hard capsules with 40 machines in three different countries, was the dominant firm in the soft capsule market. Scherer had a 60–65 percent world share in this rapidly growing segment of the capsule market.

The hard capsule factory location decision was driven mainly by transportation cost considerations. Gelatin capsules, a light, voluminous product consisting mostly of air, were expensive to transport because of their low value per unit volume. Accordingly, to minimize transportation costs, capsule factories had been located close to pharmaceutical firms' manufacturing facilities in Europe and North America. However, in recent years, pharmaceutical firms had been shifting production to developing countries to take advantage of

EXHIBIT 2   Location of Hard Capsule Factories and Machines (as of 1995)

Manufacturer	Country	No. of Machines
Capsugel	Belgium Brazil China France Japan Mexico Thailand United States	Total: 140 machines
Shinogi	Japan Spain United States	Total: 80 machines
Scherer	Brazil Canada Germany	Total: 40 machines

Source: Company records.

lower labour costs and tax incentives, and to be closer to the source of fine chemicals used as filler in encapsulated products. Indonesia, Puerto Rico, and China had emerged as popular host sites for manufacturing investments by pharmaceutical firms.

The relocation of pharmaceutical facilities created new opportunities for capsule producers. Capsule factories placed in developing countries had a transportation cost advantage in supplying these new pharmaceutical plants. Also, pharmaceutical firms from developing countries were entering the worldwide market for pharmacological products and, for similar reasons, these firms required nearby capsule factories.

Market Development

Capsule production technology became available to firms around the globe through Technophar's innovative efforts. Technophar simplified and standardized capsule production, enabling the process to be transferred with relative ease. Dube stated, "We took the production process and broke it down so that you could teach it to a 10 year old." The company developed procedures and manuals to support its simplified process. These manuals detailed the intricacies of the production process and explained machine operations, maintenance, and repair.

Technophar's innovations led to demand growth in less-developed regions of the world such as Eastern Europe, Africa, Latin America, and regions of Asia. For example, prior to Technophar's technology transfer to China, the market for hard capsules had been small because capsules were expensive to produce. Capsules were produced in a labour-intensive, hand-dipping process, which had a very low productivity. As automated capsule production technology became available to producers in China through Technophar's efforts, the market for hard capsules began to grow. Hard capsules produced with Technophar's technology became inexpensive to produce (US$3 per thousand) or purchase. As a result, developing countries could produce their own capsules, which facilitated upstream entry into the pharmaceutical industry.

Company History

Herman Victorov, president and founder of Technophar, had been a plant engineer for Scherer. During his tenure there, he developed a process modification which nearly doubled the hourly yield of capsule production from 28,000 to 48,000. In 1983, a subsequent process improvement increased output another 4,000 capsules per hour. In 1984, he left Scherer and established Multi-Motion Engineering Inc. in Windsor, Ontario, which was purchased by Cherry Burrell in 1985.

Technophar, a spin-off of the Canadian division of Cherry Burrell, came into existence as a private company in 1988. Technophar was, in the words of Dube, "a company of machine builders led by Victorov's desire to be an engineer and machine designer." Technophar employed 50 people, many of them highly skilled technicians who had worked with Victorov at Cherry Burrell's Canadian division.

Technophar, building on Victorov's experience in Bulgaria, Germany, China and Romania, quickly emerged as an international supplier of hard capsule machines. Sales, while initially slow at seven machines for the 1988–1990 period, increased dramatically in 1992 when eight machines were sold. This rapid growth rate continued, and 20 machines were sold in 1994. Revenues in 1994 were US$12 million and the company was moderately profitable.

Technophar's customers were primarily in developing countries. The company's management team, experienced in the pharmaceutical industry and in international markets, was well-suited to dealing with the uncertainty and risk in these emerging markets. Dube commented on the nature of Technophar's business:

> When you are doing business internationally, quite often you are dealing with countries that are relying on aid money, and it tends to be a feast or famine business. Our employees were either working 60 hours a week building machines, or they were painting doorknobs.

Technophar was accustomed to a high variability in orders. When the order book was empty, management was more willing to accommodate riskier contracts. Four or five contracts represented the company's annual business, and Dube was well aware of the cost of a lost contract.

> If you are planning on two or three projects and a major one crumples on you, it can be devastating to a small company like ours. With our uneven stream of revenues, we have to be a private company. We could not be a public company with quarterly reporting requirements.

Technophar manufactured hard capsule machines in its Oldcastle, Ontario, location for distribution and re-assembly in a variety of countries around the world. New capsule machines were list priced for US$535,000 to US$635,000. The company designed and constructed a number of different models for different needs, though components were readily interchangeable between models. Hence, machines tailored to specific customer needs were essentially identical across customers. The Oldcastle facility could produce 20 capsule machines annually with a single shift.

Technophar's Activities

International Operations

Technophar participated in several international alliances. Most alliances were manufacturing joint ventures, and three of these were located in Romania, Victorov's country of birth. In Bucharest, Technophar had established a model turn-key plant for prospective clients. While this plant vertically integrated the firm forward, it was not an entry into the hard capsule market. Technophar did not want to compete with its own customers in the hard capsule market. Output from this plant was used to demonstrate the quality of Technophar's machinery and hard capsule product. A second joint venture in Bucharest operated as an engineering and trading company. The third joint venture, located in Odorheiu, was a manufacturing facility which produced components used in the assembly of capsule machines.

To date, China was Technophar's largest purchaser of hard capsule machines and factories (see Exhibit 3). For that reason Technophar had devoted considerable resources to

---

EXHIBIT 3   Technophar's Worldwide Market (as of 1995)

Country	*No. of Machines Sold*
Brazil	1
Bulgaria	4
Canada	2
China	31
Colombia	1
France	5
Germany	4
Indonesia	1
Israel	2
Korea	1
Romania	4
Taiwan	3
United States	1
Venezuela	1

Source: Company records.

serving the Chinese market and was positioned to exploit the huge untapped potential (see Exhibit 4). Mark Habuda was stationed in Guangzhou, Guangdong, and two joint ventures had been established: the one in Qingdao, Shandong, assisted with Technophar's projects in China; the other located in Guangzhou, Guangdong, was a complete manufacturing facility which employed both local personnel and Canadian technicians. It produced capsule machines and support equipment for turn-key plants in China.

Turn-Key Plants

Technophar's main business was turn-key projects in developing countries. The sale of a turn-key plant was a complicated and time-consuming process: contracts were often courted for several years. Once the contract had been negotiated, a 10–15 percent deposit and a letter of credit for the balance was sent to Technophar. Because Technophar did not stock inventory, it would not begin capsule machine manufacture until these two items had been received. Technophar shipped the completed machines when it received the remaining portion of the contracted amount, less 10 percent. When the turn-key plant had been certified as fully operational, it was turned over to the purchaser in exchange for the 10 percent hold back amount.

The technology transfer consisted of four major components: preliminary building designs, the equipment necessary for the production of hard capsules, auxiliary equipment, and training in plant operations. Under the terms of the technology transfer agreement, the purchaser was responsible for the construction and cost of the Technophar-designed facility. Technophar used a standardized design which was adapted to local operating criteria. Once the facility had been constructed, a team of Technophar's technicians accompanied the machinery and equipment to the purchaser's facility.

EXHIBIT 4   Market Penetration in China
(No. of Machines as of 1995)

Province or Major Municipality	1994 Est. Population (million)	1993 GDP (US$ billion)	Per Capita GDP (US$)	GDP Annual Growth Rate (%)	Known No. of Hard Capsule Machines*
Anhui	60	28	469	17	
Beijing	11	20	1,806	0	
Fujian	31	23	744	10	
Gansu	23	10	426	18	
Guangdong	71	91	1,277	21	7
Guangxi	44	19	434	21	
Guizhou	34	9	262	8	
Hebei	64	37	577	−1	
Heilongjiang	39	26	673	11	2
Henan	89	37	417	−2	4
Hubei	57	37	649	19	
Hunan	65	29	442	13	
Inner Mongolia	23	11	492	22	
Jiangsu	73	102	1,398	10	
Jiangxi	40	18	249	11	
Jilin	27	19	720	18	
Liaoning	43	54	1,251	16	
Ningxia	5	2	516	17	
Qinghai	5	2	443	33	
Shaanxi	35	15	442	11	
Shandong	89	76	853	1	12
Shanghai	14	52	3,683	21	2
Shanxi	30	15	506	2	
Sichuan	120	52	432	15	
Tianjin	9	18	1,962	0	
Tibet	2	1	182	0	
Xinjiang	16	11	692	29	
Yunnan	39	15	393	22	
Zhejiang	47	53	1,127	5	4
Total for China	**1,205**	**882**	**743**	**11**	**31**

*Technophar machines only.

Sources: Department of Population Statistics, State Statistical Bureau, People's Republic of China, Beijing, July 1985, Table 34; *World Bank Atlas* 1995; company records.

The machines and auxiliary equipment were manufactured in one of Technophar's three manufacturing facilities. The auxiliary equipment included items such as dehumidifiers, air-conditioners, and operational controls. Half of the turn-key contract's value was in this auxiliary equipment and the other half in the hard and soft capsule machines. The machines and auxiliary equipment, once manufactured and tested, were disassembled and shipped to the purchaser's facility, where they were re-assembled by the plant set-up team.

The plant set-up team comprised five technicians. The first technician, who arrived in the purchaser's country toward the end of facility construction, inspected the new building and supervised installation of the climate control equipment. The next crew was responsible for auxiliary equipment set-up and capsule machinery installation. The final crew made the plant operational and subjected the plant to a 72-hour test run, termed the production test protocol (PTP). If the plant operated well under the PTP, Technophar completed instruction about machine operations, formulations, and gelatin preparations. Technophar's contractual obligations ended when it formally turned the plant over to the purchaser.

Service Business

Throughout the facility construction process, Technophar's technicians had the opportunity to interact with people who would be operating the plant. They emphasized to the purchaser's staff the importance of following Technophar's well-documented operating procedures. Despite this stress on conformity with procedures, factories often "went to hell in a handbasket. After the keys had been handed over, the purchaser would take shortcuts and forget about the operating rules."

Although Technophar's guarantee did not cover operational difficulties arising from equipment misuse, company technicians were available to help repair machines. This form of after-sale service was offered for a fee, but purchasers seldom took advantage of it. Plants located in developing countries typically did not have discretionary funds for maintenance and repairs. Also, the efficiency imperative found in private companies was not present in many of these state-supported plants. Thus, machines capable of operating 24 hours per day and producing 65,000 capsules per hour, were operated for 13 or 14 hours each day, and when operated, the machines ran at 60 percent efficiency.

Technophar was also engaged in the service, repair, and upgrading of existing capsule machines, a number of which had been operating for many years. These machines were much slower and produced lower quality capsules than the newer machines. Technophar had refurbished a few machines, but managers were uncertain of the size of the existing market for machine upgrades.

Auxiliary Businesses

Technophar's expertise in machine manufacture and design facilitated the company's entry into other related businesses. The company had designed and manufactured various mechanical systems and machinery for firms in the metallurgical, chemical and automotive industries. A major food processing company in North America had purchased original machines and prototypes for use in packaging. Technophar was also engaged in the manufacture of machinery for the small but rapidly expanding soft capsule industry.

Markets

Hard Gelatin Capsule

Estimates of annual worldwide capsule consumption ranged between 100 and 200 billion capsules: North America, the largest market for capsules, consumed 50 to 55 billion; Western Europe, the second-largest market, consumed 40 billion. The size of other large regional markets was uncertain. Technophar's management estimated worldwide market growth to be 3–5 percent per annum (see Exhibit 5).

EXHIBIT 5   Worldwide Capsule Consumption (as of 1995)

Region	1995 Est. Population (million)	Estimated GDP in Each Region (US$ billion)	Average GDP per Person (US$)	Capsule Consumption (Est.)
North America	300	7,350	24,500	55 billion
Western Europe	465	8,439	18,148	40 billion
Eastern Europe	447	1,879	4,203	Not known
Asia/Pacific	3,294	6,670	2,025	Not known
Latin America*	494	1,416	2,866	Not known
Africa	683	463	678	Not known
Middle East	212	1,007	4,750	Not known
World	**5,895**	**27,224**	**4,618**	**100–200 billion**

*Includes the countries of South and Central America.

Note: The worldwide market for capsules was estimated by Dube to be growing at 3–5 percent per year.

Source: *World Bank Atlas,* 1995; company records.

Gelatin Capsule Machine

Firms in developing countries and newly industrializing countries formed the large majority of Technophar's customers. One gelatin capsule plant was often sufficient to satisfy domestic demand in these countries, and Technophar was continually challenged to find new market opportunities. However, Technophar lacked formal marketing procedures and did not employ a sales force or agents dedicated to seeking and developing opportunities[1]. Trade shows, in which Technophar could display its product and meet potential customers, were deemed of little value because the North American market for gelatin capsule machines was saturated.

Technophar relied on two processes for accessing opportunities. The first was internal: managers were experienced both internationally and in the pharmaceutical industry. Dube, Victorov and Habuda had, respectively, 30, 17, and 13 years of experience in this industry and direct experience in the countries of Asia, Latin America, and Eastern Europe. Dube expanded on the importance of experience and industry contacts:

> Over a period of time we had learned who was buying capsules. When I worked at R.P. Scherer, I knew who was buying capsules because we had agents in 13 or 14 countries. We also knew where our competitors had factories.
>
> In determining opportunities for Technophar, we used our industry experience and went either through the gelatin end or through the pharmaceutical industry. We asked ourselves, "Is a pharmaceutical company interested in making capsules?" Or a group of people may leave these companies and become entrepreneurs. They would want to start a capsule-making business and would be natural customers for our product.

---

[1]An agent would travel extensively, incurring expenses of US$400 per day, and would receive salary and benefits of approximately US$60,000 per year. A secretary for this agent could be employed at an annual cost of US$30,000. (Source: John W. Wright, *The American Almanac of Jobs and Salaries,* 1995.)

In determining opportunities, these managers operated a lot on "gut feel", and each brought a unique perspective to their joint evaluation of a country. Entering into their intuitive assessment were a number of factors, one of which was the type of capsule consumption. Capsules were used for some ethical pharmaceutical products (prescription drugs and over the counter drugs), and for health food products, a rapidly growing market segment in North America and Europe. Ethical pharmaceutical consumption was multiplying in developing countries, particularly with the increased emphasis on health care.

The managers also considered the location of existing hard capsule factories. The Middle East, for example, was a promising region because only one small company produced capsules there. Other factors included the type of government in a country, its emphasis on health care (and by association, hard capsule consumption), and the openness of the country to international trade.

The second process for finding markets was also informal. Technophar gathered market information through a network of non-company agents and contacts. For example, it had an arrangement with Marubeni, a large Japanese trading company with offices around the world, to use its agents for information about potential markets. Canadian embassies and consulates had also been helpful by providing leads and by disseminating Technophar's promotional literature within their regional spheres of responsibility. American embassies, host country nationals residing in Canada, and agents within China provided an informal source of information and often approached Technophar with unsolicited orders. An agent whose efforts resulted in an actual delivery received a commission of 3–8 percent of the value of the contract. Contract values for a four-machine turn-key plant averaged US$3–4 million.

Developing Opportunities

Technophar's unblemished reputation for honesty, integrity, and reliability was instrumental in securing new contracts. The company had gone to considerable lengths in the past to protect its highly valued reputation. In 1992 for example, it had received a deposit of US$1.3 million from Saudi Arabia for a turn-key plant. Technophar had begun machine manufacture and had invested a considerable amount of time and money in bringing the deal to fruition. However, a change in priority in Saudi Arabia led to the cancellation of the contract. Technophar was under no obligation to return the deposit; nevertheless, to protect its reputation and to promote the likelihood of future business in the region, it refunded all but accrued out-of-pocket expenses. From the goodwill created by this gesture, Technophar had secured contracts with other countries in the Middle East (e.g. Jordan) and was presently speaking with representatives from the United Arab Emirates, Qatar, and a new Saudi group about capsule machine sales.

Technophar continually cultivated new clients, as winning contracts often required an extended period of negotiations. It was not unusual for managers to spend US$10,000 on travel plus weeks of management time exploring an opportunity which might not ever result in a contract. Dube and Habuda, for example, travelled more than 140 days in 1994.

During the early stages of negotiation, Technophar assisted the purchaser with market and feasibility studies for the proposed plant. Technophar had a series of standard schedules for assessing manufacturing costs, which were adaptable to factor conditions in the purchaser's country. Using these schedules, the purchaser plugged in the relevant figures to make projections of its production costs and profitability.

The Viet Nam Opportunity

Technophar received an unsolicited order for the Viet Nam contract. The deal had a Viet Kieu connection, as Mr. Ly Van Phi, the owner of an import-export business in Montreal, originally approached Technophar with officials of Cuulong about supplying hard-capsule-making equipment to Viet Nam.[2] The proposed project was valued at US$4 million, and the agreement to provide the plant and equipment was signed on November 15, 1994, during Canadian Prime Minister Chretien's two-day visit to Viet Nam.

Though Technophar had been handed this opportunity, management had to evaluate the viability of the Viet Nam technology transfer as compared with other potential projects. The company, which normally had seven or eight projects in the process of negotiation, was also developing opportunities in Russia, France, Thailand, Malaysia, India, China, and in three other countries of the former Soviet Union. An issue was: Why enter Viet Nam when other opportunities existed in China and Southeast Asia? (See Exhibits 6 and 7.)

Technophar had a number of reasons for entering Viet Nam. The central government's support was a major consideration because it was an active participant in larger projects. It supported this technology transfer because of its favourable balance of payments effects. Imports of gelatin capsules would be reduced, and exports would be upgraded in the forward integration of Viet Nam's pharmaceutical industry. Also, the government's position on health care implicitly supported the deal. A state-supported health industry was thought to lead to increased encapsulated drug consumption.

A second set of reasons for entering Viet Nam entailed a longer term perspective. Although Technophar did not perceive a market there for more than one or two capsule plants, opportunities existed for the company's related, but as yet undeveloped, businesses. Victorov, an entrepreneur and inventor, had a patent on a sugar extraction process which greatly increased the yield of sugar from sugar cane. Viet Nam had a sizable sugar cane industry, but the country's poor infrastructure hampered processing. Victorov's process was uniquely suited to the country's needs as sugar processing units could be built individually and located close to the supply of sugar cane. A second opportunity existed in the development of processing machinery for the extraction of gelatin from pig skins, beef skins, and cow bones, which were usually discarded by the Vietnamese. The introduction of this technology would enable Viet Nam's pharmaceutical industry to further integrate backwards. However, the two projects involved a much greater financial commitment and would not likely materialize in the next three to four years.

Offsetting these reasons for entering the Viet Nam market was Technophar's limited experience in this country. Previously, sales in developing markets had been to those countries in which managers had prior experience—Victorov in Romania and Bulgaria, and Habuda in China. Technophar's managers were inexperienced in Viet Nam and needed to know more about the basic characteristics of the country to which they were actually committed.

---

[2]Viet Kieu refers to members of the 1975 exodus from Viet Nam to countries such as Canada, the United States, and Australia after the collapse of South Viet Nam. The 180,000 Canadians of Vietnamese origin were, with their valuable ties and business connections, becoming increasingly important for doing business in Viet Nam. While it had been stated that Viet Kieu were welcome to assist in rebuilding Viet Nam, their exact status under Vietnamese law was still uncertain.

EXHIBIT 6   Market Penetration in Asia (as of 1995)

Country	Hard Capsule Machine
Bangladesh	No
Burma	No
Cambodia	No
China	Yes
Hong Kong	No
India	Yes (old, inferior quality)
Indonesia	Yes
Japan	Yes
Laos	No
Malaysia	No
Nepal	No
North Korea	??
Pakistan	No ?
Philippines	No
Singapore	Yes
South Korea	Yes
Taiwan	No ?
Thailand	Yes
Viet Nam	Contracted

Source: Company records.

Viet Nam—Country study[3]

Market Promise

Viet Nam was positioned in the heart of the dynamic countries of the Pacific Rim (see Exhibit 8). While slow to reach the economic growth levels of other countries in the region and saddled with a turbulent past, Viet Nam had been positioned by recent reforms to become the next tiger in the region (see Exhibit 7).

The package of economic renovations (Doi Moi) instituted in 1986 had been a turning point for the country's economy. Viet Nam had made significant progress in recent years moving away from the planned economic model toward a more effective, market-based economic system. Most prices were now fully decontrolled, and the Vietnamese currency had been devalued and floated at world market rates. In addition, the scope for private sector activity had been expanded, primarily through decollectivization of the agricultural sector and the introduction of laws giving legal recognition to private business.

Sectorally, economic growth was not evenly dispersed as industries in the economy were treated differently under the guidelines of Doi Moi. Land reforms had created more

---

[3]Sources: Joseph P. Quinlan, *Vietnam: Business Opportunities and Risks,* Pacific View Press, Berkeley, CA, 1995; The Economist Intelligence Unit reports; The Central Intelligence Agency, *The World Factbook 1995,* Internet location: www.ic.gov:80/94fact/fb94toc/fb94toc.html.

EXHIBIT 7   Characteristics of Countries in Southeast Asia and South Asia

	1994 GNP/ Capita (US $)	GNP: Growth Rate (%)	Inflation Rate, 1993 (%)	1993 Population (000)	Political Risk*	Life Expectancy (years)	Mftg. Wages (US$/hr.)
Viet Nam	170	4.8	5.2	73,103	C	67	0.24
China	743	6.5	18	1,164,908	D	69	0.37
Malaysia	3,160	5.7	3.6	19,032	B	71	1.90
Singapore	19,310	6.1	2.4	2,867	A	75	NA
Thailand	2,040	8.4	4.1	58,824	B	69	0.92
Indonesia	730	4.8	10	187,151	B	60	0.17
Philippines	830	1.6	7.6	65,775	C	65	0.67
Burma	950	5.0	30	44,277	NA	60	NA
Cambodia	600	7.5	60	10,265	NA	49	NA
Hong Kong	17,860	5.3	9.5	5,865	B	78	NA
India	290	3.0	8.0	900,543	D	61	NA

* A = Low; D = High.

Sources: *World Bank Atlas,* 1995; *The Vietnam Business Journal,* 1(3), 1993; Economist Intelligence Unit; *Business Asia,* January 16, 1995.

autonomy. Light industries, such as textiles and food manufacture, had been emphasized, as export promotion and diversification were seen to be key variables in Viet Nam's future economic success. In 1994, nearly three-quarters of export earnings were generated by only two commodities, rice and crude oil. Led by industry and construction, the economy did well in 1994 with GNP rising 4.8 percent.

In response to Doi Moi, foreign direct investment (FDI) in Viet Nam had surged dramatically in recent years. From US$360 million in 1988, FDI approvals had grown 10-fold to US$4 billion in 1994. FDI was dominated by firms from Asian countries; European and North American firms had been slow to invest in the region (see Exhibit 9). Firms from the U.S. had not been permitted to invest in Viet Nam prior to February 3, 1994, though only hours after President Clinton announced the lifting of the U.S. embargo against Viet Nam, both PepsiCo and Coca-Cola made commitments to begin bottling and distributing in Viet Nam.

Foreign investors were attracted to Viet Nam for a number of reasons. Investors were permitted to have 100 percent equity ownership in their ventures, unlike in some countries in the Asia Pacific region. Low corporate tax rates, tax holidays, potential waivers on import and export duties, and full profit repatriation were other government-centred investment incentives. Investors were also encouraged by market conditions. Wage rates were low, Viet Nam was considerably well-endowed with natural resources such as forests, marine life, minerals, crude oil, and a workforce of 32 million people. Infrastructure was poor, which hampered economic development, but created considerable opportunity for companies in this sector.

Risks

Social.   Other factors mitigated these attractions. Viet Nam was classified as a "least developed nation" by the United Nations. Malnutrition was high, double that in China, and diseases not prevalent in other countries in Southeast Asia were found in Viet Nam. Infant mortality (45.5 deaths/1000 live births) was high and literacy rates (88 percent) comparatively low. A

EXHIBIT 8   Map of Asia

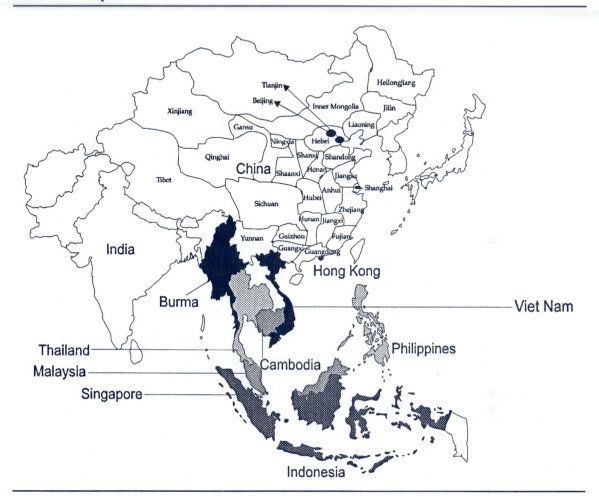

significant proportion of children did not complete secondary (high school level) school-ing. Improved living standards had been given priority, though little attention had been paid to human rights and basic freedoms. Viet Nam's natural resource advantages were suffer-ing from environmental degradation. Deforestation, water pollution, overfishing, and soil degradation were issues of concern.

Economic.   While wealthy in natural resources and people, Viet Nam was still one of the poorest countries in the Southeast Asia region. The industrial sector remained burdened by uncompetitive state-owned enterprises that the government was unwilling or unable to privatize. The economy was primarily agrarian, with 40 percent of GDP accounted for by agricultural products, and 65 percent of employment in agriculture. Eighty percent of Viet Nam's 70 million people lived as peasant farmers without the income to spend on items other than necessities such as food and shelter.

EXHIBIT 9   FDI in Viet Nam by Country (as of 1995)

	Country	No. of Projects	Total Capital Committed (US$ million)
1	Taiwan	179	1,964
2	Hong Kong	171	1,788
3	Singapore	76	1,070
4	South Korea	97	884
5	Japan	73	783
6	Australia	42	655
7	Malaysia	31	581
8	France	58	534
9	Switzerland	14	463
10	Britain	15	376
11	Netherlands	16	348
12	United States	28	270
13	Thailand	43	236
14	Indonesia	11	160
15	Russia	34	125
16	Ireland	13	81
17	Sweden	7	78
18	Canada	9	66
19	Philippines	12	58
20	Ukraine	6	45

Source: *Vietnam Business Journal*, III(1), 1995.

Unemployment loomed as a serious problem. Roughly 25 percent of the workforce was without work and population growth swelled the ranks of the unemployed yearly. The government ran a 5 percent budget deficit in 1993, and imports at US$3.1 billion exceeded exports (US$2.6 billion). Moreover, the government would issue no information on foreign currency reserves. Doubts existed as to the ability of the central government to exhibit sound fiscal management, and inflation had reached 14.4 percent by 1995.

Political.   The political risk in Viet Nam was still considerable (see Exhibit 7). Viet Nam was a one-party state in which political power came from the Communist party and its politburo. Although the Communist party enjoyed little support from the populace and was widely disliked in the south, there was no real challenge to the government's authority. However, as a vocal generation of Vietnamese emerged in the thrills and throes of economic freedom, the potential for conflict between political authoritarianism and growing market freedoms was increasing.

The central government, despite its free-market preaching, often participated overtly in markets by restricting competition and by acting as a partner in the majority of foreign ventures. Its market participation was not always valued because Vietnamese government officials had little experience in dealing with multinational agencies and corporations or in formulating and implementing projects. Also, Vietnamese security officials were suspicious of foreigners to the point of paranoia, which created apprehension in many foreign investors.

Conflict still remained between central and regional governments. Similar to the situation in China, economic power was fragmented and economic policies varied by province in their internal competition for foreign investment. Laws and regulations were interpreted differently in each region and, in cases, were disregarded. For example, officials in Ho Chi Minh City had developed their own income tax laws and had threatened to prevent foreigners from leaving the country until all personal taxes had been reconciled.

Corruption, bribery, and copyright and patent infringement were not uncommon for want of effective legal enforcement. Institutions supporting free enterprise were absent. Without a legal framework, a viable banking system or private land ownership (all land was the property of the state), business in Viet Nam involved considerable risk. Thus, the raw potential and attractiveness of the country was countervailed by these social, economic and political risk factors. Consequently, only one-third of the US$12 billion in FDI committed to Viet Nam since 1988 had been implemented and US$1 billion of projects had been cancelled.

The Viet Nam Contract

Negotiations for the Viet Nam contract transpired smoothly and quickly. The initial discussions went well when Habuda visited the Vietnamese purchasers during one of his trips to China. He returned for a second set of meetings, during which he assisted with local market and feasibility studies. Cuulong completed these evaluations and recognized the large domestic market for pharmaceuticals as well as the export potential of hard capsules. After his transfer to China, Habuda visited Viet Nam for a third time and completed the technology transfer package. The final task was to get all of the political players in place, and the contract was signed when Prime Minister Chretien's Asian trade mission arrived in Viet Nam.

The deal, though quickly negotiated, had been dragging on for a number of months. Internal changes on the Vietnamese side had caused some delays, and Technophar's costs had changed considerably since the contract had been negotiated. For example, stainless steel, a large component of the auxiliary equipment, had increased in price by 30–35 percent in the last six months. Technophar's management recognized the difficulties faced by Cuulong because of the poor infrastructure in the country, but concern about the contract became acute when the December 15 deposit did not arrive.

Management at Technophar communicated weekly with Pharmexco, the official importer of the equipment, and Cuulong. In these communications, a great deal of uncertainty began to develop about the project and the partners. Technophar's managers, who were having difficulty sorting fact from fiction in their dealings with Pharmexco and Cuulong, had no way of judging the validity of the many reasons given for the delay. Much of what was said had to be taken on faith.

Despite the increased uncertainty, Technophar's managers were reluctant to cancel the contract outright. Doing so would tarnish the company's reputation, and the contract, even with the cost increases, was still profitable. However, with additional orders coming onto the books, Technophar could keep its plant producing for at least the next six months. Thus, Technophar could legally cut the order off and renegotiate at a later date.

A more fundamental issue was Technophar's presence in Viet Nam. Largely, the company's growth had been in developing countries in markets where the managers had previous experience. Otherwise, large sales had been to developed countries such as Germany and France. The few sales that had been to riskier, developing countries involved a smaller stake: one machine had been sold to each of Brazil, Colombia, Venezuela and Indonesia. The sale of a plant, complete with four machines and auxiliary equipment, to Viet Nam, one of the least developed countries, was a considerable departure from Technophar's established practices. Dube wondered whether Technophar should even be in Viet Nam.

Technophar's entry into Viet Nam had also been one of chance. How many of these opportunities were slipping through the cracks because Technophar was not systematically seeking out and evaluating potential markets? Was the same kind of innovation which allowed for simplification and systemization of capsule production required in their approach to international markets?

24 NORA-SAKARI

A PROPOSED JOINT VENTURE IN MALAYSIA

On the morning of Monday, July 13, 1992, Zainal Hashim, vice-chairman of Nora Holdings Sdn Bhd[1] (Nora), arrived at his office about an hour earlier than usual. As he looked out the window at the city spreading below, he thought about the Friday evening reception which he had hosted at his home in Kuala Lumpur (KL), Malaysia, for a team of negotiators from Sakari Oy[2] (Sakari) of Finland. Nora was a leading supplier of telecommunications (telecom) equipment in Malaysia while Sakari, a Finnish conglomerate, was a leader in the manufacture of cellular phone sets and switching systems. The seven-member team from Sakari was in KL to negotiate with Nora the formation of a joint-venture between the two telecom companies.

This was the final negotiation which would determine whether a joint-venture agreement would materialise. The negotiation had ended late Friday afternoon, having lasted for five consecutive days. The joint-venture company, if established, would be set up in Malaysia to manufacture and commission digital switching exchanges to meet the needs of the telecom industry in Malaysia and in neighbouring countries, particularly Indonesia and Thailand. While Nora would benefit from the joint-venture in terms of technology transfer, the venture would pave the way for Sakari to acquire knowledge and gain access to the markets of Southeast Asia.

IVEY   R. Azimah Ainuddin prepared this case under the supervision of Professor Paul Beamish solely to provide material for class discussion. The authors do not intend to illustrate either effectve or ineffective handling of a managerial situation. The authors may have disguised certain names and other identifying information to protect confidentiality. Ivey Management Services prohibits any form of reproduction, storage or transmittal without its written permission. This material is not covered under authorization from CanCopy or any reproduction rights organization. Copyright © 1995, Ivey Management Services.

[1]Sdn Bhd is an abbreviation for Sendirian Berhad, which means private limited company in Malaysia.
[2]Oy is an abbreviation for Osakeyhtiot, which means private limited company in Finland.

The Nora management was impressed by the Finnish capability in using high technology to enable Finland, a small country of only five million people, to have one of the fastest-growing economies in the world. Most successful Finnish companies were in the high-tech industries. For example, Kone was one of the world's three largest manufacturer of lifts, Vaisala was the world's major supplier of metereological equipment, and Sakari was one of the leading telecom companies in Europe. It would be an invaluable opportunity for Nora to learn from the Finnish experience and emulate their success for Malaysia.

The opportunity emerged when in February, 1990, Peter Mattsson, president of Sakari's Asian regional office in Singapore, approached Zainal[3] to explore the possibility of forming a cooperative venture between Nora and Sakari. Mattsson said:

> While growth in the mobile telecommunications network is expected to be about 40 percent a year in Asia between 1990 and 1994, growth in fixed networks would not be as fast, but the projects are much larger. A typical mobile network project amounts to a maximum of a few hundred million Finnish marks, but fixed network projects can be estimated in billions. In Malaysia and Thailand, billion-mark projects are currently approaching contract stage. Thus it is imperative that Sakari establish its presence in this region to capture a share in the fixed network market.

The large potential for telecom facilities was also evidenced in the low telephone penetration rates for most Southeast Asian countries. For example, in 1990, telephone penetration rates (measured by the number of telephone lines per 100 people) for Indonesia, Thailand, Malaysia, and the Philippines ranged from 1 to 11 lines per 100 people compared to the rates in developed countries such as Canada, Finland, Germany, U.S. and Sweden where the rates exceeded 50 telephone lines per 100 people.

The Telecom Industry in Malaysia

In November, 1990, Syarikat Telekom Malaysia Sdn Bhd (STM), the government-owned telecom company, became a public-listed company, Telekom Malaysia Berhad (TMB). With a paid-up capital of RM2.4 billion[4], TMB was given the authority by the Malaysian government to develop the country's telecom infrastructure. It was also given the mandate to provide telecom services that were on par with those available in developed countries.

In a corporate statement, TMB announced that it would be investing in the digitalization of its networks to pave the way for offering services based on the ISDN (integrated services digitalized network) standard, and investing in international fibre optic cable networks to meet the needs of increased telecom traffic between Malaysia and the rest of the world. TMB would also facilitate the installation of more cellular telephone networks in view of the increased demand for the use of mobile phones among the business community in KL and in major towns.

As the nation's largest telecom company, TMB's operations were regulated through a 20-year licence issued by the Ministry of Energy, Telecommunications and Posts. In line

---

[3]The first name is used because the Malay name does not carry a family name. The first and/or middle names belong to the individual and the last name is his/her father's name.

[4]RM is Ringgit Malaysia, the Malaysian currency. As at December 31, 1991, US$1=RM2.73.

with the government's Vision 2020 program which targeted Malaysia to become a developed nation by the year 2020, there was a strong need for the upgrading of the telecom infrastructure in the rural areas. TMB estimated that it would spend more than RM6 billion between 1991 and 1995 on the installation of fixed networks, of which 25 percent would be allocated for the expansion of rural telecom. The objective was to increase the level of telephone penetration rate to 25 percent by the year 2000.

Although TMB had become a large national telecom company, it lacked the expertise and technology to undertake massive infrastructure projects. In most cases, the local telecom companies would be invited to submit their bids for a particular contract. It was also common for these local companies to form partnerships with large multinational corporations (MNCs), mainly for technological support. For example, Pernas-NEC, a joint-venture company between Pernas Holdings and NEC, was one of the companies that had been successful in securing large telecom contracts from the Malaysian authorities.

Nora's Search for a Joint-Venture Partner

In mid-1991, TMB called for tenders to bid on a five-year project worth RM2 billion for installing digital switching exchanges in various parts of the country. The project also involved replacing analog circuit switches with digital switches. Digital switches enhanced transmission capabilities of telephone lines, increasing capacity to approximately two million bits per second compared to the 9,600 bits per second on analog circuits.

Nora was interested in securing a share of the RM2-billion forthcoming contract from TMB and more importantly, in acquiring the knowledge in switching technology from its partnership with a telecom MNC. During the initial stages, when Nora first began to consider potential partners in the bid for this contract, telecom MNCs such as Siemens, Alcatel, and Fujitsu seemed appropriate candidates. Nora had previously entered into a five-year technical assistance agreement with Siemens to manufacture telephone handsets.

Nora also had the experience of a long-term working relationship with Japanese partners which would prove valuable should a joint-venture be formed with Fujitsu. Alcatel was another potential partner, but the main concern at Nora was that the technical standards used in the French technology were not compatible with the British standards already adopted in Malaysia. NEC and Ericsson were not considered, as they were already involved with other local competitors and were the current suppliers of digital switching exchanges to TMB. Their five-year contracts were due to expire by the end of 1992.

Subsequent to Zainal's meeting with Mattsson, he decided to consider Sakari as a serious potential partner. He was briefed about Sakari's SK33, a digital switching system that was based on an open architecture, which enabled the use of standard components, standard software development tools, and standard software languages. Unlike the switching exchanges developed by NEC and Ericsson which required the purchase of components developed by the parent companies, the SK33 used components that were freely available in the open market. The system was also modular, and its software could be upgraded to provide new services and could interface easily with new equipment in the network. This was the most attractive feature of the SK33 as it would lead to the development of new switching systems.

Mattsson had also convinced Zainal and other Nora managers that although Sakari was a relatively small player in fixed networks, these networks were easily adaptable, and could cater to large exchanges in the urban areas as well as small ones for rural needs. Apparently Sakari's small size, compared to that of AT&T, Ericsson, and Siemens, was an added strength because Sakari was prepared to work out customized products according to Nora's needs. Large telecom companies such as AT&T, Ericsson, and Siemens were alleged to be less willing to provide custom-made products. Instead, they tended to offer standard products that in some aspects were not consistent with the needs of the customer.

Prior to the July 1992 meeting, at least 20 meetings had been held either in KL or in Helsinki to establish relationships between the two companies. It was estimated that each side had invested not less than RM3 million in promoting the relationship. Mattsson and Ilkka Junttila, Sakari's representative in KL, were the key people in bringing the two companies together. (See Exhibits 1 and 2 for brief background information on Malaysia and Finland, respectively.)

Nora Holdings SDN BHD

The Company

Nora was one of the leading companies in the telecom industry in Malaysia. It was established in 1975 with a paid-up capital of RM2 million. In 1991, the company's paid-up capital increased to RM16.5 million and recorded a turnover of RM320 million. Nora Holdings consisted of 30 subsidiaries, including two public-listed companies: Multiphone Bhd, and Nora Telecommunications Bhd. As of August, 1991, Nora had 3,081 employees, of which 513 were categorized as managerial (including 244 engineers) and 2,568 as non-managerial (including 269 engineers and technicians).

The Cable Business.   Since the inception of the company, Nora had secured two cable-laying projects, one in 1975 and the other in 1983. For the 1983 project worth RM500 million, Nora formed a joint-venture with two Japanese companies, Sumitomo Electric Industries Ltd (held 10 percent equity share) and Marubeni Corporation (held 5 percent equity share). Japanese partners were chosen in view of the availability of a financial package that came together with the technological assistance needed by Nora. Nora also acquired a 63 percent stake in a local cable-laying company, Selangor Cables Sdn Bhd.

The Telephone Business.   Nora had become a household name in Malaysia as a telephone manufacturer. It started in 1975 when the company obtained a contract to supply telephone sets to the Telecom authority, which would distribute the sets to telephone subscribers on a rental basis. The contract, estimated at RM130 million, lasted for 15 years. In 1980 Nora secured licenses from Siemens and Northern Telecom to manufacture telephone handsets and had subsequently developed Nora's own telephone sets—the N300S (single line), N300M (micro-computer-controlled), and N300V (hands-free, voice-activated) models.

Upon expiry of the 15-year contract as a supplier of telephone sets to the government-owned Telecom authority (STM) in 1989, Nora suffered a major setback when it lost a

Exhibit 1   Malaysia: Background Information

Malaysia is centrally located in Southeast Asia. It consists of Peninsular Malaysia, bordered by Thailand in the north and Singapore in the south, and the states of Sabah and Sarawak on the island of Borneo. Malaysia has a total land area of about 330,000 sq km, of which 80 percent is covered with tropical rainforest. Malaysia has an equatorial climate with high humidity and high daily temperatures of about 26°C throughout the year.

In 1991 Malaysia's estimated population was 18 million, of which about seven million made up the country's labour force. The population is relatively young, with 40 percent between the ages of 15 and 39 and only 7 percent above the age of 55. A Malaysian family has an average of four children and extended families are common. Kuala Lumpur, the capital city of Malaysia, has approximately 1.5 million inhabitants.

The population is multiracial; the largest ethnic group is the Bumiputeras (the Malays and other indigenous groups such as the Ibans in Sarawak and Kadazans in Sabah), followed by the Chinese and Indians. Bahasa Malaysia is the national language but English is widely used in the business circles. Other major languages spoken include the various Chinese dialects and Tamil.

Islam is the official religion in Malaysia but other religions (mainly Christianity, Buddhism, and Hinduism) are widely practiced. Official holidays are allocated for the celebration of Eid, Christmas, Chinese New Year, and Deepavali. All Malays are Muslims, followers of the Islamic faith.

During the British rule, secularism was introduced to the country, which led to the separation of the Islamic religion from daily life. In the late 1970s and 1980s, realizing the negative impact of secularism on the life of the Muslims, several groups of devout Muslims such as the Malaysian Muslim Youth Movement (ABIM) undertook efforts to reverse the process, emphasizing a dynamic and progressive approach to Islam. As a result, changes were introduced to meet the daily needs of the Muslims. Islamic banking and insurance facilities were introduced and prayer rooms were provided in government offices, private companies, factories, and even shopping complexes.

Malaysia is a parliamentary democracy under a constitutional monarchy. The Yang DiPertuan Agung (the king) is the supreme head, and appoints the head of the ruling political party to be the prime minister. In 1992 the Barisan Nasional, a coalition of several political parties representing various ethnic groups, was the ruling political party in Malaysia. Its predominance had contributed to the political stability and economic progress of the country in the late 1980s and early 1990s.

The recession of 1985 through 1986 led to structural changes in the Malaysian economy, which had been too dependent on primary commodities (rubber, tin, palm oil, and timber) and had a very narrow export base. To reduce excessive dependence on primary commodities, the government directed resources to the manufacturing sector. To promote the establishment of export-oriented industries, generous incentives and relaxed foreign equity restrictions were introduced. A pragmatic approach toward foreign policy and heavy investments in modernizing the country's infrastructure (highways, air, and seaports, telecommunications, industrial parks) led to rapid economic growth in 1988 through 1991 (Table 1). In 1991 the manufacturing sector became the leading contributor to the economy, accounting for about 28 percent of gross national product (GNP). Malaysia's major trading partners were Singapore, US, UK, Japan, Korea, Germany and Taiwan.

Table 1   Malaysia: Economic Performance, 1988–1991

Economic Indicator	1988	1989	1990	1991
Per capita GNP (in RM)	5,065	5,507	6,206	6,817
Real economic growth rate	9.5%	9.3%	11.4%	9.1%
Consumer price index	2.5%	2.8%	3.1%	4.4%

Source: Ernst & Young International Ltd., 1993, *Doing Business in Malaysia.*

EXHIBIT 2   Finland: Background Information

Finland is situated in the northeast of Europe, sharing borders with Sweden in the west, Norway in the north and the former Soviet Union in the east. About 65 percent of its area of 338,000 sq km is covered with forest, about 15 percent lakes and about 10 percent arable land. Finland has a temperate climate with four distinct seasons. In Helsinki, the capital city of Finland, July is the warmest month with an average mid-day temperature of 21°C, and January is the coldest month with an average mid-day temperature of −3°C.

Finland is one of the most sparsely populated countries in Europe. In 1991 Finland had a population of five million, 60 percent of whom lived in the urban areas. Currently the city of Helsinki has a population of about 500,000. Finland has a well-educated work force of about 2.3 million. About half of the work force are engaged in providing services, 30 percent in manufacturing and construction, and 8 percent in agricultural production. The small size of the population led to scarce and expensive labour resources. Thus Finland had to compete by exploiting its lead in high-tech industries.

Finland's official languages are Finnish and Swedish, although only 6 percent of the population speaks Swedish. English is the most widely spoken foreign language. About 87 percent of the Finns are Lutherans and about one percent Finnish Orthodox.

Finland has been an independent republic since 1917, and was previously ruled by Sweden and Russia. A president is elected to a six-year term, and a 200-member, single-chamber parliament is elected every four years.

In the 1980s Finland's economy was among the fastest growing in the world, with gross domestic product increasing at an average rate of over 10 percent a year. Other than its forests, Finland has few natural resources. The country experienced a bad recession in 1991 leading to a drop in GDP (Table 2). Finland's economic structure is based on private ownership and free enterprise. However, the production of alcoholic beverages and spirits is retained as a government monopoly. Finland's major trading partners are Sweden, Germany, the former Soviet Union, and UK.

Finland's standard of living is among the highest in the world. The Finns have small families with one or two children per family. They have comfortable homes in the cities and one in every three families has a countryside cottage near a lake where they retreat on weekends. Taxes are high, the social security system is efficient, and poverty is virtually non-existent.

Until recently, the stable trading relationship with the former Soviet Union and other Scandinavian countries led to few interactions between the Finnish and people in the other parts of the world. The Finns are described as rather reserved, obstinate, and serious people. A Finn commented, "We do not engage easily in small talk with strangers. Furthermore, we have a strong love for nature and we have the tendency to be silent as we observe our surroundings. Unfortunately, others tend to view such behaviour as cold and serious." Visitors to Finland are often impressed by the efficient public transport system, the clean and beautiful city of Helsinki with orderly road networks, scenic parks and lakefronts, quaint museums, and magnificient cathedrals and churches.

TABLE 2   Finland: Economic Performance, 1988–1991

Economic Indicator	1988	1989	1990	1991
Per capita GDP (in FIM)	88,308	99,387	104,991	102,083
Increase in GDP	12.8%	12.2%	6.0%	−2.8%
Inflation	5.1%	6.6%	6.1%	4.1%
Unemployment	n.a.	3.5%	3.4%	7.6%

Source: Ernst & Young International Ltd., 1993, *Doing Business in Finland.*

RM32-million contract to supply 600,000 N300S single line telephones. The contract was instead given to a Taiwanese manufacturer, Formula Electronics, which quoted a lower price of RM37 per handset compared to Nora's RM54. Subsequently, Nora was motivated to move towards the high end feature phone domestic market. The company sold about 3,000 sets of feature phones per month, capturing the segment of the Malaysian market that needed more sophisticated sets than the ones supplied by STM.

Nora had ventured into the export market with its feature phones, but industry observers predicted that Nora still had a long way to go as an exporter. The foreign markets were very competitive and many manufacturers already had well-established brands. In 1989, exports amounted to RM2 million and were expected to increase to RM5 million after orders were filled for its N300M and N300V models from Alcatel and Tokyo Telecommunications Network. Nora's N300V had been recently approved in Germany and a shipment of 2,000 sets would be distributed through its subsidiary, Nora GmbH, to test the German market.

The Payphone Business.   Nora's start-up in the payphone business had turned out to be one of the company's most profitable lines of business. Other than the cable-laying contract secured in 1975, Nora had a 15-year contract to install, operate and maintain payphones in the cities and major towns in Malaysia. By 1992, Nora had started to manufacture card payphones under a license from GEC Plessey Telecommunications (GPT) of the UK. The agreement had also permitted Nora to sell the products to the neighbouring countries in Southeast Asia as well as to eight other markets approved by GPT.

While the payphone revenues were estimated to be as high as RM60 million a year, a long-term and stable income stream for Nora, profit margins were only about 10 percent because of the high investment and maintenance costs.

Other Businesses.   Nora was also the sole Malaysian distributor for Northern Telecom's private automatic branch exchange (PABX) and NEC's mobile telephone sets. The company had ventured into the paging market through a subsidiary, Unikom Sdn Bhd, and was capturing 50 percent of the paging business in Malaysia. It was also an Apple computer distributor in Malaysia and Singapore. In addition, Nora was involved in: distributing radio-related equipment; supplying equipment to the broadcasting, meteorological, civil aviation, postal and power authorities; and manufacturing automotive parts (such as the suspension coil, springs, and piston) for the local automobile companies.

The Management

When Nora was established in 1975, Osman Jaafar, founder and chairman of Nora Holdings, managed the company with his wife, Nora Asyikin Yusof, and seven employees. Osman was known as a conservative businessman who did not like to dabble in acquisitions and mergers to make quick capital gains. He was formerly an electrical engineer who was trained in the UK and had held several senior positions at the national Telecom Department in Malaysia.

In 1980, Osman recruited Zainal Hashim to fill the position of deputy managing director at Nora. Zainal held a master's degree in microwave communications from a British university and had several years of working experience as a production engineer at Pernas-NEC Sdn Bhd, a manufacturer of transmission equipment. In 1984, he was promoted to the position of managing director and in 1990, the vice-chairman.

Industry analysts observed that Nora's success was attributed to the complementary roles, trust, and mutual understanding between Osman and Zainal. While Osman "likes to fight for new business opportunities", Zainal preferred a low profile and concentrated on managing Nora's operations.

Industry observers also speculated that Osman, a former civil servant and an entrepreneur, was close to Malaysian politicians, notably the Prime Minister. Zainal, on the other hand, had been a close friend of the current Finance Minister since the days when they were both active in the Malaysian Muslim Youth Movement (a group that had developed a reputation for idealism, integrity and progressive interpretation of Islam). Zainal disagreed with allegations that Nora had succeeded due to its close relationships with Malaysian politicians and stressed that Nora's success was not due to its political skills. However, he acknowledged that such perceptions in the industry had been beneficial to the company.

Osman and Zainal had an obsession for high-tech and made the development of research and development (R&D) skills and resources a priority in the company. About 1 percent of Nora's earnings was ploughed back into R&D activities. Although this amount was considered small by international standards, Nora planned to increase it gradually to 5 to 6 percent over the next two to three years. Zainal said:

> We believe in making improvements in small steps, similar to the Japanese *kaizen* principle. Over time, each small improvement could lead to a major creation. To be able to make improvements, we must learn from others. Thus we would borrow a technology from others, but eventually, we must be able to develop our own to sustain our competitiveness in the industry. As a matter of fact, Sakari's SK33 system was developed based on a technology it obtained from Alcatel.

To further enhance R&D activities at Nora, Nora Research Sdn Bhd (NRSB), a wholly owned subsidiary, was formed, and its R&D department was absorbed into this new company. NRSB operated as an independent research company undertaking R&D activities for Nora as well as private clients in related fields. The company facilitated R&D activities with other companies as well as government organizations, research institutions, and universities. NRSB, with its staff of 40 technicians/engineers, would charge a fixed fee for basic research and a royalty for its products sold by clients. Thus far, NRSB had developed Nora's Network Paging System, which was the system presently used by the company's paging subsidiary, Unikom Sdn Bhd.

Zainal was also active in instilling and promoting Islamic values among the Malay employees at Nora. He explained:

> Islam is a way of life and there is no such thing as Islamic management. The Islamic values, which must be reflected in the daily life of Muslims, would influence their behaviours as employers and employees. Our Malay managers, however, were often influenced by their western counterparts, who tend to stress knowledge and mental capability and often forget the effectiveness of the softer side of management which emphasizes relationships, sincerity, and consistency. I believe that one must always be sincere to be able to develop good working relationships.

Sakari Oy

Sakari was established in 1865 as a pulp and paper mill located about 200 km northwest of Helsinki, the capital city of Finland. In the 1960s Sakari started to expand into the rubber and cable industries when it merged with the Finnish Rubber Works and Finnish Cable Works. In 1973 Sakari's performance was badly affected by the oil crisis, as its businesses were largely energy-intensive.

However, in 1975, the company recovered when Aatos Olkkola took over as Sakari's president. He led Sakari into competitive businesses such as computers, consumer electronics, and cellular phones via a series of acquisitions, mergers, and alliances. Companies involved in the acquisitions included: the consumer electronics division of Standard Elektrik Lorenz AG; the data systems division of L.M. Ericsson; Vantala, a Finnish manufacturer of colour televisions; and Luxury, a Swedish state-owned electronics and computer concern.

In 1979, a joint-venture between Sakari and Vantala, Sakari-Vantala, was set up to develop and manufacture mobile telephones. Sakari-Vantala had captured about 14 percent of the world's market share for mobile phones and held a 20 percent market share in Europe for its mobile phone handsets. Outside Europe, a 50–50 joint-venture was formed with Tandy Corporation which, to date, had made significant sales in the United States, Malaysia and Thailand.

Sakari first edged into the telecom market by selling switching systems licensed from France's Alcatel and by developing the software and systems to suit the needs of small Finnish phone companies. Sakari had avoided head-on competition with Siemens and Ericsson by not trying to enter the market for large telephone networks. Instead, Sakari had concentrated on developing dedicated telecom networks for large private users such as utility and railway companies. In Finland, Sakari held 40 percent of the market for digital exchanges. Other competitors included Ericsson (34 percent), Siemens (25 percent), and Alcatel (1 percent).

Sakari was also a niche player in the global switching market. Its SK33 switches had sold well in countries such as Sri Lanka, United Arab Emirates, China, and the Soviet Union. A derivative of the SK33 main exchange switch called the SK33XT was subsequently developed to be used in base stations for cellular networks and personal paging systems.

Sakari attributed its emphasis on R&D as its key success factor in the telecom industry. Strong in-house R&D in core competence areas enabled the company to develop technology platforms such as its SK33 system that were reliable, flexible, widely compatible and economical. About 17 percent of its annual sales revenue was invested into R&D and product development units in Finland, UK, and France. Sakari's current strategy was to emphasize global operations in production and R&D. It planned to set up R&D centres in leading markets, including Southeast Asia.

Sakari was still a small company by international standards (see Exhibit 3 for a list of the world's major telecom equipment suppliers). It lacked a strong marketing capability and had to rely on joint-ventures such as the one with Tandy Corporation to enter the world market, particularly the U.S. In its efforts to develop market position quickly, Sakari had to accept lower margins for its products, and often the Sakari name was not revealed on the product. In recent years, Sakari decided to emerge from its hiding place as a manufacturer's manufacturer and began marketing under the Sakari name.

In 1988, Sakari's revenues increased but margins declined by 21 percent when integration of the acquired companies took longer and cost more than expected. In 1989 Mikko Koskinen took over as president of Sakari when Olkkola died. Koskinen announced that telecommunications, computers, and consumer electronics would be maintained as Sakari's core business, and that he would continue Olkkola's efforts in expanding the company overseas. He believed that every European company needed global horizons to be able to meet global competition for future survival. To do so, he envisaged the setting up of alliances of

EXHIBIT 3   **Ten Major Telecommunication Equipment Vendors**

Rank	Company	Country	1992 Telecom Equipment Sales (US$million)
1	Alcatel	France/Netherlands	19,359
2	Siemens	Germany	11,877
3	AT&T	United States	10,809
4	Northern Telecom	Canada	8,029
5	Ericsson	Sweden	7,742
6	Motorola	United States	7,724
7	NEC	Japan	7,591
8	Bosch	Germany	5,221
9	Fujitsu	Japan	3,738
10	Philips	Netherlands	3,412

Source: International Telecommunication Union, 1994, *World Telecommunication Development Report 1994.*

varying duration, each designed for specific purposes. He said, "Sakari has become an interesting partner with which to cooperate on an equal footing in the areas of R&D, manufacturing, and marketing."

In 1991, Sakari was Finland's largest publicly traded industrial company and derived almost 80 percent of its total sales from exports and overseas operations. However, export sales were confined to other Scandinavian countries, Western Europe, and the former Soviet Union. Industry analysts observed that Finnish companies had a privileged relationship with the former Soviet Union, which was considered an easy market with minimal trading costs and high margins. As a result, until recently, these companies failed to invest in other parts of the world and were not making the most of their advantage in high-tech industries.

The recession in Finland which began in 1990 led Sakari's group sales to decline substantially from FIM22 billion[5] in 1990 to FIM15 billion in 1991. The losses were attributed to two main factors: weak demand for Sakari's consumer electronic products, and trade with the Soviet Union, which had come to almost a complete standstill. Consequently Sakari began divesting its less profitable companies within the basic industries (metal, rubber, and paper), as well as leaving the troubled European computer market with the sale of its computer subsidiary, Sakari Macro. The company's new strategy was to focus on three main areas: telecom systems and mobile phones in a global framework, consumer electronic products in Europe, and deliveries of cables and related technology. The company's divestment strategy led to a reduction of Sakari's employees from about 41,000 in 1989 to 29,000 in 1991.

In June 1992, Koskinen retired as Sakari's President and was replaced by Visa Ketonen, formerly the President of Sakari Mobile Phones. Ketonen appointed Ossi Kuusisto as Sakari's vice-president.

---

[5]FIM is Finnish Markka, the Finnish currency. As of December 31, 1991, US$1=FIM4.14.

The Nora-Sakari Negotiation

Since mid-May 1990, Nora and Sakari had discussed the potential of forming a joint-venture company in Malaysia. Nora engineers were sent to Helsinki to assess the SK33 technology in terms of its compatibility with the Malaysian requirements, while Sakari managers travelled to KL mainly to assess both Nora's capability in manufacturing switching exchanges and the feasibility of gaining access to the Malaysian market.

In November 1991, Nora submitted its bid for TMB's RM2-billion contract to supply digital switching exchanges supporting four million telephone lines. Assuming the Nora-Sakari joint-venture would materialise, Nora based its bid on supplying Sakari's digital switching technology. Nora competed with seven other companies short listed by TMB, all offering their partners' technology—Alcatel, AT&T, Fujitsu, Siemens, Ericsson, NEC, and Samsung. In early May 1992, TMB announced five successful companies in the bid. They were companies using technology from Alcatel, Fujitsu, Ericsson, NEC, and Sakari. Each company was awarded one-fifth share of the RM2 billion contract and would be responsible in delivering 800,000 telephone lines over a period of five years. Industry observers were critical of TMB's decision to select Sakari and Alcatel. Sakari was perceived to be the least capable in supplying the necessary lines to meet TMB's requirements, as it was alleged to be a small company with little international exposure. Alcatel was criticised for having the potential of supplying an obsolete technology.

The May 21 Meeting

Following the successful bid and ignoring the criticisms against Sakari, Nora and Sakari held a major meeting in Helsinki on May 21, 1992, to finalise the formation of the joint-venture. Zainal led Nora's five-member negotiation team, which comprised Nora's general manager for corporate planning division, an accountant, two engineers, and Marina Mohamed, a lawyer. One of the engineers was Salleh Lindstrom who was of Swedish origin, a Muslim and had worked for Nora for almost 10 years.

Sakari's eight-member team was led by Kuusisto, Sakari's vice-president. His team comprised Junttila, Hussein Ghazi, Aziz Majid, three engineers, and Julia Ruola (a lawyer). Ghazi was Sakari's senior manager who was of Egyptian origin and also a Muslim who had worked for Sakari for more than 20 years while Aziz, a Malay, had been Sakari's manager for more than 12 years.

The meeting went on for several days. The main issue raised at the meeting was Nora's capability in penetrating the South-east Asian market. Other issues included Sakari's concerns over the efficiency of Malaysian workers in the joint-venture in manufacturing the product, maintaining product quality and ensuring prompt deliveries.

Commenting on the series of negotiations with Sakari, Zainal said that this was the most difficult negotiation he had ever experienced. Zainal was Nora's most experienced negotiator and had single-handedly represented Nora in several major negotiations for the past 10 years. In the negotiation with Sakari, Zainal admitted making the mistake of approaching the negotiation applying the approach he often used when negotiating with his counterparts from companies based in North America or the UK. He said:

Negotiators from the U.S. tend to be very open and often state their positions early and definitively. They are highly verbal and usually prepare well-planned presentations. They also often engage in small talk and "joke around" with us at the end of a negotiation. In contrast, the Sakari negotiators tend to be very serious, reserved and "cold". They are also relatively less verbal and do not convey much through their facial expressions. As a result, it was difficult for us to determine whether they are really interested in the deal or not.

Zainal said that the negotiation on May 21 turned out to be particularly difficult when Sakari became interested in bidding a recently announced tender for a major telecom contract in the UK. Internal politics within Sakari led to the formation of two opposing "camps". One "camp" held a strong belief that there would be very high growth in the Asia-Pacific region and that the joint-venture company in Malaysia was seen as a hub to enter these markets. This group was represented mostly by Sakari's managers positioned in Asia and engineers who had made several trips to Malaysia, which usually included visits to Nora's facilities. They also had the support of Sakari's vice-president, Kuusisto, who was involved in most of the meetings with Nora, particularly when Zainal was present. Kuusisto had also made efforts to be present at meetings held in KL. This group also argued that Nora had already obtained the contract in Malaysia whereas the chance of getting the UK contract was quite low in view of the intense competition prevailing in that market.

The "camp" not in favour of the Nora-Sakari joint-venture believed that Sakari should focus its resources on entering the UK, which could be used as a hub to penetrate the European Union (EU) market. There was also the belief that Europe was closer to home, making management easier, and that problems arising from cultural differences would be minimized. This group was also particularly concerned that Nora had the potential of copying Sakari's technology and eventually becoming a strong regional competitor. Also, because the UK market was relatively "open", Sakari could set up a wholly owned subsidiary instead of a joint-venture company and consequently avoid joint-venture-related problems such as joint control, joint profits, and leakage of technology.

Zainal felt that the lack of full support from Sakari's management led to a difficult negotiation when new misgivings arose concerning Nora's capability to deliver its part of the deal. It was apparent that the group in favour of the Nora-Sakari joint-venture was under pressure to further justify its proposal and provide counterarguments against the UK proposal. A Sakari manager explained, "We are tempted to pursue both proposals since each has its own strengths, but our current resources are very limited. Thus a choice has to made, and soon."

The July 6 Meeting

Another meeting to negotiate the joint-venture agreement was scheduled for July 6, 1992. Sakari's eight-member team arrived in KL on Sunday afternoon of July 5, and was met at the airport by the key Nora managers involved in the negotiation. Kuusisto did not accompany the Sakari team at this meeting.

The negotiation started early Monday morning at Nora's headquarters and continued for the next five days, with each day's meeting ending late in the evening. Members of the Nora team were the same members who had attended the May 21 meeting in Finland, except Zainal, who did not participate. The Sakari team was also represented by the same members in attendance at the previous meeting plus a new member, Solail Pekkarinen,

Sakari's senior accountant. Unfortunately, on the third day of the negotiation, the Nora team requested that Sakari ask Pekkarinen to leave the negotiation. He was perceived as extremely arrogant and insensitive to the local culture, which tended to value modesty and diplomacy. Pekkarinen left for Helsinki the following morning.

Although Zainal had decided not to participate actively in the negotiations, he followed the process closely and was briefed by his negotiators regularly. Some of the issues which they complained were difficult to resolve had often led to heated arguments between the two negotiating teams. These included:

1. Equity Ownership. In previous meetings both companies agreed to form the joint-venture company with a paid-up capital of RM5 million. However, they disagreed on the equity share proposed by each side. Sakari proposed an equity split in the joint-venture company of 49 percent for Sakari and 51 percent for Nora. Nora, on the other hand, proposed a 30 percent Sakari and 70 percent Nora split. Nora's proposal was based on the foreign equity regulations set by the Malaysian government that allowed a maximum of 30 percent foreign equity ownership unless the company would export a certain percentage of its products (see Exhibit 4 for these regulations). In addition, formal approval from the Malaysian authorities would have to be obtained to enable the foreign partner to hold an equity share of more than 30 percent. Nora was concerned that this would further delay the formation of the joint-venture.

Equity ownership became a major issue as it was associated with control over the joint-venture company. Sakari was concerned about its ability to control the accessibility of its technology to Nora and about decisions concerning the activities of the joint-venture as a whole. The lack of control was perceived by Sakari as an obstacle to protecting its interests. Nora also had similar concerns about its ability to exert control over the joint-venture because it was intended as a key part of Nora's long-term strategy to develop its own digital switching exchanges and related high-tech products.

2. Technology Transfer. Sakari proposed to provide the joint-venture company with the basic structure of the digital switch. The joint-venture company would assemble the switching exchanges at the joint-venture plant and subsequently install the exchanges in designated locations identified by TMB. By offering Nora only the basic structure of the switch, the core of Sakari's switching technology would still be well-protected.

On the other hand, Nora proposed that the basic structure of the switch be developed at the joint-venture company in order to access the root of the switching technology. Based on Sakari's proposal, Nora felt that only the technical aspects in assembling and installing the exchanges would be obtained. This was perceived as another "screw-driver" form of technology transfer while the core of the technology associated with making the switches would still be unknown.

3. Royalty Payment. Closely related to the issue of technology transfer was the payment of a royalty for the technology used in building the switches. Sakari proposed a royalty payment of 5 percent of the joint-venture gross sales while Nora proposed a payment of 2 percent of net sales.

EXHIBIT 4   **An Extract of the Malaysian Government's Policy on Foreign Investment**

The level of equity participation for other export-oriented projects are as follows:

For projects exporting between 51 percent to 79 percent of their production, foreign equity ownership up to 51 percent will be allowed; however, foreign equity ownership of up to 79 percent may be allowed, depending on factors such as the level of technology, spin-off effects, size of the investment, location, value-added and the utilization of local raw materials and components.

For projects exporting 20 to 50 percent of their production, foreign equity ownership of 30 to 51 percent will be allowed, depending upon similar factors as mentioned above; however, for projects exporting less than 20 percent of their production, foreign equity ownership is allowed up to a maximum of 30 percent.

For projects producing products that are of high technology or are priority products for the domestic market, foreign equity ownership of up to 51 percent will be allowed.

Source: Malaysian Industrial Development Authority (MIDA), 1991, *Malaysia: Your Profit Centre in Asia.*

Nora considered the royalty rate of 5 percent too high because it would affect Nora's financial situation as a whole. Financial simulations prepared by Nora's managers indicated that Nora's return on investment would be less than the desired 10 percent if royalty rates exceeded 3 percent of net sales. This was because Nora had already agreed to make large additional investments in support of the joint-venture. Nora would invest in a building which would be rented to the joint-venture company to accommodate an office and the switching plant. Nora would also invest in another plant which would supply the joint-venture with surface mounted devices (SMD), one of the major components needed to build the switching exchanges.

An added argument raised by the Nora negotiators in support of a 2 percent royalty was that Sakari would receive side benefits from the joint venture's access to Japanese technology used in the manufacture of the SMD components. Apparently the Japanese technology was more advanced than Sakari's present technology.

4. Expatriates' Salaries and Perks.   To allay Sakari's concerns over Nora's level of efficiency, Nora suggested that Sakari provide the necessary training for the joint-venture technical employees. Subsequently, Sakari had agreed to provide eight engineering experts for the joint-venture company on two types of contracts, short-term and long-term. Experts employed on a short-term basis would be paid a daily rate of US$700 plus travel/accommodation. The permanent experts would be paid a monthly salary ranging from US$12,000 to US$15,000. Three permanent experts would be attached to the joint-venture company once it was established and the number would gradually be reduced to only one, after two years. Five experts would be available on a short-term basis to provide specific training needs for durations of not more that three months each year.

The Nora negotiation team was appalled at the exorbitant amount proposed by the Sakari negotiators. They were surprised that the Sakari team had not surveyed the industry rates, as the Japanese and other western negotiators would normally have done. Apparently Sakari had not taken into consideration the relatively low cost of living in Malaysia compared to Finland. In 1991, the average monthly rent for a comfortable, unfurnished three-bedroom apartment was US$920 in Helsinki and only US$510 in Kuala Lumpur.[6]

In response to Sakari's proposal, Nora negotiators adopted an unusual "take-it or leave-it" stance. They deemed the following proposal reasonable in view of the comparisons made with other joint-ventures which Nora had entered into with other foreign parties:

Permanent experts' monthly salary ranges to be paid by the joint-venture company were as follows:

1. Senior expert (7–10 years experience) . . . . RM 13,500–15,500
2. Expert (4–6 years experience) . . . . RM 12,500–14,000
3. Junior expert (2–3 years experience) . . . . RM 11,500–13,000
4. Any Malaysian income taxes payable would be added to the salaries.
5. A car for personal use.
6. Annual paid vacation of five weeks.
7. Return flight tickets to home country once a year for the whole family of married persons and twice a year for singles according to Sakari's general scheme.
8. Any expenses incurred during official travelling.

Temporary experts are persons invited by the joint-venture company for various technical assistance tasks and would not be granted residence status. They would be paid the following fees:

1. Senior expert . . . . RM750 per working day
2. Expert . . . . RM650 per working day
3. The joint-venture company would not reimburse the following:
    *   Flight tickets between Finland (or any other country) and Malaysia.
    *   Hotel or any other form of accommodation.
    *   Local transportation.

In defense of their proposed rates, Sakari's negotiators argued that the rates presented by Nora were too low. Sakari suggested that Nora's negotiators take into consideration the fact that Sakari would have to subsidize the difference between the experts' present salaries and the amount paid by the joint-venture company. A large difference would require that large amounts of subsidy payments be made to the affected employees.

5. Arbitration.   Another major issue discussed in the negotiation was related to arbitration. While both parties agreed to an arbitration process in the event of future disputes, they disagreed on the location for dispute resolution. Because Nora would be the majority stakeholder in the joint-venture company, Nora insisted that any arbitration should take place in KL. Sakari, however, insisted on Helsinki, following the norm commonly practised by the company.

---

[6]IMD & World Economic Forum, 1992, *The World Competitiveness Report.*

At the end of the five-day negotiation, many issues could not be resolved. While Nora could agree on certain matters after consulting Zainal, the Sakari team, representing a large private company, had to refer contentious items to the company board before it could make any decision that went beyond the limits authorized by the board.

The Decision

Zainal sat down at his desk, read through the minutes of the negotiation thoroughly, and was disappointed that an agreement had not yet been reached. He was concerned about the commitment Nora had made to TMB when Nora was awarded the switching contract. Nora would be expected to fulfil the contract soon but had yet to find a partner to provide the switching technology. It was foreseeable that companies such as Siemens, Samsung and AT&T, which had failed in the bid, could still be potential partners. However, Zainal had also not rejected the possibility of a reconciliation with Sakari. He could start by contacting Kuusisto in Helsinki. But should he?

25 MERCEDES COMES TO ALABAMA

In October 1993, Mercedes-Benz announced it would build a new plant to manufacture sports utility vehicles near Vance, Alabama, a small town in the southeastern United States. The state-of-the-art plant was expected to begin operation in 1997, and would produce 60,000 vehicles annually.

The announcement was warmly received in Alabama. Mercedes-Benz's chairman earned a standing ovation from local business people, and a congratulatory telephone call from President Bill Clinton. Alabama governor Jim Folsom opened his remarks with the words "*Guten Morgen.*"

Yet, this turn of events surprised many people. The move into sports utility vehicles (SUVs) marked the first time Mercedes-Benz had ventured outside its traditional strength in luxury automobiles. Whether it could succeed in a very different market segment was by no means clear. For the first time, a Mercedes-Benz automobile plant would be located outside Germany, raising questions about training a new workforce to meet exacting Mercedes standards. And if that wasn't enough, Alabama was among America's poorest and least industrialized states. For Mercedes to locate the plant in a poor state without a strong supplier base or advanced infrastructure was puzzling.

By 1998, critics and industry analysts were heaping praise on Mercedes and its Alabama adventure. Industry experts and customers liked the new car—the M-Class SUV—for its design, features, and even its price. The local workforce was meeting Mercedes' quality targets. Plans were already under way to expand the production capacity. Skepticism was replaced by applause all around.

IMD
LAUSANNE · SWITZERLAND

This case was developed by Professor Philip M. Rosenzweig as a basis for class discussion rather than to illustrate either effective or ineffective handling of an administrative situation. Copyright © 1999 by **IMD**—International Institute for Management Development, Lausanne, Switzerland. All rights reserved. Not to be used or reproduced without written permission directly from **IMD**, Lausanne, Switzerland.

Mercedes-Benz: The Rise of a Luxury Automaker

Mercedes-Benz was the automotive division of Daimler-Benz AG, Germany's largest industrial group. Daimler-Benz had been created in 1926 by two of Germany's automobile pioneers, Gottlieb Daimler and Karl Benz. Following World War I, with Germany's economy in shambles and with Ford Motor Company establishing itself as a world leader in passenger automobiles, Daimler and Benz merged their firms. Daimler-Benz prospered over the next years, and established a reputation for automobiles of high quality and superior engineering. Although many of the Daimler-Benz factories were destroyed during World War II, the company regained its health during the 1950s. Over the next decade, Mercedes-Benz automobiles became synonymous with prestige and excellence. Throughout the 1970s and 1980s, Mercedes-Benz ranked among the most prestigious luxury cars in the world.

Throughout its growth, the company followed a strategy based on German production and global exports. The vast majority of value-added activities, from research and design to procurement and manufacturing, took place in Germany. A network of foreign subsidiaries handled local sales and service. In 1973, reacting to the growing strength of the Deutsche mark (DM), Mercedes-Benz shifted the sourcing of its U.S.-destined diesel trucks to Brazil, but production of automobiles remained firmly in Germany. German engineering and German quality were hallmarks of Mercedes-Benz, and customers the world over were willing to pay the price.

By the 1990s, Daimler-Benz was a leading diversified industrial corporation, with 1991 revenues of DM 95 billion ($63 billion). Mercedes-Benz, the automobile and commercial vehicles group, contributed 69 percent of revenues; electronics and aerospace divisions accounted for the rest.

Mercedes-Benz, in turn, was organized into two divisions: Passenger Cars (with 1991 sales of DM 39 billion) and Commercial Vehicles (1991 sales of DM 27 billion). The Passenger Car Division offered three levels of luxury cars in 1991: S-Class Sedans and Coupés, including the prestigious 500 SEC and 600 SEC S-Class Coupés, Mid-Series cars including T-models, and the Compact Series, which included the popular Mercedes 190. The Commercial Vehicle Division manufactured trucks and buses, and had production broadly distributed around the world, with manufacturing sites in Mexico, Argentina, Turkey, and the United States. The U.S. operation included Freightliner, a leader in U.S. heavy-duty trucks. In 1992, 112,800 commercial vehicles were fully produced outside of Germany. The firm employed more than 300,000 German workers and more than 70,000 employees in foreign countries, for a total of 379,000. (Performance figures for Mercedes-Benz are presented in Exhibit 1 and Exhibit 2.)

Competitive Pressures in the Global Automobile Industry

Automobile companies were among the first to compete on a global basis. Some leading firms, including General Motors and Ford, had long ago set up manufacturing plants overseas, and tended to build their cars close to the point of sales. Others, including the leading Japanese automakers Toyota and Nissan, had for decades pursued an export strategy, building autos in large Japanese factories and shipping them across the oceans.

EXHIBIT 1   Financial Performance, 1982–1991

	1991	*1990*	*1989*	*1988*	*1987*	*1986*	*1985*	*1984*	*1983*	*1982*
Sales (DM million)	95,010	85,880	76,392	73,495	67,475	65,498	52,409	43,505	40,005	38,905
Net income	1,872	1,684	1,700	1,675	1,787	1,805	1,735	1,145	1,034	944
Income as % of sales	2.0%	2.0%	2.2%	2.3%	2.6%	2.8%	3.3%	2.6%	2.6%	2.4%
Earnings per share	40	36	36	40	42	43	41	27	25	23
Stock price (high)	794	955	831	772	1,220	1,256	1,041	517	524	290
Stock price (low)	507	550	626	527	575	896	481	417	277	202
P/E (high)	20	27	23	19	29	29	25	19	21	13
P/E (low)	13	15	17	13	14	21	12	15	11	9
Employees (000)	379	377	368	339	326	320	231	200	185	186

Source: Adapted from Mercedes-Benz annual reports and *Hoover Handbook of World Business, 1993.*

EXHIBIT 2   Sales and Production, 1989–1992

	1992	*1991*	*1990*	*1989*
Passenger Cars				
Sales (DM million)	39,601	39,513	35,527	32,887
Production (units)	529,428	577,990	574,227	542,160
Employees (12/31)	95,492	103,632	100,479	96,734
Commercial Vehicles				
Sales (DM million)	26,879	27,591	24,288	23,480
Production (units)	277,346	295,794	258,947	260,956
Employees (12/31)	90,786	96,762	93,920	90,663
Total				
Sales (DM million)	66,480	67,104	59,815	56,367
Net income	849	1,548	1,545	1,492

Source: Daimler-Benz annual reports.

By the 1980s, the pace of foreign investment and global expansion had quickened. Many firms that had pursued an export strategy now began to establish manufacturing plants abroad. In particular, leading Japanese firms began to invest in the U.S. and Europe. The reasons were many. Automobile manufacturing depended on inputs ranging from steel to auto parts, which could be sourced from many suppliers around the world. Labor, too, was an important component of total manufactured cost. (Refer to Exhibit 3 for a breakdown of the 1993 manufacturing cost of an average passenger car built in the U.S. compared to an equivalent car manufactured in Mexico for sale in the U.S.) Other elements of automobile cost included design and marketing. According to estimates, labor utilized in final assembly accounted for roughly 5 percent of an automobile's total cost.

EXHIBIT 3   Cost Structure of Automobile Assembly Average for U.S.-Built Automobiles

(Other Components of Value Added, Such as Design and Marketing, Are Excluded.)

	United States	Mexico
Labor	$700	$140
Parts, components, and subassemblies	7,750	8,000
Component shipping costs	75	600
Finished vehicle shipping	225	400
Inventory costs	20	40
Total	$8,770	$9,180

Source: Adapted from *Automotive News,* September 27, 1993.

Not only were firms expanding globally in the 1980s, several were broadening their product lines. A number of Japanese auto makers upgraded the quality of their vehicles and began to offer cars that were similar in quality to Mercedes but lower in price. In 1989, Japan's leading producer, Toyota, established a new luxury brand for the U.S. called Lexus; in 1992, Lexus sold 92,890 cars in the U.S. compared to 62,832 for Mercedes-Benz. Mercedes' response to the Japanese challenge was a new S-Class series. Introduced in 1992, after five years in development, the S-Class series turned out to be a two-ton automobile, bulky and out of step with demands for lean design and efficiency. Joining the chorus of critics was a report by the Massachusetts Institute of Technology, which described Mercedes automobiles as over-engineered and wasteful.

Adding to Mercedes' problems was its cost structure. The German-based strategy, once a point of strength, was now a source of weakness. German auto workers were among the highest paid in the world, yet worked the shortest work week (refer to Exhibit 4). Mercedes-Benz was not the only German automaker to be affected: its chief rival, Bayerische Motoren Werke AG (BMW), manufactured its automobiles at three German assembly plants where it, too, paid high wages and incurred high production costs. BMW found that given the strength of the DM relative to the US dollar (refer to Exhibit 5), and given a 10 percent import tax on cars costing more than $30,000 levied by the US government, its cars were becoming unaffordable for many Americans. In early 1993, BMW announced its intention to locate a new production plant in the United States, selecting a site in South Carolina.

Strategic Redirection, 1993

Beginning in early 1993, Mercedes-Benz began a major change of direction. First, chairman Helmut Werner announced that the firm would transform itself from an automaker known mainly for luxury cars into a "full-line manufacturer offering high-quality vehicles in all segments of the market."[1] As part of this new direction, Mercedes would introduce

---

[1]"Mercedes-Benz Changes Direction." *Motor Report International,* February 1, 1993.

EXHIBIT 4   **Labor Costs in Leading Industrial Nations—Approximate Average Hourly Labor Costs, Including Benefits**
($US Equivalent)

	France	Germany	Japan	United States
1970	$2.50	$3.00	$2.00	$4.50
1975	4.50	7.00	3.50	7.00
1980	9.00	12.50	7.00	10.00
1985	8.00	10.00	8.00	13.00
1990	16.00	23.00	16.00	15.00
1993	17.00	26.50	18.00	15.50

Source: Adapted from *The Wall Street Journal*, November 4, 1993.

EXHIBIT 5   **Currency Exchange Rates**

	France French Franc	Germany Deutsche Mark	Japan Yen
1970	5.52	3.65	357.6
1975	4.49	2.62	305.1
1980	4.52	1.96	203.0
1985	7.56	2.46	200.5
1987	5.34	1.58	123.5
1989	5.79	1.70	143.5
1991	5.18	1.52	125.2
1993	5.92	1.71	108.9

Note: All currency exchange rates are stated as year-end equivalent of US$1. For example, on 12/31/70, $1 = FFr 5.52. 1993 exchange rates as of 11/29/93.

Source: Compiled from *International Financial Statistics Yearbook, 1993* and *The Wall Street Journal.*

a number of new automobiles. It would offer a line of small cars aimed at mid-market consumers. Mercedes would also introduce two "lifestyle" vehicles, now increasingly popular: a minivan and a four-wheel-drive sports utility vehicle. The European market for sports utility vehicles had already reached 242,000 units in 1992, and the American market, dominated by the domestic giants GM, Ford, and Chrysler, was nearly 1 million units per year. Japanese automakers, with close to 30 percent of the U.S. market for passenger cars, had managed to gain 13 percent of the U.S. market for light trucks and SUVs. Finally, Mercedes intended to produce a low-energy, electrically powered city car.

In addition to this change in product strategy, Werner announced that Mercedes would end its exclusive reliance on German automobile manufacturing and would step up its production abroad. The minivan, set for a 1995 launch, was to be manufactured in Spain. The new line of small cars was to be built at a European site, yet to be determined.

Perhaps most dramatic was the announcement, in April 1993, that the sports utility vehicle would be built at a new plant in the United States. Although no site was announced, speculation centered on North and South Carolina, where Mercedes already had a Freightliner heavy truck operation, and where BMW was planning to build its new plant.

These announcements could do little to stem the slide in Mercedes-Benz performance. In May of 1993, the firm reported that output of passenger cars in the first quarter of 1993 was 39 percent below levels in 1992, from 153,738 units to 94,500. Even with an expected rebound in sales due to the launch in June of its new C-Class car, Mercedes expected earnings for the year to be no better than the 1992 level, which had represented a decline from the previous year. Analysts attributed much of the decline to the success of the Japanese luxury car brands: Toyota's Lexus, Nissan's Infiniti, and Honda's Acura, which had gained a large share of the US luxury car market.

In October 1993, after several months of weighing alternatives, and listening to offers from state and local authorities at more than 150 sites in 30 states, Mercedes made its surprising announcement: the new American plant would be located in Vance, Alabama, population 250. Alabama had sweetened the deal by offering an astonishing $250 million in tax abatements and other incentives.[2]

Although dramatic, the announcement did not strike most viewers as wise: Alabama consistently ranked at the bottom of the 50 states in education, income, and productivity. Furthermore, rural Tuscaloosa County had little industrial infrastructure and was located far from international air nodes, ports, canals, or even power and water supplies. Despite these drawbacks, Mercedes-Benz affirmed its commitment not only to center the production of its four-wheel-drive sports utility vehicle in Alabama, but to steer the global sales of this product line from Alabama.

Planting the Mercedes Star in Alabama

To manage the M-Series, Mercedes-Benz named Andreas Renschler president and CEO of Mercedes-Benz U.S. International Inc. (MBUSI). At 35 years of age, Renschler, a German national, was much younger than other Mercedes managers of similar responsibility. He had spent the previous years in charge of two projects in Latin America, rather than in the corridors of the Mercedes Stuttgart headquarters. Most recently, he had taken part in the feasibility study which had led to the company's entry into Alabama. Renschler was of a generation that preferred a collaborative management approach to the traditional hierarchial Mercedes ways. For all these reasons, he seemed to be the right person to head up the new venture.[3]

Mercedes managed the new SUV, called the M-Series, as an independent product line, separate from the traditional luxury lines. "We stipulated that it had to be a separate team, 12 or 13 people, with a separate budget, free from line management obligations, in separate offices, answering to a single member of the board," said one manager.[4]

---

[2]Martin, Justin. "Mercedes: Made in Alabama," *Fortune,* July 7, 1997.
[3]Muenchau, Wolfgang. "Renschler Cuts Loose," *Financial Times*, January 8, 1996, p.11.
[4]Muenchau, Wolfgang. "Renschler Cuts Loose," *Financial Times*, January 8, 1996, p.11.

Renschler quickly set up his top team, balancing four Germans with four Americans. The Americans included U.S. executives with Detroit experience as well as a few who had worked for Japanese firms in the U.S.[5] Activities proceeded along two dimensions: construction of the $300 million plant, and development of the new vehicle. Not far from the construction site, a small team of designers worked closely with their colleagues in Germany. Each day they communicated with Stuttgart for three or four hours, often by videoconference. Some managers traveled between Germany and Alabama every week.[6]

Building an American Workforce

Once construction of the plant was well under way, Mercedes-Benz began to fill 650 new jobs. More than 40,000 people applied, some from nearby communities, but many from across the country. As it reviewed candidates, Mercedes kept a specific profile in mind: strong team skills, a commitment to continuous improvement, and a determination to produce the very best quality. Mercedes subjected applicants to an intensive process of interviews, tests, and simulations, with some candidates undergoing as many as 80 hours of assessment.[7]

After their selection, many new hires were sent to a Mercedes plant in Germany. For periods ranging from one month to six months, they worked side-by-side with German employees, learning the fine points of building a Mercedes. When they returned to Alabama, they were accompanied by more than 70 Germans who continued to train the new employees on site.[8] The objective was to ensure an uncompromising attention to quality as well as a commitment to the mystique of Mercedes-Benz. "In Germany, we don't say we build a car. We say we build a Mercedes," said one German manager. "We had to train that."[9]

Forging a New Management Style

Unlike Japanese automakers, who tried to replicate their exact approach in the United States—production systems, suppliers, and philosophy—Mercedes took a different approach. "We did not have the blueprint in hand," explained one American manager. "We had to create out own plan, our own method. So this is a 'learning field' for us. We've tried to keep an open mind and do things differently so we could create a 'learning field' for ourselves and for [Mercedes-Benz in Germany]. Our production methodology is new to this company, and it is nothing like what anyone else does."[10]

Renschler explained:

> We really are a multicultural team. We are Germans, Americans, and Canadians, and we have representatives from every car manufacturer in the U.S., plus the knowledge and expertise we brought from Mercedes in Germany.

---

[5]Martin, Justin. "Mercedes: Made in Alabama," *Fortune,* July 7, 1997.

[6]Muenchau, Wolfgang. "Renschler Cuts Loose," *Financial Times*, January 8, 1996, p.11.

[7]Vlasic, Bill. "In Alabama, the Soul of a New Mercedes?" *Business Week*, March 31, 1997.

[8]Vlasic, Bill. "In Alabama, the Soul of a New Mercedes?" *Business Week*, March 31, 1997.

[9]Vlasic, Bill. "In Alabama, the Soul of a New Mercedes?" *Business Week*, March 31, 1997.

[10]Moskal, Brian S. "Not the Same Old Mercedes," *Industry Week*, October 7, 1996.

Our philosophy from the beginning was: 'There is no optimum way.' There were different optimums. We were driven to use the best of the best and define our own set of Mercedes-Benz U.S. International Inc. best practices.

This way everyone can bring their own experiences. We can combine the experiences and learn from each other. We must be open and accessible. The pillar of all this is the Mercedes-Benz tradition, and that tradition is the fundamental basis of our ability to produce a quality product here.[11]

To help employees learn from each other, Renschler forged a style that was egalitarian and informal. The new plant would have no reserved parking for executives, nor an executive dining room, nor many private offices. It would be the opposite of Mercedes-Benz' traditional style, where as Renschler recalled, "We had a canteen for workers and clerks, then we had a 'silver spoon' from a certain level onwards, and then we had a 'golden spoon.'"[12]

Renschler believed an open style was conducive to high performance. "The more barriers you erect, the less [employees] will tell you. Communication is the most important thing, no matter which company you are in."[13] Mercedes-Benz was willing to follow this new approach, Renschler commented, because top management knew that it had to change. There had been, he remarked, "not just pressure on cost savings but also cultural change. . . . Without this new mentality we would not have managed."[14]

Meanwhile, the fortunes of Daimler-Benz, which had sagged in the early 1990s, began to recover. After a loss of DM 1.8 billion in 1993, Daimler-Benz showed a net profit of DM 1.05 billion in 1994. Sales of Mercedes automobiles in 1994 rose from 1993 levels, and were higher again in 1995.[15] Improved performance could not slow down the relocation of jobs outside of Germany. Citing the impact of a strong Deutsche mark, Daimler Benz Chairman Edward Reuter announced that 13,000 jobs in Germany would be lost in 1995, bringing the total of job losses in Germany to 83,500 over a four-year period.[16]

First SUV Output in Alabama

By 1997, the Alabama plant was nearing completion. Meanwhile, nine automotive parts suppliers had located in the Vance area, bringing $225 million in additional investment and adding 1,200 new jobs.[17]

In February 1997, the first SUV rolled off the Vance assembly line. At first, only 10 were produced each day, and each was subjected to an exacting inspection. Output was expected to reach 100 per day in July 1997, and would slowly increase to 270 per day in early 1998. "Volume is not the priority here," Daimler-Benz chairman Jurgen Schrempp

---

[11]Moskal, Brian S. "Not the Same Old Mercedes," *Industry Week*, October 7, 1996.

[12]Muenchau, Wolfgang. "Renschler Cuts Loose," *Financial Times*, January 8, 1996, p.11.

[13]Muenchau, Wolfgang. "Renschler Cuts Loose," *Financial Times*, January 8, 1996, p.11.

[14]Muenchau, Wolfgang. "Renschler Cuts Loose," *Financial Times*, January 8, 1996, p.11.

[15]"Daimler Benz Plans Job Cuts of 13,500 in '95," *The Wall Street Journal*, April 13, 1995, p. A3.

[16]"Daimler Benz Plans Job Cuts of 13,500 in '95," *The Wall Street Journal*, April 13, 1995, p. A3.

[17]Vlasic, Bill. "In Alabama, the Soul of a New Mercedes?" *Business Week*, March 31, 1997.

stressed. "The priority is quality, quality, quality."[18] In May 1997, Schrempp came to Alabama to officially open the new plant. He expressed confidence that sales of the new M-Series would be excellent, and speculated that the plant might soon need to undergo a second phase of expansion. "We know that [annual capacity] of 70,000 might not be sufficient, and we may have to raise that," he said.[19]

By early autumn 1997, the first of the M-Series—the ML320—was reaching dealers. Industry analysts and consumers alike were eager to take it for a test drive. The response was overwhelmingly positive. One reviewer gushed about the ML320's smooth ride and excellent handling: "Mercedes has built a sport utility that drives like a sedan, four wheels with the best of them, and rivals the luxury of its higher-priced competitors." At $33,950, the new ML320 was firmly in the middle of the SUV range, and not at the high end.[20]

Mercedes' Continuing Expansion

While Daimler-Benz took heart from its progress in Alabama, it also pushed ahead with plans to expand abroad and into new products. In early 1997, Juergen Hubbert, the Daimler management board member responsible for automobile manufacturing, said that the firm planned to increase its foreign production from 5 percent to 25 percent in the next few years.[21] Among the countries identified for further expansion was Egypt, where Mercedes intended to assemble E-200 luxury automobiles in a new $44 million plant.[22]

---

[18]Vlasic, Bill. "In Alabama, the Soul of a New Mercedes?" *Business Week*, March 31, 1997.

[19]Simonian, Haig, and Graham Bowley. "Daimler-Benz May Increase US Output," *Financial Times*, May 23, 1997.

[20]Zesiger, Sue. "It's a Car. It's a 4x4. It's a Benz." *Fortune*, September 29, 1997.

[21]"Mercedes Sets Foreign Push in Production," *International Herald Tribune*, April 10, 1997, p. 13.

[22]"Daimler to Assemble Mercedes Cars in Egypt," *International Herald Tribune*, June 5, 1997.

26 WHERE HAVE YOU BEEN? AN EXERCISE TO ASSESS YOUR EXPOSURE TO THE REST OF THE WORLD'S PEOPLES

Instruction

1. On each of the following worksheets, note the total number and names of those countries you have visited, and the corresponding percentage of world population which each country represents. Sum the relevant regional totals on page 398.

2. If this is used as part of a group analysis, estimate the grand total for the entire group. Then consider the following questions:

   - Why is there such a high variability in individual profiles (i.e., high exposure vs. low exposure)?
   - What are the implications of each profile for one's career?
   - What would it take to get you to personally change your profile?

Region: Africa

	Country	1997 Population (in millions)	% of World Total		Country	1997 Population (in millions)	% of World Total
1	NIGERIA	117.9	2.0	29	GUINEA	6.9	.1
2	EGYPT	60.3	1.0	30	BURUNDI	6.4	.1
3	ETHIOPIA	59.8	1.0	31	BENIN	5.8	.1
4	CONGO (DEM. REP)	46.7	.8	32	LIBYA	5.2	.1
5	SOUTH AFRICA	40.6	.7	33	SIERRA LEONE	4.7	.1
6	TANZANIA	31.3	.5	34	TOGO	4.3	.1
7	ALGERIA	29.3	.5	35	ERITREA	3.8	.1
8	KENYA	28.6	.5	36	CENTRAL AFRICAN REPUBLIC	3.4	.1
9	SUDAN	27.7	.5	37	LIBERIA	2.9	
10	MOROCCO	27.3	.5	38	CONGO, REP.	2.7	
11	UGANDA	20.3	.3	39	MAURITANIA	2.5	
12	MOZAMBIQUE	16.6	.3	40	LESOTHO	2.0	
13	GHANA	18.0	.3	41	NAMIBIA	1.6	
14	CÔTE d'IVOIRE	14.2	.2	42	BOTSWANA	1.5	
15	MADAGASCAR	14.1	.2	43	GAMBIA, THE	1.2	
16	CAMEROON	13.9	.2	44	GABON	1.2	
17	ANGOLA	11.7	.2	45	MAURITIUS	1.1	
18	ZIMBABWE	11.5	.2	46	GUINEA-BISSAU	1.1	
19	BURKINA FASO	10.5	.2	47	SWAZILAND	1.0	
20	MALI	10.3	.2	48	RÉUNION (FR.)	.7	
21	MALAWI	10.3	.2	49	DJIBOUTI	.6	
22	NIGER	9.8	.2	50	COMOROS	.5	
23	ZAMBIA	9.4	.2	51	EQUATORIAL GUINEA	.4	
24	TUNISIA	9.2	.2	52	CAPE VERDE	.4	
25	SENEGAL	8.8	.2	53	SÁO TOMÉ and PRINCIPE	.1	
26	SOMALIA	8.8	.2	54	MAYOTTE (FR.)	.1	
27	RWANDA	7.9	.1	55	SEYCHELLES	.1	
28	CHAD	7.2	.1				
	Subtotal	**682.0**			**Subtotal**	**743.9**	**12.8**

Source of all statistics, except for Taiwan: *1999 World Bank Atlas.*

Region: North America and Caribbean

	Country	1997 Population (in millions)	% of World Total
1	USA	267.6	4.6
2	MEXICO	94.3	1.6
3	CANADA	30.3	.5
4	CUBA	11.1	.2
5	GUATEMALA	10.5	.2
6	DOMINICAN REPUBLIC	8.1	.1
7	HAITI	7.5	.1
8	HONDURAS	6.0	.1
9	EL SALVADOR	5.9	.1
10	NICARAGUA	4.7	.1
11	PUERTO RICO (U.S.)	3.8	.1
12	COSTA RICA	3.5	.1
13	PANAMA	2.7	
14	JAMAICA	2.6	
15	TRINIDAD AND TOBAGO	1.3	
16	GUADELOUPE (FR.)	.4	
16	MARTINIQUE	.4	
17	BAHAMAS	.3	
18	BARBADOS	.3	
19	BELIZE	.2	
20	NETHERLANDS ANTILLES	.2	
21	ST. LUCIA	.2	
22	VIRGIN ISLANDS (U.S.)	.1	
23	ST. VINCENT & THE GRENADINES	.1	
24	GRENADA	.1	
25	ARUBA (NETH.)	.1	
26	DOMINICA	.1	
27	ANTIGUA AND BARBUDA	.1	
28	BERMUDA (U.K.)	.1	
29	ST. KITTS AND NEVIS	.1	
30	CAYMAN ISLANDS	.1	
	Subtotal	**462.8**	**7.9**

Region: South America

	Country	1997 Population (in millions)	% of World Total
1	BRAZIL	163.7	2.8
2	COLOMBIA	40.0	.7
3	ARGENTINA	35.7	.6
4	PERU	24.4	.4
5	VENEZUELA	22.8	.4
6	CHILE	14.6	.3
7	ECUADOR	11.9	.2
8	BOLIVIA	7.8	.1
9	PARAGUAY	5.1	.1
10	URUGUAY	3.3	.1
11	GUYANA	.8	
12	SURINAME	.4	
13	FRENCH GUIANA (FR.)	.2	
	Subtotal	**330.7**	**5.7**

Region: Western Europe

	Country	1997 Population (in millions)	% of World Total
1	GERMANY	82.1	1.4
2	UNITED KINGDOM	59.0	1.0
3	FRANCE	58.6	1.0
4	ITALY	57.5	1.0
5	SPAIN	39.3	.7
6	NETHERLANDS	15.6	.3
7	GREECE	10.5	.2
8	BELGIUM	10.2	.2
9	PORTUGAL	9.9	.2
10	SWEDEN	8.8	.2
11	AUSTRIA	8.1	.1
12	SWITZERLAND	7.1	.1
13	DENMARK	5.3	.1
14	FINLAND	5.1	.1
15	NORWAY	4.4	.1
16	IRELAND	3.7	.1
17	LUXEMBOURG	.4	
18	MALTA	.4	
19	ICELAND	.3	
20	CHANNEL ISLANDS (U.K.)	.1	
21	ISLE OF MAN	.1	
22	ANDORRA	.1	
23	GREENLAND (DEN.)	.1	
24	FAEROE ISLANDS (DEN.)	.1	
25	MONACO (FR.)	.1	
26	LIECHTENSTEIN	.1	
	Subtotal	**387.0**	**6.6**

Region: Eastern Europe

	Country	1997 Population (in millions)	% of World Total
1	RUSSIAN FEDERATION	147.3	2.5
2	UKRAINE	50.7	.9
3	POLAND	38.7	.7
4	ROMANIA	22.6	.4
5	YUGOSLAVIA, FED. REP. OF	10.6	.2
6	CZECH REPUBLIC	10.3	.2
7	BELARUS	10.3	.2
8	HUNGARY	10.2	.2
9	BULGARIA	8.3	.1
10	SLOVAK REPUBLIC	5.4	.1
11	CROATIA	4.8	.1
12	MOLDOVA	4.3	.1
13	LITHUANIA	3.7	.1
14	ALBANIA	3.3	.1
15	LATVIA	2.5	
16	BOSNIA and HERZEGOVINA	2.3	
17	MACEDONIA, FYR	2.0	
18	SLOVENIA	2.0	
19	ESTONIA	1.5	
	Subtotal	**340.8**	**5.9**

Region: Central Asia and Indian Subcontinent

	Country	1997 Population (in millions)	% of World Total
1	INDIA	962.4	16.6
2	PAKISTAN	128.5	2.2
3	BANGLADESH	123.6	2.1
4	AFGHANISTAN	25.0	.4
5	UZBEKISTAN	23.7	.4
6	NEPAL	22.3	.4
7	SRI LANKA	18.6	.3
8	KAZAKHSTAN	15.8	.3
9	AZERBAIJAN	7.6	.1
10	TAJIKISTAN	6.0	.1
11	GEORGIA	5.4	.1
12	TURKMENISTAN	4.7	.1
13	KYRGYZ REPUBLIC	4.6	.1
14	ARMENIA	3.8	.1
15	MONGOLIA	2.5	
16	BHUTAN	.7	
17	MALDIVES	.3	
	Subtotal	**1,355.5**	**23.3**

Region: Middle East

	Country	1997 Population (in millions)	% of World Total
1	TURKEY	63.7	1.1
2	IRAN	60.9	1.0
3	IRAQ	21.8	.4
4	SAUDI ARABIA	20.1	.3
5	YEMEN	16.1	.3
6	SYRIAN ARAB REPUBLIC	14.9	.3
7	ISRAEL	5.8	.1
8	JORDAN	4.4	.1
9	LEBANON	4.1	.1
10	UNITED ARAB EMIRATES	2.6	
11	WEST BANK AND GAZA	2.6	
12	OMAN	2.3	
13	KUWAIT	1.8	
14	CYPRUS	.7	
15	QATAR	.7	
16	BAHRAIN	.6	
	Subtotal	**223.1**	**3.8**

Region: Asia Pacific

	Country	1997 Population (in millions)	% of World Total
1	CHINA	1,227.2	21.1
2	INDONESIA	200.4	3.4
3	JAPAN	126.1	2.2
4	VIET NAM	76.7	1.3
5	PHILIPPINES	73.5	1.3
6	THAILAND	60.6	1.0
7	MYANMAR	43.9	.8
8	SOUTH KOREA	46.0	.8
9	NORTH KOREA	22.9	.4
10	TAIWAN	21.8	.4
11	MALAYSIA	21.7	.4
12	AUSTRALIA	18.5	.3
13	CAMBODIA	10.5	.2
14	HONG KONG (SAR - CHINA)	6.5	.1
15	LAO PDR	4.8	.1
16	PAPUA NEW GUINEA	4.5	.1
17	NEW ZEALAND	3.8	.1
18	SINGAPORE	3.1	.1
19	FIJI	.8	
20	MACAO (PORT.)	.4	
21	SOLOMON ISLANDS	.4	
22	BRUNEI	.3	
23	SAMOA	.2	
24	FRENCH POLYNESIA (FR.)	.2	
25	NEW CALEDONIA (FR.)	.2	
26	VANUATU	.2	
27	GUAM (U.S.)	.1	
28	MICRONESIA, FED. STS.	.1	
29	TONGA	.1	
30	AMERICAN SAMOA (U.S.)	.1	
31	KIRIBATI	.1	
32	MARSHALL ISLANDS	.1	
33	NORTHERN MARIANA ISLANDS	.1	
34	PALAU	.1	
	Subtotal	**1,976.0**	**34.0**

Summary

Region	# of Countries	Which You Have Visited	1997 Population (millions)	Region's % of World Population	% of Population You Have Been Exposed To
AFRICA	55	_____	743.9	12.8	_____
NORTH AMERICA and CARIBBEAN	31	_____	462.8	7.9	_____
SOUTH AMERICA	13	_____	330.7	5.7	_____
WESTERN EUROPE	26	_____	387.0	6.6	_____
EASTERN EUROPE	19	_____	340.8	5.9	_____
CENTRAL ASIA and INDIAN SUBCONTINENT	17	_____	1,355.5	23.3	_____
MIDDLE EAST	16	_____	223.1	3.8	_____
ASIA PACIFIC	34	_____	1,976.0	34.0	_____
GRAND TOTAL	**211**		**5,819.8**	**100.0**	

27 HCM BEVERAGE COMPANY

It was 7:45 A.M. on Friday, September 19, 1997, and the marketing office was still dark. Sitting in a small adjacent conference room, Mark Johnson, age 31, General Manager of HCM Beverage Company, wondered where everyone was. Johnson had a meeting scheduled with Mr. L. M. Dinh, the Marketing Manager, at 8:00 A.M. for the first of what Johnson planned would become a routine pattern of weekly updates. At 7:55 A.M., staff members started to trickle in one by one. At slightly past 8:00 A.M., Dinh walked into his office, put his briefcase on his desk, placed his cellular phone on the charger, and walked back out of the office. As Dinh reached for the doorknob to let himself out of the building, Johnson stepped out of the conference room and waved. Dinh said he would be right back and, before Johnson could reply, was out the door. Johnson looked at his watch and shook his head. He turned to Ms. L. P. My, a member of the marketing staff, and asked, "Where is Mr. Dinh going?" "To eat breakfast," My replied.

As Johnson walked back to the conference room, he could not help thinking that Dinh's behavior was indicative of the local marketing staff's indifference to their jobs. Johnson was deeply concerned about a steady deterioration in the company's performance, but he seemed to be the only one—besides his boss, Kevin Patterson. Patterson, Asia Pacific Regional Vice President, had made it clear to Johnson that Asia had been targeted by the company for rapid growth over the next 10 years. Furthermore, Patterson stressed that this first venture into Vietnam was just the beginning of what could amount to tens of millions of dollars of investment in the country over the next several years. But despite Johnson's best efforts, sales and profits had been down every month since he arrived. In two days, Johnson was to fly to Hong Kong to review HCM's performance with his boss. He was not looking forward to the meeting.

Company Background

Formed as a joint-venture (JV) bottling company in the summer of 1994 by a large multinational food and beverage firm headquartered in the United States (49 percent equity) and a local state-owned bottling company (51 percent equity), HCM Beverage Company was the US firm's first investment in Vietnam. What the JV promised to provide to the American company was access to a potentially large and rapidly growing market. What it promised to provide to the state-owned bottler was access to Western technology, capital, and marketing savvy.

Given the mutual benefits, the JV was quickly granted a license to produce soft drinks to sell in the Vietnamese market. During the first year, the US firm invested just over $US 2 million in new bottling equipment. By 1996, HCM Beverage Company had become the second-largest bottler of carbonated beverages in Vietnam. The largest bottling company in Vietnam, and HCM Beverage Company's major competitor, was Vietnam Beverage Company (VBC), a state-owned company located in Hanoi.

HCM Beverage Company was headquartered in a small town on the outskirts of Ho Chi Minh City (HCM City). This was also where the factory was located. To ease distribution problems, the warehouse and the sales and marketing departments were located about 25 miles away inside HCM City.

HCM Beverage Company had 300 full-time factory employees and about 200 additional temporary factory workers. The factory ran 24 hours a day with three eight-hour shifts, each with a one-hour break for meals. Because there was no place to eat within the vicinity of the plant, meals were served free at HCM Beverage Company's cafeteria inside the factory. Due to poor public transportation from the city out to the factory, a company bus picked up employees at one central location in the city, dropped them off at the plant, and took them back after their shift.

Top management of HCM Beverage Company consisted of five full-time managers, three of whom were members of the Board of Directors. (See Exhibit 1 for HCM Beverage Company's organizational chart.) The management team held staff meetings once a week to provide updates on their department's current activities and future plans. Given that the general manager, plant manager, and vice president of accounting all had offices either at or adjacent to the plant, staff meetings were typically held in a boardroom at the plant.

Mr. P. V. Luong was Chairman of the JV's Board of Directors. He was a government official who had worked in the Ministry of Industry prior to being appointed as chairman of the JV. During the JV negotiations in Hanoi, Mr. Luong had been a key representative for the government. Johnson commented on the Chairman's involvement with day-to-day operations:

> Normally, Mr. Luong doesn't involve himself in daily operating decisions. In general, he seems to be largely uninterested in the JV. However, with declining operating results, Mr. Luong had

Exhibit 1   HCM Beverage Company's Organization Chart

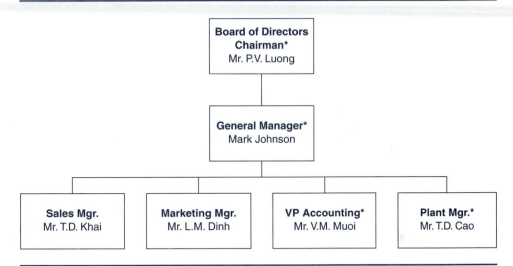

*Members of the Board of Directors.

become more involved of late. More precisely, he has complained louder and more frequently at board meetings. Still, he is not active in the management of the JV, nor can we rely on him for unique insights relating to our problems.

Mr. T. D. Cao, age 47, was a senior operations manager of the state-owned bottling company prior to the JV's formation. He had been with the company for over 20 years, and his family had lived in the south of Vietnam for several generations. When the JV was formed, HCM Beverage Company took over control of the former state-owned facility, and Mr. Cao was named plant manager. In addition to serving as plant manager, Mr. Cao also supervised the personnel department, covering not only the plant but the company's accounting, marketing, and sales activities. Since the formation of the JV, Mr. Cao had made significant increases in overall output and efficiency of the plant. He readily acknowledged that the new equipment supplied by the US partner had made a major difference in both quality and production capacity.

Mr. L. M. Dinh, age 51, had come to the JV soon after its formation. From 1963 to 1990, Mr. Dinh worked in Hanoi for VBC in a range of mid-to-upper-level management jobs. From 1990 to 1994, he worked as a regional bureaucrat in the Ministry of Industry in the south of Vietnam. His appointment in late 1994 as marketing manager for HCM Beverage Company had been championed by Chairman Luong.

Mr. T. D. Khai, age 42, was the sales manager and, in theory, reported directly to Johnson. However, he was several years junior to Mr. Dinh, and Mr. Dinh treated him as though Mr. Khai was a direct report.

Mr. V. M. Muoi, age 38, was the VP of accounting. Mr. Muoi had little professional training, but had worked in the accounting section of the Vietnamese partner before the formation of the JV.

Mark Johnson had been in Vietnam as the General Manager for about six months. He had joined the U.S. parent in 1992, fresh out of graduate school with an MBA from a well-known U.S.-based business school. After a series of promotions, he was most recently national brand manager for the company's fifth-best-selling soft drink product. HCM Beverage was his first international assignment. He explained the circumstances surrounding his appointment as the JV's general manager.

> I had been searching for an unusual assignment for the past couple of years. When I heard about the opening in Vietnam, I was intrigued. I contacted Kevin Patterson, Asia Pacific Regional Vice President of Marketing—someone I had known for a few years—about the position. He told me that despite a successful start-up, performance at the Vietnamese JV had begun to slip. He seemed very excited to learn I might be interested in the position.
>
> With nearly 80 million people, Vietnam seemed like a huge potential market. I really wanted some international experience. Asia was a strategic growth area for the company and I wanted some P&L responsibility to add to my marketing background.
>
> I met with my boss, Frank Carpano, and told him about the opening. He told me he thought I had great potential to move up in marketing and asked me if I was sure I wanted to leave headquarters to run some JV half way around the world. I gave him my rationale, and arranged for him and Patterson to talk. Within a few days, Kevin [Patterson] called me and offered me the job. The package was excellent—a 30 percent pay raise, cost of living adjustment, a furnished three-bedroom apartment in an upscale, Western-oriented compound in HCM City, a new Mercedes and full-time driver, maid service, paid home leave. The works.
>
> My wife was excited by the opportunity. Neither of us had lived overseas. She had taken the past six months off to stay at home with our new daughter and seemed happy to stay out of the corporate grind for two or three years.
>
> The move happened so fast. Between the time we made the decision and when we arrived in Vietnam, we had just eight weeks. We barely had time to put our furniture in storage and contract with a property management company to take care of renting our house while we were gone.
>
> When we arrived here in February, our driver met us at the airport. The ride in from the airport was an eye opener. Bicycles and mopeds were everywhere. The heat and humidity were stifling. We had been warned about it, but until you experience it, you can't quite imagine it. Good thing our apartment was nice. Thank heavens for air-conditioning.

Johnson had felt he had no time for training prior to his departure for Vietnam and thought he had been too busy since his arrival for any follow-up. He had picked up a couple of books on the country, but one was tough reading and went into all sorts of details about the economic and political history of the country that Johnson felt were a bit removed from his day-to-day management challenges.

Vietnam

Vietnam's history and strong Chinese cultural influences date back to the third century B.C., when early ancestors from China migrated into the Red River Delta. Located in the Indochina peninsula, Vietnam in 1996 had a population of just over 75 million people. In modern times, its people had experienced rule as a former French colony, the tragedy of the Cultural Revolution of 1945, the frustration of being a divided nation at the 17th parallel for 30 years (1945 to 1975), the devastation of the "Vietnam War" until the fall of Saigon in 1975 (renamed Ho

Chi Minh City to honor the country's founding father, Ho Chi Minh), and the challenges of being reunited as an independent country and member of the United Nations since 1977.

Although Vietnam had been reunited almost as long as it was divided, many of the effects of the division remained. For almost 30 years, the North practised socialism with support from the former Soviet Union while the South followed capitalism with the support of the United States. The differences in these systems and their impact on the people of Vietnam had been profound.

Vietnam's Economic System

From 1945, the North operated a centrally planned economy modelled on those of the Soviet Union and Eastern Europe. The North's leaders believed that a centrally planned system was essential for war conditions, because resources were scarce and consumption had to be limited, stable, and equitable. The system allowed the state to control all land and natural resources and maintain ownership of virtually all productive activities; the state allocated equipment and raw materials for production, and it organized agriculture under a collective system, meaning no private ownership of agricultural land. The state, under a system of egalitarian rationing, also controlled the distribution of agricultural products and consumer goods for personal consumption. It created monopolies in foreign trade and in critical industries. Central plans set production quotas, ignored the requirements for profit-making and eliminated competition among enterprises. Managers were considered effective if they met state quotas regardless of the quality of the product or whether it simply sat in warehouses after it was finished.

Jobs were guaranteed for everyone willing to work, but severe restrictions were placed on the size, number of employees, and capitalization of non-state enterprises. As a consequence, most factory employees worked in state-owned and controlled enterprises and most "private" enterprises were small in size.

The implementation of the centrally planned system to mobilize human and material resources during the 30-year battle for national independence and reunification resulted in economic distress and hindered economic growth. Large enterprises were run like government agencies, with little concern for profits and losses. Virtually no incentives existed to develop management skills in marketing, quality control, product development, or finance. In most enterprises, labor surpluses were retained even if there was no work for employees to perform. State enterprises were vertically integrated and accumulated large inventories in the face of chronic uncertainty.

For nearly 10 years after reunification in 1975, the North tried to impose its centrally planned system on the whole country. To some extent, the North was successful in creating an "iron rice bowl" mentality throughout the whole country. People came to see a job, and more particularly a certain level of income, as an entitlement. However, while neighboring countries such as Taiwan, Hong Kong, and Singapore were growing and prospering, Vietnam stagnated economically.

As a result of problems arising from central planning and state ownership, in 1986 the Congress of the Vietnam Communist Party adopted the policy of restructuring (*doi moi*) in order to turn the country from a bureaucratic centralized state-subsidy system to a regulated market economy. In the late 1980s, the government began deregulating the state-owned industrial sector and moving toward privatization.

A lack of capital and hard currency for the economic restructuring forced the government to welcome foreign investors. As a result of these policy changes, foreign direct investment flows into Vietnam rose to an estimated $US 6.3 billion in 1994 from an estimated $US 3.5 billion in 1993. Most foreign investments took the form of JVs, with local partners typically contributing about 30 percent of the capital and foreign investors kicking in about 70 percent. These capital contributions, however, did not directly reflect equity ownership. In many of the JVs, local Vietnamese partners retained 51 percent ownership even if their capital contributions were less. Often plant, equipment, land, and "goodwill" were assigned valuations that made up the difference.

After the implementation of *doi moi* in 1986, Vietnam experienced rapid economic growth. In 1992, for example, Vietnam's gross domestic product (GDP) grew by 8.7 percent and real national income increased by 5.3 percent. Vietnam expanded its industrial sector by 14.5 percent and its agricultural output by 4 percent. The country stabilized its currency, the *dong,* and reduced inflation to 38 percent in 1992 from more than 67 percent the previous year. Inflation had remained basically between 8 percent and 9 percent through 1996.

The government expected this economic growth to continue. (See Exhibit 2 for data on the Vietnamese economy.) However, the government also realized that rapid growth would only be possible with continuing international aid, improved access to international borrowing, reductions in the country's massive budget deficit, and improved controls over inflation. Another roadblock to continued economic growth was government bureaucracy. The government was prone to assess high taxes on foreign investments, which had driven some foreign companies out of Vietnam. Most Western economists believed that Vietnam's long-term development depended on the government's ability to create a favorable trade and investment environment, stable economic conditions, and an improved general standard of living.

Infrastructure

Vietnam's infrastructure had suffered from years of inadequate investment and before that, decades of war. Geography also added to the problem. Vietnam stretches 1,600 kilometers from north to south and from a temperate climate in the North to a tropical one in the South (see Exhibit 3). The central areas of the country are covered with dense forests. Vietnam

---

EXHIBIT 2   Vietnam Economic Data, 1990 to 1996

	Measure	*1990*	*1991*	*1992*	*1993*	*1994*	*1995*	*1996*
Population	Millions	67.7	68.6	70.4	72.0	73.5	73.9	75.1
Labor Force	Millions	37.6	38.8	39.9	40.8	41.8	42.8	43.1
GDP (current price)	Trillions Dong	38.2	70.0	101.9	136.0	174.0	222.8	254.5
GDP (constant '89 price)	Trillions Dong	27.0	28.6	31.0	33.3	36.0	39.3	43.1
Industrial Output ('89 constant price)	Trillions Dong	14.0	15.5	17.8	19.7	21.9	21.5	22.3
Exchange Rate (D:$US)	Thousands Dong	N/A	N/A	11.18	10.64	10.98	11.04	11.05

EXHIBIT 3   Map of Vietnam and Area

---

has more than 2,000 rivers over 10 kilometers long. In the early 1990s, only 10 percent of Vietnam's 105,600 kilometers of roads were sealed with asphalt or concrete, and even the best roads were considered to be of very low quality. Given the poor infrastructure, national distribution companies were virtually nonexistent. Moving products from the south to the north or vice versa was expensive and time-consuming.

Labor Structure

In 1996, the minimum wage for laborers working in enterprises with foreign invested capital was $US 35 per month for Hanoi and HCM City and $US 30 per month for other areas of the country. Companies with more capital tended to offer higher salaries to attract the best people. In addition to wages, most enterprises with foreign invested capital were expected to provide employees a daily food allowance, transportation to and from work (if the company was located outside of Hanoi or HCM City), and work clothes.

Organized labor was increasingly making its presence known in both state-controlled and private enterprises. Workers were demanding better working conditions and higher pay and were increasingly using strikes in state and foreign enterprises to make management take their demands seriously. Most of the recent strikes had been over salary disputes and higher productivity demands by firms. In an effort to control labor unrest, the most recent draft of the labor relations bill (in thirtieth revision) passed by the National Assembly in 1996 stated that strikes could only be used as a "last resort." However, the success of recent strikes in gaining workers' demands encouraged their use of it as a "weapon of first resort."

As state-owned enterprises privatized and streamlined their workforce, national unemployment had risen from 5.8 percent in 1992 to 6.7 percent, or 2.2 million people in 1993. The government figures for 1996 put unemployment in the urban areas at 13.2 percent and about 4 percent in the rural areas. However, these figures were believed by most independent experts to understate the true unemployment rate in both the urban and rural areas.

The Vietnamese labor force was relatively young and literate. The literacy rate was about 88 percent for the working age population. The largest group in the labor force, accounting for 53 percent of the total labor force and nearly 29 percent of the total population, was between the ages of 15 and 29. While Vietnam did not face a general labor shortage, skilled workers were in short supply.

Cultural Environment

Generations of Vietnamese had lived through communism, socialism, civil war, and now a type of controlled capitalism. With the exception of farmers, most people were not used to working eight-to-ten-hour days, six days a week. The effect was especially pronounced in the North.

The effects of the war and socialist system also affected mid-day activities. At the office, many workers turned off the light to take a nap around noon. Most shops also closed during this time and business usually picked up again by 2:00 P.M. This practice came about during the years of war when the fighting disrupted normal work schedules and activities. Sleeping also served as a coping mechanism and as a means of dealing with hunger and difficult working conditions. Although conditions had much improved, taking mid-day naps had remained popular.

Another interesting phenomenon was the emerging inequity gap between "office" workers and "factory" workers as the country moved toward industrialization. Most office workers were required to have college degrees, whereas factory workers had no educational requirements. This differential in education was beginning to show up in workers' compensation. Factory workers were increasingly uncomfortable with this rising wage gap. After all, office workers had nice air-conditioned offices to work in, while factory workers had to deal with noise, heat, cold, and humidity, as well as physically demanding and dangerous tasks.

The Vietnamese Soft Drink Industry

The Vietnamese soft drink industry dated back to the pre-1975 era when soft drinks were imported from the United States, France, and other nations. During this time, several foreign companies sold licenses to Vietnamese bottlers to produce their drinks locally. The most widely recognized brand during the 1960s and 1970s was Coca-Cola. Soft drinks were considered a luxury item during that time and were available mostly in Saigon, where the French and later Americans troops were stationed.

After the fall of Saigon, all foreign companies pulled out, and soon Vietnam was left with musty factories and rusty equipment. In the early 1980s, Vietnamese chemists began to formulate their own cola concentrates. However, these beverages were not very successful, and the soft drink market did not pick up again until the implementation of new economic reforms.

Once the Vietnamese government began to change its economic policies and governments such as the United States lifted their restrictions on doing business in the country, foreign investment and interest in Vietnam exploded. To keep themselves from being pushed out of the industry by foreign competition, most locally owned bottling companies began forming JVs with the foreign investors. They sought foreign investors to contribute capital and resources in order to upgrade the neglected facilities, equipment, and technology.

The tropical climate made the soft drink market one of the more attractive investment opportunities in Vietnam. In urban cities in 1997, the average selling price for bottled water was 2,000 dong per bottle.[1] Soft drinks cost between 900 to 2,000 dong. A bottle of beer could run between 2,000 and 5,000 dong.

In 1997, about 80 percent of the soft drinks sold in Vietnam were through large accounts—government ministries, state-owned enterprises, hotels, and restaurants. As economic conditions improved, the consumer segment of the Vietnamese soft drink market started to pick up. Both HCM Beverage Company and VBC had begun to actively target this segment. The keys to winning over consumers were branding and distribution. Despite rising consumer demand, distribution channels were not well developed. Most consumers purchased soft drinks from tiny "hawker stalls" and "mom and pop" stores. Servicing these highly fragmented vendors was difficult and expensive.

HCM Beverage Company's Problems

Dinh finally returned to his office at 8:30 A.M. Johnson was impatiently waiting for him. "We had a meeting scheduled for 8:00, not 8:30," Johnson commented in a stern and disapproving voice. Dinh explained that he understood but he was too hungry to wait and did not want to have another ulcer attack. Puzzled, Johnson asked what the normal starting hours were for the marketing staff. Dinh responded in halting English,

> Well, I have been a little lenient on my staff lately because they've been overworked during the last couple of months. We've been understaffed here in this department. I need at least two more people, but I haven't heard anything from Mr. Cao. He keeps telling me that he's looking but I don't see anyone at my doorstep. You know, having the personnel department located out at the factory and reporting through Mr. Cao is a little inconvenient. So, sometimes I let my kids leave early or take longer lunches.

After an abbreviated meeting, Johnson made a mental note to himself to tell his assistant to keep an eye on Dinh and his department.

Johnson's main concern right now was to address the question of declining sales. At the last staff meeting, the sales manager, Mr. Khai, explained that there were several reasons for the sales decline. "First," he explained, "it's the rainy season. People don't drink as much when it rains. Second, it is hard for all salesmen to reach their target accounts in one day because of bad road conditions."

While there was some truth to Mr. Khai's concerns, Johnson believed that the real problem was increasing competition, not a little rain and muddy roads. The decline in sales and profits had been apparent since before he arrived. While Johnson had expected a short-term

---

[1]Exchange rate as of September 1, 1997, was 12,100 VND to US$1.

decline in profits as a result of the new focus on the consumer market segment and spending some extra money on marketing, sales, and promotional activities, the overall decline in sales revenues had been unexpected.

Johnson began to seriously question the level of loyalty among HCM Beverage Company employees. He wondered if perhaps some were being contacted by the competition to jump ship. He also wondered why some of the larger institutional accounts were slipping in sales volume. When he asked Mr. Khai specifically about the drop in volume from large accounts, Mr. Khai simply repeated his rainy season explanation.

Privately, Johnson suspected it was more closely tied to employee motivations. He had heard rumors that some managers and salespeople were complaining that they were paid too little. Consequently, in August 1997, Johnson had put together a proposal to raise wages for supervisors, managers, senior managers, and directors (see Exhibit 4).

When he had floated the idea past Mr. Cao, he expected significant support because, as a senior manager, Mr. Cao's compensation would significantly increase with the plan. Instead, Mr. Cao gave Johnson a perplexed look and a statement that factory workers were hinting about striking to get higher wages. When Johnson pointed out that HCM Beverage Company factory workers were already being paid more than workers in other factories, Mr. Cao simply stated that now was "not a good time to unsettle the workers." The discussion was left there.

EXHIBIT 4   Monthly Wage Distribution for Vietnamese Employees

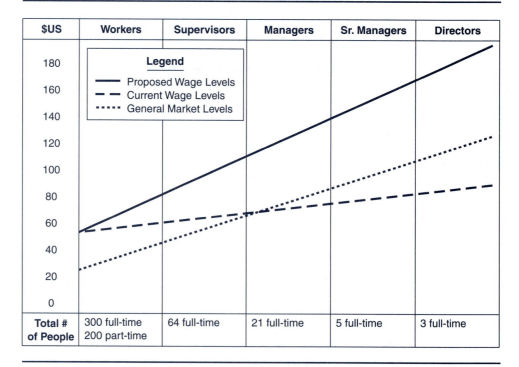

Upcoming Meeting with Patterson

While 1997 year-to-date sales were down by 15 percent, profits were down by nearly 40 percent. The fact that the JV was still profitable would be of little consolation to Kevin Patterson, with whom Johnson had a meeting in two days. Not only were sales down, but Johnson was concerned that Coca-Cola—even though it got a late start re-entering Vietnam—was on the verge of announcing major new investments in Vietnam. With Coca-Cola's much higher brand recognition, Johnson knew that Patterson would want some answers.

With JV profits down, Johnson felt there was no way he could significantly raise factory worker wages in addition to those of management. Although raising the wages for a total of about 30 supervisors, managers, senior managers, and directors would also hurt profit margins in the short run, Johnson thought it was necessary to hold onto managerial talent over the long run.

As Johnson contemplated a course of action, a memo arrived from his assistant, Ms. Tracy Nguyen. Johnson had asked Nguyen, a second generation Vietnamese who was working for HCM Beverage as an intern from a US MBA program, to make an independent assessment of the marketing and sales staffs. In her memo, she reported the following:

> Marketing and sales staff members continue to trickle in after 8:00 A.M. The day normally begins with everyone at their own desk doing their own thing. By 10 or 11 o'clock, the department is almost empty. Some will be out running personal errands. The ones left behind are either sitting behind a computer playing computer games or socializing.
>
> My lunches with them have been most useful. I found out that they feel the pay is too low at HCM Beverage Company. Also, most are not happy with how things are run. Many of the newcomers (those who have been with the company for less than one year) say that there is no room for personal growth. Of the new people hired in these two departments, three have resigned within the last three months. People say they are tired of putting in extra hours. They feel that they are overworked and underpaid.

In preparing for his meeting with Kevin Patterson in Hong Kong, Johnson had pretty much determined that the pay increase plan was necessary. However, he was not convinced that it alone would solve the sales problem—and it would only worsen the JV's profitability.

> I can't see any way to avoid a pay increase for the office staff. People like Dinh are worked too hard for what they get. It's no wonder they don't show up for meetings on time. Paying them a competitive salary can only help them take their jobs more seriously. Of course, it won't solve all our problems, but I don't think there's any way to avoid a pay increase.

Johnson was also concerned about Mr. Cao's warning to "avoid unsettling the workers." He had talked with Mr. Cao several times since that first statement without much progress as to what was really behind it. Whether the lack of progress was due to reluctance on Mr. Cao's part to talk with Johnson, Mr. Cao's limited English skills, or something else, Johnson was just not sure. Despite Mr. Cao's concern, Johnson just did not feel it was possible from a profitability perspective or necessary from a competitive comparison perspective to significantly raise workers' wages. Still Johnson worried. The company could not afford a strike. The economic and reputational effects could be devastating. If a strike happened, they might as well send out announcements to foreign firms to pick off their dissatisfied employees. Also, the company could not afford to continually spend time and money recruiting and training staff, only to lose them.

As the meeting with Patterson approached, Johnson could feel the knot in his stomach getting tighter and bigger. A marketing job back home seemed awfully appealing at the moment.

> Thinking about this meeting with Patterson has caused me to be more introspective. I realize that the longer I live here, the more frustrated I have become. When I was back home in the States, I could always find a way to make things happen. Here, it sometimes feels as though I'm trying to push water uphill. I also find myself missing things back home more. For example, every Monday night a bunch of us guys used to gather at Joe's [a sports bar] and watch Monday Night Football. Now I get to read about the game a week later.
>
> Back home, I worked hard but I could leave my job at the office most days. Here my job has become everything. I seem to go from one problem to the next. Even my wife has commented that I seem unhappy and a bit more irritable. In some ways she is doing better than I am. She hasn't gotten over being fascinated with the place. I have.
>
> Anyway, I have to decide what to do. Patterson will want answers, not excuses.

With less than two days to finalize what he was going to present to Patterson, Johnson had little time to spare.

28 WIL-MOR TECHNOLOGIES, INC.

In February 1997, David McNeil, CEO of Wilson Industries Inc. (Wilson) met with Ron Berks, the President of Wilson's North American Automotive Division. "Ron, the situation with the Wil-Mor joint venture (JV) does not seem to be improving," said McNeil. "After three years it is still losing money. What's going on down there?" Berks, a JV board member and the Wilson executive who initiated the JV formation, realized there was a problem but was not sure what to do. Not only were the JV managers not concerned, but they were talking about expansion. Wilson's Japanese JV partner did not even want to discuss profitability; all they seemed to care about was lowering costs and keeping the JV's largest customer happy. McNeil emphasized that something had to be done, adding, "When we formed this venture you predicted it would reach break-even by the second year of operation. We are not even close to that after three years."

Wilson Industries Inc.

Wilson, a Detroit-based company founded in 1923, was a manufacturer of plastic and metal parts for the automotive and appliance industries. Total sales in 1996 were $480 million of which $290 million came from the North American Automotive Division. The Automotive Division produced components for engines, transmissions, and power steering systems.

IVEY   Andrew C. Inkpen prepared this case solely to provide material for class discussion. The author does not intend to illustrate either effective or ineffective handling of a managerial situation. The author may have disguised certain names and other identifying information to protect confidentiality. Ivey Management Services prohibits any form of reproduction, storage or transmittal without its written permission. This material is not covered under authorization from CanCopy or any reproduction rights organization. Copyright © 1999, Ivey Management Services.

Ford and Chrysler accounted for 80 percent of Wilson's sales with the remainder going to General Motors. For several years, the Automotive Division's sales had remained flat and profits had been decreasing.

In recent years, Wilson had taken steps to internationalize its automotive operations. In 1986, exports began to Germany and a small plant was purchased in England. Besides Wil-Mor, a JV was launched in 1990 to distribute Wilson products in Australia.

The Automobile Industry

The North American automobile industry changed dramatically in the last two decades of the 20th century. The primary impetus for much of the change was the emergence of the Japanese automakers as leading competitors and domestic producers. In 1981, there were no Japanese assembly plants in North America. In 1990, there were nine Japanese-operated assembly plants in the United States and three in Canada. These plants produced 1.8 million cars in 1990, more than 20 percent of total North American production. By 1997, output from the Japanese assembly plants, referred to as transplants[1], was getting close to three million cars per year. Including imports, the three largest Japanese firms, Honda, Nissan, and Toyota, collectively had a 27 percent share of the U.S. passenger car market. In contrast, the Big Three (Chrysler, Ford, and General Motors) had seen a steady decrease in share. From 1993 to 1997, the Big Three share had dropped from 66 percent to about 61 percent.

Although Nissan was experiencing financial difficulties and was rumored to be a takeover candidate, Honda and Toyota continued to increase capacity and establish new industry standards for design and production efficiency. Both firms were becoming full-fledged North American producers capable of designing, engineering, and assembling vehicles entirely in North America. In 1998 Toyota planned to introduce a U.S.-designed full-size pickup truck produced in a new plant in Indiana. This truck would attack the Big Three in their primary profit sanctuary of light trucks. In late 1997 Honda expected to introduce the newest iteration of the best-selling Accord model. The new Accord was planned to arrive exactly four years after the previous new model, a consistent development cycle that none of the Big Three had yet managed to imitate.

All of the Japanese producers in North America were committed to increasing local content and reducing reliance on imported parts. By the mid-1990s, with the Japanese yen appreciating more than 50 percent since 1990, the Japanese producers were ramping up their efforts to increase their number of U.S. suppliers.

Automotive Suppliers

The typical car is made up of more than 10,000 parts. In the initial years of the automobile industry, carmakers tried to produce as many parts in-house as possible. By the 1950s, outsourcing of parts from independent suppliers had become commonplace. Suppliers were given blueprints and asked to bid on parts contracts. The lowest bidder generally was

---

[1]Transplant was the generic term used for foreign direct investment in the automotive industry. Besides the Japanese firms, BMW (in South Carolina) and Mercedez-Benz (in Alabama) also had transplant operations.

awarded the contract, usually for one year. In the 1990s, the world's automobile companies were all using outsourcing as an increasingly important element of production.

The shifting importance of outsourcing developed in the 1980s as the Big Three increased their outsourcing and made substantial cuts in the number of suppliers they dealt with. The customer-supplier relationship shifted to a structure based on tiers of suppliers. The first tier suppliers dealt directly with the vehicle manufacturers and, increasingly, participated jointly in the design of new systems and parts. The first tier suppliers coordinated the operations of many smaller second tier suppliers who, in turn, worked with their own sub-suppliers. The advantage of this multi-layer approach, used by the Japanese producers for many years, was that the automakers could deal with a limited number of companies and work closely with them in design and engineering.

Besides the move toward outsourcing and multi-tiered supplier arrangements, several other trends characterized the supplier industry. One, automakers were pushing their suppliers toward just-in-time delivery systems and increased investment in design and engineering capabilities. Two, mergers were becoming prevalent in the supplier sector, largely because of the heavy demands for research and development, new equipment, and employee training. This trend was reflected in the increasing international consolidation of automotive suppliers. Large suppliers, such as Johnson Controls, Lear, Magna, and Bosch, were increasingly focused on automotive systems, rather than just parts. With systems, such as seats or car interiors, suppliers took on more responsibility for design and engineering and worked closely with the automakers throughout the design and development product life cycle stages. Three, suppliers were moving away from their traditional focus on home markets toward foreign investment. For example, close to 300 Japan-based supplier firms had operations in North America, most of which had arrived in the late 1980s and early 1990s.

The arrival of the transplant automakers was the major reason Japanese suppliers were locating in North America. However, many of the Japanese suppliers were making inroads into the domestic automakers as well. The implications were clear: like the situation with automaking capacity, excess capacity at the supplier level was becoming a reality. The overcapacity and competition from foreign-based component suppliers were creating increasingly difficult conditions for North American automotive suppliers, and particularly smaller suppliers, like Wilson. The industry view was that over the next few years, many of the remaining smaller suppliers would either be acquired by the large multinational firms or forced to exit the automotive industry.

The Japanese Transplants

With their traditional North American market eroding, many suppliers, including Wilson, saw a potentially lucrative market in supplying the transplants. The transplants were committed to North American content and were rapidly building up their manufacturing capacity. Unfortunately, becoming a supplier to a transplant firm had proved to be very difficult for many North American–based firms. North American companies were often unfamiliar with the rigors of Japanese just-in-time inventory systems and demands for flexible production. A further problem frustrating the efforts of North American suppliers was that unlike their North American competitors, the Japanese automakers rarely changed suppliers. For example, Toyota's supplier base in Japan had remained virtually unchanged since the 1950s. Many of the Japanese suppliers were partially owned by the automakers and, as part of a keiretsu, had a relationship that was much stronger than a North American supplier relationship. The president of Nissan's U.S. operations explained:

> Nissan's mix of U.S. suppliers and Japanese suppliers is not likely to change much. Given our philosophy, once you become our supplier you're our supplier forever on that part, unless you mess up so bad we can't fix you.[2]

The Japanese firms put much more emphasis on trust and cooperation in the supplier relationship. As one supplier executive commented:

> The North American supplier relationship is often adversarial. The supplier usually works with the blueprint provided by the automaker. You manufacture according to the blueprint and if the part doesn't fit, "you tell your customer to stuff it." With Honda our relationship is supportive as long as we deliver the product. And, the blueprint is only the starting point. The part must fit the car; if it doesn't, Honda will say, "What can we do together to make it fit?" If you ship 150 bad parts to General Motors, they will tell you that you have a problem and you better fix it fast. Honda may say you have a problem, but they will also say, "How can we help you fix it?" The Japanese customer will not use its power to threaten or harass the supplier. Once the marriage is formed, they will try to make it work.

In North America, the threat that supplier contracts could be cancelled or moved in-house had created a system in which, according to some observers, neither party fully trusted the other. By contrast, the Japanese approach was based on long-term relationships, mutual discussion and bargaining. While suppliers were expected to decrease prices over the term of the contract, joint activities between supplier and automaker were critical to the relationship. According to one study, "The (Japanese) system replaces a vicious circle of mistrust with a virtuous circle of cooperation."[3]

Of course, the Japanese automakers could, and did, fire their suppliers. When it became obvious that a supplier could no longer meet the exacting quality standards or improve on cost and quality, the Japanese customer was as likely to look for a new supplier as an American customer. The difference was that the Japanese automaker would expend more effort in assisting the supplier than was typical in the North American context. In addition, the Japanese companies usually kept their suppliers better informed about their performance relative to other suppliers.

The JV Formation

In the early 1990s, Ron Berks was convinced that the transplant share of the North American market would continue to grow. He began to explore the possibility of becoming a supplier to the transplant firms. He made several trips to Japan and initiated discussions with Honda America in Ohio. However, after several years of fruitless efforts, he became convinced that without an established reputation, access to the Japanese transplants was very difficult. One way to speed up this access was to establish a relationship with a Japanese firm.

---

[2]*Ward's Auto World*, February 1991, p. 29.
[3]James P. Womack, Daniel T. Jones, and Daniel Roos. *The Machine That Changed the World*. (New York: Rawson Associates, 1990), p. 150.

In the meantime, the Japanese presence in the automobile industry continued to grow. The transplant automakers encouraged their Japanese suppliers to build plants in North America in order to maintain established customer relationships; also, because of political pressure, increased domestic content was a priority. Trepidation about starting a new facility in North America and pressure from the Japanese automakers to involve local firms in the supply chain encouraged many Japanese suppliers to form JVs with American partners. As well, a large number of Japanese suppliers entered the North American market on their own.

Nevertheless, through the early 1990s, the Japanese automakers continued to source components from Japan. But with the continuing rise in the value of the yen, there was a new effort to localize the supplier base. The strengthening of the yen made it more economical to produce in the United States and local production supported the Japanese automakers' commitment to lean production and just-in-time delivery. All of the Japanese producers were carefully reviewing their purchasing programs to determine what component production could be shifted out of Japan. For example, Toyota's Georgetown, Kentucky, facility increased its purchases of U.S.-made parts from $700 million in 1990 to more than $2 billion in 1995.

In late 1991, Berks first considered the feasibility of forming a JV. An obvious choice for a JV partner was Morota Manufacturing Company Ltd. (Morota). For several years, Wilson had been involved in a licensing agreement with Morota. Morota, founded in 1950, was a manufacturer of small electric motors for products such as sewing machines and small appliances and also produced various components for engines and transmissions for the automobile industry. Morota had sales of $480 million in 1996 with $276 million to the automobile industry. About 70 percent of the automobile sales were to Toyota with the remainder going to Nissan, Honda, and Mitsubishi. Although Toyota did not own equity in Morota, the two firms had a very close relationship that had begun in the 1950s. Except for a JV in Korea, Morota had limited international experience.

Berks knew that Morota wanted a plant in North America because Toyota could no longer justify importing Morota components from Japan. In early 1992, he contacted the president of Morota and set up a meeting in Japan for July. Berks learned at the meeting that Morota was being encouraged by Toyota to form a JV in North America. He also learned that Morota was "internationally naive and probably scared to death to come to the U.S. They were particularly worried about dealing with an American workforce." At the meeting, the two firms agreed to work toward forming a JV.

The JV Agreement

JV discussions between Wilson and Morota started in late 1992 and six months later a JV agreement was signed. The JV was named Wil-Mor Technologies, Inc. (Wil-Mor). Initially, Berks had hoped that Wilson would have about 70 percent ownership. However, although the Morota executives would not say so explicitly, Berks sensed that there would be problems with Toyota if Wilson had a majority position. Berks, therefore, agreed to 50/50 ownership. The JV agreement specified that Wilson would be responsible for locating a plant site and managing the workforce. Morota would be responsible for the equipment acquisitions and installation. Morota would provide initial engineering support and help train the workforce, both in Japan and the U.S. Morota would also work with Toyota to ensure that the JV had contracts when the JV became operational.

The JV president would be nominated by Morota and the general manager would be nominated by Wilson. These two managers would be responsible for the JV startup. The JV board would include three executives from each firm. From Wilson, there would be Berks, an Automotive Division vice president, and the JV general manager. Morota's representatives would include Morota's president, its executive vice president, and the JV president.

Berks was very enthusiastic about the JV's potential. After the JV announcement in early 1993, his opinion was that the joint venture was a very important strategic move for Wilson. The JV was seen as an extension of Wilson's existing operation that would help increase market share and provide access to a growing segment of the market. The JV would also help Wilson learn from its Japanese partner. There was even some thought that in a few years, the JV would be able to export parts back to Japan.

Startup

Berks thought that an experienced American manager should be general manager. He selected 58-year-old Dan Johnson, a Wilson employee for 30 years and most recently a plant manager. The president, Akio Sakiya, was 55 years old and had spent his entire career with Morota. Although an engineer by training, he was vice president finance prior to becoming the JV president.

Johnson was given the task of selecting the plant site. He chose Elizabethtown, Kentucky, a small town south of Louisville and close to the Toyota plant in Georgetown. The initial investment in the JV was $20.2 million. Each partner contributed $4 million; the other $12.2 million was borrowed by the JV and guaranteed by the partners.

The JV plant was based on the manufacturing system used by Morota. Most of the equipment in the plant was Japanese. Morota put together a Japanese team of engineers and technical specialists. This team was responsible for installing the equipment, getting the process started, and training the workforce. The workforce was hired by Johnson and Sakiya. Their emphasis was on young people with little or no manufacturing experience (from Morota's perspective, "no bad habits."). Both partners wanted to keep the JV union-free.

The JV began operations in early 1994 with contracts from Toyota. All contracts were for engine component parts, identical to parts made in Japan by Morota and functionally similar to parts made by Wilson for its Big 3 customers. The initial startup was done very slowly and for some months there was only enough work for about two–three days a week. The startup, slower than Wilson would have liked, was based on Morota's attitude of "training before operating."

JV Management

Besides the president and general manager, JV management came from both partners. Wilson provided the operations manager, human resource manager, controller, and a marketing manager. None of these managers had any Japanese language capability or experience with the transplants. Morota provided the engineering manager, the quality manager, and a marketing manager (see Exhibit 1 for an organization chart). None of these managers had any prior international experience and, except for the marketing manager, had only limited English language skills. The Japanese managers, including the president, had three- to five-year visas. At the end of the visa terms these managers would be rotated back to the

EXHIBIT 1 Organizational Chart

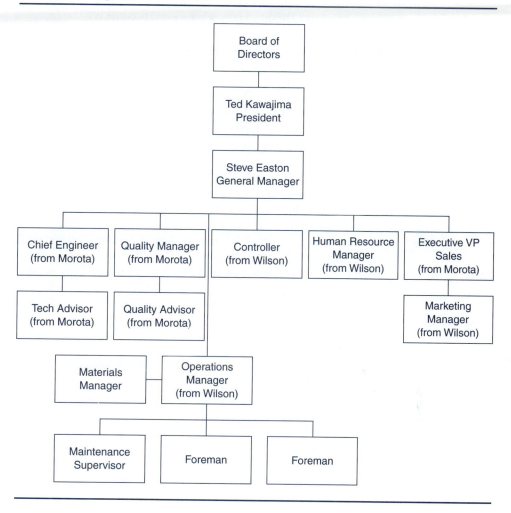

Japanese parent. The American managers were in the JV for an indefinite period. The partners hoped that eventually the Japanese managers could be replaced by American managers promoted from within the JV.

The JV did not begin smoothly. The Japanese managers insisted on complete technical responsibility. Johnson, the general manager, was not allowed to assist in the technical setup. This caused several problems because the Japanese were unfamiliar with many of the basic aspects of establishing a new plant, especially one in North America. The Japanese insisted on running the operation their way. They used a Japanese approach in selecting suppliers. Johnson estimated he could have saved the JV about $300,000 a year if a North American approach had been used to select suppliers. However, the Japanese insisted that, if possible, suppliers should be selected not just on the basis of price but because they had established themselves as capable suppliers to Wilson or Morota.

When the JV started, the Japanese managers were initially skeptical about the ability of an American workforce to produce a quality product. They wondered: Can they run the machines properly? Do they know what a good product is? The Japanese managers drove the workers very hard at the outset. Several times Sakiya became furious with what he saw on the shop floor and berated the workers in Japanese.

Johnson became convinced that the Japanese managers were deliberately excluding him from the management process. The Japanese managers would regularly hold meetings and exclude the Americans. When meetings were held with both Americans and Japanese present, they would last for hours because of the necessity to translate from English to Japanese. In addition, the Japanese managers corresponded daily by fax with their head office in Japan and would meet socially in the evenings and on weekends. The inevitable result was two distinct management "camps": the Americans and the Japanese.

By March 1995, it was obvious to Ron Berks that there were serious management problems in the JV. Although the contracts with Toyota seemed to be working out well, the plant was still running at far less than capacity. Very few decisions in the JV were "joint" because the Americans and Japanese rarely talked to each other. The American managers were looking after areas such as materials sourcing, human resources, accounting, and finance. The Japanese managers concentrated on product design, quality, pricing, and sales.

Berks discussed the situation with Morota's president. They decided to replace the JV president and the general manager. The new general manager, Steve Easton, was 46 and a former Wilson plant manager who had recently been working at Wilson headquarters in an international development position. The new president was 51-year-old Ted Kawajima, an engineer with several years of international experience and an excellent command of English.

The New Management Team

The new management team got off to a much better start than the previous one. Both Easton and Kawajima were avid golfers. They began playing golf together regularly and involved several of the other managers. Gradually, the tension between the American and Japanese "camps" began to ease. Although the regular faxing between the JV and Japan continued, meetings of Japanese managers became less frequent.

The JV was also successful in winning new contracts with Toyota and was quoting on some work for Mazda and Ford. By early 1996, Wil-Mor had successfully bid on several General Motors contracts. The JV customer mix was now about 80 percent Toyota and 20 percent General Motors. The JV was actively seeking new customers and was encouraged by Toyota to do so.

Annual sales in the JV were now close to $30 million. Employment had reached 300 and the plant was close to capacity. Although the JV was still losing money, Easton and Kawajima were considering a possible expansion.

Head Office Concerns

Ron Berks was pleased by the improved managerial situation in the JV but was troubled by a financial situation that did not seem to be improving. He knew at the outset that it would take a few years for the JV to become profitable. However, based on Morota's estimates, he thought that the JV could at least be at breakeven by the end of 1995 and making a profit by 1996. In early 1997 the JV was still losing about $100,000 a month.

Even more troubling was the fact that at the most recent JV board meeting in November 1996, the Morota executives did not seem concerned that the JV was losing money. In fact, they seemed pleased that the losses were not greater. At the board meeting, when Berks questioned the JV's performance, Kawajima replied that the JV was meeting expectations and was exceeding Toyota's quality standards. He went on to say that the JV still had to get its costs down and had some way to go before quality was at a level consistent with that in Morota's Japan plants. When Berks angrily asked how many years it would be before there was a profit, Kawajima replied that:

> Profit is obviously important but to achieve profitability there has to be a satisfied base of customers. We have achieved a good record with Toyota and now we are trying to build a relationship with General Motors. I think that we are in a very strong position.

Berks left the board meeting without a clear understanding of the Japanese expectations about profits in the JV. They seemed concerned only about the quality of the product and not about making money.

Easton's Perspective

Steve Easton knew that Berks, his boss, was concerned about the JV performance. He explained:

> There is an unresolvable conflict in the relationship between the partners. Morota is willing to lose money in the JV for as long as it takes to build up market share and quality in North America. Right now, their primary focus is on customer service and product improvement, not profit. They intend to be in this market for the long term and they know that Toyota plans to increase its North American capacity. Morota is determined to make money in North America but is willing to be patient. They believe that if there is a quality product and low costs, profit will take care of itself. They cannot answer the question about when the JV will be profitable because it is not consistent with their philosophy. Their approach is that prices are not the issue; costs must be improved first.
>
> When the JV was formed, the partners thought that they were in sync about prices and profit margins that might be expected. Clearly, that was an incorrect assumption. Wilson wanted to make a quick buck; they were skeptical of making long-term investments. They saw the JV as a way to make some money. They expected a profit in two or three years. Morota expected the JV to lose money for about five or six years. However, they never communicated this to Wilson and the business plan was very unclear on partner expectations. Wilson prepared the pro-formas and based on my conversations with Ron Berks, no one at Morota raised any serious objections when we were negotiating the final agreement.

This perspective was echoed by an industry analyst's comments:

> The Japanese invest in a country first and anticipate the payoff later. They have staying power.

Easton suspected that part of the problem was that Berks did not do his homework when the JV was formed. He commented:

> The JV was started on blind faith. Each partner had some expectations about the other which have not been met. Wilson expected faster production and higher efficiency. The only thing certain at the outset was that Toyota would be a customer. Berks expected that a share of Toyota's business would be great to have and that it would be profitable. Unfortunately, nobody in Wilson had any idea of the potential profitability of supplying the transplants.

The reality is that we are unable to get the same kind of profit margins with Toyota as we can with the Big 3. We make more money on the parts we sell to GM than on the parts we sell to Toyota. A lot of suppliers are starting to say that transplant business is not good business because the prices are too low.

Easton also sensed that there was some resentment in Wilson toward the JV and an unwillingness to acknowledge openly that the JV provided an excellent learning opportunity:

I have given other Wilson managers an open invitation to visit the JV and see what we are doing. There has been some response to my invitations but there seems to be some resentment toward us. When I attend corporate meetings at Wilson, I show people what we are doing and it is clear that the JV is outperforming the other Wilson plants on a quality basis. In terms of reject rates, we beat Wilson by 10 times. Wilson talks about quality but we do it. I don't like to brag about our success in the JV, but what I would like to see is an interest by the other Wilson managers in finding out why the JV is able to do so well.

The JV and the relationship with Toyota has put Wilson in a position to start questioning their capabilities. Berks would like to have Toyota as a customer so he invited Toyota purchasing managers to visit the Wilson plants. Toyota reported back to Wilson and the report was scathing. Berks's attitude was "these guys are just unreasonable."

Berks has acknowledged that some changes at Wilson may be necessary but he has avoided the serious questions. The reality is that Wilson would have to cross a lot of hurdles to get any Toyota business. However, the senior management at Wilson don't know that and would be surprised to find out. They have not addressed it and it is not a priority because of their existing business. My own belief is that Wilson has not grasped what world class manufacturing is.

On the relationship between the partners, Easton commented:

Kawajima and the Morota executives realize that Berks is not pleased with the JV performance. However, they view their relationship with Wilson from a long-term perspective. They intend to succeed in North America and assume that Wilson thinks the same way. Should Wilson express some desire to end the JV, Kawajima and the other Morota executives would be shocked and take it as a serious affront. From their perspective, strengthening the relationship between the partners is critical to the success of the JV.

The Current Situation

The meeting with David McNeil left Berks in a difficult position. Berks was aware that at Wilson headquarters, there was growing opposition to the JV because it was not making money. Some managers were even starting to question Morota's capabilities, arguing that if they can't make money when they have a new plant and a guaranteed customer, how can we ever hope to learn anything from them?

McNeil wanted to see a JV return on investment at least as high as the other Wilson plants but Berks did not know when that would happen. At a meeting with Easton the previous week, Easton had assured him that Wil-Mor had the potential to be a leading supplier to both the transplants and the Big 3. Easton had also said that an expansion would soon be necessary. Berks knew that McNeil would never approve further capital investment until the JV started showing a profit. However, Easton argued that without expanding, the JV would lose market share and would probably take even longer to become profitable.

Ron Berks wondered what should be done about the JV. Maybe Wilson should cut its losses and get out of the JV. Or perhaps it would be better if Wilson lowered its ownership interest to about 20 percent. That would reduce Wilson's share of the losses and would allow Wilson to maintain its relationship with Morota. Whatever the decision, Berks knew that McNeil was expecting something to be done very soon.

III Multinational Management

29 MATRA-ERICSSON TELECOMMUNICATIONS 1990

*There are two arrogant peoples in the world: the French and the Swedes. As Swedes,
we think we are the owners of the truth. The French think the same way.*
Swedish Manager in MET

We are impervious to the Ericsson and Swedish culture; we are French.
French Manager in MET

When Lars Jarnryd accepted the position of president of Matra-Ericsson Telecommunications (MET), the joint venture between LM Ericsson (Ericsson) and the French company Matra S.A. (Matra), he was unaware of the extent to which the relationship between Ericsson and Matra had deteriorated. Now, in October 1990, Jarnryd wondered what steps should be taken to get the relationship back on track. The most recent event in the strained relationship involved Jarnryd's status as president. At a MET board meeting a few days earlier, Jacques Payer, MET's Chairman and a Matra appointee, said that he would not accept Jarnryd as the new representative from Ericsson and that Jarnryd would not be allowed on MET premises. As a result, Jarnryd was working out of an office near the Arc de Triomphe, a long way from MET's suburban Paris offices. Although an optimist by nature, Jarnryd saw this latest salvo in the Matra-Ericsson battle as a clear sign that events were looming out of control. The question now was what should be done to rebuild the relationship so that the partners could capitalize on the very lucrative French market.

This case was prepared by Andrew Inkpen for the sole purpose of providing material for class discussion. It is not intended to illustrate either effective or ineffective handling of a managerial situation. Any reproduction, in any form, of the material in this case is prohibited unless permission is obtained from the copyright holder. Copyright © 1999 Thunderbird, The American Graduate School of International Management.

LM Ericsson

Ericsson's history goes back to 1876, when Lars Magnus Ericsson opened a repair shop for telegraph equipment. He soon realized that there was a need for improvements in the telephones then available, and began manufacturing them himself. In 1892, Ericsson launched its first major international product. Early in the 20th century, the company expanded internationally with businesses established in Mexico in 1905, Thailand in 1908, and Paris in 1911. Over the next century, Ericsson established itself as a major telecom equipment supplier. In 1975 the company introduced its digital AXE switch, which would become the world's single best-selling telephone system.

Switches were designed to route a telephone call from one place to another. The principal customers for public network, or central office, switches were the telecommunications companies that provided services for resale. Switches were connected to transmission lines that were linked to hundreds or thousands of local lines extending to the customer premises. Switches varied in size and design and were made up of a series of refrigerator-size boxes of wiring. Using complex software, digital switches relayed data and voice signals and could provide billing information, specialized services such as call waiting, conference calling, and data transfer.

By the mid-1980s, Ericsson had established itself as one of the world's leading suppliers to public telephone companies (PTTs). The firm was strong in Latin America (Brazil, Mexico), the Middle East (Egypt, Kuwait, and Saudi Arabia), the Far East (Malaysia, Thailand, and Singapore) and Australia. The only European markets of importance were the Nordic countries and Ireland. Ericsson was a minor supplier in the Netherlands, Spain, and Italy in continental Europe. Ericsson was also one of the first telecom firms to recognize the importance of China. In 1989, Ericsson sales were $6.3 billion, net income was $297 million, and the company had about 70,000 employees. Ericsson invested heavily in technical development and had an R&D budget of about 20 percent of sales.

Ericsson was considered a strong technical company with very reliable products. As one manager put it:

> We didn't make a lot of money but we could deliver and our products worked. We were like an old Volvo that just kept working. In our international businesses we were very good at building local relationships and when we entered a market we persevered. People liked Ericsson.

In most of the major industrialized markets, there were strong national telecom firms such as AT&T in the United States, Northern Telecom in Canada, Siemens in Germany, Philips in the Netherlands, and various ITT companies across Europe. These markets were tightly controlled and Ericsson was effectively shut out. In the 1980s, the doors began to open for Ericsson with gradual liberalization, de-monopolization, deregulation and eventually privatization of telecommunications services. New technology, new economies of scale, and errors by European equipment firms in choosing technologies resulted in the decline of the British, Dutch, and Swiss industries and eventually caused the ITT Group to exit telecommunications. For Ericsson, the AXE switch emerged as a competitive and attractive technology. However, because Ericsson had been focused on developing countries, there were fears that the company might be poorly positioned in the increasingly competitive North American and European markets. Therefore, the opportunity in France that emerged in 1986 was viewed as critical to Ericsson.

The French Government Proposal

France's state-owned telegraphic service, established in 1851, became part of the French Post Office in the 1870s at the same time that Alexander Graham Bell was perfecting the telephone. The French government licensed three private companies to provide telegraph service, and during the 1880s these companies merged to form the Societé Genérale de Telephones (SGT). In 1883 the country's first exchange was started. Four years later an international circuit was installed connecting Paris and Brussels. The government nationalized SGT in 1889.

After years of neglect, the French state-owned PTT, the Direction Genérale des Telecommunications (the name France Telecom was adopted in 1990), launched a massive upgrading program in the early 1970s. In about 10 years, the number of telephone lines increased from three million to 22 million in a system with state-of-the-art technology. By 1985 this number increased to 25 million phone lines connecting more than 95 percent of France's households.

During this period of upgrading, the primary equipment supplier was ITT. A few other firms also competed, including Ericsson, which had been in France for many years. Within the French PTT there was increasing dissatisfaction with the reliance on foreign technology, particularly since the PTT labs were devoting substantial resources to research and development. The French government decided that explicit steps had to be taken to ensure French control over the telecom equipment industry. Ericsson was an initial target. In 1976, Ericsson was forced to sell its French subsidiary, Societé Francaise des Teléphones Ericsson, to Thomson-CSF, a large defense firm with no history in telecommunications. At the same time, ITT sold a division to Alcatel Alsthom (Alcatel), the large French technology company. This left the French market dominated by three firms: Alcatel, Thomson, and Compagnie Genérale des Construction Telephoniques (CGCT), which was still owned by ITT.

A senior Ericsson manager involved in public switching at the time described Ericsson's reactions to these events:

> Ericsson developed a deep suspicion about French industrial and telecommunications policy. We saw favors granted here and there by different governments, an inefficient industry and PTT, irrational price levels, and low telephone density despite public statements about priority. It was simply a market that foreigners could not master or manage, fully proven to be true when the socialist government nationalized the remaining ITT company and then threw it out to the private market a few years later.

In 1982 French elections, the socialist party won a majority. One of their election promises was to nationalize ITT's remaining French operations. So, in 1982, much to the dismay of the firm's management, CGCT was nationalized. In 1983, Thomson sold its telecom business to Alcatel. This left the French PTT with only one technology source, since CGCT was then manufacturing under license from Alcatel. This sole supplier situation was deemed unsatisfactory by the French government. In early 1986 the government began a process of evaluating alternative technologies. In late 1986 the government decided to privatize some of the companies that were nationalized in 1982, including CGCT. For some time, CGCT management had been pressing the government to be privatized. The view in CGCT was that without privatization, the company would die. From 1982 to 1986 CGCT had shed more than 4,000 employees and lost all of its export customers.

Also in 1986 and following the decision to privatize CGCT, a formal bidding process for new suppliers to the French PTT was announced. The winning supplier would be guaranteed a 16 percent share of the French PTT business for ten years. Even though a 16 percent share of the French PTT business was too small to warrant a fully integrated manufacturing unit in France, the artificially high price level created by Alcatel provided an attractive opportunity for the major equipment firms. The government decided that the privatization of CGCT's public network business and its remaining 1,800 employees would be linked with the call for supplier bids. The firm that won the proposal would, with its partner, assume control of CGCT and its public network business. Bidding guidelines required that the winning firm have a French partner and that the non-French company have a minority ownership position. Four companies bid for the French business: AT&T (United States), Ericsson, Northern Telecom (Canada), and Siemens (Germany). Northern Telecom dropped out quickly, leaving three firms, none of which were willing to consider a licensing agreement. So the three firms found JV partners and submitted bids.

Ericsson teamed up with Matra. For many years, Matra had been one of the French government's largest defense suppliers. In the 1960s, Matra entered the space systems markets (missiles and satellites) and also produced race cars. In the 1970s, Matra began producing transit systems and in 1979, entered the telecommunications industry with acquisition of Compagnie des Telephones Depaepe. In 1984 Matra consolidated its telecom activities within a subsidiary called Matra Communication (MatraCom). Until late 1987, Matra was 51 percent owned by the French government. Matra was run by Jean-Luc Lagardère, one of France's most powerful industrialists. In addition to Matra, Lagardère controlled Hachette, a large newspaper, publishing, and broadcasting company. In 1987, CGCT's telephone and private branch exchange businesses were privatized and acquired by MatraCom.

Ericsson and Matra had known each other for several years and knew Jean-Luc Lagardère as an ambitious person prepared to work with foreigners only on the basis of control and independence. The foreign company would provide Matra with the credibility for entering a new business. Ericsson knew that Matra would never have the resources to internally develop an independent technological position in the public switching sector of the telecom industry.

Ericsson's Successful Bid

During the bidding process, the U.S. government was rumored to be considering legislation that would bar the U.S. market to foreign suppliers whose home markets were closed to U.S. competitors. This put tremendous pressure on the French government to select AT&T. The German government was lobbying for Siemens. In the technical evaluation of the proposals, Ericsson and AT&T were ranked the highest. A few factors helped shift the balance in favor of the Ericsson bid. According to French PTT sources, AT&T had better switch technology. However, Ericsson's offer of a mobile phone partnership with Matra was critical. As well, Ericsson priced its switches lower than AT&T. Perhaps most important, in the telecom supplier industry, Ericsson was considered to be the most successful marketer in politically driven international switch markets. In France, the company skillfully sold itself as a noncontroversial alternative to both AT&T and Siemens. The result was that Ericsson was declared the winner, surprising the industry and establishing Ericsson as a major player in France. An Ericsson manager described the 1986 negotiations with the French government:

We were used to negotiating with developing countries where flexibility was critical. We were surprised by the meticulous way in which they were negotiating. The negotiations were very difficult and very tedious. Every word was examined. The proposed exports were broken down into very minor details. But, we were desperate to win this contract.

The view at Ericsson headquarters was that winning the privatization process created little risk and various benefits:

- Prestige for having beaten AT&T and Siemens and one more Swedish flag in Europe.
- Participation in a cash cow that agreed to pay a generous license fee for Ericsson technology.
- Future opportunities in a new market that would eventually be deregulated.

As well, it was recognized within Ericsson that Matra would be a difficult partner to work with on a daily basis.

The Formation of MET

As the successful bidder, Ericsson was required to form a JV and absorb the CGCT public network operation into the new company. In the new JV, Matra controlled 50.01 percent of the equity and Ericsson 49.99 percent. Other important conditions were:

- The board would comprise five members appointed by each partner. The JV board would be the primary vehicle for interaction between the firms.
- Ericsson would be responsible for technical issues.
- The JV would sell public network switches based on current Ericsson technology. Three years were required to adapt the switches for France. By 1991, all MET switches would be based on Ericsson technology.
- Components for the switches would primarily be transferred from Ericsson in Sweden.
- Ericsson would receive a fee of 7 percent of sales revenues.
- The JV would be committed to developing export markets.

In one key area, MET was different from other Ericsson JVs formed to gain market entry. Most of Ericsson's JVs were with silent partners. The partners provided non-executive chairmen acting primarily as figureheads. During the MET negotiations, a great deal of time was spent on defining the roles of the Président Directeur Générale (PDG) and the Directeur Générale (DG). Both the PDG and the DG would be on the MET board. The MET shareholder agreement specified that Matra would provide the PDG and Ericsson the DG. Ericsson's understanding was that the PDG would primarily deal with the board and would not actually run the company. The PDG would attend and chair the board meetings, use his prestige and influence to help with the business, and help with business relations in Parisian circles. The company would be run by the Ericsson appointed DG who would act as president.

Ericsson appointed a French-speaking Swede, Nils Söderquist, in what was assumed to be the president's position. Söderquist had not been involved in any of the earlier negotiations. Matra appointed Jacques Payer as the PDG. Payer was involved in the MET negotiations and had proven to be a very skilled negotiator with the French government. Payer was also the PDG of Matra's other telecom equipment company, MatraCom. MatraCom was not a competitor of MET because MET was to produce switches for the French PTT (i.e., public networks) while MatraCom was involved in PBXs and telephones.

In many French companies, the PDG had almost complete authority and acted as both chairman and CEO/president. Although the Ericsson side understood the French PDG position and the power that a PDG could exercise, they did not expect Payer to act with such suspicion and force and, after a while, with such contempt for Söderquist. According to an Ericsson-appointed manager in MET:

> Even though we say that we are an international company, we are really a company run by Swedes. Our partner said you don't understand this country. This is my country. I decide if you want to make money. Yes or no. But if you want to make money, do it my way.

Initially, Payer was willing to let Söderquist manage day-to-day operations. However, when it became apparent that MET was struggling, Payer decided to get more involved. Payer was an imposing figure, as described by an Ericsson manager:

> He is a tall man and a very strong and dominating personality. He would pound the table. He was very authoritarian. He wanted to change everything. He was also very practical. He said we have to fire 800 people, bingo. The Swedes said no, no—that is not the Swedish way. We can't do that. And that started the non-conversation between Payer and the Ericsson man. They really had a non-conversation.
>
> Payer's personality was consistent with his being PDG. He was even more French than the French themselves. In France, everything the PDG says goes. If he doesn't say anything, nothing gets done. That was very difficult for us because the Swedish way, like the Japanese, is more about consensus.

Very quickly, Payer and Söderquist were in disagreement over a number of different issues, some important and some trivial. Clearly, the relationship between Payer and Söderquist showed poor "chemistry." In each significant disagreement, the issue would go before the partners and Payer would get his way. Even though Söderquist challenged Sweden to confront Matra about who should actually be governing MET, Ericsson chose not to. According to one of the French managers, "The Swedes did not like conflict and Payer thrived on conflict."

An initial disagreement between the partners involved the issue of how much local added value the switches would have. Many of Ericsson's subsidiaries were selling products produced in other countries, or selling a mix of local and foreign produced products. Although the MET shareholder agreement made a commitment to increased local manufacturing, Ericsson was resisting because of the profitability of selling equipment and components. After the JV was formed, the French managers and Payer insisted that MET would assemble and test in France all the switches sold in France. Reluctantly, Ericsson agreed to this request.

Another element of the shareholder agreement would also prove controversial. When the JV was negotiated, European digital mobile telephone standards had not been implemented. The telecom community knew that a technical standard called GSM would be adopted in Europe. Ericsson was emerging as a strong firm in digital mobile telephony

---

(Note: A PBX (private branch exchange) is a multiline business telephone system that routes calls among extensions within a system, or between an extension and an external line.)

infrastructure and the French PTT was interested in having that technology in France. Matra was also involved in mobile but the French government was concerned that Matra was too small to be a major mobile competitor and its technology would likely not be exportable. And, at the time, Alcatel was not in the mobile business. This potential connection in mobile was one of the reasons why Matra and Ericsson became partners.

The result was that Matra and Ericsson agreed to cooperate in France and worldwide in the development of GSM mobile telephony. After the JV was formed, the two sides began to work together. The agreement proved to be very unpopular with Swedish engineers at Ericsson because their view was that the Ericsson technology was superior and would win the standards battle. They were very reluctant to expose their technology to Matra. The Matra engineers also thought they had strong technology. Compounding the problem was that when GSM did emerge as the standard and mobile succeeded far beyond expectations, it became clear that Ericsson would become one of the dominant mobile firms. The initial agreement with Matra would, in retrospect, look like a serious mistake. As a result, when it came time to convert the Ericsson-Matra agreement into real partnerships, nothing much happened.

Increasing Dissatisfaction at Matra

Over the next few years, the relationship between the partners remained strained. Payer was becoming more powerful but Ericsson was unable to do anything about it:

> The Swedes hated conflict and did not want to see the business go downhill. But, Payer was clearly exceeding what Ericsson thought he would do. They first tried to persuade him gently. That did not succeed. They talked to the Matra Group—nothing happened. The Ericsson vice president in Sweden who was in charge of MET soon saw that Payer was really good as a financial manager and the Ericsson manager was rather weak. Payer did things for the bottom line of the company. But, things got worse and worse in relations between Payer and Ericsson managers.

R&D payments from MET to Ericsson became a major issue. The JV was paying about 7 percent of sales to Ericsson for technology. Payer thought this amount was too high. In Ericsson's view, 7 percent was reasonable given that the company was spending about 18–20 percent of sales on R&D. There were also concerns about the level of transfer payments for components used by MET and manufactured by Ericsson. Although the shareholder agreement specified what Ericsson could and could not do, Payer was convinced that Ericsson was over-charging the JV and questioned why Ericsson should make money from R&D fees *and* transfer payments. Payer threatened to go outside Ericsson for components if the transfer fees were not reduced.

> Payer made a huge fuss. He said my God, I don't accept this. I'm going to build up my own business. So enormous amounts of time were dedicated to negotiating the details of transfer prices. Payer said, "if I don't get this, I close down the factory." It was very drastic.

On the Ericsson side, there was a very different view about transfer payments. According to an Ericsson manager based in Stockholm and involved in transfer pricing decisions:

> Matra kept asking for too much. We had the technology; they had nothing except for some connections in France.

The issue of transfer prices was complicated by the fact that CGCT was formerly a separate French company. The French MET managers below Payer knew what the real costs for Ericsson components were. These managers got caught in the middle because as a former CGCT manager explained:

> To Ericsson, MET was an embarrassing partner because unlike other Ericsson local companies, MET was a company [CGCT] that existed before the JV was formed. We had purchasing people and industrial engineering people. We were in a position to question procedures between the Ericsson central body and the local companies. When Ericsson said, "you buy this and this is what it costs," we had the means to figure out the real cost. We were able to figure this out in less than a year. Seen from Matra, whenever we were not shouting loud enough at Ericsson, we were suspected of being too lenient with them. From Ericsson's viewpoint, we were treacherous.
>
> So this has led to very heated debates. But it never led to a crisis in the board. There were four board meetings a year. The week before the board meeting, Payer would say, "if you don't settle this issue before the board meeting, I will put it on the table at the meeting." Every time agreements were found.

Another issue was that Payer proposed a merger between MET and MatraCom. One of MatraCom's businesses was telephone handsets, at that time based on fixed wires. With mobile starting to grow, Payer saw that handsets based on the GSM standard would become a huge business. Since Ericsson was becoming the GSM leader and Matra was in the handset business, combining MET and MatraCom could make strategic sense. Ericsson management, seeing that the JV was running into difficulties, said no to the merger.

Compounding these problems, Payer thought that Ericsson was not living up to the specific terms of the shareholder agreement. In his view, the JV was exporting less than what was acceptable. In addition, because Ericsson considered itself an emerging leader in mobile, Ericsson was unwilling to make a major commitment to work with Matra in developing GSM.

Ericsson's Perspective

From an Ericsson headquarters perspective, Payer was unrealistic and exceedingly difficult to work with.

> We were used to partners being nice guys. If the business is very profitable, he gets a good return on his money. But he doesn't meddle in the business because that is my problem. Mr. Payer says, "Hey, I'm in charge." That was really the big issue—the lack of understanding between nations about who runs the business.
>
> We knew that Matra was trying to take the best out of Ericsson for the French market and exploit our international position. That was part of the government's original plan. We also knew that transfer prices and royalty fees were quite high. There was foundation for Payer's suspicion that Ericsson was exploiting the high prices in the French market by making MET pay excessive prices for Ericsson equipment.
>
> At the same time, the GSM business was growing and they said, "What about the GSM partnership?" Because we underestimated the growth in the mobile business, we just could not combine with Matra in GSM because if we did, we would be giving away billions. For us that was not a problem. In many of Ericsson's international markets, particularly those in developing

countries, flexibility was critical. As a result, we believed that we could control things later. So we signed the agreements and expected the counterpart to be flexible, since the future is impossible to forecast. We reserved the right to be flexible in case the environment changed. That is the way business is done in places like Mexico and Brazil. It is not dishonest; it is the way things work for everybody. Matra was trying to hold us to every specific element of the original deal. We decided on a "go slow" policy on resolving the transfer prices, exports, and GSM cooperation issues until the full launch of GSM and until the abuses and insults from Matra stopped.

As for exporting, Ericsson's position was that while exporting was fine in principle, it was politically very difficult. All of the major telecom deals to developing countries involved French financing. If MET was competing for a contract it was likely that Alcatel also was involved. Not surprisingly, as a 100 percent French-owned company, Alcatel had certain advantages over MET.

The Situation in 1990

Despite the problems between the partners, MET was profitable. France Telecom was a reliable customer and the 16 percent market share was generating strong profits. After an initial loss for eight months of operations in 1987, net income after tax in France was FF66 million in 1988 and FF112 million in 1989. Sales were FF1,084 million in 1988 and FF1,133 million in 1989. Based on France Telecom projections, sales and net income would continue to increase steadily. However, Nils Söderquist, the Ericsson appointed manager, was disillusioned by his lack of influence and seemed unable to deal with Payer. The two were constantly disagreeing. Ericsson decided that a new and stronger Ericsson presence was necessary in the JV. In 1990 Lars Jarnryd was selected as the new president of the JV. Jarnryd, a managing director in one of Ericsson's U.S. operating companies at the time, spoke French and had some JV experience. His initial assignment in France was to work on the export issues and determine exactly how MET would meet its export commitments in the future. During this time, Jarnryd was working in an office in downtown Paris. In September, when the time came to join MET as president, Payer said Jarnryd could not enter MET premises. According to Jarnryd:

> Payer's position was "As a person we accept him. As a representative of Ericsson, we say no. We forbid him to go to the office." So, I was forbidden to enter the office. But, this being France, I was given a nice office near the Arc de Triomphe. They said, "We're not against you so we'll give a very nice office and see you now and then." Their view was "This is only way to make those guys [Ericsson] understand the problem. You have promised exports. You have not done that. Show me exactly how you will do it. And finally, you promised me GSM cooperation and it has not happened."

To Jarnryd it was clear that there were some deep undercurrents of conflict between the partners. In the opinion of the French managers of MET, the Swedes simply did not understand France or the French culture. According to one French manager:

> The Swedes view France as a Mediterranean country, which we are not. The Swedes have no difficulty dealing with the other Nordic countries, the UK, Germany, or America. With the French it is different.

30 Toppan Moore

In the summer of 1991, the semi-annual meeting of the Board of Toppan Moore, a joint venture between Toppan Printing of Japan and Moore Corporation of Canada, took place in Tokyo. With sales exceeding US$1 billion, Toppan Moore was a leader in the Japanese business forms industry and widely considered one of the most successful international joint ventures in Japan. While pleased with the venture's recent results, the issue for the Board members was how to ensure continued prosperity.

The Parent Companies: Toppan Printing

Founded in 1900, Toppan Printing was one of the world's largest printing companies, with 1990 revenues of US$6.7 billion. The organization had been listed on the Tokyo Stock Exchange since 1908 and had grown through merging several small printing companies and vertically integrating operations. By 1942, Toppan had established a number of wholly owned subsidiaries in China and southeast Asia. Mr. Inoue, who was President at the time, explained:

> We do not construct new plants to fulfill existing and anticipated demands. We establish a plant first and then find clients.

Ivey   Professor Paul Beamish and Mr. Shigefumi Makino prepared this case with the assistance of Joyce Miller solely to provide material for class discussion. The authors do not intend to illustrate either effective or ineffective handling of a managerial situation. The authors may have disguised certain names and other identifying information to protect confidentiality. Ivey Management Services prohibits any form of reproduction, storage or transmittal without its written permission. This material is not covered under authorization from CanCopy or any reproduction rights organization. Copyright © 1992, Ivey Management Services.

Toppan Printing's growth was halted during World War II when air raids by allied forces caused extensive damage and destroyed its head office and several major plants. The company recovered its momentum in the post-war period when the demand for general printing increased dramatically. With its superior technology and full line of printing methods, Toppan Printing was able to capture the bulk of orders for colour printing. The company subsequently founded a Technology Institute to create innovative printing technologies, and it established the Toppan Service Centre in 1961 to enhance customer service. Over the following decades, Toppan Printing strengthened its marketing channels throughout Japan and aggressively expanded its business to direct mail, point-of-purchase displays, magnetic printing for credit cards, and so on. By 1991, Toppan Printing operated nine plants in Japan and had subsidiaries in Australia, England, Hong Kong, Indonesia, Korea, Singapore, and the United States.

Moore Corporation

With 1990 sales of over US$2.7 billion, Toronto-based Moore Corporation was the world's largest manufacturer of business forms and a leader in new product development. The company traced its beginnings back to 1882 when Samuel J. Moore acquired the rights to produce a "manifold copying" book that he thought would revolutionize sales management. Inserting a carbon sheet into the binding of accounting books provided receipts for both the customer and the store. This ensured the accurate recording of transactions and represented the birth of the modern business forms industry.

By 1928, nine companies formed the Moore Group, which became Moore Corporation in the following year. While financial issues were discussed in Toronto, the individual companies continued to implement their own marketing and production plans. This autonomy was seen as a strong factor in the organization's growth although it did create some inefficiency in coordinating similar activities. Over time, there were joint efforts in purchasing, human resources, and research and development. However, as most of the affiliated companies produced business forms, they tended to compete with each other. In 1941, Moore saw the need to strengthen the Corporation's control over the various companies and integrated their individual activities into a new organizational structure called Moore Business Forms.

Through the 1960s and 1970s, the business forms industry in North America enjoyed real growth rates of roughly double the Gross National Product, due largely to purchases by business and government of computers that used continuous feeding forms. Numerous small printing companies began producing forms, particularly low value added stock items. In the 1980s, the industry's growth slowed with the increased penetration of computers, together with the shift towards personal computers and workstations that used fewer conventional forms products. New printing technologies, plain paper substitution, computer output onto microfilm, and electronic data storage also worked to displace the demand for conventional business forms. At present, the North American forms industry was highly fragmented and was characterized by persistent overcapacity. There were some 550 companies in the United States alone (18 were national in scope) manufacturing and selling over US$7 billion worth of these products. Increasingly, the industry had become more oriented toward satisfying changing customer needs and less towards producing traditional forms products.

Moore responded to the gradual maturing of the North American forms industry by emphasizing high value added products and diversifying into ancillary fields. While conventional business forms still accounted for the lion's share of sales in 1991, 10 percent of the Corporation's revenues were generated from sales of direct marketing products, printing equipment, and database services. Exhibit 1 provides an overview of the current financial status of both parent companies and Toppan Moore.

The Birth of Toppan Moore

Saburota Yamada, Toppan Printing's Managing Director, first became interested in the business forms area in 1953 when he saw continuous feeding serial forms being used in computers at a U.S. Air Force base in Japan. At the time, Toppan's R&D division concluded that the company did not have the technology to manufacture a product of comparable quality. A few years later, Toppan Printing purchased forms processing equipment from a German firm and began producing simple business forms in a range of sizes, largely for banks and security companies. One such company, Daiwa Security, subsequently established a subsidiary called Asia Business Forms (ABF) to produce its own forms. In 1962, Toppan Printing obtained a 55 percent share in ABF.

In the following year, Yamada travelled to North America with two of his managers to research the business forms industry, which was then worth about US$500 million. Analysts estimated that the Japanese market had the potential to grow to at least one-tenth the size of the American market. After visiting several business forms producers, Yamada approached Moore Corporation, the industry's leading manufacturer, about negotiating a joint venture. Yamada believed that the companies had complementary interests. Such an arrangement would enable Toppan Printing to introduce new products into an existing market, while Moore would be able to create a new market with its existing products. Exhibit 2 sets out the initial agreement and Exhibit 3 contains extracts from the final agreement.

At first, it was envisioned that a joint venture would use Moore's technology and equipment to produce business forms, which Toppan Printing's salesforce would sell in Japan and other Asian markets. Toppan Printing contended that it had an extensive distribution network, a knowledge of the market, and a well-qualified sales staff. Moore countered that the salesforce of the new company should be independent from Toppan Printing because Moore intended to bring its own sales methods into the venture. Upon further discussion, Toppan Printing acknowledged that the marketing of new products would be quite different from that of existing products. However, Moore recognized that consumer behaviour in Japan might be very different from that in North America and that its methods could not always be applied. In the end, an agreement was reached whereby the sales method and production planning would be independent of both parent companies, while cost and pricing principles would generally follow Moore's methods.

In June 1965, Toppan Moore was established as a 55:45 joint venture between Toppan Printing and Moore Corporation. Although Moore had initially insisted on an equal partnership, Japan's Ministry of International Trade and Industry (MITI) was reluctant for a foreign company's ownership to exceed 50 percent. The capital structure chosen reflected the agreement that the venture would use Toppan Printing's salesforce (initially) and sell products to Toppan Printing's major customers.

EXHIBIT 1   Overview of Parent Company and Joint Venture Activities

Moore Corporation	
Total Sales: U.S.	$2.77 billion
Total Assets:	$2.17 billion
Net Income:	$ .121 billion
No. of Employees:	25,021
Shareholders' Equity:	$1.54 billion
Established:	1928

Sales Breakdown

• Business forms   90%
• Data management service
• Direct marketing products   10%
• Packaging

Toppan Printing	
Total Sales:	¥781 billion
Total Assets:	¥928 billion
Net Income:	¥ 31 billion
No. of Employees:	12,393
Shareholders' Equity:	¥425 billion
Established:	1900
Export Ratio:	3%

Sales Breakdown

• General printing   48%
• Books and periodical printing   21%
• Wrapping papers   27%
• Securities paper printing   4%

Toppan Moore

Total Sales:	¥146 billion
Total Assets:	N.A.
No. of Employees:	2,774
Shareholders' Equity:	¥ 5 billion
Established:	1965

Sales Breakdown

• Business forms 77% (1985)	• Data entry
• Forms processors	• Dispatch or computer staff
• System supply service	• Form processing
• Computer/system machines	• Computer training software
• Cards/related equipment	• Video Tex display production
• System houses	• Video software production

Development of the Internal Organization

Yamada took on the presidency of Toppan Moore after retiring from his position as Managing Director at Toppan Printing in 1965. Yamada's management team was drawn almost exclusively from Toppan Printing. A vice president was appointed from Moore, but this person remained in Toronto and did not have any substantive responsibility for managing the venture. The Moore Vice President explained:

> I act as a "communications pipeline" between Moore and Toppan Moore. This position was stipulated as part of the joint venture agreement, and my role is to review the venture's results semiannually, independent of Toppan Moore's management, and present a report to the Board. I am

---

EXHIBIT 2   The 1963* Agreement between Toppan Printing and Moore Corporation

---

1. Toppan Printing and Moore will set up a new company to produce business forms and sell business machines.
2. The new company's name is "Toppan Moore Business Forms Company, Ltd." The stock of this company will be listed in the security market.
3. The new company will become effective after Asia Business Forms, Inc. (ABF), increases its stock up to ¥150 million.
4. The breakdown of ABF's capital will be assigned as below so that the ownership of the new company will be equal:

Toppan Printing	¥52.2 million (35%)	(+ ¥8.5 million)
Moore Corporation	¥52.5 million (35%)	(+ ¥52.5 million)
Daiwa Security	¥45.0 million (30%)	(+ ¥9.0 million)
Total	¥150.0 million (100%)	(+ ¥70.0 million)

5. Toppan Printing has responsibility for the venture's operation and developing its business plan, while Moore is responsible for supplying the production technology for making business forms.
6. There should be two senior managers from Moore.
7. The royalty allocation will be discussed later.
8. Moore will provide technical assistance and instruction for all of its products.
9. This tie-up is effective in perpetuity, with equal partnership. Either company should not establish relationships with other organizations without the permission of the other company.
10. Moore will provide the venture with printing machines, process machines, and other related equipment.
11. The venture will sell its products with the assistance of Toppan Printing's sales force, at least initially.
12. The sales area includes Japan, Hong Kong, and Asian markets in the ASEAN group.

---

*These agreements were superseded by agreements in 1965 and later. For example, Toppan Moore is not a publicly traded company, the two parents own all of the voting stock, and the royalty rate payable to Moore was later reduced.

---

also one of Moore's five voting members on the Board. Actually, the Board is dominated by Toppan Moore people, and there are even fewer representatives on the Board from Toppan Printing than from Moore.

Moore accepted not having a bigger formal role in the joint venture because we didn't know a lot about the Japanese market in the beginning. We knew that for Toppan Printing, the joint venture was an outgrowth of what they were doing with Asia Business Forms. We saw our role as bringing proven sales and production methods into the venture, and we were willing to allow Toppan Moore to operate fairly autonomously. Because of the royalty arrangement, we were confident that the people in the joint venture would feel compelled to make it a success.

In the initial stage of operation, Yamada saw the joint venture as being two to three decades behind Moore in terms of technological development. To bridge this gap, Toppan Moore asked its Canadian parent to provide it with a business forms processor. Moore had developed proprietary technology, and both its equipment and production system were highly regarded within the industry. Yamada remarked:

Moore sent us their newest machine, a high performance press that cost almost ¥75 million, more than the cash assets (¥70 million) of the whole company. Even though Moore knew that we couldn't afford this, they didn't send a cheaper, lower performance model. Our general managers

---

EXHIBIT 3   **Excerpts from the Final Agreement in 1964* between Toppan Printing and Moore Corporation**

- The new company is responsible for marketing the products that have never been produced by Toppan Printing, such as regi-forms, etc.
- The control centre of the new company is responsible for product price and production cost.
- Discounts above 20% should be reported to and authorized by Moore.
- There will be a royalty of 2% of total sales to Moore during the first five years of operation.

---

*These agreements were superseded by agreements in 1965 and later. For example, Toppan Moore is not a publicly traded company, the two parents own all of the voting stock, and the royalty rate payable to Moore was later reduced.

were very impressed that Moore sent us their best equipment when they didn't have to, and they didn't expect quick payment. In the end, we did somehow raise enough money to pay for it.

Moore was generous with their technology. Over the years, they made a great contribution to Toppan Moore's production technology and production-management skill. The company showed very human feelings. Everyone knows the 1941 story where Moore sent a letter to one of its Japanese salesman who was incarcerated during the war saying "don't worry, we are watching over you; Moore will remain your friend". This is symbolic of the way Moore has always worked. Developing strong human relationships is the most important key to business success.

Moore transferred forms-processing technology and equipment to Toppan Moore under a Technology Assistance Agreement signed in 1965. This agreement also stipulated shared budgets for common R&D activities. Joint efforts on product design, quality, and the manufacturing process resulted in frequent communication at every level between the companies on a whole range of issues. On occasion, engineers were exchanged between the two companies for short periods. A Toppan Moore manager commented:

Moore had particular ideas that they wanted to bring into the joint venture, regarding both sales and production methods. Moore wanted the salesforce to work under a territory coverage system based on commissions. As well, Moore wanted to introduce a 3-shift system and to control production using cost-based pricing. There was some minor resistance from the plant workers when we added a third shift, but this was largely because of a reduction in net wages.

Moore was a well-established company with good standing in the industry, and we realized there was much to learn from them. We did have some early disagreements over pricing, however. Moore used a highly disciplined pricing scheme based on formal planning and cost-benefit analysis. In Japan, many companies put priority on expanding market share, and prices tended to fluctuate. Under Moore's system, we did much less price cutting. This is just one aspect where we adapted our operating methods. We were never forced. As the company developed, we were able to select which methods we wanted to incorporate into our own practices.

Toppan Printing's contributions were more in the way of intangible assets, the social credit associated with the Toppan name. By comparison, we have less interaction with our Japanese parent. In a sense, there is nothing to learn from Toppan Printing. In the case where we have common clients, there is some opportunity to cooperate; however, there is seldom any sharing of technology. We are not targeting the same markets; therefore, the technology is not so overlapped and the concepts often do not translate back to Toppan Printing. We know Toppan Printing very well; we know our partner's heart. All of our senior managers have come from Toppan Printing. In some instances, it may be that we know too much.

Shortly after Toppan Moore was established, several of the joint venture's managers visited two of Moore's US plants to assess their sales and production systems. Mr. Kawai, who made this trip, offered his impressions:

> Moore has achieved the position of being the leading business forms manufacturer in the world through a step-by-step process. Overall, Moore is a well-structured company. The president and plant managers act according to a shared business policy. They do their clearly assigned duties and communicate well with each other and between and across sections. I realized that Moore has a different style than the typical Japanese organization, and although I didn't totally agree with Moore's methods, there were some principles that could be applied to our new organization, such as the emphasis on low waste and high productivity in their production system.

Company Pledge

During the startup phase, Toppan Moore's management began looking for a way to bring people together under the same purpose. Mr. Matsuda, the Hino plant manager, suggested using a company pledge:

> Since Adam Smith, it has been thought that the goal of the company is to maximize its profitability. But I believe the time has come to rethink this attitude. I think that the goals of a modern corporation should be to serve the public, to develop the company in a sound way, and to support the employees. Moreover, we have to think of these concepts as inseparable.

Matsuda's basic idea, "tria juncta in uno" (three contributions), was to focus on:

1. Social Community: Let us always be pioneers in the development of Business Forms, and play an important role in the growth of Japan's economy.
2. Company: Let us always be pioneers in the development of Business Forms, and devote ourselves to the prosperity of our Company.
3. Personal Happiness: Let us always be pioneers in the development of Business Forms, and endeavour to achieve the happiness of our people.

This pledge was recited each morning by all employees in every office and plant. Jiro Miyazawa, who succeeded Yamada as president in 1967, was seen as having a strong role in inspiring this philosophy both inside and outside of the company. Moore's vice president remarked:

> Miyazawa was a natural leader and he thrived on being a public figure. In fact, over time, he garnered something akin to a cult following in Japan. At one point, he organized an informal association with members from both inside and outside of the company called 'Seishun', after Samuel Ullman's poem, "Youth", for people who believed that 'youth is not a time of life—it is a state of mind'. Miyazawa was an inspiration to many people. He was an extraordinary man, and he was quite driven. He had an eye for detail, and he was very skilled interpersonally. Miyazawa was employee-oriented, and he understood and rewarded superior behaviour. He often gave out awards, not for years of service, but to those people who went the extra mile by working on the weekend or calling a customer from home.

TOMOMI-kai: The Employees' Association

Miyazawa believed that having a cooperative relationship between management and labour was critical for the venture. Consequently, Miyazawa and two of his senior managers sketched out the idea of forming a employees' association, TOMOMI-kai ("TO" from Top-pan, "MO" from Moore, (TOMO, a combination of "TO" and "MO", means "friendship" in Japanese), "MI" was another Japanese pronunciation of "BU", meaning beautiful, from Business Forms, and "kai" meaning organization or society). Toppan Moore's managing director, Mr. Ogura, and five other managers were appointed to a Steering Committee and had the responsibility for the overall management of TOMOMI-kai.

All employees, including top management, joined this association. A company song was composed by one employee, Miyazawa designed a company flag, and several internal statutes were enacted, including the "Ringi rule". A Steering Committee member explained:

> The Ringi rule is a typical style of decision-making in Japan. If someone has an idea, he documents it and passes it up to his boss who checks it. Depending on the issue, the boss may talk to his colleagues in other divisions before handing the paper up to the next level. This consensus approach is used throughout the company.
>
> TOMOMI-kai acts somewhat like a labour union, but the major difference is that where a union typically has a position against management, this organization is a place to have communication between managers and employees. The role of the Steering Committee is to oversee these developments. Often, we find ourselves heatedly discussing what employees really hope for from TOMOMI-kai and why this association should exist.

The Division Control Department and Project Teams

Since its formation, Toppan Moore had focused on expanding its market share, and concentrated its capital on establishing plants and merging small, local printing firms. Initially, all sales and production activities were controlled by headquarters in Tokyo. Sections were subsequently established in each plant to coordinate conflicts between the production and sales divisions.

By 1969, Toppan Moore had 850 employees, twice as many as when the venture was established. Many of these people worked in local offices, which operated increasingly independent of the central sales department. In fact, the distinction between headquarters and the local offices had become quite pronounced over the years. Miyazawa worried about this segregation between "brain and body" and thought that a new organizational structure was required. He remarked:

> The growth process of a company resembles that of a child. The whole body does not grow in perfect harmony with its individual parts. Muscles grow rapidly at one time and bones at another time. Because of this, children are more vulnerable to disease during this period. When a rapidly growing company concentrates its resources on particular functions, the organizational structure grows disharmoniously as a whole. As a result, the company faces many issues of coordination among functions. Our company has reached this stage. The time has come to introduce a control department to overcome the disharmony.

The Division Control Department was formed in 1969. Miyazawa served as the Department's director, and together with several senior functional managers and two management directors, coordinated cross-functional issues. The Division Control Department had an important role in establishing the company's budget control system and developing five-year business plans. This group was also involved in areas as diverse as devising Toppan Moore's employment exam, selection procedures, and managing the company dormitory.

In May 1970, Miyazawa established a project team within the Division Control Department to look at organizational issues. Miyazawa explained:

> I feel there is a need to restructure, but I'm not sure how to change the organization, so I set up a group of senior managers to look at the issues. I think the project team will become one of the most important functions within the company.

Project teams worked on issues like office work rationalization, research and development, and employee welfare. These teams were required to submit a report within a three-month period. Proposals for office automation, a five-day work week, and the standardization of business forms were subsequently adopted within the company.

Development of the Sales Organization

Early on, Toppan Moore sent several employees to its Canadian parent company as short-term trainees. Moore provided them with information on effective promotion and sales strategy. Moore's sales director, Mr. Seabury, subsequently conducted a training seminar at Toppan Moore for the salesforce and managers. One of the participants explained:

> We were not familiar with selling forms. A business form was quite a new product to us. We saw this as an expendable supply for a computer system and focused just on its price. I must admit that we didn't have the attitude that we should join in the customer's form-producing process. We learned that we needed much more "thinking" in our sales activity. Seabury emphasized that Moore did not sell a "thing", but rather the company sold the "value" of a product. He believed that a person selling business forms should, therefore, be a consultant, not merely an order taker. Moore's sales methods emphasized product knowledge, and the company concentrated on educating its salesforce. Generally, we continued using the sales methods brought over from Toppan Printing, but with Moore's help, we changed the tools that our salespeople went out with.

Seabury also introduced Territory Sales and the Sales Coverage Plan (SCP) as methods to control and implement sales activities. The SCP stressed new orders and new products. Using SCP, Toppan Moore was able to significantly rationalize its salesforce. However, some Japanese marketing managers were uneasy about adopting Moore's philosophy and the Territory Sales method, particularly the "door-to-door" and "walk-in" sales styles that Seabury emphasized. One of the managers elaborated:

> The business environment in Japan is different from North America. Our salespeople were used to selling continuous forms for computers in big volumes to large clients who had several regional offices, whereas Moore's clients were typically smaller, family firms. It has been said that the Japanese market is two decades behind the forms industry in North America, and Moore seemed to look upon our market as the same one it faced 20 years ago.

The North American approach is to build business on the basis of market coverage, whereas the Japanese focus on key customers. This is a different task. The approach in North America is different because, for the most part, these firms are not under the same pressure to develop close relationships with customers.

A system of Preferred Sales was later brought in by Mr. Spencer, who joined Toppan Moore in 1966 after spending 12 years in sales at U.S. Steel. This system focused sales activity on major clients without the territorial constraints of the previous approach.

A Period of Growth

When Toppan Moore was established, the Japanese economy was in a period of unprecedented prosperity. An observer commented:

> The 1950s and 1960s were a time of growth in Japan. GNP was increasing and every economic index was rising. Every industry was growing and every company was aggressively exporting. If a company could make a product, it could sell it. At this time, Japan was seen as a mass producer of low cost goods. MITI encouraged growth through export sales, and Toppan Moore was among the many companies that benefitted from its protectionist policies.

The demand for business forms increased dramatically, driven largely by the increasing use of American-made computers that used continuous forms. Over time, developments in information technology created a need for higher quality forms and more diverse products. Because commercial customs varied across regions, the Japanese forms industry became highly fragmented with many family companies responding to local needs. Toppan Moore succeeded, to some degree, in standardizing the specifications for business forms and was essentially the only company in the industry that operated on a national scale. Given the strength of the Toppan name in Japan, the salespeople saved time and effort explaining who Toppan Moore was, and they could gain the trust of new prospects more readily. The company experienced a dramatic growth in sales: 136 percent in 1967, 146 percent in 1968, 140 percent in 1969, and 150 percent in 1970. Local offices were added to cover the cities of Sapporo, Sendai, Nagano, Saitama, Chiba, and Kobe (see Exhibit 4). Three regional sales departments were subsequently formed to control the local offices in Western Japan, Eastern Japan, and the Tokyo area.

A Changing Environment

Toppan Moore's sales growth slowed in the early 1970s due to the "Dollar Shock". The uncertainty created by U.S. President Nixon's August 15, 1971, announcement that the U.S. dollar would no longer be linked to the gold standard resulted in an appreciation of the Japanese yen. As many Japanese companies depended heavily on exports to the North American market, the strong yen (against the dollar) acted as a brake on the Japanese economy, and the country experienced its first recession in the post-war era. During this time, Toppan Moore's orders and sales fell far short of plan, and the company took emergency

EXHIBIT 4   Toppan Moore Facilities in Japan

measures that had never been used before. All employees who had sales experience, including senior managers, were asked to call on clients. By March 1972, the company finally saw orders increase. In the following year, however, a pulp shortage increased the price of paper. This set off a chain reaction in the other basic materials used to produce forms, such as inks, and Toppan Moore was again obliged to raise the price of its products.

The early 1970s was also a time of rising oil prices, commonly referred to as "Oil Shock". On October 17, 1973, six Middle East oil producers announced price increases, together with a 5 percent decrease in production levels. Japan had no domestic energy source and the economy was highly dependent on oil imports. These six countries supplied over 90 percent of the oil imported into Japan. As a result, product prices increased across the board. Toppan Moore's prices were soon three times the level they were a year earlier. In 1974, the Japanese government implemented a "Total Demand Control Policy" aimed at controlling price increases. Although this policy reduced inflation, it also dampened demand and increased inventories. At this time, Miyazawa appealed to all Toppan Moore employees to "provide customers with more valuable products than a price increase". A sales manager reflected:

> Miyazawa kept telling us that the hard times wouldn't last and that the customer had to be the priority for all actions. A lot of business forms users looked to Toppan Moore to provide a stable supply, but this was something no manufacturer could guarantee. Many forms makers were, in fact, breaking up with some clients to satisfy the demands of others on more favourable terms. We made a great effort to keep our existing clients. The sales managers, and even Board members, called clients to explain the situation we faced and request a 10–20 percent reduction in orders. Most of our clients agreed to this. In daily meetings, our salespeople were told never to show arrogance to the customer, the kind of arrogance that can come from being in a seller's market.

Toppan Moore subsequently established several subsidiaries to disperse headquarters functions and to increase the responsiveness to local markets. These are described in Exhibit 5. Toppan Moore had also entered a number of joint ventures in southeast Asia and became an important link in the global product/service network of Toppan Printing and Moore Corporation.

Once each year, managers from Toppan Moore and Moore met for an open sharing of technical information. Although the joint venture had initially depended heavily on Moore's forms production technology, and still did to some degree, it had altered products to meet the specific requirements of Japanese customers, developed its own production knowhow, and was bringing new products to market such as magnetic forms, single cut forms, set forms, delivery forms, non-impact printing forms, envelopes, postcards, and labels.

A notable example of new product innovation was the development by Toppan Moore in cooperation with Moore of a hand-held, intelligent data entry terminal that has been highly successful in eliminating paperwork in the North American parcel delivery market.

Over the years, Toppan Moore had aggressively integrated its operations and automated its manufacturing process. Its system facilitated small lot production without sacrificing product quality, and the company was able to satisfy diverse customer requirements. Toppan Moore also began manufacturing business forms processors and computer supply equipment. In fact, Moore purchased a forms-processing machine developed by Toppan Moore.

As well, the company had built up a strong service business which involved dispatching computer operators to customer sites, developing computer software, and processing output forms. A fully automated Distribution Centre was established in 1982 near Tokyo. The Centre was connected with every sales department to enhance the company's delivery capability. By 1990, more than 30 such centres operated throughout Japan, and Toppan Moore had reached over US$1 billion in sales (see Exhibit 6). At this time, the company had about 70,000 customers, although 80 percent of its business was generated by 150 accounts.

EXHIBIT 5   Toppan Moore's Subsidiaries and Joint Ventures

Toppan Moore Operations (1975) was founded to send skilled operators, programmers, and system engineers to client companies. As well as managing and operating computer systems, this company offered computer programming services on a commission basis and also provided consulting services.

Toppan Moore Learning (1980) was a joint venture between Toppan Moore and Applied Learning International, Inc., a U.S.-based educational information processing company. Several media, including videotapes and textbooks, were used in products aimed at both general and specialized education programs for system engineers.

Toppan Moore-Deltak Company, Ltd. (1980) was a joint venture established between Toppan Moore and Deltak, an American computer training company. This venture offered training packages at both the beginner and advanced levels.

Toppan Moore Systems, Ltd. (1981) offered development services for software systems and application software and assisted clients with hardware selection. The organization provided support on a global scale to Japanese companies setting up overseas operations. As well, Toppan Moore Systems offered services to companies throughout Asia and in Europe and the United States.

Data Card Japan, Ltd. (1981) was established as a joint venture between Toppan Printing Company, Ltd., and U.S.-based Data Card, the leading global manufacturer of card-issuing equipment. This venture had developed a "laser graphic system" and was regarded as the world's first supplier of ID card systems. As well as having a network within Japan, the company operated throughout southeast Asia.

Toppan Moore Forms Handling Centre, Ltd. (1983) was established to process printed business forms on a commission basis. Processing included cutting, binding, sealing, and inserting. The company provided a broad range of support for computer data processing.

A New President

In 1990, Miyazawa retired as chairman (Mr. Kinami became president in 1987), but continued to hold an advisory function within the company. This was a common practice in Japan for retiring executives. Mr. Ogura, who had been Toppan Moore's managing director since 1968, took over as president. There was a great deal of consultation with Moore over Miyazawa's successor. Although Ogura was less of a public figure than Miyazawa had been, he knew the organization and worked well within the company. Ogura considered that he "managed by logic and by developing a network within the company."

Ogura had some strong ideas about the continued evolution of Toppan Moore:

So far, Toppan Moore has enjoyed immense success. This is not the norm for many joint ventures in Japan. One of the reasons is that Moore provided good circumstances for the development of the company. Moore is a very caring parent. They made a sincere effort to launch the company. They gave us a lot of autonomy. They didn't interfere. We were able to adopt certain managerial methods and arrange them to fit with Japanese business customs. Moore looks at Toppan Moore as a young company, and they have a long-term view of its growth. For instance, Moore has never asked us to have a detailed strategic plan. We make decisions on personnel, investment, and fund raising without detailed consultation. We are able to manage freely, and

---

Exhibit 6   **Japan's GNP and Toppan Moore's Sales and Number of Employees**

Year	1965	1970	1975	1980	1985	1990
GNP*	100.7	171.2	212.9	266.5	321.3	404.5
Sales†	8	63	203	433	863	1,485
No. of employees	410	1,028	1,797	1,667	2,229	2,774

*GNP: 100 billion yen.

†Sales: 100 million yen.

we have adopted many Japanese principles, such as a long-term focus, interdependence among companies, business diversification, and a management style based on loyalty and human feeling. Toppan Moore is very much a traditional Japanese company.

Our good relationship with Moore is based on personal communication. A formal agreement is not enough without having good intentions behind it. I believe that the most important way to develop a good relationship is to make the partner company a personal friend. We always try to find opportunities to shake hands with our parent companies. Shaking hands and communicating with partners are the first steps for making a good friend.

There are many examples where Moore and Toppan Printing are learning from Toppan Moore, and we are still learning from our partners. But the relationship between Toppan Printing and Toppan Moore needs to be changed. It is tough for an operating company to manage another operating company. You can't have the manager of a fish shop trying to control the manager of a vegetable shop. An operating company doesn't have an organization to manage a joint venture, and it doesn't have the whole picture, the broader perspective. We should be managed through a holding company, more like how Moore Corporation is set up. But the Japanese government legally prohibits establishing such a structure.

Another important issue is understanding the current product line. Some aspects are maturing, and we need to think about how to maintain growth.

James Saunders, the president and chief operating officer of Moore International Latin America and Pacific, who was in Tokyo for the semi-annual meeting of Toppan Moore's Board, shared Ogura's concern for ensuring the venture's continued prosperity. It had been an enormously successful partnership, and recently Saunders had been thinking a lot about the relationship between Moore and the joint venture. Saunders, 62, had first visited Toppan Moore in 1970 and since 1980 had made at least two trips a year to Japan. Among other possible ideas, Saunders was considering sending Dick Jones, a marketing manager at Moore, into the joint venture for a five-year period. Jones would remain on the Moore payroll. This would presumably provide the opportunity for increased knowledge of, and interaction between, the two organizations.

Twenty-six years of joint venture operations in Japan had resulted in both profits and goodwill. Ultimately for both Ogura and Saunders, the challenge was to build upon the success experienced to date.

31 BLACK & DECKER-EASTERN HEMISPHERE AND THE ADP INITIATIVE (A)

In late April 1996, Bill Lancaster, president of Black & Decker-Eastern Hemisphere, faced a difficult decision. Should he accept a new performance appraisal and management development system presented to him by Anita Lim, manager of Human Resources, or should he introduce a U.S.-designed Appraisal Development Plan (ADP) throughout the Eastern Hemisphere? ADP had been launched in the U.S. a few years earlier, and Lancaster, who had recently arrived in Singapore, had been very impressed with its impact on management development. A key feature of ADP in Lancaster's mind was a 360° performance instrument which provided each employee with feedback from subordinates, peers, and supervisors.

Before moving forward with ADP in the Eastern Hemisphere, Lancaster had asked for feedback from a number of local managers. Several expressed concern that 360° feedback might not work in Asia. To counter these concerns, Lim had proposed a modified version of ADP that included many of the features that Lancaster believed in and wanted to see, but lacked the 360° feedback element that he thought had been critical in ADP's success in the U.S. Lancaster was torn. On the one hand, he believed strongly in ADP and had seen it change the management and culture of Black & Decker in the U.S. On the other hand, he knew that 360° feedback might not be universally embraced because of cultural differences.

IVEY   Drs. Allen Morrison and Stewart Black prepared this case solely to provide material for class discussion. The authors do not intend to illustrate either effective or ineffective handling of a managerial situation. The authors may have disguised certain names and other identifying information to protect confidentiality. Ivey Management Services prohibits any form of reproduction, storage or transmittal without its written permission. This material is not covered under authorization from CanCopy or any reproduction rights organization. Copyright © 1998, Ivey Management Services.

Black & Decker Corporation

Black & Decker was founded in 1910 by Duncan Black and Alonzo Decker who invested $1,200 to start a company that manufactured industrial machinery. In 1914, the partners patented a drill with a pistol grip and trigger switch that revolutionized the power tool industry. By 1918, the partners had opened representative offices in Canada, England, Russia, Australia, and Japan. Seventy-eight years later, Black & Decker had sales offices in 109 countries and was the world's largest producer of power tools, electric lawn and garden tools, and related accessories. By 1996, Black & Decker's sales had reached $4.9 billion, net income was $229.6 million, and the company employed just over 29,000 people. Headquartered in Towson, Maryland (just outside Baltimore), Black & Decker was noted for its stable of well known brands including DeWalt™ and Black & Decker power tools, Dustbuster™ portable vacuums, Kwikset™ (locks and security hardware), Price Pfister™ (faucets), Emhart (glass and fasteners), and Black & Decker brand household products (irons, mixers, food processors, coffee makers, toasters, and toaster ovens). Under the direction of Nolan Archibald, Black & Decker's Chairman, President and CEO since 1986, recognition of the company's brand had grown to such an extent that in a survey of 6,000 brands in the early 1990s, Black & Decker was ranked seventh in the U.S. and nineteenth in Europe.

Despite major successes in North America and Europe, Black & Decker continued to face challenges in Asia and Latin America. By the early 1990s, senior corporate executives began to refocus efforts on strengthening the company's position in these emerging markets. Lancaster explained the situation in the early 1990s:

> During the early 1990s, there was a separate North American Group [located at corporate HQ in Towson] and a separate European Group [located in London]. Everything else was part of the International Group [located at corporate HQ in Towson]. At the time, International was thought of as mostly an opportunistic, export business. In Asia, we had a small team in Singapore on the Black & Decker payroll and that was it for the entire region. Not surprisingly, whereas Black & Decker was number one in market share in the U.S., we were a weak number five in Asia.

In 1993, there was a major reorganization of Black & Decker's operations. The International Group was split into Latin America, and the Eastern Hemisphere. Latin America's headquarters was moved to Miami; Eastern Hemisphere's headquarters was moved to Singapore. The territory covered by the Eastern Hemisphere office included the Middle East, Africa, India, Pakistan, and all of Asia-Pacific including China, Japan, Korea, the Philippines, Indonesia, Malaysia, Thailand, Singapore, Australia, and New Zealand.

Both the Eastern Hemisphere and Latin America offices reported to Black & Decker's Worldwide Power Tools Group. In the Eastern Hemisphere, about 70 percent of sales were power tools or accessories. The remainder of sales included such products as small appliances, fasteners, and security hardware. Power Tools was Black & Decker's largest single business and represented the "spiritual heart" of the company. Reporting through the Power Tools organization was viewed as an effective way of avoiding the duplication of infrastructure that would be necessary if multiple business unit headquarters were established in the Eastern Hemisphere.

Bill Lancaster Appointed as President of Eastern Hemisphere

In October 1995, Bill Lancaster was appointed President of Black and Decker Eastern Hemisphere. Although new to Singapore, Lancaster had held senior administrative positions for Black & Decker in Australia from 1988 to 1990. From 1990 to 1995, he was Vice President Marketing and Sales, Professional Products for the North American Power Tools group.

Lancaster worked closely with Jim Barker, Executive Vice President and President of Worldwide Power Tools. Under Barker's lead, the two undertook extensive market research in the early 1990s on the professional-industrial power tool segments. DeWalt had been purchased by Black & Decker in the 1970s and was known for large stationary tools, including radial arm saws. Recognizing the potential of the professional-industrial and professional-tradesmen segments, DeWalt was repositioned as Black & Decker's answer for these markets. An entirely new line of professional quality power tools was launched with a bold and innovative marketing strategy. DeWalt tools were yellow in color (a symbol of safety often found on job sites) and were introduced to potential buyers at construction sites. A fleet of yellow DeWalt vans was set up, and "events" were staged at major construction sites. The events included product demonstrations and free give-aways (T-shirts, hats, etc.). Putting the tools in the hands of professionals, it was believed, would give them first-hand experience of the quality, durability and innovative features of the DeWalt product line. The strategy was a huge success. DeWalt sales in North America went from essentially nothing to $300 million in a little over two years. In October 1995, Lancaster was promoted to run the Eastern Hemisphere.

By the time Lancaster arrived in Singapore, Black & Decker had either spent or had committed to spend nearly $80 million to set up its Singapore headquarters and build new factories in Singapore, India and China. In early 1996, the Eastern Hemisphere had nearly 1,000 employees. Growth plans called for employment to increase significantly by 2001, of which a large percentage would be new managers.

Lancaster's Initial Impressions

When Lancaster first arrived in Singapore, he spent a lot of time talking to employees throughout the organization. He started with members of the Eastern Hemisphere's Management Advisory Council (MAC). The MAC was composed of Lancaster's direct reports—eight vice presidents or directors, seven of whom were expatriates. He also spent considerable time talking to rank and file employees throughout the Eastern Hemisphere organization. He summarized his conclusions:

> I found that there was a major disparity in the management styles of people here. Some had styles that emphasized employee empowerment. Others were of the old authoritarian school. Some, quite frankly, were bad managers.
>
> I also ran into a lot of people who had been doing the same jobs for five or more years. They didn't seem to be growing or developing. About 70 percent of management and supervisory jobs were being filled by outsiders. Something wasn't right about this. We weren't growing our own people and needed to do something about it.

Finally, I felt uncomfortable with the existing management assessment and development system and thought that it needed to be changed. Managers were using a MBO-type system that had been replaced in the U.S. some time ago.

Management Appraisal and Development

ADP was first introduced in the U.S. in 1992 as a replacement for the company's Management by Objective (MBO) plan. Under the previous MBO program, superiors would meet individually with each subordinate to discuss the subordinate's performance and jointly establish clear and comprehensive objectives for the subordinate for the coming year. During the review session, criteria would also be set for assessing the subordinate's progress on the agreed-upon objectives and a schedule for follow-up meeting(s) would be set. Managers were encouraged to have at least one interim meeting with subordinates during the year to review progress and provide coaching.

MBO systems were widely used by Western businesses. During the late 1980s, for example, it was estimated that slightly less than half of the *Fortune 500* companies were using MBO-type systems. Yet, despite their widespread use, not everyone was happy with the results. Bill Lancaster commented on his U.S. experience with Black & Decker's MBO system:

> It had some good components. But it didn't seek input from others in the organization. This is important because as a boss, I was only seeing my subordinates doing their job maybe 10 percent of the time. Either I was gone or they were gone. I would see reports, maybe hear a few things in terms of their performance, but that's about it.
>
> Under the MBO system, I used to dread having to give performance reviews. In many cases, I wouldn't have a lot to say. If someone wasn't making their numbers, I often wouldn't really know why. So I would make up a list of suggestions. It probably wasn't very helpful, but it was the only feedback I could give. Sometimes the sessions got contentious. People would argue against my assessment saying that I didn't know enough about what they were doing to form an accurate opinion. Maybe they were right.

Casey Chan, Singapore-based Senior Brand Manager for Black & Decker Eastern Hemisphere, shared some additional insights into the MBO system:

> A MBO system has the advantage of making you be responsible to your boss. He knows you best and best understands the business objectives. Unfortunately, if you don't get along with your boss, your reviews might be bad. But it also goes the other way. If you are friends with your boss, you might get great reviews. It can be difficult to make the system objective.

The Appraisal Development Plan

In the U.S., ADP included six major steps. *First,* the appraising manager requested input from between three and six of the employee's peers (see Exhibit 1 for a sample of the form they receive). *Second,* the appraising manager requested input from between three and six of the employee's subordinates (see Exhibit 2 for a sample of the form they receive). *Third,*

EXHIBIT 1   Peer Review
Sample ADP Template

Name of employee to be assessed: _____

Period under review: From _____ To _____ (DD/MM/YY)

Please answer the following questions as objectively as possible with reference to the above employee's performance under the review period.

   i. What do you see as this person's key contributions over the period under review (as applies to you)?

  ii. What activities should be continued to maintain effectiveness?

  iii. What activities should be minimized to increase effectiveness?

  iv. What new activities will increase his/her effectiveness over the next 12 months?

  v. Has the performance of this employee under the above review period met the stated team objectives? Why, why not?

  vi. In your opinion, has this employee performed as a team player under the above review period?

  vii. What skills should be further developed?

  viii. Is this employee meeting his customer's requirement? Explain.

  ix. Should his/her role change in order to better meet/exceed customer requirements over the next 12 months? Explain.

---

the appraising manager asked the employee to perform and submit a self-review. The self-review included a document covering the employee's background, past year's performance, job function and other feedback (see Exhibit 3) as well as a nearly blank form for each employee to summarize his/her objectives and accomplishments for the year. *Fourth,* the appraising manager reviewed all of the submitted forms and prepared a formal assessment of the employee. Managers considered 14 different performance dimensions in assessing each employee (achievement orientation, interpersonal communication, conceptual thinking, analytical thinking, initiative, decisiveness, job knowledge, teamwork, customer-focused, focus on quality, organization commitment, leadership, developing others, and adaptability). After preparing a written assessment, the appraising manager then destroyed all peer and subordinate reviews. *Fifth,* the manager and employee met together. During the meeting, the manager discussed his/her written report with the employee. Then, the manager and employee agreed in writing on the employee's performance objectives, measurement criteria and weights, and future career development plans. *Sixth,* these written objectives and plans were summarized in a separate short form that also included comments from the employee, manager, and the manager's boss. These summary forms were kept on file in the local human resource manager's office. The entire ADP process ran from November 1 to the end of February each year.

EXHIBIT 2   Subordinate Review
Sample ADP Template

Name of manager to be assessed: _____

Period under review: From _____   To _____ (DD/MM/YY)

Please answer the following questions as objectively as possible with reference to the above employee's performance under the review period.

  i. How has your immediate manager helped you in meeting your performance expectations during the period under review?

 ii. How have you helped your immediate manager in meeting his/her performance goals during the period under review?

iii. What would you like your immediate manager to do more of in the next 12 months in order for you to be more effective?

 iv. What would you like your manager to do less of?

  v. Other feedback.

ADP's Acceptance in the U.S.

ADP was generally well received when it was introduced in the U.S. Bill Lancaster was a big fan.

> After ADP was introduced in the U.S., reviews became something I looked forward to. With all the feedback I got, I could add real value in the review sessions. I was very impressed by what ADP did for people in the U.S.
>
> ADP was designed as a tool to develop people. Another big benefit that came from ADP was the potential to build a highly functional, high performance team. ADP encouraged people to work together, to build one another. People who were good at managing ADP also got noticed. People wanted to work for them because they saw how successful they were at building people and strengthening a team.

Nicholas Levan, Vice President-Marketing for the Eastern Hemisphere, was one of the senior expatriates in the region and a member of the MAC. His experience with ADP in the U.S. was also positive.

> In the U.S., managers understood that peer reviews were invaluable. They made the job of doing assessments much easier. The reason is that managers don't see their subordinates as much as their peers do. Under the ADP, about 80 percent of evaluating subordinates is done for the manager. As a manager, I like that. But it is also good for employees. For example, the emphasis on self-assessments and career planning is a great development exercise and tool for building future leaders. Peer feedback and employee self-assessments add significant value to ADP as a development tool and ease the evaluation burden on management.

EXHIBIT 3   Self-Review
Sample ADP Template

Name: _____ Date of ADP Review: _____

Period under review: From _____ To _____ (DD/MM/YY)

The questions given below are intended to help you clarify your ideas about your job in preparation for the discussion. For your past year's performance, please prepare a document covering the following areas. This document must be returned to your manager by

_____
(to be completed by appraising manager)

A. BACKGROUND
  i. Career background (hire date, position(s) held).
  ii. Education/training background (company training and external training).
  iii. Other elements of your background (optional).

B. PAST YEAR'S PERFORMANCE
  i. Performance versus stated objective.
  ii. Performance versus on-going accountabilities.
  iii. Key achievements.
  iv. Key strengths.
  v. Areas needing further improvements to achieve maximum effectiveness.

C. JOB FUNCTIONS
  i. Brief summary of major job responsibilities.
  ii. Brief summary of other secondary duties.
  iii. What frustrates you?
  iv. What do you enjoy doing most?
  v. Do you see among your main activities any that should be modified, supplemented, or adopted?
  vi. Do you think that the scope of the job itself should be reconsidered?
  vii. What do you consider should be the main targets and tasks for the next review period? List clearly any new targets, priorities, and methods or means to achieve them. Consider any training or course required.
  viii. What kinds of support, special skills, and experiences do you need to do your job?
  ix. Where do you see yourself progressing in the job?
  x. What can I (we) do better as your manager to help you do your job or achieve your goals?

D. OTHER FEEDBACK

Despite the benefits of ADP, there were detractors. Bill Lancaster explained:

> At the senior levels, ADP was embraced quickly. This was less the case the further down you went in the organization. I think it safe to say that there were real concerns when ADP was first introduced in the U.S. Some people were very worried that 360° feedback would open up the evaluation process to bias. If they weren't popular, some managers feared that perhaps subordinates would gang up on them. There was also real concern about the amount of work involved in filling out, collecting and processing the forms. If you managed 10 people, you might have 120 forms to go through. Finally, people complained that there was no reward for doing a good job at ADP. What was the payback for spending so much time on a HR function?

Notwithstanding these concerns, ADP had earned wide support and acceptance in the U.S. by 1996. Worry over potential abuses diminished over time, and the process was gradually refined to accommodate the additional time required to make ADP work.

ADP in the Eastern Hemisphere

When Lancaster arrived in Singapore, the Eastern Hemisphere was using its own MBO system. A hybrid of the system which ADP had replaced in the U.S., the Eastern Hemisphere's MBO consisted of a simple rating scale that was completed solely by the appraising manager. A little digging convinced Lancaster that most managers in the Eastern Hemisphere were not using the MBO for joint goal setting. Instead, most were using it only as a simple performance evaluation instrument.

To test out ADP's potential in the Eastern Hemisphere, Lancaster met with Anita Lim, the Singapore-based Manager of Human Resources. Lim, aged 32, had been with Black & Decker for six years, longer than almost anyone else in the office. She had risen from an entry level human resource position to one of considerable authority in Asia Pacific. Her insight into the mind-sets of Asian workers was viewed as critical.

Lim was opposed to the introduction of the U.S. version of ADP in the Eastern Hemisphere. She had three primary, inter-related concerns. First, she argued that Asian people might not willingly open up the way Americans do. "If you ask them to provide candid feedback on their boss, they are likely to say something polite but won't be critical." Second, she asserted that Asians might not believe in the confidentiality of the ADP system. "No matter what a boss says about feedback being anonymous, Asians won't believe him or her. Somehow he or she will find out who said what about whom and there will be negative consequences for that person." Third, she believed that a change from MBO to ADP might be too radical. In her words, "Asians will not support radical change of this nature."

Sharon Seng, a Singaporean who reported to Lim as a Human Resource officer, had her own views. Seng had recently joined Black & Decker after having worked for the Singapore Broadcasting Corporation and Sony.

> As a HR professional, I have always wanted something that allowed people to increase communication and set objectives. When I arrived, I was quite shocked by the existing performance appraisal and development tool we were using.
>
> Many of the people being hired at Black & Decker are young. We are the MTV generation. We can be a lot franker than the earlier generation. For example, if I have a problem with my boss, I'll tell him or her. I don't need an annual review to raise concerns. I think if you have gone to university or spent much time overseas, you are much more likely to accept ADP. For me personally, it would not be that big of a deal.
>
> My biggest concern is the staff. Some of the managers have been here a long time and have rigid views. If their boss has been afraid to tell them something negative for five years, he or she is not going to change because of ADP. Another concern is over language. The ADP booklets from the U.S. are all in English. Many lower level employees don't speak English. Even some of our more senior people in Korea, Taiwan, and China don't speak good English. What do we do for them? Even if we translate the material, you have to wonder if they are translating the words or the meanings. It will take a lot of time and energy. I wonder if it is something we should be spending all of our time on right now.

Lancaster decided to talk to more people. He approached other members of the MAC for their reactions. Lancaster summarized their input:

> Those who had seen it work in the U.S. were excited and supportive. Those who had come to the Eastern Hemisphere from Europe [where ADP had not been adopted] were less convinced. I found that those who were opposed to ADP were mostly concerned about maintaining confidentiality. I heard someone say that only "an act of God" would convince people that the ADP results would be confidential.

Lancaster pressed on, meeting with other managers in Singapore and wherever he travelled. Their reactions were mixed. Eric Ang, Commercial Director for Black & Decker in Singapore and Malaysia, explained his perspective:

> In this part of the world, we have three percent unemployment. Because of this, growing people and building people are essential. ADP, as I understand it, forces your boss to look at your career path. What are your gaps and how do you fill these gaps? In theory, this should help us build the next generation of managers. But the problem is that in Asian cultures, people don't tend to open up. They will never say that their career's ambition is to have their boss's job. As a result, while ADP is designed to build commitment and develop managers, it may backfire. People may quit if they are pressed to open up in ways that make them uncomfortable.

Kevin Ip, Finance Director for China and Hong Kong, was concerned about the ability of ADP to assist in developing people.

> Here in the field, I think ADP will be much more difficult to implement than in Singapore. Although I am based in Hong Kong, I work with three representative offices in China. Trying to effectively communicate ADP to these people will be very difficult. For one thing, virtually none of these people speak English. But also, most people in the representative offices are working very hard. We are so focused on building sales, that I wonder if it is important or even possible to really develop people with broader skills. If you are making the numbers, some people believe that's all that is important.
>
> It is one thing for HQ to use ADP, but another for the country offices. There are not many developmental opportunities in China. If you want a promotion here, where do you go? You can change someone's title, but that's about it. They are still going to be doing the same things with the same colleagues.

Casey Chan, a Singapore-based Senior Brand Manager for Black & Decker, commented on the amount of time required to make ADP work:

> ADP seems to have a lot of open-ended questions that are general. It will take a lot of thinking to fill out the forms for an individual. I think it will likely take me three to four hours per person to do an appraisal. And I have five people who report to me. That's almost 20 hours of work. And it comes at the end of the year when we are busiest.

Liew Mee Salamat, Methods & Process manager and a Malaysian national, was concerned about cultural barriers to implementing ADP:

> I used to work for a large Japanese MNC. There, we didn't use a formal evaluation system. I didn't know how I was evaluated. The only way I found out I was doing a good job was by the size of the pay raise I got. There, if you question your boss, it is a lose-lose situation. You lose because you question him. He loses because he loses face.
>
> My worry about ADP is that if, in your peer review, you criticize someone whom your boss likes, you are really criticizing your boss. I think if my boss were American, I could be more

open in an evaluation session. But if he is Japanese, I don't think I could open up. I could never disagree with him or criticize someone he likes because he will hold a grudge against me. Having said this, ADP is an American system and American systems are generally regarded here as being fair. I would like to give it a try.

Milind Kapoor, Group MIS Manager for the Eastern Hemisphere, was an Indian national who had been at Black & Decker since mid-1995. He also had some interesting insights into ADP:

What I like about ADP is that it promises to give me feedback from in-house MIS customers. I want to know how we are doing and ADP promises to be much better than our existing performance appraisal system.

Despite this positive point, I think that in India, ADP would need to be modified. In my opinion, peer reviews won't work in India. If you have a job opening in India, 10,000 people apply. It is very different than here in Singapore where it is difficult to hire strong information technology people. Because of the tight labor market, I just can't seem to find or retain good people in Singapore. In India, there is so much more competition between peers that peer reviews would be very suspect. Everyone is competing for that one job. We are also so busy in India. We are very put off by the paper work. I am afraid that over time, ADP might not work in India.

If ADP were implemented in Singapore, my guess is that everyone would get an average rating. That is how people seem to do things. So if everyone gets an average rating, what kind of raise do you give people? I believe that the job market in Singapore is so tight right now that whether we do ADP or not, everyone will get about the same raise. In Singapore, if people don't get a 7 to 8 percent raise, they'll quit and take another job. So, is all the work associated with ADP really going to be worth it?

The feedback for Lancaster was sobering.

Here I was, relatively new in the job, wanting to change the culture and more effectively develop our people, and everyone was telling me that ADP may not be the way to go at the present time. I really believe in participative management. You can't railroad people. And yet, I still thought ADP could work wonders in the Eastern Hemisphere.

Lancaster had become increasingly worried about the lack of management strength in his organization. The brutal competition the company was facing throughout the region made him particularly sensitive to the need for more and better managers. For him, ADP was an ideal tool for developing these people.

As I contemplated a course of action, I took a closer look at our management needs in the Eastern Hemisphere. The intensity of the competition over here has surprised me. Our big competitors view Asia as the last frontier. To win the battle here, we need excellent management. I was convinced that ADP was one the best tools we had.

A Hybrid Plan Is Proposed

In March 1996, Lancaster asked Anita Lim to develop an ADP implementation plan. One month later, in April 1996, Lim presented a hybrid performance evaluation and management development system to Lancaster. Her plan was similar to the ADP in terms of its emphasis on career planning and goal setting, but without 360° feedback. Instead, Lim's plan relied on 180° feedback only (no peer or subordinate feedback). She suggested assessing the hybrid plan for a year. This would let people try it out and get comfortable with it. After a year, if it had been accepted, they could then add peer reviews, and then after another year, go to the full 360° ADP plan by adding subordinate reviews. Lim believed that a step-wise introduction of the plan would allow people to gradually buy into the change while at the same time allowing revisions where called for by cultural realities.

Betty Rong Rong, Human Resource Manager for Training, worked with Lim in developing the hybrid proposal. She commented on Lim's proposal:

> Anita put in a lot of work developing the hybrid model. We didn't know a single other company in Asia that had been successful with 360° feedback. IBM came the closest, but eventually shifted to a 180° plan. Most Asians don't like criticism or praise. Peer reviews are particularly unpopular because we are competing with each other for the same promotion.

Moving Forward

With Lim's new hybrid plan, Lancaster began to have concerns about moving forward. On the one hand, he was convinced that ADP could provide significant benefits in terms of management training and development. On the other hand, he knew he would need the human resource staff's full support if ADP were ever to be successfully implemented.

As he contemplated a course of action, Lancaster was also feeling increasing pressure from Jim Barker to improve results in the Eastern Hemisphere. The Eastern Hemisphere Group's year-end results for 1995 were disappointing and Lancaster needed to ensure that the breakeven point for the company's investments was achieved on schedule.

By late April 1996, Lancaster was considering three different options involving ADP. The first option was to do nothing. Despite the need for action, Lancaster appreciated that this option, like the others, required serious evaluation of its benefits and consequences. Perhaps the cultural gap between East and West was so great that ADP should be put on hold and they should just stick with what they were already using. Implementing ADP would require a huge effort that perhaps would be better spent building sales and focusing on figuring out the external market place.

Part of Lancaster's concern was that for ADP to be most effective, it would have to be accompanied by a huge new commitment to training and development. As a result of ADP sessions, many bosses would almost certainly encourage subordinates to take additional university courses or in-house training programs. Unfortunately, the money and infrastructure to arrange outside courses or design and put on in-house programs were limited. Whereas in the U.S., managers could put much of the onus on the employee, Lancaster realized that such an approach might be problematic in Asia. Lee Kwang Chian, Engineering Manager at the Eastern Hemisphere Design Center, explained:

> The problem is that in an Asian culture people believe that it is up to the company to look after them. If I suggest to one of my subordinates that he or she take a certain university course, he or she will take the course, but only after we arrange it all for him. People take what you give them but complain when it's not given to them on a spoon. With ADP, their expectations may only rise.

These issues were very real to Lancaster. By waiting, he would be able to ensure that the right infrastructure and follow-up programs were in place, and he would avoid shaking up such a delicate organization.

A second option for Lancaster was to go ahead with Lim's hybrid ADP. Clearly, she understood the culture better than he did. By moving forward more slowly, ADP could evolve over time. Iterative change was always less threatening, particularly when the perceived change agent was viewed by so many as an outsider. As he reflected on the input he had received, he had a growing realization that the Eastern Hemisphere was not one culture but many cultures. While he knew this intellectually before, he now had a much better "feel" for the cultural morass he was now working in. Could a single program work in such a diverse part of the world? Perhaps Lim was right and the step-wise introduction of ADP was the best way forward.

Lancaster's final option was to go forward full speed ahead. This had been his initial plan. His logic seemed impeccable. The region clearly needed shaking up. He wanted a new high performance organizational culture in the Eastern Hemisphere. He wanted to hire and support the type of employee who embraced rather than shunned change. He needed management strength now and ADP was the best tool he had. If ADP was imperfect, so be it.

With these arguments swirling through his mind, Lancaster was facing one of the toughest decisions in his career.

> Building managers here has been difficult. In part, it is because there is a limited supply of truly talented managers available. Our people need business skills, leadership skills, and industry knowledge. How do you get this in an organization that is really only a couple of years old? We must grow our people. But how should we begin and what role should ADP play?

32 GLOBAL ENTERPRISES, INC.

February 17, 1995

As she prepared for the next day's meeting of the Board of Directors, Jennifer Copperman-Williams, the 49 year old president and CEO of GLOBAL Enterprises, had never felt more frustrated. Despite years of work restructuring the company, GLOBAL had just reported a loss of $99 million on sales of $2.55 billion. While Copperman-Williams continued to enjoy the confidence of the Board, she knew that the next day could bring questions for which she did not have answers. In preparing for her presentation, she wondered whether to downplay the company's current problems or turn to the Board for real direction. Almost certainly the Board would push for significant changes in leadership, including the removal of several senior managers. It had become increasingly clear that key individuals stood in the way of the integration efforts that had been ongoing in the company. What was less certain to Copperman-Williams was whether the company's restructuring in fact made sense. As the architect of the company's current integration efforts, Copperman-Williams was clearly in a tough position. With the Board meeting less than 24 hours away, she had little time to spare.

The Early Years—1948 to 1970

GLOBAL traced its roots back to 1948 in Los Angeles, when Benjamin Copperman started a small company, named Precision Devices, shortly after earning a Ph.D. in Mechanical Engineering at the California Institute of Technology. During its early years, Precision focused exclusively on designing and manufacturing diagnostic and control equipment for the medical industry. As a result of several patents, sales grew rapidly, making Copperman a millionaire before he reached the age of 28.

This fictional case was prepared as the basis for class discussion by Mr. S. M. Steele, Program Director, IBM Leadership Institute, with the assistance of Professor Allen Morrision, American Graduate School of International Management. No part of this case may be reproduced, stored in a retrieval system, used in a spreadsheet, or transmitted in any form without the express written permission of the IBM Leadership Institute, 20 Old Post Road, Armonk, NY 10504. Phone 914/765–2000.

In 1956, Precision acquired Professional Services, Inc. (PSI), for $500,000. PSI provided temporary and contract personnel to the accounting and data processing industry. Jeremy "Joco" Morris, the 26 year old owner and close personal friend of Copperman's, stayed on as President. In 1959, Precision spent $2.6 million to buy Best Brands, a Canadian automotive electronics product design and manufacturing company. Best Brands had lucrative OEM contracts with Ford and American Motors for controls, sensors, and sound systems. They also supplied a national chain of retail/wholesale automotive parts stores with after-market products. John Michaels, the owner of Best Brands, also continued as President. In 1963, Copperman paid $11.6 million for New Horizons, a Princeton, New Jersey, company that designed and manufactured flight simulators and high resolution video display devices for the aerospace industry. New Horizons also held and licensed key patents for the manufacture of solid state silicon and germanium circuits. The president of New Horizons was Carl Rose, a 34 year old with separate Ph.D.'s in physics and mathematics. Although somewhat eccentric, he was highly respected in his field and had been able to attract and retain what many regarded as a brilliant young staff.

While Copperman maintained ultimate control of each company, they continued to be managed largely as autonomous ventures. These companies, combined with Precision's core medical equipment operation, generated Group sales of $168 million in 1968.

International Expansion—1970 to 1975

In the early 1970s, the strong market and growing demand in Europe and Asia began to exceed the distribution capability of Precision's predominantly U.S.-oriented companies. Growth in these geographies seemed to require a dedicated manufacturing, marketing, and service presence. As such, Copperman began a search for international partners.

In 1975, he formed two international partnerships. One was with Nitta Nippon Electronics, a $115 million Japanese distribution company owned by Shinichi Nitta, the 53 year old founder. The other was with Rhine Mark Products, a $112 million German medical supply company owned by Friedreich Schuller, a hard driving 50 year old. The key terms of the agreements were as follows:

1. Precision Enterprises gained 50 percent ownership of both partner companies and the right to purchase the remaining 50 percent when the current owner "retired" or reached the age of 70. For Precision, the purchase price amounted to $31 million over 6 years for one-half of Nitta Nippon's equity and $24 million over 4 years for one-half of Rhine Mark's equity.

2. Nitta Nippon Electronics and Rhine Mark Products were each granted unlimited use of Precision Enterprises' patents, brand names, and technology.

3. Each partner was given exclusive distribution and manufacturing rights for the following geographic areas:

   Rhine Mark Distributors—Europe, Middle East, and Africa.

   Nitta Nippon Electronics—Asia, South Pacific, and Australia.

   Precision Enterprises—The Americas.

Upon ratification of the partnership agreement, GLOBAL Enterprises, Inc., a private holding company, was formed (Exhibit 1).

The Fast Growth Years—1975 to 1990

Precision Enterprises.   By 1990, Precision Enterprises had become a $702 million business. Under the direction of Jennifer Copperman-Williams throughout much of the 1980s, Precision was widely regarded for providing excellent installation, maintenance, and facility operations services in the health care industry. In 1988, Precision Enterprises won the prestigious Deming Quality Award and in 1989 the U.S. Commerce Department's Baldrige Award.

Copperman-Williams was generally regarded as a hard working, no-nonsense manager. She joined the company in 1969 after receiving an MBA (with an emphasis in International Management) from U.C.L.A. and an undergraduate degree in political science from Georgetown University. She worked in a variety of marketing and finance positions and in 1975 was appointed vice president of administration for Precision Devices. Over the next nine years she also served as vice president of marketing and vice president of operation for Precision Devices. In 1984 she was named as President of Precision Enterprises.

Rhine Mark Products, Inc.   By 1990, Rhine Mark had grown to $648 million in sales and $44 million in profits. With the political assistance of the European Development Council, the company opened manufacturing facilities in Germany, Italy, and France. In 1986 and again in 1988, it was honored as the "most admired" company by the European Asso-

EXHIBIT 1   Organization Chart, 1975

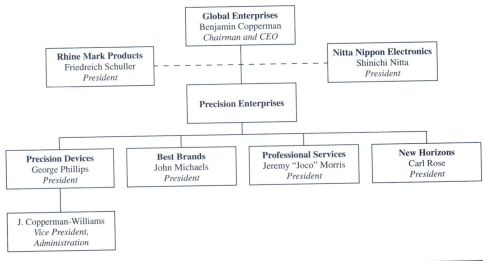

ciation of Manufacturers. In 1987 Friedreich Schuller was appointed as a commissioner to the European Common Market and, in 1989, was elected to the board of directors of the European Bank of Commerce.

Schuller believed a strong centralized management system should develop strategic direction and control capital investment. He ruled with what many regarded as an iron hand, and on more than one occasion had summarily fired plant managers and vice presidents who questioned his direction or failed to produce results. Ironically, at the same time, he fiercely defended his independence from GLOBAL. He was once quoted as saying, "*We have to send them half our profits, but we don't have to accept their advice or return their phone calls.*"

Nitta Nippon Electronics.   Initially, the growth in the Asia/Pacific geography outstripped GLOBAL's ability to ship product from the U.S. Over time, Nitta Nippon opened manufacturing facilities in Japan, Korea, and Singapore. In each country it was able to negotiate significant concessions on local tariffs, taxes, and administrative regulations. In return, they agreed to limit the import of components and subassemblies. By 1990, Nitta Nippon had profits of $50 million on sales of $670 million.

Shinichi Nitta was a role model for a participative management culture that valued consensus and long-term success over short-term gains. Nitta put a premium on loyalty, quality, and teamwork. He encouraged employees and suppliers to view Nitta Nippon Electronics as part of their family, and routinely sent personal notes and gifts when an employee married or had a child. In 1988 he was named as one of the "Outstanding Asian Entrepreneurs" by *Fortune* magazine. The company was also voted "the most desired place to work" by the Japanese Association of Student Engineers in 1986, 1987, and 1989.

GLOBAL Enterprises.   Throughout most of the 1980s, Ben Copperman devoted considerable time to helping Schuller and Nitta establish manufacturing operations in their respective geographies. Despite his best efforts, he continued to find that nationalism represented an enormous barrier to integration. To those who knew him, his biggest disappointment was his inability to effectively exploit the broad geographic scope of GLOBAL. By 1989 the relationship between the partners deteriorated to the point where they frequently would not return each other's phone calls.

Somewhat out of frustration, Copperman began to withdraw from the day to day operations of GLOBAL. He became active on several U.S. Presidential Commissions and served on the board of AMTRAK, Bankers Trust, the International Red Cross, and Brunswick.

GLOBAL Goes Public—1990 to 1991

In January 1990, Friedreich Schuller suffered a massive heart attack and died in his office on a Sunday afternoon. GLOBAL acquired the outstanding 50 percent ownership of Rhine Mark for $109 million and named Peter Notehelfer, the former Vice President of Manufacturing, as President.

In September 1990, Shinichi Nitta was appointed as a member of the Japanese delegation to the International Commission on Trade and Tariffs. He retired and quickly reached an agreement to sell GLOBAL the outstanding 50 percent interest in Nitta Nippon Electronics for $124 million. Hajime Takeuchi, the former Director General of Operations, was appointed President.

GLOBAL engaged Goldman-Sachs to take the company public in order to finance the buyouts. The IPO of 25 million shares at $25 was oversubscribed and on January 1, 1991, the stock was trading at $30/share. When the smoke cleared, the Copperman family had received $255 million in cash and was left with 3 million shares, or 12 percent of the outstanding stock in GLOBAL.

On March 1, 1991, Copperman addressed a special meeting of the top 95 managers where he announced his retirement from GLOBAL in order to accept an appointment as the Chairman of U.S. Presidential Commission on Productivity and Quality. In a brief statement he thanked them for their support and said,

> Your dedication to providing value to the customer, value to the stakeholders, and value to each other has been the foundation for GLOBAL's past success. The future, like the past, will require strength of character and leadership. My legacy to you is my deep faith in your ability to be guided by an unswerving commitment to the GLOBAL Common Values. (See Exhibit 2.)

Following his announcement, Jennifer Copperman-Williams was named by the board as the new President, CEO, and Chairman of GLOBAL.

The New GLOBAL—1991 to Present

Copperman-Williams' succession to the CEO job, while not unexpected, was not particularly celebrated in EMEA or Asia/Pacific. Although she was highly regarded as a capable and strong leader, she was generally perceived to have a "U.S.-centric" focus. This perception was reinforced by her announcement on April 23, 1991, that GLOBAL would reorganize into international product groups with independent geographic marketing and distribution companies (see Exhibit 3). The product groups were as follows:

> *Best Brands*—specialized in OEM and after-market automotive sound systems, speakers, and gauges. These were manufactured in the United States, Germany, and Singapore.

EXHIBIT 2   GLOBAL Common Values

The customer is the center of everything we do.
Performance in the marketplace is the measure of our success.
We work together as a team to provide our customers with the most competitive products
  and values in the industry.
We act with integrity.
We value diversity and treat each other with respect.
We provide our shareholders, partners, associates, and suppliers with a fair deal and a fair
  return on their investments.

New Horizons—built its proprietary visual display and simulation technology into a leadership position in the multimedia entertainment and communications industry, with manufacturing facilities in Mexico, Italy, and Korea.

Precision Devices—specialized in "big ticket" customized medical diagnostic and process control systems with design and manufacturing facilities in the United States, Japan, and France.

Professional Services—provided consulting, programming, and facilities management services to the medical and data processing industries. This product line tended to be regionally unique and, as such, would continue to report directly to the geographies.

Under the new organization, Product Line Managers (PLMs) were paid on Market Share and Sales Operating Profit. PLMs controlled investments in R&D and all aspects of production. Country-based General Managers (GMs) were evaluated on Net Profit, Customer Satisfaction, and Employee Morale. They controlled all marketing, sales, and service activities.

Not surprisingly, many GMs were frustrated because they had lost control of product development and production. Notehelfer and Takeuchi were particularly upset at the perceived loss of power and prestige associated with the reorganization. They were also angry that their input on the restructuring had, for the most part, been ignored.

During this period, the patents on several "cash cows" and New Horizons' licenses on proprietary manufacturing processes expired. This caused intense pressure on prices and manufacturing costs and opened the door to new competition. In 1993, for the first time in history, GLOBAL lost $71 million on $2.4 billion in sales.

Key events from the perspective of the GMs and PLMs include the following:

EXHIBIT 3   Organizational Chart, April 23, 1991

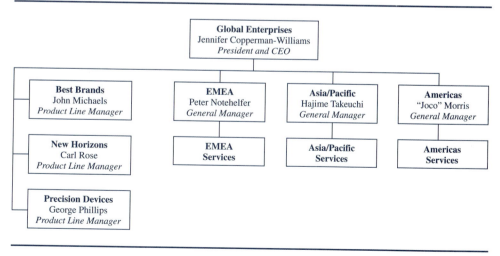

John Michaels, PLM of Best Brands

Sales of cars and trucks and the profits of the companies that make them are hitting new highs every quarter. Unfortunately, this is happening at the expense of the independent suppliers who have had to increase productivity and cut costs just to squeeze out razor thin margins. This is particularly true in the automotive sound systems industry, which has gone through a blood bath and continues to be a basket case.

The products are all the same under the covers and the only purchase criteria are price and delivery. Brand name, while important in the after-market, is of no value in the OEM market. Hell, there are times when I could make more money buying stuff in bulk from our competitors and putting it out under our name then I could by building it in our own factories.

If we are going to succeed in this business, we must consolidate our manufacturing and cut our costs. Unfortunately, it has been almost impossible to get the geography GMs to accept this. They give it lip service until it comes time to face the music and close a plant in one of their countries. Then they cry like babies. . . . "it will kill morale, the government will go nuts, I am not going to be the GM to have the first layoff."

We need to face the facts. This is a flat commodity market where we can make some money if we are the low cost producer and pay attention to balancing demand and production. The first step was closing down our antiquated plant in Europe and doubling our production capacity in the U.S. It was painful and expensive, but we are now positioned to be much more competitive and profitable. The next step will be to close the plant in Singapore. I know it will take some time and investment capital, but if we are serious about this market we must do it. If not, we should hand out the pink slips and turn the plants into shopping malls.

Carl Rose, PLM of New Horizons

The marketplace for interactive entertainment, virtual reality, and multimedia communications is going to explode. It will dwarf the PC boom and the developing nations of Asia and eastern Europe will lead the way The beauty of it is that we don't have to worry about the infrastructure—cable, optic, glass, cellular, satellite, laser, magnetic, digital, etc.—it doesn't matter. The value added in this market is all in the application. The winner will be the company that can integrate multiple independent complex virtual worlds in a way that brings value to the user, improves the quality of life, and helps people rediscover fun. I call it "reengineering life", the ultimate thrill in cyberspace.

We have a good start on this thing, but like any huge new market, it is crowded with deep pocket wanna-be winners. While we fight it out, the demand is going to continue to grow at a 15 percent a year with no end in sight. Anyone who misses this, or stands in the way, should be summarily executed. That includes the nay sayers in GLOBAL who just don't get it. I can't ever remember it being so hard getting funding as it is now. The future of GLOBAL is in New Horizons, and getting there faster, with more for less, is my mission.

George Phillips, PLM of Precision Devices

The aging Precision Devices product line, although approaching end of life, continues to be the most profitable for GLOBAL. Over the last four years the impact of managed health care and hospital cost constraints has slowed the industry growth rate from 12 percent per year to 5 percent. Precision has held on to 25 percent of the market by combining continued investment in R&D with highly visible, personalized, value added marketing. I could grab another 15 points of the market if we had the capital to expand production capacity and took a more aggressive pricing posture.

Unfortunately, I have not been able to convince Jennifer or the GMs to make a major investment in Precision Devices. After all, it is a cash cow and is supposed to generate the capital to invest in New Horizons, not consume it. This difference of opinion has become a source of constant frustration and frequent angry debate. I feel that Rose spends too much time in fantasy land, where the rubber meets his dreams, and never comes to grips with the fact that he has yet to show a profit. We have reached the point where continuing with New Horizons is throwing good money after bad.

Jeremy "Joco" Morris, GM, Americas

You know, at 65, I am one of the youngest senior managers in GLOBAL and although I hate to admit it, I am running out of steam. This business is beating me up. The profit margins are way down and the competition has become fierce. We are all holding our breath for Rose to ride in on his white stallion with another New Horizons blockbuster but, so far, it is not happening. Thank goodness for the services business. While it might not be the most profitable, it is surely the most fun. I really enjoy the personal relationships that have been built over the years.

Despite that, if the truth be known, I want to spend more time being a grandfather and plan to retire as soon as I have finished helping Jennifer clean up the mess that Notehelfer made when he closed his Best Brands plant. I owe her old man that much and, anyway, she has been like a daughter to me.

Peter Notehelfer, GM, Europe, Middle East, Africa

There is an old German saying, "the devil is in the details." That goes to the heart of the problem with the way GLOBAL has gutted the power and capability of the country organizations in favor of centralized U.S. control. Neither Jennifer nor her PLMs have ever had a job outside of the U.S. What do they know about our culture, about our customers, about our unique market requirements?

Case in point, look at the decision to close my Best Brands plant in favor of doubling capacity in the U.S. Michaels thought I should be a good team player and jump at the opportunity to ring up Bonn to tell them we are going to throw a bunch of Germans out of work so that we can import products from America. It sure was convenient that he wanted to double the capacity in Joco's territory and that Joco has an almost mystic ability to influence Jennifer. The whole thing was a little too cozy for me.

To top it off, we lost $58 million on the sale of the plant and paid out another $71 million in severance payments and other extraordinary charges. It was the first layoff in the history of GLOBAL, even dating back to the days of Rhine Mark. It has left me with a huge political problem and has impacted the morale of the entire European operation. It was, in my opinion, one of the dumbest business decisions you could make.

Hajime Takeuchi, GM, Asia/Pacific

We have a long and proud history of association with GLOBAL from the early days when Nitta-San formed his partnership with Copperman-San. Over the years we have seen the roots of that partnership intertwine and enrich the lives of our employees and their families. Recently, however, the pressure of being a public corporation has caused us to take the seductive road to short-term success at the expense of long-term opportunity.

Perhaps the cultural gap between Japan and the U.S. is too wide for us to understand each other. We appreciate the pressure to show profits every quarter, but we must not do so at the expense of missing the emerging opportunity in the New Horizons line. We must be patient and make personal sacrifices until we can put these hard times behind us. It is most important during these times that the young woman, who is our CEO, has the wisdom to seek guidance from Copperman-San and Nitta-San as she moves forward on the competitive battlefield.

February 17, 1995

Copperman-Williams met with her father over dinner to give him a personal preview of the 1994 business results (see Exhibits 4–7). With the Board meeting the next day, she had little choice but to brief her father. Although now 72 years old, Ben Copperman remained the company's biggest single shareholder and a strong supporter of his daughter. Jennifer ran through the events of the last year.

> I backed Michaels' plan to consolidate the production of Best Brands to get a cost advantage which would help them grow and become profitable. The gamble worked out well and helped the Best Brands product line show a small operating profit of $30 million on sales of $628 million. In Europe, Notehelfer dragged his feet on closing his Best Brands plant and ended up paying almost $100 million dollars in separation packages and extraordinary charges. As a result, EMEA ended the year with a $115 million loss on sales of $833 million. Thank heavens for George Phillips. He milked the Precision product line to a $106 million in profit on sales of $757 million. This all went to help finance Rose, who had promised this would be the year of the big win for New Horizons. The big win turned out to be a $100 million loss on sales of $530 million. Joco squeaked in at $16 million in profit on sales of $857 million in the Americas and Takeuchi-San barely broke even in Asia/Pacific with $2 million in profit on $854 million in sales.
>
> The PLMs have never been more at each other's throats. The restructuring was supposed to have clarified organizational responsibilities, reduced duplication of effort and cost, and leveraged our global size to make us more competitive. Yet it has only created more conflict. The PLMs and the geographies are ready for war. It's starting to show on the bottom line.

She ended the meeting by asking her father if he thought she was doing the right thing. Copperman listened quietly as his daughter finished speaking. As they stood to leave he said,

> You know, I built this company by taking risks and making investments to bring new technology to the marketplace, faster and better than the competition. That is what you have been doing and it is too early to know if it will pay off. I would say you are in Act II of the opera and the fat lady is scheduled to sing next year. You know I'll support you. But I'm not sure of the other directors. You'll do what's right. Give 'em hell.

Once her father left she returned to the task at hand, which meant preparing a statement for the board. By 8:30 P.M., alone in her office, she had penned the following remarks.

> In 1994, GLOBAL generated $2.5 billion in sales and posted a loss of $97 million. I am not here to offer excuses; however, there are several items that need to be brought to your attention to help you put this record in perspective. First, we incurred a one time $130 million extraordinary charge for closing our Best Brands plant in Germany. Second, we invested an additional $100 million in our continued development of the New Horizons interactive multimedia product. If we had ducked these two tough but strategically necessary investments, we would have shown an annual profit of $130 million, or 5.5 percent net return on sales.
>
> I want to make it very clear that I am personally responsible for our 1994 business results. While disappointing in the short term, they represent an investment in the future and are a tribute to the courage, commitment, and support of my colleagues. Despite the problems we encountered last year, GLOBAL is now well positioned in every market and has the potential to generate a 10 percent net return on sales in 1995.

Exhibit 4   Global Enterprises Consolidated Income Statement—1994 (in millions)

	Americas	EMEA	Asia/Pacific	Total
Sales revenue	$858	$833	$855	$2,546
Cost of products & services	480	467	487	1,434
Depreciation & inventory charges	65	55	68	188
Gross margin	313	311	300	924
Expenses	288	288	288	864
Operation profit	25	23	12	60
Quality programs	10	10	10	30
Extraordinary charges	0	129	0	129
Net earnings before taxes	15	(116)	2	(99)
Taxes	0	0	0	0
Net earnings	15	(116)	2	(99)

Exhibit 5   Global Enterprises Consolidated Product Income Statement— 1994 (in millions)

	Best Brands	New Horizons	Precision Devices	Services	Total
Sales revenue	$628	$528	$757	$633	$2,546
Cost of goods sold	450	349	251	384	1,434
Depreciation	23	34	108	18	183
Inventory charges	1	3	1	0	5
Gross margin	154	142	397	231	924
Marketing expense	108	198	216	161	683
Research & development	15	46	75	45	181
Operating profit	31	(102)	106	25	60
Quality programs	10	10	10	0	30
Extraordinary charges	129	0	0	0	129
Net earnings before taxes	(108)	(112)	96	25	(99)
Taxes	0	0	0	0	0
Net earnings	(108)	(112)	96	25	(99)

I do, however, believe that our potential can best be realized by an infusion of new ideas and new leadership. As such, I have proposed an amendment to our by-laws that would require the retirement of all officers, General Managers, and Product Line Managers upon reaching age 65. In anticipation of board approval of this amendment, I have asked for, and received, the undated letters of resignation of all the GMs and PLMs. I plan to take action later today on several of them. The others, if they are over age 65, will take effect on July 1.

EXHIBIT 6   Global Enterprises Consolidated Sources & Uses of Cash—1994 (in millions)

	Americas	EMEA	Asia/Pacific	Total
Sources:				
Starting cash	$588	$509	$521	$1,618
Sales & receivables	895	759	812	2,466
Extraordinary cash in	0	237	0	237
Loans in	150	0	0	150
Uses:				
Production costs	458	343	449	1,250
Inventory charges	0	1	3	4
Operating expenses	288	288	288	864
Quality programs	10	10	10	30
Investment in plant	556	217	146	919
Loans out	0	150	0	150
Extraordinary cash out	0	71	0	71
Taxes	0	0	0	0
Current cash	321	425	437	1,183

On a personal note, last month marked my 26th year with GLOBAL. I am thankful for the opportunity I have had to work with such a distinguished group of people. However, I too, have reached a point where it is time to move on. Therefore, I am offering my resignation to the board, to become effective on whatever date you choose. In the interim, I will continue my commitment to helping GLOBAL achieve sustained profitability and market leadership.

As Jennifer closed her note pad, she realized that a statement of this sort would provide no opportunity for turning back. Lesser action would no doubt be acceptable to the Board. Would this statement, she wondered, go too far? Or, would it not go far enough?

EXHIBIT 7   Global Enterprises Consolidated Balance Sheet—1994 (in millions)

	Americas	*EMEA*	*Asia/Pacific*	*Total*
Assets:				
Cash	$321	$425	$437	$1,183
Intercompany loans	0	150	0	150
Product inventory	5	57	134	196
Receivables	826	794	761	2,381
Plant and services fixed assets	1,695	1,075	1,285	4,055
Total assets	2,847	2,501	2,617	7,965
Liabilities:				
Bank loans	1,000	850	700	2,550
Payables	914	726	826	2,466
Intercompany loans	0	150	0	150
Stockholders' Equity:				
Common stock, par value $25.00 per share				
25 million authorized and issued	208	208	208	624
Accumulated retained earnings	725	567	883	2,175
Total liabilities	2,847	2,501	2,617	7,965

33 HONEYWELL INC. AND GLOBAL RESEARCH & DEVELOPMENT

In mid-1997, Steve Wilson, a Honeywell Technology Center (HTC) manager, thought back to the previous week's visit from a Chinese delegation interested in Honeywell Inc. (Honeywell) technology and products. These visits were becoming increasingly frequent. Wilson and other HTC managers were certain that there were many international opportunities for Honeywell, not just in China but throughout Asia and Eastern Europe. The dilemma was that HTC, Honeywell's research and development R&D organization, was centralized in Minneapolis, a long way from the potential new markets.

Recently, a Honeywell manager based in Asia had raised the following issues:

There are several reasons for spreading R&D capability around the world. One, time to market in today's world is probably the most significant competitive advantage a company can have. One way to get quicker time to market is to do R&D in multiple locations around the world so you have a 24-hour R&D process. Second, there are talented people around the world and by not taking advantage of those skills and talents that may exist in China or India or other places, a company is putting itself at a competitive disadvantage. Third, in many countries, including China, personal contacts and connections are invaluable in the business world and there is a great loyalty among alumni of certain institutions. American companies that have established relationships with these institutions may get access to alumni in important government positions down the road. Fourth, its much easier to understand the unique product requirements of a country or region of the world if you spend time there. It's very hard to sit in Minneapolis and figure out the cooling control requirement for a Chinese air conditioning system if you have never been in an apartment building in China that has poured concrete walls that you can't run thermostat wire through.

There was a growing consensus that HTC had to become more international to support Honeywell's growth opportunities. However, before anything could be done, many issues had to be addressed. How should Honeywell attempt to build effective global R&D capabilities? HTC had developed a unique entrepreneurial, interaction-based culture. Could this culture be replicated outside the United States? How quickly should HTC move? Who would manage new R&D organizations? How would these organizations be funded? Should international R&D sites be centers of excellence for specific technologies, or should they be application centers using technology developed in Minneapolis, or should they be a combination of both?

Honeywell Background

Honeywell had a long history of engineering and scientific achievement. In 1885, Albert Butz invented the damper flapper, a device that opened furnace vents automatically. Butz formed the Butz Thermo-Electric Regulator Co. in Minneapolis to market the product. In 1927, the firm, now known as the Minneapolis Heat Regulator Company, merged with its main competitor, Honeywell Heating Specialties of Wabash, Indiana. The new public company, named the Minneapolis-Honeywell Regulator Co. and headquartered in Minneapolis, became the leading U.S. firm in home heating controls.

Throughout the 1930s, Minneapolis-Honeywell expanded and diversified. In 1930, the first international subsidiary was opened in Toronto and in 1934, the first European subsidiary was established in the Netherlands. Between 1900 and 1937, the company evolved from manufacturing one thermostat to producing more than 3,000 control devices and its engineers received more than 1,000 patents. During World War II, Minneapolis-Honeywell became involved in mass-production of military instruments and equipment. This work led to the development and production of an aircraft autopilot, positioning Minneapolis-Honeywell in the aeronautical engineering business. After the war, the firm reorganized its various defense-related businesses into the Military Products Group, and by the late 1950s, military business represented one-third of the company's sales. By the 1960s, the firm, now called Honeywell Inc., had become an important supplier for the U.S. space program.

In 1955, Honeywell formed a division called Datamatic to build computers. This division would eventually have a 10% market share. Honeywell's controls business also grew rapidly in the post-war period. In 1950, the firm acquired the Micro Switch Corporation, a manufacturer of switches, sensors, and manual controls used in myriad products such as cars, airplanes, appliances, air conditioning systems, and factory equipment. In 1953, Honeywell introduced its famous round thermostat, the Honeywell Round. Much of Honeywell's growth between 1960 and 1980 was the result of international growth and, in particular, demand from developing nations for home, building, and industrial controls.

The 1980s and early 1990s was a period of restructuring for Honeywell. Total employment dropped from 94,000 in 1985 to 50,000 in 1995. Cutbacks in U.S. defense spending had a dramatic effect on Honeywell's Space and Aviation Division. During a three-year period from 1991 to 1994, space and aviation revenue declined by $700 million to $1.4 billion. Space and aviation employment declined by half to about 11,000 and 3 million square feet of plant space was closed. In 1990, the defense business, which a few years earlier had accounted for almost half of total revenues, was spun off into a new organization. In 1986, Sperry Aerospace, a Phoenix-based firm manufacturing flight instrumentation, advanced avionics, and other electronics systems was acquired for $1.03 billion. The acquisition solidified Honeywell's position as the leader in aircraft navigation systems and flight controls. Also in 1986, after its market share dropped to 2 percent, the computer business was spun off into a joint venture of Compagnie des Machines Bull of France and NEC Corp. of Japan. In 1991, Honeywell exited the computer business.

Honeywell Sectors in 1997

Honeywell was organized around three industry sectors: home and building control, industrial control, and space and aviation control. Exhibit 1 shows summary financial information for Honeywell, Exhibit 2 shows a list of products, customers, and competitors, and Exhibit 3 shows segmented financial information by division and geographic region.

The home and building control division manufactured controls for heating such as thermostats, ventilation, humidification, and air-conditioning equipment, home automation systems, lighting controls, building management systems and services, and home consumer products such as air cleaners and humidifiers.

The industrial control sector produced systems for the automation and control of process operations in industries such as oil refining, oil and gas drilling, pulp and paper manufacturing, food processing, chemical manufacturing, and power generation. For example, Honeywell controls were used in 24 of the world's 25 largest oil refineries. The industrial control sector also produced switches, sensors, and solenoid valves for use in vehicles, consumer products, data communication, and industrial applications.

The space and aviation sector was a leading supplier of avionics systems for the commercial, military, and space markets. Honeywell systems could be found on virtually every commercial aircraft produced in the Western world and were aboard every manned space flight launched in the United States. Products included automatic flight control systems, electronic cockpit displays, flight management systems, navigation, surveillance, and warning systems, and severe weather avoidance systems. In 1995, the Boeing 777 was launched, marking the successful launch of a new suite of Honeywell integrated avionics controls.

Of the three product sectors, home and building control was the most international because its products had potential applications in every country. The end customer was the homeowner, and housing needs differed in every country. Most of the home and building control products sold in Europe were engineered and manufactured in European factories. For example, German homes were usually heated with hot water, whereas in the U.S. forced air was the norm. As a result, various valves and boiler parts were developed in Germany for the German heating market. In other cases, the European products were close adaptations of products sold in the United States. There were also products, such as thermostats sold in the Netherlands, that were imported directly from the United States.

With its worldwide standards, space and aviation was the best defined international sector. Aviation products did not have to be localized, which meant that aviation could be operated as a centralized global business. Industrial control products, although not standard worldwide, tended to be less localized than home and building products because customers wanted similar controls worldwide in their plants.

EXHIBIT 1   **Honeywell Inc. Financial Information**
(Dollars and Shares in Millions Except Per Share Amount)

	1996	1995	1994	1993	1992
Sales					
Home and Building Control	$3,327.1	$3,034.7	$2,664.5	$2,424.3	$2,393.6
Industrial Control	2,199.6	2,035.9	1,835.3	1,691.5	1,743.9
Space and Aviation Control	1,640.0	1,527.4	1,432.0	1,674.9	1,933.1
Other	144.9	133.3	125.2	172.3	152.0
Total sales	$7,311.6	$6,731.3	$6,057.0	$5,963.0	$6,222.6
Operating Profit					
Home and Building Control	$345.8	$ 308.6	$ 236.5	$ 232.7	$ 193.4
Industrial Control	254.9	233.8	206.6	189.7	156.9
Space and Aviation Control	163.3	127.6	80.9	148.1	175.8
Other	6.2	2.8		(1.8)	(9.5)
Total operating profit	770.2	672.8	524.0	568.7	516.6
Operating profit as a percent of sales	*10.5%*	*10.0%*	*8.7%*	*9.5%*	*8.3%*
Interest expense	(81.4)	(83.3)	(75.5)	(68.0)	(89.9)
Litigation settlements				32.6	287.9
Equity income	13.3	13.6	10.5	17.8	15.8
General corporate expense	(91.9)	(97.6)	(89.3)	(72.6)	(95.7)
Income before income taxes	$610.2	$ 505.5	$ 369.7	$ 478.5	$ 634.7
Assets					
Home and Building Control	$2,144.3	$1,727.2	$1,529.8	$1,327.3	$1,302.4
Industrial Control	1,376.1	1,307.2	1,273.3	1,059.8	1,057.5
Space and Aviation Control	1,037.3	971.1	1,174.9	1,219.6	1,403.6
Corporate and Other	935.6	1,054.7	907.9	991.4	1,106.6
Total assets	$5,493.3	$5,060.2	$4,885.9	$4,598.1	$4,870.1
Additional Information					
Average number of common shares outstanding	126.6	127.1	129.4	134.2	138.5
Return on average shareholder's equity	*19.7%*	*17.1%*	*15.6%*	*18.4%*	*13.8%*
Shareholders' equity per common share	$ 17.44	$ 16.09	$ 14.57	$ 13.48	$ 13.10
Price/Earnings ratio	20.7	18.6	14.7	14.3	11.5
Percent of debt to total capitalization	31%	28%	32%	28%	28%
Research and development					
Honeywell-funded	$ 353.3	$ 323.2	$ 319.0	$ 337.4	$ 312.6
Customer-funded	$ 341.4	$ 336.6	$ 340.5	$ 404.8	$ 390.5
Capital expenditures	$ 296.5	$ 238.1	$ 262.4	$ 232.1	$ 244.1
Depreciation and amortization	$ 287.5	$ 292.9	$ 287.4	$ 284.9	$ 292.7
Employees at year-end	53,000	50,100	50,800	52,300	55,400

Source: Honeywell 1996 Annual Report.

EXHIBIT 2 **Honeywell Products, Customers, and Competitors**

Sector	Representative Customers	Competitors
HOME AND BUILDING CONTROL. **Home and Building Products: *Consumer Products.*** Heaters; fans; humidifiers; vaporizers; electronic air cleaners; water filtration products; thermostats and home security systems. ***Control Products.*** Perfect Climate Comfort Center® System; SYSNet™ Facilities Integration System; thermostats; TotalHome® home automation system; HVAC equipment controls; integrated furnace and boiler controls; demand-side energy management systems; energy-efficient lighting equipment; utility services; water controls; direct-coupled actuators; zoning systems; media controls; heat recovery and energy recovery ventilators. **Building Solutions:** Installed systems; HVAC solutions (EXCEL 5000®); fire solutions (Excel Life Safety); security solutions (Excel Security Manager); open systems technology; performance contracting; compressed air management; isolation room controls; remove HVAC monitoring (ServiceNet®); and maintenance services.	Architects and developers; building managers and owners; consulting engineers; contractors, distributors and wholesalers; hardware and home center stores; heating, ventilation and air conditioning equipment manufacturers; home builders; physicians; consumers; airports; hospitals; hotels; manufacturing facilities; office and government buildings; restaurants; retail stores; education facilities; utilities; and security directors.	Johnson Controls; Siebe; Landis & Staefa; Emerson; White Rodgers; Holmes; Alerton; Siemens, ADT and regional companies such as Andover.
INDUSTRIAL CONTROL **Industrial Automation and Control Products and Solutions:** Advanced control software and industrial automation systems for control and monitoring of continuous, batch and hybrid operations; process control instrumentation; industrial control valves; recorders; controllers; flame safeguard equipment; supervisory cell controllers; product management software; equipment controls; programmable controllers; communications systems for industrial control equipment and systems; and professional services, including consulting, networking, engineering and installation. **Sensing and Control Products and Solutions:** Solid-state sensors for position, pressure, airflow temperature and current; vision-based sensors; precision electromechanical switches; PC-based device level control.	Chemical plants; computer and business equipment manufacturers; data acquisition companies; food processing plants; medical equipment manufacturers; oil and gas producers; pharmaceutical companies; pulp and paper mills; refining and petrochemical firms; textile manufacturers; heat treat processors; utilities; package and material handling operations; appliance manufacturers; automotive companies; and aviation companies.	Asea Brown Boveri; Elsag-Bailey; Fisher-Rosemount; Siebe (Foxboro); Siemens; Yokogawa; Allen-Bradley; Banner; Cherry; Omron; Sprague; Telemecanique; Turck.
SPACE AND AVIATION CONTROL **Major Products:** Integrated cockpit avionics, including automatic flight controls, electronic display systems, flight management systems; Global Positioning Systems (GPS) based avionics; communications systems; Traffic Alert and Collision Avoidance Systems (TCAS); automatic test systems; helmet-mounted display and sighting systems; space instruments and sensors; and data management and processing systems.	Airframe manufacturers; international, national, and regional airlines; corporate operators; NASA; prime U.S. defense contractors; and the U.S. Department of Defense.	Allied Signal; Litton; Kaiser; Rockwell International; Sextant.

EXHIBIT 3   Segmented Financial Information

Home and Building Control

1996 Sales Mix

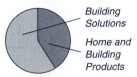

Building Solutions

Home and Building Products

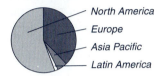

North America

Europe

Asia Pacific

Latin America

Financial Results
(Dollars in Millions)

	1996	1995	1994
Sales	$3,327.1	$3,034.7	$2,664.5
Operating Profits	$345.8	$308.6	$265.2*
Margin	10.4%	10.2%	10.0%

*Excluding special charges.

Industrial Control

1996 Sales Mix

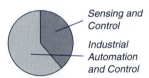

Sensing and Control

Industrial Automation and Control

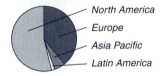

North America

Europe

Asia Pacific

Latin America

Financial Results
(Dollars in Millions)

	1996	1995	1994
Sales	$2,199.6	$2,035.9	$1,835.3
Operating Profits	$254.9	$233.8	$221.0*
Margin	11.6%	11.5%	12.0%

*Excluding special charges.

Space and Aviation Control

1996 Sales Mix

Space Systems

Commercial Flight Systems

Military Avionics Systems

International (destination basis)

North America

Financial Results
(Dollars in Millions)

	1996	1995	1994
Sales	$1,640.0	$1,527.4	$1,432.0
Operating Profits	$163.3	$127.6	$100.5*
Margin	10.0%	8.4%	7.0%

*Excluding special charges.

Source: 1996 Honeywell Inc., Annual Report

International Opportunities

Honeywell's international organization is shown in Exhibit 4. European operations were headquartered in Brussels and the Asia-Pacific region was based in Hong Kong. Non-U.S. sales were $2.8 billion, equal to 39 percent of 1996 total sales. By the year 2000, non-U.S. sales were expected to increase to 45 percent. Much of this growth was projected for China and Eastern and Central Europe. With their high levels of air and water pollution and poor record of energy efficiency, these areas were large potential markets for Honeywell home and building and industrial controls. As one HTC researcher indicated, "the mess in Eastern Europe is a huge market for us."

In particular, the area of district heating was a large potential market for Honeywell. In Eastern Europe and China, most people had never used a thermostat in their homes. Apartments generally had no heating controls and their temperatures were determined by outputs of a central district heating facility. During the winter it was not unusual to see open windows in apartment buildings as residents tried to cool their apartments. Hot water for domestic radiators was provided by a central boiler in each region. On a designated day of the year, an official turned the heating on for the whole city; on another, it was turned off. Often, there were no valves on the radiators. The plumbing was often arranged so that if one occupier turned down the heating, the entire building would be affected. With district heating, Honeywell's goal was to provide a complete system from the boiler to the individual apartment unit. Honeywell could provide monitoring and control systems to improve productivity, save energy, reduce air pollution and provide better temperature control. To do this would require Honeywell home and building control and industrial control units to work closely together as a team. As an early entrant, Honeywell, which opened a Moscow office in 1974, was a major supplier of district heating controls in Eastern Europe.

Although Honeywell's Asian business accounted for only about 8 percent of sales, CEO Michael Bonsignore indicated that "Asia represents the greatest growth opportunity for Honeywell in the next 20 years."[1] Bonsignore added that he would like Asian businesses to reach $1 billion in sales by 2000 and to grow at a 20 percent compound rate or better. Honeywell's Asia/Pacific business had operations in 17 Asian countries and Hong Kong. Its joint ventures included partnerships with South Korean conglomerate Lucky-Gold Star Group and China National Petrochemical, the world's third-largest petroleum refiner. About half of Honeywell's Asian sales were in China. Honeywell generated about $250 million in revenue in China and expected sales of at least $500 million by the end of the decade. In 1997, Honeywell began working with Beijing District Heating Co. to improve heating services for 20 percent of the capital's buildings, with the potential for expansion. As well, China needed more than 1,000 new aircraft over the next 15 years, which created opportunities for Honeywell avionics products.

Competition

Honeywell's home and building and industrial control competitors ranged from diversified global giants like Siemens and Asea Brown Boveri to small, specialized firms such an Andover Controls, a $70 million manufacturer of programmable, network-based building

---

[1]DeSilver, D., "Honeywell Plans Asian Forays," *Minneapolis-St. Paul City Business*, June 21, 1996, p. 11.

EXHIBIT 4   Honeywell International

President, Honeywell Asia Pacific	President, Honeywell Europe	Vice President and GM, Latin America	President, Honeywell Canada
HQ, Hong Kong	HQ, Brussels	HQ, Sunrise, Florida	HQ, North York, Ontario

Asia Pacific (HQ, Hong Kong):

Affiliates: Australia, China, Hong Kong, Malaysia, New Zealand, Pakistan, Singapore, Taiwan, Thailand

Manufacturing: Sydney, Auckland, Taipei, Shenzhen, Tianjin

Joint Venture Manufacturing: Pune (India), Fujisawa, Hadano, Kamata, Isehara, Shanan (Japan), Bupyong (South Korea)

Europe (HQ, Brussels):

Affiliates: Austria, Belgium, Bulgaria, Czech Republic, Denmark, Egypt, Finland, France, Germany, Hungary, Italy, Kuwait, The Netherlands, Norway, Oman, Poland, Portugal, Romania, Commonwealth of Independent States (Russia), Saudi Arabia, Slovak Republic, South Africa, Spain, Sweden, Switzerland, Turkey, Ukraine, United Arab Emirates, United Kingdom

Centers of Excellence and Manufacturing: Brussels, Belgium; Varkaus, Finland; Amiens and Grenoble, France; Amsberg, Maintal, Mosbach, Neuwied and Schönaich, Germany; Den Bosch and Emmen, The Netherlands; Porto, Portugal; Newhouse, Scotland; Geneva and Zurich, Switzerland

Latin America (HQ, Sunrise, Florida):

Affiliates: Argentina, Brazil, Chile, Mexico, Panama, Puerto Rico, Venezuela, Colombia, Ecuador

Centers of Excellence and Manufacturing: Caracas, Venezuela; Chihuahua, Ciudad Juarez, Districto Federal and Tijuana, Mexico; São Paulo, Brazil

Canada (HQ, North York, Ontario):

Manufacturing: Ontario, Quebec

---

automation systems (see Exhibit 2). In the space and aviation control sector, the set of competitors was much smaller and primarily U.S.-based.

Competitors in the home and building and industrial control sectors were, like Honeywell, intent on international growth. For example, Johnson Controls, Honeywell's largest U.S.-based competitor in home and building controls, had recently announced an R&D partnership with a Hong Kong university. In 1997, U.K.-based Siebe announced plans to establish a wholly owned subsidiary in India, which would include engineering centers for industrial process control equipment. White-Rodgers, a division of Emerson Electric with a worldwide base of 23 sales, distribution, and manufacturing sites, had made a commitment to expand its international presence. Even tiny Andover, based in Andover, Massachusetts, operated three technical centers outside the United States in the United Kingdom, Germany, and Hong Kong.

In addition to increasing internationalization, the controls industry had seen a wave of mergers, acquisitions, and alliances. In 1996, Electrowatt Group, a Swiss-based holding company, announced the formation of Landis & Staefa, Inc., a worldwide combination of Landis & Gyr and Staefa Control System. Landis & Staefa competed with Honeywell in home and building controls. Later in 1996, it was announced that Siemens AG was acquiring a 44.9 percent share in Electrowatt Group. Siemens, a Honeywell competitor in various product markets, was one of the world's largest organizations. Siemens had sales of more than $60 billion, 250 manufacturing sites in 42 countries, and subsidiaries and affiliates in more than 190 countries. In the United States alone, Siemens had more than 46,000 employees in over 400 office locations, 40 research and development facilities, and 80 manufacturing and assembly plants. In 1991 Siebe acquired U.S.-based Foxboro for $656 million. The Siebe group employed over 42,500 people and consisted of more than 150 companies located in 40 countries. In 1992, Emerson Electric bought Fisher Controls for $1.4 billion, forming the Fisher-Rosemount family of companies.

Research and Development

R&D was a focal point throughout Honeywell with technology seen as the key to marketplace differentiation. About 30 percent of Honeywell's current sales were from products introduced in the past five years. Honeywell was involved in two main R&D activities: R&D that supported Honeywell's worldwide product divisions and contract research funded by outside government agencies and firms. Including R&D done both in the product divisions and by HTC, Honeywell funded $353 million of R&D in 1996 and contract work generated revenue of $341 million. Until the cutbacks in U.S. military spending in the early 1990s, most of the contract research was for military purposes. Although a significant amount of contract research still involved the Dept. of Defense, other funding agencies included NASA, Department of Commerce, and the Electric Power Research Institute. Increasingly, non-defense firms were forming alliances to jointly develop new technologies through contract research. Cooperative research with OEM customers also occurred. All of the outside contract funding was from U.S. sources, although several project applications were targeted outside the United States, such as a Dept. of Commerce power plant upgrade project in Ukraine.

Honeywell Technology Center

The Honeywell Technology Center (HTC) was Honeywell's primary research organization and supported the worldwide product divisions. As a corporate service organization, HTC's mission was to support the product divisions and develop technologies that had the potential to benefit multiple product divisions. This mission was expressed as:

> In partnership with Honeywell's businesses, we provide world-class technologies, processes, and product concepts that fuel Honeywell's global growth and profitability.

HTC, based in Minneapolis, employed about 575 people, including 300 engineer/ scientists. Of these 300, 100 had Ph.D.'s, and 180 had Bachelor or Master's degrees. With the exception of about 40 employees in Phoenix and five in Prague, all HTC employees were in two locations in the Minneapolis area. In 1996, HTC's spending was $90 million, which came from several sources: 50 percent from outside contracts, 40 percent allocated to HTC by Honeywell corporate management, and 10 percent funded directly by divisions for near-term projects.

HTC Organization

Exhibit 5 shows the Honeywell corporate organization and Exhibit 6 shows the HTC organization. Prior to 1993, Honeywell operated two corporate R&D organizations: the Sensors and Systems Development Center (SSDC) for home, building, and industrial R&D and the Systems and Research Center for space and aviation R&D. The Systems and Research Center was primarily involved in military research and was oriented to outside contracts. Because there was comparatively less outside contract work in the non-defense-related controls area, SSDC R&D was focused on commercial applications and product division problems. In 1993 the two R&D groups were merged for both cost and synergy reasons. There was also a realization that with government military spending declining, Honeywell-funded R&D had to become more application-oriented.

About 350 HTC technical employees worked in one of the four technology areas whose managers reported to the HTC technology director. These four areas, controls and navigation, sensors, information processing and displays, and systems and software, were in turn broken down into 19 subareas headed by section heads. For example, controls and navigation R&D was divided into home and building control systems, industrial control systems, space and aviation guidance and control systems, and navigation systems. The role of the technology section head was to facilitate interaction between the product divisions and corporate R&D performed by the HTC. As one section head indicated, "I try to be a broker of technology to the product divisions."

R&D development cycles and the maturity of technologies influenced HTC's organization. Because commercial control technologies were more mature than the space and aviation technology, research in this area was more oriented towards how to apply the technology in existing and new products. As a result, the controls and navigation group was organized around markets and product lines. The other three groups were organized around technologies and engineers and scientists in these groups tended to identify with technologies rather than products.

HTC had two additional groups of managers, called Business Development Managers and Divisional Technology Managers (DTMs). The five Business Development Managers were responsible for generating outside contracts. Six DTMs provided an interface between the divisions and HTC, working closely with the technology section heads and the product divisions. The DTMs had two main responsibilities: (1) to understand the divisional business strategy; translate that strategy into short- and long-term technology needs; and disseminate that information in HTC as the basis for influencing investments in R&D and (2) to establish mechanisms for the transfer of mature technology from HTC to divisions. According to a DTM, the DTM's role was "to be a funnel for information transfer and dissemination."

EXHIBIT 5   Honeywell Organization

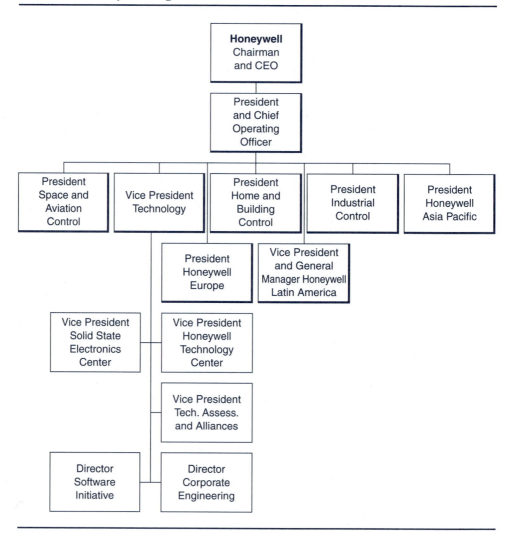

Although HTC had a structure and clear lines of authority, HTC management believed that to operate effectively, the structure had to exist as a loose framework in order to support interaction among the engineers, scientists, and product divisions. According to an HTC manager:

> We are very good at quite a number of areas. I can bring together researchers in sensors, control theory, information processing, real time software and those are the guts of Honeywell products. We need to work from a systems perspective, which means we have to have interaction and networking.

EXHIBIT 6   HTC Organization

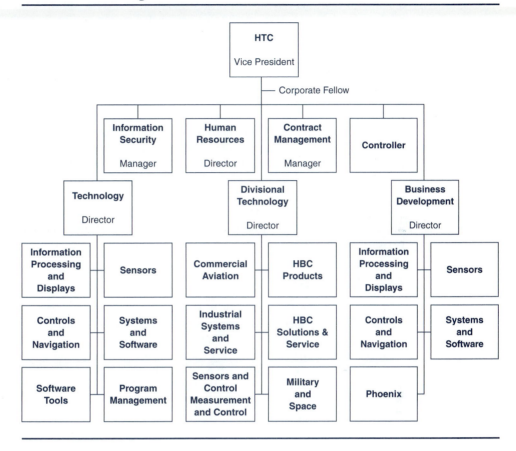

HTC management saw their key role as ensuring that the interaction occurred.

> The researchers are the people that really make things happen here. As managers, our job is to make sure they have lights, food, and water to get things done.

The Research Process

Very little product development or product testing was done at HTC. HTC supported divisional product development by providing new technologies that could be incorporated into products and by developing concepts for new products. The actual development of new products was a divisional responsibility and each of Honeywell's product divisions had active engineering organizations. It was a divisional responsibility to turn new technology into something that was producible and salable. As such, most of the R&D done at the division level was product development and engineering work using existing technologies.

Occasionally, if HTC was convinced a product should be developed immediately to create a market window and no division had the resources to react quickly, HTC might initiate product development. HTC might also approach a customer directly as the basis for generating divisional interest in a technology. As well, technology that would benefit only one division was normally viewed as R&D that should be funded at the division level rather than at corporate.

Within HTC, scientists and engineers competed for funding via various funding programs. The Home Run Program supported projects with low technical risk, an established market need, a large funding requirement, and an expectation of a rapid capital return. The Initiatives Program focused on innovative, technology-based funding with high risks and longer term payoffs. Technology Base Funding supported longer range division needs. Joint Projects provided for matching funds from divisions tied directly to divisional products needs.

There were many and varied linkages between HTC and the product divisions. In some cases, HTC engineers were assigned to divisions to support product development. The assignments could range from several weeks to a year. Nevertheless, it was acknowledged that it was difficult to get people to accept short-term assignments because of family and personal constraints.

Technology Transfer

Within the divisions, the perception of HTC had shifted in recent years as HTC increasingly stressed the importance of relevance and pushed this message deep within the organization. Relevance meant that HTC's goal should be to help the divisions serve their customers, as a manger remarked: "Our job in HTC is to transfer technology but we don't really transfer technology, we transfer solutions." As well, Honeywell was committing greater funds to technology transfer. Ten years ago, technology transfer was more ad hoc with fewer specific funding mechanisms available. This commitment to technology transfer was evident in the following comment from an HTC manager:

> We know that whatever we do is worthless until a division makes money from it. If they don't want the technology, we can't force them to take it.

The underlying philosophy of technology transfer was consistent throughout HTC. First, technology transfer required funding, which occurred through different mechanisms. Second, technology transfer was rarely a function of "how incredible the technology is." The technology had to be mature and its transfer had to be economically feasible in terms of cost effectiveness and ROI. Some successful technology transfers involved technology that had been developed five to ten years earlier. Third, there had to be an emotional commitment to the technology within a product division. The challenge for all technology transfers was to convince the product divisions that the technology was relevant and could provide customer solutions. The highest probability technology transfer occurred when HTC and a division identified a specific divisional need that HTC could meet. An HTC manager described the difficulty in transferring technology:

> Half the battle is how badly the product division managers and engineers want the technology. If they don't want it, they aren't going to get it. Tech transfer is about interaction and begins with trust between two people. . . . Some of the best engineers in Honeywell divisions think they

don't need HTC because they can do it themselves and because they think HTC gets to do all the fun stuff. There is some implication that I [as a division engineer] am not capable of getting my part of the job done so the hired guns from HTC are being brought in to get it done for me. And, I have to pay for it.

The key to establishing a successful match between HTC and the division was the network and personal contact-based system that allowed individual researchers to determine the technological needs of Honeywell. Researchers were expected to generate funding for their projects, which could be either internal or external funding. This forced researchers to be in close contact with the divisions, the customers, other researchers, funding agencies, and so on. By getting an outside research sponsor, researchers could control the support for their research. The same held true for Joint Projects funded by divisions and HTC. For example, researchers might go to a divisional engineer and convince him(her) of the relevance of a project; the engineer might interact with the HTC DTM; and the DTM would work between the division and HTC to ensure that the project was funded. An HTC manager offered this view:

> The real success stories come out of these contact scenarios where a researcher sells an idea either internally or externally. If they sell it externally, it is with the end goal of eventually selling it internally. We don't do research for the good of science. We do research that will lead to customer solutions.

For software, technology transfer often involved transferring individuals to teach the software and adapt it to applications. For home and building controls and its more mature technology, technology transfer often meant the transfer of hardware solutions. For space and avionics applications, the cost of the technology might be less important than the contribution of the technology to safety or reliability. For home and building controls, the cost of the technology was always an issue since there was a belief that customers were very reluctant to spend more money for basic controls such as thermostats, even if the technology was significantly better.

Technology Transfer Example

Technology transfer occurred in many different forms depending on the technology, the product division involved, project funding, and so on. The following discussion illustrates one example of a successful technology transfer. The project began with an idea from a university student intern working at HTC. The project was initially funded under the Initiatives Program, the internal HTC funding mechanism for advanced, long-range thinking. The project involved fuzzy control theory that was not initially directed at a product. As the project progressed, the Home and Building Control Systems Group saw some potential applications for the technology in the boiler control area. Some additional internal funding of around $50,000 was provided to do some modeling and simulation of the concept. Although discussions with the product divisions had not yet occurred, there was a belief that the technology could be useful to one of the European divisions.

The next step was to show some examples of the technology to product divisions. The initiation of the HTC-division interaction could occur in various forms, such as a monthly HTC report on internally developed HTC programs, a DTM presentation to the divisions, or a specific request from a division for a particular technology. The HTC objective in interacting with the divisions was to develop divisional interest for the project. In this example, a division in the Netherlands was interested. This division sold valves and other components for boilers used in homes for heating and hot water. Based on a proposal prepared by HTC engineers, the division agreed to participate in a Joint Project, which meant that the division and HTC would share project funding equally. By getting the division involved, product and market specifications could be developed. At this point, the personnel involved in the project included the Home and Building Control Systems Group section head, HTC engineers, a division development engineer, and a DTM. At the division level, the engineer would work with sales and marketing people to justify the funding.

The next phase was called build-and-test and could have been done at HTC or in the division. This decision was negotiated based on various constraints: scheduling, funding, personnel, and R&D skills. In this example, the build-and-test phase was carried out in the division. Initial results were promising and it was hoped that the product could be marketed to boiler OEMs by the end of 1997. If so, the entire phase from idea to market would be about five years. From the time that the division became aware of the technology and saw it as a potential product application was about two years.

HTC's Relationship with Honeywell Europe

Technology transfer to the Honeywell Europe divisions had always been problematic. While the European divisions expected HTC to develop new technology, European managers often complained about the irrelevance of the technology for their markets, the cost of HTC, and their lack of contact with HTC. Although 25 percent of Honeywell sales were in Europe, a much smaller percentage of R&D was carried out either in Europe or in Minneapolis for European solutions. Until about 1990, there was very little Honeywell R&D being done for Europe even though Europe was supporting central R&D financially, creating some bitterness in the European operation. Central R&D was primarily focused on the U.S. market. New product development in Europe was originating in the European divisional engineering groups.

An HTC manager recounted his experience in making a presentation to a group of Honeywell mangers in Brussels. After making the presentation and outlining current technology initiatives in HTC, the Europeans indicated that they were unaware that HTC was working on such leading technologies. The manager continued:

> When I first went to Europe a few years ago it was clear to me how angry they were at the U.S. notion that HTC was going to provide good stuff. They also believed that most of the Honeywell resources were being harbored in the United States. There was not a feeling that they were equal members in getting the same resources for development as the U.S. divisions. That said, in the past few years there have been some very good technology transfer projects, and they were done in the same way as in the United States—personal interaction, people spending time in the divisions, some short-term relocations to Europe. Increasingly, there is acceptance that the paradigm of R&D jointly sponsored by HTC and the divisions is the best approach.

Over the past few years, relationships with Europe had begun shifting and HTC was becoming more responsive in addressing the needs of European businesses. The current

Honeywell COO was an Italian who was previously head of Honeywell Europe and the CEO had also been the head of Europe. The head of Divisional Technology responsible for the DTMs was also spending a great deal of time in Europe. As well, there was now an HTC organization based in Europe, HTC Prague.

HTC Prague

In the early 1990s SSDC (the R&D organization that preceded HTC) managers were considering how to strengthen European R&D. With the collapse of the Iron Curtain and expectations of new Honeywell markets developing in Eastern Europe, the viability of an R&D organization somewhere in Eastern Europe was being debated. There was a belief that very strong technical skills could be found in countries like Poland and Russia. In 1992 an HTC scientist and former university professor in Czechoslovakia was attending a conference in Tampa. He met a Czechoslovakian from a research institute in Prague. With the Czech economy in transition and research funding drying up, the Czech scientist was interested in new opportunities. The HTC scientist returned to Minneapolis with reasonable assurance that a partnership with the Czech scientist could work. HTC Prague began with five former Czech university professors hired on a contract basis to do research in two areas: computational fluid dynamics, a technology area important for evaluating control product designs, and advanced boiler control technology. Honeywell's Eastern Europe office was moved from Vienna to Prague, and by 1997, the Honeywell sales organization in Prague had grown to more than 60 employees. Prague was viewed as an excellent entry point for what could be a huge business in controls for district heating.

In 1995 the Prague professors became Honeywell employees. The professors were very entrepreneurial and had established a reputation for getting things done. Compared to their counterparts in the universities, they were pleased to have access to funding and equipment to continue their research. In 1997, one of the Prague researchers came to Minneapolis for nine months to work on a district heating project. All of the HTC senior management team had been to Prague.

Several objectives were established for HTC Prague: (1) to develop specific technologies for Europe; (2) to assist in HTC technology transfers to Europe; (3) to provide access to activities and opportunities in Eastern Europe; and (4) to help alleviate Honeywell Europe concerns about the lack of support from HTC. Projects in HTC Prague were to be coordinated through HTC to ensure that Prague became an integral part of HTC and not a separate entity.

In 1997, HTC management conceded that it was too early to make an evaluation of HTC Prague's viability and future within Honeywell. For one thing, HTC Prague consisted of only five researchers, which limited the potential impact. As a manger indicated, "With only five people, it is not clear what Prague really is or can be." There were concerns that HTC Prague might become an application center rather than a true R&D center. One manager suggested that the Europeans were too accustomed to looking to the United States for new technology and, therefore, HTC Prague would have trouble building legitimacy. Still, other European divisions had questioned the decision to start an R&D organization in Prague rather than in, say, Germany or Belgium. Other European managers offered a different perspective, suggesting that European divisions were already taking ownership of the technology being developed in Prague and viewed Prague as "their" technology center.

Several HTC managers were emphatic that Prague had to be expanded if it was to remain relevant. But if Prague were to be expanded, when should it happen and could additional high quality technical talent be found for Prague? The model for HTC in the United States was to rely heavily on outside contracts. Would Prague be able to develop outside funding? Should Prague be given the tools and skills necessary to bid on outside contracts? If Prague were to be expanded, who would pay for the expansion: Honeywell Europe or HTC? Other managers suggested that perhaps Prague should remain at 5–6 people and additional R&D centers should be established close to other Honeywell operations, perhaps in Germany, Scotland, or the Netherlands.

Reasons for Centralized R&D

Within Honeywell, reasons for and against centralized R&D were being actively debated. Reasons supporting centralized R&D included the following:

1. The complexity of Honeywell products and systems is such that a large team of R&D people is needed in one location to ensure interaction occurs between scientists. For example, the control system for a refinery incorporated hundreds of other products. It is easy to share information when almost all HTC employees are in the same building and see each other regularly. Decentralization would reduce interaction and personal contacts.

   Technology transfer is based on personal contacts. This is one of the biggest challenges we have in trying to operate on a global basis. We have a system in HTC that works quite well and we are comfortable with it. What does it mean to deal with things around the world when we need to maintain our contact-based system?

   The strength of HTC is the world-class people we can bring to bear on a problem. How do we connect these people with the far-flung empire of Honeywell in order to bring together the expertise, know-how, and ability to make money?

   The biggest logistical issue is communications. You can't invent science with only one scientist. You need multiple disciplines and interaction. The various distributed R&D organizations must communicate with each other the same way they would if they were all in Minneapolis and could meet in the hallways or the cafeteria. That is extremely difficult to do. We are looking at new information technology but you also have to have interchanges of people. Without communication, remote R&D will only work for a little while because people will get out of touch. Once people go native they lose the advantage of outside views and new ideas coupled with the connection with the marketplace.

2. One of the main functions of Honeywell's central R&D is to move ideas around the world. Decentralizing R&D would jeopardize this central dissemination function.

3. When the product is a system comprising various parts, a team can be built using people from different areas. Scattering people geographically would make this difficult.

   A product like abnormal situation management for oil refineries requires sensors, controls, human interface, and so on. We have all the people in one place to put these technologies together. No division of the company has all these parts.

4. If R&D scientists are too far from the central labs, they risk becoming obsolete, migrating from R&D to the product divisions, or losing contact with central R&D. They may even think they are competing with central R&D.

   We have a group in Plymouth, which is only 15 miles from the Minneapolis location. When I talk to those guys, they feel like they are cut off from all kinds of things. To a degree, they are correct. We have a group in Phoenix that sometimes feels like they are in yonder land.

5. If R&D is tied too closely with a division, there is the risk that the division will not have the long-term orientation necessary for R&D, which could lead to complacency. Or, after assuming ownership of the R&D, the division may decide that a particular technology is no longer necessary and R&D efforts could decline. A central R&D organization can ensure stability in research efforts and implement controls to keep people motivated.

6. Engineers and scientists interested in R&D prefer to work in a central R&D organization.

7. What the non-U.S. and non-European divisions need now is localization of existing products, not new technology.

8. The HTC culture would be difficult to transfer.

   How do you transfer the HTC culture outside the United States? HTC has developed a unique culture based on openness and interaction across different levels and technologies. The kinds of people we hire and attract are very entrepreneurial down to the youngest engineers. How do you duplicate this culture in a place like like Prague? It is tough enough to do it in Phoenix.

9. Before R&D could be localized, Honeywell had to develop more incentives to transfer technology.

   Although a few years ago I was committed to the idea of global technology management, I am not so sure now. The problem is that within Honeywell there are still expectations that solutions will come from the United States. Until that changes and funding is in place to support technology transfer outside the United States, creating new R&D organizations makes no sense. Right now, we do not have the financial incentives in place to transfer technology to Europe.

Reasons for Decentralized R&D

1. Central R&D is too far removed from the customer, particularly customers outside the United States. It is impossible to develop customer solutions if you do not understand customer problems. The current remote sites in Phoenix and Prague benefit from being close to the divisions. Different parts of the world should logically be the focus for problems unique to their area. For example, tropical Asia has unique air conditioning requirements because of the heat and humidity.

   You need people immersed in all aspects of the culture to communicate with customers and other parts of Honeywell. There is a whole lot of networking that has to happen and it has to involve people from the HTC culture who know what is going on. People of this culture have to see with their own eyes what is going on outside the United States. We are not going to sell U.S. thermostats in Beijing. What they need and want is different, the amount of money the Chinese have to spend is different.

You have to live with the culture to understand the opportunities. You cannot simply transfer technologies and product designs that are used in the United States. There have to be different solutions because the business models in different countries are different. Right now, the paradigm says that products come from the United States. There is a strong mix of prejudice and ignorance about international markets. For example, in the United States, air conditioning is the focus for home and building controls. In Europe, central air conditioning is much less common. We have a huge opportunity in district heating in Eastern Europe. In the United States, Honeywell has limited knowledge about district heating because it is hardly used here.

2. If the technology does not require interaction with other technologies, like the development of a particular sensor or flat panel displays, it may be better to have it located where the local support structure is strongest. The support could come from the product division or in a geographic area known for a particular technology.

3. Application developments may require close interaction with a customer in the customer's facility.

4. Putting R&D people in geographic business units would increase the relevance of R&D and increase the information flow from business units to R&D.

5. Future sales will be growing faster outside the United States and, therefore, people from all parts of Honeywell must be in the growing areas of the business.

6. Traveling to Europe, China, and other locations outside the United States is expensive and time consuming. It would be better to have people on the ground in these locations.

7. Remote R&D facilities would facilitate technology transfers outside the United States.

8. Remote locations in countries like China provide a foothold that gives Honeywell credibility and makes it look like a committed Chinese business. It could also help in hiring local engineers and scientists.

9. Remote locations show the product divisions that Honeywell is serious about a particular region.

Along with the basic question of centralized versus decentralized R&D, there were additional issues associated with R&D:

- Would remote locations have to focus on unique technologies? How would those technologies be identified? Are there technologies that are unique to specific locations?

- Outside funding was critical to HTC. As part of a U.S. corporation, could a remote location gain access to outside funding? With greater R&D presence, could HTC gain access to funding from agencies such as the World Bank and the Asian Development Bank?

- What kind of controls must be in place to ensure that a remote location remained part of *central* R&D rather than becoming an offshoot of a product division?

- In Europe and Asia, with its diversity of countries and markets, where should HTC have a stronger presence?
- With an increasing shift to software as the key to product differentiation, how would this influence future Honeywell R&D?
- Within Honeywell, the allocation of HTC costs was based on divisional revenues. Was this allocation system appropriate given that some regions within the firm were growing faster than others?
- How would remote R&D locations be staffed? Would it make sense to move HTC people out of Minneapolis to new locations? If not, were skilled scientists available in other parts of the world? As an HTC manager commented:

> The key thing about our culture is networking and sharing and bringing together different technologies. The only way you can create that culture in a remote R&D center is to take some of the HTC people and put them in China or Russia for a while. This would infect the new hires with "the way we do business." Then we will bring them back. We have had good luck getting people to go to different places.

Future Opportunities

In view of Honeywell's international growth opportunities, the issue of international R&D was becoming a high priority issue in HTC. For example, China's economy was growing so rapidly that some sort of HTC presence seemed inevitable. One line of thinking was that HTC should have employees based in China with a broad learning and exploration agenda. Another view was that until there was a clear understanding of the opportunities in China, it would not make sense to commit to expensive expatriate employees. A further issue was that in China, and Asia in general, there were no engineering staffs to adapt technologies for the local market. For the most part, products manufactured and sold in Asia were products transferred from America or European Honeywell divisions. Without an engineering staff in Asia, technology could not be transferred.

Further issues are evident in the following comments from HTC managers:

> By the year 2000, sales outside the United States could be 60 percent of our business. At HTC we have to start experimenting in other parts of the world. Our mission is to help the divisions understand what they can do with our technology. If you ask them what they want, you will get the most ordinary ideas. If we work with their customers and understand that environment, we can link customers with our technology and come up with something completely different. If we are not out here looking at the world we will never grow the company. And, I can't hire someone in China to do this for me; someone from here has to go over there and get the HTC culture going.

> Technology is technology; it is physical principles and science—there is nothing unique about the technology needed in Europe or Asia. However, the application needs seem to vary from region to region. Perhaps we should set up application groups around the world. The technology engine will remain in Minneapolis and Phoenix. These groups will be the selectors and appliers of those technologies given their knowledge of the region. If we go this way, we won't need the best researchers in Prague and other regions. We will need people who can apply technology and gain access to technology sources outside the United States. We have really not tapped into these non-U.S. sources.

The notion of distributed R&D is very important to me. I am convinced that HTC is going to become more distributed, not less. How can we create one large, global R&D organization and not 12 small ones is a big issue. Strategically, putting together other R&D centers in Beijing or Eastern Europe is going to become a way of life at HTC.

It is difficult enough making HTC work. Trying to replicate it somewhere else in the world is even more difficult. This is one of the reasons that Prague has remained small—we are not sure what to do with it. My view of what Prague should be will probably be radically different from other people's. In the United States, 20 years of evolution has allowed HTC to develop some unique capabilities. Can we wait for Prague or some other remote R&D center to naturally evolve over 20 years? What is the best way for a non-U.S. R&D organization to have an impact?

34 HILTI CORPORATION (A)

In the summer of 1993, the new executive board of Hilti Corporation, led by Dr. Pius Baschera, was meeting to discuss the less than satisfactory operations of the Hilti company in Hong Kong. Dr. Baschera and the other three members of the board would not officially take up their new positions until January 1994, but to ensure a smooth transition, the group began functioning in mid-1993. Whatever decision they came to about Hong Kong would have to be agreed to by Michael Hilti, the current CEO, and other members of the outgoing executive board.

The way forward in Hong Kong was not clear. The country manager was proposing a course of action that was a marked deviation from Hilti's well proven worldwide strategy of selling construction tools and fasteners directly to end users. Yet something had to be done. In a market that was growing at least 10 percent per year, it appeared that Hilti Hong Kong would have 1993 sales and profits 5–10 percent lower than 1992.

Hilti Corporation

The Hilti company was founded in 1941 by Martin and Eugen Hilti in the Principality of Liechtenstein, which is nestled between Austria and the eastern border of Switzerland. The Hilti brothers laid the foundations for the company when they obtained an order to manufacture threaded studs and nails for a pistol-like tool that was intended for fastening work in construction. Although not fully developed, this tool was recognized by the Hiltis as having great potential for the rebuilding of Europe. Patents were obtained, and a product line centred on high velocity tools was created. (Refer to Exhibit 1 for a selection of products from Hilti's line of drills, anchoring systems and direct fastening systems.)

IMD — This case was prepared by Professor Peter Killing as a basis for class discussion rather than to illustrate either effective or ineffective handling of a business situation. Copyright © 1997 by **IMD** – International Institute for Management Development, Lausanne, Switzerland. All rights reserved. Not to be used or reproduced without written permission directly from **IMD**, Lausanne, Switzerland.

EXHIBIT 1   The Hilti Product Line

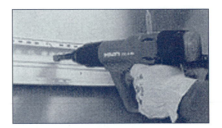

Sources: Top left, 1994 Hilti Corporation Annual Report; others, 1996 Hilti Corporation Catalogue, "Kompakt-Katalog Producte und Anwendungen."

By 1960, Hilti had a major production facility in Liechtenstein and was well established in European markets. Martin Hilti's belief that "market share is more important than factories" had led to a great emphasis on understanding and responding to customer needs. Recognizing that customers would value knowledgeable advice on how to best use Hilti tools, the company had established a direct sales force, rather than using distributors or dealers.

The 1960s and 1970s were years of strong growth for Hilti, as construction in the company's major markets of Europe and the United States was booming. Key to Hilti's success were the strong-willed entrepreneurs running each country operation who pushed their sales forces for ever better results. As sales and profits grew, production facilities were added throughout Europe, and a plant was built in the U.S.A.

In the early 1980s, however, Hilti was hard hit by a worldwide recession in the construction industry. Sales and profits slumped, and the managers in major markets like Germany, France, and the U.S. informed the head office that little could be done in this adverse economic environment. Market shares were already high, so growth was not an option: they would just have to ride out the storm and wait for better times. One younger manager commented:

> When the markets turned down, we began to realize that these Hilti "country kings" were not very complete managers. They successfully grew sales volumes in boom times, but they had failed to develop their organizations and their people.
>
> I have to give credit to Schaan [Hilti's head office], as they recognized the problem, and in the next few years replaced most of the country kings. They promoted or brought in from the outside younger managers, better educated, with broader skills.
>
> Of course simply changing the senior managers was not enough, as there were many others in the country organizations also used to doing things their own way. So we brought in McKinsey to perform an overhead value analysis, which resulted in changes in our processes and structures that gave us more flexibility. And we were not happy with central research and development—it seemed to be an empire unto itself—so we also brought in BCG (Boston Consulting Group), and created four divisions at head office that were responsible for developing, manufacturing, and sourcing products that were then sold to the country units for resale to final customers.
>
> These changes went some way to curbing the power of the countries, and improving the innovation process in the company.

Strategy 2000—The Beginning

In 1984, for the first time, a week-long meeting was held to bring together all senior Hilti managers from around the world. As the 30 or so country managers made presentations on their business, it became clear that, in the words of one of the attendees, "we had no vision, no strategy, no coherence. We were simply a collection of countries each doing its own thing, and the results were not nearly as good as they could have been."

A decision was made to begin a major strategy review, again with the help of BCG. The work began in the United States, where Hilti's performance had been suffering. The challenge was both to increase profitability and return to higher rates of growth. A close examination of Hilti customers and their needs made it clear that Hilti's policy of selling direct to end customers should be maintained. It was also decided that telephone-based customer service should be instituted. Thus, a customer could contact Hilti by phone, or by direct contact with the salesman.

Hilti USA was divided into three business units, each to serve a particular customer segment for the whole country. This was a sharp change from the previous area-based organization in which a salesman sold all Hilti products to all customers in his geographic region. A senior manager commented:

> A change like this is dramatic, because it means that many of our customers are now dealing with a new salesman, and they have to get to know each other. Remember that we are not just selling products; we are also giving advice and training—and it is those things and our product quality that allow us to price our products 20–30 percent above competitors like Bosch or Makita. So the salesman has to learn his product line in depth, and a market segmented approach encourages that. Once the salesman understands the applications of his product line in the trades he serves very well, he will begin to demand modifications and new products from our product development people.

With the U.S. model in place by the late 1980s, attention turned to Europe. Pius Baschera, head of Hilti's operations in Germany at the time, recalled the situation:

> Germany was (and still is) Hilti's largest operation, and we were performing well. The country was divided into five geographic regions, and within each region the sales force was segmented by trade group—plumbers, electricians, and so on. So we could see the U.S. rationale for dividing the sales force—although we thought they had the trades segmented incorrectly—but we could not see the rationale for creating whole business units for each trade. Our plan was to keep the sales force specialised by trade, but at the management levels above the sales force, we did not see the need for specialization.
>
> There was a lot of pressure on the German management team to make a quick transition to the U.S. model, however. The president of Hilti Western Hemisphere was given the responsibility for the total core business worldwide, and as a member of the executive board, he worked with the new head of Germany (Baschera's successor) to push changes through. There was a lot of resistance: almost no one, for example, thought that the quick move to set up a central customer service function and closing all the regional sales offices was a good idea. Several key managers left the German company.

The Evolution of Strategy 2000

As the roll out of Strategy 2000 continued in Europe, adjustments were made in a number of areas. Agreement was reached on the best way to segment the sales force, for example, which meant that the U.S. adopted the trade segments used in Europe. The German drive for maintaining regional centres was not supported, however.

In the early 1990s, a diagram was created that captured the heart of the Hilti 2000 strategy on a single page. This chart, shown in Exhibit 2, became known in the company as the "mother of all charts" and was widely displayed in company facilities all over the world. The

EXHIBIT 2   Global Strategy

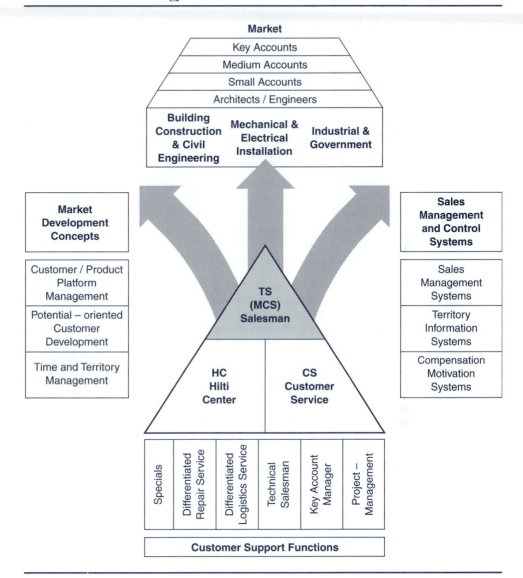

Source: Hilti Corporation Company Document.

creation of a common, simply communicated strategy was seen by employees at all levels as extremely valuable, and the items on the chart became a part of everyday communication.

As European countries gradually moved to implement Strategy 2000, the resistance in Germany continued. In the early 1990s, with East Germany opening up, Germany was growing at 20 percent per year. Instituting a program of major change did not make sense to many people in the German operation. But by 1991, it was clear that the change would happen; by early 1993, it was largely complete.

A Challenge for New Management

In mid-1993, significant changes were taking place at the most senior levels of Hilti. Michael Hilti, the son of Martin, was to become Chairman of the Board; and Pius Baschera, aged 44, would be the first nonfamily member to take over the CEO role. At the same time, the other two members of the executive board would also change, as Hilti's mandatory age limit of 55 necessitated their retirement.

The Hong Kong situation was the first major issue addressed by the new management team. Pius Baschera commented:

> In 1991, dealer sales accounted for one third of our total sales in Hong Kong. But in 1992, this figure fell to 19 percent, and is heading for zero in 1993 as Strategy 2000 is fully implemented. To compensate, we have increased our direct sales force, but sales are not increasing yet. Without dealers, we find it difficult to access the small customers—and they are growing in number. We estimate that there were about 6,000 construction companies in Hong Kong in 1983, with an average of about 16 employees. Today, there are closer to 13,000 with an average of fewer than 10 employees. So there are more and more small guys in this business, and at the moment, they account for at least 15–20 percent of the Hong Kong market. In the West, small operators play a less important role.
>
> What the Hong Kong general manager is proposing is that we use a controlled number of "local sales elements" (the name he gave to dealers) to carry a limited number of our product lines most suitable for small customers. In this way, he argues, we can regain our lost ground, and participate fully in the growth of the market.
>
> Taking a broader perspective, we must remember that while approximately 60 percent of our two billion Swiss francs of annual revenue comes from Europe, and only about 12 percent from Asia, our greatest growth prospects are in Asia and Eastern Europe. And we are not currently meeting our targets of double digit growth in sales and profits—so we need to get our approach to Asian markets just right.

Another member of the executive board added the following:

> We must bear in mind that there are good reasons for our direct sales approach. First, we are not just selling products. We add value by giving advice and training. Our customers trust us. We can only create such relationships by selling direct. Second, by working with customers, we get valuable ideas for new products and applications. Third, if we have two competing channels, we hurt our salesforce. And remember, of the 12,000 people in this company, 4,000 are salesmen! These people live on their commissions, and being an exclusive channel for Hilti products is very much part of their livelihood. We do not want to set up a conflict in the company.

The *other* risk of using dealers is that we lose control of pricing. We have international customers who can quite effectively take advantage of any global anomalies in our pricing policies. And of course, we lose some of our profit margin by selling to dealers.

And if we do this in Hong Kong, it will only be the beginning. I can name at least three other countries that are just implementing Strategy 2000 who will argue that they too should be allowed to use "local sales elements."

A third board member commented:

We will never survive if we just copy what other people are doing. Bosch uses dealers and is very good at it. They have drill bits packaged nicely to be displayed in dealer premises. They have point of purchase material, incentive programs for dealers, and so on. We have none of this. It is not our way of doing business. We need to stick with our unique Hilti strengths and approach to doing business wherever we can.

Secondly, I must stress that while the roll out of Strategy 2000 in Asia is extremely important, we *also* need to extend out Hilti culture to the Asian region. As our small country operations in Asia grow, we need to ensure that we manage our people there the same way as we do elsewhere. We must emphasize worldwide training programs, for example, which will stress the Hilti values of self responsibility, freedom to take risks, openness, commitment and freedom of choice.

As he sat at the board table with his new team, Pius Baschera reflected on the views of Michael Hilti and his executive team, the people to whom he had to make his new management group's recommendation.

Michael and his executive team have been working very hard to put Strategy 2000 in place. It has not always been easy, as the struggle in Germany shows, but they have been firm and persistent. If we come in as the new management team and as our first act encourage Hong Kong to walk away from Strategy 2000, I do not know how it will be received.

35 BRISTOL COMPRESSORS, ASIA-PACIFIC

On Monday, August 4, 1997, Trevor Woods, President of Bristol Compressors, Asia-Pacific, chaired a meeting of his top management team to discuss the company's on-going management challenges in the region. The Hong Kong-based team, known as the Management Committee (MC), included Woods, aged 46, and seven other senior functional managers. Despite attractive markets in the region, Bristol Compressors' growth in Asia-Pacific had not met expectations. A broad consensus had emerged among MC members that lack of management depth was a major factor contributing to the company's weak performance. Although everyone present was convinced that something had to be done, a specific plan had not yet been developed. Woods' charge to MC members was to come up with a set of recommendations to increase significantly management bench strength in the region.

Company Background

Bristol Compressors was founded in 1913 by Peter Watson, who invested £4,000 to set up a machine shop on the eastern outskirts of Bristol, England. Watson, who was just 26 years old at the time, was heavily involved in purchasing equipment for a new steel fabrication plant and had been shocked at the prices of air compressors. After some research, he became convinced that existing suppliers were inefficient and that the industry had huge growth prospects. With borrowed money, Peter set out on his own and Bristol Compressors was born.

The company initially manufactured air-compressing machines that were used as a blast for iron forges. In 1923, Bristol Compressors began what would become a tradition of aggressive product and international expansion by acquiring a Swiss company that specialized in the production of hammer tools used in tunnelling. By 1996, Bristol Compressors had sales revenues of £2.1 billion, and operating profits of £94 million. The company had 17 manufacturing plants in nine countries, sales and service offices in 42 countries, and over 22,000 employees worldwide. In two-thirds of its product lines, Bristol Compressors was either number one or number two in worldwide market share, making it the largest compressor manufacturing company in the world.

Bristol Compressors was organized into four product divisions. These included: (1) AirCom, which manufactured portable and stationary air compressors used in powering pneumatic tools such as wrenches and drills; (2) CleanCom, which made oil-free compressors that eliminated hazardous contaminants in the gas stream. Oil-free compressors were most commonly used in food production, scientific laboratories, hospitals, and the military, as well as in filling Scuba and fire-fighting tanks; (3) FrigCom, which made condensing equipment used in large air conditioning units for apartment, commercial, and industrial buildings. The division also made evaporative coil units and condensers for commercial refrigerators and freezers; and (4) DrillCom, which developed, manufactured and marketed a range of pneumatic tools including jackhammers and mechanical boring machines used in rock drilling, tunnelling, quarrying, and well-drilling.

A division president who had full, worldwide profit and loss responsibility ran each of these four divisions. Although divisional headquarters were located in the same corporate offices in Bristol, each division operated with a relatively high level of autonomy. Product development, manufacturing, sales, and marketing activities were all run independently. In 1989, purchasing activities and core research were centralized.

Until the late 1980s, the company's efforts to expand outside Europe centered almost exclusively on North America. In 1989, 84 percent of Bristol Compressors' sales came from Europe and North America. Under the direction of Stewart Egan, Bristol Compressors' Chairman and Managing Director since 1987, the company began seriously exploring market opportunities in Asia-Pacific. It was believed that the easiest way to enter new Asian markets was through the sale of portable and stationary compressors. In 1992, the Asia-Pacific region was formally organized in Hong Kong and given responsibility for the company's operations in India, Pakistan, Bangladesh, China, Taiwan, Japan, Korea, the Philippines, Vietnam, Indonesia, Malaysia, Thailand, and Singapore. The president of Asia-Pacific reported to Clive Brooks, 49, who was the president of AirCom. The thinking was that AirCom would take the lead in setting up manufacturing plants and representative offices throughout the region. Initially, the representative offices would also help sell and manage the importation of CleanCom, FrigCom, and DrillCom products. In due time, it was anticipated that each of these divisions would establish its own facilities in the region.

Initial Expansion Efforts

In 1994, Bristol Compressors spent £11 million on a 50/50 joint venture factory in Indonesia with the Modir Group. In 1995, approximately £7 million was spent to renovate Asia-Pacific's existing headquarters and upgrade the company's Hong Kong warehouse facilities. In addition, in 1995, another £9 million was spent setting up a new compressor plant in Hong Kong.

In October 1995, Trevor Woods was appointed President of Bristol Compressors, Asia-Pacific. Before his appointment, Woods had served as Vice President Marketing and Sales for AirCom Europe (1992 to 1995), and senior marketing executive for AirCom Canada (1988 to 1990). Overall, he had spent 19 years with the company.

In AirCom Europe, Woods worked closely with Clive Brooks (and would continue to do so in Hong Kong). Woods' promotion to President, Asia-Pacific was in part a recognition of his work launching the LiteCom line of highly portable compressors for use on construction sites. The compressors were used to power a wide range of pneumatic tools and were noteworthy for their lightweight, quiet operation and highly efficient gasoline-powered engines. To promote LiteCom compressors, AirCom organized a small army of field representatives that visited construction sites and offered convenient product demonstrations. In 1994, LiteCom was AirCom's number-one selling product line in Europe with sales of £72 million.

Asia-Pacific Infrastructure Is Established

Woods continued with the on-going expansion efforts in Asia-Pacific. In 1996, £4 million was invested in a 50/50 joint venture with Zhou Ling Industries in Shekou, China (near Hong Kong). An additional £20 million was authorized for a second joint venture compressor plant in Shanghai, China. The output from these manufacturing plants (as well as the earlier investments in India and Hong Kong) was largely intended to meet anticipated demand from Asia-Pacific countries. A modest amount of exports to Europe and North America was also planned.

To build revenues, representative offices were also opened up throughout the region. From 1995 to 1997, offices were opened in Malaysia, Thailand, Taiwan, Korea, South Africa, and Hong Kong/China. Each office had between 25 and 50 employees who focused on marketing, sales, and service.

Slow Beginnings

Despite promising market research and substantial new plant capacity, Bristol Compressors' sales growth in the Asia-Pacific was slower than expected. By the summer of 1997, the company's manufacturing plants throughout Asia were operating at less than 30 percent capacity. Opinions varied as to why sales had not met expectations. With four years of service in Asia (and 17 years of experience with the company), Bombay-based Charles Withers, General Manager of Bristol Compressors India, had been in the Asia-Pacific region longer than any other expatriate manager in the company. He provided some important background on the investment decisions.

> We wanted to invest in Asia for global strategic purposes. We all knew doing business here would be hard. But if we had let our competitors continue to grow as they had in Asia, Bristol Compressors would have lost its number one position in worldwide compressor sales by 2005. We also thought that strength in Asia would help in the development of lower cost products for Europe and North America.
>
> Despite the strategic logic, you cannot get capital in this company without showing a three-to-four-year payback. So that is what the budget numbers reflected. You cannot fault Woods for this. Most of the investment decisions were made before he arrived in January 1996.

Numerous formal and informal discussions were held within the MC over the cause of weak sales. Most discussions centered on three factors: (1) weaker markets than anticipated in the region, (2) unexpectedly fierce competition, and (3) ineffective strategy and execution.

Weak Markets

While sales of stationary compressors to factories had largely met projections, sales of portable compressors had been very weak in the region. By 1997, marketing managers had become leery of the earlier research that showed booming markets for portable compressors in Asia. In China, for example, it was believed that huge sales would be generated by the enormous construction projects underway in boom cities like Shanghai, Beijing, and Guangzhou. For example, in 1996 it was estimated that there were more construction cranes operating in Shanghai than in the entire U.S. How could there not be a gigantic market for portable compressors? However, further investigation revealed that many of the buildings were empty, unfinished shells. Unfortunately, compressors were more often used in interior finishing work than in heavy construction. Even when interior work was being done, compressors were rarely used in countries like China where labor was cheap compared to capital or where full employment was more important than labor productivity.

Fierce Competition

Others felt Bristol Compressors' disappointing performance was the result of fierce competition. Most company veterans underestimated the competitive response in Asia. Philip Dewer, Vice President of Marketing for Asia-Pacific and a member of the MC, put it this way:

> Competition in Asia has been brutal. We have been successful taking share from our competitors in Europe and North America and they are bound and determined not to let it happen again in Asia. Asia has become a fierce battleground in the global compressor industry.

Bristol Compressors' key competitors in the region included two Japanese companies, a Korean company, a German company, and two U.S. companies. Each was either a stand-alone multi-billion dollar company or a division of an even larger multinational corporation. In most Asian countries, local companies held between 25 percent and 35 percent of the market. Local manufacturers were generally viewed as relatively unsophisticated and vulnerable to the aggressive moves of multinational competitors.

The competition was unrelenting. For example, in 1996, one major competitor unilaterally cut its prices in Japan on stationary compressors by 20 percent. Bristol Compressors followed with a similar price cut. The competitor then cut prices by another 15 percent and signaled more cuts if Bristol Compressors followed. In addition to dramatic price cuts, competitors used a range of blocking strategies that, while perfectly legal in Asia, would be against the law in many of Bristol Compressors' traditional markets. For example, one competitor was notorious for shutting off supplies or cutting advertising incentives to distributors that added Bristol Compressors' products. This created substantial barriers to entry in distribution.

Strategy and Execution Missteps

Initially, Bristol Compressors sought to end-run the competition by downplaying distribution channels in favor of the pull strategy it perfected in Europe. When Woods first arrived in Hong Kong, he pushed the national sales and marketing offices to focus on the LiteCom brand of portable compressors and build sales by sending teams to construction sites and auto repair shops. Initially, the strategy seemed immensely successful. Local workers loved the site visits and seemed eager to try the pneumatic equipment and receive free tee shirts and key chains emblazoned with the LiteCom logo.

Surprisingly, though, few sales materialized. After months of tinkering with the concept, the national marketing and sales staffs began to realize that the way portable compressors were purchased in some parts of Asia was fundamentally different from Europe. In Europe, professional users typically either owned their own business or knew the owner. As a result, they either bought LiteCom products themselves or were influential in buying decisions. In contrast, in many parts of Asia, professional users had limited influence on buying decisions. In Singapore, for example, the vast majority of construction workers came from countries like India, Pakistan, and the Philippines. These people had no direct input in buying decisions. In other parts of Asia, construction workers or auto repair technicians were employed by large corporations or government-owned enterprises with independent buying offices. As a result, in many cases, worker interest in the "events" might have been driven more by curiosity and handouts than by an interest in actually purchasing compressors.

To complicate matters, the actual buyers were often large distributors. In China, for example, Bristol Compressors worked with approximately 20 distributors who handled the importation and distribution of portable and stationary compressors in different local markets. Not only were these distributors far removed from end users, but also compressors represented a fraction of each distributor's product line. As a result, it was often difficult to gain their full attention.

As their understanding of the buying criteria increased, Bristol Compressors' managers began to shift their emphasis towards developing deep relationships with major buyers. The "pull" strategy that was so effective in moving the LiteCom line in Europe was gradually de-emphasized in several major Asian markets. With this change in strategy came the need for sales people with different skills than had been anticipated. Winston Baxter, Sales Manager for China and Hong Kong, explained:

In Asia, we need sales people who are skilled at finding the decision-makers. The decision-makers are not typically hanging around construction sites and auto repair shops. Once they find them, our people need to be excellent at building relationships with senior business people. These are different skills than we are promoting in our European sales people.

Although Bristol Compressors' strategy was still being sorted out, sales throughout Asia-Pacific had risen steadily over the past two years. In many Asian countries, Bristol Compressors was the only compressor manufacturer that was increasing its market share. In China, Bristol Compressors climbed to number four in market share for both portable and stationary compressors. However, despite encouraging growth, it still had a long way to go to match the market share it enjoyed in Europe and North America.

Increasing Management Bench Strength

In order to accelerate sales and better manage existing business, members of the MC were convinced that Bristol Compressors, Asia-Pacific had to significantly increase both the number and quality of managers in the region. Better management would help Bristol Compressors find new markets, compete more effectively, and avoid strategy missteps.

The challenge was to determine the best approach to increasing management bench strength. Three options had begun to emerge: developing managers from within, hiring skilled local managers, and significantly increasing the number of expatriate managers in the Asia-Pacific. Each option had supporters and detractors.

Developing Managers from Within

Developing managers from within primarily meant working closely with employees to mold and shape their skills and abilities so that, over time, they would be competent in managing critical activities. In Europe as well as North America, Bristol Compressors hired most of its future leaders out of graduate schools. It then spent 10 or more years developing them through a combination of in-house training, teamwork, travel, and new assignments. Exposure to these different developmental activities tested and developed managers and virtually guaranteed the company a steady stream of loyal and competent managers.

A similar approach to management development was thought by some to be essential if Bristol Compressors was ever to develop a strong market position in Asia-Pacific. The advantage of this approach was that it was built on the natural strengths of host country nationals. These were the people who knew the markets, spoke the language, and had the local connections. Over time, they could develop a deep understanding of Bristol Compressors' products, values, culture, and policies. They could also establish long-term relationships with other managers throughout Bristol Compressors' regional and global organization. Such relationships were essential in establishing and maintaining quality, two-way communications and in effectively formulating and implementing country and regional strategies.

Margaret Reeve, Director of Marketing for China and Hong Kong, believed Bristol Compressors had an excellent track record in developing people.

A lot of people in Hong Kong and China want to work for an MNC because they generally provide good training. Bristol Compressors is very good at giving people significant responsibilities early in their careers. We are also a very good marketing company. People can learn an awful lot about marketing by working for us.

Despite the advantage of developing people from within, several senior Asia-Pacific managers were concerned that this approach was too little, too late. Charles Withers was one of them.

It takes time to develop local people. The competition won't give us five years to get our act together.

Bristol Compressors has a company culture that encourages people to develop themselves, to take personal responsibility for their own career progress. In Asia, the culture is "company, look after me. Tell me what to do." The model we have used to develop people in Europe and North America will likely fail in Asia.

Others cited different concerns with a "build from within" strategy. Hong Kong–based Anthony Yip was the Human Resource Manager responsible for management training in the Asia-Pacific. His major concern was attrition:

Job turnover is high in Hong Kong and Singapore because demand exceeds supply. Losing people through poaching is a very big problem at all levels of the company. Lower level employees switch easily. If you fire them, they can find a job in a day. They will quit if the working conditions aren't perfect or for a little more money. Senior people also quit because they want a promotion or a better working environment.

Once trained, local managers faced attractive opportunities outside the company. Poaching was a huge problem for Bristol Compressors throughout Asia. Hong Kong–based Henry Lee, Director of Logistics for Bristol Compressors China and Hong Kong, explained that the situation in China was particularly tough:

Our biggest problem in China is retaining quality people. The Chinese think out one to two years into the future only. They want immediate rewards—pay, power, and benefits. Senior Chinese managers, in particular, are very mobile. Typically, when we train these people, we put them under a contract to continue working for us for a certain period of time after the training is over. However, even when they are bound by a contract, some still leave. There is essentially no way to track them down or to enforce the contract in a Chinese court. One of our competitors sent 24 Chinese managers to the U.S. for a 6-week, intensive training course. The course cost $20,000 per person. After two years, only one person was still with the company. The other 23 quit and got better offers with other companies in China.

Another reason for the high turnover is that many people—Chinese, in particular—don't like working under pressure. If the company pushes too hard to make the numbers, many Chinese get uncomfortable. They do not think the company should be that concerned with making the numbers but instead should focus on building relationships where things get worked out more slowly. Many expatriates we have over here do not understand this and are surprised when people simply quit. The Chinese will never complain and the reason they leave will never be brought up.

Others believed that the retention of trained managers was not as serious a concern as it might appear. Winston Baxter argued:

Retention is currently a problem for Bristol Compressors throughout the region. However, it is not as big a problem with some of our customers. Many of our customers have employees who have worked for them their entire careers. People want to work for a company they can count on. They want to be proud of their company. Bristol Compressors is new here. It does not have a track record. In time, it will, and the retention problem will largely look after itself.

Some questioned whether Bristol Compressors was starting off with the right group of local managers. Many of the best and the brightest were attracted to the large multinational companies like Sony, General Motors, Coca-Cola, and Unilever. These companies tended to have substantial national organizations that offered distinct career tracks and household names that looked good on a résumé. Some wondered whether Bristol Compressors' existing local management pool was strong enough to support a "build from within" strategy.

Cultural differences also raised serious questions about the efficacy of management development programs. Many potential Asia-Pacific managers were ethnic Chinese; in some cases, Chinese cultural norms interfered with Bristol Compressors' efforts to accelerate management development. The way in which many ethnic Chinese often approached decision making and delegation illustrated the issue. The typical structures of Western and Chinese business organization are shown in Exhibit 1. In most cases, Western business organizations were built on the principles of delegation and teamwork. Typical Chinese organizations followed very different principles. They tended to have large numbers of people who reported directly to the General Manager. Power was tightly guarded at the top of the organization and teamwork was not valued to the same degree it was in most Western organizations. It was not unusual for general managers in Chinese organizations to nominally supervise hundreds or even thousands of employees including drivers, loading dock workers, and clerical staffs. The problem was that Bristol Compressors' approach to management development placed a high emphasis on experiential learning through delegation and teamwork. As a result, some argued that Bristol Compressors faced huge cultural barriers in quickly developing large numbers of ethnic Chinese managers.

Some also pointed out that accelerating the development process was inherently risky. The more rapid the learning process, the less grounded any individual would be in his or her current assignment. Costly mistakes would almost certainly follow. Several members of the MC wondered whether Bristol Compressors actually had the forbearance required to develop managers effectively. Hong Kong–based Paul Wang, Director of Finance for Asia-Pacific and the only non-British national on the MC, explained this concern:

> If you take a guy with no general management experience and put him in a job, and six to nine months later sales are still flat and nothing is happening, we'll likely replace him. Competition is so severe and members of the MC are so preoccupied putting out fires that we don't have the time or the attention span to effectively develop our replacements. It is a real problem. The question is, does Bristol Compressors have the patience to actually develop people?

One final obstacle to management development was the seeming unwillingness or inability of many Asians to move away from their countries of birth. Because developmental opportunities were limited in any one country, local managers often needed foreign assignments to gain exposure to the full array of issues facing Bristol Compressors in Asia-Pacific. While some welcomed the opportunities for promotions or lateral transfers outside their home countries, most were very hesitant to move. Woods explained:

EXHIBIT 1   **Building Bench Strength in Bristol Compressors–Asia-Pacific**

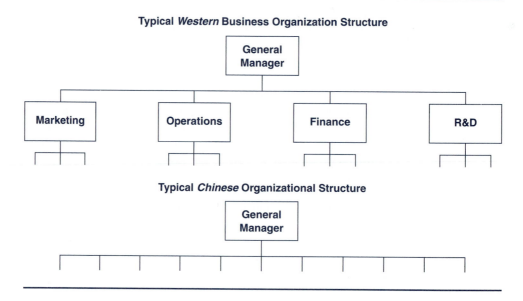

Typical *Western* Business Organization Structure

Typical *Chinese* Organizational Structure

Most local nationals are much less mobile than Americans and Europeans. Many don't want to leave their home countries. Family is a big reason. In many cases, parents put huge pressures on them to stay nearby. In addition, religion can be a factor. For example, Muslims from Malaysia may be uncomfortable moving to countries where Islam is not generally practised. Others simply fear the unknown. Short-term assignments and travel help but are usually not enough. We have developmental opportunities for people outside their home countries, but are restricted as to what we can do within the country.

Paul Wang had another perspective of developmental opportunities in the region:

Hong Kong is a great place to live. Who wants to give this up to move to Manila or Shanghai? Furthermore, Hong Kong nationals get much smaller relocation "packages" when they move to mainland China than the British. There is less incentive for us to move.

Hiring the Best and the Brightest Local Managers

A second option to building management bench strength was to simply hire the best local managers. This would circumvent the five-to-ten-year management development cycle and allow Bristol Compressors to build sales volumes in the region more quickly.

Paying top dollar for the best and the brightest local talent had many advantages. First, even the most expensive local managers were cheaper than expatriates. Elizabeth Higgens, Director of Human Resources for Asia-Pacific and a member of the MC, estimated that top talent in Singapore and Hong Kong would cost between £60,000 and £100,000 per year in 1997.[1] This was higher than Bristol Compressors paid for UK-based managers with

---

[1] in September 1997, one British pound was equal to approximately 1.60 US dollars.

comparable skills (about £40,000 to £55,000 per year). However, when a British national was brought to Asia as an expatriate, his or her total compensation package averaged about three times base salary (£120,000 or much more, depending on the position). As a result, hiring local talent was much more cost effective than using expatriates. The compensation differential was even more pronounced in countries like China where top local people cost between £20,000 and £35,000 per year.

The best and the brightest local managers often had established relationships with customers, distributors, and government officials. They also frequently had relationships with competent workers in other companies who could be tapped to join Bristol Compressors. Finally, they had the potential to serve as credible role models for other local employees.

Despite the clear advantages of this approach, several shortcomings were evident. Philip Dewer shared his views:

> When you pay serious money to hire someone, you often don't get the experience required. They may have been great working as part of a big team in a well-established company with proven processes and Asian strategic experience. However, will they be effective as part of our team to develop the appropriate new strategies and processes Bristol Compressors needs to be capable and achieve success in Asia?

Margaret Reeve was also concerned that while Bristol Compressors could always hire top people, no one really knew what they were getting until it was too late.

> It's hard to find talented people here in Hong Kong. I hired a guy who has worked in the compressor industry for many years. He had been a manager for one of our competitors. We are paying him about £65,000 per year and so far, I am not very happy with his performance. I have to follow up with him every day on what he is doing. It seems that he needs to be told what to do all the time.

Charles Withers had a similar story:

> We had a great guy we hired into the China/Hong Kong office. We hired him away from another large MNC. He was a Hong Kong national with an MBA from the London Business School. He looked great on paper. Unfortunately, he didn't last long. We had to let him go. He did not know either the industry or Bristol Compressors. We need a balance of both to succeed.

Winston Baxter felt that many of those who wanted to hire senior local managers were motivated by the desire to hire someone who "looked" as if they could do the job. The thinking was that if they wore a suit and had a good education they could be trusted. Baxter explained:

> I have a fabulous sales representative who barely graduated from high school, speaks no English, has never worn a tie, has grease under his fingernails. I know some expats here are bothered by his appearance. But, he is great. He works extremely hard and is very successful. What I've found is that while hiring a "suit" may be consistent with Bristol Compressors' culture, it doesn't always get the job done.

Flooding the Asia-Pacific with Expatriate Managers

The third option under consideration was the most aggressive. The thinking went along the following lines. Bristol Compressors dominated the portable and stationary compressor industry in Europe and North America. Some competitors had been seriously hurt in these markets and were now focusing on Asia, the last major competitive battleground in the global compressor industry. Bristol Compressors could not permit these companies to succeed in the booming economies of Asia. To do so would allow the competition to build production volumes that would underwrite research and development and produce economies of scale that would lower per unit costs. If the company's competitors were allowed to dominate the growing markets of Asia, AirCom's established markets would eventually be at risk. In addition, Asian profits in portable and stationary compressors would strengthen competitors in market share battles with Bristol Compressors' other lines of business.

In order to ensure that this never happened, some argued that Bristol Compressors should flood Asia-Pacific with expatriates. Although expensive, expatriates had proven highly valuable throughout the Asia-Pacific. They had excellent functional skills; they knew how to run a marketing campaign and organize a sales force; they could efficiently run factories, they understood international logistics, and so on. They had considerable industry knowledge. They knew who the competitors were, what their strategies were, etc. They were also familiar with Bristol Compressors' products including how compressors worked and how they could be used in a range of industries. They understood Bristol Compressors' values, culture, policies, and organization structure. Finally, Bristol Compressors' expatriates were highly loyal employees. The poaching of expatriates had never been a major problem.

At any point in time, Bristol Compressors had about 20 expatriates working in the Asia-Pacific region. Their contributions had proven invaluable. Charles Withers had seen this first hand. He believed that "well prepared expats can have a huge impact." Margaret Reeve concurred, "I would feel a lot better with 10 more expatriates here. Things would happen much faster." Others shared similar views.

Under an expatriate strategy, Bristol Compressors would literally flood Asia-Pacific with professionals from outside the region. It was estimated that an additional 40 to 50 expatriates would profoundly impact operations in the region. Less experienced locals would be moved out and would be replaced with seasoned expatriates. Under this scenario, all country general managers and virtually all of their direct reports would be expatriates. Local assistants would help in matters of cultural interpretation, language, cross-cultural negotiations, and so on.

Although this would be a novel strategy for Bristol Compressors, Japanese companies had for decades relied heavily on expatriates in managing international operations. Paul Wang had spent considerable time observing how Japanese firms were using expatriates:

> Some of our Japanese competitors are filling management bench strength in Asia with expatriates. An advantage Japanese companies have over us is that their expats are cheaper than British expats. They cost less, in part, because Japanese managers will go where they are told to go and, in part, because they are coming from Japan, which is far more expensive than most countries in the region. In many cases, Japanese companies pay less keeping expats in China or Indonesia than they would keeping them in Tokyo.

No one who promoted the expatriate strategy option believed that local managers were not needed. Rather, it was an issue of timing. The view was, "Let's first win the war. In five years, then we'll get serious about developing local management."

Although the expatriate strategy seemed to have a certain logic, it had numerous detractors. Charles Withers identified a range of concerns.

There are a number of reasons why relying on expats isn't a good idea. First, expats are very expensive. On average, each expat costs us well over £140,000 fully loaded. Second, I don't think we could find 40 quality expats in either Europe or North America who would come over here. Just because we ask doesn't mean they will come. Third, what do we do with the expats who go home? We don't have a program to deal with mass repatriation. Fourth, Bristol Compressors is essentially a marketing and sales company. To be effective, we need to understand local customers. No matter what is said about the strengths of expats, locals are far better at understanding customers.

Philip Dewer strongly agreed with Withers.

We need quality management at home. Europe and North America would suffer if we moved 40 to 50 people overseas. Even if we had plenty to spare, many don't want to go overseas. They are comfortable with their familiar business environments and personal lifestyles. Some do not desire an international assignment for personal or family reasons. Finally, neither British nor Americans are insiders in Asia. Many of our skills simply don't work here.

Frank Lau, Finance Director for China and Hong Kong, was equally skeptical of the potential contribution of expatriates. From his perspective, expatriates were largely a negative influence:

People in Hong Kong and China quit, in part, because they see such high turnover of expats. They get disoriented with such turnover. Sometimes people also feel disillusioned when they don't get the job but the company brings in another expat to the job that the local feels he or she could do better. It is bad for morale.

Moving Forward

The stakes for Bristol Compressors were enormous. With substantial assets now in the region, every member of the MC was under mounting pressure to aggressively move the organization forward. All agreed that a new generation of competent, savvy managers was required.

Management bench strength affected each MC member personally. Seven of the eight members of the MC were British nationals. While most would eventually return home, they all shared a strong desire to build bench strength and nationalize management in Asia-Pacific. They also all understood that the greater the quantity and quality of local managers, the greater the impact each MC member could have on his or her own organization. Where they disagreed was over the timing and approach to be taken.

The August 4, 1997, meeting of the MC brought no clear solutions to a huge challenge for the Asia-Pacific region. With the meeting drawing to a close, everyone present had a new awareness of the need for a unifying approach to building management bench strength. After summarizing the discussion, Woods proceeded with the following request:

The time for action is upon us. I want from each of you a two-page summary of the bench strength issue and a set of recommendations. You have two weeks to get me your input. Once I've heard from all of you, we can make some decisions and move forward.

36 MATSUSHITA ELECTRIC INDUSTRIAL LTD. EUROPE

SALES AND MARKETING, 1994

Matsushita Electric Industrial Co. Ltd. (MEI) was one of the leading electronics firms in the world, well-known for its Panasonic, National, Technics, and Quasar brands. It was a leader in many industry segments, including video-equipment (such as televisions, video cassette recorders, and camcorders); audio equipment (radios, tape recorders, and compact disk players); home appliances (refrigerators, air conditioners, and home laundry equipment); communication and industrial products (facsimile equipment, personal computers, and copying machines); as well as electronic components, batteries, and assorted other products. (A breakdown of sales by major product segment is shown on Exhibit 1.) While Matsushita was at the forefront of new product technology, it was best known for excellence in manufacturing, rather than for its product innovation or marketing flair.

Matsushita had grown rapidly and prospered in the 1980s, and reached sales of more than ¥7 trillion, or almost $60 billion, by 1990. In the early 1990s, however, a combination of factors led to a dip in revenues and profits. By 1994, revenues stood at ¥6.6 trillion, down 12 percent from its 1992 level. (A summary of recent financial performance is provided on Exhibit 2.)

In response to this shift in fortunes, Matsushita embarked on a three-year Revitalization Plan aimed at restoring profitability and boosting sales. As one part of the Revitalization Plan, key managers were rethinking MEI's approach to European sales and marketing. Matsushita had traditionally conducted sales and marketing in Europe through a series of autonomous country organizations, known as Sales Companies. Now, under a new program called Vision 35, a team had been assigned to recommend better ways to manage these efforts.

EXHIBIT 1   **Matsushita Electric Industrial Ltd.:   Revenues by Major Product Segment**

	¥ 6,599	¥ 7,056 (−5%)	¥ 6,624 (−6%)	
Video Equipment	26%	20%	20%	Traditionally strong business areas 39%
		8%	8%	
Audio Equipment	9%	14%	13%	
Home Appliances	14%			
Communication & Industrial Equipment	23%	24%	25%	New business areas 61%
Batteries & Kitchen Related Products	5%	5%	5%	
Electronic Components	13%	12%	12%	
Entertainment		8%	9%	
Others	10%	9%	8%	
	1991	**1993**	**1994**	

Note: In billion yen.

Source: Matsushita Electric company document, 1996.

Matsushita Electric Industrial: An Overview

Matsushita Electric Industrial Ltd. was founded in 1918 by Konosuke Matsushita, then a 23-year-old inspector with the Osaka Electric Light Company. In its early years, MEI manufactured battery-powered lamps, electric irons, and small radios. As the company grew it expanded into other electrical products. In the years following World War II, MEI was a leading company in the rapidly growing industry of consumer electronics, first producing black and white televisions, then transistor radios, tape recorders, home stereo units, and color televisions. By the 1960s, MEI was also active in home appliances such as dishwashers, ovens, dryers, and kitchen disposal units.

The company's growth was guided by the vision and business philosophy of its founder. In 1932, Konosuke Matsushita articulated a corporate mission statement, or

EXHIBIT 2

MATSUSHITA ELECTRIC INDUSTRIAL LTD:
Financial Performance, 1992–1994

	(Millions of yen, except per share information)		
For the year	*1994*	*1993*	*1992*
Net sales	¥6,623,586	¥7,055,868	¥7,449,933
Operating profit	173,606	235,830	383,272
Income before income taxes	128,223	162,207	356,920
Net income (loss)	24,493	37,295	133,904
Capital investment	¥ 266,097	¥ 309,097	¥ 543,223
Depreciation	317,283	355,535	342,852
R&D expenditures	381,747	401,817	418,071
At year-end			
Long-term debt	¥1,260,387	¥1,201,228	¥1,227,642
Total assets	8,192,632	8,754,979	9,149,243
Stockholders' equity	3,288,945	3,406,303	3,473,496
Number of shares issued at			
year end (thousands)	2,095,679	2,094,946	2,094,946
Stockholders	217,539	222,436	220,317
Employees	254,059	252,075	242,246
Overseas employees	98,639	94,779	92,238
Per share data (Yen)			
Per share of common stock:			
Net income (loss)	¥ 11.67	¥ 17.66	¥ 61.13
Cash dividends	12.50	12.50	12.50
Stockholders' equity	1,569.39	1,625.96	1,658.04
Per American Depositary Share,			
each representing 10 shares of common stock:			
Net income (loss)	¥ 117	¥ 117	¥ 611
Cash dividends	125	125	125
Stockholders' equity	15,694	16,260	16,580
Ratios (%)			
Operating profit/sales	2.6%	3.3%	5.1%
Income before income taxes/sales	1.9	2.3	4.8
Net income (loss)/sales	0.4	0.5	1.8
Stockholders' equity/total assets	40.1	38.9	38.0

Source: Matsushita Electric 1996 Company Annual Report.

Meichi, which emphasized the objective of "helping society to achieve happiness by providing an abundance of material goods." Over the next five years, the company's philosophy was codified into Seven Principles:

1. Contribution to society.
2. Fairness and honesty.
3. Cooperation and team spirit.
4. Untiring effort for improvement.
5. Courtesy and humility.
6. Adaptability.
7. Gratitude.

Matsushita's philosophy was translated into a set of Basic Business Principles, which included an emphasis on profitability as the measure of contribution to society, a respect for competition as the stimulus of improvement, and a belief in autonomous business units. Matsushita's belief in autonomy was reflected in its multidivisional organizational structure, with each division operating as a separate business unit, responsible for the full range of activities from product design to manufacturing, and fully accountable for its results.

Over the years, the Basic Business Principles remained an integral part of the company, and provided a common set of values for behavior and decision making. One manager noted that the Principles were broad enough to serve as effective guidelines, yet also allowed differences in interpretation. He added: "The principles do not change, although interpretations and implementation naturally evolve to fit changing circumstances."

Matsushita's International Expansion

During its early years MEI operated exclusively in Japan. International expansion had always been an important element in Matsushita's long-term vision, and as the company grew following World War II, it began exporting consumer electronics products such as radios and tape recorders. Revenues from exports were soon an important part of the company's business, and MEI, like other Japanese firms in the same industry such as Sony Corporation, set up sales offices abroad. Matsushita's first overseas sales office, the Matsushita Electric Corporation of America (MECA), was established in 1959 in New York.

In the next years, MEI continued to expand internationally, and soon established Sales Companies in Europe. In 1962, MEI opened its first Sales Company in Europe, Panasonic Deutschland GmbH, in Hamburg, Germany. Over the next two decades, additional European Sales Companies were set up in France (1968), the United Kingdom (1972), Sweden (1972), Belgium (1973), Italy (1980), Denmark (1980), Norway (1980), Spain (1981), Austria (1982), and Ireland (1985). In several other countries, MEI relied on distributors and sales agents. (Refer to Exhibits 3A and 3B for the list of sales companies and sales agents.)

MEI also set up numerous factories overseas. Like many other Japanese electronics firms, MEI in the 1970s found it important to set up manufacturing operations in local markets. At the outset this was due to fears of protectionism, but as the yen strengthened in the 1980s, it became economical to locate production in other countries. In Europe, MEI first

EXHIBIT 3A   Matsushita Electric Industrial Ltd.: Sales Companies in Europe

	Country	Company	Employees	Initials	Year
1	UK	Panasonic UK Ltd	(650)	PUK	1972
2	Germany	Panasonic Deutschland GmbH	(900)	PDG	1962
3	France	Panasonic France SA	(250)	PFS	1968
4	Italy	Panasonic Italia SpA	(200)	PIT	1980
5	Spain	Panasonic Sales Spain SA	(250)	PSS	1991
6	Sweden	Panasonic Svenska AB	(130)	PSA	1972
7	Denmark	Panasonic Denmark A/S	(50)	PAD	1980
8	Norway	Panasonic Norge A/S	(50)	PNA	1980
9	Belgium	Panasonic Belgium NV	(100)	PBN	1973
10	Belgium	Panasonic Battery Sales Europe NV	(15)	PBSE	1974
11	Austria	Panasonic Austria GmbH	(90)	PAG	1982
12	Ireland	Panasonic Ireland Ltd	(25)	PIR	1985

Note: Employee numbers are casewriter estimate.
Source: Matsushita Electric company document, 1996.

EXHIBIT 3B   Matsushita Electric Industrial Ltd.: Sales Agents in Europe

	Sales Agent	Country	Initials	Notes
1	Kaukomarkkinat Oy	Finland	KAUKO	Sales of both living & systems products
2	Haagtechno bv	Netherlands	HATO	Sales of both living & systems products
3	John Lay Electronics AG	Switzerland	JLE	Sales of both living & systems products
4	Intertech SA	Greece	INTERTECH	Sales of systems products
5	Viane SA	Greece	VIANE	Sales of living products
6	Uniclima Grissin-Pappas	Greece	UNICLIMA	Sales of air conditioning equipment
7	Sonicel	Portugal	SONICEL	Sales of living products
8	Papelaco	Portugal	PAPELACO	Sales of systems products

Source: Matsushita Electric company document, 1996.

established manufacturing plants in Belgium (1970), Spain (1973), and the UK (1974). Over the next decades MEI added several more plants, and by 1993 had 19 manufacturing companies in Europe (refer to Exhibit 4). From an organizational standpoint, these factories reported directly to their respective business units in Japan, and were entirely separate from the growing network of Sales Companies.

As Matsushita became an increasingly global company, it articulated a set of principles regarding the conduct of its overseas operations (refer to Exhibit 5). It stressed that

EXHIBIT 4   Matsushita Electric Industrial Ltd.: Manufacturing Companies in Europe, 1993

	Country	Company Name	Initials	Year Founded	Production Items
1	Germany	MB Video GmbH	MBV	1982	VTRs, CD Players, Mini Hi-Fi
2	Germany	Matsushita Video Manufacturing GmbH	MVM	1986	VTR Mechanisms
3	Germany	Matsushita Electronic Components (Europe) GmbH	ECOM	1984	VTR Tuners, RF Converters, Remote Controls, etc.
4	Germany	Matsushita Communication Deutschland GmbH	MCD	1985	Car Audio, CCTV Cameras
5	Germany	Matsushita Business Machine (Europe) GmbH	MBM	1986	Plain Paper Copiers
6	Germany	Matsushita Electronics (Europe) GmbH	EMEC	1995	Cathode Ray Tubes
7	Germany	Siemens Matsushita Components GmbH & Co	S+M	1989	Passive Components
8	UK	Matsushita Electric (UK) Ltd	MELUK	1974	Color TVs, Microwave Ovens
9	UK	Kyushu Matsushita Electric (UK) Ltd	KMEUK	1986	Electronic Typewriters, Printers, PBX Telephone Equipment
10	UK	Matsushita Communication Industrial (UK) Ltd	MCUK	1988	Mobile Telephones
11	UK	Matsushita Electronic Components (UK) Ltd	UKCOM	1988	MWO Transformers, etc.
12	UK	Matsushita Graphic Communication Systems (UK) Ltd	MGUK	1989	Facsimiles
13	UK	Matsushita Electronic Magnetron Corporation (UK) Ltd	MMUK	1989	Magnetrons
14	UK	Matsushita Industrial Equipment CO (UK) Ltd	MIECOUK	1992	Flyback Transformers
15	France	Panasonic France SA	PFS	1987	VTRs
16	Belgium	Philips Matsushita Battery Corporation NV	PMBC	1970	Dry Cell Batteries
17	Spain	Panasonic Espana SA	PAES	1973	Vacuum Cleaners, Hi-Fis
18	Ireland	Ireland Kotobuki Electronics Industries Ltd	IKEI	1992	3.5" Hard Disc Drives
19	Poland	Philips Matsushita Battery Poland SA	PMBP	1993	Dry Cell Batteries

Source: Matsushita Electric company document, 1996.

EXHIBIT 5   Matsushita Electric Industrial Ltd.:   Overseas Operations

---

Objectives: "To contribute to the society of our host countries"
1. To conduct operations welcomed by host countries.
2. To operate within principles of host governments, while fostering understanding of our company's beliefs.
3. To promote transfer of technology.
4. To manufacture competitive products.
5. To establish profitable operations.
6. To develop local employees' abilities.

Source: Matsushita Electric company document, 1996.

operations should be welcomed by the host country, and that they should be internationally competitive, profitable, and able to generate sufficient capital for their own expansion. Matsushita also emphasized the need for training and development of local personnel, referred to as "localization" of management.

MEI grew rapidly in the 1980s, with annual sales rising from ¥2,916 billion ($13.7 billion) in 1980 to ¥5,291 billion ($24.9 billion) in 1985. Sales climbed in the late 1980s despite the sharp appreciation of the yen, and reached ¥6,003 billion ($37.7) in 1990. Profitability remained healthy and consistent: in 1990, pre-tax profit was 9.5 percent, and net income stood at 3.9 percent.

Although MEI operated globally, with sales companies and manufacturing facilities spread across the world, it retained a strong base in Japan. More than half of its revenues were generated in Japan; the rest was spread across the world. Of its 1993 workforce of 252,000 employees, 157,000 (62 percent) were based in Japan, while 95,000 (38 percent) were overseas. All of its board members and senior executives, and virtually all top managers in the company, were Japanese nationals.

Matsushita's European Sales Companies

As Matsushita created Sales Companies in Europe, it gave the Managing Directors (MDs) of those companies full responsibility for sales and marketing. One manager suggested that each Sales Company was like a castle, with its Managing Director the "king." Whether the country was large, like Germany or the United Kingdom, or whether it was small, like Austria or Denmark, each "castle" was self-sufficient, and performed the full range of activities from purchasing products from Japan, to marketing and sales, technical support, logistics and warehousing, and supply of spare parts.

Sales Companies worked directly with factories in Japan to develop variations for their local markets, usually related to voltage or broadcast specifications in each country. Occasionally a Sales Company also asked for products to be developed to meet local tastes in design and styling, but in general Matsushita products were similar in appearance and design across Europe.

Each Sales Company ordered its products directly from the factories in Japan, Singapore, or Europe. Because Sales Companies varied in size and order volume, they received different prices from the factories. Products were shipped directly from Japan to each Sales Company, which had its own warehouses and spare parts centers. By 1994, there were 22 separate warehouses in Europe, plus a spare parts center in each country.

Marketing was also handled locally, resulting in a variety of marketing campaigns for the same product. Matsushita's leading consumer electronics brand, Panasonic, was perceived differently across Europe. One manager lamented that "a wide variety of messages are being transmitted in all parts of Europe, and this is working adversely to weaken the influence of the messages and confuse our customers." Sales promotions and merchandising, too, were handled by each Sales Company, with each one deciding whether to use cash rebates, interest free financing, or some other approach. By 1994, Matsushita's European Sales Companies had offered more than 100 different types of cash discount schemes and more than 300 different sales promotion programs.

Each Sales Company had its own administrative support structure, with its own Finance Department, Human Resource Department, and its own Information System Department. There were, by one estimate, 170 employees in the various European Sales Companies involved in finance alone. The workforces of the Sales Companies were comprised of local nationals with some Japanese expatriates, usually in management roles. There was little or no movement of managers among the European Sales Companies. Human resource policies were tailored to each country, and as a result performance evaluation, salary administration, and benefits differed among countries.

Creation of Panasonic Europe (Headquarters) Ltd.

By 1988, MEI had 11 Sales Companies in Europe, managed from Matsushita's head office in Osaka. With its European presence growing, Matsushita decided to create a parallel oversight office in Europe, and establish Panasonic Europe (Headquarters) Ltd. (or PEHQ) near London. In large part, PEHQ was formed to help prepare for the single European market, due in 1992. As one manager recalled, PEHQ was intended to coordinate the several Sales Companies, but not to manage them as an integrated whole. One example of coordination was the establishment of an intra-European invoicing system that handled the movement of products from European factories to European sales companies, and handled foreign exchange risk management. PEHQ also acted as a point of collection of information from Sales Companies, forwarding that information to Japan but not performing much analysis. It also housed a team of internal auditors who worked with many of the sales companies.

In the years following the creation of PEHQ, Sales Companies continued to operate in a largely autonomous manner. Unlike in the United States, where a single country operation had been created first, the tradition in Europe had been one of local autonomy. Bringing about greater integration was therefore a difficult matter. "The role of the European headquarters was never really clarified," explained one manager. "The role was basically one of providing support for the sales companies." In addition to PEHQ, a variety of other support activities, such as training, export promotion, and legal affairs, were distributed throughout Europe (refer to Exhibit 6).

Following the fall of communism in 1989, Matsushita planned to set up Sales Companies in central and eastern Europe. The first one was opened in Poland in 1993, with additional Sales Companies planned for Hungary and Czech Republic.

EXHIBIT 6 **Matsushita Electric Industrial Ltd.: Group Support Offices in Europe**

Country		Company Name	Employees	Year Founded	Function
1 UK	(PE)	Panasonic Europe (Headquarters) Ltd	(40)	1988	European Headquarters
1 UK	(PE)	Panasonic Euro-Settlement Centre	(4)	1979	Settlement between manufacturing and sales
1 UK	(PE)	Production Support Centre	(2)	1989	QC, materials, etc.
1 UK	(PE)	Panasonic Training Centre Europe	(2)	1989	Training and seminars
2 UK	(PIF)	Panasonic International Finance (UK) plc	(7)	1986	Finance
3 UK	(OWL)	Office Workstations Ltd	(20)	1984	R&D
4 Germany	(PEL)	Panasonic European Laboratories	(20)	1991	R&D (new AV technology)
5 Germany	(EPC)	Export Promotion Centre	(4)	1973	Export promotion to Japan
6 Belgium	(BLO)	Brussels Liaison Office	(4)	1983	Legal and EC affairs

Note: Employees are casewriter estimate.

Source: Matsushita Electric company document, 1996.

Matsushita Electric Industrial Ltd. in the 1990s

In the 1990s, Matsushita's performance began to level off. A few reasons explained the shift in fortune. First, the consumer electronics industry as a whole was reaching maturity. Many of the products that had fuelled the industry's rapid growth—such as color TVs, VCRs, and CD players—were now widely owned. New products, such as camcorders, were not reaching the same level of acceptance. Second, the combination of economies of scale and growing competition among global firms led to intense pressure on prices and margins. The prices of consumer electronics products fell year after year, squeezing profit margins.

As a result, MEI's revenues fell from ¥7,450 billion in 1992 to ¥7,055 billion in 1993, a drop of 5 percent. The next year revenues fell an additional 6 percent, to ¥6,623 billion in 1994. The decline in net income was even more serious, from ¥133 billion in 1992 to ¥24 in 1994. Deeply concerned by its faltering performance, Matsushita announced in 1994 a three-year Revitalization Plan. Under this Plan, the company vowed to restore cost competitiveness, to work aggressively to shift from mature segments to segments of higher growth, and to emphasize new production innovation.

Rethinking European Sales and Marketing

The renewed emphasis on cost reduction and effective marketing stimulated new thinking about MEI's approach to sales and marketing. In particular, a few new developments forced a reconsideration of the autonomous Sales Companies.

Mature Market, Falling Margins.   In Europe, the sales volume of TVs, VCRs, and other key products was roughly flat after 1990, but a continuing erosion in price per unit drove down margins. As margins shrank and profits fell, Matsushita felt a special imperative to cut costs. Since the European structure of autonomous Sales Companies involved substantial overlap, there might be some benefits from consolidation.

Cross-National Customers.   A second important development was the increasingly multinational nature of MEI's European customers. Many key customers were now operating on a regional basis, and were increasingly looking to MEI for a single approach to pricing, sales terms, and technical support.

Some of these customers were end-users with multinational operations. Such firms would approach MEI with a single European bid, and expected a single unified reply. In one such instance, a bid from a major industrial firm called for a great amount of communication among autonomous Sales Companies, and ended up taking more than a year to coordinate internally. Although MEI eventually won the contract, the lesson was a sobering one.

Other customers were dealers, and it was here that the advent of regional integration was most dramatic. A large share of MEI's sales went to retail chains, buying groups, and hypermarkets which were themselves operating in more than one country. For example, the retail chain Dixon's had expanded from its UK base and now operated retail outlets in the Netherlands. FNAC had expanded from France into Belgium, Germany, and Spain. The buying group Expert operated in 12 European countries, from Finland to Spain. These and several other dealers did not have to place a separate order for product in each country, but could consolidate their orders and place them in the country which offered the lowest price, then ship product to other countries for sale.

MEI's Sales Companies, which offered different trade prices and repayment plans, found themselves played off against each other. As an example, because Panasonic Austria ordered a lower volume from Japan than Panasonic Germany, it was charged a higher price by the factory. Dealers with retail outlets in both Austria and Germany now tended to place a single large order with Panasonic Germany at the more attractive price, then ship inventory from Germany to retail outlets in Austria. This practice, sometimes referred to as the "grey market" but officially known as "parallel imports," was entirely legal within the laws of the European Union, and MEI could do nothing to prevent it. The result for small Sales Companies such as Panasonic Austria: many final sales of MEI products on Austrian soil were recorded as sales for Panasonic Germany, not Panasonic Austria. Yet when consumers had problems with their products, they naturally contacted Panasonic Austria for service and support.

Vision 35

The combination of a more intense business climate and the emergence of cross-border customers led some executives at MEI to reconsider the country-by-country approach to sales and marketing. Taking the lead was Seinosuke Kuraku, Managing Director of PEHQ, whose vantage point gave him a clear overview of Matsushita's European activities.

In October 1994, Mr. Kuraku announced a new initiative called Vision 35, so named because it was to be implemented in 1997, the 35th anniversary of MEI's first European Sales Company. Mr. Kuraku stated:

> We have to change the ways in which we do business in Europe and cannot simply continue on the same path. . . . Europe is changing rapidly, with a large growth in cross-border dealers and increasing requests for central purchasing by large retail groups.

Mr. Kuraku concluded that it had become "necessary for us to establish a Panasonic identity throughout Europe and further promote our marketing function to open the way for better sales achievements." Toward this end, he appointed a six-person Vision 35 team, consisting of four Japanese nationals and two Europeans, one from Germany and one from the United Kingdom. In January 1995, they met for the first time to consider specific actions.

37 DSL DE MEXICO S.A. DE C.V.

In late April 1996, Lane Cook, the 28-year-old General Manager of Distribution Services Limited de Mexico (DSL), had just finished a meeting with José Hernandez, the traffic manager of SuperMart, a medium-sized Mexican retail company. DSL, a U.S.-based freight consolidator, had spent two years trying to build a business in Mexico. Despite initial successes, the collapse of the Mexican economy hit DSL's business hard. Faced with falling revenues and substantial overhead costs, Cook began an all out effort to attract new business. SuperMart seemed like an ideal prospect.

After several weeks of negotiations, Cook believed that he had won Hernandez over and that SuperMart would soon sign a contract turning all of the company's Asian shipping business over to DSL. Prices had been agreed upon, and Hernandez gave every indication of wanting to work with DSL. Cook scheduled one last meeting in anticipation of finalizing all arrangements. As the meeting was drawing to a close, Hernandez brought up one last request. He insisted that he, not DSL, select DSL's trucking company subcontractor for all of SuperMart's business. Although this condition would not be included in the written contract, Hernandez made it clear that Cook's cooperation would be essential to cement the deal. Although surprised by the request, Cook asked for time to think about it. After the meeting Cook did some investigating and through a contact learned that the company Hernandez wanted to use had made arrangements to funnel payments back to Hernandez on every shipment DSL managed. Cook realized that Hernandez was waiting for a response and wondered what action to take.

Company Background

Distribution Services Limited was founded in 1978 by Philip Clarke, Sr., and Cobb Grantham. The men served together in the Korean War and worked in Asia after the war for Sea-Land Corp., a major U.S.-based shipping company. While at Sea-Land, Clarke and Grantham recognized a potential trans-Pacific market for ocean freight consolidation. Although commonly used for shipments between North America and Europe, in the late 1970s the consolidation business had not been developed across the Pacific. Believing that the Pacific shipping market presented great opportunity, Grantham and Clarke left Sea-Land in 1978 and started DSL. Based in Hong Kong, DSL focused on consolidated orders for U.S.-based retail companies which were interested in accessing Asian markets.

Freight consolidators act as agents for either buyers or sellers interested in moving partial container loads of goods. Rather than pay for full container load volumes, customers could work with a consolidator who could pool these smaller sized orders. Consolidators could also save customers money by pre-purchasing, often at substantial discounts, large volumes of capacity with one or more shipping companies. These pre-purchases represented considerable exposure for consolidators; many lost money when anticipated demand did not materialize. However, if demand could be accurately forecast and if operations could be run smoothly, consolidators could make considerable profits. Grantham and Clarke quickly learned that the key to DSL's survival was volume. The more volume they could guarantee, the lower the rates with the shipping lines. It became clear very early on that developing and maintaining an active and healthy client base with steady transportation needs would be critical.

Working with Retailers

Retail shipping needs from Asia to the U.S. included such products as apparel, toys, shoes, electronic components and the like. The norm for U.S. retail companies was to negotiate prices that were FOB at the supplier's dock. By taking ownership of the goods overseas, retailers could handle negotiations with the freight companies themselves. For large retailers like Sears, Wal-Mart, and J.C. Penney, substantial volume discounts could be secured on massive volumes of goods being shipped. Retailers could also control shipping schedules and manage priority freight more effectively. Finally, FOB contracts enabled U.S. retailers to perform full quality inspections prior to shipping. Not only would they avoid shipping costs for inferior or damaged goods, but feedback to Asian suppliers could be immediate. This feedback minimized longer-term quality problems and increased the overall buying power of the U.S. retail companies.

To facilitate shipping and manage inspections, most large retailers established buying agents or representative offices throughout Asia. These agents or offices negotiated essentially all container load rates with shipping companies. As a result, consolidators relied on two types of retail customers: (1) small customers, including trading companies, that rarely ordered large volumes, and (2) larger retailers who, because of precise sales projections and sophisticated inventory tracking systems, ordered mixed sized lots. For example, Wal-Mart might order 8½ container loads of radios and, rather than wait to consolidate its own shipment, call in a consolidation company to expedite shipment of the half-size load.

DSL's Growth

In the late 1970s and early 1980s, DSL was one of the few consolidators working the Hong Kong–Southern California route. Over its first 10 years, sales grew by an average rate between 15 and 20 percent. Gross margins hovered in the 15 percent range, a rate which was considered very healthy in the industry. Over time, DSL opened offices in Taiwan, Korea, China, Singapore, and many other Asian origins.

DSL benefited greatly from a close relationship with Wal-Mart. Both Cobb Grantham and Philip Clarke, Sr., had known Sam Walton since the mid-1960s when he was just establishing his first Wal-Mart stores in Arkansas, and Clarke and Walton's simple and modest personalities produced a strong friendship. Because of this relationship DSL became Wal-Mart's principal consolidator out of Southeast Asia. DSL grew as Wal-Mart grew.

DSL's work with Wal-Mart proved to be fortuitous along a number of other dimensions as well. Wal-Mart was an industry leader in inventory management. In the mid-1970s, Wal-Mart began to invest lavishly on an electronic inventory and purchasing system that would help it reduce order costs, increase its bargaining power with suppliers and better manage inventories. In 1977, it began using electronic data transmission technologies to link its major trading partners with its order desks. The system, which became known as Electronic Data Interchange (EDI), grew to include an elaborate network that linked suppliers, shippers, warehouses, and individual stores. Wal-Mart insisted that all vendors and shippers upgrade their computer systems so they were compatible with Wal-Mart's state-of-the-art system. By following Wal-Mart's lead, DSL became entrenched in Wal-Mart technology and learned many key advantages in just-in-time (JIT) and inventory management earlier than many competitors. Skills in managing sophisticated tracking and pricing systems provided the company a source of competitive advantage. Not only would such systems raise barriers to entry in the industry, but they also made large customers like Wal-Mart more dependent on a smaller group of dedicated suppliers.

By the end of 1995, DSL had grown to a $200 million company. Of this amount, about $80 million was derived from Wal-Mart; another $50 million came from Target Stores. The balance was derived from such retailers as Edison Brothers, J.C. Penney, Fingerhut, Shopko, Hills Department Stores, the American Retail Group, as well as various U.S.-based trading houses.

As DSL grew, it began to encounter increasing competition. By the late 1980s a number of freight carriers began to move into the consolidation business. More efficient inventory management by the retailers also squeezed consolidators. One senior DSL manager commented on the evolution of the business in the 1980s and early 1990s:

> In the early days the margins were great. Business was sweet. But there are essentially no barriers to entry in the consolidation business. Logistics companies don't require a lot of capital investment. In reality, the freight business is more like a commodity business than anything else. At the drop of a hat, you could find yourself in a bidding war. Anybody could become your competitor. By the late 1980s, our gross margins before administrative costs had dropped to between 8 and 10 percent. In 1994 and 1995, they were down to about 4 percent. Our overall profits in 1995 were about 1 percent of revenue. That's still $2 million. Not bad, but not good enough.

Although Wal-Mart was DSL's largest account, the profit margin on the account was not the largest. Wal-Mart was relentless in pushing its cost down. Despite this, DSL made substantial "indirect profits" through Wal-Mart. Wal-Mart's volume covered a disproportionate amount of DSL's overhead costs. It also allowed DSL to negotiate substantial rate reductions when buying shipping space. As a result, DSL's biggest margins were actually recouped via its smaller customers. And finally, DSL charged back receiving fees to Asian manufacturers that delivered to its warehouse facility in Hong Kong. Although the margins were thin, Wal-Mart's high volume made them a very attractive account. One DSL manager explained how receiving fees worked:

> In many cases we may have a single vendor delivering 50 boxes of Wal-Mart merchandise to our dock in Hong Kong. In addition to charging Wal-Mart our consolidator fee, we charge the vendor a handling fee—in cash, right there on the spot. For 50 boxes we received, the vendor might pay us $30 in handling charges. On some days we get hundreds of vendors each paying $30. After a while it all adds up. The money is not from Wal-Mart, but it's all attributed to the Wal-Mart business.

With increasing competition across the Pacific, DSL focused on providing greater service to its customers and on developing new international markets. The emphasis on service was strongly encouraged by large retailers who were increasingly outsourcing non-core activities. In its early days, DSL would simply inform customers that their shipments had arrived in Long Beach and give directions for pick-up. Over time, retailers demanded a wider range of U.S.-based services including full logistics support in shipping goods to final destinations throughout the U.S. DSL soon began breaking up orders at its Long Beach warehouse and shipping directly to retail distribution centers around the country. By the mid-1980s, DSL had set up support offices in several large U.S. cities, including Dallas, San Francisco, New York, Chicago, and Miami.

Expansion to Mexico

In 1988, DSL's regional director in San Francisco made contact with a large Bay-area trading company that did considerable business with a major Mexican retailer. The trading company, which was buying goods in Asia and selling them to the Mexican retailer, asked DSL to assist in shipping, customs clearances, and the like. In response, DSL in 1990 formed a joint venture with a Mexico City–based shipping agent to assist in managing the new business. DSL viewed the joint venture as a stand alone entity and initially provided little attention or investment.

Throughout the early 1990s trade between the U.S. and Mexico flourished in part because of the establishment of maquiladora industries. In August 1992, the Prime Minister of Canada and Presidents of Mexico and the U.S. announced the North American Free Trade Agreement (NAFTA), which would come into effect on January 1, 1994. The passage of NAFTA clearly caught DSL's attention as it promised a dramatic increase in trade between the U.S. and Mexico.

In 1992, Troy Ryley, a recent graduate from The American Graduate School of International Management-Thunderbird, was hired by DSL to examine the company's joint venture in Mexico. Ryley recommended that DSL break off the relationship with its partner and establish a wholly-owned affiliate in Mexico that would pursue more aggressive growth objectives. A small office was set up in Mexico City and Ryley began the DSL effort. Initial discussions with the largest retailers in Mexico—Gigante, Comercial Mexicana, and Grupo Cifra—appeared promising. Gigante had the largest number of grocery and merchandise stores (over 100) in Mexico; Cifra had approximately 80 grocery and merchandising stores but also owned restaurants and a variety of smaller specialty retail chains. Cifra's total retail revenues of over $US 1.2 billion placed it as the largest overall retailer in Mexico. Cifra was also regarded as the best run and most financially sound retailer in the country.

DSL de Mexico S.A. de C.V.

In October 1993, Wal-Mart opened its first store in Mexico as a 50–50 joint venture with Cifra. Within the month, DSL became incorporated in Mexico and began handling not only Wal-Mart's consolidated freight from Asia, but also its domestic consolidation of Mexican suppliers for delivery to its new Mexico Supercenters. In November 1993, DSL subcontracted the use of a small warehouse in Mexico City. DSL placed two employees in the facility to do administrative work but relied on subcontractors for equipment and manual labor. DSL's main accounts were Gigante, Comercial Mexicana, and the newly arrived Wal-Mart. For each of these accounts, DSL acted as the sole consolidator of shipments from Asia to Mexico. To assist, DSL established a small operation in Laredo, Texas, that would help process trans-shipments through the U.S. and coordinate customs crossings to and from Mexico. In addition, DSL acted as Wal-Mart's sole consolidator within Mexico, a role that included working with Wal-Mart's Mexican vendors by consolidating their small orders and sending full truck loads to the Mexican stores.

In the Summer of 1994, Wal-Mart announced an aggressive expansion plan that called for the opening of 100 stores in Mexico by late 1996. Shortly thereafter, DSL rented a larger, 15,000 square foot warehouse facility in Mexico City.

In November 1994, Lane Cook was appointed General Manager of DSL de Mexico. Cook, 28, was hired by DSL in 1994 when he graduated with a Master's degree from The American Graduate School of International Management-Thunderbird. DSL had been impressed with Cook's experience in Latin America, his Spanish skills, and his ability to work independently under difficult conditions. A native of Phoenix, Arizona, Cook had worked for several years in Argentina and had done consulting work in Mexico prior to going back to school. Cook's first position with DSL was in operations in Mexico. When Troy Ryley returned to the U.S. in November of 1994, Cook was asked to take over as DSL de Mexico's General Manager.

By early 1995, Wal-Mart had 33 stores in Mexico, including 22 Sam's Clubs and 11 Wal-Mart Supercenters. In March 1995 DSL moved into a 75,000 square foot, two-year-old warehouse facility located in the northern outskirts of Mexico City. The new facility was near the main north-south highway connecting Mexico City with Laredo, Texas, and could effectively handle the loading and unloading of 25 trucks. It was leased with the intention of enabling DSL to grow with Wal-Mart demand. Cook commented on the choice of the facility:

> Here it was early December of 1994, and our year-end results were looking very good. It was Christmas time, and our warehouse was overloaded with cargo, and Wal-Mart was demanding that if we were going to continue, we needed a better facility. We were also very positive on the outlook for Mexico and our ability to generate new customers through premium service. When

I went to the ownership and gave them my proposal, the Wal-Mart business clinched it. They saw that we were shipping 240 truckloads a month out of a 15,000 square foot warehouse. Our people were putting in 18 and 20 hour days, week after week because the old warehouse couldn't handle the volume. It was time to move.

Hard Times for DSL de Mexico: The Devaluation

Two days after DSL signed a contract on the new warehouse, Mexico moved to devalue the peso. Between December 20, 1994, and February 1, 1995, the peso's value fell close to 40 percent against the U.S. dollar, and caused what most Mexican experts call the worst economic crisis in Mexico's history. (See Exhibit 1 for a review of the devaluation of the Mexican peso.) Given that the lease was denominated in pesos, the devaluation substantially lowered DSL's warehouse cost in U.S. dollar terms. However, the devaluation also paralyzed the Mexican economy. Imports went into a tailspin, drying up DSL's Asian consolidation business. Purely domestic business also suffered. Cook reflected back on the impact of the devaluation:

> Imports died. So did disposable income. DSL's business was general, non-food merchandise, and after the devaluation all people were buying was food. That's all they could afford. January through June are typically our off months. We would normally expect to move about 180 truckloads a month. In January 1995, we handled 80 truckloads. After that it went up to 125 truckloads per month and it hasn't really changed. The devaluation cost us between 20 and 30 percent of our domestic volume, and over 50 percent of our import volume. The only positive effect was that our exports are on the rise. It has been a challenge to get senior management in the U.S. to understand the extent of our problems because they are so busy, and they have other priorities at present. Also, DSL de Mexico is still comparatively small—pocket change in comparison to Asian business.

Cook Responds

Cook had considerable latitude in responding to the crisis in Mexico. As General Manager, Cook reported to C.J. Charlton, DSL's regional director of Texas, Arkansas, and Mexico. Charlton, 58, was based in Bentonville, Arkansas, and had been an active supporter of DSL's Mexican investments. Charlton, in turn, reported to Executive Vice President Darse Crandall, who was based at Corporate Headquarters in Long Beach, California. DSL's management philosophy was founded strongly on the importance of delegation. Cook saw Charlton three or four times per year—either in Mexico or in the U.S. Cook commented on their organizational ties:

> In general, he knows a lot that's going on. I give him a weekly activity report via our e-mail system. Even more important is the fact that most of the truckloads coming into or out of Mexico go through one of DSL's sister companies—a truck brokerage firm called ETA.. Charlton is the president of ETA. This means we are in continuous contact over mutual clients and operations. We also end up talking on the phone about twice a week. But his hands-off approach has helped me develop skills and experience a lot faster than any other way.

EXHIBIT 1   The Devaluation of the Mexican Peso

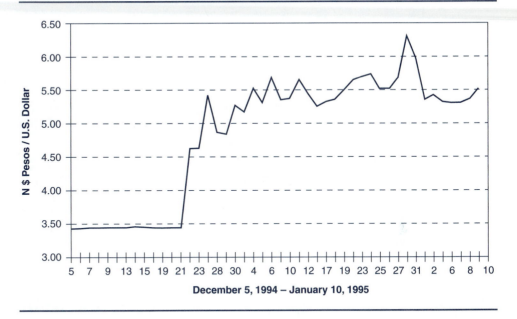

December 5, 1994 – January 10, 1995

With business hurting, Cook moved quickly to cut costs. In May of 1995, the only other American manager (running operations) at DSL de Mexico was transferred back to the U.S. By Summer 1995, DSL de Mexico's staff had been drastically reduced. The office staff shrunk from nine to seven people: an accountant and an assistant who managed billings, three people who ran import/export traffic and customer service, a messenger, and Cook. Cook described his job as a cross between being operations manager, financial officer, sales director, and warehouse manual laborer. The DSL de Mexico warehouse staff went from 48 people on two shifts to a single shift of 14. The company also contracted external firms to provide security. DSL de Mexico's financial statements are found in Exhibits 2 and 3.

Wal-Mart Goes It Alone

By late Summer of 1995, the Mexican economy was beginning to show signs of stability. Many at DSL believed that the worst was over. These hopes were shattered when, in July 1995, Wal-Mart broke ground on its own distribution and warehouse facility only 1.5 miles from DSL's building. In establishing an in-house distribution system, Wal-Mart turned to its wholly owned affiliate, McLane. Based in Temple, Texas, McLane, a national distribution and food processing company, was purchased by Wal-Mart in 1990. With 1995 sales approaching $8 billion, McLane owned a nationwide trucking operation, four food processing plants and two food storage warehouses. McLane had little international experience and none at all in Latin America.

EXHIBIT 2

DSL de MEXICO S.A. de C.V., BALANCE SHEET
DECEMBER 31, 1995 (N$ Pesos)

Current Assets

Cash	112,390
Investments	1,138,744
Accounts Receivable	4,705,728
	5,956,862

Fixed Assets

Transportation Equipment	127,272
Warehouse Equipment	305,852
Office Equipment & Furniture	410,976
Accrued Depreciation	(188,044)
	656,056

Deferred Assets

Guarantee Deposits	243,200
Advance Payments	57,654
Installation Expenses	483,482
Amortization-Installation	(19,780)
	764,556
Total Assets	7,377,474

Current Liabilities

Suppliers	1,500,716
Allowance for Profit Sharing	22,234
Allowance for Income Tax	62,774
Taxes Payable	365,746
Accounts Payable-DSL*	5,585,606
Other Creditors	160,260
Total Liabilities	7,697,336

Capital

Capital Stock	100,00
1994 Loss	(557,188)
Current Profit	137,326
Total Capital	(319,862)
Total Liabilities and Capital	7,377,474

*Dollar denominated

As Wal-Mart grew in Mexico, it first invited McLane to assist with grocery distribution. McLane did a surprisingly good job with groceries and soon pushed for the entire Wal-Mart distribution account. The decision to turn the entire distribution operation over to McLane clearly caught DSL by surprise. Another surprise came in late 1995 when Wal-Mart

EXHIBIT 3

DSL de MEXICO S.A. de C.V., INCOME STATEMENT
JANUARY 1–DECEMBER 31, 1995 (N$ Pesos)

	Amount	*Percentage*
Net Sales	21,479,002	100%
Sales Cost	0	
Gross Income	21,479,002	100%
Minus		
General Office Expenses	3,947,252	18.38%
General Warehouse Expenses	16,082,538	74.88%
Financial Income	(423,926)	(1.96%)
Foreign Exchange Losses	1,712,536	7.97%
Other Revenues and Expenses	(61,730)	(0.29%)
Operating Earnings	222,332	1.00%
Minus		
Allowance for Profit Sharing	22,234	0.10%
Allowance for Income Tax	62,772	0.29%
Net Profit	137,326	0.64%

and Cifra agreed to merge their distribution systems in Mexico. The new joint venture distribution company, DCW, would be managed entirely by McLane. Some observers predicted that Wal-Mart would eventually purchase all of Cifra's grocery and merchandise stores.

By the summer of 1996, DCW was managing all of Wal-Mart's and Cifra's grocery and general merchandise distribution in Mexico. DSL continued to act as a consolidator for Asian goods purchased by both companies but lost its domestic consolidation business. Lane Cook reflected on the loss of business:

> The Wal-Mart domestic consolidation account was a huge percentage of our business in Mexico, as we hadn't had much time to diversify. We put a lot of investment in our new warehouse facility for the account. We put $100,000 into capital improvements—office space, telephone lines (which are very expensive in Mexico), computers, furniture, and so on. We modified some of the facilities as well to better handle their freight. We also signed a two-year lease on the new facility—equivalent to U.S. $210,000 per year in rent. As long as you're just coordinating movements you have no fixed costs or no big capital frontage. Getting into a warehouse you've got fixed costs . . . So all of a sudden, we have a huge fixed cost that we could do five times as many international movements and we still couldn't pay the rent because coordinating movements is a tiny portion of revenues; the real earnings come from warehouse handling—inventory. With the loss of Wal-Mart, we are down from about 80 percent capacity to about 35 percent capacity in our facility.

Pressure to Raise Revenues

With so much unused capacity and costs cut to the bone, Cook was under enormous pressure to raise revenues. DSL's U.S. offices helped considerably here. By the summer of 1996, DSL had 20 offices in the U.S. and many of these had large accounts that did business in Mexico. The collapse of the peso brought about a significant increase in U.S. imports from Mexico. DSL de Mèxico regularly received requests for transport price quotes from DSL U.S. offices.

Despite this ongoing interest, Cook believed that the key to growth lay within developing local business, including warehouse accounts. Here, the company faced steep competition.

> Service is essentially a misunderstood concept in Mexico. We have trucking companies in Mexico that are slow, often late, and prone to lose some of the boxes on the way. This is actually a common occurrence here and this is what many customers are used to. If most customers can find a shipper who can move $100,000 of cargo for 300 pesos cheaper (under $40 U.S.), they'll switch. They don't view quality service as a tangible value. Part of the reason is that many Mexican companies only look at direct costs—they throw all the rest in administration and overhead. They don't quantify what good service could actually do for them. So, if we are ever going to be successful, we have to educate and convince our customers that time, accuracy and information can save them money. Probably our biggest challenge is that we sell a very ambiguous service. We are not the cheapest. We use a lot of computers and special tracking systems. We have systems that our competitors and many customers don't have. The market in Mexico is probably 10 years behind the U.S. in terms of service technology, so this is new to them.

The Supermarket Issue

With business off and significant overheads to cover, Cook began working overtime to build sales. In May 1996, Cook approached SuperMart, a medium-sized, Mexico City–based general merchandise retailer. SuperMart had a 60-year history in Mexico and revenues in excess of $US 150 million. Initially Cook proposed that DSL engage in a broad array of services with SuperMart. After several meetings with José Hernandez, SuperMart's 58-year-old traffic manager, Cook switched the proposal to the management of SuperMart's import shipments from Asia. Cook estimated that this would be a $US 60,000–70,000 business for DSL.

Under normal practices, SuperMart would take possession of the goods in Asia and contract with DSL for shipping to Mexico via the United States. DSL would in turn buy freight space across the Pacific to Long Beach, California, and then arrange ground transportation for the shipments through Laredo, Texas, and on to Mexico City. As a result, DSL's Hong Kong, Long Beach and Laredo offices would all be involved in managing the shipments. Cook's office in Mexico City would select the transportation company that would bring the freight from the Laredo border to Mexico City and track the shipment for SuperMart.

Hernandez seemed convinced of DSL's capabilities and he and Cook spent considerable time negotiating fees and other arrangements. Cook explained what happened next.

After about three weeks of meetings and several late night dinners, Hernandez promised us the contract at an agreed upon price but only on the condition that he select the trucking company in Mexico. I later found out through a mutual contact that Hernandez had a bank account here in Mexico City as well as a bank account in Laredo and that the trucking company he selected promised to make a payment to his American bank account whenever a shipment was made. The Laredo bank would then wire the money to Hernandez's Mexico City account. I am sure he didn't want this in the contract because he was worried his boss would find out.

I have thought long and hard about this. On the one hand, the Mexican trucking company he suggested quoted me competitive rates. I am not sure we could do much better. As a result, part of me says, who cares? It's his problem. On the other hand, I am thinking that if they can spare kickback payments to Hernandez, they should be able to lower their prices by that amount to make DSL that much more competitive.

If I don't respond favorably, I am pretty sure that SuperMart will take its business elsewhere. Unfortunately, this is the type of account that we need to see DSL through the tough times here in Mexico. Although there definitely are a lot worse things we could be involved with, I am still troubled by it and wonder what exactly to do. Maybe we should abide by the norms of business here in Mexico. What Hernandez asked for is not that unusual.

38 LARSON IN NIGERIA—1994

David Larson, Vice-President of International Operations for Larson Inc., was mulling over the decisions he was required to make regarding the company's Nigerian operation. He was disturbed by the negative tone of the report sent to him on January 4, 1994, by the Chief Executive Officer of the Nigerian affiliate, George Ridley (see Exhibit 1). Larson believed the future prospects for Nigeria were excellent and was concerned about what action he should take.

Company Background

Larson Inc. was a New York–based multinational corporation in the wire and cable business. Wholly owned subsidiaries were located in Canada and the United Kingdom, while Mexico, Venezuela, Australia, and Nigeria were the sites of joint ventures. Other countries around the world were serviced through exports from the parent or one of its subsidiaries.

The parent company was established in 1925 by David Larson's grandfather. Ownership and management of the company remained in the hands of the Larson family and was

IVEY Professor I.A. Litvak of York University prepared this case solely to provide material for class discussion. It was revised by Professor Paul W. Beamish of The University of Western Ontario, with the assistance of Mr. Harry Cheung. The author does not intend to illustrate either effective or ineffective handling of a managerial situation. The author may have disguised certain names and other identifying information to protect confidentiality. Ivey Management Services prohibits any form of reproduction, storage or transmittal without its written permission. This material is not covered under authorization from CanCopy or any reproduction rights organization. Copyright © 1995, Ivey Management Services.

Exhibit 1

The Ridley Report

In response to the request from head office for a detailed overview of the Nigerian situation and its implications for Larson Inc., George Ridley prepared the following report in December 1993. It attempts to itemize the factors in the Nigerian environment that have contributed to the problems experienced by Larson's joint venture in Nigeria.

The Nigerian Enterprises Promotion Decrees

1. There can be no doubt that the Nigerian Enterprises Promotion Decree of 1977 represents very severe and far-reaching indigenization legislation. The cumulative damaging effects of the decree have been exacerbated by some aspects of its implementation. In particular, the valuation of companies by the Nigerian Securities and Exchange Committee has in many cases been unrealistically low. This has represented substantial real-capital asset losses to the overseas companies concerned, which had no opportunity of appeal to an independent authority. Although the Decree was amended in 1989 to remove some of these problems, companies have experienced difficulties and delays in obtaining foreign currency for the remittance of proceeds from the sale of shares. A disquieting feature has been the enforced imposition, in certain cases, of a requirement to issue new equity in Nigeria instead of selling existing shares, with the consequent ineligibility to remit even part of the proceeds from Nigeria and dilution of value to both Nigerian and foreign shareholders. Another aspect causing great concern is related to the time constraint for compliance, particularly as the Nigerian authorities concerned appear to be literally snowed under with applications.

Remittance

2. In addition to the problems of remittances of the proceeds from the sale of shares, there has been a steadily increasing delay in the granting of foreign exchange for remittances from Nigeria, such as payment for supplies and services from overseas. Whereas early this year delays of about one year were being reported, delays of up to five years or even more are now not unusual. Larson Nigeria cannot continue to operate effectively if it is unable to remit proceeds and pay bills in a reasonable time frame. It is in the position of importing $5.5 million in products and services annually. These delays in remittances, coupled with delays in payments (see paragraph 4 (a) below), also raise problems related to export guarantees, which normally are of limited duration only.

3. A problem regarding remittances has arisen as a result of the Nigerian Insurance Decree No. 59, under which cargoes due for import to Nigeria have to be insured with a Nigerian-registered insurance company. For cargoes imported without confirmed letters of credit, claims related to cargo loss and damage are paid in Nigeria; however, foreign exchange for remittance to pay the overseas suppliers is not being granted on the grounds that the goods have not arrived.

Exhibit 1 continued

Problems Affecting Liquidity and Cash Flow

4. A number of problems have arisen during the last two years that are having a serious effect upon liquidity and cash flow, with the result that local expenses can be met only by increasing bank borrowing, which is not only an additional cost but also becoming more difficult to obtain.

   (a) Serious delays exist in obtaining payment from federal and state government departments for supplies and services provided, even in instances where payment terms are clearly written into the contract concerned. This is particularly true for state governments where payment of many accounts is 12 months or more in arrears. Even after payment, further delays and exchange-rate losses are experienced in obtaining foreign currency for the part that is remittable abroad. This deterioration in cash flow from government clients has, in turn, permeated through to the private clients.

   (b) There is a requirement that a 100 percent deposit be made on application for foreign currency to cover letters of credit.

   (c) In order to clear the cargo as soon as possible and to avoid possible loss at the wharf, importers normally pay their customs duty before a ship arrives.

   (d) Under the current FIFO inventory system, net earning after tax (35 percent income tax + 2 percent education tax) is insufficient to cover increased working capital requirements and to maintain an adequate inventory.

Incomes and Prices Policy Guidelines

5. Many of the guidelines issued by the Productivity, Prices, and Incomes Board are of direct discouragement, as they make operations in Nigeria increasingly less attractive in comparison with other areas in the world. Although these guidelines were removed in 1987, increases for wage, salary, fees for professional services, and auditing are still subject to final government approval.

Dividends

6. While Larson Inc. welcomed the raising of the level of dividend restriction from 30 percent gross (16.5 percent net) to 40 percent gross (20 percent net) of issued capital, the exclusion of script/bonus issues past October 1, 1976, is still a matter of concern where profits that would otherwise have been available for remittance have been reinvested. It seems inequitable that investors, both indigenous and foreign, should not receive a return on this reinvestment. Furthermore, it results in an artificial dilution of share value for both indigenous and overseas shareholders.

7. The regulations regarding interim dividends are also a matter of concern. The requirement to pay advance income tax on such dividends prior to the due date for payment of tax on the full year's income is unreasonable, and the rule under which remittance to overseas shareholders has to await final account is discriminatory.

Exhibit 1 continued

Offshore Technical and Management Services

8. Restrictions on the reimbursement of expenses to the parent company for offshore management and technical services are a cause of great concern, since such services are costly to provide.

Professional Fees

9. The whole position regarding fees for professional services provided from overseas is most unsatisfactory. Not only are the federal government scales substantially lower than those in most other countries, but also the basis of the project cost applied in Nigeria is out of keeping with normally accepted international practice. The arbitrary restriction on the percentage of fees that may be remitted is a further disincentive to attracting professional services. Moreover, payment of professional fees in themselves produces cash flow problems exacerbated by long delays in payments and remittance approvals (referred to above).

Royalties and Trademarks

10. The Nigerian government's apparent unpreparedness to permit payment of royalties for the use of trademarks for a period of more than 10 years is out of keeping with the generally accepted international practice.

Quotas, Work Permits, and Entry Visas

11. It must be recognized that expatriate expertise is a very important element for this business, but expatriate staff is very costly. Unfortunately, at the present time there are a number of difficulties and frustrations, such as the arbitrary cuts in expatriate quotas, the delays in approving quota renewal, and, in some cases, the refusal of entry visas and work permits for individuals required for work in Nigeria.

Expatriate Staff

12. In general, the conditions of employment and life in Nigeria are regarded as unattractive when compared with conditions in many other countries competing for the same expertise. These differences are due to: the general deterioration in law and order; the restrictions on salary increase and home remittance; the difficulties in buying air tickets; the poor standard of health care; the unsatisfactory state of public utilities such as electricity, water, and telecommunications; the harassment from the police, airport authorities, and other government officials; the general frustrations related to visas and work permits mentioned above. The situation has now reached a stage where not only is recruitment of suitably qualified skilled experts becoming increasingly difficult, but we are also faced with resignations and refusals to renew contracts even by individuals who have worked and lived here for some years.

Furthermore, the uncertainty over the length of time for which employment in Nigeria will be available (due to doubts whether the necessary expatriate quotas will continue to be available to the employer) is most unsettling to existing staff. This and the restriction of contracts to as little as two years are important factors in deterring the more highly qualified applicants from considering posts in Nigeria. These factors are resulting in a decline in the quality of expatriate staff it is possible to recruit.

Local Staff

13. Nigeria has one of the strongest national unions in Africa. Its National Labor Congress (NLC) basically operates in every joint venture employing over 100 workers. It is almost impossible to discipline a worker without attracting confrontation with the union. On certain occasions, some union members can be very militant. The union is also continuously attacking the employment of expatriates and trying to replace them with Nigerian staff.

14. Inadequate local technical training leads to low quality workers who tend to be lazy and not quality conscious.

15. The desirability of maintaining a tribal balance in the work force limits the options in recruiting the best workers.

16. Nigerian companies suffer heavily from pilferage, which normally accounts for 2 percent of sales.

Public Utilities

17. The constant interruption in public utility services not only affects the morale of all employees but also has a very serious impact upon the operation of the business itself. Unless reasonable and continuing supplies of electricity, water, petroleum products and telecommunications can be assured, and the highway adequately maintained, the costs related to setting up and operating escalate.

Continuity of Operating Conditions

18. The general and growing feeling of uncertainty about the continuity of operating conditions is a matter of considerable concern. It would seem that this uncertainty is engendered by a whole range of matters related to: short notice changes (sometimes even retrospective) in legislation and regulations; imprecise definition of legislation and regulations, which leads to long periods of negotiation and uncertainty; delays between public announcement of measures and promulgation of how they are to be implemented; and sometimes inconsistent interpretation of legislation and regulations by Nigerian officials.

Exhibit 1 concluded

Government Officials

19. Foreign partners have to rely on their Nigerian counterpart to handle the government officials. But it is impossible to measure its performance nor to control its expenses in these activities. In addition, carefully cultivated relationships with officials could disappear, as they are transferred frequently.

Bribery

20. Surrounding many of the problems previously listed is the pervasive practice of bribery, known locally as the *dash*. Without such a payment it is very difficult to complete business or government transactions with native Nigerians.

highly centralized. The annual sales volume for the corporation worldwide approximated $575 million in 1993. Revenue was primarily generated from the sale of power, communication, construction, and control cables.

Technical service was an important part of Larson Inc.'s product package; therefore, the company maintained a large force of engineers to consult with customers and occasionally supervise installation. As a consequence, licensing was really not a viable method of serving foreign markets.

Background on Nigeria

Nigeria is located in the west-central part of the African continent. With 105 million people in 1993, it was the most populous country in Africa and the ninth-most-populous nation in the world. From 1970 to 1993, population had grown by 2.4 percent annually. About 47 percent of the population was under 15 years of age.

Seventy-five percent of the labour force in Nigeria worked in agriculture. About 20 percent of the population lived in urban centres.

The gross national product in 1993 was about $33 billion. While per capita GNP was only about $310, on a purchasing power parity basis it was substantially higher at $1,480. GNP had grown from 1987 to 1993 at over 5 percent annually—one of the highest rates in the world. This increase was fuelled in part by the export sales of Nigeria's large oil reserves.

During the 1988 to 1992 period, Nigeria's annual inflation rate had ranged between 8 and 51 percent. This fluctuation had contributed to the change in the value of the naira from 4.5 to the U.S. dollar in 1988 to 17.3 to the U.S. dollar in 1992.

The Nigerian Operation

Larson Inc. established a joint venture in Nigeria in 1984 with a local partner who held 25 percent of the joint venture's equity. In 1989, Larson Inc. promised Nigerian authorities that the share of local ownership would be increased to 51 percent within the next five to seven years. Such indigenization requests from developing country governments were quite common.

Sales revenue for the Nigerian firm totalled $28 million in 1993. Of this revenue, $24.5 million was realized in Nigeria, while $3.5 million was from exports. About 40 percent of the firm's Nigerian sales ($10 million) were made to various enterprises and departments of the government of Nigeria. The company was making a reasonable profit of 10 percent of revenue, but with a little bit of luck and increased efficiency, it was believed it could make a profit of 20 percent.

The Nigerian operation had become less attractive for Larson Inc. in recent months. Although it was widely believed that Nigeria would become one of the key economic players in Africa in the 1990s and that the demand for Larson's products would remain very strong there, doing business in Nigeria was becoming more costly. Furthermore, Larson Inc. had become increasingly unhappy with its local partner in Nigeria, a lawyer who was solely concerned with quick "paybacks" at the expense of reinvestment and long-term growth prospects.

David Larson recognized that having the right partner in a joint venture was of paramount importance. The company expected the partner or partners to be actively engaged in the business, "not businesspeople interested in investing money alone." The partner was also expected to hold a substantial equity in the venture. In the early years of the joint venture, additional funding was often required and it was necessary for the foreign partner to be in a strong financial position.

The disillusionment of George Ridley, the Nigerian firm's CEO, had been increasing since his early days in that position. He was an expatriate from the United Kingdom who, due to his background as a military officer, placed a high value upon order and control. The chaotic situation in Nigeria proved very trying for him. His problems were further complicated by his inability to attract good local employees in Nigeria, while his best expatriate staff requested transfers to New York or Larson Inc.'s other foreign operations soon after their arrival in Nigeria. On a number of occasions, Ridley was prompted to suggest to head office that it reconsider its Nigerian commitment.

The Decision

David Larson reflected on the situation. He remained convinced that Larson Inc. should maintain its operations in Nigeria; however, he had to design a plan to increase local Nigerian equity in the venture to 51 percent. Larson also wondered what should be done about Ridley. On the one hand, Ridley had been with the company for many years and knew the business intimately; on the other hand, Larson felt that Ridley's attitude was contributing to the poor morale in the Nigerian firm and wondered if Ridley had lost his sense of adapt-ability. Larson knew Ridley had to be replaced, but he was unsure about the timing and the method to use, since Ridley was only two years away from retirement.

Larson had to come to some conclusions fairly quickly. He had been requested to pre-pare an action plan for the Nigerian operation for consideration by the board of directors of Larson Inc. in a month's time. He thought he should start by identifying the key ques-tions, whom he should contact, and how he should handle Ridley in the meantime.

39 MABUCHI MOTOR CO., LTD.

In September 1995, a full year had elapsed since Mabuchi Motor Co., Ltd., the world's most successful producer of small electric motors, had implemented a new management training program at one of its foreign operations in China. The program, called New Integrated Headquarters And Overseas Operations (NIHAO), was intended to improve the management skills of local managers in Mabuchi's foreign operations to enable the corporation to maintain its strategy of cost minimization and to allow continued aggressive production expansion. The Manager of Mabuchi's Internal Affairs Department, Nobukatsu Hirano, was responsible for the development and implementation of NIHAO.

A Brief History of Mabuchi Motor Co., Ltd.

(see Exhibit 1 for an overview)

After founding Kansai Rika Kenkyusho, a scientific research institute, in 1946, Kenichi Mabuchi invented the world's first high performance horseshoe-shaped magnetic motor, a significant improvement over prior technology. In the coming years, this product was refined and experiments were undertaken to develop the process of mass production of these small motors.

EXHIBIT 1   Summary of Important Events in Mabuchi's History

1946	K. Mabuchi designed the world's first horseshoe-shaped magnetic motor.
1954	Tokyo Science Industrial Co. is established to begin production.
1957	Mabuchi Shoji Co. Ltd. is established to undertake export operations.
1958	Mabuchi Industrial Co. is established.
1964	Factory is constructed in Kowloon, Hong Kong.
1965	Sales office is established in the U.S.
1966	Sales office is established in Germany.
1969	Factory is constructed in Taipei, Taiwan.
1978	Factory is constructed in Hukou, Hsinchu, Taiwan.
1979	Factory is constructed in Kaohsiung, Taiwan.
1984	Mabuchi stock is listed for public sale via the over-the-counter market.
	Technical Center is established in Japan to centralize R&D activity.
1986	Mabuchi becomes a member of the Tokyo Stock Exchange second section.
	Factory is constructed in Dongguang, Guangdong, China.
1987	A representative office is established in Singapore.
	Factory is constructed in Dalian, China.
1988	Mabuchi becomes a member of the Tokyo Stock Exchange first section.
1989	Factory is constructed in Chemor, Perak, Malaysia.
1992	New Technical Center is completed.
	Sales office is established in China.
1993	Factory is constructed in Wu Jiang, Jiangsu, China.
1994	Factory is constructed in Wangfandian, Liaoning, China.

In 1954, Kenichi and his brother, Takaichi Mabuchi, set up a workshop within a toy company to begin production of small electric motors under the name of Tokyo Science Industrial Co. for the Japanese toy industry. In an effort to diversify from the toy business and into emerging markets for small motors, the Mabuchi brothers established their own trading company in 1957 under the name of Mabuchi Shoji Co., Ltd.

Their modest business continued to grow when, in 1964, Mabuchi established a production facility in Hong Kong despite the fact that the yen was very weak, trading at the time at ¥360:$US 1. Subsequently, in 1969, a second offshore facility was constructed in Taiwan. These early investments in foreign production were rather unusual for a Japanese company; already by that time, most buyers considered goods produced in Asia outside of Japan to be of inferior quality. Nonetheless, by the end of the 1960s, Mabuchi had established sales offices in both Germany and the U.S. to manage its developing markets.

In the following decade, the markets for small motors grew significantly in Europe, the U.S., and Japan. Mabuchi was encouraged to continue its strategy of production expansion, establishing new plants in Taiwan in 1978 and 1979. By this time, many of the firms that had previously manufactured small motors had fallen away, leaving Mabuchi as the dominant world force commanding about 60 percent of total international demand. Although Mabuchi's main customers were the Japanese manufacturers of audio and visual equipment (i.e., CD players, camcorders, VCRs, etc.), the company also had strong sales positions in Europe and in North America. As Japan's producers became dominant in the expanding world market for consumer electronic products, Mabuchi also enjoyed significant growth in sales and profitability. Throughout the period of 1970–1980, in fact, sales multiplied more than six-fold.

Throughout the 1980s, Mabuchi continued to expand production with a focus on China in order to take advantage of the low cost of Chinese labor. In 1986, Mabuchi constructed a firm in the southern Chinese city of Dongguang. It also expanded its production base by subcontracting its requirements on a commission basis to a collection of firms in the free trade zone near Shenzhen, Guangdong, just over the border from Hong Kong. In 1987, Mabuchi made headlines in the popular press by establishing in Dalian, Liaoning, the first Japanese wholly owned subsidiary in China. By 1988, Mabuchi relied on Chinese operations to supply over 40 percent of its total output of small motors. Therefore, in an attempt to diversify from this reliance on China, Mabuchi added a fifth wholly owned production unit in 1989, this time in Malaysia. During this period, Mabuchi's main market remained the audio and visual equipment manufacturers but it was also enjoying strong growth in the automotive and precision tool markets. Just as the Malaysian plant reached full capacity in 1990, Mabuchi's consolidated sales totalled over ¥60 billion and net income reached a new high of nearly ¥7 billion.

From record highs in 1991 of net income (almost ¥10 billion) and earnings per share (¥230 per share), these indicators dropped in 1992 and 1993 due to the depreciating Japanese currency and high capital depreciation costs. In 1993, net income and EPS were 64 percent and 57 percent, respectively, of what they had been two years prior. Nonetheless, Mabuchi continued along its path of expansion, constructing a plant in 1993 in Wu Jiang, Jiangsu, China, and following with another Chinese plant in the next year in Wangfandian, Liaoning. At this point, the share of Mabuchi's production that came from China exceeded 70 percent. To diminish its reliance on Chinese output, Mabuchi began actively seeking another production base outside China as established markets continued to grow and new markets were being developed. By 1995, producing over 1 billion motors a year, Mabuchi's forecast for all markets was bullish and its overall demand figure was projected at double-digit growth. In the view of senior management, there was still a lot of potential to be developed in the small motor business.

The Electric Motor Industry

In the 1950s and 1960s, the main markets for small electric motors were toys and games including racing cars and model airplanes although, towards the end of this period, the audio and timepiece markets were beginning to emerge. In the 1970s, new applications for small electric motors were being found in household electronics such as blenders and shavers as well as other applications such as hand-held power tools including circular saws, hedge trimmers, and drills. Throughout the 1980s, the audio and visual markets for motors were very strong as consumer electronic goods firms successfully developed new markets for VCRs, cameras, and camcorders. At the same time, the market for small motors in the automotive industry began to expand rapidly when options such as power windows, power locks, and cruise control became standard features on new cars. By this time, the average car contained between 15 and 20 micro motors, while many luxury cars contained three times that number. In the 1990s, with toys becoming more sophisticated (and, hence, requiring more motors), household electronics, audio, and visual equipment becoming increasingly common possessions of the average consumer, and automobiles becoming more automated, demand for motors continued to be great. At the same time, new markets for small motors emerged in such areas as personal computers, computer peripherals, and communication technology including pagers and cellular phones. The market for small electric motors had been very strong for many years and expectations were bullish for the foreseeable future.

Despite its strong worldwide position, Mabuchi was still not free to pick and choose its markets. Johnson Electric, also a well-established and successful family-owned business, was an aggressive competitor absorbing the 35 to 40 percent balance of market share not occupied by Mabuchi. A Hong Kong company established in 1959, Johnson Electric had accumulated over HK$1.5 billion in sales and profits of HK$350 million. With over 90 percent of its production capacity in technically sophisticated but low cost operations in southern China, Johnson Electric tried to take away any developing or established markets over which Mabuchi did not have firm control.

Mabuchi Management Style and Organizational Structure

Mabuchi's management philosophy was based on the assumption that all people are essentially the same, having similar needs and wants. Whether in an affluent developed country or faced with the struggles that are part of everyday life in less developed economies, people have a common longing for security, peace, ease of living, and freedom from want. In Mabuchi's view, the small electric motor had the capacity to contribute to the fulfillment of these desires by freeing people from the demands and dangers that come with physical labor. It was also believed that the motor had the capacity to increase productivity to the point where these common goals were easier to achieve. This attempt to lift the activities of the firm out of the everyday and onto a higher plane was common for Japanese firms. Traditionally, Japanese firms had placed a greater emphasis than many of their western counterparts on finding ways to encourage employees to take on the organization's goals as their own.

In certain ways, Mabuchi was not a typical Japanese organization. Partial evidence of this can be found in the firm's early willingness to develop offshore production capability. However, Mabuchi's management style was, nonetheless, more or less characteristic of Japanese companies. There was a great respect for hierarchy and the lines of authority were very clear (see Exhibit 2). Throughout its history, Mabuchi's head office had always firmly controlled the activities of its subsidiaries, setting standards for both product quality and work practices.

Mabuchi Corporate Strategy

The cornerstones of Mabuchi's strategy were the diversification of both production bases and markets, the maintenance of high quality standards, and the minimization of production costs. Since small motors had become a low technology item that could be easily reproduced by new or established competitors, Mabuchi also believed that, tactically, it was very important to move quickly once an opportunity emerged. In other words, quick response time to market opportunities could enhance competitive advantage by simply occupying the maximum amount of competitive space.

Exhibit 2   Mabuchi Motor Co., Ltd. Organizational Structure

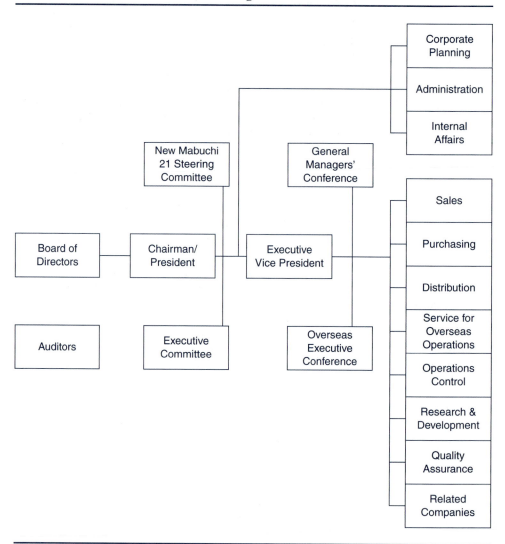

Diversification

Although a single product company, Mabuchi had always been concerned with diversification of both markets and production locations. In its earliest days, the company moved away from excessive dependence on the toy industry, stretching instead for other markets. By 1995, Mabuchi divided its markets for small motors into four basic segments: audio and visual equipment, automotive products, information and communication equipment, and home and industrial equipment. One of the significant benefits of its diversified market position was that since the demand cycles of these market segments were not closely related, when one market slowed, others tended to pick up, thus smoothing the demand. The fact was, however, that in many years the demand from all segments was up at the same time.

Similarly, Mabuchi's ongoing effort was to maintain a diverse base of production facilities. While it might have been easier to locate all plants in China, where costs of labor were among the lowest in the Asian Pacific region, Mabuchi attempted to reduce its dependence on a single country by maintaining facilities in other locations such as Taiwan, Hong Kong, Malaysia; in addition, it was searching for another non-Chinese location in 1995. While this aspect of its market strategy may have been more difficult to implement, the company believed it added a measure of security to its long-term plans.

Quality

In the view of top management, one of the responsibilities of running a worldwide production network was to guarantee an identical level of high quality product no matter where that particular product came from. The primary method of maintaining quality control was to ensure that all operations adhered to the standards set by the head office Technical Center. As early as 1984, Mabuchi had established the Technical Center, relocated and refurbished in 1992, where new technologies were tested and new products were developed. In general, technical service and the management of the international network of subsidiaries were centrally located and, once a new product or work practice was devised, it was then introduced to Mabuchi affiliates as quickly as possible by head office personnel. The various plants were expected to attempt to implement as closely as possible the patterns and processes devised in corporate headquarters.

Cost Minimization

Mabuchi endeavoured to maximize its competitiveness by minimizing its costs of labor, making its work practices more efficient, reducing the variety of products offered, and streamlining its administration.

Cost of Labor.   Since small electric motors were a labor-intensive product, one of the key competitive considerations was, of course, the relative cost of labor. It was this factor that led to the establishment of Mabuchi's first offshore production facility in Hong Kong in 1964 where, at the time, labor rates were low. By 1995, all of Mabuchi's production capability had been shifted outside of Japan to take advantage of the low cost labor available elsewhere. In fact, since labor rates in the 1990s in Taiwan and Hong Kong had become expensive relative to those available in other East Asian countries, Mabuchi was forced to begin realigning its production distribution away from these locations in order to stay cost competitive. Rather than abandoning these high cost facilities, however, the sites that were experiencing escalating costs of labor were made to change their focus, concentrating instead on higher value-added operations such as the fabrication and maintenance of production equipment for other plants.

Efficient Work Practices.   Mabuchi's top management clearly believed that there was one best way to build small motors. These methods were developed over years of experience with new methods being tested in the Technical Center. One of the many roles of expatriate managers was to ensure that the methods of production designed in Japan were mirrored in their foreign locations.

Reduction of the Variety of Products Offered.   While many organizations worldwide had attempted to satisfy their increasingly demanding customers by offering tailor-made products, Mabuchi steadfastly resisted this trend. Senior management believed, instead, that customers cared more about price than selection. Although selling about 4 million motors a day, at least 70 percent of total sales were made up of no more than 20 models. Further, about 55 percent of total sales consisted of 10 models. In general, Mabuchi concentrated on producing as few models as possible in order to achieve greater speed of production and, hence, lower average costs.

Streamlining of Administration.   In 1971, Mabuchi reorganized its administration of marketing and production to concentrate responsibility for these functions in the head office. Since then, Japanese personnel had always been in firm control over the activities of all subsidiaries. This initiative was originally an effort to reduce duplication of effort and inefficiency in management control. However, beginning in the early 1990s, the firm began to try to shift many of these responsibilities back to the individual subsidiaries. Given the rapid growth in production over the 1970s and 1980s, Mabuchi's centralized, multilingual organization had become cumbersome and difficult to manage for the head office administrative staff. Mabuchi management felt that their organization resembled a train where the head office was the locomotive, the only source of power, pulling the totally dependent subsidiaries behind. As a result, Mabuchi began to encourage subsidiary managers to communicate directly with their counterparts in other subsidiaries in an effort to attain greater corporate-wide administrative effectiveness and operational efficiency.

Strategic Initiatives at Mabuchi

In 1992, in the spirit of Kaizen (continuous improvement), Takaichi Mabuchi announced the formulation of the New Mabuchi 21 Steering Committee made up of a select group of 20 young (under 35 years) Mabuchi managers under the leadership of Executive Vice President Akira Ohnishi. This committee was charged with the task of examining and making recommendations on three key aspects of Mabuchi's business:

1. Product quality.
2. Delivery lead time.
3. Costs of production.

To address the product quality issue, the New Mabuchi 21 Steering Committee recommended implementing ISO 9000 standards at all plants. To reduce delivery lead-time, the Committee introduced the Coordinated Mabuchi Production and Sales System (COMPASS) program, a computer-based management information system designed to improve and quicken the transfer of information between departments and between subsidiaries. Finally, the Steering Committee determined that in order to decrease costs of production, the number of Japanese managers posted to foreign subsidiaries must be reduced.

The Plan to Develop a Training Program for Foreign Managers

In many East Asian countries, the cost of maintaining a Japanese expatriate (salary, travel allowances, accommodation, etc.) was 10 to 20 times that of a local manager. According to a major U.S.-based institution that focused on international human resource management, the all-inclusive cost of maintaining a senior-level Japanese manager in China was no less than US$400,000 annually and approximately US$325,000 for a mid-level Japanese manager. Even a lower-level technician from Japan would cost at least US$175,000 annually including salary, bonus, and travel allowances. In 1995, Mabuchi had 84 expatriates in various locations abroad (see Exhibit 3). Notwithstanding the cost, there did not exist a large pool of local management talent that Mabuchi could draw on in its foreign locations; therefore, a program had to be implemented to train local personnel to enable them to achieve Mabuchi's standards of production efficiency and product quality.

Mabuchi's corporate strategy included aggressive plans to continue expansion of production to reduce the possibility of the emergence of new competition or, for that matter, the loss of developing markets to current competitors. Further, since Mabuchi's market position was based on a reputation for supplying high quality products on a timely basis, all established plants were required to continue to run at a steady state and new plants had to be brought on stream without major difficulties.

EXHIBIT 3   Mabuchi Motor Co., Ltd.
Local Management/Expatriates Levels
(As of December 1995)

Plant Location	Workers	Group Leaders	Foremen	Section Chiefs	Factory Managers	Managing Directors	Total Employed
Wangfandian	214	12/0	2/0	6/0	1/0	0/1	236
Guang Dong 1	5,407	288/0	58/0	5/5	0/1	0/1	5,765
Guang Dong 2	6,378	340/0	68/0	5/9	0/1	0/1	6,802
Guang Dong 3	4,877	260/0	52/0	14/4	0/1	0/1	5,209
Guang Dong 4	1,405	75/0	15/0	11/0	0/1	0/1	1,508
Guang Dong 5	6,947	370/0	74/0	5/9	0/1	0/1	7,407
Taipei	1,889	101/0	20/0	15/4	0/1	0/1	2,031
Hukou	1,716	92/0	18/0	9/10	0/1	0/1	1,847
Dalian	7,605	405/0	81/0	5/18	1/0	0/1	8,116
Chemor	3,848	205/0	41/0	9/3	0/1	0/1	4,108
Wu Jiang	1,942	104/0	21/0	11/2	0/1	0/1	2,082
Total	42,228	2,252/0	450/0	95/64	2/9	0/11	45,111

Therefore, in late 1992 it became the responsibility of Nobukatsu Hirano, Manager of Internal Affairs, to oversee the establishment of detailed plans to fulfill these important and related goals. Since Mabuchi had limited previous experience in developing corporate training programs for foreign personnel, Andersen Consulting was retained to assist in elaborating a detailed plan. Under the direction of Mr. Hirano, a team of five Mabuchi employees and two Andersen Consulting people worked out a plan they named the New Integrated Headquarters And Overseas Operations (NIHAO). It was decided that the Dalian plant would be the first to go through the NIHAO program.

A Review of NIHAO

Fundamentally, the training program was intended to reinforce the hierarchical notion of management control where each management level was expected to play a specified role. The standardization of management practice was emphasized where tasks were to be divided between management levels so that there was no overlap or omission of duties. Further, it was clearly spelled out that there should be no individual differences in tasks or procedures when comparing personnel in similar positions; in other words, Mabuchi saw little room for individual interests or capabilities when it came to the fulfillment of managerial tasks. Overall, management was seen as a generalist task that was suited to some people and not to others and, if an individual could not complete the tasks as per company policy, he or she should be reassigned to a more suitable, perhaps more specialized, task.

A second major element of the training program was the requirement for regular performance evaluation of all employees. The belief at Mabuchi was that if an individual was not evaluated and challenged to improve, then morale would inevitably decline. All managers were, therefore, required to formally evaluate their subordinates twice a year. In actual practice, the subordinate was required to evaluate himself/herself and the manager was then required to review this self-criticism and formalize the process with a signature. Repeated unsatisfactory performance evaluations were expected to lead to demotion, whereas satisfactory evaluations usually resulted in significant bonuses. Regular workers and group leaders were often awarded bonuses of as much as 150 percent of salary and higher-level managers (i.e., factory and section managers) were commonly given bonuses of up to 300 percent of regular salary.

While it was a common experience for foreign-owned companies to lose valuable employees once improved management skills made the individual more marketable, Mabuchi did not expect to encounter this problem. First of all, to reduce the attractiveness of other employers, the corporate policy was to pay at levels higher than the local average as well as to provide all benefits required by Chinese labor regulations. Further, Mabuchi believed it could offer the sort of upward mobility necessary to retain capable young managers. In fact, Mabuchi could point to the fact that the President of its Taiwanese subsidiary, a local manager from Taiwan, had even been appointed to the corporate board of directors in 1993. An explicit goal of the NIHAO training program was to allow local managers to take over key positions as their skills developed to sufficient levels.

The Implementation of NIHAO

With five different training manuals designed to address the concerns of each level of management (see Exhibit 4), a delegation of Mabuchi staff traveled to Dalian to commence the training program. In a series of seminars that were given in Japanese and then translated into Chinese, the sessions began with the upper levels of the hierarchy and then proceeded to include lower echelons on a level-by-level basis. After each session, a short test was administered to determine whether the main points were being grasped. In cases where test results were not satisfactory, remedial sessions were offered. Subsequent batteries of seminars were held to enhance and reinforce the understanding of the management trainees regarding the basic concepts of the division of labor and the responsibilities of management. These later sessions, however, were led by a Mandarin-speaking Mabuchi employee and a Chinese Andersen Consulting employee to improve the level of comprehension.

EXHIBIT 4   Mabuchi Motor Dalian Ltd. Organizational Structure
Title (number of positions)

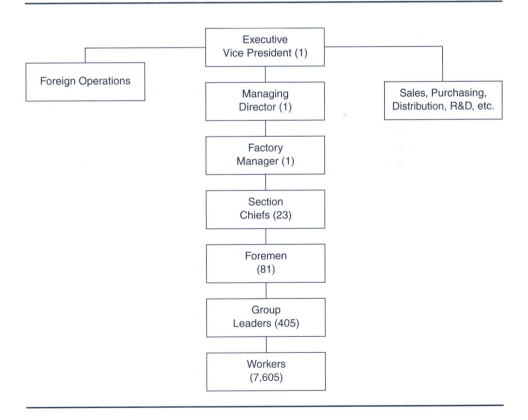

In order to determine to what extent Mabuchi's management training program had an impact, Andersen Consulting was asked to conduct periodic follow-up tests. It was soon realized that the trainees in Dalian were having great difficulty in internalizing some of the essential aspects of Mabuchi's requirements of management, personnel management in particular. It seemed that the Chinese managers, regardless of prior experience, were either not capable of, or perhaps simply not accustomed to, controlling their subordinates. The clear division between subordinate and superior was not being manifested in actual practice. Mabuchi was convinced that it had hired the best managerial talent that Dalian had to offer— yet perhaps the prior exposure of these people to the methods of management in Chinese state-owned enterprises made them poorly suited to the demands of a capitalist enterprise.

Similarly, the performance evaluations were not being completed with the rigor required by Mabuchi where less than satisfactory performance was not being met with remedial action or demotion. Evaluations were a central component of Mabuchi's management incentive system; however, the Chinese were more sensitive to personal networks and were also accustomed to a more collective approach to compensation. For example, after a particular foreman had been awarded a performance bonus, the foreman's subordinates demanded a similar bonus in keeping with what had become a Chinese custom— when one person in a work group receives a reward, the entire group shares the benefit. However, this was not Mabuchi corporate policy and, in fact, went counter to the concept of isolating people for individual reward in order to encourage everyone to attempt to achieve their personal best. The discontented employees were eventually pacified when a subsidiarywide raise was given, although the situation was not formally resolved.

The corporation's future plans for expansion hinged on its ability to move quickly into new markets, producing high quality micro motors efficiently. NIHAO was expected to play a central role in Mabuchi's process of organizational development.

40 Scotch-Brite (3M)

In June 1990, the 3M operating committee met in world headquarters in St. Paul, Minnesota, to consider a proposal to rationalize the North American production and distribution of "SCOTCH-BRITE" hand scouring pads. Due to increased consumer demand, the decision had been made to upgrade the equipment that converted the jumbo-sized rolls into consumer and industrial-sized packages and quantities. At issue was where this upgraded processing equipment would be located.

Currently, most of the conversion took place in Alexandria, Minnesota, from jumbo rolls supplied from Perth, Ontario. The Alexandria facility then shipped finished goods to eight distribution centres around the United States. (See Exhibit 1.)

The Canadian division of 3M was now proposing that all production and distribution for "SCOTCH-BRITE" hand pads take place from Perth. This would mean $4 million in new equipment would go to Perth, the current "SCOTCH-BRITE" workforce in Alexandria would be shifted to different responsibilities, and Perth would now ship directly to the various distribution centres. (See Exhibit 2.) This proposal to grant a regional product mandate to Perth had not gone unopposed. The Alexandria plant felt it would be preferable to place the new converting equipment in their facility, and to maintain the existing relationship with Perth.

IVEY Professor Paul Beamish prepared this case solely to provide material for class discussion. The author does not intend to illustrate either effective or ineffective handling of a managerial situation. The author may have disguised certain names and other identifying information to protect confidentiality. Ivey Management Services prohibits any form of reproduction, storage or transmittal without its written permission. This material is not covered under authorization from CanCopy or any reproduction rights organization. Copyright © 1993, Ivey Management Services.

EXHIBIT 1   Present SCOTCH-BRITE Product Flowchart

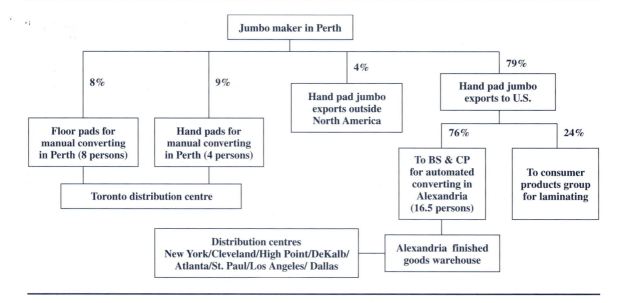

3M Background

3M was a multinational enterprise with 80,000 employees, subsidiaries and operations in 50 countries, and worldwide annual sales in excess of US$10 billion. During the past decade, 3M's outside-the-U.S. (OUS) sales had climbed from about one-third to nearly one-half of total sales. This growth was a result of a conscious strategy of global expansion. The company was organized into four divisions: Industrial and Consumer, Electronic and Information Technologies, Life Sciences, and Graphic Technologies.

Among the more familiar products were "SCOTCH" Brand transparent tapes, magnetic tapes, cassettes, and cartridges. Abrasives and adhesives were early products of the company and still formed a very important portion of the business.

Developing other technologies and applying them to make problem-solving products was the basis on which 3M had been able to grow. So many new products were produced on an ongoing basis that 25 percent of any year's sales were of products that did not exist five years before.

Like its parent company, 3M Canada Inc. was a highly diversified company that manufactured thousands of different products for industry, business, the professions, and the consumer. The head office and main plant were located in London, Ontario, with sales and service centres across the country. 3M Canada was established as part of the newly founded International Division in 1951. Additional subsidiaries were set up at that time in Australia, Brazil, France, West Germany, Mexico, and the United Kingdom. 3M Canada employed about 2,000 people. In addition to operations in London and Perth, the company had manufacturing plants in Toronto, Havelock, and Simcoe, Ontario, and Morden, Manitoba. Canada was the sixth-largest of 3M's subsidiaries.

Exhibit 2 Proposed SCOTCH-BRITE Product Flowchart

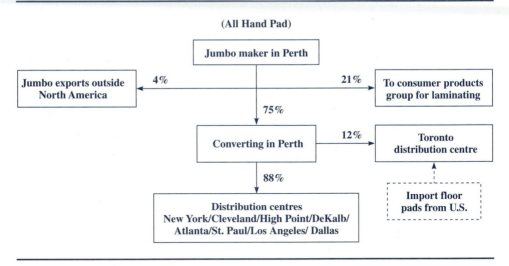

With the exception of two or three people from the worldwide organization, everyone working for 3M Canada was Canadian. The Canadian subsidiary annually lost 10–15 people to the worldwide organization. Although a high proportion of the professional management group in Canada had a career goal to work in the worldwide organization at some stage, this was not a requirement. For example, several managers at the plant manager level and above had indicated a preference to stay in Canada despite offers within the worldwide organization.

The Canadian subsidiary, under the direction of its president, Jeffery McCormick, was expected to generate sales growth and to produce an operating income on Canadian sales. Increasingly, emphasis was being placed on achieving certain target market share levels.

Within Canada, the 25 individual business units were split among 8 groups, each of which operated as a profit centre. Variability existed in each with respect to the amount of divisional input from the United States.

The headquarters perception of the competencies of the Canadian subsidiary varied according to the business and functional area. For example, Canadian manufacturing and engineering had a solid reputation for getting things done.

In terms of research, Canada specialized in three somewhat narrow areas. These dealt with polymer chemistry, materials science, and electro-mechanical telecommunications. Several dozen scientists pursued research in these areas within Canadian laboratories.

The Canadian subsidiary did not have a critical mass in R&D for all the technologies necessary to support "SCOTCH-BRITE". In addition it was not deemed feasible to move (or build) a pilot plant to Canada for "SCOTCH-BRITE" testing purposes since pilot plants tended to serve a multitude of products.

Partly as a consequence of the 1988 Canada-U.S. Free Trade Agreement, the overall level of company harmonization between the two countries had risen. Some U.S. divisions were asking for more direct control over their businesses in Canada. The Canadian president needed to deal with these issues and to develop the necessary organizational response.

The Canadian subsidiary had placed a lot of importance on building intercompany sales. Over 20 percent of its sales were of this type, and further increases were intended.

3M Canada sales in 1990 were over $500 million while after-tax earnings were in the range of 10 percent. (See Exhibits 3 and 4 for financial statements.)

The Perth SCOTCH-BRITE Plant

The $5 million Perth plant went into operation in 1981, employing 22 people. The plant covered 36,000 square feet on a 78-acre site and was the first Canadian production facility for this product line. It was built to supplement the jumbo output of Alexandria, which was nearing capacity. The plant was designed with sufficient capacity to produce enough hand pads and floor pads to eliminate imports, but with exports in mind. In 1981, the Canadian duty on shipments from the United States to Canada was 13.5 percent, while shipments from Canada could enter the United States duty free.

EXHIBIT 3

3M CANADA INC.
CONSOLIDATED STATEMENT OF EARNINGS AND RETAINED EARNINGS
FOR THE YEAR ENDED OCTOBER 31, 1989

	1989	1988
	(Dollars in Thousands)	
Revenue		
Net sales*	$561,406	$516,663
Other income	8,823	3,536
	570,229	520,199
Costs and Expenses		
Cost of goods sold and other expenses	451,298	412,826
Depreciation and amortization	16,908	15,921
Interest	312	239
Research and development	1,876	2,010
	470,394	430,996
	99,835	89,203
Provision for Income Taxes	41,636	38,339
Net Earnings for the Year	58,199	50,864
Retained Earnings—Beginning of Year	215,960	185,496
	274,159	236,360
Dividends	28,046	20,400
Retained Earnings—End of Year	246,113	215,960
*Includes Net Sales to Parent and Affiliated Companies	$106,773	$ 89,709

EXHIBIT 4

3M CANADA INC.
CONSOLIDATED BALANCE SHEET AS AT OCTOBER 31, 1989

Assets

	1989	1988
	(Dollars in Thousands)	
Current Assets		
Interest bearing term deposits	$ 66,998	$ 52,896
Accounts receivable	73,524	69,631
Amounts due from affiliated companies	18,050	13,670
Other receivables and prepaid expenses	5,472	4,592
Inventories—		
Finished goods and work in process	67,833	63,745
Raw materials and supplies	9,321	10,601
	241,198	215,135
Fixed Assets		
Property, plant and equipment - at cost	180,848	164,313
Less accumulated depreciation	85,764	75,676
Other Assets	9,590	8,856
	$345,872	$312,628

Liabilities

	1989	1988
Current Liabilities		
Accounts payable—trade	$ 21,600	$ 18,388
Amounts due to affiliated companies	18,427	17,985
Income taxes payable	9,394	12,437
Deferred payments	1,437	1,422
Other liabilities	20,832	18,367
	71,690	68,599
Deferred Income Taxes	14,669	14,669
	$ 86,359	$ 83,268

Shareholders' Equity

	1989	1988
Capital Stock		
Authorized—		
Unlimited shares		
Issued and fully paid—		
14,600 shares	13,400	13,400
Retained Earnings	246,113	215,960
	259,513	229,360
	$345,872	$312,628

Over the next decade, the plant was expanded several times, and employment grew to 80 people. Throughout this period, the plant exclusively produced "SCOTCH-BRITE". "SCOTCH-BRITE" was a profitable, growing product line in a core business area. The total scouring pad market in which "SCOTCH-BRITE" competed was estimated to be $60 million in the United States and nearly $5 million in Canada.

"SCOTCH-BRITE" material was a web of nonwoven nylon or polyester fibres impregnated throughout with abrasive particles. The result was a pad, disk, or wheel used to scour, clean, polish, or finish materials such as wood, metal, plastic, and many other surfaces.

As "SCOTCH-BRITE" material wears down it exposes more abrasives so that it continues to be effective all through its life. Because it is made of a synthetic fibre it does not rust or stain. Some types of "SCOTCH-BRITE" have a sponge backing so that both scouring and washing can be done with the one product. Other versions of this material have integral backing pads and handles made of strong plastic to enable the user to scour and clean flat surfaces and corners with ease.

"SCOTCH-BRITE" products were made in sheet, roll, and wheel shapes, and used in a wide variety of applications in the metal-working, woodworking, and plastics industries, as well as in the hotel and restaurant trade, and the home.

Floor and carpet cleaning companies, schools, hospitals, and building maintenance personnel used a wide variety of "SCOTCH-BRITE" disks and pads for floor maintenance. Other smaller handheld pads were used for cleaning painted surfaces such as door frames, stairs, walls, sinks, and tiles surfaces. "SCOTCH-BRITE" products were used in hotels and restaurants for griddle and grill cleaning, deep fat fryer scouring, as well for carpet and floor maintenance. Several types of "SCOTCH-BRITE" products were available for home use. These ranged from a gentle version designed for cleaning tubs, sinks, tile, and even fine china, to a rugged scouring pad with a built-in handle for scouring barbecue grills.

The Perth Proposal

During the 1980s as the Perth plant grew in size and experience, its reputation as a workforce with a demonstrated ability to work effectively began to develop. With increased confidence came a desire to assume new challenges. An obvious area for potential development would be to take on more of the SCOTCH-BRITE value-added function in Perth, rather than to ship semi-finished goods to the United States.

In the mid-1980s, the Perth managers advocated that they should now supply finished goods to the U.S. for certain mandated products. The SCOTCH-BRITE Manufacturing Director during this period opposed this approach. He claimed that nothing would be saved as all the finished goods would have to be sent to Alexandria anyway, for consolidation and distribution to the customer.

The U.S.-based manufacturing director also argued that mandating products could reduce the utilization of the larger, more expensive maker at Alexandria which would increase the unit burden costs on other products there. During this period, the Perth maker operated as the swing maker with utilization cycling in order to keep the Alexandria maker fully loaded.

With a change in management came a willingness to take a fresh look at the situation. The new manager, Andy Burns, insisted that a more complete analysis of all the delivered costs be provided. To that end, a study was initiated in December 1989 to determine the cost of converting and packaging SCOTCH-BRITE hand pads in Perth, rather than shipping jumbo to Alexandria for converting and packaging.

The task force struck in Canada was led by Len Weston, the Perth Plant Manager. Procedurally, any proposal would first go to Gary Boles, Manufacturing Director for Canada, and Gord Prentice, Executive Vice President of Manufacturing for Canada. Once their agreement had been obtained, the Perth plant manager would continue to champion the project through the 3M hierarchy, although people such as Prentice would facilitate the process.

The proposal would next go to the Building Service and Cleaning Products (BS 1 CP) division for review and agreement. If successful, the proposal would then be sent back to Canadian engineering to develop an Authority for (capital) Expenditure, or AFE. It would then be routed through senior Canadian management and U.S. division and group levels. The final stage was for the AFE to go to the Operating committee at the sector level for assessment. See Exhibits 5 and 6 for partial organization charts for 3M Worldwide and International.

The Perth proposal acknowledged that Alexandria was a competently managed plant and that putting the new equipment in either location would reduce costs from their current levels. At issue was where the greater cost savings would be generated. The Perth proposal argued that these would occur in Perth (see Exhibit 7) through a combination of

EXHIBIT 5   3M International—Partial Organization Chart

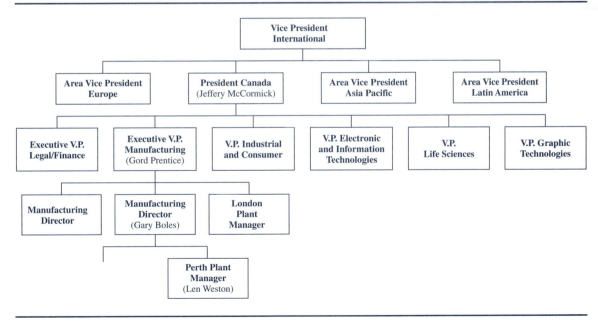

EXHIBIT 6   3M Worldwide—Partial Organization Chart

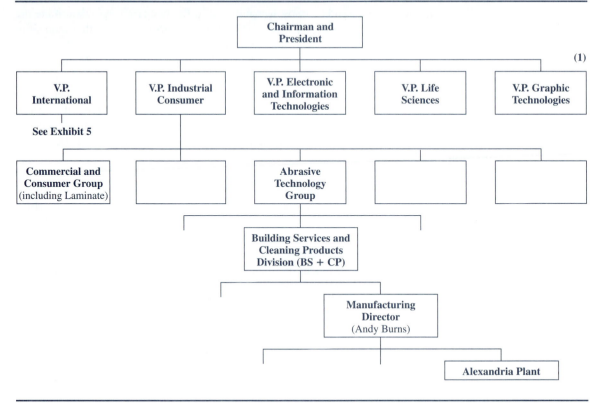

Note: (1) Operating Committee made up of the 4 sector vice-presidents, the V.P. International, and several other key executives.

reduced freight and storage costs, and faster and more efficient manufacturing. The Perth proposal's overall approach was to emphasize what was best for shareholders on the basis of total delivered costs.

Overall employment needs were expected to increase by 8 in Canada yet decline by at least double that in Alexandria. (See Exhibit 8.)

Some of the modest employment increases in Canada could be traced to the fact that the small amount of manual converting in Perth would now be automated. It had been viable to convert a small quantity of hand pads in Canada, even manually, when shipping costs and duties were factored in.

The biggest reason for the small number of proposed new hires in Canada was the plan to discontinue floor pad manual converting in Perth and to shift those operators to the auto-mated hand pad area. The initial response to this in Canada, in several quarters, had been less-than-enthusiastic.

The Canadian floor pad business manager felt that he might now have to pay a premium if purchasing from the United States. As well, he was concerned that some of his customers might notice a difference in performance. He felt the manually converted floor pads from

EXHIBIT 7   Sample Unit Cost Comparison (U.S. Dollars per Case)

	Current Alexandria Operation	Upgraded Cutter Alexandria	Upgraded Cutter Perth
Jumbo Cost Ex Perth	$6.20	$6.20	$6.20
Jumbo Freight to Alexandria	$0.70	$0.70	—
Jumbo Storage	$0.70	$0.70	$0.05
Jumbo Burden Absorption	—	—	($0.20)[1]
Input Cost to Converting	**$7.60**	**$7.60**	**$6.05**
Converting Waste	$0.95	$0.65	$0.45
Converting Labour	$1.35	$0.30	$0.15[2]
Variable Converting Overhead	$0.60	$0.45	$0.30
Fixed Converting Overhead	$1.00	$0.55	$0.85[3]
Packaging Supplies	$1.20	$1.20	$1.20
Fin Goods Whse/Mat Hand	$0.45	$0.45	$0.25
Fin Goods Direct Charges	$1.15	$1.15	$0.90
Cost Including Converting	**$14.30**	**$12.35**	**$10.10**
Freight to Branch	$0.90	$0.90	$1.05
Cost Delivered to Branch	**$15.20**	**$13.25**	**$11.15**

[1]Volume savings through equipment usage.
[2]Lower than Alexandria due to faster equipment speed and smaller production teams.
[3]Higher than Alexandria due to larger investment in equipment.
Source: Perth proposal.

EXHIBIT 8   Changes in Staffing for Each Proposal

Perth Proposal

Add in Perth	1 Maintenance
	3 Shippers
	4 Production Operators *
Total	8 Persons @ Labour Rate U.S. $13.18/hr
Delete in Alexandria	Maintenance ?
	Shipping / Receiving ?
	16.5 Production Operators

Alexandria Proposal

Add in Alexandria	6 Operators @ $15.43

*In addition, 8 persons in floor pad manual conversion and 4 persons in hand pad manual conversion would now be shifted to hand pad automated conversion in Perth.

Perth were of a slightly higher quality than the automatically converted ones from Hutchison, Minnesota. The Canadian business manager had built a higher market share for 3M floor pads in Canada than his U.S. counterparts, and he did not wish to see this jeopardized.

A shift from floor pad manual converting to hand pad automated converting would also have immediate implications for the operators. Currently most of the manual floor pad (and hand pad) jobs were on a one shift (day) basis. A second, evening shift was sometimes required, but no one worked the midnight-to-morning shift. With automation, all operators would now need to work a three shift rotation in order to maximize machine utilization. In a nonunion plant, with a 10-year tradition of day jobs in converting, and with a no-layoff policy, this could be an emotional issue. The task of selling it to the operators would fall to Weston.

The Alexandria Response

The Alexandria response was less a proposal, and more a reaction to the Perth initiative. A variety of concerns, some old and some new, were raised.

- First, the increased production volume in Canada and the resultant re-exports to the United States would cause an increased vulnerability to currency fluctuations.
- Second, lengthening the supply distance would make it more difficult to guarantee delivery to U.S. customers.
- Third, the Perth plant would now need to be interfaced with the 3M-USA computer-based materials management system in order to have effective transportation. This would require the Canadian information technology group to work with the logistics people in order to develop a program which would allow for cross-border integration of information.
- Fourth, cost of shipping finished goods to the branches would increase in both Perth and Alexandria. In Perth it would be due to the smaller volumes and increased distances associated with shipping a single product line. In Alexandria it would now take longer to make up a truckload without the hand pads.
- Fifth, since SCOTCH-BRITE converting was already well established in Alexandria, and there would be savings wherever the new equipment was located, it was safer to keep it where the manufacturing experience already existed rather than to rely on optimistic projections from Perth.

Conclusion

In part, due to the distances involved, regional production mandates on various products had been granted as early as the 1970s by 3M in Europe. SCOTCH-BRITE, in fact, was already also being produced in Europe, Asia, and Mexico. However, unlike these other production mandates, the Perth proposal was to supply the core U.S. market. For the operating committee, the decision would come down to how much confidence they had in the Perth proposal.

41 ENRON DEVELOPMENT CORPORATION

On August 3, 1995, Rebecca Mark, chairman and CEO of Enron Development Corporation (EDC), hurried to the airport to catch the first leg of a flight from Houston to Bombay. Earlier that day she had received word from India that EDC's $2.8 million Dabhol power plant project had been canceled. Given the political situation in the state of Maharashtra, the cancellation was not completely unexpected. However, if the decision could not be reversed, EDC's potential financial losses were significant. More importantly, EDC was counting on Dabhol as a beachhead that would lead to further projects in India. India's power-generating capacity was forecast to triple in the next 15 years. The cancellation of the Dabhol project could seriously undermine EDC's participation in this massive development.

Enron Corporation

Houston-based Enron Corporation (Enron), formed in 1985 in a merger between Inter-North, Inc. and Houston Natural Gas Corp., was a leading firm in the worldwide energy industries. The firm's new slogan was "Creating Energy Solutions Worldwide" and its stated vision was to become "The World's Leading Energy Company—creating innovative and efficient energy solutions for growing economies and a better environment worldwide."

Enron was the largest natural gas company in the United States and operated the largest gas pipeline system in the world outside of Gazprom in Russia. The firm was involved in developing more natural-gas-fired independent power plants than any other company in the world. Enron owned and operated energy facilities in 15 countries and had projects under

563

way in 15 additional countries. In 1994, the firm had revenues of $9 billion and an operating profit of $944 million. Enron's international operations had earnings before interest and taxes of $148 million in 1994, an increase of 12 percent over the previous year. International operations represented 15 percent of the company's total sales and operating income. Exhibit 1 provides a financial summary for Enron.

Enron had five operating divisions:

- Enron Operations Corp. was responsible for U.S. interstate natural gas pipelines, operated the company's worldwide physical assets (except those owned by Enron Oil & Gas), and provided engineering, construction, and operating services expertise across all business lines.
- Enron Capital & Trade Resources Corp. conducted the majority of the firm's worldwide marketing activities for natural gas, liquids, and electric power and was responsible for U.S. power development.
- Enron Oil & Gas was involved in exploration and production activities in natural gas and crude oil.
- Enron Global Power & Pipeline (EPP) owned and operated natural gas pipelines in emerging market countries. Enron Corporation held a 52 percent ownership interest in Enron Global Power & Pipelines.
- Enron Development Corporation (EDC) was involved in the development of international energy infrastructure projects such as power plants, pipelines, fuel transportation, and natural gas processing plants.

Enron Development Corporation.   EDC's focus was on natural gas projects. The firm had an international reputation as a reliable provider of turnkey natural gas projects on a

EXHIBIT 1   Enron Financial Summary

(Dollars in Millions, Except per Share Amounts)	Year Ended December 31				
	1994	1993	1992	1991	1990
Revenues	$ 8,894	$ 7,986	$ 6,415	$ 5,698	$5,460
Income Before Interest, Minority Interest and Income Taxes	944	798	767	715	662
Income Before Extraordinary Items	453	332	328	232	202
Total Assets	11,966	11,504	10,312	10,070	9,849
Long Term Debt	2,805	2,661	2,459	3,109	2,983
Shareholders' Equity	3,257	2,837	2,518	1,929	1,856
Earnings per Common Share	1.70	1.46	1.21	0.98	0.86
NYSE Price Range					
High	$ 34⅝	$ 37	$ 25	$ 19⅛	$ 15⅝
Low	27	22⅛	15¼	12⅜	12½
Close December 31	30½	29	23³⁄₁₆	17½	13⅝

Source: Enron financial statements

timely basis. All of EDC's projects were project-financed and had long-term contracts with pricing agreements reached in advance. Revenues were tied to the U.S. dollar and the host government or an outside agency held responsibility for currency conversions.

EDC's projects spanned the globe. On Hainan Island in China, EDC was constructing a $135 million 150-megawatt (MW) power plant. This independent power plant was the first developed by a U.S. company in China. After completion by late 1995, Enron would be the operator and fuel manager. In the Dominican Republic, EDC was completing the first phase of a 185MW power plant. This project had a 20-year power purchase agreement with the government. In Colombia, EDC was constructing a 357-mile natural gas pipeline for the state-owned oil company. Other projects in active development included a 478MW gas-fired power plant in Turkey, a 1,120-mile natural gas pipeline from Bolivia to São Paulo, Brazil, a 500MW gas-fired power plant in Java, Indonesia, and a $4 billion liquefied natural gas processing plant in Qatar.

There was a close relationship between EDC and Enron Global Power & Pipelines (EPP). The parent firm had granted EPP a preferential right to acquire all of EDC's ownership interests in completed power and gas projects outside the United States. The projects under construction in which EPP had preferential rights included the firm's interest in the Dominican Republic power project, the Hainan Island power project, the Colombia pipeline, and the first and second phases of the 2,015MW Dabhol project in India.

Market Reform in India

India's population of more than 900 million inhabited the seventh-largest country in the world. Issues of language and religion played a major role in Indian culture, politics, and business. Fifteen national languages were recognized by the Indian constitution and these were spoken in over 1,600 dialects. India's official language, Hindi, was spoken by about 20 percent of the population. English was the official working language and for many educated Indians, English was virtually their first language. Hinduism was the dominant religious faith, practiced by over 80 percent of the population. Besides Hindus, Muslims were the most prominent religious group, making up 11 percent of the population.

On a purchasing power parity basis, the Indian economy was the fifth-largest in the world. Gross domestic product per capita was $1,300. After India gained its independence from Great Britain in 1947, and until the mid-1980s, the government pursued an economic policy of self-sufficiency. This policy was often referred to as *swadeshi*, a Hindi word meaning indigenous products or made in India. The term was first used by Mahatma Gandhi during the independence movement to encourage people to buy native goods and break the British economic stranglehold on India. To many Indians, *swadeshi* evoked images of patriotism and Indian sovereignty.

After decades of socialist-oriented/statist industrial policy focused on achieving self-sufficiency, India was financially strapped and bureaucratically bloated. High tariffs kept out imports and official government policy discouraged foreign investment. In the 1970s, Coca-Cola and IBM were among the multinational firms that pulled out of India. During the period 1985 to 1990, foreign investment in India averaged only about $250 million annually.

Efforts to reform the Indian economy began after the 1991 federal elections. The Indian government was on the verge of bankruptcy and foreign exchange reserves were sufficient for only three months of imports. After considerable prodding by the IMF and Finance Minister Manmohan Singh, Prime Minister Rao introduced free-market reforms in July 1991. Singh urged that India follow the free-market models of South Korea and Taiwan in achieving rapid economic development. India's economic liberalization plan moved the economy away from its traditionally protectionist policies toward actively encouraging foreign participation in the economy. As part of the plan, the Prime Minister's office set up a special "fast track" Foreign Investment Promotion Board to provide speedy approval for foreign investment proposals. In October 1991, the government of India opened the power industry to private sector foreign direct investment. In February 1992, the Indian government allowed the rupee to become partially convertible. In 1994, India ratified the World Trade Organization agreement on intellectual property laws.

The economic reform program had a powerful effect. By 1995, the Indian economy was growing at an annual rate of more than 8 percent, although from 1991 to 1993 growth averaged only 3.1 percent. Exports were up by 27 percent over the previous year in the April-June quarter. The country had more than $20 billion in foreign reserves, up from $13.5 billion in 1994 and only $1 billion in 1991. Food stocks were at an all-time high and inflation was under 10 percent. Tariffs, while still high and ranging from 30 to 65 percent, were only about one-fifth what they were before liberalization. By some estimates, the government's policies had produced up to $100 billion in new entrepreneurial projects in India since 1992. In January 1995, a delegation of U.S. executives accompanied U.S. Commerce Secretary Ron Brown on a visit to India. During the trip, Brown was asked if the CEOs from the energy sector had expressed any fears about doing business in India. Brown replied, "if they had any [fears] before they came, they certainly have been dissipated by this visit."[1]

Despite these efforts to encourage market reform and economic development, many hurdles remained. In 1995, foreign direct investment in India was only $1.3 billion, as compared to $33.7 billion in China. About 40 percent of the industrial economy remained government-owned. Perhaps the greatest impediment to both rapid growth and attracting foreign investment was the lack of infrastructure that met international standards. In particular, India suffered from a substantial electricity shortage.

Demand for Electricity

The Indian population was starved for electricity. It was estimated that many of India's industries were able to operate at only half their capacity because of a lack of electric power. Frequent power outages were taken for granted. In New Delhi, the government-owned power company imposed rotating one to two hour blackouts periodically during the summer, when demand for electricity peaked and temperatures were often as high as 115 degrees Fahrenheit. More remote areas had no power at all. India's current annual electrical generating capacity was about 80,000MWs. Demand was expected to nearly triple by 2007, as Exhibit 2 shows.

---

[1]N. Chandra Mohan, New Beginnings, *Business India*, January 30–February 12, 1995, p. 135.

EXHIBIT 2   Power Demand Projections (at March 1995)

Current capacity	78,900 MWs
Estimated growth rate of demand to 2007	Approximately 9% per year
Total requirements by 2007	220,000 MWs
Likely rate of addition to 2007	3,000 MWs per year
Total capacity by 2007	115,000 MWs
Likely shortfall in 2007	107,000 MWs
Additional investment needed	Rs 5 trillion ($160 billion)

Source: The Economist Intelligence Unit, *India: 3rd Quarter Report. EIU*, 1995.

Virtually all of India's power was generated and managed by state-owned electricity boards (SEBs). It was widely acknowledged that these boards suffered from chronic managerial, financial, and operational problems.[2] As much as a quarter of the electricity generated was stolen. Government-run power plants typically operated at about 50 percent capacity. In comparison, the private power plants run by Tata Steel, an Indian company, operated at around 85 percent.

Indian power rates were among the lowest in the world. Farmers paid less than 15 percent of the cost of electricity generated by new thermal power plants. In several states, small farmers paid nothing for electricity. Although the SEBs had been trying to raise rates, this had proved to be very difficult. In 1994, in the state of Gujarat, the opposition government encouraged farmers to blockade roads and burn government property after rural power rates were increased. The government was forced to back down and lower the amount of the increase.

Because of these problems and because all levels of government were so short of funds, the Central Government decided to turn to the private sector. The Electricity Act was amended in October 1991 to make this possible. However, the response from the private sector was poor. The act was amended again in March 1992 to provide further incentives, including a 16 percent rate of return to investors. In comparison, the Chinese government in 1994 announced a 12 percent rate of return cap on private power projects.

Still, potential investors remained skeptical of the central government's commitment to reform and were doubtful of the SEBs' ability to pay for privately generated power. The government took one more step. In May 1992, a delegation of Indian central government officials visited the United States and the United Kingdom to make a pitch for foreign investment in the power sector. The delegation included then power secretary S. Rajagopal, finance secretary K. Geethakrishan, and cabinet secretary Naresh Chandra. The visits were a major success. Many independent power producers (IPPs) immediately sent executives to India. By July 1995, more than 130 Memorandums of Understanding (MOUs) had been signed by the Government of India with IPPs. Twenty-three of the 41 pending electricity projects bid on by non-Indian companies were led by American firms.

---

[2]Michael Schuman, India Has a Voracious Need for Electricity: U.S. Companies Have a Clear Inside Track, *Forbes*, April 24, 1995.

The Dabhol Project

In turning to the private sector for power plant development, the Indian government decided to give the first few private sector projects the status of pioneer projects; later these projects became known as "fast track" projects (of which eight such projects were eventually signed). For the fast track projects, the central government decided not to follow the standard public tendering process. Instead, it would negotiate with IPPs for individual projects. The rationale was that the government was not in a strong negotiating position, and therefore the financial risk to the IPPs had to be reduced to entice them to invest in India. At a press conference, power secretary S. Rajagopal said the first few projects "would not be allowed to fail."

EDC's Rebecca Mark met with the Indian delegation when it visited Houston. In June 1992, Mark and several other EDC managers, at the Indian government's invitation, visited India to investigate power plant development opportunities. Within days, Enron had identified a potential site for a gas-fired power plant on the western coast of India in the port town of Dabhol, 180 miles south of Bombay in the state of Maharashtra (see map in Exhibit 3). Maharashtra was India's richest state and the center of Indian industrialization. The huge port city of Bombay was the capital and the headquarters of most of India's major companies, including Air India and Tata Enterprises, the largest Indian industrial conglomerate. Firms based in Bombay generated about 35 percent of India's GNP.

EDC, acting on the government's assurances that there would not be any tendering on the first few fast track projects, submitted a proposal to build a 2,015MW gas-fired power plant. The proposed project would be the largest plant EDC had ever built, the largest of its kind in the world, and at $2.8 billion, the largest foreign investment in India. The liquefied natural gas needed to fuel the Indian power plant would be imported from a plant EDC planned to build in Qatar. The proposal was very favorably received by both the central government and officials in the Maharashtra state government. The Maharashtra State Electricity Board (MSEB) had long wanted to build a gas-fired plant to reduce its dependence on coal and oil. Other countries with limited petroleum reserves, such as Japan and Korea, had followed a similar strategy and built coastal gas-fired power plants.

EDC was the first IPP to formally submit a proposal. Later in June 1992, EDC signed an MOU with the MSEB. A new company called Dabhol Power Company (DPC) was formed. Enron held 80 percent of the equity in Dabhol and its two partners, General Electric and International Generation Co., each held 10 percent. International Generation was a joint venture between Bechtel Enterprises Inc. (Bechtel) and San Francisco-based Pacific Gas & Electric formed in early 1995 to build and operate power plants outside the United States. General Electric was contracted to supply the gas turbines and Bechtel would be the general contractor. Exhibit 4 lists the various individuals involved with the Dabhol project, and Exhibit 5 shows the timing of the various events.

Following the signing of the MOU, EDC began a complex negotiation process for proposal approval, followed by more negotiations on the actual financial details. Officially, no power project could be developed without technical and economic clearance from the Central Electricity Authority. Typically, this process could take many months, or possibly years. The Foreign Investment Promotion Board (FIPB) was the central government's vehicle for a speedy approval process. The FIPB asked the Central Electricity Authority to give initial clearance to the Dabhol project without the detailed information normally required. However, final clearance would still be necessary at a later date.

EXHIBIT 3   Map of India

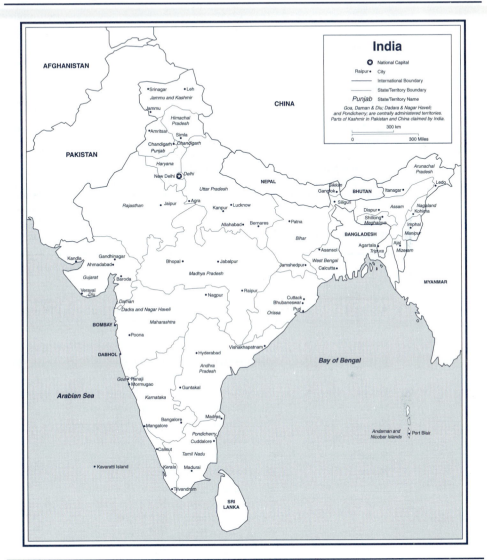

In November 1992, EDC made a detailed presentation at a meeting chaired by the central government finance secretary and attended by various other senior government officials, including the chairman of the MSEB. (Note: The finance secretary was the senior civil servant in the finance department and reported directly to the Finance Minister.) From this meeting came a recommendation to the FIPB to approve the project. In turn, the Central Power Ministry, acting on the advice of the FIPB, asked the Central Electricity Authority to expedite the approval process. The Central Electricity Authority gave an in-principle (not final) clearance to proceed with the project since the Ministry of Finance had found the project satisfactory.

EXHIBIT 4   Individuals Involved in the Dabhol Project

Name	Title and/or Role
Lal Krishna Advani	President of the Federal BJP Party
Manohar Joshi	Chief Minister of Maharashtra, deputy leader of Shiv Sena
Kenneth Lay	CEO of Enron Corporation
Rebecca Mark	Chairman and CEO of EDC
Gopinath Munde	Deputy Chief Minister of Maharashtra with direct responsibility for the state energy ministry, BJP party member
Ajit Nimbalkar	Chairman and Managing Director of Maharashtra State Electricity Board
Sharad Pawar	Former Chief Minister of Maharashtra, voted out of office March 1995; known as the Maratha strongman
P.V. Narasimha Rao	Prime Minister of India.
N.K.P. Salve	Federal Power Minister
Manmohan Singh	Federal Finance Minister, architect of free market reforms and economic advisor to PM Rao
Robert Sutton	EDC Managing Director
Balashaheb "Bal" Thackeray	Leader of Shiv Sena

EXHIBIT 5   Timing of Events Associated with the Dabhol Project

October 1991	Government of India invites private sector participation in the power sector.
May 1992	Indian delegation visits UK and U.S.; EDC invited to India by government of India.
June 1992	Maharashtra State Electricity Board signs MOU with EDC.
February 1993	Foreign Investment Promotion Board (FIPB) grants approval.
March 1993	Power Purchase Agreement negotiations start.
November 1993	Central Electricity Authority clears Dabhol project.
February 1994	Government of Maharashtra signs guarantee.
September 1994	Government of India signs guarantee.
March 1995	Dabhol financing completed.
March 1995	Maharashtra State election results announced.
April 1995	Construction begins; Government of Maharashtra orders a review; Munde Committee set up to investigate Dabhol Project.
August 1995	Project canceled by Government of Maharashtra.

In March 1993, with the necessary government approvals largely in place, EDC was in a position to negotiate the financial structure of the deal. The most critical element was a Power Purchasing Agreement (PPA) with the MSEB. The PPA was the contract under which EDC, as the owner of the power plant, would supply power to the MSEB electric grid. Over the next year or so, Rebecca Mark visited India 36 times. Ajit Nimbalkar, chairman and managing director of MSEB, described the negotiations:

This is the first project of this kind that we are doing. MSEB did not have any experience in dealing with international power developers. It was a complicated exercise, for the money involved is large, and so the negotiations took a long time.[3]

MSEB turned to the World Bank for advice in the negotiations. The World Bank offered to fund a team of international consultants. The MSEB chose Freshfields, a British law firm, and the British office of the German Westdeuche Landesbank Girozentale as consultants in the PPA negotiations.

In addition to negotiating the project financial structure and gaining state and central government approvals, EDC had to obtain dozens of other government approvals, some of which were based on regulations dating back to British colonial times. For example, to get permission to use explosives on the construction site, EDC had to visit the western Indian town of Nagpur, where British Imperial forces once stored munitions.[4]

In November 1993, the Central Electricity Authority officially cleared the Dabhol project. In December 1993, the MSEB signed the Dabhol PPA. The state government of Maharashtra signed a financial guarantee in February 1994 and the central government signed a guarantee in September 1994. These guarantees provided financial protection for EDC in the event that the MSEB was unable to make its payments. The central government's guarantee, which was to become very controversial, was signed with EDC before the government's guarantee policy was announced publicly.

Structure of the Dabhol Project

Although the original plans were for a 2,015MW project, the Maharashtra government decided to break the project into two phases. Phase I would be a 695MW plant using distillate fuel instead of natural gas and Phase II would be a 1,320MW gas-fired plant. The capital cost for Phase I would be $920 million, with an estimated turnkey construction cost of $527 million.[5] The second phase would cost about $1.9 billion.

Dabhol was broken into two phases because EDC had been unable to finalize its gas contracts and because the government had become concerned about the mounting criticism of the project. The shift from gas to distillate was done because distillate could be sourced from local refineries, helping deflect the criticism that gas imports would be a persistent drain on India's foreign exchange. Furthermore, using distillate instead of gas eliminated the need to build a port facility for Phase I.

The capital cost for Phase I included some costs for infrastructure items that would normally have been provided by the state, such as a pipeline. If these costs were deducted from the total capital cost, the cost per MW was comparable with the other fast track power plant projects. However, Dabhol was the only project that had been finalized. The other projects were still going through planning and approval stages.

---

[3]Bodhisatva Ganguli & Tushar Pania, The Anatomy of a Controversial Deal, *Business India*, April 24–May 7, 1995, p. 57.

[4]Marcus W. Brauchli, A Gandhi Legacy: Clash Over Power Plant Reflects Fight in India For Its Economic Soul, *Wall Street Journal*, April 27, 1995, p. A6.

[5]Ganguli & Pania, p. 59.

The Indian government generally followed what was known as a fixed rate of return model. Investors were assured a 16 percent rate of return on net worth for a plant load factor of up to 68.5 percent. Beyond the 68.5 percent, the rate of return on equity would increase by a maximum of 0.70 percent for each 1 percent rise in the plant load factor. Net worth was based on the total costs of building the power plant. The main objection against this model was that it provided no incentive to minimize the capital costs of investment.

The Dabhol project used a different model. A tariff of Rs2.40 ($1 equaled about 36 rupees) per unit (kilowatt/hour) of electricity was established. The tariff, fixed in terms of U.S. dollars, consisted of a capacity charge of Rs1.20 based on the capital cost of the plant and an energy charge of Rs1.20 for the price of fuel. It was estimated that the plant would run at 80 percent capacity. By using a fixed tariff, the problems of a cost-plus system were eliminated and consumers would not be affected by increases in the capital cost of the project. For EDC and its partners, there was an incentive to become more efficient to improve shareholder returns. Based on the capital costs per MW, Dabhol was comparable to other proposed projects in India. As to the tariff of Rs 2.40, other fast track power projects had similar tariffs, as did several recently approved public sector projects. Several existing public sector plants were selling power in the Rs2.15 range (although the average tariff for state electricity boards in India was Rs1.20). Enron's projected internal rate of return on the project was 26.5 percent before tax. Dabhol was granted a five-year tax holiday and the initial purchase agreement was for 20 years. Failure to achieve electricity targets would result in substantial penalty payments by the DPC to the MSEB. In the event that MSEB and DPC could not settle disagreements, international arbitration proceedings in London would be possible as specified in the PPA.

Nevertheless, because there was no competitive bidding on the Dabhol project, critics argued that the Rs2.40 per unit was too high and that the company would be making huge profits. Kirit Parekh, director of the Indira Gandhi Institute of Development and Research, was an ardent critic:

> In the United States, power generated from gas-based plants is sold to utilities at 3–4 cents while Enron is charging 7 cents. It is a rip-off. The China Power Company, which is setting up a 2000MW power plant in Hong Kong, and which will go on stream in 1996, is doing so at 15 percent less capital than Enron.[6]

Further criticism was directed at the company's lack of competitive bidding for its principal equipment supplier, General Electric, and its construction partner, Bechtel. Although General Electric and EDC had worked closely in the past, some critics suggested that foreign equipment suppliers were favored over Indian suppliers. EDC countered with the argument that is had awarded more than 60 contracts worth more than $100 million (Rs3.6 billion) to Indian companies.

EDC was also subject to criticism because of its plan to import gas for Phase II from its gas processing plant in Qatar. When completed, this plant would be owned by a joint venture between Enron Oil & Gas and the Qatar government. Although Enron vigorously denied it, critics suggested that Enron would make excessive profits through transfer pricing and charging arbitrary prices for the fuel. From EDC's perspective, taking responsibility for fuel

---

[6]Ganguli & Pania, p. 58.

supply was a means of reducing its risk, since the contract specified penalties when the plant was not able to generate electricity. Fuel supply failure would not constitute sufficient grounds for being unable to generate electricity.

The federal guarantee also came in for criticism. A World Bank report questioned the guarantee arrangement because in its opinion, it was nothing more than a loan made by the federal government on behalf of the MSEB if it could not cover its payments to Enron. EDC's Sutton countered:

> It is only after the government of India decided as a policy to give guarantees that we also decided to ask. It would have been impossible to raise money from international bankers at competitive rates without the guarantee when others are approaching the same bankers with guarantees in their pockets.[7]

The Political Situation in India

India's political process was based on a parliamentary system. At the national, or Central, level, as it was referred to in India, the Congress (I) party formed the current government and its leader, P.V. Narasimha Rao was Prime Minister. The Congress (I) party was the descendant of the Indian National Congress, which was formed in 1855 and became the major vehicle of Indian nationalism. From 1947 to 1989, some form of the Congress party ruled India in an unbroken string of governments. Indira Gandhi, who had been Prime Minister since 1964, founded the Congress (I) party after her defeat in the 1977 election. In 1980, Indira Gandhi and the Congress (I) party regained power. After Indira Gandhi was assassinated in 1984, her son Rajiv became Prime Minister. In the 1989 election, Congress (I) lost and turned power over to a minority Janata Dal government. During the 1991 election campaign, Rajiv Gandhi was assassinated and P.V. Narasimha Rao became Congress (I) party leader. Congress (I) regained power in a minority government and although Rao was not considered to be a strong leader by opponents or supporters, he had proven to be surprising resilient. The next election was scheduled for May 1996. Predictions in August 1995 were that three parties, Congress (I), Left Front, and the Bharatiya Janata Party (BJP), would each get about 150 of the 543 available seats in the Lok Sabha (House of the People).

The official opposition party was the BJP. In English, this translated to the Indian People's Party. The BJP platform emphasized support for traditional Hindu goals and values, making the party less secular than the Congress (I) party. Many of its members belonged to the urban lower middle class and distrusted the free market reforms and modern cultural values. The BJP believed it could build support among the business community that sought decentralization and deregulation but resented intervention on the part of foreign multinationals. The BJP was considered to be the front party for a Hindu fundamentalist movement led by Rajendra Singh, known as Rashtriya Swayamsevak Sangh (RSS; translation: National Volunteers Core). The RSS supported economic nationalism and promoted anti-Muslim, anti-feminist, and anti-English language views. In 1990, the RSS formed the Swadeshi Jagaran Manch, or National Awakening Forum, to promote economic nationalism. The Forum

---

[7]Ganguli & Pania, p. 56.

deemed the marketing of Western consumer goods frivolous and wasteful ("India needs computer chips, not potato chips"). According to the Forum's Bombay representative, "Soft drinks and instant cereals do not serve the mass of Indian people. We are not pleased with the way [Coke and Pepsi] are demolishing their rivals."[8]

The Maharashtra Election.   The political parties in the 25 Indian states level mirrored those at the Central level, although the Congress (I) was less dominant. Only five states had a majority Congress government. In two states, West Bengal and Kerala, politics had long been dominated by the Communist Party. The BJP was particularly strong in the industrial, heavily populated, and largely Hindu northern states. Decision making was decentralized in India, and many of the states had a substantial amount of power and autonomy. For example, the World Bank had secured an agreement to lend directly to individual states.

On February 12, 1995, a state election was held in Maharashtra. Results were to be announced about four weeks later because the chief election commissioner in Maharashtra had a policy of delinking voting from the counting of votes. The incumbent Congress (I) party and an alliance between the BJP and Shiv Sena Parties were the primary contestants. State elections were normally held every five years. In the previous election in 1990, the Congress (I) party had formed a majority government under Chief Minister Sharad Pawar. Pawar was confident of retaining power in the 1995 election.

The BJP was closely aligned with the national BJP. Shiv Sena was a Maharashtra-based party with the stated objective of protecting the economic interests and identity of Maharashtrians and safeguarding the interests of all Hindus. The official leader of Shiv Sena was Manohar Joshi but he had limited power and openly admitted that the real authority was Bal Thackeray (sometimes referred to as Mr. Remote Control for his ability to control the party from an unofficial capacity). Thackeray was a newspaper cartoonist before he became a right-wing activist. A talented organizer and rousing orator, he set up the Shiv Sena Party in the mid-1960s to appeal to poor Hindus who resented the influence of foreigners and non-Maharashtrians, particularly those from South India. Thackeray was prone to provocative and somewhat threatening statements. He wanted to change the name of India to Hindustan and during the Maharashtra election, talked about chasing non-Maharashtrians out of the state.

The Dabhol power project was a major campaign issue leading up to the election. Election Commission norms in India prohibited a state government from taking decisions on vital matters in the run-up to an election. However, the BJP and Shiv Sena did not make this an issue in February. Had they done so, the Election Commission might have ordered the state government to defer the decision on Dabhol.

The BJP/Shiv Sena election campaign rhetoric left little doubts as to their sentiments—one of their slogans was "Throw Enron into the Arabian Sea." The BJP platform promoted economic nationalism and sovereignty and denounced the Dabhol project. The BJP attempted to isolate Chief Minister Pawar as the only defender of Enron. The Dabhol project was described as a typical case of bad government—the failure of the ruling party to stand up to pressure from multinationals, corruption, and compromising on economic sovereignty.

---

[8]*Asia Week*, India Power Down: A Major Blow to Rao's Reform Drive, August 18, 1995.

The BJP had always been opposed to the project for various reasons: the social and environmental aspects, alleged bribes, the project's cost, and the lack of competitive bidding. The BJP/Shiv Sena campaign strategy painted the Congress (I) party as anti-poor, corrupt, and partial to foreign firms. This platform evidently appealed to Maharashtrians. On March 13 the election results were announced. The BJP/Shiv Sena coalition won 138 of 288 seats in the election and, with the help of several independent members, formed the new government. The Shiv Sena's Manohar Joshi became the new Chief Minister.

Not long after the election, Enron CEO Kenneth Lay noted, "If something happens now to slow down or damage our power project, it would send extremely negative signals to other foreign investors."[9] Other firms with power projects under way or in planning included the Swiss firm ABB, the U.S. firms AES Corp. and CMS Energy, and Hong Kong's Consolidated Electric Power Asia.

Construction Begins

On March 2, 1995, EDC completed the financing for Phase I of the Dabhol project. Phase I financing would come from the following sources:

- A 12-bank syndication led by the Bank of America and ABN-Amro (loans of $150 million).
- U.S. Export-Import Bank ($300 million; arranged by GE and Bechtel).
- The U.S.-based Overseas Private Investment Corp. ($298 million).
- Industrial Development Bank of India ($98 million).

Construction was soon under way. But, almost simultaneously, the new state government in Maharashtra, in keeping with its campaign promises, decided to put the project under review.

The Munde Committee

One week after coming to power, deputy chief minister and state BJP president Gopinath Munde ordered a review of the Dabhol project. The committee formed to carry out the review had two members from the BJP and two from the Shiv Sena. Munde, a known critic of Dabhol, was the Chairman. An open invitation to individuals to appear before the committee was followed up by letters to the MSEB and Dabhol Power Company. The committee was scheduled to submit its report by July 1.

Over the next few months, the committee held more than a dozen meetings and visited the site of the power plant. The committee was assisted by five state government departments: energy, finance, industries, planning, and law. All requests for appearances before the committee were granted. Among those making depositions were: environmental groups, energy economists, a former managing director of the Bombay Suburban Electric Supply Company,

---

[9]Emily MacFarquhar, A Volatile Democracy, *U.S. News and World Report*, March 27, 1995, p. 37.

representatives of other IPPs, and representatives of the IPP Association. The Industrial Development Bank of India, a prime lender to the project, representatives from the former state government, and the Congress (I) party did not appear before the committee.

During the committee hearings, the BJP continued its public opposition to Dabhol. The issue of irregularities—a euphemism for bribes—was raised. According to a senior BJP official:

> Though it is impossible to ascertain if kickbacks were paid to [former Maharashtra chief minister] Pawar, even if we can obtain circumstantial evidence it is enough. The project has been padded up and if the review committee can establish that, it is sufficient to cancel the project.[10]

Allegations of bribery were vigorously denied by EDC. Joseph Sutton, EDC's managing director in India, had told delegates at India Power '95, a conference on the power sector held in New Delhi in March, "during the three years we have been here, we have never been asked for, nor have we paid any bribes."[11]

On June 11, the RSS (the Hindu fundamentalist group) issued a directive to the BJP that it would like the party to honor its commitment to the *swadeshi* movement. The economic advisor to the central BJP, Jay Dubashi, said:

> We think canceling this project will send the right signals. It will demonstrate that we are not chumps who can be taken for a ride. Enron probably never imagined that Sharad Pawar [former Maharashtra Chief Minister] would go out of power. They thought he would see the deal through.[12]

Pramod Mahajan, the BJP's all-India secretary, was also fervently against Dabhol, stating that "we will go to court if necessary and decide in the long-term interest of the country."[13] Mahajan also ruled out paying penalties to EDC if the project were scrapped.

Meanwhile, EDC officials were shuttling back and forth between New Delhi and Bombay, trying to convince the press and the government of the viability of the Dabhol project. At one point, the U.S. ambassador to India, Frank Wisner, met with BJP president, L. K. Advani. Advani refused to meet Enron officials. The issue was even discussed during U.S. Treasury Secretary Robert Rubin's visit to India in April. According to the Assistant Secretary of the Treasury, "we pushed for resolution of the issue."[14] In May 1995, the U.S. Department of Energy warned that failure to honor the contract would jeopardize most, if not all, other private projects proposed for international financing in India. Maharashtra had attracted more than $1 billion of U.S. investment and more than half of all foreign direct investment projects in India were in this state. Furthermore, more than 25 percent of all FDI in India was from the United States.

In the meantime, Bechtel had not stopped construction. A spokesman for Bechtel said the company can't afford to have its 1,300 workers idled during a month-long review. "We have to meet a schedule; we have to provide power according to the power purchase agreement."[15]

---

[10]Ganguli & Pania, p. 56.
[11]Ganguli & Pania, p. 55.
[12]Ganguli & Pania, p. 55.
[13]Ganguli & Pania, p. 55.
[14]Ganguli & Pania, p. 55.
[15]*San Francisco Business Times*, May 5, 1995, Sec. 1, p. 1.

Cancellation of the Dabhol Project

The Munde Committee report was submitted to the Maharashtra government on July 15, 1995. Prior to the release of the report, N.K.P. Salve, India's power minister, stressed that the "Enron contract can be canceled only if there is a legal basis for doing so, not for any arbitrary or political reason."[16] On August 2, the Indian Supreme Court dismissed a petition by a former Maharashtra legislator challenging the Dabhol project on the grounds of secrecy.

On August 3, Chief Minister Joshi (who had visited the United States in the previous month to attract investment to India) announced to the Maharashtra legislature that the cabinet unanimously agreed to suspend Phase I of the project and scrap Phase II. The following are excerpts from Chief Minister Joshi's lengthy statement in the Assembly:

> The Enron project in the form conceived and contracted for is not in the best interests of the state. . . . Being conscious of the deception and distortion in the Enron-MSEB deal which have caused grave losses, the subcommittee is clear that the project must not be allowed to proceed. The subcommittee wholeheartedly recommends that the Enron-MSEB contract should be canceled forthwith. . . . Considering the grave issues involved in the matter and the disturbing facts and circumstances that have emerged pointing to extra-commercial considerations and probable corruption and illegal motives at work in the whole affair, immediate action must be initiated under the penal and anti-corruption laws by police.
>
> The wrong choice of LNG [liquefied natural gas] as fuel and high inflation in capital costs, along with unprecedented favours shown to Enron in different ways, including in the fuel procurement [had all resulted in an] unreasonable fuel cost to the consumers. . . . The documentary evidence obtained by the committee shows beyond any reasonable doubt that the capital cost of Enron Plant was inflated and jacked up by a huge margin. The committee believes that the extent of the inflation may be as high as $700 million. . . . Being gas-based, this project should have been cheaper than coal-based ones but in reality, it turns out to be the other way about.
>
> I am convinced that Enron, Bechtel, and GE will sell off at least 50 percent of their equity for the recovery of their expenditures on the project plus profits and the government would be a helpless spectator. The government should have sought some part of this for itself. . . . This contract is anti-Maharashtra. It is devoid of any self-respect; it is one that mortgages the brains of the state which, if accepted, would be a betrayal of the people. This contract is no contract at all and if by repudiating it, there is some financial burden, the state will accept it to preserve the well-being of Maharashtra.[17]

Other grounds were given for cancellation: there had been no competitive bidding; EDC held secret negotiations and used unfair means to win its contract; there was potential environmental damage to a region that was relatively unpolluted; the guaranteed return was well above the norm; and concerns about the $20 million earmarked by EDC for education and project development. The BJP government charged that concessions granted to EDC would cause the state of Maharashtra to lose more than $3.3 billion in the future. The committee was also outraged that loose ends in the Dabhol project were being tied up by the Maharashtra government as late as February 25, almost two weeks after the state election. In effect, the contract had been made effective by an administration that had already been rejected by voters.

---

[16]Foreign Investment in India: The Enron Disease, *The Economist*, July 29, 1995, p. 48.

[17]"Indian State Axes $2.8 BN Dabhol Power Project", in *International Gas Report, The Financial Times*, August 4, 1995; Mahesh Vijapurkar, Enron Deal Scrapped, Ongoing Work Halted, *The Hindu*, August 4, p. 1.

When the decision was announced, Prime Minister Rao was on a trade and investment promotion trip to Malaysia. He indicated that the economic liberalization policies initiated by his government would not be affected by this decision. Sharad Pawar, the chief minister of Maharashtra at the time the original agreement was signed with Enron, criticized the BJP's decision to cancel the Dabhol power project:

> If the government of Maharashtra was serious about the industrialization of Maharashtra, and its power requirements for industrialization and agriculture, they definitely would have appointed an expert group who understands the requirement of power, about overall projection, about investment which is coming in the fields of industry and agriculture, legal sides, but this particular angle is totally missing here and that is why I am not so surprised for this type of decision which has been taken by the government of Maharashtra.[18]

On the day after the government's cancellation announcement, the *Saamna* newspaper, known as the voice of the nationalist Shiv Sena Party, published a headline that read, "Enron Finally Dumped into the Arabian Sea." Later that week, *The Economic Times* in Bombay reported that local villagers celebrated the fall of Enron (See Exhibit 6).

EDC's Next Steps

About 2,600 people were working on the Dabhol power project and it was nearly one-third complete. More than $300 million had been invested in the project and estimated costs per day if the project were shut down would be $200,000 to $250,000. Cancellation of Phase II was less critical because EDC had not yet secured financing commitments for this portion of the project.

A few days before the Munde Committee report was made public and anticipating a cancellation recommendation, Rebecca Mark had offered publicly to renegotiate the deal. She told the media that the company would try to meet the concerns of the MSEB. On August 3, EDC announced that while it was aware of the reported announcement in the Maharashtra Assembly on the suspension of Dabhol, the company had received no official notice to that effect. The statement, issued in Houston, said:

> [EDC] remains available for discussions with the government on any concerns it may have. . . . [EDC] has very strong legal defenses available to it under the project contracts and fully intends to pursue these if necessary. The DPC and the project sponsors would like to reiterate that they have acted in full compliance with Indian and U.S. laws.[19]

[18]All-India Doordarshan Television, 3 August 1995.
[19]Vijapurkar, p. 1.

Exhibit 6

Excerpts from *The Economic Times*, Bombay, August 7, 1995

Villagers Celebrate 'Fall' of Enron

The 'Fall' of Enron was celebrated with victory marches, much noise of slogans, firecrackers and dancing outside the gates of the Dabhol Power Project and in the neighboring villages of Guhagar, Veldur, Anjanvel and Katalwadi on Sunday.

The march was led by local BJP MLA, the boyish Mr. Vinay Natu, whose father, a former MLA, is said to have originally brought the Enron project to its present site. The younger Natu denies this and says it is Enron propaganda to defame his father.

Much action was expected at the project site by the accompanying police escort. If nothing else, the celebrators were expected to pull down the Dabhol Power Company signboards on the gates of the high fence. They had earlier trailered this in Guhagar when women pulled down a DPG signpost indicating the way to the site and trampled it with fury.

Instead, the processionists danced, threw gulai in the air, and burst long strings of firecrackers before moving on to the next gate. Behind the wire fences at the site stood the tense security staff of the project; in the distance on higher ground could be seen site engineers observing the proceedings through binoculars.

Lining the fence inside were hundreds of construction workers who came to see the show. These workers too come from the neighboring villages, including those where the celebrations were being held. And even among the processionists were many who on other days worked inside the fence area on pay much higher than anything they can get in their villages. The paradox of benefiting by the Enron project as well as protesting against it has been the most striking aspect of the controversy.

The local Congress leader, 'Mama' Vaidya, was most unimpressed by the show or the opposition to the project. "This backward area needs the project," he said. As to any Congress efforts in the area to muster support for the project or economic development of the area, Mr. Vaidya said there was infighting in the party and coordinated action was not possible.

At DPC itself work goes on. There's worry on the faces of engineers, but they are determined to go on until they are told by their bosses to stop. No such order has been served yet.

42   CRISIS AT RENAULT

THE VILVOORDE PLANT CLOSING (A)

The news took almost everyone by surprise. Late in the afternoon of February 27, 1997, Renault S.A., France's second-largest auto maker, announced that it would close its plant in Vilvoorde, Belgium, effective July 31. Vilvoorde's 3,100 employees would be out of work in just five months.

According to a Renault spokesperson, the move was necessary in order to "streamline its industrial facilities." Production at Vilvoorde would be transferred to existing plants in France and Spain, where only 1,900 workers would be needed to produce the same number of autos that had been built in Belgium. By consolidating production at fewer plants, Renault expected an annual savings of FFr850 million ($160 million) beginning in 1998.

Reaction to the Vilvoorde plant closing was swift and angry. Labor unions, politicians, and community leaders in Belgium and France expressed outrage at Renault's sudden and "brutal" decision. Vilvoorde's workers were stunned, not only because they had received no advance warning of the closure, but because by all indications their plant was profitable and running well. As recently as 1995, Renault had spent $226 million to modernize the plant—hardly an indication of impending closure.

Over the next months, repercussions of the Vilvoorde plant closure dominated European economic news. By May, initial shock had given way to deeper questions about the future of European employment in an era of intense global competition, especially in industries with substantial overcapacity. Questions were also raised about the responsibility of corporations towards their employees and other stakeholders.

Renault S.A.: A Brief Company History

Renault S.A. traced its origins to 1898, when 21-year old Louis Renault assembled a motor vehicle in the Paris suburb of Billancourt. Along with his brothers, Marcel and Fernand, Louis Renault established Renault Frères and produced the world's first sedan in 1899. Over the next decades the company prospered, selling automobiles, trucks, tractors, and aircraft engines. In the 1920s and 1930s the company expanded into neighboring countries, building new plants close to local markets. One such plant was built in Vilvoorde, a few kilometers north of Brussels.

Renault grew steadily until the 1940s. During World War II, Louis Renault operated the Paris facilities for the occupying Germans. Accused of collaboration and jailed after the war, Louis Renault died in prison, and his company was nationalized by the French government in 1945. It remained nationalized until the 1990s.

In the post-war years, Renault achieved its greatest success with several popular and low-cost cars, including the 4CV in the 1950s, the Renault 4 in the 1960s and 1970s, and the Renault 5 in the 1970s and 1980s. By the mid-1980s, however, Renault's performance began to falter. Although revenues remained strong, the company was losing money due to the high costs of a bloated workforce and inefficient manufacturing operations.

Turnaround in the 1980s

Beginning under new CEO George Besse, and then under his successor, Raymond Lévy, Renault began to improve its performance. From 1985 to 1995, Renault steadily increased revenues and returned to profitability (refer to Exhibit 1). The number of automobiles produced remained steady, but the automobile workforce declined from 140,000 in 1986 to 102,000 in 1995 (refer to Exhibit 2). At the same time, Renault continued to modernize its plants, investing in new technology and emphasizing simplicity in manufacture. The result was an improvement in quality and cost.

Renault also improved its product line, offering more imaginative and attractive cars. The Twingo, introduced in 1992, was one of a new generation of minicars aimed at young buyers. The round-bodied car came in bright colors and featured gaily printed fabric seats. It was simple to build, requiring only 18 labor hours, about the same as small Japanese cars. Another new model, the Espace, was the first minivan in Europe. These and other new models helped boost Renault's image and improved its market position.

Leading many of these initiatives was Renault's chairman, Louis Schweitzer. The Swiss-born great-nephew of famed doctor and Nobel Prize Winner Albert Schweitzer, he had graduated from the prestigious Ecole Nationale d'Administration. During the 1970s and 1980s Schweitzer held a series of government positions, where he gained a reputation for diligence and pragmatism.[1]

In the early 1990s, the French government began to privatize a number of state-owned companies, many of which had been nationalized under Socialist president Francois Mitterand in the early 1980s. In 1994, it sold 47 percent of Renault's shares to a variety of

---

[1]"An aggressive driver," *Financial Times*, March 8/9, 1997.

EXHIBIT 1   Selected Consolidated Financial Data, 1986-1995

Financial Data in Millions of Francs		*1986*	*1987*	*1988*	*1989*	*1990*	*1991*	*1992*	*1993*	*1994*	*1995*
Revenues	(1)	122,317	147,510	161,438	174,477	163,620	165,974	179,449			
	(2)						171,502	184,252	169,789	178,537	**184,065**
	(7)										
Operating income (loss)	(1)	3,542	9,204	14,385	12,944	6,299	4,663	7,920			
	(3)						4,813	7,734	609	2,317	**1,259**
	(7)										
Pretax income (loss)	(4)	(4,916)	3,562	8,975	9,725	1,380	4,109	6,313			
	(5)						3,969	6,481	1,094	3,485	**1,976**
Net income (loss) excluding minority interest		(5,847)	3,256	8,834	9,289	1,210	3,078	5,680	1,071	3,636	**2,139**
Cash flow from operations	(1)	2,240	10,010	15,260	15,050	7,919	10,113	13,149			
	(2)						12,305	16,117	11,017	12,145	**11,669**
Investments	(1)	5,157	7,021	7,295	10,361	13,213	21,554	11,685			
	(2)						20,637	13,565	12,043	16,050	**15,499**
Net financial indebtedness for industrial and commercial activities	(6)	54,346	46,377	23,786	17,593	27,110	15,528	12,549			
								8,727	7,851	(1,458)	**3,368**
Shareholders' equity		(11,433)	(7,811)	14,012	22,466	17,014	31,331	33,965	33,877	42,784	**43,796**
Workforce	(2)	182,448	188,936	178,665	174,573	157,378	147,185	146,604	139,733	138,279	**139,950**

Source: 1995 Renault Annual Report.

investors, retaining a 53 percent majority ownership. A further sale in 1996 reduced the government's holding to 46 percent (refer to Exhibit 3). Successful privatization was due in large measure to investor confidence in Renault's ability to bring its costs into line. Renault had cut about 1,500 jobs in France during each of the last five years, largely through attrition, early retirement, and part-time work plans.

Renault in 1995

By 1995, Renault was operating profitably, with sales of FFr184 billion ($33.4 billion). Passenger cars accounted for more than 80 percent of revenues (refer to Exhibit 4). In terms of geography, almost half of revenues were from Renault's home market, with the remainder largely in Western Europe (refer to Exhibit 5). In addition to its strong market position in France, where Renault held 29.2 percent of the passenger car market, it had strong positions in Spain (13.9 percent), Portugal (12.8 percent), and Belgium-Luxembourg (11.1 percent) (refer to Exhibit 6). Overall, Renault had a 10.3 percent share of the Western Europe passenger car market.

Renault operated a large network of automobile plants, with nine large factories in France and others in Belgium, Spain, and Turkey (refer to Exhibit 7). There was considerable overlap among plants, with some models manufactured in more than one plant.

EXHIBIT 2   Renault: Automobile Production and Workforce, 1986–1995

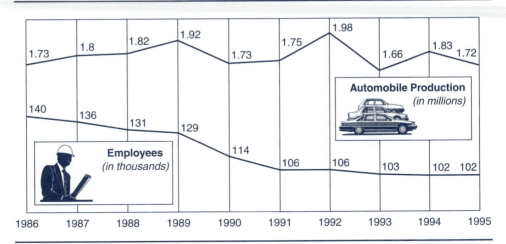

Source: *L'Express,* March 13, 1997, p. 32.

EXHIBIT 3   Principal Shareholders and Voting Rights at December 31, 1995

	%
French government[1]	52.97
AB Volvo	11.38
Templeton Group[2]	1.49
Protocol shareholders	
Lagardère Groupe	1.50
Sogepaf (Elf-Aquitaine group)[3]	1.50
Banque Nationale de Paris	1.00
Rhône-Poulenc Finance	1.00
Public including Group employees and others[4]	29.16
	100.00

[1]Includes shares reserved for distribution of bonus shares (2.87 percent).

[2]U.S. pension fund manager (exceeds the 1 percent statutory threshold).

[3]The Elf-Group, in addition to its interest as a protocol shareholder, holds 0.68 percent of Renault's equity capital.

[4]To the knowledge of the company, no other shareholder owns more than 1 percent of the equity at December 31, 1995. At that time, employees and former employees of the Group held 2.50 percent of the equity capital in the form of collectively managed and non-transferable shares. Cofiren, a 100% subsidiary of the Renault Group, holds 0.69 percent of the capital. These shares come from the stabilization funds of the market of investment certificates held by employees and former employees before the public offering of Renault capital.

Source: 1995 Renault Annual Report.

EXHIBIT 4

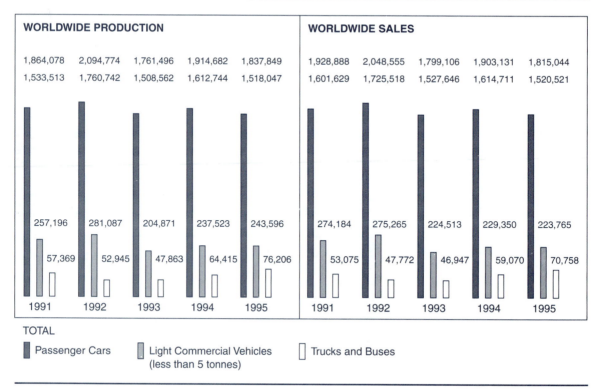

WORLDWIDE PRODUCTION

| 1,864,078 | 2,094,774 | 1,761,496 | 1,914,682 | 1,837,849 |
| 1,533,513 | 1,760,742 | 1,508,562 | 1,612,744 | 1,518,047 |

| 257,196 | 281,087 | 204,871 | 237,523 | 243,596 |
| 57,369 | 52,945 | 47,863 | 64,415 | 76,206 |

| 1991 | 1992 | 1993 | 1994 | 1995 |

WORLDWIDE SALES

| 1,928,888 | 2,048,555 | 1,799,106 | 1,903,131 | 1,815,044 |
| 1,601,629 | 1,725,518 | 1,527,646 | 1,614,711 | 1,520,521 |

| 274,184 | 275,265 | 224,513 | 229,350 | 223,765 |
| 53,075 | 47,772 | 46,947 | 59,070 | 70,758 |

| 1991 | 1992 | 1993 | 1994 | 1995 |

TOTAL

■ Passenger Cars   ▨ Light Commercial Vehicles (less than 5 tonnes)   ▯ Trucks and Buses

Source: 1995 Renault Annual Report.

The Belgian plant, at Vilvoorde, had been operated by Renault since the 1930s. Generations of residents from Vilvoorde and surrounding communities had worked at the plant. Its workforce was thought to be among the hardest working in Renault's production network.[2] In 1995, Renault invested $226 million to install an entirely new assembly line at Vilvoorde. By 1996, the plant turned out 143,342 cars, but was operating well below its full capacity of 1,000 per day.

The European Automobile Industry in 1996

Despite its many improvements in recent years, it was apparent in 1996 that Renault still faced major difficulties. Greater competition from a variety of rivals threatened Renault's position. New minicars, including the Opel Corsa, VW Polo, and Ford Ka, all took sales from the Twingo. The lead enjoyed by the Espace was wiped out as virtually all European automakers introduced their own minivans, including the Opel Sintra, the VW Sharan, and

---

[2]"Renault's plant closing mirrors industry woes," *The Wall Street Journal*, March 6, 1997, p. B4.

EXHIBIT 5   Geographic Distribution of Renault Revenues, 1991–1995

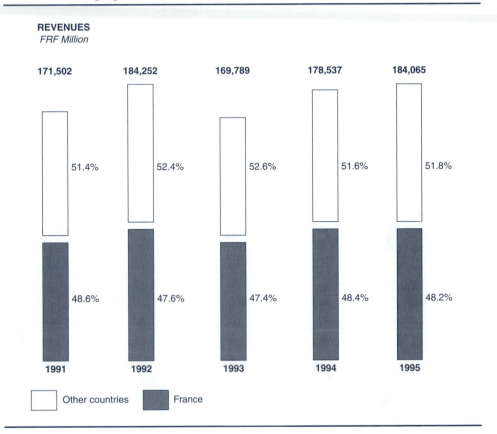

REVENUES
FRF Million

| 171,502 | 184,252 | 169,789 | 178,537 | 184,065 |

51.4%	52.4%	52.6%	51.6%	51.8%
48.6%	47.6%	47.4%	48.4%	48.2%
1991	**1992**	**1993**	**1994**	**1995**

☐ Other countries   ■ France

Source: 1995 Renault Annual Report.

the Ford Galaxie. Renault's Megane sedan, introduced in 1995, found itself stacked against four new cars: Fiat Bravo and Brava, Opel Vectra, and Ford Fiesta.

Adding to Renault's challenges was a general problem facing the entire European auto industry. Until the 1990s, European automakers had been able to survive by relying on sales in their home markets. The gradual introduction of the single European market meant that cars could more easily cross borders, allowing major auto companies to compete for sales in other markets. Facing greater competition at home, companies like Fiat could no longer rely on Italian sales to survive, nor could Renault rely on French sales. The more open market, plus investments into Europe by Japanese and Korean automakers, led to a growth of productive capacity and a resulting intensification of competitive pressure. *The Wall Street Journal* summed it up simply: "The problem is overcapacity, combined with a breakdown of traditional national markets."[3]

---

[3]"Renault's plant closing in Belgium reflects industry overcapacity," *The Wall Street Journal Europe*, March 4, 1997, p.1.

EXHIBIT 6   Renault in Western Europe—Passenger Cars

	% Change in Registrations		Renault Market Share (%)			*Renault Registrations 1995*
	M.T.M.[1]	*Renault*	*1993*	*1994*	*1995*	
France	−2.1	−4.9	30.6	30.0	29.2	**563,712**
Germany	+3.3	+4.6	5.2	5.1	5.2	**170,916**
United Kingdom	+1.8	+6.9	5.2	5.9	6.2	**120,485**
Spain	−8.4	−16.9	16.3	15.3	13.9	**115,906**
Italy[2]	+4.1	−11.0	7.3	7.0	6.0	**104,400**
Belgium-Luxembourg	−7.1	−13.8	11.7	12.0	11.1	**43,026**
Netherlands	+2.9	−9.7	7.3	8.3	7.3	**32,590**
Portugal	−13.6	−25.4	14.2	14.8	12.8	**25,782**
Austria	+2.2	−1.1	6.4	6.7	6.5	**18,264**
Switzerland	−0.0	−10.2	6.4	7.4	6.7	**17,856**
TOTAL Western Europe[3]	**+0.8**	**−5.2**	**10.6**	**11.0**	**10.3**	**1,240,972**

[1]Total new car market.

[2]The figures have been established in accordance with the new method of counting registrations introduced in Italy in 1994.

[3]EU, Iceland, Norway, and Switzerland.

Source: 1995 Renault Annual Report.

EXHIBIT 7   Renault: Major Production Sites and Models, 1995

Flins	Clio, Twingo
Douai	Renault 19 then Mégane
Sandouville	Safrane, Laguna, Laguna Nevada
Maubeuge	Renault 19 convertible, Express
Vilvoorde (Belgium)	Clio, Renault 21 Nevada, Mégane
Palencia (Spain)	Laguna, Renault 19 then Mégane
Valladolid (Spain)	Twingo, Clio, Express, engines
Bursa (Turkey)	Renault 9/11/12/21
Cléon	Engines, transmissions, aluminum castings
Le Mans	Front/axle assemblies, mechanical parts, iron castings
Lorient (S.B.F.M.)	Iron castings

Source: 1995 Renault Annual Report.

Some companies, notably General Motors and Volkswagen, moved deliberately to reduce capacity and better match their output to demand. In early 1997, Ford Motor Company, having lost $291 million in Europe in 1996, announced the closure of its plant in Halewood, England, with the loss of 1,300 jobs. Jac Nasser, chairman of Ford Europe, said that auto companies could not merely trim prices to increase demand; they also had to reduce capacity. The present situation of overcapacity in Europe, he observed, "is not sustainable in the long run."[4] Fiat, too, made clear that it would take steps to reduce capacity.[5]

As for Renault, it was becoming clear that its output was not sufficient to justify its network of plants. One analyst estimated that Renault's plants were operating at just 78 percent of capacity.[6] Furthermore, a comparison of leading plants showed that Renault's efficiency lagged behind major rivals (refer to Exhibit 8).

Renault and Vilvoorde: Chronology of a Crisis

1997 began with a sense of gloom in the French auto industry. On February 14, Peugeot announced that 1996 sales had declined from 1995 levels, and indicated it would report a loss for the year. Many analysts speculated that Renault, too, would soon report weak performance for 1996.

Faced with declining performance and under pressure to reduce costs, Renault's chairman, Louis Schweitzer, and his counterpart at Peugeot, Jacques Calvet, jointly proposed a plan to the French government in which 40,000 employees would receive state-funded early retirement in return for hiring 15,000 younger, cheaper workers. The government of Prime Minister Alain Juppé was wary of appearing to support the growing calls for retirement at 55, a key policy of the Socialist opposition. On February 26, after extensive consideration, the government officially rejected the plan. The very next day, Renault announced it would reduce employees in another manner—by closing the Vilvoorde plant.

Thursday, February 27.   Late in the afternoon, Renault issued a brief statement that the Vilvoorde plant would close on July 31. The announcement also stated that Renault expected to report "a very significant loss" for 1996, its first loss in 10 years.

The announcement caught the town of Vilvoorde completely unaware. Some employees learned of the news on the radio as they arrived at work for the evening shift. "I heard it on TV," said one shocked worker. "I couldn't catch my breath."[7] The plant closure was especially grim news given that unemployment in Vilvoorde was already more than 12 percent.

---

[4]"Europe's great cars wars: The fracas over Renault's closure of its Belgium factory is an indication of the rotten state of Europe's car industry," *The Economist*, March 8, 1997.

[5]"Europe's great cars wars: The fracas over Renault's closure of its Belgium factory is an indication of the rotten state of Europe's car industry," *The Economist*, March 8, 1997.

[6]"Euro automakers catch up as Renault's downfall sparks fears for auto markets," *USA Today*, March 7, 1997.

[7]"Renault's plant closing in Belgium reflects industry overcapacity," *The Wall Street Journal Europe*, March 4, 1997, p.1.

**EXHIBIT 8   Major Automakers in Europe: Number of Automobiles Produced
per Year per Employee at the Most Productive Factories**

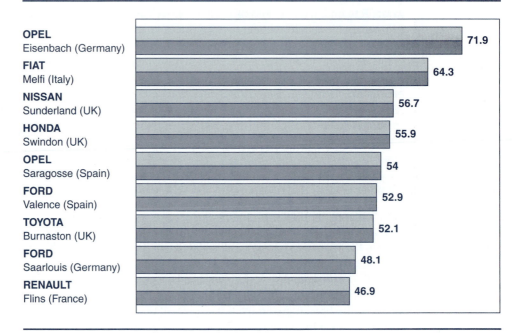

OPEL Eisenbach (Germany)	71.9
FIAT Melfi (Italy)	64.3
NISSAN Sunderland (UK)	56.7
HONDA Swindon (UK)	55.9
OPEL Saragosse (Spain)	54
FORD Valence (Spain)	52.9
TOYOTA Burnaston (UK)	52.1
FORD Saarlouis (Germany)	48.1
RENAULT Flins (France)	46.9

Source: *L'Express,* March 13, 1997, p. 30.

"We never expected such a brutal decision," said Vilvoorde Mayor Willy Cortois. "It's a total surprise." Cortois said that the total number of jobs lost in the Vilvoorde area could reach 6,000 because many local firms relied on the Renault factory.[8]

Friday, February 28.   The news in Belgium was dominated by the plant closure. Eric Van Rompuy, a minister in the Flanders regional government, denounced the closing as "an act of terrorism against the Flemish economy." Belgian Prime Minister Jean-Luc Dehaene said his government was "concerned and stupefied" by the "brutal and unilateral decision . . . which took no account of the social repercussions." Dehaene, himself a resident of Vilvoorde, called French Prime Minister Alain Juppé in view of the French state's 46 percent ownership of Renault to register his strong protest.[9]

The Belgian response was particularly intense because of the country's heavy reliance on the automobile industry for employment and export earnings. On a per capita basis, Belgium was the biggest car producer in the world, operating plants for five companies: Ford,

---

[8]"Dehaene lambastes 'brutal' decision," *Dow Jones News Service*, February 28, 1997.

[9]"Renault workers protest, Belgians angered by plant closure," *USA Today*, March 4, 1997.

Volkswagen, General Motors, Volvo, and Renault. These plants employed 34,000 people and turned out 1.2 million cars a year, accounting for 15 percent of the country's export earnings. Although the Vilvoorde plant was the smallest of the five, many Belgians were fearful that other plant closures might follow.[10] With unemployment in Belgium already at 13 percent, the prospect of further job losses was of grave concern.

In Brussels, a spokesperson for the European Union Commission said Renault appeared to have broken two E.U. laws. One law, a 1975 agreement (revised in 1992) on collective redundancies, said that firms considering a reduction in employment were required to consult workers "in good time with a view to reaching an agreement." The other law, a 1994 E.U. works council directive, stipulated that company management had to "inform and consult with employees" on all important decisions. The spokesperson noted that although Renault had been among the first large companies to set up a works council, doing so in 1993, it had apparently not fulfilled its duty to consult with the council.

Meanwhile, angry Vilvoorde employees occupied the plant, shutting down all production. They also prevented the shipment of 5,000 finished cars worth BFr3 billion ($86 million), and threatened to hold "hostage" 2,000 partly assembled cars.[11]

News of the plant closure was greeted positively by shareholders. Renault shares jumped 13 percent on the Paris Bourse, reaching 146.9 Francs.

Sunday, March 2. Public opposition grew stronger and louder over the weekend. Protests spread into the streets of Brussels, where 3,500 people staged a peaceful march to denounce the plant closure. Elsewhere in Belgium, union leaders urged a boycott of Renault cars.

Responding to the public outcry, Renault chairman Louis Schweitzer met with Belgian government officials. Schweitzer explained the rationale for the closure, and reaffirmed his intention to close the Vilvoorde plant on July 31. He also indicated that Renault expected to take a FFr2.4 billion (approximately $400 million) provision in 1997 to cover severance pay and other costs associated with the plant closure.

Monday, March 3. The Belgian Employment Minister, Miet Smet, said the government would bring formal legal action against Renault for failure to inform and consult with employees. Under Belgian law, the maximum penalty for breaching such rules was BFr20 million, or about $580,000. "It's largely symbolic," a spokesman conceded. King Albert II of Belgium added his voice to the public debate, visiting the European Commission to express his concern about the plant closure.

The European Union Competition Commissioner, Karl Van Miert, stated his belief that Renault had failed to respect the E.U. directives on worker consultation. He added: "I don't understand Renault's decision because it is closing a very profitable plant in which it has invested a lot in recent years."[12]

---

[10]"Europe's great cars wars: The fracas over Renault's closure of its Belgian factory is an indication of the rotten state of Europe's car industry," *The Economist*, March 8, 1997.

[11]"Belgium set to sue Renault over factory closure," *Financial Times*, March 4, 1997, P1.

[12]"Belgium set to sue Renault over factory closure," *Financial Times*, March 4, 1997, P1.

The Belgian government asked for a meeting of the Organization for Economic Cooperation and Development to determine if a code of conduct for multinational corporations had been broken. Breaching an OECD code did not, however, carry any financial penalty.

In France, Renault's labor unions expressed concern that the closing at Vilvoorde was only the beginning of further cutbacks. "The problem will expand in France with the announcement of draconian job cuts," warned France's *Force Ouvrière* union.

Tuesday, March 4.   Fears of further job cuts were well-founded. A source close to Renault said the firm intended to eliminate 2,764 French jobs, or nearly 2.8 percent of its French workforce, by the end of the year. These reductions would take place mainly through attrition, and would not involve the closing of any French plants.

Following this latest announcement, France's Industry Minister, Franck Borotra, summoned Renault's top management to new talks about their restructuring plans. He emphasized, however, that the government would not seek to intervene in exchanges between the company and Belgian authorities.

In a public statement, Renault chairman Louis Schweitzer characterized the Vilvoorde plant closing as "grave and painful," but maintained that it had been examined "attentively to make sure the need for it was incontestable on a strategic and economic level."[13] Renault also clarified the shift in jobs resulting from the closure. Production of Megane and Clio models would be shifted to plants in Spain and France. Although 3,100 jobs in Belgium would be lost, 1,900 jobs would be added at other Renault plants, primarily the Spanish plants of Palencia and Valladolid. Unemployment in Spain stood at 21 percent.

Separately, industry analysts noted that the average after-tax take-home pay of Vilvoorde workers was similar to that of French Renault workers—about $1,700 per month—but was considerably more expensive to the company because of higher social charges and tax rates in Belgium. Some estimates placed the total cost of employing a Renault worker in Belgium as 30 percent more than in France and 48 percent more than in Spain.[14]

Wednesday, March 5.   In Paris, French President Jacques Chirac added his voice to the chorus of criticism, saying he was "shocked by the method" by which Renault had announced the closure at Vilvoorde. Prime Minister Alain Juppé similarly criticized the way the decision had been communicated, and summoned Louis Schweitzer to his offices at Matignon to complain about the abrupt announcement. One newspaper described the meeting as a "tongue-lashing session" with a "livid Prime Minister Alain Juppé." Schweitzer once again explained his reasons for the plant closure, adding: "I also indicated that Renault wishes to start as soon as possible talks with Vilvoorde employees on aid measures and the possibility of converting the factory for other uses."[15]

Some of Renault's Vilvoorde workers wondered openly whether Renault would have treated them differently if they were French-speaking Walloons rather than Flemish speakers. One Vilvoorde resident voiced the widely shared belief that: "Of course they closed the plant in Belgium to save jobs in France."

---

[13]"Paris calls Renault chiefs to new talks on job cuts," *Financial Times,* March 5, 1997, p. 14.

[14]"Renault workers despair for Europe's job security," *Financial Times*, March 6, 1997.

[15]"Euro automakers catch up: Renault's downfall sparks fear for auto markets," *USA Today*, March 7, 1997, p. 10B.

The leader of France's opposition Socialist Party, Lionel Jospin, called on Juppé to intervene in the closure, describing Renault's decision to close the Vilvoorde plant as "financially, industrially, and socially aberrant." He added: "Trying to play off workers from one country against those of another is not worthy of a great French and European enterprise." France's Minister of Labor and Social Affairs, Jacques Barot, took a different tack, noting that "Renault's closure is not against Belgium. Competition is raging. We realize that to be a player in this globalization of the economy we have to fight."

Industry analysts, meanwhile, took a favorable view of Renault's actions, although some claimed that the job cuts at Vilvoorde and in France represented only about 4 percent of Renault's total workforce. One analyst suggested that Renault would have to lay off as many as 10,000 employees in order to regain competitiveness, meaning another 4,000 in addition to the Vilvoorde and French cutbacks.[16]

Analysts also made clear that other automakers would have to pare their workforces, too. By one estimate, European automakers would produce 16.5 million cars and vans in 1997, but would sell only 13 million. "This looks like the beginning of a squeeze that happens periodically in the European motor industry," commented one expert.[17] An international economist in London concurred, saying that "the likelihood is that [European automakers] are going to continue pruning workforces for some time to come." These words were of scarce comfort in France, where unemployment had already reached a record level of 12.8 percent.

Friday, March 7.   Renault's plan to shift production to one of its Spanish plants was dealt a blow when the European Commission blocked subsidies to Renault's Valladolid plant as long as Renault did not reverse its decision regarding Vilvoorde. In response, Renault's chairman Schweitzer repeated that the decision to shut down the Belgium plant was "irrevocable."

Thursday, March 13.   Despite the public criticism levelled at Renault by French President Chirac and Prime Minister Juppé, some French press reports suggested that the French government had known of the Vilvoorde closure in advance and had given a "tacit backing" to the move. One analyst stated that the French government, still by far Renault's biggest shareholder, had "given the industry carte blanche to go ahead and restructure."[18]

Sunday, March 16.   Public demonstrations in Belgium continued for the third consecutive weekend, this time involving organized labor from all over Europe. More than 50,000 European trade unionists converged on Brussels, venting their anger at job losses and what was termed "inhumane companies and uncaring governments." Delegations were present from France, Spain, Portugal, Great Britain, Germany, Luxembourg, the Netherlands, Italy, Greece, Austria, Hungary, Slovenia, and the Czech Republic. "It is a show of solidarity," said one auto worker from England. "We are all workers. We are all in the struggle."

---

[16]"The skid at Renault: Once a star, the carmaker may lose $1 billion," *Business Week*, March 17, 1997.

[17]"Renault's plant closing mirrors industry woes," *The Wall Street Journal*, March 6, 1997, p. B4.

[18]"The skid at Renault: Once a star, the carmaker may lose $1 billion," *Business Week*, March 17, 1997.

The demonstration featured red, green, and yellow union banners, as well as noisy chants, firecrackers, and sirens. One banner read: "They follow more rules for swine fever than for us." Another said: "Renault is developing turbo-charged unemployment." French Socialist Party leader Lionel Jospin observed: "We need a better balance in the European economic and social model. It has gone too far [toward the economic]." The head of Belgium's Christian Democratic CSC trade union, Willy Pierens, exclaimed to the assembled thousands: "This is a signal of anger and indignation. A signal of solidarity against brutality. We don't want to be lied to again. We won't be cheated again."[19]

Wednesday, March 19.   Renault chairman Louis Schweitzer and eleven union leaders from the Vilvoorde plant met face-to-face for the first time since the February 27 announcement. The meeting was held on neutral ground at Beauvais, north of Paris, after workers refused to travel to Renault headquarters at Boulogne-Billancourt, and Schweitzer refused to attend a meeting at Vilvoorde. In a meeting that lasted more than two hours, the union proposed a 10 percent reduction in working hours as an alternative to a full shutdown. Schweitzer rejected any such proposal, telling union leaders that the decision to close the plant was irrevocable and could not be delayed beyond July. He stated, however, his willingness to discuss the terms of the shutdown so as to reduce the impact on workers. Union leaders termed Schweitzer's position "unacceptable" and said they were very disappointed by his unwillingness to consider their proposal.[20]

Friday, March 21.   After weeks of hints and speculation, Renault reported its 1996 results. It showed a loss of FFr5.25 billion ($925 million), its first loss in 10 years. Analysts were unsurprised with the figures, noting they were "pretty much bang in line" with expectations. Renault chairman Louis Schweitzer commented simply: "1996 was, as you know, a difficult year."[21]

Schweitzer also reported Renault's restructuring plan had been approved "by a very large majority" of the board of directors, and stated his expectation that with the steps it had taken, the firm would return to an operating profit by year end. With the closing of the Vilvoorde plant, said Schweitzer, "Renault has an industrial structure and plant distribution that won't require any further plant closings until 2000." He added that the Vilvoorde plant would have been closed at some point given its location, and that "the 1996 results convinced us that we could not delay the closing."[22]

Meanwhile, workers at Vilvoorde continued to occupy the plant. At Wavrin, in northern France, workers clashed with police as they occupied a Renault distribution center. Workers at Renault plants in France, however, rejected calls for a companywide strike and remained on the job.

---

[19]"The skid at Renault: Once a star, the carmaker may lose $1 billion," *Business Week*, March 17, 1997.

[20]"Renault tells unions: Closing of Belgian plant is 'irrevocable,'" *International Herald Tribune*, March 20, 1997; *Financial Times*, March 20, 1997, p.2; "A Beauvais, Louis Schweitzer face a onze syndicalistes de Renault," *Le Monde*, March 20, 1997.

[21]"Renault posts yearly loss as workers protest job cuts," *Wall Street Journal Europe*, March 21–22, 1997, p.3.

[22]"Renault earnings—In line with expectations," *Dow Jones News Service*, March 20, 1997.

Friday, March 28.   Protests continued as 900 demonstrators clashed with police outside the headquarters of the Flemish regional government and the office of the European Union. Protesters threw cans, stones, and eggs at police.

Thursday, April 3.   In the first legal ruling on the case, a Belgian court ruled that the Vilvoorde plant closure was illegal because Renault had failed to consult its workers. The Brussels labor court said Renault had breached labor consultation rules and called it to restart discussions with its workforce. The court did not have the power to force Renault to reverse its decision, but could fine the company up to BFr20 million ($580,000) if the company did not promptly reopen talks with workers. Labor unions welcomed the court's ruling. "It is good that the judicial power in Belgium is bringing Renault back into line," said Denis de Meulemeester, a spokesperson for the Belgian metals union.[23]

Responding to the court ruling, a Renault spokesperson said: "We respect Belgian law, but economic reality being what it is" the company expected to proceed with the shutdown.[24]

Friday, April 4.   One day after the Belgian ruling, a French court found that Renault had failed to consult properly with its workers and imposed a fine of FFr15,000 ($2,600) to be paid to the worker consultation body.

Legal analysts commented that neither the French nor the Belgian ruling could stop Renault from actually closing the plant. Renault chairman Schweitzer again reiterated his intention to close the plant, stating that "the ruling doesn't change the economic reality." He told one French newspaper that Vilvoorde might have to close earlier than July 31 if its workers, still on strike and occupying the factory, did not soon return to work.[25]

In a separate development, the Citroen division of Peugeot announced that it would cut 800 of its 28,400 jobs during 1997. The company added that it would present its layoff plans to employee representatives on April 15.

Friday, April 11.   Nearly 69 percent of the Vilvoorde workforce voted to return to work, bringing to an end the six-week strike that began with the announced plant closure. "Work will start on Monday," said a union official, Hendrick Vermeersch. Some workers said they were still angry with Renault, but reasoned they were better off returning to work than forgoing the wages they could earn until July 31. The union warned, however, that assembly work would be difficult if almost one-third of workers wanted to continue the strike. Moreover, workers continued to occupy the factory's parking lot, where 5,000 finished cars had been blocked since the plant closure was announced.[26]

On the Paris Bourse, Renault stock closed at FFr154, reaching a 52-week high, up almost 50 percent from its 52-week low of FFr103.

---

[23]"Court finds Renault's plan illegal," *International Herald Tribune*, April 4, 1997, p. 13.

[24]"Renault still planning to close plant," *The New York Times*, April 4, 1997.

[25]"Unions win Renault suit," *International Herald Tribune*, April 5–6, 1997, p. 9; "Renault to appeal on consultation ruling," *Financial Times*, April5/April 6, 1997, p. 2.

[26]"Renault strike in Belgium to end," *International Herald Tribune*, April 11, 1997, p. 11.

Tuesday, April 15.   Employees at Vilvoorde resumed work in both morning and afternoon shifts. The resumption of production had been delayed one extra day as a small number of workers had refused to start production on Monday.

Wednesday, May 7.   A French appeals court reversed the lower court's ruling that Renault had been obliged to notify its unions before deciding to close the Vilvoorde plant. Renault said that the closing had been an "industrial and economic necessity," and once again confirmed it would go ahead with the closure as planned.[27]

Thursday, May 22.   A wildcat strike at the Vilvoorde plant blocked production for the second day in a row. Despite the earlier vote to return to work, a small group of disgruntled workers had been able to effectively block production.[28]

Renault management, acting in compliance with the rulings of Belgian and French courts, agreed to meet with representatives of the Vilvoorde workforce on June 3 to discuss the plant shutdown. A spokesperson for Renault maintained, however, that the plant still needed to be closed as part of a vital streamlining of operations.

Sunday, May 25.   In the first round of French parliamentary elections, voters repudiated the center-right government of Prime Minister Alain Juppé. The leftist coalition of Socialists, Communists, and Greens captured 42.1 percent of votes against 36.2 percent for the ruling coalition of President Chirac's Gaullists and the centrist Union for French Democracy. Several factors explained the ruling party's unpopularity, including a 12.8 percent rate of French unemployment, concerns about government support for European monetary union, and opposition to further cuts in social spending.

Thursday, May 29.   Campaigning in the north of France for the second round parliamentary voting, Socialist leader Lionel Jospin met with a delegation of workers from the Vilvoorde plant. Jospin said that if he became prime minister, he would intervene in the Renault affair and force a reconsideration of the Vilvoorde plant closure. "Representatives of the state on Renault's board will demand other measures" be taken regarding Vilvoorde, said Jospin.[29] Renault workers cheered his words, and presented him with a Renault Megane.[30]

Renault headquarters retorted that a new prime minister could not overturn the decision to close the plant. A spokesperson stated: "On March 20, the board of directors voted by a large majority to support the chairman, Louis Schweitzer. Only he can change the decision." Whether a new prime minister might be able to replace Schweitzer as chairman was open to discussion, as the French state held only 46 percent of the voting shares.[31]

---

[27]"Renault/Court: Vilvoorde closure costs 3,100 jobs," *Dow Jones News Service*, May 7, 1997.

[28]"Renault to sell 0.9% stake in Elf back to company," *The Wall Street Journal Europe*, May 23–24, 1997, p. 8.

[29]"The political lesson: forward to the past," *The International Herald Tribune*, June 2, 1997.

[30]Reported on Radio France Info, May 30, 1997.

[31]"M. Jospin veut faire revenir la direction de Renault sur la fermeture de Vilvoorde," *Le Monde*, June 2, 1997.

Sunday, June 1.   The French Socialists swept to power in parliamentary voting, taking a solid majority of more than 300 seats in the National Assembly. One news account said that French voters had "delivered a powerful rejection of the performance of the center-right governing coalition in trying to push through changes to make the economy more competitive and French society less dependent on jobs and benefits provided by the government."[32]

Monday, June 2.   At 9:15 A.M., Prime Minister Alain Juppé met with President Jacques Chirac to offer his resignation. Less than two hours later, Lionel Jospin arrived at the Elysée and was asked by President Chirac to serve as France's next prime minister. Later that day, he moved into the prime minister's office at Matignon.

On the Paris Bourse, French stocks stablized after losing more than 4 percent of their value over the previous week. Renault shares closed at FFr126.

---

[32]"Socialists recapture power in France," *International Herald Tribune*, June 2, 1997.

43 THE BRENT SPAR PLATFORM CONTROVERSY (A)

April 30th, 1995

Top executives at Shell UK had just learned that Greenpeace activists—accompanied by journalists—had boarded a Shell platform in the North Sea to protest its scheduled disposal in the Atlantic.

Apparently, four protesters had scaled the platform using ropes and winches. They then notified vessels in the area that they were protesting Shell's plan to sink the Brent Spar at sea. Their communiqué stated that Greenpeace would remain on board until Shell or the UK government "came to its senses" and reversed its decision. The protesters were well provisioned—apparently they intended to stay.

Since receipt of approval for the platform's disposal at sea in February 1995, this was the first protest of any kind that Shell management had encountered.

Shell Expro and the North Sea Oil Fields

Since the early 1960s, the North Sea oil and gas fields (refer to Exhibit 1) had been a major source of revenue for the United Kingdom, the Netherlands, Norway, and Denmark. The UK was the country with the highest production (refer to Exhibit 2), having derived some US$ 130 bn in revenue since 1964. As of 1995, the UK oil and gas industry employed approximately 300,000 workers.

By the 1990s, the production of the giant first-generation North Sea fields, with billions of tons of recoverable oil and gas reserves, was starting to decline. The aging facilities had become costly to maintain and the few newly found reserves were increasingly located in

This case was prepared by Research Associates Matthias Winter and Mary Schweinsberg under the supervision of Professor Ulrich Steger and Professor Peter Killing as a basis for class discussion rather than to illustrate either effective or ineffective handling of a business situation. Copyright © 1996 by **IMD** – International Institute for Management Development, Lausanne, Switzerland. All rights reserved. Not to be used or reproduced without written permission directly from **IMD**, Lausanne, Switzerland.

NORTH SEA, (GP) Greenpeace today scaled and took up residence on an old North Sea oil platform to stop its owner, Shell, from dumping the rusting hulk and its highly toxic contents to the sea bed. Four climbers used ropes and winches to scale the Brent Spar, which is the first of the 400 North Sea oil platforms to be dumped at sea. The climbers have food and supplies for what is expected to be a long occupation. The Greenpeace ship Moby Dick is standing by as a safety vessel. The activists first climbed the steel ladders on the installation, then scaled the outer part of the rig, 28 metres high above the waterline. After Moby Dick captain Pelle Pettersson notified the five other rig support vessels in the area, stating that Greenpeace was protesting the dumping of the Brent Spar, a Shell standby vessel then sailed very close to the Moby Dick and the inflatables, harassing them.

The Brent Spar contains over 100 tonnes of toxic sludge—including oil, arsenic, cadmium, PCBs and lead—including more than 30 tonnes of radioactive waste left over from oil drilling and storage operations on the Brent Oil Field. The UK Government's decision to allow Shell to dump the Brent Spar was based on information supplied and paid for by Shell. Ironically, the planned dump comes just one month before North Sea environment ministers meet in Denmark in June to discuss measures to eliminate the discharge of hazardous substances from all sources into the North Sea and the marine environment. "The decision is short-sighted and the latest example of governments allowing industry to treat the seas as a toxic dump," said Greenpeace's Tim Birch onboard the Moby Dick. "Greenpeace will remain on Brent Spar until the UK Government or Shell comes to their senses and revokes the decision to dump it," Birch said. (…)

small fields which were difficult to exploit economically (in 1995, a barrel of oil was one-third its 1980 price in real terms). Additionally, gas production had gained more importance and platforms in the North Sea were being modified to produce gas rather than oil.

Shell UK Limited was engaged in the exploration and production of oil and natural gas, in oil refining, chemicals manufacturing and in the marketing of the resulting products. Shell's UK main oil and gas producing subsidiary, Shell Exploration and Development (Shell Expro), was a joint venture between Shell and Esso. Shell UK acted as the operating partner and the company's main operational base was located in Aberdeen, Scotland. The venture, which was started in the 1960s, operated in the British sector of the North Sea; in 1994, Shell Expro was responsible for roughly one-quarter of all UK oil and gas production.

The Brent Spar

The Brent oil and gas field in the northern North Sea was Britain's largest producer—accounting for more than 10 percent of British oil and gas production—during the two decades following its discovery in the early 1970s. Shell and Esso had spent some £7 billion developing and operating it. In 1995, however, they were investing a further £1.3 billion to redevelop the field so that its productive life could be extended well into the next century. This project involved changing the management of the reservoir so that the field would increasingly produce gas rather than oil. To this end, Shell Expro's three production platforms in the Brent Field would require extensive modifications, and its storage platform, the Brent Spar, would need to be scrapped all together.

Exhibit 1   North Sea Map

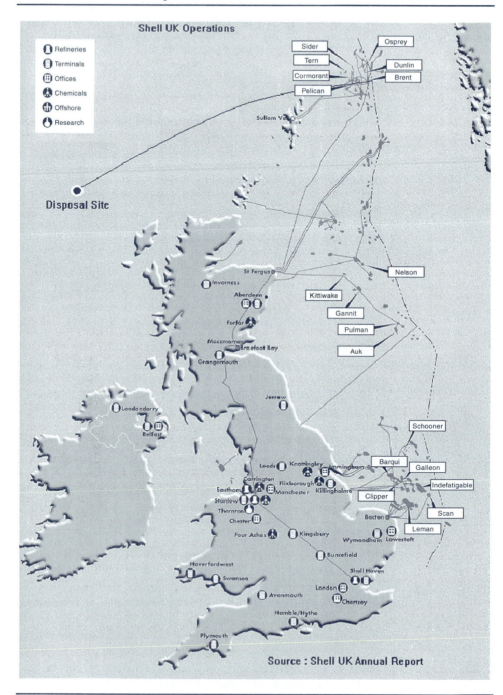

Exhibit 2   1994 Gas and Oil Production in the North Sea

Country	Oil Revenue in US$ Millions	Oil: Millions of Tons per Year	Number of Platforms	Gas in Billion Cubic Meters per Year
Norway	12,157	91.0	71	25.0
UK	11,220	84.0	208	45.0
Denmark	800	6.0	31	5.1
Netherlands	255	1.9	106	17.3

Source: *Der Spiegel* 25/1995, p. 29.

The Spar was located in the British block of the North Sea, 190 km north-east of Shetland.[1] Originally built as a storage tank in the mid-1970s, the Brent Spar had been operational between 1976 and 1991 and was subsequently substituted by pipelines. Shell Expro used it to store crude oil prior to distribution to refineries. The Spar was 137 meters deep, the steel construction weighed 14,000 tons and was originally designed to contain 300,000 barrels of oil (1 barrel = 159 litres) in its six main tanks. The platform included a topside with a helideck and accommodation for workers (refer to Exhibit 3).

Shell Disposal Options for Brent Spar

Shell Expro closed down the platform in 1991. The Spar had been designed to act solely as a storage facility. Its six storage tanks and complex structure made the disposal especially problematic. The Brent Spar was the first North Sea storage facility necessitating disposal. Beginning in 1991, Shell undertook some 30 studies on possible disposal options. One of these studies, done by the consulting company Rudall Blanchard Associates Ltd., examined six options for the disposal of the Brent Spar:

Option 1:   Disposal on land horizontally.[2] If the platform should break during the dismantling, risk of environmental damage and human injury was considerable: the probability of a lethal accident was estimated at 0.03 to 0.09 percent. The cost was estimated to be around £46 million.

Option 2:   Disposal on land vertically. This option had a higher risk than option 1 and was therefore not further considered.

Option 3:   Blasting the platform in the oil field ("Walk-away Strategy"). This would be the least costly solution. It was never seriously considered since Shell thought it was unlikely that the UK government would give permission.

---

[1] Accidents were not uncommon in at-sea oil production, especially in the North Sea where weather conditions made operations more problematic than average. Over the 15 year life of the Brent Spar, two workers were killed in accidents.

[2] Horizontal disposal would entail turning the Spar on its side and dismantling it section by section. This could be done either on land or in shallow water.

EXHIBIT 3

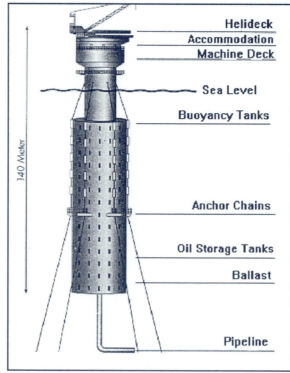

Option 4:   Disposal in the deep sea. The consultants had considered this to be an environmentally acceptable strategy. Studies showed that if the rig was sunk in water more than 1,500m deep, it would have minimal environmental impact as there was little aquatic life beyond that depth. The risk of accident was very low (between 0.005 and 0.014 percent). Cost calculations were around £11.8 million.

Option 5:   Restoration and use of the platform on another production site. The problem with this solution was that Shell would need to find a site where they could use the Brent Spar. No such place was found. No detailed cost calculations were made.

Option 6:   Continuous maintenance of the platform and further use in the Brent field. This solution was not of interest to Shell, as Brent Spar had been made obsolete by the Brent Pipeline.

The studies concluded that Brent Spar should be sunk at the North Feni Ridge, where the Atlantic was more than 2,000m deep. At that depth, contamination would neither enter the food chain nor cause other environmental harm. Shell UK had the explicit assurance from geologists at the University of London that the sinking of a platform at such a depth would have no environmental impact.[3] They pointed out that natural physical processes on the sea floor produced more dangerous substances than the whole of Brent Spar and its contents. The studies argued that the quantities of metals in the platform were very small compared to the releases from natural sources such as the Broken Spur hydrothermal vent field in the North Atlantic, which emitted between 500,000 and 5 million tons a year.

Some scientists even suggested that "the bacteria of the ocean-floor would have greeted the arrival of Brent Spar as if all their Christmases had come at once." Many deep-sea microbes require heavy metals as electron or energy sources in their metabolism.

Shell Expro director Heinz Rothermund was convinced that compared to the usual emissions from a platform, the amount and effect of environmentally harmful material inside Brent Spar with its 100 tons of sludge was very limited. Recent estimates concluded that the oil emissions caused by exploration in the North Sea were between 86,000 and 210,000 tons per year. In other words, on any one working day, the 200 British platforms leaked more oil than could be found in the tanks of the Brent Spar. Shell Expro estimated the platform contained 10 tons of unrecoverable crude oil, 6 kg of cadmium, 9 kg of lead, 43 kg of copper, some minor amounts of chrome, nickel, and mercury and 30 tons of weak radioactive salts which came from natural sources.

Laws Pertaining to Platform Disposal

The International Maritime Organisation (IMO) guidelines for the removal and disposal of redundant offshore petroleum installations stated that any installation in waters shallower than 75 meters must be totally removed. For installations in deeper waters, the guidelines stated that the decision should be made on an individual basis, taking into account such

---

[3]These findings were to be published on June 29th, 1995, in the British scientific journal *Nature,* Vol. 375, p. 715: "Is metal disposal toxic to deep ocean?"

factors as environmental impact, safety, occupational health, other marine users, and economic considerations. Furthermore, the 1992 Oslo-Paris-Convention[4] stated that sea disposal would be allowed in exceptional cases. However, the IMO guidelines are not legally binding. Another international law, the United Nations Convention on the Law of the Sea (UNCLOS Treaty), which requires the removal of redundant structures, was not ratified by the British government.

Under the UK legislation on abandonment—covered by the 1975 Petroleum and Submarine Act—operators must submit their abandonment proposal for government approval, together with full supporting documentation and a review of the other options considered. The petroleum taxation system required the cost of abandonment to be borne by the filed licensees, who could then offset part of the cost against tax. Where Petroleum Revenue Tax had been paid, reimbursements of previous payments could meet between 50 percent and 70 percent of the cost of abandonment. Should approval be granted, countries with boundaries onto international waters would need to be informed of the decision, but they would have no right to intervene.

Permission for Deep Sea Disposal

After carefully weighing its choices, Shell Expro decided to apply in September 1992 for sea disposal. Both Shell UK and Royal Dutch in The Hague approved this decision. Shell reasoned that the Brent Spar could qualify for special status due to the estimated high risk of accident in a land disposal. Deep sea disposal was, according to Shell executives and independent scientists, a responsible balancing of all environmental, safety, health, and economic factors.

On February 17, 1995, the British energy minister Tim Eggar announced the British government's intention to approve Shell's plan to sink the platform and informed his European counterparts accordingly. Eggar made clear that the Brent Spar disposal would not be a precedent for further platform dumping into the sea, but an exception to the rule of land disposal.

That same day, Shell issued a press release announcing its decision. The announcement received little or no attention. No country objected to the plan.

Greenpeace

Founded in 1971 and then reorganised by Canadian environmentalist Dave McTaggart in 1976, Greenpeace had become synonymous with bold environmental activism. From its "Save the Whales" campaigns to its protests of French nuclear tests in the South Pacific, Greenpeace members were seen—via television and newspapers—selflessly and bravely putting their lives on the line for environmental causes. With virtually every campaign, they gained public support and credibility.

---

[4]Signing countries were Belgium, Denmark, Finland, France, Germany, Iceland, Ireland, Luxembourg, Netherlands, Norway, Portugal, Spain, Sweden, Switzerland, UK.

Yet in recent years, Greenpeace had been changing its strategy to include more passive techniques of activism, such as using scientific studies and dialogue to influence the governments and corporations it targeted. The new director of Greenpeace International (GPI), Thilo Bode, had a reputation for trying to cooperate with industry. Bode explained:

> We don't lose our ability to confront and attack by talking to them. On the contrary, they know us better and we know them better. It is important to know your adversary. But it is not just a cynical exercise in getting to know the enemy.

Still, Greenpeace was not ready to entirely abandon their old tactics, Thilo Bode explained:

> We can intervene physically, without violence, against environmental destruction, such as the killing of the whales. This holds true where the destruction is visible. But you can't see global warming, so here we have to find the most effective confrontation.

Furthermore, Greenpeace knew there was a direct relationship between media coverage of its protest and the amount of contributions it received. Between 1991 and 1995, worldwide donations had dropped from US$ 178 million per year to US$ 142 million. At the same time, the number of donors declined from 5 million to 3 million. In recent years, Greenpeace had been looking for ways to improve its structural effectiveness. Bode once commented to a German newspaper:

> The organization Greenpeace is like a medium-sized business and has all the sorts of problems of a business this size.

By 1995, it had more than 40 offices, with its headquarters (Greenpeace International) based in Amsterdam. Greenpeace employed some 900 people worldwide. Countries who contributed the most (Germany, U.S.A. and Netherlands) played the biggest role in selecting the personnel for the international positions. In recent years, Greenpeace had reorganized itself several times so that many of its resources had been spent resolving internal issues, while environmental actions with strong press coverage were reduced. Decision making in Greenpeace was concentrated within a small group of elected representatives; for example, the German organization's steering committee consisted of 40 voting members, in contrast to its countrywide membership of 507,000.

Greenpeace country organizations were highly autonomous and were linked to GPI primarily through a licensing agreement. They often focused their efforts on national issues. In recent years, the organization had suffered a number of defeats. A lack of a strong leadership meant, for example, that the major environmental dramas in Russia were never tackled by Greenpeace. In the United States, the organization had become involved in women's rights, Native American issues, and Gulf War protest, topics that did not build public support. As a result, U.S. Greenpeace was experiencing financial difficulties.

Clashes with Shell

Greenpeace and Shell were well acquainted. Greenpeace had often castigated Shell for its role in the Global Climate Coalition, an industry alliance which lobbied successfully against tighter emissions controls both in the U.S. and internationally. Greenpeace argued that since oil-based energy was responsible for 44 percent of carbon dioxide emissions, Shell should shift its emphasis away from fossil fuel towards the development of renewable resources.

In January 1995, Gijs Thieme, a Dutch Greenpeace member, stumbled onto a scientific study from the University of Aberdeen that evaluated different options for disposal of the Brent Spar platform. The study concluded that sea disposal in the Atlantic would be environmentally the best possible solution. Thieme was involved in Greenpeace's action planning for the North Sea Conference (which would take place the first week of June); he took the study to Tim Birch, who was coordinating the North Sea Conference protest. Thieme told him:

> We have to do something here. This will be a big story for the summer. It has everything you need for a real scandal: visually interesting, symbolic and a strong opponent.

Birch was not convinced. They had decided that Greenpeace would focus its efforts on chlorchemical dumping in the North Sea. But Thieme did not give up, making a journey through Greenpeace offices in London, Amsterdam, Copenhagen, and Hamburg in order to find activists who would support him.

Bode, who was head of Greenpeace Germany at the time and scheduled to become GPI's director in April, liked the scenario. This was a move away from the more scientific work in the last years and back into the heat of battle. Bode said:

> We have a check-list at Greenpeace that helps us evaluate potential campaigns. There are 15 possible requirements and the Brent Spar fulfilled all of them. There was a clear goal with a feasible solution; the issues were easy to understand; the Spar was a powerful visual symbol; the protest would destroy the image of the opponent; and so on. . . . I still had my doubts though. It looked like we would have to invest DM 2 million just to get the activists on the platform, and there were no guarantees that it would work.

The action-oriented members of Greenpeace were happy that after all the theoretical discussions in recent months, the group could start another major confrontation. Members speculated that there were two possible options: First Greenpeace would set up a radio/television broadcast station on the platform, relaying and promoting environmental causes in a dramatic way, or second, they could focus a campaign against Shell. GPI's communications director, Ulrich Jürgens, believed that a highly visible campaign would spur new donations. He commented on Shell's study:

> I don't care about scientific arguments. I don't care if there are 10 or a thousand tons of hazardous waste on the platform. The question is, how does our society cope with their waste? And our message is: don't litter!

After discussing the matter internally, Greenpeace activists came to the conclusion that they had two strategic options to prevent the dumping:

1. *Pressure the UK government* to rescind its permission. This option had two disadvantages: First, revoking its permission would leave the UK government open to a lawsuit brought by Shell. Second, Greenpeace had no direct means of putting much pressure on the government.

2. *Pressure Shell UK* to rescind its decision voluntarily. Shell would have no direct legal recourse and could be hurt financially more easily than the UK government.

Because of the size and location of Brent Spar, the activists realised that boarding the rig would be a difficult task. They also felt it was possible that Shell would learn of the plan beforehand and try to stop them, as Greenpeace planning was always well observed.

Furthermore, Greenpeace decided to focus their public relations efforts on the UK and Germany[5] since Germans had a reputation for being sensitive to environmental issues. In addition, the German population had no direct economic ties to the situation, as Germany was not involved in North Sea oil production. It seemed probable that Germans would sympathise more with Greenpeace than would the populations in Norway, Denmark, or the Netherlands, and Shell Germany could be a good target.

Shell Germany was one of the most important country organizations in the Royal Dutch/Shell group. With a turnover of DM 21 billion (US$ 15 billion), it accounted for roughly 11.5 percent of the total group turnover. Its net income in 1994 was DM 531 million (US$ 350 million). Shell Germany had only a limited involvement in production and distribution of oil and gas products.

In early discussions, Greenpeace members decided not to focus their criticism only on the environmental impact of Brent Spar's disposal; instead, they also brought into question whether the Spar would serve as a precedent for the large number of North Sea platforms to be decommissioned in the coming years. The activists who would capture the platform were carefully selected. In order to generate maximum media coverage, they were chosen from four different countries. Also, in the case of legal action against the activists, four embassies would become involved.

Publicly, Greenpeace decided to base its action on the following arguments:

1. There was no formal inventory of the Brent Spar's contents, so the environmental impacts could not possibly be properly assessed.

2. There was insufficient understanding of the deep sea environment, and it was therefore impossible to predict the effects of the proposed dumping on deep sea ecosystems.

3. The documents which supported Shell's license application were highly conjectural in nature; they contained numerous unsubstantiated assumptions, minimal data, and extrapolations from unnamed studies.

4. Dumping the Brent Spar would create a precedent for dumping other contaminated structures in the sea and would undermine current international agreements. The environmental effects of further dumping would be cumulative.

5. Dismantling the Brent Spar *was* technically feasible and offshore engineering firms believed it could be done safely and effectively. The necessary facilities were already in routine use and the decommissioning of other oil installations had already been carried out elsewhere in the world.

---

[5]The strongest contributing country for Greenpeace was Germany, where donations reached USD 40 million in 1994.

6. To protect the environment, the principle of minimising the generation of waste should be upheld and harmful materials should always be recycled, treated, or contained.

7. Greenpeace suggested that the dumping was either illegal under international law (the Geneva convention), or contrary to a series of decisions taken at international convention meetings.

8. The UK government (namely the Right Honourable Tony Benn MP, who was Secretary of State for Energy in the Labour Government at the time) had promised, when opening up the North Sea oil fields, that all structures would be removed at the end of their working lives.

The Royal Dutch/Shell Group

The alliance between Shell and Royal Dutch dated back to 1907 when the two companies decided to merge their interests while keeping their identities separate. In 1995, Shell Petroleum N.V. and The Shell Petroleum Company Limited between them held all the shares in the Service Companies and, directly or indirectly, all interests in the Operating Companies (e.g., Shell Germany and Shell UK). The parent companies did not engage directly in operational activities (refer to Exhibit 4).

The country subsidiaries were relatively autonomous, as long as the financial results were satisfactory. Since 1960, Shell had operated with a matrix structure through which each operating company reported to a regional coordinator supported by a functional coordinator (chemicals, oil products, or such). The heads of operating companies were akin to local barons, free from much interference from the parent company, which acted almost like an internal shareholder only. In recent years, this decentralisation had spawned layers of regional bureaucracy.

Shell companies were engaged in oil, natural gas, chemicals, coal, and other businesses throughout the world. The total company turnover was US$ 116 billion in 1994 with earnings of US$ 6.3 billion. The company employed some 106,000 people worldwide, with US$ 69.2 billion invested in over 130 countries. Nevertheless the company's performance had begun to slip in recent years in terms of return on equity compared to its competitors. In addition, Shell's underlying return on equity of about 10 percent was insufficient to sustain its long-term plans. Royal Dutch chairman Cor Herkströter's goal was 12 percent return on equity—15 percent on older assets, less on investments just coming into operation. Shell expected a continuation of flat oil prices and growing competition; changes would be required in order to meet the parent company's financial targets.[6]

The Royal Dutch/Shell Corporation did not set environmental strategies for its subsidiaries; it allowed individual companies to decide their own goals, "reflecting the national and cultural background in which they work." Shell believed that putting the

---

[6]*Forbes,* February 27, 1995, p. 64.

EXHIBIT 4   Legal Structure of the Royal Dutch/Shell Corporation

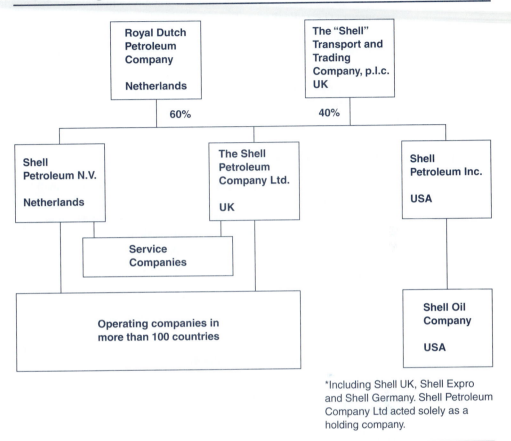

*Including Shell UK, Shell Expro and Shell Germany. Shell Petroleum Company Ltd acted solely as a holding company.

responsibility at a country level encouraged a sense of ownership, which in turn encouraged innovative thinking. Also, there was no organizational unit assigned to handling public relations issues on an international level.

In early 1995, Herkströter began a massive restructuring of the global organization. The new structure would reduce the importance of country management and concentrate on functional results. Shell would be grouped by five lines of business: exploration and production, oil products (refining and marketing), chemicals, gas, and coal. Each line of business would have its own business organization managed by a business committee consisting of appropriate senior managers. The committees would be chaired on a nonexecutive basis by one of the group's four managing directors. The overseeing committees would ensure that the Shell group's collective interests were better met than in the past, but still, consensus would stay one of the top priorities. For example, Shell wanted to avoid past mistakes, where purchasing prices for identical material from the same supplier differed up to 30 percent depending on the country organization who bought it. Therefore, Herkströter had to concentrate his efforts on restructuring the company, which demanded much of his time and resources. The radical reshaping of the headquarters would eliminate roughly 1,000 of the 3,900 jobs in the headquarters in the Hague and London. Herkströter, a stolid, mild-mannered accountant by training and president of Shell's managing director's committee in The Hague, announced the changes:

> I am confident the new organization will give us as good a platform as is possible to achieve the sustainable performance we require. Of course, it is up to us to make it happen.

Shell UK and Its Stakeholders

Shell UK was a company with a number of sensitive problems. Shell UK's exploration subsidiary Shell Expro faced a steady decline of exploitable resources in the North Sea as well as an aging fleet of platforms. The downstream oil business in the UK was experiencing declining sales and increasing competition, particularly with the entry of supermaket chains into gasoline retailing. Nevertheless, in 1994 Shell UK had earnings of £453 million, which accounted for around 10 percent of the Royal Dutch/Shell Group's total. The businesses of Shell UK employed nearly 8,000 people.

The United Kingdom had the reputation of being an environmental holdout in Europe. The British government had traditionally justified itself by stating that its environmental policies set realistic targets. Concerning Shell Expro's Brent Spar, the UK government maintained that their decision to allow Shell to sink the platform was correct and that it was in their general interest that the disposal of old platforms should be done in an environmentally friendly yet cost effective way.

Nevertheless the government realised that they had to be sensitive to the European environmental conscience, especially when it came to questions concerning the sea. In the past, many of the cases where popular opinion had overridden official positions were connected with the oceans. The British government had long been under pressure to accelerate the clean-up of beaches and inland waters—even though strict cost/benefit analysis suggested that the full investment was not worthwhile. The UK had also come under criticism in the past for dumping radioactive waste at sea. More recently, the UK had held off signing the latest convention phasing out disposal at sea on the grounds that the alternatives to dumping were far too costly.

In addition to contracting a number of technical feasibility studies of the disposal options, Shell Expro had consulted a number of not-for-profit-organizations in the consulting process, including the Scottish National Heritage, the Joint National Conservancy Committee (however, these two organizations are funded by the British government) and five different commercial fishing associations. All of these stakeholders accepted the position of Shell UK: deep sea disposal would be favorable over land disposal in environmental terms.

44 Sicom GmbH and CD Piracy

"As far as I am concerned, it is not an issue we need to worry about," said Josef Radler in April 1997. Radler was the chief executive of the German firm Sicom GmbH (Sicom). Sicom, the leading firm in the compact disc (CD) equipment industry, produced CD replicators. CD replicators were used to produce copies of CDs from master versions. According to Radner:

> We are the world's leading manufacturer of CD replicators. When you are the biggest player, you have the biggest chance of supplying people who infringe on other people's rights. I am not going to stop selling replicators in Asia. How can I control who uses our product? What about the manufacturers of photocopiers? They must know that sometimes their machines are used to illegally copy books and other printed materials and even money. Should these companies be held responsible for illegal photocopying?

Radler had recently discussed the issue of CD piracy in China with Sicom's managing director for Asia, John Thomson. Thomson, based in Hong Kong, was adamant that CD piracy was not Sicom's concern. According to Thomson:

> I am not here to enforce the law. My job is to sell products. If I sell you a car, do I ask if you have a valid driver's license? No. It is not our responsibility to determine if our Chinese customers have licenses to import CD replicators. Sometimes we ask them and sometimes we don't. When we ask them, they just say they applied and expect to get one soon. What more are we supposed to do?

Sicom GmbH

CD replicators are used to reproduce CDs from master copies. A decade before 1997, producing CDs required large clean rooms that sealed out dust and other substances that could damage disk quality. The equipment used in these clean rooms was very expensive, required great technical expertise to operate, and cost about $30 million. In 1987, Josef Radler developed technology that greatly simplified CD manufacturing. This technology resulted in glass-enclosed units that were much smaller than the clean rooms and could be used as self-contained assembly lines. Radler's machines were easy to use and transport and, most important, were priced at about $2.5 million. On the basis of the new technology, Radler had built a successful business based in Rosenheim, a small town near Munich. Sicom became the world's largest producer of CD replicators. Sales in 1996 were $120 million, 45 percent in Asia. Sicom had a reputation for high quality and timely delivery and was recognized as the industry technology leader.

Most of Sicom's replicators destined for the Asian market were air-freighted to a Hong Kong agent for shipment to final destinations. Because Hong Kong, due to become part of China in July 1997, was a free port, there were no import or export restrictions on replicators. When CD replicators arrived at a customer's premises in China, Sicom engineers were called in to set up the equipment. Sicom engineers did not attempt to determine whether the CD production line was legal or illegal.

CD Piracy

According to one estimate, nearly 200 million pirate CDs were produced annually, with 60 percent coming from China.[1] The International Federation of the Phonographic Industry (IFPI) claimed losses of $2.2 billion due to CD piracy. Although precise data were unobtainable, the largest market for pirate CDs was thought to be Russia, mainly imported from China and Bulgaria. Despite new intellectual property laws introduced on January 1, 1997, piracy in movies, computer software, and CDs was rampant in Russia. In dollar terms, the second-largest market for pirate CDs was thought to be the United States.[2] In Western Europe, Italy was considered the largest market for pirate CDs.[3] Significant declines in the sale of pirate CDs had occurred in a number of countries, including the United Kingdom, South Korea, and Thailand.

As a measure to reduce piracy, a coding system (called SID codes) was introduced in 1992 as a joint initiative by Philips Consumer Electronics, which issued licenses to use its CD manufacturing technology, and the IFPI, which oversaw the code-monitoring system. The coding system involved two code numbers applied to the silver inner part of the disc. One number identified the plant that manufactured the master CD and another number

---

[1] R. S. Greenberger and C. S. Smith, "Double Trouble: CD Piracy Flourishes in China and West Supplies Equipment," *The Wall Street Journal*, April 24, 1997, pp. A1, A13.

[2] "Stolen Melodies," *The Economist*, May 11, 1996, p. 64.

[3] "One in Every 5 Music Recordings Sold in 1995 Was Pirated Copy," *Audio Week*, May 20, 1996.

identified the plant where the disc was replicated. The latest IFPI figures estimated that 68 percent of all CD production plants worldwide were using the codes.[4] In China, the coding system became mandatory for all CD production in 1995.

CD Piracy in China.   CD piracy in China began to flourish in the early 1990s when other Asian countries took steps to curb the piracy within their borders. In particular, when the government of Taiwan shut down pirate CD plants, Chinese CD piracy took off. Despite the efforts of the Chinese government to crack down on piracy by closing CD plants and destroying illegal CDs, piracy continued to flourish. It was estimated that about 90 percent of the CDs purchased in China were counterfeit. Many of the illegal factories reportedly were joint ventures with Taiwanese businesses, which helped finance the equipment used to produce counterfeit CD product. By early 1994, China had at least 25 CD plants with a total capacity of about 75 million CDs, at a time when demand for legitimate CDs in China amounted to no more than three million units.[5]

The majority of pirate CD plants were believed to be located in the South China province of Guangdong, often operating with the cooperation and support of provincial officials. Until the development of replicators like those produced by Sicom, China-based pirate CD manufacturers struggled to deal with the environment and, in particular, the high humidity prevalent in South China. Pressing digital discs of any quality required sterile temperature-and humidity-controlled conditions that were difficult to create. The new replication equipment overcame this problem with self-contained manufacturing systems that could be operated virtually anywhere. One report suggested that with a reliable, portable power supply, pirates could produce CDs from the back of container trucks in the near future, perpetually and untraceably roving the countryside like truck-mounted Cold War Soviet missiles.[6]

Many of the pirate CDs produced in China were shipped around the world through Hong Kong. Given the huge volume of goods that passed through Hong Kong, there was little customs inspectors could do to stem the flow of illegal goods. Each day, more than 15,000 trucks and 300 container ships moved from the Chinese border to Hong Kong. Random checks were carried out only on goods destined for the Hong Kong market and on those that had to be off-loaded and stored in Hong Kong for more than 24 hours.

One of the complaints of the music industry was that Chinese restrictions against the importing of legitimate CDs contributed to the growth of the pirate industry. The situation with respect to imported music seemed to be changing. According to the IFPI, the number of titles approved for import to China had grown from 150 in 1992 to 300 in 1995 to about 450–600 in 1996.[7] Nevertheless, although official import quotas for recordings had been abolished, significant hurdles remained for the music companies trying to develop the Chinese market. The many steps involved in getting a license for the sale of a music recording included: identifying a Chinese record company as a business partner, showing proof

---

[4]T. Heath, "A Safer World For Replicators," *Billboard*, August 24, 1996, p. 41.

[5]J. Berman, "Chinese Piracy Reform Still Murky In '96," *Billboard*, January 6, 1996.

[6]B. Atwood and G. Burpee, "War On Piracy Continues In China," *Billboard*, July 20, 1996.

[7]T. Duffy, "Music Imports Increasing In China," *Billboard*, June 1, 1996.

of copyright ownership of the recording to be licensed, discussing trade terms, signing a letter of intent, providing a sample of the recording and translation of the lyrics for censorship review, signing a contract and registering the deal with the national copyright-administration officials, and providing a master recording once approval was obtained. Compounding the difficulties of licensing was a royalty rate as low as 10 cents per cassette or $1 per CD, long waiting periods for payment, the lack of promotion and marketing for releases, the restricted sale of products through only a single company; and the virtual impossibility of verifying sales figures.[8]

A further issue associated with the sale of legitimate CDs in China was that only about 10 percent of the population had enough disposable income to spend on consumer products such as audio recordings. Nevertheless, 10 percent of the population represented a potential market of 120 million, predominately in the country's major cities. With the growth of satellite television, Chinese consumers were becoming more aware of different forms of entertainment.

The Policies of Piracy

The issue of piracy had become a contentious political issue. In 1994, the Recording Industry Association of America began to pressure the Chinese government to deal with the pirate CD operations. On February 26, 1995, after the threat of sanctions by the U.S. government, the Chinese government, in a 6-page agreement and 22-page action plan, agreed to the following:[9]

- To investigate all CD production lines.
- To seize and destroy all infringing products, as well as the machinery used to manufacture such products.
- To revoke business permits for factories involved in illegal production.
- To ban the export of infringing products.
- To introduce a copyright verification system that would prevent manufacture and export of CDs that had not been cleared by the Chinese government and representatives of affected copyright owners.
- To monitor CD plants for compliance and to revoke business permits of companies operating without SID codes or outside of approved verification channels.
- To abolish all quotas or other restrictions on the importation of audio products.
- To permit U.S. record companies to enter into joint ventures for the production and reproduction of audio products.

In the aftermath of the agreement, few of the provisions were implemented. CD piracy continued to grow in scale and American record companies were making only limited progress in gaining entry to China. In late 1995, the IFPI closed its branch office in

---

[8]*Billboard*, June 1, 1996.
[9]Berman, 1996.

Guangzhou because of reports that CD pirates had hired hit men and taken out contracts on the IFPI office staff.[10] The director-general of IFPI promised to reopen the office as soon as Chinese authorities could guarantee his staff's safety. The IFPI was also trying to stop the pirates by blocking their supplies of raw material. CDs are pressed from polycarbonate plastics. Only five companies in the world produced polycarbonate with the purity and thermal and optical characteristics necessary for CDs.

In 1996, the U.S. government once again threatened to impose trade sanctions on China if the Chinese government did not clamp down on the illegal production of U.S. films, music, and computer properties. Under an intellectual property rights agreement negotiated between the United States and China in June 1996, China agreed that imports of CD replicators would require a license. The Chinese government promised that no new licenses would be issued. The government also agreed to the prosecution or investigation of about 70 individuals involved in the pirate trade and committed to "special enforcement" periods in which actions would be taken on illegal products already in the marketplace.

In 1997, according to Chinese government officials, no new licenses for the importation of replicators had been issued. Since signing the intellectual property rights agreement, the Chinese government had closed dozens of illegal CD operations and destroyed hundreds of thousands of pirate CDs. In December 1996, 20 illegal production lines were closed and the Chinese government indicated that new pirate plants would be shut down as they were discovered. However, the U.S. State Department estimated that at least 27 production lines with the capacity to produce 150 million CDs annually were set up in China in the second half of 1996.[11] It appeared that as the Chinese government clamped down in one region, the illegal and easily transferable factories moved to other parts of China. Within China, it was suspected that there was a market for used CD replicators. Equipment was also being moved out of China to Macau and Hong Kong.

Officials from the United States were putting pressure on their European counterparts to deal with the piracy problem at the source, which meant going after the manufacturers of CD replication equipment. Most of these firms were in Germany, Holland, and Sweden. EU officials insisted that the problem was in China and must be solved by the industry and by China. In reaction, U.S. Trade Representative Charlene Barshefsky publicly stated:

> The focus is to do whatever we can to help ensure that CD presses do not go into China. So far, in spite of our repeated efforts, the EU and member states take a see-no-evil attitude.[12]

Sicom's Situation

Josef Radler recognized that his company could get caught in the middle of a battle between U.S. and EU government officials. Publicly, his position was that Sicom should not be held accountable for the actions of others:

---

[10]B. Fox, "Chinese Pirates Target CD Police," *New Scientist,* January 6, 1996, p. 7.

[11]*The Wall Street Journal,* April 24, 1997.

[12]*The Wall Street Journal,* April 24, 1997.

If CDs are being made illegally with Sicom equipment, it is up to the various countries to enforce their laws. In a free market, Sicom should be able to sell to any customer that wants the product and has the money to pay for it. We are a small company with limited resources in a highly competitive industry. If I refuse sales because I am concerned about possible illegal use of the equipment, I can assure you there are other CD equipment firms who would gladly take the orders. I have to keep my costs down and improve my technology. I cannot afford to cut my sales back. If I do, I might as well shut my business down. How am I supposed to explain that to my employees? I have worked hard to build this business and support my community. My replication equipment is the best in the industry. Why should I stop selling to certain customers just because of rumors that my customers are not using the equipment properly?

619

ACRONYM	PROPER NAME
ADB	Asian Development Bank
AfDB	African Development Bank
AFIC	Asian Finance and Investment Corporation
AFTA	Asian Free Trade Agreement
ASEAN	Association of Southeast Asian Nations
ATPA	Andean Trade Preference Act
BIS	Bank for International Settlements
BOP	Balance of Payments
CIM	Computer-Integrated Manufacturing
CIS	Commonwealth of Independent States
CISG	UN Convention on Contracts for the International Sale of Goods
CEMA	Council for Mutual Economic Assistance
CRA	Country Risk Assessment
DB	Development Bank
DC	Developed Country
DFIs	Development Finance Institutions
DISC	Domestic International Sales Corporation
EBRD	European Bank for Reconstruction and Development
ECOWAS	Economic Community of West African States
EMU	Economic and Monetary Union
EEA	European Economic Area
EFTA	European Free Trade Association
EMs	Export Management Companies
EMCF	European Monetary Cooperation Fund
EMS	European Monetary System
EPO	European Patent Organization
ETC	Export Trading Company
ETUC	European Trade Union Confederation
EU	European Union
FCPA	Foreign Corrupt Practices Act
FDI	Foreign Direct Investment
FSC	Foreign Sales Corporation
FTAA	Free Trade Agreement of the Americas
FTZ	Foreign Trade Zone
Fx	Foreign Exchange
G7	Group of Seven
GATT	General Agreement on Tariffs and Trade
GC	Global Company
GDP	Gross Domestic Product
GNP	Gross National Product
GSP	Generalized System of Preferences
IAC	International Anti-counterfeiting Coalition
IC	International Company
IDA	International Development Association
IDB	Inter-American Development Bank
IEC	International Electrotechnical Commission
IFC	International Finance Corporation
IMF	International Monetary Fund
IPLC	International Product Life Cycle
IRC	International Revenue Code
ISA	International Seabed Authority
ISO	International Organization for Standardization
ITA	International Trade Administration
JIT	Just-in-Time
JV	Joint Venture
LAIA	Latin American Integration Association (formerly LAFTA)
LDC	Less Developed Country
LIBOR	London Interbank Offer Rate
LOST	Law of the Sea Treaty
MERCOSUR	Free Trade Agreement between Argentina, Brazil, Paraguay, and Uruguay
MNC	Multinational Company
MNE	Multinational Enterprise
NAFTA	North American Free Trade Agreement
NATO	North Atlantic Treaty Organization
NIC	Newly Industrializing Country
NTBs	Nontariff Barriers
OECD	Organization for Economic Cooperation & Development
OPEC	Organizational of Petroleum Exporting Countries
PPP	Purchasing Power Parity
PRC	People's Republic of China
PTA	Preferential Trade Area for Eastern and Southern Africa
SACC	Southern African Development Coordination Conference
SBA	Small Business Administration
SBC	Strategic Business Center
SBU	Small Business Unit
SDR	Special Drawing Rights
SEZ	Special Economic Zone
TQM	Total Quality Management
UN	United Nations
UNCTAD	UN Conference on Trade and Development
VAT	Value Added Tax
VER	Voluntary Export Restraint
VRAs	Voluntary Restraints Agreements
WEC	World Energy Council
WIPO	World Intellectual Property Organization
WTO	World Trade Organization